CIVIL WAR CLAIMS IN THE SOUTH

An index of Civil War damage claims filed before

the Southern Claims Commission, 1871-1880.

Gary B. Mills

ISBN: 0-89412-047-6

AEGEAN PARK PRESS
P.O. Box 2837
Laguna Hills, California 92653
(714)586-8811

Manufactured in the United States of America

INTRODUCTION

Many conscientious Americans of the 1960's were disturbed by the outbreak of a protest movement against an unpopular war in which their nation was then involved. Surely, such opposition on the home front was believed by many persons to be "disloyal" and "demoralizing," as well as unprecedented in the course of American history.

But was it really unprecedented? The answer is no! It is perhaps surprising how few people are aware that in every war there have been at least two divergent viewpoints on both sides of the battle line. This has been true of every conflict in which the United States has been involved, from the American Revolution to the Vietnam Conflict. But, in many respects, the War Between the States, because of its very nature, serves as the quintessential example of divided loyalty.

In its eighth decade of existence, the United States was very definitely a divided nation, and not solely along geographical lines. Sectionalism was not only physical, it was also ideological; it was not only the North versus the South, but it also included Northerner versus Northerner and Southerner versus Southerner. Struggles between Piedmont and Tidewater, Black Belt and Mountains, Delta and Hills are interwoven throughout American history; and this on-going conflict came to a head in the course of the Civil War... especially in the South. Complicated by such other elements as economic, social, and even cultural differences, the Southern States between 1861 and 1865 were far from being a united Confederacy.

The myth of Southern Solidarity has been perpetuated by and large by two elements. There are traditional "flag wavers" or "die hards" who have considerable difficulty in seeing or appreciating more than one interpretation of historic "patriotism;" and there are those outside of the South who seek to analyze, interpret, and/or criticize the Southern States without fully understanding them. These outsiders are prone to simplify Southern society in order to explain it. This is unfortunate, however, because Southerners, like other segments of American society, are too complex to be lumped into neat little categories and assigned specific behavioral patterns.

In short, Southerners between 1861 and 1865 were not a steadfast legion of saintly patriots, fighting a noble, but losing war. There were many who opposed the Confederacy. The Confederate States of America, very simply, was a political union imposed upon men and women of different origins, different hearts, and different minds.

Those "Confederates" who did not support the ideals of the Confederacy were a cross-section of all economic, social, and racial segments of the society. There were some pro-Unionists who were wealthy planters and slave-owners; there were laborers who sincerely felt that the conflict was a "rich man's war and a poor man's fight"; there were free blacks who owned slaves themselves, but who were willing to forfeit this accumulated "property" in exchange for the equality which the Federal government seemed to promise. There were many Southerners who felt that the slave issue was the least important one at stake, an issue far less urgent than the need to preserve the new nation which many of their grandfathers had sacrificed their lives to establish.

In some areas of the South, the "loyal to the Union" Southerners were even in the majority. North Alabama, for example, not only opposed secession but reputedly tried to form the free states of Winston and Nickajack. In East Tennessee, in western Virginia (now West Virginia), and along the Red River of Louisiana, the populace voted strongly against secession, and these areas continued to be "hot beds of Union activity" throughout the war.

Those "loyal to the Union" Southerners who resided in areas that were predominantly secessionist in sympathy were in a tenuous position. Most of the pro-Unionists were forced to fall into line with their neighbors in support of the Confederacy, even prior to the outbreak of hostilities. A few fled the South, leaving property behind. Others tried to co-exist without making an issue of their loyalty.

A small but surprising number of Southerners were openly Unionist in sentiment, yet remained unharmed — probably because of their forceful personalities or their long-term community standing. Perhaps this phenomenon has been best explained by the contemporary Georgia senator, Ben Hill. Such outspoken Unionists, Hill pointed out, were often able to resist conformity because "everybody knew from their character that they would not be treacherous; that is, they would not subject themselves to criminal prosecution for infidelity to the Confederate Government."[1]

The Union invasion of the South served to create still more problems for the pro-Union Southerners. Federal troops were not able to distinguish between pro-Union and anti-Union Southerners. Much property was officially and unofficially confiscated for use by the federal forces, and much more was wantonly destroyed. Union officers sometimes paid for supplies or animals taken from Southerners who professed loyalty to the Union. More often, however, only receipts were given and promises made that at the close of the war the Federal Government would make appropriate restitution. In the meanwhile, the Union sympathizers suffered just as heavily at the hands of the Union Army as did their Confederate neighbors.

It was not until March 3, 1871, that Congress enacted legislation which opened official channels through which pro-Union Southerners could apply for reimbursement of their losses. Congress had already, seven years before, in fact, passed an enabling act for repayments to "loyal citizens in states not in rebellion," and this earlier act set an undeniable precedent which Southerners used to support their demands for reimbursement. Yet, lingering hostilities of Northerners for Southerners in general and a power struggle between Southern Radicals and Moderate Democrats delayed the extension of justice to those "loyal to the Union" Southerners who had braved the antipathy of their "rebel" neighbors and who were still suffering from the losses inflicted upon them by the Union that they had supported.

The Southern Claims Commission, a three-man board, was finally authorized by Congress on March 3, 1871. Its purpose, explicitly, was to consider the war claims of loyalists who resided in states which had been "proclaimed as in insurrection against the United States." According to the terms of the original act, reparations were to be considered for those commissary and quartermaster goods taken by or supplied to the United States Army; and a special act passed the following year (May 11, 1872) extended coverage of goods taken by the United States Navy.

---

[1] Frank W. Klingberg, The Southern Claims Commission (Berkeley: University of California Press, 1955), 13-14.

The response from Southern "pro-Unionists" was overwhelming. Some 22,298 cases were filed by individuals, family groups, churches, and businesses. The total amount of damages that were claimed was staggering: $60,258,150. The original enabling act had allowed two years for the adjudication of the claims. The deadline, however, was extended at intervals, until March, 1880. Ultimately, only 7,092 claims, amounting to $4,636,929.69, were able to withstand the intense, minute, and often absurdly rigid, investigation and qualifying tests that were administered.

Basically, the 22,298 war claims can be grouped under the following four classifications:

(1) Property destroyed out of military necessity. Such claims were disallowed as being "the fortunes of a war for the public defense."

(2) Goods officially contracted for by the Federal Government. In these cases the various departments who had contracted for the goods were authorized to pay the claims.

(3) Stores and supplies officially taken or furnished "on the spot" for the Union war effort. These claims were based on agreements, both verbal and written, between civilians and Federal officers. The legality of the claims were questioned extensively and it eventually took another act of Congress to straighten out the problems involved.

(4) Losses occasioned by unofficial acts taken by Union troops, i.e., destruction of homes and other buildings, theft of personal belongings, and so forth, that were not included among ordinary Commissary or Quartermaster supplies. Such losses were categorized as "pillage by unauthorized soldiers" and no damages were paid. Eventually, disallowed claims for some of these losses were refiled with the United States House of Representatives' Court of Claims where some were allowed and some were not.

The adjudication of these 22,298 claims created a vast store of historical data that is now on file in the National Archives in Washington, D.C. Aside from a general monograph prepared some two decades ago by Frank W. Klingberg, these records have been by and large neglected by the very people to whom they would be the most service.

The documents filed in these 22,298 claims, and the testimony given by some 220,000 witnesses, are of tremendous value to family historians; and, in the case of estates, where the original pro-Unionist died after the loss was incurred, but prior to the settlement of the claim, the degree of supporting genealogical material is even greater. In order to prove their relationships, as well as their rights to share in the claims, legal heirs filed such documents as wills, birth records, and lists of children and other family members. All claimants filed sundry, and often extensive, material relating to their activities during the war and to the effect of the war upon them and their families. There are household inventories, travelogues, military records, family letters, and personal descriptions, all routinely filed in these claims.

The testimonies of witnesses often were even more revealing. As part of the case proceedings, "knowledgeable parties," both friends and enemies, employers and employees, and even former slaves, were sought out and asked to testify as to the loyalty of claimants and their family members as to the circumstances and events surrounding the loss of property or the extent of property, and as to the degree and cause of their interest in the claim or of the interest of others (i.e., family ties, business relationships, etc.).

The index which follows is an index to claimants only. Family historians would do well to search not only for the names of specific ancestors who are believed to have supported the Union, but also for the names of other family members, even in-laws, who might have filed a claim as administrator of that ancestor's estate. Indeed, so much information was so often given on neighbors, friends, community leaders, local politicians, and even enemies, that a family researcher would do well to examine as many of the files within a particular community as he finds possible. For example, descendents of the Rapides Parish, Louisiana, family of Bynum will find vital family information in the case of a non-relative, General William Bailey; and this is information no longer available elsewhere, since public records of that parish were destroyed by fire in the course of the Civil War.

For the professional historian, the files of the Southern Claims Commission offer a wide variety of material that to date has only superficially been investigated and utilized. The documents frequently reflect upon politics, especially political struggles within the states over secession and reconstruction. There is considerable treatment of slave life and welfare: new material appears concerning slave housing, slave ownership of property, and slave relations with their white or black master appear frequently in claims not only filed by whites (for or against whom the freedmen were testifying), but also in claims filed by ex-slaves themselves for property they owned while still in bondage. Quite a few of the claimants were free Negroes or free people of color in the antebellum era, and their files are a rich source of data that has not yet been fully explored by black historians.

The yield is somewhat lower for the historians who focus exclusively upon the military, but there are still few such historians who would not glean significant new data from the use of these "claim" files. Most of the Southern Claims Commission cases provide behind-the-scenes material on units, commanders, encampments, advances and retreats, forages, and personal insights into relationships between the citizenry and the military. Testimonies by various officers, often key officers, for example, might be of considerable value and use to their biographers.

It must, however, be kept in mind, particularly by those who are involved in researching individual claimants, that the use of these records must be tempered by a realization that the claimants had something very important at stake: MONEY. While many of the claimants were basically honest and set forth their claim in a manner they felt just, there were still extenuating factors that might have affected the claim filed. The American judicial system, for example, had already established the precedent of "compromising" in damage claim cases; consequently, it would have been a naïve claimant who did not adjust his losses upward in anticipation of that compromise.

Moreover, there were many Southerners who had suffered heavily at the hands of both opposing armies. The Confederacy was now defunct and could not reimburse them, but the Union would. Many of these Southerners were staunch Confederates who felt that the Union justly owed them much, if not for anything else than the lost slaves and the hardships and deprivations of war. Since the Union was not paying for these items, some Southerners rephrased their losses into commodities that the Union would consider paying for; and they justified their misrepresentations on the premise that the Union had been, still was, and ever would be their enemy. In some of the claims on file such fraud is clearly apparent.

For further detail on the scope of material available and where it can be found, the researcher is referred to three sources: Frank W. Klingberg's The Southern Claims Commission (previously cited) which is an excellent scholarly study of the Commission and its activities; Pamphlet Describing M87 (Washington, D.C.: The National Archives, 1972) lists various groups of the records that are now available from the archives on microfilm; and Donald M. Zahn's "Special Report on Records Pertaining to the Southern Claims Commission," which was compiled in June 1955 for the Archives, but has not yet been published, though a photocopy can be ordered by researchers who will find it to be of tremendous help in using Archives files.

The general observations made in this introduction are based, in part, on a study of the three above-named works, and in part on a detailed personal examination of several thousand of the claim files themselves. The compiler of the accompanying index has found that the index has been of tremendous value in leading to documents which have greatly assisted him in preparing several books and articles on Southern history; and it is hoped that the publication of this index will assist other students of history to find valuable new sources of information concerning the Civil War era.

The accompanying index has been carefully reconstructed from two primary sources: (1) National Archives Microfilm Publication 87, Roll 13, Geographical List of Claimants; and (2) Annual Report of the Commissioner of Claims, House Miscellaneous Documents, 42d Congress, 2nd Session, and 46th Congress, 2nd Session (Washington, D.C., 1871-1880).

It must be noted that a number of discrepancies or variations in the spelling of names appear in these two sources. The compiler has used the most frequent or most logical spelling of each name. Researchers are urged to check all possible variant spellings, and should bear in mind that the "county" given for each claimant is not necessarily the county in which the claimant may have resided; occasionally the identifying county used for the claim file was the county in which the loss occurred.

It must also be noted that one page of the M87 list of Cherokee County, Alabama claimants has somehow been lost through the years. An attempt has been made to identify the "lost" claimants through the Annual Reports, but the format of the reports do not permit identification without some element of doubt. Consequently, "Cherokee?" appears after some of the claims in Alabama, indicating that these claimants probably, but not conclusively resided or suffered a loss in Cherokee County.

Researchers will also discover that in some states there are one or more counties listed that do not appear on modern maps. In some cases, the names of counties have undergone a change. In other cases, this researcher has not been able to determine that counties by those names ever existed. Two possible explanations exist: either those counties have been "forgotten" by history or else a government clerk erred in recording the name of the county. He might have recorded, for example, the town in which the claimant resided, rather than the <u>county</u>. In any case, such entries have been left "as is," since this might provide a more exact clue than would the editor's speculation.

Microfilm or photocopies of any desired claim(s) can be ordered at a nominal fee from the National Archives. Although the various claims are somewhat scattered in several division files of the Archives (i.e., Record Group 56, Records of the Treasury; RG 233, Records of the U.S. House of Representatives; RG 217, records of the U.S. Court of Claims), an inquiry directed to the Legislative, Judicial and Fiscal Branch of the Archives, citing RG 56, would be the most expeditious. The researcher should also provide the name of the claimant, as it appears in this index, the state and county given for the claimant, and the specific claim number.

GBM

INDEX

ALABAMA

Case Number	Name of Claimant	County
3,184	Aaron, Sam	*Cherokee?
9,095	Abbott, Hill	Walker
7,829	Abernathy, David W.	Jefferson
4,806	Abernathy, Mial S.	Limestone
5,802	Abernathy, Miles J.	Fayette
777	Abney, William T.	Cleburne
6,802	Acker, Lucy C.	Cherokee
11,119	Adams, Charles	Colbert
9,821	Adams, David	Lauderdale
12,969	Adams, Mila	Jefferson
2,274	Adare, John B.	Madison
2,164	Addison, Marian M.	Winston
4,085	Adkins, James	Jackson
8,335	Aikins (Akins), Nathan B.	Jefferson
7,363	Alberti, Ernestine	Cherokee?
4,805	Albright, Jacob	Cherokee?
21,244	Alexander, James M.	Macon
3,959	Alexander, John, Estate of	Colbert
3,958	Alexander, John F.	Colbert
9,365	Alexander, Price M. & Widow Susan	Lauderdale
989	Alexander, Thos. J.	Lawrence
193	Alexander, William R.	Colbert
19,878	Alexander, Woodruff W.	Madison
6,241	Alford, John	St. Clair
783	Allbright, Jacob	Cleburne
781	Allbright, William H.	Cleburne
9,446	Allen, Asa F.	Limestone
11,424	Allen, Henry D.	Lauderdale
19,213	Allen, Isaac	Limestone
15,443	Allen, Lindsey	Franklin
5,803	Allen, Nelson	Lauderdale
13,106	Allen, Robert	Lawrence
17,287	Allen Sarah	Tallapoosa
4,086	Allen, Simeon F.	Jackson
8,715	Allen, William	Jackson
5,406	Allington, Thomas C.	Lauderdale
1,650	Allison, James L.	Jackson
19,869	Allison, John	Madison
20,979	Almour, Caroline *et al*	Mobile
20,146	Alsobrooks, William B., Estate of (Abner W. Ligon, Adm.)	Colbert
2,337	Alvis, Elizabeth	Walker
20,119	Alvis, F.N.	Fayette
6,891	Amberson, John D.	Blount
7,531	Amerson, Young R.	Fayette
21,941	Amos, Ada E.	Conecuh
8,248	Anderson, Albert G.	Colbert
1,755	Anderson, Frederick H.	Franklin
7,532	Anderson, Catharine, Adm. of Est. of Horatio Anderson	Jackson
2,307	Anderson, Jane	Monroe
6,851	Anderson, John C., Estate (Jacob W. Whorton, Adm.)	Cherokee?
5,405	Anderson, William	Colbert
9,447	Anderton, C.C.	Lawrence
16,343	Anderton, William P.	Morgan
5,612	Andrews, James T. (or P.)	Limestone
14,451	Angle, Malinda	Cherokee
14,449	Angle, Permelia	Cherokee
14,450	Angle, Rebecca	Tuscaloosa
11,881	Appling, Francis B.	Tuscaloosa
9,843	Appling, Richard	Tuscaloosa
3,184	Aran, Samuel	Walker
8,247	Armistead, Vincent	Lauderdale
3,957	Armistead, Woodson	Lauderdale
11,606	Armstrong, James Estate of	Cherokee?
19,870	Armstrong, James H., Administrator of Estate of Wilson Turbyfill	Madison
5,604	Armstrong, James S.	Winston
4,192	Armstrong, Lorenzo D.	Marshall
6,700	Arnold, Jeremiah	Jackson
3,108	Arthur, Hamilton F.	Limestone
20,836	Asforth, Caroline T.	Limestone
5,251	Ashcraft, Thos.	Walker
20,944	Asher, Montgomery P.	Lauderdale
6,011	Ashford, Harriet	Lawrence
16,931	Ashley, Benjamin F.	St. Clair
7,195	Ashley, Jane	Cherokee
7,196	Ashley, Robinson	Cherokee
5,801	Atchly, William	Madison
6,788	Atkins, Madison	Cherokee
12,374	Atkinson, Caroline H.	Colbert
17,075	Attaway, Isiah	Macon
6,803	Austell, Meredith T.	Jackson
6,888	Austin, John H.	Morgan
1,343: 1,346: 1,348:	Austin, William A., Estate of (Thos. G. Rucker, Adm.)	Jackson
13,105	Auten, John	Colbert
8,386	Bagley, Minas	Jefferson
7,198	Bagwell, Littleberry	Cherokee?
6,085	Bagwell, Wiley G.	Tuscaloosa
13,825	Baily, John T.	Cherokee
6,676	Bain, Richard C.	Cherokee
5,805	Baker, Alvin R.	Walker
10,506	Baker, Hetta Ann	Walker
6,804	Baker, James	Cherokee
6,086	Baker, James	Tuscaloosa
11,526	Baker, James C.	Tuscaloosa
6,671	Baker, Joseph	Cherokee
5,806	Baker, Joseph	Walker
3,555	Baker, Thomas B.	Jackson
18,694	Baker, Thomas W.	Marion
6,790	Baker, William	Cherokee
6,482	Baker, William	Walker
14,955	Balch, Hezekiah	Madison
3,111	Ballinger, Claborne C.	Walker
3,109	Ballinger, William M.	Walker
16,067	Barclay, William	Madison
12,970	Barclift, Joseph C.	Blount
599	Barden, Earl D.	Jackson
5,509	Barksdale, Alfred S.	De Kalb
4,811	Barksdale, Thomas M.	Limestone
2,309	Barlow, Ann	Monroe
18,891	Barnard, Eliza	Cherokee
17,122	Barnes, Benj.	Dallas
5,605	Barnes, Ephraim	Winston
17,225	Barnes, Jasper N.	Dallas
4,195	Barnes, Jehu	De Kalb
4,194	Barnes, John	De Kalb
3,554	Barnes, Rebecca A.	Jackson
22,702	Barnett, Geo. W.	Lauderdale
3,536	Barriere, Maria	Jackson
2,165	Barton, Gifford M.	Winston
5,258	Barton, Hiram, I	Walker
5,256	Barton, Hiram, II	Walker
5,257	Barton, Hiram, III	Walker
2,166	Barton, James A.	Winston
13,567	Barton, Jane	Colbert
5,254	Barton, John M.	Walker
2,167	Barton, Jonathan	Winston
5,255	Barton, Moses	Walker
5,259	Barton, Nathaniel, Sr.	Walker
13,566	Barton, Pleasant B.	Colbert
2,168	Barton, Willis	Winston
18,928	Barrett, Charles	Frankin
12,226	Barrett, James	Colbert
5,804	Barron, John	Lauderdale
9,845	Bates, David F.	Limestone
8,342	Bates, Levi	Walker
7,963	Bates, Martha A.	Limestone

*See Introduction for explanatory note on Cherokee County claims.

7,092	Batson, Geo. W.	Jefferson
1,366	Battle, John W.	Lawrence
3,351	Battles, Caswell	St. Clair
14,452	Battles, Wm.	Cherokee
11,756	Batts, George W.	Limestone
4,081	Baugh, Richard B. *et al*	Lauderdale
7,089	Baugh, William	Lauderdale
3,116	Baugher, Woodward H.	Madison
2,310	Baulkman, Elizabeth	Monroe
6,506	Bean, Armistead, Estate of (Abner W. Ligon, Administrator)	Franklin
18,013	Bean, John W.	Morgan
20,864	Beard, Andrew, Estate of	Madison
4,095	Beard, John G.	Jackson
2,056	Beard, Nancy	Walker
2,169: 21,108:	Beard, William W.	Walker
12,946	Beasley, Elizabeth	Jefferson
6,247	Beason, Curtis G.	St. Clair
17,967	Beaty, William M.	St. Clair
21,109	Beaver, Mary & Henry R., Estate	Jackson
6,805	Beaver, Milla, Adm. of Estate of William Beaver	Jackson
9,882	Beckham, Anna	Lauderdale
9,824	Beckham, William	Lauderdale
9,096	Beckwith, Alfred	Lauderdale
1,753	Beckwith, Lewis	Lauderdale
12,947	Belcher, John	Jefferson
5,982	Bell, James H.	Cleburne
17,413	Bell, James M.C.	Dallas
7,962	Bell, James T.	Madison
776	Bell, John H.	Cleburne
19,474	Bellamy, David R., Adm. of Estate of John C. Tinney	Jackson
5,398	Belote, Joshua L.	Cherokee?
4,081	Benham, Vincent M. *et al*	Lauderdale
7,200	Bennett, Martha, Widow of Wm.	Cherokee?
7,201	Bennett, Martha A., Widow of Moses H.	Cherokee?
6,087	Bennett, Phoebe	Walker
4,024	Bennett, Wm. H.	Cherokee?
15,567	Bennett, William W.	Tuscaloosa
1,370	Bentford, David	Limestone
723	Benton, Joseph	Randolph
9,295	Berry, John H.	Madison
2,640	Berry, Rachel A.	Winston
10,544	Berry, Richard, Estate of	Cherokee?
3,560	Berry, William C.	Jackson
19,438	Best, Geo. M.	Cherokee?
19,780	Bevins, Robert	Jefferson
6,806	Bevis, James	Lauderdale
9,982	Bevis, Martha A.	Lauderdale
7,961	Bibb, Elizabeth C.	Madison
19,871	Bibb, Porter, Estate of	Limestone
21,355	Bibb, William J.	Montgomery
13,824	Biggers, Robert P.	Cherokee?
7,320	Biggs, Archibald	Monroe
7,319	Biggs, Sarah	Monroe
7,088	Binford, John H. (John L.), Anne H., Asa, Burton, & Henry N. and Ann Eliza Thorne, wife of R.G. Thorne	Limestone
6,756	Bird, Ezekiel	Cherokee?
6,249	Bishop, John H.	Cherokee?
2,648	Bishop, Sampson	Jackson
19,780	Bivins, James A., Adm. of Robert	Cherokee?
8,343	Black, John	Walker
8,716	Black, John W.	Jefferson
14,453	Black, P.T.F.	De Kalb
14,454	Black, P. Truett	De Kalb
5,253	Black, Samuel, Sen.	Walker
3,114	Blackburn, Andrew J.	Blount
19,982	Blackburn, Elizabeth	Perry
18,890	Blackburn, Jeremiah	Cherokee?
8,717	Blackburn, John	Lauderdale
3,961	Blackburn, Robert	Blount
6,635	Blackwell, Davidson	Walker
5,187	Blackwell, James M.	Walker
2,338	Blackwell, John P. & Margaret H.	Walker
20,120	Blackwell, Joshua	Winston
2,338	Blackwell, Margaret H. & John P.	Walker
17,042	Blake, Allen	Cleburne
16,066	Blake, Joseph	Dallas
7,197	Blakemore, Elizabeth	Cherokee?
6,696	Blakemore, Joseph	Cherokee?
5,510	Blancit, William A.	De Kalb
395	Blankenship, Jesse	Lawrence
3,110	Blanton, Isaac	Walker
2,313	Boatright, Ruffin	Monroe
17,530	Bodiford, Alexander, Estate of (Wm. Johnson, Adm.)	Crenshaw
12,480	Boggs, John B.	Lauderdale
12,479: 12,481:	Boggs, John B. and Mary A. Houston	Lauderdale
18,990	Bogus, Lewis	Madison
6,481	Bolt, Berry	Randolph
4,046	Bolton, James	Jackson
6,699: 7,953:	Bolton, Sevier	Jackson
21,107	Bonner, Fannie R.	Clay
21,106	Bonner, Thomas, Jr.	Clay
21,105	Bonner, Thomas, Sr.	Clay
6,682	Booker, Elizabeth	Cherokee?
6,760	Booker, Jefferson G.	Monroe
6,744	Booker, William B.	Monroe
6,742	Booker, Willis, Estate of (Wm. B. Booker, Adm.)	Mobile
4,907	Booth, Jeptha	Cherokee?
6,396	Borden, Nancy	Walker
779: 780:	Borden, John	Cherokee?
13,826	Boring, Isaac J.	Cherokee?
3,112	Boshell, Andrew J.	Walker
1,438	Boshell, John	Walker
6,088	Boshell, Mack M.	Walker
6,483	Boshell, Sarah E.	Walker
6,257	Boswell, Miles B.	St. Clair
18,289	Bostick, Mathew D.	Madison
8,985	Boteler, Thos.	Winston
5,511	Bouldin, Elijah	De Kalb
14,457	Bouldin, Reuben	De Kalb
3,352	Bowen, Catherine	Walker
19,475	Bowen, Wilkerson C.	Colbert
9,984	Bower, Luna	Jackson
8,088	Bowers, Lemuel	Cherokee?
10,244	Bowhannon, Mary J.	Madison
8,188	Bowman, John	Cherokee?
7,090	Boyce, Cyrus L.	Limestone
9,098	Boyd, T., Dr.	Walker
2,749	Bradford, Charles W.	Lauderdale
7,270	Bradley, Margaret	Walker
5,252	Brake, John	Walker
7,093	Brakefield, Robert	Walker
7,533	Branan, Daniel F.	Walker
11,458	Brandon, Jerry	Cherokee?
18,663	Brandon, Robert	Madison
11,458	Brandun, Jerry	Limestone
6,747	Brantley, Lucy	Monroe
2,308	Branton, Robert S.	Monroe
6,013	Braselton, Elizabeth A.	Tuscaloosa
1,765	Bratton, Alex	De Kalb
1,766	Bratton, Mary E.	De Kalb
21,968	Bray, Shadrack	De Kalb
14,459	Brazeal, Elias	Blount
6,807	Brewer, Chas B.	Jackson
6,485	Brewer, Christopher	Lauderdale
14,458	Brewer, Elizabeth	Cherokee?
17,075	Brewer, Wm. G., Adm. of Estate of Isaiah Attoway	Macon
10,659	Bridgeforth, James W.	Limestone
21,110	Bridgeforth, John W.	Limestone

5,287	Briggs, John W., Estate of (James McPeters, Adm.)	Lauderdale
5,188	Broach, William T.	Walker
2,749	Broadfoot, Chas. W.	Cherokee?
2,281	Brocker, Ernest C.	Cherokee?
22,015	Brooks, C.C., Estate of (Julia A. Fuller, Adm.)	Russell
6,798	Brooks, George	Marshall
4,342	Brooks, Rose C.	Cherokee?
4,808	Brooks, Samuel	Lauderdale
4,807	Brooks, William, Estate of	Lee
16,132	Brown, Andrew J.	Lawrence
20,837	Brown, George, Estate of	Marion
9,844	Brown, James	Blount
5,832	Brown, John, Estate of (Archer A. Snead, Adm.)	Madison
5,189	Brown, John, Sen.	Walker
20,979	Brown, John M., Caroline W. Almour & Matilda H. Johnson, Administrator of Wm. H. Johnson	Mobile
11,445	Brown, John U.	Macon
3,185	Brown, Lovey	Walker
4,809	Brown, Martha	Walker
3,537	Brown, William R.	Jackson
12,483	Bruce, Murphy	Limestone
3,960	Brumley, James, Adm. of Estate of Jos. Brumley	Lawrence
1,459	Brunston, Isaac	Marshall
9,097	Bruton, Marvil M.	Colbert
2,339	Bryan, Wallis M.	Walker
8,986	Bryant, Phoebe	Winston
6,808	Bryant, Thos. J.	Jackson
4,193	Bryant, William	Marshall
5,407	Buchanan, James M.	Jackson
13,009	Buchanan, Thomas F.	Colbert
6,757	Buffington, T.P.	Monroe
8,864	Bull, Dempsey D.	Lauderdale
9,448	Bull, Russell S.S.	Marion
5,512	Bullard, Henry H.	De Kalb
21,969	Bundren, James	De Kalb
19,235	Burford, Emily H.	Jefferson
12,971	Burford, James H.	Jefferson
7,091	Burford, Washington C.	Jefferson
7,535	Burgess, Benjamin	Franklin
19,473	Burgess, Jonathan M.	Jackson
4,081	Burham, V.M., Estate of (John Shaw Morrow, G.W. Evans, Richard B. Baugh and W.B. Wood, Administrators)	Lauderdale
7,087	Burkhead, Cornelius	Cherokee?
4,556	Burleson, Ann	Morgan
18,991	Burleson, John	Franklin
5,807	Burlison, Jackson	Limestone
5,864	Burnett, Lemuel	Marion
18,417	Burnett, Peyton	Fayette
20,121	Burnum, Simpson A.	Morgan
4,810	Burrow, George W.	Jackson
2,671	Burrow, Jasper	Franklin
5,804	Burrow, John	Cherokee?
9,983	Burrow, V., Dr.	Lauderdale
11,120	Burton, Cader	Walker
3,115	Burton, Peter S.	Walker
8,249	Busbee, James J.	Jackson
7,202	Busbin, Harriet A.	Cherokee?
9,158	Busby, Derrell	Jackson
987	Butler, Darius H.	Lauderdale
2,661	Butler, Henry W.	Lauderdale
3,113	Butler, John T.	Walker
21,717	Butler, Margaret	Shelby
6,014	Butler, Nancy A.	Marshall
22,003	Butler, William	Madison
5,260	Butt, William	Walker
16,932	Byers, Alemeth	St. Clair
13,948	Bynum, Oakley H.	Lawrence
6,484	Bynum, Oakley H., Guardian of Walter S. Sherrod	Lawrence
19,605	Bynum, Robert, Estate of (John P. Bynum, Adm.)	Jackson

14,648	Bynum, Sandy	Madison
2,311	Byrd, Arthur P.	Monroe
722	Byrd, Bolling, Estate of (Samuel T. Torian, Adm.)	Lawrence
7,534	Byrd, Eli	De Kalb
6,756	Byrd, Ezekial	Monroe
1,367	Byrd, Martha	Lawrence
2,312	Byrd, Stephen, Sen.	Monroe
9,007	Cabbell, Moses	Dallas
2,170	Cagle, Aleas	Winston
2,225	Cagle, Benj. A.	Winston
2,171	Cagle, Ephraim	Winston
555	Cagle, John F.	Winston
2,172	Cagle, Loyd H.	Winston
15,659	Cagle, Valentine	Jackson
7,207	Cahoon, Lucy A.	Cherokee?
21,743	Cain, Carolina A.	Monroe
13,472	Cain, William L.	Etowah
12,949	Caldwell, Alexander	Jefferson
3,980	Caldwell, David K., Adm. of Estate of Benj. Snodgrass	Jackson
18,667	Calhoun, Frederick	Madison
18,668	Calhoun, Sandy	Madison
18,669	Calhoun, Tazewell	Madison
6,258	Callan, James A.	Cherokee?
21,117	Callen, William L.	Shelby
3,117	Calvert, Robt.	Winston
21,118	Camak, Moses	Walker
1,347	Cameron, Daniel	Jackson
19,593	Cameron, Elizabeth	Cherokee?
11,527	Campbell, Adam	Walker
5,515	Campbell, Eli A.	Cherokee?
18,180	Campbell, Emeline S.	Montgomery
16,907	Campbell, Geo. M.	Dallas
2,756	Campbell, Geo. W.	Madison
20,122	Campbell, Isaac	Jackson
20,840	Campbell, James, Estate (Wm. W. Campbell, Adm.)	Jackson
13,107	Campbell, James F.	Randolph
9,449	Campbell, John R.	Walker
2,396	Campbell, Leroy P.	Madison
14,460	Campbell, M.G.J.	Cherokee?
12,972	Campbell, Thomas	Jefferson
9,533	Camron, William J.	Franklin
1,756	Canian, James B. & Mary E. Darwin	Madison
21,114	Cannon, Jabez, Estate of	Lauderdale
1,148	Cannon, James M.	Lauderdale
18,014	Cantrell, Dennis C.	Winston
6,486	Capehart, Thomas A.	Jackson
21,116	Card, Elizabeth A.	Jackson
14,503	Carden, Christopher C., Estate (John G. Winston, Exec.)	De Kalb
3,468	Cardin, Leonard W.	Jackson
13,285	Cargile, James	Jackson
1,651	Cargile, Jesse	Jackson
3,538	Cargile, Lewis	Jackson
3,539: 291:	Cargile, Plesant	Jackson
17,149	Carlisle, Robt., Estate of (Moody H. May, Adm.)	Dallas
4,467	Carmichael, Alex	Madison
12,973	Carmichael, James F.	Jefferson
5,808	Carpenter, John C.	Madison
21,994	Carpenter, John R.	Greene
11,605	Carpenter, Walter O.	Madison
6,811	Carr, Ann	Cherokee?
8,719	Carr, Ann	Lauderdale
7,204	Carr, Melville B.	Cherokee?
8,251	Carrithers, John	Colbert
15,568	Carroll, Christopher C.	Tuscaloosa
15,569	Carroll, Daniel	Tuscaloosa
2,641	Carroll, Thos.	Winston
18,666	Carter, Benj.	Madison
12,375	Carter, Charles W.	Colbert
5,616	Carter, David H.	Montgomery
20,279	Carter, Jane R.	Jackson
3,861	Carter, J.H.	Colbert
12,376	Carter, Mary Roberta	Colbert

4,815	Casey, Robert	Lauderdale
17,231	Castle, Berry (or Benj.)	Jackson
13,839	Cavin, John	Cherokee
19,872	Cawthorn, Marius B.	Madison
18,589	Chadrick, Isaac	De Kalb
18,993	Chambers, Jonathan	Franklin
21,115	Chanlder, Elijah G.	Lauderdale
1,760	Chandler, Garret S.	Lauderdale
7,203	Chandler, Milton	Cherokee?
5,337	Chandler, Nicholas	Cherokee?
2,280	Chandler, William R.	Madison
4,814	Chaney, John	De Kalb
19,783	Chapman, James	Jefferson
7,205	Chapman, Sarah	Cherokee?
6,743	Chapman, Wm. R.	Monroe
12,033	Chappell, E. P.	Mobile
2,642	Cheatham, Wyatt D.	Walker
192	Cheek, Randal, Estate of	Lowndes
6,680	Chesnut, Jonathan	Cherokee?
9,099	Childers, Lewis	Walker
9,100	Childers, Nelly	Walker
3,789	Childress, John, William *et al*	Baldwin
6,769	Childs, Willis	Monroe
14,461	Chisolm, Patrick J.	Cherokee?
6,089	Christian, Thos. A.	Walker
9,145	Christian, W.H.	Jackson
5,645	Clardy, Pendleton	Morgan
2,340	Clark, James W.	Walker
5,613	Clark, Joseph A.	Madison
2,341	Clark, Mary A.	Walker
19,476	Clarke, Joseph S.	Jackson
14,903	Clarke, James S., Adm. of Robt. M.	Lawrence
6,809	Clarke, Robert A.	Cherokee?
8,727	Clay, Philip	Lawrence & Limestone
5,514	Clayton, Charles A.	Etowah
6,235	Clayton, Solomon H.	Etowah
5,409	Cleere, David	Cherokee?
18,701	Clem, Anderson A.	Limestone
16,848	Clem, Joseph M.	Limestone
6,017	Clements, Gabriel, Estate of	Tuscaloosa
5,656	Clemmons, Mary A.	Lauderdale
2,284	Clemmons, William M.	Pickens
2,124	Clendenin, James	Jackson
7,094	Click, Susan	Jefferson
6,785	Clifton, Lovin A.	Cherokee?
25,614	Cloud, James M.	Jackson
16,371	Cloud, Jerry T.	Macon
5,409	Clure, David	Franklin
2,283	Coady, James A.	Pickens
1,342	Coates, Minerva	Jackson
3,531	Coats, J.T.	Jackson
5,070	Cobb, Bryant	Madison
20,123	Cobb, Christopher C.	Jackson
6,749	Cobb, John W.	Conecuh
5,071	Cobb, W.R.W., Estate (Bryant Cobb, Adm.)	Madison
21,672	Cocks, David	Walker
1,349	Coffee, Rice A.	Jackson
7,965	Coffee, Webb	Lauderdale
4,816	Coffey, Absalom	Jackson
6,810	Coffman, James D.	Limestone
3,353	Cohen, Philip	Dallas
6,758	Coker, Tabetha	Monroe
19,782	Coker, Thompson H.	Monroe
12,329	Cole, Alice	Calhoun
18,376	Cole, Rachel R.	De Kalb
9,807	Cole, Robert	Butler
8,150	Cole, Sophia	Watson
20,144	Coleman, Daniel & Heirs Elizabeth L & James L. Coleman	Limestone
19,606	Coleman, Elizabeth L.	Limestone
19,663	Coleman, James L.	Chambers
5,809	Coleman, Stephen	Lauderdale
1,653	Coley, William	Jackson
8,250	Collier, Scipio	Lauderdale
5,517	Collins, Alfred	De Kalb
6,015	Collins, David A.	Tuscaloosa
1,879	Coman, James L.	Limestone
20,841	Coman, Joshua P.	Limestone
6,787	Comer, Charles A.	Cherokee?
6,773	Comer, Nancy C.	Cherokee?
7,209	Compton, Eli	Cherokee?
401	Commons, Joseph	Madison
15,481	Congleton, Luke	Conecuh
19,566	Conley, Morris J., Estate of	Montgomery
5,810	Conn, James	Walker
8,720	Conner, John A.	Jefferson
21,671	Cook, Goe. W.	Fayette
14,462	Cook, Mathis	Cherokee?
3,118	Cooner, Samuel E.	Walker
18,665	Cooper, Haywood	Madison
5,518	Cooper, James	De Kalb
1,762	Cooper, John	Lauderdale
14,463	Copeland, James	Cherokee?
20,839	Copeland, James	Madison
5,617	Copeland, Reuben	Franklin
5,190	Copeland, Washington	Walker
7,830	Cordel, Jackson	Walker
6,260	Cordell, Susannah	De Kalb
9,985	Corum, Lemuel	Lauderdale
7,964	Cosby, John W.	Madison
7,966	Cosby, William J.	Madison
12,220	Cossler, A.M.	Mobile
7,208	Cothran, John A.	Cherokee?
3,571	Coulson, Henry H.	Jackson
1,884	Coulson, Jacob	Jackson
3,573	Coulson, W.C.	Jackson
852	Cowan, Elizabeth	Jackson
3,540	Cowan, Malinda	Cherokee?
12,948	Coward, George	Jefferson
7,687	Cowen, Sarah L.	Blount
19,802	Cowles, George	Cherokee?
18,992	Cox, James B.	Limestone
8,478	Cox, Larkin M.	Cherokee?
5,513	Crabtree, Warren	De Kalb
18,695	Craig, Miles S., Estate (Reuben Craig, Adm.)	Limestone
6,487	Craig, William K.	Colbert
7,381	Crain, James	Cherokee?
8,189	Crane, Clarissa	Cherokee
8,345	Cranford, Chesley H.	Walker
7,206	Crawford, Frances J.	Cherokee?
5,399	Crawford, Jesse F.	Cherokee?
18,474	Crawford, Peter A.	Limestone
19,781	Crawford, William G., Estate of	Macon
1,759	Creamer, G.W.	Cherokee?
17,043	Crider, David V.	Cleburne
11,604	Criner, Isaac	Madison
4,812	Crittenden, Moses H.	Lauderdale
1,759	Cromer, Geo. W.	Colbert
10,202	Cromer, Philip	Cherokee?
3,541	Cross, Clark	Jackson
4,047	Cross, George	Jackson
4,049	Cross, Mary A.	Jackson
4,050	Cross, Melinda	Jackson
3,532	Cross, Sandifer	Jackson
4,048	Cross, Wiley	Jackson
18,664	Crow, David	Madison
5,615	Crow, David M.	Morgan
5,408	Crow, John	Lee
19,477	Crow, Washington D.	De Kalb
11,882	Crump, William M.	Tuscaloosa
21,113	Crutcher, Mary R.	Limestone
7,555	Culbert, Matthew, Estate of (Elizabeth A. Wright, Adm.)	Marshall
11,528	Cummings, John H.	Tuscaloosa
13,742	Cunningham, Ebenezer	Cherokee?
9,818	Cunningham, P.H.	Lauderdale
2,281	Curtin, Lewis, Estate of	Lawrence
557	Curtis, Benj. F.	Winston
10,339	Curtiss, William V.	Winston
19,983	Dana, Miles	Limestone
20,866	Dandrige, John T., Estate of & Octavius A. Van Hook, Guardian of Dandrige Infant	Lawrence

3,962	Danforth, James	Cherokee?
5,191	Danforth, William	Limestone
14,464	Daniel, Cynthia	Cherokee?
14,958	Daniel, Daniel	Madison
14,957	Daniel, Jackson	Madison
14,465	Daniel, Leonard F.	Cherokee?
17,529	Daniel, William J.	Crenshaw
1,752	Danley, William	Lauderdale
1,756	Darwin, Mary E. & Jas. B. Canian	Madison
16,368	Daugherty, Mary	Macon
17,018: 18,590:	Davenport, Arthur	De Kalb
4,196	Davenport, Joseph	De Kalb
20,145	Davenport, Orville J.	De Kalb
16,933	Davenport, Rodophus R., Estate	De Kalb
5,192	David, Dempsey	Limestone
6,248	Davidson, Elizabeth	De Kalb
6,253	Davidson, Francis M.	De Kalb
8,865	Davidson, Nora	Colbert
16,867	Davidson, Wm. C.	Jackson
8,344	Davis, Anna	Walker
12,522	Davis, Daniel	Walker
19,066	Davis, David M.	Cherokee?
14,649	Davis, Dennis	Colbert
6,090	Davis, George	Walker
3,122	Davis, Henry	Madison
10,035	Davis, James	Cherokee?
7,967	Davis, James B.	Limestone
2,493	Davis, Joseph H., Jr.	Randolph
2,059	Davis, Lucinda A.	Morgan
12,093	Davis, Mary A.V.	Randolph
3,120	Davis, Richard S.	Winston
11,630	Davis, Van Buren T.	Walker
2,342	Davis, William L.	Walker
18,586	Dawson, Henry	Jackson
19,784	Dawson, Jack	Limestone
18,015	Dawson, James J.	Limestone
3,119	Day, William B.	Walker
17,077	Dean, Maria	Bibb
18,786	Dean, Mary Eliza	Mobile
4,341	Dearing, Mary Ann	Cherokee?
5,619	De Arman, John A., Estate, & Newton B.	Calhoun
18,762	Deason, Absalom	Tuscaloosa
984	DeGraffenried, Mary	Lawrence
8,190	Dendy, Joel	Cherokee?
20,939	Dennis, Joel	Lauderdale
11,121	Dennis, Robert	Shelby
14,956	Denton, William	Franklin
5,621	Derrick, David	Jackson
5,620	Derrick, Sarah	Jackson
6,741	Devane, Felix	Monroe
6,488	Devaney, Alfred	Franklin
19,236	Deviney, Samuel A.	Colbert
17,076	Dexter, Emeline	Bibb
5,865	Dickinson, John J.	Marion
9,450	Dickinson, Wiley R.	Marion
3,354	Dill, Joseph	St. Clair
15,471	Dill, Uriah	Franklin
6,019	Dillard, Elizabeth	Jackson
20,078	Dillard, Francis W., Heirs of	Lee
5,622	Dillworth, Nancy	Cherokee
2,053	Dobbs, Eliza	De Kalb
7,211	Dockray, Ephraim	Cherokee?
12,292	Dodd, Mary	Winston
3,081	Dodd, Wiley	Winston
2,173	Dodd, William, Sr.	Winston
17,325	Dodd, William, Jr.	Winston
6,812	Dolberry, Absalom	Jackson
18,475	Donald, Jackson, Estate of	Limestone
16,934	Donivan, Martin	Jackson
3,356	Donley, James L.	Colbert
7,382	Dorsey, James R.	Cherokee?
20,871	Dorsey, Rebecca E.	Jackson
16,368	Dougherty, Mary	Cherokee?
6,018	Doughty, Mordecai F., Estate	Tuscaloosa

15,570	Dowdle, Sarah S., Widow of James	Tuscaloosa
7,212	Downey, James M.	Cherokee?
13,754	Downey, Peter, Estate of (Wm. C. Eubanks, Adm.)	Jefferson
16,844	Doyle, John M., Adm. of Estate of Eber S. Gossett	Blount
5,812	Drain, Nancy A.	Jackson
13,089	Drake, John	Marion
13,827	Drake, John C.	Cherokee?
9,846	Draper, John B., Estate of (Geo. H. Draper, Executor)	Jefferson
12,950	Draper, Philip M.	Jefferson
19,478	Draper, William E.	Morgan
20,280	Drennon, Walter B., Estate of (Daniel D. Drennon, Adm.)	Walker
8,122	Drew, Amelia A.	Monroe
13,502: 13,534:	Drew, Wm.	Cherokee?
3,121	Drummond, Freeman R.	Walker
5,811	Dublin, Elanor	Madison
6,020	Dublin, Wesley M.	Madison
20,110	Dulaney, William	Jackson
10,815	Dunken, Samuel W.	Chambers
9,101	Dunlary, Braxton	Walker
12,974	Dunn, Ann	Blount
4,817	Dunn, Henry	Lauderdale
6,093: 20,126:	Dunn, James T.	Tuscaloosa
2,332	Dunn, Nancy	Lauderdale
20,125	Dunn, Thos. D. (or T.)	Tuscaloosa
9,760	Dupree, John N.	Lauderdale
2,752	Dupree, William M.	Madison
2,393	Durando, Edward P.	Madison
7,095	Durham, Osborn	De Kalb
3,186	Dutton, James	Walker
2,060	Dutton, William	Walker
7,096	Dutton, William M.	De Kalb
6,092	Earnest, Burrell	Walker
3,123	Easley, Pleasant E.	Walker
18,995	Eason, Henry	Madison
18,994	Eason, Jeff	Madison
12,951	Eastis, Daniel	Jefferson
6,490	Eaves, Margaret	Limestone
8,389	Echols, John	Jefferson
8,387	Echols, John W.	Jefferson
8,388	Echols, Louisa A.	Jefferson
3,675	Eddins, Christiana	Monroe
9,451	Edgar, James	Marion
1,350	Edwards, Daniel (or David)	Jackson
1,345	Edwards, David	Jackson
1,344	Edwards, David, & Nathaniel A. Johnson	Jackson
5,421	Edwards, Henderson	Lauderdale
14,467	Edwards, James	Cherokee or De Kalb
14,466	Edwards, John	De Kalb
9,847	Edwards, John	Morgan
3,543	Edwards, Sarah	Jackson
5,813	Eldridge, Jno. R.B.	Madison
6,022	Elkins, Nancy K.	Jackson
18,016	Elkins, William G.	Colbert
7,097	Ellard, John	Jefferson
7,213	Ellenburg, Alex E.	Cherokee?
16,358	Ellenburg, James J.	Cherokee?
16,357	Ellenburgh, Deborah A.	Cherokee?
18,670	Ellett, Malinda	Madison
18,388	Ellington, John M.	Macon
11,842	Elliott, Lindsey F.	Shelby
4,306	Elliott, Patrick B.	Cherokee?
6,091	Ellis, James	Walker
9,374	Ellis, James S.	Lauderdale
20,127	Ellis, Richard	Winston
9,376	Ellis, Templeton E.	Lauderdale
2,061	Ellis, William	Walker
9,814	Emerson, Martha Jane	Lauderdale
2,645	England, Tilman	Lauderdale
6,869	English, John	Cleburne
16,908	English, Sarah A.	Dallas

6,021	Espey, Thomas	Walker
14,959	Esslinger, Andrew J.	Madison
21,229	Eudy, Ishmael	Marshall
20,112	Evans, Ellen	Jackson
4,081	Evans, George W. *et al*	Lauderdale
6,491	Evans, Thomas	Franklin
1,120	Evins, Claiborne	Jackson
14,468	Ewing, Rhoda	Cherokee?
2,017	Farmer, William H.	Lauderdale
12,952	Farrington, Willis A.	Jefferson
10,034	Farrow, Elihu	Cherokee?
6,093	Faught, James A.	Walker
2,062	Faught, J.J.	Walker
2,063	Faught, Nancy	Walker
6,024	Faught, Sarah E.	Tuscaloosa
6,816	Faulkner, James H.	Limestone
2,314	Feagin, John W.	Monroe
2,315	Feagin, T. E.	Monroe
21,232	Feemster, John B.	Cherokee?
21,233	Fellows, Wm. H., Guardian of Sally A. & Wm. Fair Jones	Dallas
20,128	Feltman, Isham B.	Winston
20,281	Fennell, Francis M., Estate of (Isabella Fennell, Exec.)	Jackson
2,343	Fergerson, Joseph	Walker
6,813	Ferguson, Aquilla	Cherokee?
11,118	Ferguson, Henry	Walker
8,346	Ferguson, Henry, Sen.	Walker
3,187	Ferguson, Mary	Walker
22,107	Ferris, Amand L.	Madison
17,123	Fielder, Anderson	Colbert
14,416	Fielding, N.R.	Morgan
8,390	Fields, Nancy M.	Jefferson
8,391	Fields, William C.	Jefferson
11,631	Files, Jeremiah F.	Fayette
6,492	Files, Richard	Walker
10,349	Files, Richard, Adm. of Louisa C. Stevenson	Walker
7,537	Files, Thos. B.	Winston
5,261	Filkins, John M.	Walker
2,651	Findley, John B.	Marshall
4,818	Finley, James	Limestone
21,348	Fiquet, William	Dallas
6,815	Firestone, Wm.	Cherokee?
18,746	Fitch, Henry	Dallas
2,769	Fitzpatrick, William J.	Lauderdale
6,023	Flanagan, John M.	Limestone
14,470	Flanagan, Mary	Cherokee?
6,689	Flemming, David B.	Cherokee?
6,679	Fleming, Wm.	Cherokee?
2,755	Flippen, Francis	Jackson
20,255	Floyd, Ann	Montgomery
5,770	Floyd, Sallie	Elmore
19,785	Foote, Sarah E.	Mason
15,310	Forbes, Arthur	Lauderdale
10,367	Force, Lewis M.	Cherokee?
3,019	Ford, Jane	Morgan
11,108	Ford, Jonathan	Morgan
5,262	Ford, William C.	Walker
3,124	Foster, John F.C.	Walker
576	Foulk, Joshua	Cherokee?
18,369	Fountain, Green K.	Montgomery
6,814	Fowler, Chauncy	Macon
10,017	Fowler, William	Fayette
7,098	Franklin, John N.	De Kalb
20,842	Franklin, William	Madison
19,479	Fraser, Emily (or Fraizer)	Limestone
8,252	Freeman, Benjamin F.	Tuscaloosa
18,017	French, Jeremiah W.	Limestone
16,726	Friday, Henry, Estate of (Leroy Friday, Adm.)	Dallas
19,664	Friend, Anthony	Limestone
18,475	Friend, Caroline, Adm. of Estate of Donald, Jackson	Limestone
6,636	Frost, Edward	Walker
2,174	Fry, Thos. W.	Winston
12,291	Fry, William	Winston
16,909	Fulford, Philip S.	Dallas
19,437	Fuller, Abner T.	Cherokee?
18,671	Fullerton, Sarah C. (or Fullington)	Madison
13,006	Fulton, David	Shelby
13,282	Fulton, James M.	Shelby
19,797	Fulton, Rutha E.	Jefferson
21,232	Fumster, John B.	Marshall
14,413	Gaither, Richard H.	Blount
21,699	Gamar, Elizabeth	Walker
16,675	Gambill, Thomas T.	Lawrence
5,195	Gargis, Henry	Colbert
5,196	Gargis, Henry, Sr., Adm. of Estate of Wm. King	Colbert
6,493	Garland, E.C.	Jackson
19,481	Garland, Joseph	Jackson
6,494	Garland, William	Jackson
11,014	Garner, Alice	Walker
13,132	Garner, Argy L., Estate of (John D. Inman, Adm.)	Colbert
9,986	Garner, Enoch H.	Lauderdale
11,883	Garner, Reuben A.	Tuscaloosa
13,568	Garner, Richard	Colbert
18,018	Garner, Samuel F.	Madison
2,272	Garner, Susan B., Adm. of Wm. F.	Madison
7,831	Garnett, Peter F. (or Garrett)	Limestone
2,317	Garrett, Caswell	Monroe
4,340	Garrison, Levi	Cherokee?
5,606	Garrison, John S.	Winston
15,549	Gasque, John M.	Jackson
3,365	Gaston, James	Madison
9,848	Gautney, William	Lauderdale
11,122	Gaylord, Thomas W.	Bibb
14,472	Gaza, Frederick L.	Cherokee?
3,125	Gentle, Thos.	Winston
6,739	George, John H.	Monroe
14,965	Geron, John W. (Am., Morris K. Taylor)	Madison
9,850: 16,188:	Gibbs, Thos.	Morgan
3,020	Gibson, David D.	Morgan
3,355	Gilbert, Elizabeth	Tuscaloosa
14,471	Gilbreath, Dicy A.	De Kalb
11,606	Gilbreath, M.M.	Jackson
17,655	Gilder, Joseph	Mobile
7,832	Gill, Josephy M.	Jefferson
1,968	Gill, William B.	Dallas
16,734	Gilliland, Robert S.	Jackson
21,104	Gilmer, Elizabeth H.	Chambers
10,543	Gilreath, Lacinia, Estate of (Lydia Matthews, Adm.)	Cherokee?
3,127	Givens, Samuel H.	Winston
4,339	Givins, John C.	Cherokee:
8,370	Glascock, Bazel G. & Ellendar D.	Jackson
15,976	Glasgow, John F.	Jefferson
11,757	Glass, William W.	Macon
1,751	Glaze, Benjamin H.	Limestone
8,392	Glenn, Elias	Jefferson
12,954	Glenn, Esther	Jefferson
19,786	Glenn, Joseph B.	Jefferson
11,836	Glover, Lewis A.	Walker
3,082	Glover, Richard W.	Walker
17,481	Godbold, Olivia	Mobile
7,218	Godfrey, Freeman	Cherokee?
1,771	Goggin, Edward T.	De Kalb
16,050	Goggins, William D.	Jefferson
3,126	Goin, James	Lauderdale
6,025	Goin, Susan	Tuscaloosa
20,129	Goins, Sarah A.	Colbert
20,865	Golden, Shadrach, Estate of	Madison
8,371	Gonce, Mary	Jackson
6,495	Good, William	Lauderdale
9,452	Goode, William	Jefferson
4,348	Goodloe, John C.	Colbert
2,653	Goodloe, King	Colbert
1,969	Goodwin, Aquilla M.	Dallas
1,920	Goodwin, Henry W.	Lawrence
12,096	Gordon, Abraham, Estate of	Randolph

14,650	Gordon, Caroline M.	Morgan
16,844	Gossett, Eber, S., Estate of (John M. Doyle, Adm.)	Blount
19,439	Gordon, Thos. F.	Cherokee?
3,985	Gouch, Caswell	Lauderdale
3,188	Grace, John	Walker
4,819	Grady, Douglas	Morgan
3,787	Graham, Elijah	Baldwin
5,197	Graham, Malcolm G.	Lawrence
7,100	Graham, Nancy Ann	Jefferson
9,849	Graham, Priscilla	Jefferson
5,198	Graham, Sarah J.	Limestone
7,099	Graham, William	Jefferson
6,261	Graves, Hiram	De Kalb
6,256	Graves, Joshua	De Kalb
7,101	Gravlee, John	Morgan
1,197	Gray, Bethany	Lauderdale
18,348	Gray, John H.	Limestone
8,253	Gray, Lucy Ann	Limestone
7,968	Gray, Terrell, Executor of Jesse T. Price	Cherokee?
19,482	Green, Asa R., Estate of	Jackson
5,866	Green, E.C.	Marion
1,823	Green, Elias and Samuel H.	Cleburne
3,623	Green, Samuel	Madison
1,823	Green, Samuel H. and Elias	Cleburne
4,347	Green, Thos. W. (or U.)	Madison
20,843	Greene, Amanda J., Estate of (John P. Timberlake, Adm.)	Jackson
10,346	Greenhill, Samuel (of Barton Station)	Colbert
14,651	Greenhill, Samuel (of Cherokee)	Colbert
20,256	Greenwood, Unity E.	Macon
5,193	Gresham, Jared	Cherokee?
6,817	Gresham, Thomas	Lauderdale
4,197	Grey (Gray), George W., Adm. of Estate of Quinn Gray	Lawrence
18,672	Griffin, Daniel	Madison
6,230	Griffin, James M.	Etowah
2,316	Griffin, John	Monroe
7,217	Griffin, John N.	Cherokee?
12,953	Griffin, Phillip T.	Jefferson
20,844	Griffin, Richard S.	Fayette
8,674	Griffin, Richard S.	St. Clair
16,068	Griffith, Ezekial	Madison
19,665	Grigsby, George	Limestone
613	Grimes, Pleasant O.	Dallas
21,120	Grimmet, Matthew N.	Madison
5,193	Grisham, Jared	Lauderdale
12,484	Grisham, Willis P.	Limestone
19,480	Gross, John V.	Jackson
3,963	Gullott, William	Jackson
6,739	Gurgee, Desdemonia, Estate of	Monroe
2,175	Guthrie, Edwin	Winston
6,695	Guthrie, Stephen B.	Cherokee?
2,176	Guthrie, William E.	Winston
6,094	Guttery, Isham	Walker
18,720	Guttery, Isham, Jr.	Walker
3,129	Guttery, John	Walker
20,130	Guttery, Johnson	Walker
3,128	Guttery, Robert	Walker
3,130	Guttery, William	Walker
2,345	Guttry, Benj. F.	Walker
18,696	Hackett, James C.	Winston
2,751	Hackworth, Johnson	Jackson
1,655	Hackworth, Lydia C.	Jackson
1,654	Hackworth, Newton	Jackson
17,603	Haden, Caroline M.	Dallas
3,135	Haden, Horatio H.	Madison
4,350	Haden, John T.	Madison
19,873	Hafley, John W.	Limestone
2,387	Hailey, William	Lauderdale
21,998	Hairson, Sarah J.	Madison
13,914	Halcomb, Littleberry B.	Calhoun
2,177	Haley, Green M.	Marion
7,103	Hall, Chas. G.	Limestone
18,746	Hall, Henry	Dallas
5,410	Hall, Lewis F.	Limestone

19,237	Halbrooks, Ezekial J.	Morgan
18,020	Halloway, Margaret	Madison
3,986	Ham, John M.	Lauderdale
8,721	Ham, Jordan	Lauderdale
12,975	Hamaker, Samuel	Jefferson
21,124	Hambrick, Alfred	Madison
3,134	Hambrick, Francis D.	Madison
19,230	Hamer, Anderson	Madison
21,997	Hamer, Ann E.	Madison
22,001	Hamer, John M.	Madison
15,260	Hames, Andrew	Cherokee
2,227	Hames (Hanes), Hiram	Winston
3,131	Hamilton, Andrew J.	Walker
11,633	Hamilton, Harvy W.	Walker
5,330	Hamilton, Jacob B.	Walker
5,264	Hamilton, James J.	Walker
43	Hamilton, Robert, Adm.	Cherokee?
6,498	Hamilton, William	Colbert
6,499	Hamilton, William G.	Colbert
3,358	Hamm, James R.	Lauderdale
11,632	Hamner, John	Tuscaloosa
12,228	Hamner, William T.	Tuscaloosa
14,475	Hampton, Ellen	Cherokee?
14,476	Hampton, Moses	Cherokee?
12,977	Hanby, Lucretia	Walker
9,853	Hand, Simeon	Jefferson
2,227	Hanes (Hames), Hiram	Winston
6,250	Haney, Nancy	De Kalb
3,357	Hanna, Lemuel	Madison
9,759	Hannah, Thompson	Lauderdale
5,624	Hanola, William	Madison
21,125	Hanserd, William R.	Limestone
11,817	Hanson, William	Colbert
2,399	Haraway, Geo. M.	Lauderdale
2,226	Harbin, Mary	Winston
9,210	Harbin, Thos. M.	Cherokee?
3,133	Harbison, Martin T.	Winston
19,787	Hardee, Joel	Monroe
6,759	Hardee, John	Monroe
12,976	Hardin, Elizabeth	Jefferson
3,250	Hardman, John B.	Cherokee?
9,103	Hardwick, Joseph A.	Lauderdale
4,820	Hardyman, Uriah	Limestone
6,496	Hargiss, Thomas J.	Jackson
22,002	Harlass, Thos. S.	Madison
14,011	Harless, Geo. R.C.	Shelby
4,822	Harper, Andrew	Jackson
1,747	Harper, Benjamin, Estate of	Limestone
11,190	Harper, Jasper	Marshall
12,313	Harper, Matthew	Shelby
3,582	Harper, Robert F.	Jackson
16,069	Harris, Bartley	Madison
18,291	Harris, Bartley, Jr.	Madison
13,088	Harris, David S.	Marion
2,228	Harris, Francis C.	Winston
18,675	Harris, Mansfield	Madison
15,640	Harris, Melville	Dallas
19,483	Harris, Spencer	Limestone
18,676	Harris, Stephen	Madison
20,027	Harrison, B.H., Exec. of Estate of Jesse Stephens	Cherokee?
18,677	Harrison, David H.	Limestone
4,824	Harrison, Lenanzy	Limestone
2,657	Harrison, Perry (Percy?) L.	Madison
16,727	Harrison, Sarah H.	Dallas
5,624	Harrold, Wm.	Cherokee?
9,102	Hart, Henry	Lauderdale
9,851	Hartzell, George	Morgan
6,786	Harwell, Francis A.	Cherokee?
6,394	Harwood, Philip	De Kalb
18,290	Haslett, Eliza J.	Morgan
6,823	Hassell, Miles B.	Fayette
19,851	Hatchett, Wm. T. & Benjamin Trimble	Montgomery
4,201	Hawkins, Alexander	De Kalb
16,925	Hawkins, Benjamin	Jefferson
4,200	Hawkins, James	De Kalb
4,199	Hawkins, John	De Kalb
7,538	Hawkins, William (Mary Ann Hawkins, Adm.)	De Kalb

8,650	Hawkins, Wm. H.	Cherokee?
14,652	Hawkins, Williamson	Jefferson
11,233	Haws, George W.	Jackson
16,404	Hayes, John B.	Limestone
11,255	Hayes, John S.	Walker
14,477	Haynes, B. Tolbert	Cherokee?
18,674	Haynes, Benjamin	Madison
4,221	Haynes, James H.	Lauderdale
18,721	Haynes, John	Madison
4,357	Haynes, Stephen and John Ogden	Madison
4,881	Hays, Sarah L.	Blount
4,248	Hays, William	Jackson
5,546	Hazlewood, Thos. (Samuel Hazlewood, Adm.)	Lawrence
20,282	Head, Mary C.	Morgan
19,631	Heald, Henry P.	St. Clair
14	Heflin, Robt. S.	Randolph
6,825	Heinshaw, Geo. W.	Jackson
7,969	Heinshaw, Nancy	Jackson
14,178	Helms, John	Cherokee?
14,479	Helms, Winnie	Cherokee?
1,351	Helton, P.H., Dr.	Jackson
6,875	Henderson, Ezekiel	Cleburne
6,686	Henderson, James M.	Cherokee?
5,265	Hendon, James Al.	Walker
7,219	Hendricks, Laurette	Cherokee?
18,962	Hendricks, Madison	St. Clair
6,820	Hendrix, Avilla	Cherokee?
6,819	Hendrix, Samuel	Lauderdale
8,724	Hendrix, Zenas N.	Lauderdale
6,500	Herman, William	Lauderdale
3,987	Herndon, Horace	Lauderdale
6,675	Herron, Andrew J., Adm. of Estate of Samuel H. Herron	Cherokee?
8,004	Herston, William C.	Lauderdale
12,978	Hewett, Nancy J.	Walker
6,026	Hewitt, Isaac	Tuscaloosa
2,397	Hewlett, Augustine M.	Madison
3,965	Hewlett, Narcissa V.	Madison
11,759	Hicks, John	Cherokee?
11,760	Hicks, Isaac M.	Bibb
17,017	Hicks, Matilda	De Kalb
20,014	Hiern, Roger A., Estate of (Robert Otis, Administrator)	Monroe
9,815	Higgins, Calvin	Lauderdale
10,246	Higgins, James M.	Limestone
14,222	Higgins, John	Lauderdale
17,659	Hightower, James W.	Lee
21,122	Hightower, Thomas	Lauderdale
8,393	Hightower, William	Lawrence
1,626	Hill, Calvin Smith	Lauderdale
17,754	Hill, C.B., Estate of (Wm. R. Hill, Administrator)	Jackson
11,075	Hill, Elizabeth C.	Cherokee?
7,790	Hill, Isabella B.	Cherokee?
5,199	Hill, Louisa	Lauderdale
9,808	Hill, Lucy	Butler
6,497	Hill, Orin	Jackson
19,789	Hill, Reuben T.	Jefferson
4,821	Hill, William H.	Lauderdale
1,627	Hindman, Daniel	Lauderdale
6,825	Hinshaw, G.W.	Cherokee?
9,852	Hine, Randal	Limestone
10,505	Hisan, William	Walker
137: 17,252:	Hobart, Lewis	Morgan
1,825	Hobbs, John N.	Cleburne
14,960	Hobbs, Joseph A., Adm. of Harriet B. Stokes	Madison
2,650	Hobgood, Martha A.	Colbert
1,212	Hocut, Robert T.	Walker
3,964	Hodge, John K.	Cherokee?
9,825	Hodges, William	Franklin
2,346	Hogan, James	Walker
1,767	Hoge, John J.	De Kalb
1,657	Hogwood, Mary S.	Jackson
1,656	Holden, Mary E., Adm. of Estate of John Holden	Jackson
10,158	Holland, Jack	Jackson
5,815	Holland, James L., Estate of	Lauderdale

7,970	Holleman, Merit	Lauderdale
20,845	Hollingsworth, John	Limestone
12,979	Hollis, Aliza M. (Elijah M.?)	Jefferson
12,981	Hollis, Elizabeth Jane	Walker
12,980	Hollis, John H.	Walker
12,982	Hollis, Mary L.	Walker
18,020	Holloway, Margaret E.	Cherokee?
4,823	Holmes, Thomas	Lauderdale
8,866	Holmes, Thos. H.	Limestone
7,337	Holsonback, James	De Kalb
6,818	Holt, Amelia H.	Limestone
5,607	Holt, Geo. W.	Franklin
19,170	Holt, Jessie	Limestone
1,746	Holt, John D.	Limestone
8,723	Holt, John W.	Limestone
6,782	Hood, Benj. F.	Cherokee?
19,614	Hood, Celinda	Cherokee?
201	Hood, Sarah C.	Montgomery
4,349	Hooks, William	Lawrence
8,722	Hooper, Edward W.	Franklin
18,673	Horton. Elizabeth	Madison
4,198	Houk, Hopkins L., Estate of (Archimedes Houk, Adm.)	Limestone
15,312	Howard, Hardin	Lauderdale
21,999	Howard, Jane	Madison
8,479	Howard, Maria L.	Cherokee?
2,278	Howard, Michael	Madison
3,544	Howard, Nancy J.	Jackson
7,102	Howell, Burrill	Marion
1,825	Howle, John N.	Cleburne
17,045	Howle, Sarah A.	Cleburne
17,044	Howle, Mack G.	Cleburne or Cherokee?
17,609	Huckabee, Caswell C.	Perry
21,123	Hudson, Hugh B.	Limestone
5,200	Hudson, Martha E.	Walker
5,625	Hudspeth, Giles	Limestone
5,401	Huff, William H.	Etowah
2,625	Huggins, Andrew J.	Jackson
16,607	Hughes, Albert H.	Limestone
5,626	Hughes, Anderson E., Estate of	Limestone
18,019	Hughes, Asbury T.	Elmore
15,607	Hughes, Catharine	Limestone
8,254	Hughes, Geo. W.	Lauderdale
3,132	Hulsey, Kenion T.	Jefferson
21,121	Humphrey, William D.	Madison
6,027	Hundley, John H.	Limestone
19,484	Hunt, Archey C.	Lauderdale
22,171	Hunt, George E.	Madison
10,245	Hunt, Jerry	Madison
18,389	Hunt, Stephen A.	Limestone
11,758	Hunter, Robert S.M.	Randolph
6,793	Hurley, Stephen	Cherokee?
19,788	Hurst, Edward	Jefferson
16,605	Hurst, John	Colbert
19,388	Huer, Wm. F.	Jackson
6,501	Husky, Hartwell	Colbert
5,867	Huston, Andrew J.	Marion
4,120	Hutton, John	Jackson
12,227	Hyatt, Jerome B.	Colbert
13,973	Hude, Louis	Colbert
16,226	Hyde, Samuel M.	Lauderdale
21,126	Ikelheimer, Edward	Dallas
2,178	Ingle, Andrew J.	Winston
3,048	Ingle, Katharine, Estate of	Winston?
3,048: 2,179:	Ingle, Paul	Winston
4,042	Ingle, Peter	Marion
12,293	Ingle, Sarah C.	Winston
6,746	Ingraham, Mary J.	Monroe
13,505	Ingram, Henry	Monroe
18,292	Ingram, Henry P.	Lee
13,132	Inman, John D., Adm. of Estate of Argy L. Garner	Colbert
20,846	Irion, Philip J.	Lauderdale
20,847	Irvin, Milton V.	Limestone
1,369	Irwin, William B.	Lawrence
8,394	Isaacs, A. Morgan	Jefferson
6,028	Isbell, Allen	Jackson

5,885	Isbell, James R.	Marshall
11,809	Isbell, Lewis	Colbert
6,502	Isbell, Miller	Jackson
5,816	Isom, Emanuel	Limestone
7,104	Isom, John C.	Cherokee? Limestone?
5,423	Isom, Mathew	Limestone
5,422	Isom, Sylvester B.	Limestone
6,826	Isom, William S.	Limestone
19,984	Ivey, Sarah	Dallas
14,480	Jack, Jeremiah R.	Cherokee?
11,981	Jackson, Jacob	Tuscaloosa
6,503	Jackson, Jesse	Fayette
13,705	Jackson, John	Limestone
8,008	Jackson, William	Lauderdale
2,180	Jackson, William M.	Winston
11,839	James, Francis B.	Clark
8,821	James, Mary	Jackson
7,105	James, Thomas	Jefferson
13,741	James, Wm	Cherokee?
20,618	James, William P.	Jackson
7,540	Jarrett, William	Limestone
18,678	Jefferson, Jessie	Madison
19,874	Jenkins, Mills	Madison
5,266	Jetton, Ephraim	Walker
8,255	Johns, Square A.	Tuscaloosa
7,973	Johnson, David B.	Morgan
5,338	Johnson, Edwin	Cherokee?
9,453	Johnson, George	Walker
6,692	Johnson, Henry F.	Cherokee?
9,813	Johnson, James	Lauderdale
1,460	Johnson, James R.	Marshall
612	Johnson, Jeremiah	Dallas
18,021	Johnson, John B.	Colbert
21,674	Johnson, John C.	Walker
280	Johnson, J.V.	Colbert
6,238	Johnson, Lucretia C., Adm. of Estate of Richmond Johnson	De Kalb
1,352	Johnson, Lysander	Jackson
20,979	Johnson, Matilda H. *et al*	Mobile
21,673	Johnson, Milton	Fayette
11,634	Johnson, Moses L.	Fayette
7,221	Johnson, Nancy	Cherokee?
1,344	Johnson, Nathaniel A. & David Edwards	Jackson
7,220	Johnson, Parks J.	Cherokee?
1,461	Johnson, Pleasant F., Estate of	Marshall
16,070	Johnson, Richard M.	Madison
6,238	Johnson, Richmond, Estate of (Lucretia C. Johnson, Adm.)	De Kalb
4,030	Johnson, William, Estate of (Wm. H. Fellows, Adm.)	Dallas
20,979	Johnson, Wm. H., Estate of	Mobile
3,359	Johnston, Eveline	Walker
7,971	Jolley, Benjamin	Madison
6,029	Jones, Alfred A.	Lawrence
3,137	Jones, Anthony	Madison
14,138	Jones, Asa	Shelby
10,247	Jones, Cyrus	Madison
9,104	Jones, Dandridge	Limestone
21,675	Jones, Elias A.	Jefferson
19,790	Jones, Garland	Jefferson
14,012	Jones, James	Shelby
17,078	Jones, James A. Estate of	Bibb
7,972	Jones, James A.	Walker
18,681	Jones, James D.	Limestone
12,485	Jones, John W.	Shelby
12,812	Jones, Jordan	Shelby
2,753	Jones, Nancy	Madison
18,679	Jones, Rachel	Madison
21,233	Jones, Sally Ann & Drury Fair (Wm. H. Fellows, Guardian)	Dallas
19,875	Jones, Seaborn, Estate of (Wm. B. Jones, Adm.: Allen, Decherd, Martha, Margaret, Susan, Trenton & Vina Jones, Heirs)	Madison

19,876	Jones, Seaborn M., Jr.	Madison
9,105	Jones, Shandy	Limestone
18,680	Jones, Shandy	Madison
10,158	Jones, Sidney, Mrs.	Lee
2,667	Jones, Sidney A.	Franklin
5,627	Jones, Thos. W.	Madison
13,503	Jones, Wiley	Blount
18,997	Jones, William	Madison
19,875	Jones, Wm. B., Adm. of Estate of Seaborn Jones (Heirs: Allen, Decherd, Martha, Margaret, Susan, Trenton & Vina Jones)	Madison
2,273	Jones, Zachariah	Madison
5,628	Jordan, Elisha	Limestone
8,192	Jordan, Geo.	Cherokee?
7,609	Jordan, Solomon E.	Randolph
12,098	Jordan, William	Randolph
2,663	Kachelman, John	Lauderdale
2,750	Kahelman (Kakleman), Harris	Lauderdale
7,222	Keaton, Harriet	Cherokee?
5,629	Keel, Moses B.	Jackson
11,637	Keeton, Archibald	Walker
11,636	Keeton, Sarah F.	Walker
2,066	Keeton, William	Walker
8,031	Keith, Wm. R.	De Kalb
2,655	Keller, Henry	Colbert
14,961	Kelley, Hampton W., Estate of	Madison
6,798	Kelly, Seneca J.	Cherokee?
17,364	Kelly, William A.	Dallas
11,123	Kendrick, Palmer A.	Bibb
3,139	Kennamer, David, Jr.	Marshall
3,161	Kennamer, Demarius	Marshall
3,138	Kennamer, John B.	Marshall
3,361	Kennamer, John S.	Marshall
5,630	Kennamer, Nathaniel	Jackson
3,140	Kennamer, Seaborn F., Adm.	Marshall
3,360	Kennamer, Stephen D.	Marshall
7,871	Kennamore, David	Marshall
7,541	Kennamore, David, Sen.	Marshall
616	Kennamore, Jacob L.	Marshall
617	Kennamore, Keziah	Marshall
11,816	Kennard, George W.	Madison
6,031	Kennemer (Kennemore), Sophia M.	Madison
4,351	Kent, William M.	Lawrence
4,352	Kerr, William S.	Madison
19,488	Key, Charles	Lauderdale
2,758	Keys, Jesse	Madison
17,153	Kidwell, Peter	Fayette
1,974	Kiker, John	Walker
2,019	Kilburn, Russel M.	Lauderdale
6,505	Kilgore, George	Fayette
3,189	Kilgore, William	Walker
19,791	Killough, Allen	Jefferson
2,379	Kimball, Franklin G.	Mobile
19,489	Kimbrough, James M.	Franklin
19,989	King, Charles L.	Morgan
20,508	King, Guilford D., Estate of	Lauderdale
18,998	King, James C.	Colbert
146	King, Low	Cherokee?
19,487	King, Meredith, Estate of (Susan King, Adm.)	Cherokee?
6,511	King, Robt., Estate of	Lawrence
19,487	King, Susan, Adm. of Estate of Meredith King	Cherokee?
11,635	King, Thomas J.	Walker
4,493	King, Ursula	Conecuh
5,196	King, William, Estate of (Henry Gargis, Sr., Adm.)	Colbert
6,504	King, William R.	Walker
21,127	Kington, Martin	De Kalb
5,201	Kiper, Elizabeth	Cherokee?
15,064	Kirby, Andrew J.	Jackson
20,131	Kirby, Clinton	Jackson
20,849	Kirby, Elizabeth	De Kalb
15,660	Kirby, Mary J.	Jackson
19,486	Kirby, Richard L., Jr.	Jackson
10,834: or : 10,334:	Kirk, Leacy (Lucy)	Cherokee?

986	Kirk, William L.	Lawrence
8,725	Kirkland, David H.	Lauderdale
6,030	Kirkpatrick, John	Jackson
6,012	Kitchin, James M., Estate of	Walker
12,523	Knight, Davis, Estate of (Martin D.L. Knight, Adm.)	Walker
2,067	Knott, Franklin S.	Randolph
16,189	Knowles, Thos. R.	Cherokee?
11,179	Koger, Wm.	De Kalb
2,660	Krastle, Barbara	Lauderdale
6,032	Kyle, Nelson	Jackson
849	Ladd, Bayless E.	Jackson
9,147	Ladd, E.T. (or C.T.)	Jackson
21,525	Ladd, Louise	Jackson
2,391	Lamberson, Leonard F.	Madison
4,354	Lamberson, Leonard F. (Adm. of Estate of John Lamberson)	Madison or Cherokee?
9,854	Land, Luvenia J.	Jefferson
615	Landers, Allen B.	Lawrence
14,481	Landers, Talafero L. (or Palo F.L.)	De Kalb
21,130	Landers, Woodson C.	Limestone
5,827	Lane, Isaac, Estate of	Colbert
3,083	Langerds, Francis M.	Walker
8,917	Langford, John	Madison
22,295	Lanston, Spire A.	Morgan
22,170	Lanier, Adams	Madison
18,722	Lansden, Martha W.	Madison
4,828	Lassiter, James L.	Morgan
18,370	Latham, Cornelius	Bibb
17,079	Latham, Jane	Bibb
11,499	Latham, John	Cherokee?
6,827	Lauderdale, Robt.	Limestone
2,400	Lawler, Benjamin, Estate of (Rhoda Lawler, Adm.)	Madison
2,394	Lawler, Jehu	Madison
2,275	Lawler, John	Madison
2,395	Lawler, William J., Estate of (John Lawler, Adm.)	Madison
5,128	Lawless, Augustine	Cherokee?
4,309	Lawrence, G.W.	Cherokee?
5,424	Lawson, John M.	Lauderdale
21,128	Laxson, William G.	Madison
5,817	Layne, Reuben	Morgan
6,259	Lea, William	De Kalb
4,831	Leach, Cain	Lauderdale
18,023	Leach, John M.	Dallas
6,791	Leath, Ebenezer	Cherokee?
6,688	Leath, Mary	Cherokee?
18,927	Lee, Francis	St. Clair
16,910	Lee, James H.	Dallas
11,885	Lee, Susan	Tuscaloosa
19,985	Lee, Zachariah S.	Limestone
6,109	Leeth, Napoleon B.	Cherokee?
4,825	Lefan, Thomas	Lauderdale
4,826	Legg, Celia	Limestone
4,353	Legg, David (Daniel) M.	Limestone
4,827	Legg, Edward	Limestone
18,682	Legg, Joel E.	Limestone
7,108	Legg, Lovil	Limestone
20,518	Lemaster, John W.	Lauderdale
5,631	Lemly, Rueben, Jr.	Marshall
5,632	Lemly, Reuben, Sr., Dr.	Jackson
17,146	Lemons, David J.	Fayette
5,412	Lentz, James H.	Limestone
4,832	Lentz, Sarah E. & Estate of J.W.	Limestone
5,202	Lentz, Solomon	Limestone
10,248	Lesley, John L.	Madison
19,490	Lettuce, Benjamin	Lauderdale
15,917	Levy, Harris	Lee
18,911	Lewallen, Madison	Jackson
4,829	Lewis, Burwell	De Kalb
7,223	Lewis, Eliza	Cherokee?
2,627	Lewis, John T.	Jackson
10,203	Lewis, Thos., Adm. of Barbara Patty	Cherokee?
11,884	Lewis, Thos. P.	Tuscaloosa
16,370	Lightfoot, Phillip	Macon

20,146	Ligon, Abner W., Adm. of Wm. B. Alsobrooks	Colbert
6,506	Ligon, Abner W., Adm. of Armistead Bean	Franklin
13,924	Ligon, James W.	Colbert
20,132	Ligon, Thomas H.	Colbert
12,662	Lile, Thos., Estate of (Thos. A. Lile, Adm.)	Morgan
4,830	Liles, Amos & Widow Elizabeth	Lauderdale
6,033	Liles, William	Lauderdale
854: 856: 13,829:	Lilly, Jesse	Jackson
16,521	Lindsey, Miles R.	Franklin
14,226	Lindsey, Philip	Lauderdale
3,967	Lindsey, William	Walker
9,454	Linn, Andrew J.	Jefferson
8,395	Linn, Samuel (Lum)	Jefferson
3,676	Linom, John B.	Wilcox
3,677	Linom, Wm. H.	Wilcox
20,461	Litten, Julius B.	Lauderdale
18,888	Little, Sarepta C.	Cherokee?
988	Littleton, Charles E.	Lauderdale
11,982	Lock, Jane W.	Limestone
9,166	Logan, John C.	Jackson
21,129	Logwood, Delia	Lawrence
3,533	Lollar, Jane	Jackson
3,141	Lollar, William	Walker
3,966	Loller, Jenetta (Adm. of Estate of Joab Loller)	Walker
19,852	Long, Albert (Alfred), Estate of (James Long, Adm.)	De Kalb
9,466	Long, James	De Kalb
18,022	Long, William R.	Marion
20,462	Lorance, Andrew J.	Lauderdale
5,520	Low, Thomas	Etowah
7,833	Lovett, Elijah B.	Jefferson
2,229	Lovett, Elizabeth	Winston
12,097	Loveless, William	Randolph
7,107	Lunceford, Cullen H.	Tuscaloosa
1,770	Luttrell, John B.	De Kalb
11,074	Lynch, Eda	Cherokee?
13,007	Lyon, John	Shelby
3,363	Lyons, Daniel	Madison
20,850	Lyons, John	Marion
9,135	Lyons, Margaret	De Kalb
3,146	Macbee, Martin	Walker
3,148	Mace, Ezekiel	Sanford
4,835	Macklin, Reuben	Limestone
6,507: 6,588:	Madison, Susan	Fayette
21,373	Maguire, M.C.	Lauderdale
19,853	Mahaffy, William	De Kalb
11,124	Mahan, Jesse W.	Bibb
6,510	Mahan, Matthew	Morgan
18,024	Malone, Benj.	Limestone
8,256	Malone, George	Limestone
20,853	Malone, Geo. W.	De Kalb
19,491	Malone, Henry	Limestone
10,028	Malone, James Bass	Mobile
18,027: 18,301:	Malone, James Bass & Henrietta N.; Richards, Charles G.; and Steele, Lafayette D.; Heirs of Stephen Steele	Mobile
20,283	Manasco, David C.	Walker
5,373	Manasco, Wiley B.	Winston
3,144	Manning, James	Jefferson
3,364	Manning, Thomas	Jefferson
5,268	Mannon, T.C.B.	Walker
22,000	Mans, Geo. W.	Cherokee?
16,930	Manscill, Benjamin	Franklin
3,395	Mansell, Samuel J. (Lemuel G.)	Conecuh
1,914	Maples, James N.	Jackson
6,690	Maples, Josiah	Cherokee?
2,384	Maples, Moses	Jackson
14,482	Mapp, Margaret	Cherokee?
4,911	Marshall, Absalom	Cherokee?
21,700	Martin, Barton	Walker
21,135	Martin, Francis C.	Limestone

3,080	Martin, Jas. R.	Walker
19,494	Martin, John	Jackson
1	Martin, John J.	Macon
2,072	Martin, John W.	Randolph
22,294	Martin, Joseph A.	Jackson
4,807	Martin, Lyman W., Adm. of Wm. Brooks	Cherokee?
21,133	Martin, Maria	Jackson
16,728	Martin, Robt. M.	Dallas
14,849	Martin, Thos. L.	Montgomery
2,231	Martin, Thos. M.	Winston
5,143	Mason, E.W.S., Estate of	Jackson
6,740	Mason, Franklin A.	Monroe
21,132	Mason, John R., Estate of (Glorvinia Mason, Adm.)	Limestone
19,492	Mason, Nelson, Estate of (Matilda Mason, Adm.)	Limestone
2,157	Massey, Elizabeth	Lawrence
4,355	Massingall, Marcus M.	Madison
990	Masterson, James N.	Lawrence
18,025	Mathews, Thos. M.	Dallas
21,348	Mathews, William	Dallas
7,233	Matthews, John	Cherokee?
6,822	Matthews, Joseph	Cherokee?
10,543	Matthews, Lydia, Adm. of Estate of Lavinia Gilreath	Cherokee?
6,830	Matthews, Mary	Marion
3,142	Matthews, Philip	Lawrence
2,499	Matthews, Stephen J.	Lauderdale
6,828	Matthews, Wm.	Cherokee?
18,697	Maxwell, Thos. W.	Winston
18,763	Mayfield, Rebecca	Tuscaloosa
20,854	Mayhew, Jonathan	Madison
17,149	May, Moody H., Adm. of Estate of Robert Carlisle	Dallas
3,247	Mays, David	Marion
7,227	McAbee, Barnett G.	Cherokee?
7,225	McAbee, James	Cherokee
7,231	McAbee, James R.	Cherokee
396	McAllister, Joseph L.	Winston
16,227	McBride, John	Limestone
14,962	McBroom, Hannah	Madison
5,819	McBroom, Susan	Madison
4,356	McBryde, William P.	Madison
12,920	McBurnett, Albert	Randolph
2,495	McCafferty, Amanda M.	Lauderdale
10,348	McCaleb, John P.	Fayette
12,095	McCarley, Robert A.	Randolph
5,634	McCarley, Thos. J.	Morgan
7,230	McCarley, Thos. N.	Cherokee
2,495	McClafferty (McCafferty), Amanda M.	Lauderdale
18,684	McClelland, Senia	Cherokee?
19,607	McClendon, Malinda	Jackson
8,397	McClintock, John A.	Jefferson
2,665	McCluskey, J.C.	Lawrence
17,148	McCollum, Joseph	Fayette
2,070	McCollum, Moses C.	Cherokee?
2,349	McCollum, William	Walker
8,257	McComak, Chas.	Limestone
12,984	McComak, (McCormak), William and Widow Delphina	Jefferson
6,110	McConnell, Joseph H.N.	Cherokee
7,228	McCord, Robert	Cherokee
5,204	McCorkle, Sarah	Lauderdale
9,823	McCorkle, Thomas T.	Lauderdale
9,811	McCorkle, Thomas T., Adm. of R.H. Rawlings	Lauderdale
19,000	McCorkle, Wm.	Colbert
12,095	McCorley, Robert A.	Cherokee
15,231	McCoy, Birdin	St. Clair
2,353	McCracken, David	Walker
822: 8,221:	McCrary, Benj. P.	Madison
6,254	McCrary, John W.	St. Clair
7,610	McCrary, Sam	Cherokee?
6,251	McCrary, Thos. P.	St. Clair
3,084	McCredie, Nelson A.	Walker
8,987	McCullars, Andrew	Winston
2,070	McCullom, Moses C.	Walker
18,390	McCullough, James	Cherokee
2,351	McDade, Geo. W.	Walker
2,352	McDade, James	Walker
9,929	McDavid, Albert	Madison
20,240	McDaniel, Armistead	Cleburne
14,227	McDaniel, Mary A.	Lauderdale
10,347	McDonald, Alexander	Fayette
19,793	McDonald, Jacob	Jefferson
2,350	McDonald, James	Walker
2,069	McDonald, Lucy J.	Morgan
5,267	McDuff, Richard	Walker
10,249	McFarland, Thomas	Madison
11,607	McGaha, Robert S.	Madison
4,617	McGaughy, John H.	Cherokee?
2,654	McGee, Abraham	Lauderdale
2,385	McGee, Jacob	Lauderdale
3,969	McGee, John	Lauderdale
21,134	McGehee, William E.	Macon
21,223	McGhee, Barclay, Estate of	Monroe
7,232	McGill, John	Cherokee
2,071	McGough, William	Walker
3,528	McGray, Caroline	Jackson
7,610	McGray, Samuel	Jackson
7,226	McGriff, Thomas	Cherokee
8,259	McGuire, James	Lauderdale
3,043	McGuire, John L.	Marion
2,386	McGuire, John W.	Lauderdale
12,230	McGuire, L.T.	Bibb
11,886	McGuire, Moses	Tuscaloosa
21,112	McGuire, Wm. B., Estate of (Murphy Bruce, Adm.)	Limestone
8,258	McGwinn, Jane	Jackson
4,885	McHaffey, Gustavus A., Estate of	Madison
19,792	McIntyre, Sterling C.	Jefferson
16,159	McKay, Johnson	Jackson
2,748	McKelrey, John	Lauderdale
7,234	McKelvey, George	Cherokee
29,463	McKinney, Brooks S.	Limestone
4,834	McKinney, James, Estate of (John McKinney, Adm.)	Limestone
4,833	McKinney, John	Limestone
991	McKnight, Elizabeth	Lauderdale
1,758	McKnight, Samuel J.	Lauderdale
18,684	McLelland, Senia	Madison
8,867	McMahan, John C., Estate of (Margaret D. McMahan, Adm.)	Lauderdale
6,035	McMillion, Amon	Tuscaloosa
7,229	McNeely, O.D.	Cherokee
19,493	McNelly, Henry	Jackson
6,683	McNew, Elijah	Cherokee
18,698	McNutt, Henry	Winston
2,230	McNutt, Winston	Cherokee?
6,111	McPeters, James	Lauderdale
5,287	McPeters, James (Adm. of Estate of John W. Briggs)	Lauderdale
6,833	McWilliam, William	Limestone
7,977	McWilliams, Andrew	Limestone
15,230	McWilliams, Denis	Limestone
5,203	Meals, James A.	Limestone
15,958	Meals, John, Estate of	Madison
2,967	Meede, Alexander	Madison
9,456	Messer, William Estate of	Jackson
18,026	Metcalf, Eliphalet H.	Montgomery
20,510	Michael, John W.	Lauderdale
2,320	Middleton, Henry C.	Monroe
2,319	Middleton, John G.	Monroe
2,318	Middleton, Martin	Monroe
5,818	Middleton, Shugar B.	Madison
6,034	Miles, John	Tuscaloosa
2,181	Miles, William	Marion
7,974	Miller, Corland M.	Madison
7,234: 14,484:	Miller, Elizabeth	Cherokee
16,847	Miller, Erastus W., Adm. of Zachary White	Cherokee?
5,889	Miller, John	Marshall
6,669	Miller, John L.	Cherokee

6,036	Miller, Lucinda	Madison
3,143	Miller, Lucus C.	Walker
6,831	Miller, Sarah	Jackson
21,677	Miller, Thos. B.	Shelby
8,260	Miller, Wiley J.	Tuscaloosa
6,832	Millican, Elizabeth	Cherokee
1,761	Milligan, Martin	Lawrence
16,911	Milling, Robt.	Dallas
18,029	Milner, Catharine R.	Tallapoosa
8,261	Mingea, Micajah	Limestone
5,270	Minor, Mary A.	Walker
7,235	Minshew, E.P.	Cherokee
8,726	Minton, John	Lauderdale
7,975	Mitchell, A.S., Estate of	Jackson
18,288	Mitchell, Helen T.	Colbert
16,566	Mitchell, Leroy P.	Colbert
10,660	Mitchell, Lion	Franklin
11,830	Mitchell, Martha	Marion
1,908	Mitchell, Robert, Estate of	Macon
4,052	Mitchell, Susan	Jackson
7,834	Mitchell, Thos. J.	Jackson
20,855	Montgomery, Eliza	Madison
21,698	Montgomery, Nathan	Winston
21,131	Montgomery, William A.	St. Clair
6,252	Moody, Benjamin E.	St. Clair
7,835	Moody, Reuben	Franklin
5,820	Mooney, Elbert	Walker
8,396	Moore, David H.	Jefferson
18,683	Moore, Edward	Madison
20,856	Moore, Harry	Madison
18,999	Moore, Henry	Madison
8,193	Moore, James M.	Cherokee
20,751	Moore, James S.	Lee
16,340	Moore, John	Jackson
18,238	Moore, John C.	Fayette
12,229	Moore, Louisa F.	Tuscaloosa
4,475	Moore, Richard H.	Baldwin
3,147	Moore, Squire	Madison
9,132	Moore, William	Jackson
11,500	Moreland, Nathaniel	Bibb
3,145	Morgan, David	Walker
5,269	Morgan, Ezekial	Walker
982	Morgan, James T., Adm. of Sidney C. Posey	Lauderdale
4,836	Morgan, Jeremiah T., Estate of (Delila Morgan, Adm.)	De Kalb
2,321	Morgan, John W.	Monroe
1,748	Morgan, Joseph	Jackson
5,428	Morris, Andrew J.	Lawrence
18,293	Morris, James Henry	Marshall
3,856	Morris, John W.	Colbert
2,073	Morris, Martha	Morgan
16,190	Morris, Peter	Lauderdale
12,983	Morrison, James E.	Jefferson
1,161	Morrow, John Shaw	Lauderdale
4,081	Morrow, John Shaw; Baugh, Richard B.; Evans, G.W.; and Wood, W.B., Adm. of V.M. Burham	Lauderdale
3,968	Morrow, Orson H.	Marshall
20,851	Morrow, William	Morgan
1,749	Morton, Martin W.	Sanford
2,271	Mosely, William F.	Lawrence
21,676	Moss, Edmond	Shelby
7,110	Mulberry, R.D.	Tuscaloosa
18,929	Mullens, Joshua	Franklin
9,455	Mullens, William S.	Marion
2,735	Mulloy, Asenith	Cleburne
4,883	Murphree, Margaret	Blount
6,509	Myers, Abraham	Walker
13,985	Myers, Nicey D.	Walker
17,147	Myers, Russell J.	Walker
3,190	Myers, Thornton	Walker
2,018	Myrick, James C.	Lauderdale
8,868	Nabers, William F.	Jefferson
8,044	Nabors, William	Tuscaloosa
4,837	Nail, Emanuel	Lauderdale
8,262	Nance, William P.	Colbert
11,189	Nation, Thomas	Blount
5,272	Nations, Joseph	Walker
5,271	Nations, Nancy J.	Walker
3,149	Navemore, Polly	Tuscaloosa
14,485	Naylor, Jere	De Kalb
17,414	Nell, Elizabeth	Dallas
3,789	Nelson, D.W., *et al*	Baldwin
3,787	Nelson, Elisha & James R., *et al*	Baldwin
21,678	Nelson, Hardy S.	Shelby
5,822	Nelson, Isaac S.	Walker
5,821	Nelson, James	Lawrence
12,986	Nesmith, John N.	Blount
12,987	Nesmith, N.W.	Blount
20,464	Newby, James M.	Limestone
5,245	Newby, Sarah J.	Limestone
16,157	Newcomer, Geo. W.	Jackson
14,229	Newman, Ann	Lauderdale
9,987	Newsome, Whitmel R.	Colbert
3,789	Nichols, Mary, *et al*	Baldwin
6,229	Nicholson, Mary B.	Etowah
10,159	Nobles, Absalom	Russell
7,355	Noles, William	Limestone
2,182	Norris, Martha A.	Winston
5,608	Norris, Reuben	Walker
10,250	Norris, Robert S.	Madison
2,232	Norris, William Y.	Winston
8,953	Norville, Edward & Widow Anna E.	Mobile
20,465	Oakley, James P.	Lauderdale
19,678	Oates, David C.	Colbert
7,236	Odell, Rebecca	Cherokee
7,111	Odom, Jennings	Jefferson
4,357	Ogden, John & Stephen Haynes	Madison
2,669	Oliver, Jane R.	Lauderdale
12,955	Oliver, John	Jefferson
7,542	Orear, Elijah	Walker
1,980	O'Rear, Jerry	Walker
5,205	Osborn, Hiram	Colbert
20,014	Otis, Robert, Adm. of Roger A. Hiern	Monroe
18,856	Owen, Chas. P.	Walker
17,326	Owen, Lewis	Montgomery
7,112	Owen, Robert	Jefferson
4,838	Owens, Alfred	Jackson
14,486	Owens, Belson	Cherokee
4,839	Owens, F.C., Estate of	Lawrence
16,356	Owens, Harriet	Cherokee
9,107	Owens, Samuel	Morgan
7,237	Owens, Sarah	Cherokee
6,698	Owens, William B.	Cherokee
13,008	Ozley, Thos.	Shelby
12,814	Ozley, William	Shelby
3,604	Pace, Joseph B.	Jackson
20,858	Paine, Benj. F.	De Kalb
6,239	Painter, James	De Kalb
19,986	Painter, James	De Kalb
5,206	Palmer, Elizabeth A.	Walker
14,964	Palmer, Sarah A.	Madison
20,950	Palmer, William	Lauderdale
20,466	Parham, William	Limestone
21,228	Parker, Elenor, Adm. of Estate of Rodney Parker	Marshall
14,214	Parker, Elizabeth	Lauderdale
14,230	Parker, Jasper N.	Lauderdale
11,557	Parker, John W.	Morgan
3,150	Parker, Thos. B.	Walker
3,971	Parker, William	Morgan
11,446	Parker, Zachariah	Morgan
1,924	Parsons, Abia	Lauderdale
2,322	Pate, Elijah	Monroe
10,572	Patterson, David N.	Franklin
8,869	Patterson, James A.	Colbert
2,977	Patterson, John	Mobile
4,358	Patterson, Wasington	Morgan
5,426	Patton, Henry	Lauderdale
5,414	Patton, William	Limestone
10,203	Patty, Barbara, Estate of (Thos. Lewis, Adm.)	Cherokee?
18,294	Payne, William E.	Madison
20,859	Peacock, Henry	De Kalb
11,286	Peacock, Jourdan	Jackson

11,288	Peakcock, Martha Ann	Jackson
2,668	Peerson, William W.	Franklin
5,823	Peevey, Robert W.	Madison
19,877	Peevy, Leroy M., Adm. of Estate of Solomon Smith	Cherokee?
3,211	Pemberton, Mary J.	De Kalb
21,136	Pemberton, Mary J.	Jackson
8,398	Pendergrass, Joseph	Marshall
3,970	Penn, John B.	Madison
2,389	Penney, John	Madison
19,001	Penny, Samuel	Madison
7,238	Pennington, Margaret	Cherokee
16,729	Peoples, Jesse H.	Dallas
7,836	Pepper, Edwin	Limestone
21,755	Perkins, Bettie F.	Madison
21,131	Perkins, Williams	Marshall
7,543	Perryman, John	Lauderdale
19,495	Peters, Hiram	Jackson
1,458	Peters, Naomi S.	Lawrence
19,496	Peters, Phil	Lauderdale
7,545	Pettipool, John	Lauderdale
9,148	Pettitt, Thomas	Jackson
5,415	Phillips, Absalom T.	Lauderdale
12,990	Phillips, Bruton	Walker
12,989	Phillips, Chas.	Walker
12,988	Phillips, Elizabeth	Jefferson
8,870	Phillips, Elijah, Estate of	Jackson
12,991: 18,857:	Phillips, Geo. W.	Walker
18,793	Phillips, J.R.	Lauderdale
20,833	Phillips, James M.	Russell
5,824	Phillips, Lucinda	Marshall
1,592	Phillips, Pleasant D.	De Kalb
9,388	Phillips, Robert	Lauderdale
7,241	Phillips, Sarah	Cherokee
8,727	Phillips, Thos.	Limestone
20,857	Phillips, Warren G.	Limestone
15,557	Phillips, Wiley	Butler
19,283	Phillips, William H.	Franklin
10,160	Phillips, William N.	Lauderdale
5,829	Phillips, Wilson	Lauderdale
5,635	Phipps, Susan K.	Madison
4,652	Picard, J.J.	Mobile
2,398	Picard, Henry J.	Madison
8,263	Pieper, Eliza & George, Adm. of Estate of Charles A. Tenge	Lauderdale
14,904	Pierce, James J.	Lawrence
16,935	Pierce, Thos. B.	Dallas
8,151	Pike, Joseph C.	Walker
9,457	Pike, Mary	Walker
6,112: 7,544:	Pike, Philip P.	Walker
17,151	Pike, Reuben A.	Walker
17,212	Pilant, Caldonia G.	Limestone
6,789	Pinkston, James	Cherokee
14,487	Pinson, Loueza	Cherokee
2,664	Pitt, Charles W.	Lawrence
7,493	Pitts, Elizabeth	Cherokee
7,979	Pledger, Pleasant W.	Jefferson
4,036	Plowman, George W.	Talladega
6,037	Poe, Wyatt	Tuscaloosa
7,114	Pointer, Philip, Estate of	Lawrence
20,133	Pointer, Samuel C.	Lawrence
14,488	Pollard, Caroline	Cherokee
4,359	Pollard, Susan	Madison
5,413	Pool, Edmund H.	Lauderdale
14,231	Pool, James J.	Lauderdale
19,497	Pope, William J.	St. Clair
7,113	Posey, Charles	Lauderdale
5,828	Posey, Napoleon B.	Walker
982	Posey, Sidney C., Adm. of Estate of James T. Morgan	Lauderdale
637	Potter, Wade L.	Escambia
3,191	Potts, James T.	Walker
12,231	Potts, Thos. E.	Bibb
3,151	Powell, Jane	Madison
2,390	Powell, Jeremiah	Madison
14,963	Powers, Daniel	Madison
10,258	Powers, William, Estate of (F.P. Ward, Exec.)	Madison

11,983	Prewett, John W.	Tuscaloosa
5,521	Prewett, William W.	Etowah
5,825	Prewitt, Geo. W.	Lauderdale
7,493	Price, Elizabeth	Cherokee
7,968	Price, Jesse T., Estate of (Terrell Gray, Executor)	Cherokee?
17,150	Price, Reuben	Dallas
12,023	Price, Sarah A.	Butler
21,530	Price, William C.	Jackson
7,239	Pridgeon, Josiah E.	Cherokee
10,816	Prince, James H., Adm. of Estate of Isham Prince	Walker
2,971	Pruitt, Robert	Calhoun
1,368	Pugh, Nathan N.	Lawrence
8,871	Pullum, Litha	Jackson
2,200	Pusser, John	Lauderdale
1,768	Putnam, David L.	De Kalb
638	Rabb, Robert S.	Conecuh
4,361	Ragsdale, Edward	Limestone
19,855	Raily, Mahala	De Kalb
7,546	Raney, Jane	Limestone
11,501	Rapier, James T.	Montgomery
1,658	Rash, Laxon	Jackson
9,811	Rawlings, R.H., Estate of (T.T. McCorkle, Adm.)	Lauderdale
611	Ray, Daniel J.	Lauderdale
11,761	Ray, H.B.	Bibb
9,812	Rayburn, Howell J.	Lauderdale
9,458	Raynes, Samuel	Jackson
11,638	Raymines, William C.	Walker
6,098	Read, Sidney	Walker
6,677	Redden, Martin	Cherokee
19,667	Redus, Alfred H. (Elizabeth B. Redus, Adm.)	Limestone
6,231	Reed, Sarah	Etowah
5,376	Reed, William	Walker
8,480	Reeves, Louisa	St. Clair
5,771	Reeves, Richard	Monroe
7,115	Reid, Benjamin F.	Limestone
15,977	Reid, Daniel, Estate of (Tabitha Reid, Widow)	Jefferson
5,208	Reid, Lucyntha	Walker
4,843	Reid, Robert C.	Franklin
6,255	Respess, Ransom	St. Clair
2,800	Reynolds, James	Butler
8,090	Reynolds, Memory C.	Cherokee
3,152	Reynolds, Thos. H.	Lauderdale
12,992	Rice, Cherry E.	Walker
721	Rice, Henry C.	Lawrence
19,229	Rice, Sousaner	Madison
18,027: 18,301:	Richards, Charles G.; Steele, Lafayette D.; and Malone, James B. & Henrietta N., Heirs of Stephen Steele	Mobile
3,192	Richardson, Jabe	Walker
19,679	Richardson, John	Limestone
5,418	Richardson, Joseph	Walker
19,498	Richardson, Milly	Limestone
8,015	Richardson, Samuel H.	Lauderdale
20,134	Richardson, William	Limestone
2,666	Ricks, Olivia	Colbert
2,020	Riddle, Robert P.	Limestone
20,468: 20,111:	Ridge, Geo. W.	Jackson
20,467	Ridge, William, Estate of (Geo. W. Ridge, Adm.)	Jackson
5,416	Rikard, Henry F.	Franklin
3,155	Rikard, Nancy	Franklin
5,637	Rikard, William	Franklin
7,548	Rigney, Penelope	Madison
6,113	Rinehart, Enoch	Cherokee
12,993	Ritchards, Geo. W.	Walker
19,499	Rivers, William E.	Madison
6,834	Rives, William	Etowah
4,054	Roach, Dennis	Jackson
3,546	Roach, Margaret W.	Jackson
4,053	Roach, Perkins	Jackson
12,995	Robbins, Elizabeth A.	Jefferson
7,117	Robbins, E.N.	Jefferson
3,154	Robbins, John B.	Jefferson

11,837	Robbins, Levi M.	Jefferson
11,838	Robbins, Thos. B.	Jefferson
15,444	Roberson, John P.	St. Clair
18,925	Roberson, Richard K.	St. Clair
2,074	Roberts, E.M.	Walker
3,973	Roberts, Geo. W.	Morgan
20,860	Roberts, Howard, Estate of	Marion
7,549	Roberts, Jesse	Jackson
5,417	Roberts, John	Jefferson
5,207	Roberts, Julia A.	Walker
1,196	Roberts, Nancy C. & Estate of James (Elias Thrasher, Adm.)	Lauderdale
3,789	Roberts, Owen *et al*	Baldwin
20,861	Roberts, Samuel C.	Marion
1,922	Roberson, Absalom, Estate of	Lawrence
9,988	Roberson, Margaret A.	Limestone
614	Roberson, William F.	Lawrence
6,513	Robertson, Robert	Franklin
19,854	Robertson, Samuel M.	De Kalb
4,841	Robinson, Caroline	Lauderdale
11,639	Robinson, Geo. H.	Walker
2,754	Robinson, John	Madison
5,831	Robinson, Little	Lauderdale
19,666	Robinson, Richard G.	Limestone
8,264	Robinson, Silas F.	Lauderdale
2,324	Robinson, William	Monroe
12,524	Rockett, Thos. W.	Jefferson
14,490	Roden, Benj. H.	De Kalb
14,492	Roden, Jere	De Kalb
13,706	Roden, John M.	Marshall
14,491	Roden, Walton W.	De Kalb
14,489	Roden, William B.	De Kalb
7,497	Rodgers, Jane	Cherokee
3,512	Roe, Thos. W.	Marshall
2,757	Rogers, Benj. B.	Madison
7,242	Rogers, J.J.B. William	Cherokee
2,772	Rogers, Julius M.	Lauderdale
6,099	Rogers, Richard A.	Walker
10,542	Rolater, John	Cherokee
10,257	Rolfe, Oscar, Estate of	Morgan
8,246	Rollins, Mary	Cherokee
5,375	Romine, James	Walker
4,360	Romine, William L.	Morgan
7,116	Ross, Andrew C.	Jefferson
4,840	Ross, Irvin	Lauderdale
2,323	Ross, Sarah	Monroe
3,972	Ross, William	Lauderdale
857: 292:	Rosser, Walter	Jackson
9,759	Rotonberry, William A.	Limestone
2,388	Rountree, William	Madison
12,994	Row, John	Jefferson
18,764	Rowan, James	St. Clair
5,636	Rowan, Jordan	Jackson
7,980	Rowan, Thos.	Jefferson
1,348	Rucker, Thomas G. (Adm. of Wm. A. Austin)	Jackson
6,234	Rudd, Iaiah	Cherokee
6,701	Rudder, Eliza J.	Jackson
5,339	Rush, Frederick	Cherokee
6,038	Rush, Moses	Madison
2,183	Rush, William A.	Winston
1,923	Russel, Alexander, Sen.	Lauderdale
6,039	Russell, Archibald H.	Madison
6,512	Russell, Daniel C.	Shelby
14,493	Russell, Elizabeth	Cherokee
7,547	Russell, Geo. W.	Shelby
13,816	Russell, Henry C.	Barbour
7,958	Russell, Israel P.	Jackson
12,996	Russell, Litha J.	Madison
3,153	Russell, Nancy A.	Blount
19,500	Russell, Sarah C.	Jackson
4,804	Russell, William	Jackson
3,529	Rutherford, Archibald	Jackson
19,608	Ryan, John	Jackson
2,960	Ryan, Miles	Conecuh
10,255	Saffold, Mary E.	Dallas
5,935	Sammons, Grove	Jackson
2,961	Sampey, John	Conecuh

6,843	Sanders, Benj. V.	Jackson
13,775	Sanders, Elbert L.	Marion
8,678	Sanders, Elbert L.	St. Clair
1,915	Sanders, John	Jackson
8,348	Sanders, Moses	Walker
8,349	Sanders, Nathaniel	Walker
1,356	Sanders, William	Jackson
9,108	Sandlin, Daniel	Walker
3,979	Sandlin, Joel W.	Morgan
5,638	Sanford, Allen	Madison
6,835	Sanford, Henry C.	Cherokee
3,372	Sanford, John	Madison
10,253	Sanford, Joseph K.	Madison
6,836	Sanford, Lemuel J.	Cherokee
2,075	Satterwhite, Sarah E.	Randolph
11,447	Saunders, Margaret	Morgan
3,362	Sawyer, Thomas G.	Blount
7,837	Scarboro, Martha Ann	Jackson
10,254	Schrimsher, Andrew J.	Madison
21,252	Schrimsher, James E.	Madison
4,849	Scidmore, Jane C.	Morgan
11,015	Scott, Carter	Walker
19,502	Scott, James, Estate of	Limestone
2,277	Scott, James B.	Madison
12,997	Scott, John	Jefferson
14,234	Scott, John, Sen.	Lauderdale
14,233	Scott, John M.	Lauderdale
9,820	Scott, Polly	Lauderdale
2,021	Scott, Silas H.	Limestone
12,420	Scott, Thos. Lee	Lee
7,244	Scroggins, John C.	Cherokee
12,930	Scroggins, Richard J.	Lawrence
2,392	Scruggs, Alfred	Madison
1,881	Scruggs, Thos. J.	Jackson
1,754	Seal, John E.	Colbert
1,145: 18,239:	Sears, John L.	Autauga
4,845	Sego, Chapman L.	Lauderdale
7,248	Sego, Marzy	Cherokee
5,209	Sego, Rebecca	Lauderdale
4,846	Sego, William G.	Lauderdale
15,918	Selby, John	Jackson
16,768	Selby, Walter	Jackson
9,109	Self, John Clayton	Walker
12,998	Sellers, Emanuel	Shelby
7,838	Shackleford, Daniel	Lawrence
13,111	Shackleford, Edward P.	Lawrence
5,836	Shackleford, Susan A. & Sam W.	Lawrence
15,571	Shamblin, Thos. L.	Tuscaloosa
3,978	Shanks, William W.	St. Clair
7,551	Sharp, Adrian	Lauderdale
16,054	Sharp, Reddin A.	Cherokee
19,239	Sharp, Robert, Sr.	Colbert
15,959	Sharp, Wilson L.	Madison
7,243	Shaw, R.W.	Cherokee
3,615	Shelton, Alfred M.	Jackson
3,617	Shelton, William	Jackson
3,616	Shelton, William F.	Jackson
20,137	Shelton, William L.	Jackson
16,913	Shener, John	Dallas
16,912	Shener, Martha A.	Dallas
7,981	Shepherd, Jeremiah, Estate of (Isham H. Shepard, Adm.)	Walker
20,621	Sherley, Elizabeth	Jackson
6,100	Sherly, A.	Walker
18,731	Sherman, William D.	Lowndes
18,930	Sherrill, John	Colbert
6,516	Sherrod, Archie	Lawrence
13,110	Sherrod, Coleman	Lawrence
13,109	Sherrod, Cyrus	Lawrence
6,484	Sherrod, Walter S., Estate of	Lawrence
6,842	Shields, Geo. W.	Cherokee
2,282	Shields, James M.	Limestone
3,977	Shields, William C.	Limestone
10,020	Shipp, Joseph R.	Walker
11,506	Shooks, Arminda	Jackson
1,750	Shugart, John	Jefferson
2,025	Sides, Andrew A.	Walker
11,641	Sides, Andrew A., Adm. of Richard Townley	Cherokee? or Walker?

2,024	Sides, Benjamin	Walker
2,027	Sides, Elijah	Walker
5,271	Sides, James	Walker
4,847	Sides, Jonathan	Walker
5,210	Sides, Joseph D.	Walker
2,026	Sides, Susan	Walker
5,639	Sides, Thos. A.	Colbert
3,988	Simmons, Geo. S.	Lauderdale
11,608	Simmons, Scipio	Madison
6,517	Simmons, William	Jackson
3,370	Simmons, William T.	Lawrence
9,819	Simons, William	Lauderdale
2,325	Simpkins, John J.	Monroe
16,052	Simpson, B.J.	Tuscaloosa
12,663	Simpson, Eleazar	Shelby
8,728	Simpson, Randolph	Tuscaloosa
21,995	Simpson, Sawyer	Madison
16,051	Simpson, Thos. B.	Tuscaloosa
6,041	Simpson, Wyatt	Tuscaloosa
6,016	Simpson, Zachariah S.	Tuscaloosa
3,051	Sims, John W.	Winston
2,234	Sims, Martha E.	Winston
15,661	Sims, Matthew	Jackson
7,550	Sisk, Wesley	Jackson
21,680	Skelton, James F.	Jackson
8,266	Skillington, Milton J.	Morgan
5,640	Skillington, John A.	Morgan
8,265	Skillington, William H.	Morgan
319	Slaughter, Henry	Morgan
1,764	Sloan, William	De Kalb
3,371	Small, Stephen T.	Winston
6,845	Smart, John W.	Jackson
16,676	Smith, Aaron G.	Limeston
17,152	Smith, Daniel	Fayette
2,356	Smith, Edward B.R.	Walker
4,851	Smith, Gentry	Lawrence
6,237	Smith, Henry H.	De Kalb
3,367	Smith, Jacob	Walker
20,136	Smith, James	Walker
6,839	Smith, James	Cherokee
19,337	Smith, James	Limestone
6,792	Smith, James M.	Cherokee
17,226	Smith, James M.	Limestone
15,136	Smith, Jesse	Marshall
3,369	Smith, John	Walker
6,837	Smith, John	Cherokee
10,251	Smith, John	Jackson
17,080	Smith, John, Estate of	Bibb
5,427	Smith, John A.	Lauderdale
6,837	Smith, John C.	Cherokee
6,043	Smith, John P.	Madison
3,156	Smith, John T.	Blount
3,976	Smith, John W.	Lauderdale
5,211	Smith, John W.	Limestone
16,424	Smith, Joseph C.	Limestone
14,504	Smith, J.W.	De Kalb
17,227	Smith, Lewis	Limestone
14,494	Smith, Margaret E.	Cherokee
19,503	Smith, Patsey A.	Winston
19,425	Smith, Rebecca J.	Mobile
7,248	Smith, Rebecca S.	Cherokee
8,152	Smith, Simeon A.	Walker
19,877	Smith, Solomon, Estate of (Leroy Peevy, Adm.)	Cherokee?
7,249	Smith, T.J.	Cherokee
6,245	Smith, William	De Kalb
4,850	Smith, William B.	Limestone
7,247	Smith, William I.	Cherokee
6,650	Smitha, William	Barbour
17,081	Smitherman, Jesse	Bibb
16,071	Smithers, James	Madison
5,832	Snead, Archer A., Adm. of Estate of John Brown	Madison
3,980	Snodgrass, Benjamin, Estate of	Jackson
19,504	Snodgrass, John, Sr.	Jackson
11,505	Snow, Levi	Jackson
15,978	Snow, William H.	Jefferson
10,415	Snyder, Sophia C.	Dallas

16,053	Southerland, James	Walker
4,848	Southern, Alfred B.	Marion
2,184	Spaine, Samuel D.	Winston
1,880	Spangler, Elizabeth, daughter of Gideon	De Kalb
5,274	Sparks, Eli A.	Walker
3,193	Sparks, Elizabeth	Walker
20,139	Sparks, Louisa E.	Colbert
6,840	Sparks, Mary M.	Cherokee
18,562	Sparks, Riley	Franklin
4,162	Sparks, Samuel, Estate of	Walker
6,515	Sparks, Thomas	Walker
8,399	Spaulding, Nancy E.	Jefferson
3,974	Speaks, Hansford	Lawrence
19,795	Spencer, Alfred S.	Jefferson
17,359	Spencer, Thomas	Colbert
15,979	Spradling, William	Jefferson
7,245	Spraggins, Nancy	Cherokee
15,463	Springer, Josiah	Madison
6,042	Squires, Alexander	Tuscaloosa
21,670	Stacks, Mathew	Walker
20,140	Stacks, William	Walker
21,350	Stacy, John H.	Montgomery
20,135	Stafford, Samuel C.	Lauderdale
2,043	Staggs, John, Jr.	Walker
2,023	Staggs, John, Sr.	Walker
19,002	Stallings, Lemuel D.	Colbert
8,091	Stallings, William	Cherokee
625	Stadefer, Lemuel J.	Etowah
5,522	Standifer, Franklin H.	Cherokee
6,040	Stanley, E.H., Mrs.	Tuscaloosa
12,933	Stanley, Francis M., Adm. of Estate of Joshua M. Stanley	Walker
5,275	Stanley, John T.	Walker
12,933	Stanley, Joshua M. (Francis M. Stanley, Adm.)	Walker
10,252	Stapler, Rebecca	Madison
14,654	Star, Eliza	Mobile
6,242	Starling, Abram H.	Cherokee
6,233	Starling, John A.	De Kalb
6,246	Starling, Nancy	Cherokee
6,240	Starling, Wiley B.	Cherokee
15,384	Starnes, John, Estate of	Marshall
15,383	Starnes, John A.W.	Marshall
11,640	Stavall, Green P.	Fayette
19,505	Stearns, Frederick	Jackson
15,137	Stearns, Isham R.	Marshall
20,138	Stedman, James	Walker
18,031	Steed, A.M.	Clay
5,276	Steedman, Elias	Walker
2,652: 5,834:	Steele, Archibald J.	Madison
4,362	Steele, James W.	Madison
18,027: 18,301:	Steele, Lafayette D.; Malone, James Bass & Henrietta N.; and Richards, Charles G.; Heirs of Stephen Steele	Mobile
3,366	Steely, James P.	Jackson
18,295	Steen, Curtis, Estate of	Lowndes
18,295	Steen, Margaret E., Adm. of Estate of Curtis Steen	
3,975	Stephens, Henry	Marshall
20,027	Stephens, Jesse, Estate of (B.H. Harrison, Exec.)	Cherokee?
3,368	Stephenson, Robt. S.	Madison
13,504	Sterne, Henry	Bullock
5,837	Sterns, Peter C.	Marshall
20,113	Stevens, Jesse	Jackson
8,400	Stevens, Tabitha	Jackson
4,145	Stevens, Nicholas	Jackson
10,349	Stevenson, Louisa C.	Walker
1,340	Steward, Claiborne	Jackson
19,680	Steward, John	Walker
5,838	Stewart, Duncan	Lauderdale
18,296	Stewart, James W.	Lauderdale
2,233	Stewart, Jacob S.	Walker
21,996	Stewart, John	Madison
6,847	Stweart, Thomas	Limestone
10,333	Stinson, William	Cherokee

6,514	Stoddard, Samuel	Fayette
16,706	Stogsdill, Elisha	Jackson
14,960	Stokes, Harriet D., Estate of (Joseph A. Hobbs, Adm.)	Madison
13,108	Stokes (Stoker), Henry	Chambers
2,185	Stokes, William	Winston
1,661	Stoltz, John	Jackson
192	Stone, G.W., Adm. of Randall Cheek	Lowndes
6,844	Story, Calvin	Cherokee
10,161	Stovall, David L.	Walker
5,278	Stovall, Elizabeth	Walker
18,685	Street, Reuben	Madison
18,765	Strickland, Lloyd	Fayette
7,251	Stricklin, Eliza	Cherokee
7,250	Stricklin, James	Cherokee
7,252	Stricklin, Joseph	Cherokee
5,374	Stringer, David	Colbert
17,713	Stringer, Robert J.A.	Crenshaw
20,862	Strong, Robert H.	Madison
3,787	Strong, Samuel S., Heirs of (Widow Mary, Gilbert, Charles, Washington & Edward)	Baldwin
9,461	Studdard, David	Fayette
1,198	Stutts, Geo. W.	Lauderdale
1,199	Stutts, Henry	Lauderdale
1,200	Stutts, Jacob	Lauderdale
985	Stutts, John R.	Lauderdale
1,201	Stutts, Walter F.	Lauderdale
983	Stutts, William	Lauderdale
3,789	Styson, Abisha *et al*	Baldwin
2,662	Sullivan, Charles	Lauderdale
4,055	Sullivan, John	Jackson
5,833	Sullivan, Mary A.	Madison
2,022	Sumner, James	Walker
9,760	Surber, Miranda J.	Limestone
6,670	Sutterlin, Charles & Widow Joanna	Cherokee
18,723	Sutton, William A.	Marshall
19,856	Swader, Thomas	De Kalb
14,496	Swansey, William	Cherokee
19,609	Swift, John H.	Madison
11,887	Swindle, Jesse	Tuscaloosa
16,228	Sykes, Jonas	Lawrence
3,373	Sykes, Matilda	Lawrence
14,235	Tacker, Riley	Lauderdale
13,828	Tallent, William	Cherokee
7,457	Talley, J.B.	Jackson
6,520	Tanner, David M.	Colbert
10,256	Tanner, John D.	Madison
17,415	Tanner, William P.	Limestone
12,999	Tate, Francis	Jefferson
13,000	Tate, James W.	Walker
19,796	Tatom, Abel	Lee
3,982	Tatum, Menafee	Macon
256: or 556:	Taylor (Tayloe), Benj. Ogle, Estate of	Cherokee or Winston?
556	Taylor, Chas. A.	Winston
21,230	Taylor, Creed L.	Marshall
8,139	Taylor, David	St. Clair
1,769	Taylor, John	De Kalb
2,643	Taylor, John	Winston
9,464	Taylor, John E., Estate of (Wm. B. Taylor, Adm.)	De Kalb
6,044	Taylor, John W. (or James W.)	Madison
7,253	Taylor, Lucy	Cherokee
12,094	Taylor, Matilda	Cleburne
14,965	Taylor, Morris K., Adm. of Estate of John W. Geron	Madison
6,525	Taylor, Paschal H.	Randolph
256	Taylor (Tayloe), Phebe Warren	Marengo
2,670	Taylor, Pleasant	Franklin
17,714	Taylor, Randall & Widow Thyrza	Crenshaw
5,213	Taylor, Richard	Franklin
17,046	Taylor, Sarah E.	Cleburne
9,465: 12,145:	Taylor, William B.	De Kalb
6,244	Templeton, James H.	Etowah
8,263	Tenge, Charles A., Estate of	Lauderdale
5,214	Terry, Joseph	Lawrence
15,329	Terry, Thos. L.	Limestone
5,839	Teters, Martha A.	Jackson
19,682	Thack, Thomas	Limestone
19,003	Tharp, Robert, Jr.	Colbert
10,239	Tharp, Robert, Sr.	Colbert
3,157	Thomas, David	Jefferson
16,196	Thomas, Jesse	Lauderdale
4,852	Thomas, John D.	Limestone
5,215	Thomas, Joseph	Jackson
6,521	Thomas, Phineas	Lauderdale
3,374	Thomas, William	Blount
2,401	Thomas, William C.	Jackson
9,989	Thomason, Anderson C.	Morgan
19,987	Thompson, Benj.	Colbert
17,124	Thompson, Daniel	Colbert
18,476	Thompson, James M.	Colbert
13,286	Thompson, Meredith	Colbert
8,872	Thompson, Samuel	Jefferson
12,232	Thompson, Thomas	Randolph
9,110	Thompson, William	Limestone
10,893	Thorn, Pleasant S.	Colbert
15,769	Thorn, Presley S.	Colbert
13,974	Thorn, William H.	Colbert
7,088	Thorne, Ann Eliza Binford (Wife of R.G. Thorne, and Heir of John H. Binford)	Limestone
855	Thornton, Mary	Jackson
3,530	Thornton, William A.	Jackson
5,216	Thrasher, Elias	Lauderdale
18,264	Thrasher, Geo.	Lawrence
3,981	Thrasher, Susan Y.	Lauderdale
3,158	Thrasher, Thomas	Lauderdale
4,202	Thrasher, William B.L.	Lauderdale
7,552	Tiara, Jesse V.	Fayette
6,519	Tiara, Martha	Fayette
3,989	Timberlake, John P. & Joel S.	Jackson
20,843	Timberlake, John P., Adm. of Estate of Amanda Greene	Jackson
1,772	Tiner, Stephen J.	De Kalb
19,474	Tinney, John C., Estate of (David R. Bellamy, Adm.)	Jackson
16,405	Tinsley, Peter	Limestone
14,497	Tipton, Mordecai	Cherokee
19,506	Tipton, Vance B.	Jackson
10,162	Todd, Jacob W.	Limestone
6,045	Tompkins, Christopher C.	Franklin
16,084	Tompkins, Marion, Estate of (Sarah J. Tompkins, Widow)	Franklin
4,363	Toney, Edmund	Madison
16,858	Toney, Margaret	Madison
6,702	Tonner, Evaline & Lucy	Jackson
19,507	Toon, Ellison	Jackson
16,133	Toone, William	Limestone
722	Torian, Samuel T., Adm. of Estate of Bolling Byrd	Lawrence
11,641	Townley, Richmond, Estate of, Andrew A. Sides, Adm.	Walker
20,142	Townley, Richmond, Jr.	Walker
6,101	Townley, Susannah	Walker
5,419	Townsley, Stephen, Estate of (Sarah Townsley, Adm.)	Lauderdale
8,651	Tramel, Levi	Cherokee
7,968	Trice, Jesse C., Estate of	Jackson
1,921	Trim, John H.	Fayette
13,675	Trimble, Thomas C.	Sumter
2,276	Trousdale, Sarah E.	Lawrence
22,172	True, Rutha	Madison
8,351	Tubbs, Daniel	Walker
11,609	Tuck, John	Madison
10,018	Tucker, Charles	Walker
18,931	Tucker, Charles E.	Limestone
20,863	Tucker, Geo. S.	Marion
18,297	Tucker, James, Estate of	Limestone
19,338	Tucker, Thos. G.	Limestone

5,279	Tuggle, James B.	Walker
19,870	Turbyfill, Wilson, Estate of (James H. Armstrong, Adm.)	Madison
8,729	Turner, Ann D.	Lauderdale
285	Turner, Benjamin Sterling	Dallas
2,235	Turner, Celia	Winston
12,931	Turner, Nelson	Madison
6,612	Turner, Prior	Madison
2,076	Turrentine, Charity W.	Morgan
2,276	Tweedy, Robert E.	Lawrence
6,518	Tyner, Jackson H.	Russell
20,284	Underwood, Alexander, Estate of	Marion
5,868	Underwood, Jesse	Marion
3,789	Underwood, M.	Baldwin
6,849	Underwood, Matilda	Cherokee
12,932	Underwood, Nimrod T.	Colbert
7,254	Underwood, Theron	Cherokee
5,280	Underwood, William M.	Walker
17,834	Utter, Annie	Jackson
8,374	Utter, Harriet Ann & John W.	Jackson
3,159	Vandeford, James	Jefferson
7,256	Vandevier, Ambrose	Cherokee
7,255	Vandivier, John D.	Cherokee
13,001	Vann, Margaret E.	Jefferson
21,137	Vann, Robert J.	Jefferson
7,839	Vaughan, Philip	Lawrence
14,498	Vaughn, Hartwell, Jr.	Cherokee
14,499	Vaughn, Hartwell, Sr.	Cherokee
15,662	Vaught, Hiram	Jackson
14,500	Ventress, Mary E.	De Kalb
9,111	Vest, William A.	Walker
21,138	Vickers, Thomas G.	Montgomery
10,350	Vince, James	Limestone
18,686	Vincent, David	Madison
6,522	Vineyard, James L.	Randolph
19,240	Vinson, Allen	Limestone
16,085	Wade, Sarah	Lawrence
10,163	Wade, William N.	Lauderdale
14,236	Wadkins, Margaret L.	Lauderdale
2,285	Wales, Thos. J.	Limestone
5,642	Waldrep, James S.	Morgan
18,032	Walker, Buckner	Winston
3,033	Walker, Elethan, Estate of	Cherokee
7,840	Walker, Hamilton	Limestone
11,762	Walker, John F.	Bibb
18,687	Walker, Lovel	Limestone
18,418	Walker, Thaddeus	Fayette
17,360	Walker, William A.	Colbert
17,479	Walker, William W.	De Kalb
7,982	Wall, Alfred	Madison
3,548	Wall, Joshua C.	Jackson
4,056	Wallace, Elizabeth	Jackson
4,369	Wallace, James M.	Lauderdale
5,524	Wallace, John	De Kalb
5,420	Wallace, John B.	Lauderdale
2,326	Wallace, Luarcha	Monroe
4,368	Wallace, Samuel W.	Lauderdale
7,118	Wallace, Thomas A.	Lauderdale
4,859	Wallace, William	Lauderdale
16,730	Waite, John C.	De Kalb
554	Ward, Anderson	Winston
10,258	Ward, F.P., Exec. of Wm. Powers	Madison
6,855	Ward, Henrietta	Cherokee
6,854	Ward, Newton C.	Cherokee
13,002	Ward, Reuben R.	Walker
11,815	Ward, Samuel, Estate of (George W. and Fleming B. Ward, Execs.)	Madison
6,853	Ward, Samuel F.	Cherokee
7,119	Ward, Sarah A.	Jackson
21,141	Ware, James A., Estate of	Montgomery
7,841	Ware, Jeptha M.	Jefferson
20,147	Ware, Mary E.	Jefferson
19,510	Warren, Charlotte A.	Jackson
18,700	Warren, James M.	Lawrence
7,121	Warren, Samuel D.	De Kalb

4,914	Warrington, Sarah A. & Wm. B.	Jackson
18,299	Washburn, John	Madison
19,988	Washington, Samuel	Madison
6,672	Waters, Claborn C.	Cherokee
9,817	Waters, Nancy	Lauderdale
1,757	Watkins, E.A.C.	Lawrence
6,858	Watkins, George W.	Limestone
2,659	Watkins, John S.	Lauderdale
19,798	Watson, John T.	Jefferson
19,214	Watson, Williams	Montgomery
8,153	Watt, William	Walker
17,125	Weaver, Leroy G.	De Kalb
7,506	Weaver, Mary	Cherokee
17,360	Weaver, William W.	Colbert
18,577	Webb, Alexander P.	Colbert
9,810	Webb, Henry	Lauderdale
6,440	Webb, Margaret T.	Jackson
6,523	Webb, Nancy M.	Walker
6,232	Webb, Thomas	Cherokee
20,870	Webster, James L.	Madison
6,857	Wedgeworth, Francis M.	Limestone
7,554	Weems, Joseph	Lauderdale
5,846	Weir, Leonard L.	Limestone
5,525	Wells, Andrew	De Kalb
5,929	Wells, Elizabeth	Jackson
14,502	Wells, Milly	Cherokee
20,143	Welsh, Emily M.	Colbert
1,763	Wesson, John W.	De Kalb
4,855	West, George W.	Limestone
21,681	West, John S.	Walker
2,186	West, William	Winston
7,257	Wester, George	Cherokee
14,501	Wester, James	Cherokee
2,649	Wheat, Moses K.	Macon
558	Wheeler, Calvin M.	Cherokee
20,868	White, Benega	De Kalb
20,869	White, John, Estate of (John G. White, Adm.)	De Kalb
20,867	White, Joseph	De Kalb
17,082	White, Michael K.	Bibb
3,378	White, Thomas	Lauderdale
5,643	White, Thos. J.	Limestone
4,856	White, Thomas J.	Lauderdale
19,508	White, Wm. H.	De Kalb
6,856	White, William M.	Cherokee
16,847	White, Zachariah, Estate of	Winston
5,845	Whitefield, John	Jackson
4,856	Whitehead, Jacob	Lauderdale
17,405	Whiteside, Margaret	Calhoun
8,927	Whitlock, Elizabeth	Colbert
4,370	Whitlock, John K.	Cherokee
9,816	Whitsett, Wilson	Lauderdale
8,049	Whitson, Thos. J.	Tuscaloosa
10,662	Whittier, Simeon, Adm. of Nathaniel Whitticur	Marshall
9,855	Whittle, Nancy	Lauderdale
6,851	Whorton, Jacob W., Adm. of Estate of John C. Anderson	Cherokee
6,850	Whorton, Nancy	Cherokee
2,968	Whorton, Solomon	Madison
17,154	Widman, Susan	Fayette
5,201	Wiker, Elizabeth	Walker
3,375	Wilaby, Winchester	Tuscaloosa
7,553	Wilborn, Elias, Estate of (James Wilborn, Adm.)	Jackson
19,759	Wilburn, Samuel	Madison
2,646	Wilder, Mary J.	Jackson
19,241	Wildsmith, Thomas	Jefferson
22,263	Wiley, Amy	Jefferson
7,120	Wilkes, John H.	Jefferson
4,479	Wilkinson, Algernon L., for Heirs of Laura	Madison
21,139	Wilkinson, Laure E., Heirs of	Madison
16,013	Wilkinson, Robert	Lauderdale
18,699	William, Sally	Winston
7,258	Williams, Howell	Cherokee
1,662	Williams, Jacob M.	Jackson
9,112	Williams, John	Walker
18,858	Williams, John H.	Walker

4,447	Williams, Littleton P.	Lauderdale
19,683	Williams, Lucinda	Walker
21,142	Williams, Martha R.	Madison
18,298	Williams, Melvina E., Estate of (Wm. S. Williams, Adm.)	Lawrence
9,567	Williams, Milton	Madison
16,369	Williams, Priscilla A.	Lee
4,857	Williams, Salina	Walker
13,569	Williams, Thomas	Colbert
9,462	Williams, William	Walker
5,217	Williams, William W.	Walker
954	Wialliamson, A.O.	Madison
775	Williamson, Asa	Cleburne
11,310	Williamson, Russell B.	St. Clair
18,708	Willis, Adeline M.	Butler
10,122	Willman, Xavier	Talladega
7,389	Wilson, Benj. I.	Cherokee
3,990	Wilson, Cassius	Lauderdale
8,481	Wilson, Danl. H.	Cherokee
2,236	Wilson, James M.	Winston
9,758	Wilson, John	Lauderdale
8,362	Wilson, John H.	Colbert
8,352	Wilson, John H.	Walker
5,281	Wilson, Lewis	Walker
5,641	Wilson, Mariah	Jackson
17,416	Wilson, Martha, Estate of	De Kalb
3,085	Wilson, Philip	Winston
21,140	Wilson, Robt. D.	Winston
6,395	Wilson, Sarah E.	Walker
13,003	Wilson, Washington	Walker
2,080	Wilson, W.W.	Walker
15,287	Wilson, William	Dallas
6,045	Windham, E.H.	Tuscaloosa
10,190	Wingo, George L.	Colbert
18,766	Winn, Jack, Estate of (Jesse Winn, Adm.)	Tuscaloosa
2,656	Winston, John G.	Marshall
14,503	Winston, John G., Exec. of Christopher C. Cardon	De Kalb
3,984	Winston, John N. (or W.O.)	De Kalb
2,279	Wishard, Olive E.	Madison
18,889	Witt, Nancy S.	Cherokee
10,661	Womble, Cynthia	Lauderdale
3,376	Wood, Abner	Jefferson
13,004	Wood, Elias	Walker
16,677	Wood, James P.S.	Limestone
700	Wood, Robert	Cherokee
3,169	Wood, Robt. J.	Walker
6,524	Wood, Thos. J.	Jackson
5,841	Woodall, P.S.	Jackson
4,366	Woodall, Pleasant	Jackson
5,401	Woodall, Pleasant S., Adm. of Estate of Presley R. Woodall	Jackson
2,647	Woodall, Silas P.	Jackson
9,463	Woodard, Sarah A.	Walker
19,318	Woodroof, J.W.	Limestone
14,966	Woodson, James	Madison
14,967	Woodson, Robert	Madison
4,367	Woody, Geo. W.	Madison
4,365	Woody, Robt. W.	Madison
16,191	Woolsey, William, Estate of	Jackson
3,983	Wornack, Martha	Limestone
5,840	Wortham, William H., Estate of	Madison
17,363	Wren, James S.	De Kalb
13,005	Wright, Elias	Walker
5,282	Wright, Elias W.	Walker
6,745	Wright, Ellander	Monroe
6,048	Wright, Francis C. (or Thomas A.)	Madison
5,842	Wright, James	Madison
6,859	Wright, John W.	Jackson
3,626	Wright, Lavinia, James K.P. & Estate of John L.	Jackson
15,599	Wright, Moses R., Estate of	Cherokee
19,509	Wright, William C.	Jackson
18,591	Wright, William H.	De Kalb
3,625	Wright, Zachariah J.	Jackson
3,789	Wroten, William	Baldwin
9,990	Wylie, William	Lauderdale
5,844	Wynn, John, Estate of (Margaret Wynn, Adm.)	Jackson
958	Yarbrough, Samuel H.	Madison
3,379	Yielding, John	Blount
7,122	York, Andrew Y.	Limestone
5,644	York, Tapler T.	Tuscaloosa
11,984	York, William E.	Limestone
21,143	Young, Isaac	Clay
19,215	Young, James C.	Lauderdale
4,854	Young, John	Lauderdale
15,472	Young, John T.	Jackson
8,401	Young, Lawson	Jefferson
2,658	Young, Samuel	Lauderdale
3,473	Yocum, Sarah	Colbert
18,300	Yuckley, George W.	Madison

ARKANSAS

11,359	Abbott, Elisha G.	Arkansas
768	Abel, Lindley	Sebastian
17,983	Adams, Mary S.	Franklin
7,635	Adams, W.C., Estate of	Franklin
5,743	Aday, B.W.	Crawford
14,032	Addy, Jerusha C.	Saline
22,157	Adney, James D.	Yell
15,205	Agent, Nathan	Franklin
12,470	Agery, John	Pulaski
9,877	Aiken, John	Prairie
10,772	Alderson, Jesse W.	Benton
19,195	Aldridge, Alfred	Franklin
21,489: 21,778:	Aldridge, Milton	Franklin
20,345: 12,421:	Alexander, Andrew	Pulaski
22,025	Alexander, David	Desha
10,855	Alexander, Wm. L. and Cate, Henry T. and Obed	Washington
9,920	Alfrey, Absalom H.	Benton
14,280	Allcock, Wm. J.	Johnson
11,522	Allen, Abijah, Estate of	Cross
10,783	Allen, Abraham	Independence
826	Allen, Elijah	Conway
6,422	Allen, Elizabeth A.	Hot Springs
11,768	Allen, Fannie	Cross
2,701	Allen, John	Marion
3,177	Allen, Jethro M.	Clark
7,925	Allen, John D., Estate of	Clark
14,506	Allen, Lucinda	Jefferson
3,037	Allen, Russel	Crawford
2,106	Allen, Moses S.	Monroe
4,280	Allen, William	Independence
4,462	Allen, William D.	St. Francis
12,638	Alston, Thomas M.	Phillips
20,205	Anderson, A.J.M.	Carroll
711	Anderson, Archie	Pulaski
13,179	Anderson, Charles V.	Hot Springs
9,591	Anderson, Jackson	Benton
16,342	Anderson, James R.	Monroe
11,021	Arbaught, Francis	Johnson
13,832	Arbuckle, John D.	Sebastian
9,240	Arendale, Richard	Benton
4,279	Armistead, Emanuel W.	Pulaski
5,930	Armstrong, Elijah	Benton
5,760	Arnold, Elisha	Izard
9,592	Arnold, William	Boone
21,539	Arthur, Subrina	Benton
4,741	Ashley, Austin	Grant
9,593	Atchley, Clayborn	Boone
19,649	Atkins, John	Scott
11,413	Atwood, Thomas J.	Arkansas
18,012	Austin, Andrew W.	Craighead
710	Austin, Henry	Pulaski

20,220	Austin, John K.	Madison
5,776	Austin, Thomas & John N. Curtis	Benton
19,652	Awalt, Michael	Scott
7,037	Axum, Nelson	Clark
13,141	Ayliff, Charles	Pulaski
10,798	Bailey, Mary	Sebastian
6,605	Bailey, Wiley	Sebastian
18,710	Baird, Abner	Jackson
19,658	Baird, Wm.	Sebastian
18,703	Baker, A.P.	Benton
3,443	Baker, Andrew C.	Drew
18,087	Baker, Arthur A.	Carroll
11,182	Baker, Isaiah	Sebastian
1,609	Baker, Maria	Benton
4,281	Baker, Peter K.	Independence
9,594	Baker, Richmond	Washington
18,694	Baker, Thomas W.	Marion
4,786	Baldwin, Lewis	Pulaski
13,278	Ballard, Margaret	Phillips
14,033	Ballard, Moses	Pulaski
18,725	Ballard, Sallie	Benton
11,163	Ballou, R.M.	Woodruff
8,693	Bancroft, Cora C. & Edwin	Prairie
14,540	Banks, Mary E.	Washington
22,088	Barhyte, Maria	Sebastian
15,223	Barker, James M.	Arkansas
12,011	Barker, Wm. E., Estate of	Washington
17,532	Barnard, Louisa	Sarber
2,876	Barnes, Claiborne	Pulaski
13,674	Barnes, Geo. W.	Madison
9,217	Barnes, Sarah	Washington
8,423	Barnes, William	Sebastian
9,568	Barnett, James	Crawford
10,858	Barr, John F.	Washington
14,888	Barrington, Margaret I.	Washington
17,115	Barron, Ann	Phillips
1,319	Barron, Hiram H.	Washington
9,218	Barron, Wm.	Washington
15,265	Barrow, Thomas	Phillips
11,670	Bartow, John W.	Clark
2,766	Bastion, Solomon	Conway
12,439	Bates, Henderson	Washington
9,595	Bates, James F.	Washington
5,610	Baxter, Arabella V.	St. Francis
20,039	Baxter, Elgira P.	Monroe
19,657	Baxter, Patience	Scott
17,418	Bean, Caesar	Crawford
20,052	Bean, John W.	Washington
9,699	Bean, Joseph	Nevada
18,039	Beasley, Eveline T.	Monroe
817	Beatie, Alexander	Washington
13,705	Beard, Daniel Y.	Crawford
12,552	Bearden, Mary	Pulaski
9,256	Beasley, Quinton B.	Johnson
1,165	Beaver, John M.	White
11,162	Becton, John W.	Woodruff
9,596	Bedingfield, James M.	Carroll
11,360	Belknap, Chas. W.	Arkansas
12,679	Bell, Elizabeth	Fulton
20,556	Bell, Jesse H.	Scott
6,269	Bell, John M., Estate of	Prairie
13,640	Bell, Tilitha	Pulaski
22,011	Bender, David	Pulaski
20,197	Benham, Ada	Pulaski
9,554	Bennett, D.D., Mrs.	Monroe
9,249	Bennett, David	Johnson
20,062	Benson, Wm. F.	Washington
16,859	Benton, Jesse H.	Benton
9,023	Berna, Francis H.	Crawford
4,863	Berna, Henry C.	Crawford
13,641	Berry, Nancy	Pulaski
10,781	Berry, Wm. P.	Independence
10,529	Bevins, Nancy Ann	Saline
22,086: 19,315:	Billingsly, John	Washington
8,107	Bingham, Nathan	Crawford
8,214	Bingham, Sarah J.	Saline
9,599	Black, Alexander & William	Benton
9,599	Black, William & Alexander	Benton
682	Black, William W.	Benton
18,597	Blackburn, Churchill H.	Desha
11,151	Blackman, Nancy	Sebastian
4,888	Blackwell, Clement	Johnson
7,664	Blackwell, Nancy	Crawford
14,645	Bladgett, Noah H.	Pulaski
13,979	Blake, Samuel	Washington
9,600	Blanset, Archibald	Benton
22,291	Bledsoe, Eli	Montgomery
20,151	Blevins, John W.	Benton
9,024	Blevins, Pleasant	Crawford
9,601	Blevins, Squire	Boone
9,697	Block, Solomon	Ouachita
4,465	Bloom, Jacob, Jr.	Jefferson
3,632	Bloom, Jacob, Sr.	Jefferson
1,098	Bloyd, Wm.	Washington
18,783	Blythe, James M.	Washington
11,684	Bogan, Timmy	Clark
9,694	Boggs, Wm. R.	Clark
21,799	Bolin, John	Crawford
11,003	Bolinger, H.H.	Madison
19,192	Bolinger, Mary A.	Franklin
14,007	Bonds, Robert E.	Monroe
5,779	Bone, Martha A.	Benton
9,236	Bonham, George	Washington
9,598	Bonham, Jesse	Washington
9,597	Bonham, John	Washington
1,174	Bonnell, Ann E.	Jefferson
14,173	Bonner, Charles S.	Phillips
16,331	Boon, John	Crawford
20,369	Boone, Edmond	Washington
15,216	Boone, Nicholas T.	Franklin
12,433	Booth, Robert, Jr.	White
20,213	Boothe, John M.	Washington
20,244	Boren, Joshua	Madison
17,519	Bostick, J.S.	Pulaski
19,462	Bostick, Sarah A.	Crawford
20,348	Bott, Isaac	Pulaski
21,082	Bowen, Hiram	Johnson
6,416	Bowen, William D.	Hot Springs
19,610	Bowen, Wm. R.	Sebastian
17,855	Bowers, L.G.	Monroe
22,005	Bowlin, Jane	Crawford
1,085	Bowlin, William	Crawford
15,835	Bowser, Nancy	Madison
12,580	Box, Martha	Boone
9,602	Boyd, Willis	Washington
12,067	Boyer, Elizabeth	Crawford
19,670	Boyett, Thomas	Sebastian
18,398	Bracket, James	Boone
13,259	Bradford, D.M.	White
5,745	Bradford, John	Crawford
9,688	Bradley, Wm. L., Estate of	Ouachita
16,329	Bradner, Alonzo	Crawford
9,022	Bradshaw, Elisha J.	Sebastian
17,621	Branch, James H., Estate of	Monroe
14,139	Branham, Isom M.	Crawford
8,106	Branham, William	Crawford
15,742	Brashears, Eliza	Saline
21,516	Brazil, Moses	Saline
21,540	Breeden, Lindsey O.	Conway
5,577	Brents, William	Saline
5,576	Brewer, Elvy	Saline
15,836	Brewer, John	Madison
12,594	Brewer, Mary Jane	Pulaski
901: 902:	Brewer, Mathias	Washington
12,595	Brewer, Nathan T.	Pulaski
12,551	Brewer, Sampson	Pulaski
21,939	Brewer, Wm. L., Estate of	Sebastian
3,326	Brickey, David	Washington
4,568	Brickey, James N.	Benton
12,617	Brickley, John	Pulaski
7,927	Bridges, John	Clark
7,926	Bridges, Martha & Newton	Clark
7,928	Bridges, Wm. J.	Clark
19,348	Bridgman, James, Estate of	Crawford
8,424	Briggs, Archibald	Sebastian

21,661	Bringle, Mary	Arkansas
10,051	Brisick, Owen J.	Hot Springs
1,840	Bristow, William G.	Johnson
11,846	Britton, James M.	Pulaski
22,074	Brodie, Wm. B.	Washington
12,592	Brogan, Joseph	Sebastian
13,949	Brooks, Lafayette	Washington
14,711	Brooks, Lucy W.	Phillips
14,201	Brooks, Newell P.	Nevada
19,429	Brooks, Thomas	Washington
22,085	Brotherton, Benjamin H.	Washington
9,603	Brown, Alfred	Benton
9,283	Brown, Emily A.	Johnson
21,308	Brown, George H.	Sebastian
19,736	Brown, George W.	Washington
10,146	Brown, Jackson	Pulaski
17,622	Brown, Jacob	Monroe
15,714	Brown, James A.	Pulaski
21,807	Brown, John, Estate of	Washington
1,893	Brown, Jno. G.	Johnson
21,492	Brown, Josephys	Sebastian
13,357	Brown, Marquis D.	Sarber
22,037	Brown, Martha	Sebastian
18,269	Brown, Mary A.	Monroe
1,841	Brown, Sallie	Johnson
5,531	Brown, Thomas, Estate of	Monroe
13,950	Brown, Thomas F.	Washington
20,470: 21,496:	Brown, Wm.	Franklin
12,482	Brunk, Phoebe	Crawford
11,872	Bryant, Berry	Crawford
11,870	Bryant, Elijah	Crawford
15,837	Bryant, William	Madison
17,166	Bryson, Andrew J.	Sarber
13,457	Bryson, John	Sarber
1,612	Bryson, Samuel	Benton
5,298	Buchanan, Jason	Clark
13,980	Buchanan, John	Washington
19,450	Buchanan, Leander	Washington
5,297	Buchanan, Robert & William F.	Clark
21,085	Buck, Archibald	Franklin
18,785	Buck, Henderson	Benton
6,107	Buckingham, Frederick	Perry
4,282	Bullington, John J.	Independence
11,411	Bullington, Wm. B.	Arkansas
19,273	Bumpass, Pleasant	Pulaski
5,781	Burgin, Elijah P.	Benton
17,623	Burns, Sarah Ann	Monroe
8,108	Burriss, Mary	Crawford
19,751	Burrow, Isaac	Washington
11,619	Burton, Shadrach W.	Madison
12,548	Bushong, James S.	Crawford
4,866	Bushong, Mary	Crawford
5,018	Butler, George B.	Pulaski
21,536	Butler, Israel S. & Spurgeon, Greenberry J.	Sebastian
11,755	Butler, James A.	Phillips
16,091	Butler, Nancy	Crawford
9,266	Buttram, Elijah H.	Benton
5,780	Buttram, Eliza	Benton
2,408	Buttram, Joel	Saline
9,604	Buttram, Wm. D.	Benton
9,278	Buttry, John	Benton
6,939	Bybee, Rosa A.	White
17,905	Byers, Meekness M.	Arkansas
17,812	Bynum, Geo. W.	Conway
2,957	Bynum, James M.	Johnson
11,709	Byrd, Edward	Washington
9,027	Byrne, Charles, Estate of	Sebastian
9,349	Byrne, James	Calhoun
15,217	Cagle, Green L.	Franklin
19,428	Cagle, Jacob	Polk
16,394	Cain, Cornelius	Montgomery
9,725	Calahan, Abram M.	Crawford
15,178	Caldeleugh, Alexander B.	Arkansas
14,186	Caldwell, Lucy A.	Jefferson
15,389	Caldwell, Wm. H.	Washington
15,743	Cale, Wm. H.	Saline
13,952	Caler, Wm.	Washington
14,986	Calhoun, Hugh	Montgomery
6,570	Callahan, Andrew	Marion
9,246	Callahan, Kelsey H.	Johnson
13,563	Campbell, Harriet A.	Pulaski
9,605	Campbell, J.M.	Washington
21,635	Campbell, John	Independence
9,542	Campbell, Joseph M.	Pulaski
17,879	Campbell, Thomas M.	Washington
5,369	Campbell, Wm.	Washington
17,984	Campbell, William W.	Franklin
18,909	Cannon, David J.	Pulaski
20,500	Cannon, John	Washington
5,730	Cappock, Olive	Saline
20,565	Capps, Benjamin F.	Sebastian
9,607	Cardwell, Hosea G.	Washington
1,301	Cardwell, Wm. H.	Washington
18,554	Carlile, J.D.	Washington
2,201	Carlile, J.T.	Washington
4,153	Carlisle, Jasper M.	Washington
1,090	Carney, George G.	Washington
1,089	Carney, James W.	Washington
9,606	Carney, N.A.	Washington
21,782	Carr, Jane	Franklin
12,437	Carr, Mary	Sebastian
9,608	Carrigan, Patrick M.	Washington
10,052	Carson, Calvin H.	Grant
13,953	Carter, David	Washington
21,811	Carter, Elum	Washington
9,149	Carter, Henry H.	Clark
7,027	Carter, John B.	Clark
7,026	Carter, Littleton N.	Clark
4,203	Carter, Samuel	Washington
20,948	Carter, Wm.	White
18,910	Carver, John M.	Grant
13,642	Carver, Marina	Grant
4,283	Case, George, Estate of	Independence
1,842	Casey, Anthony	Newton
10,043	Cash, Martin	Hot Springs
16,215	Cason, Jesse	Ashley
4,154	Cate, Henry T.	Washington
10,855	Cate, Henry T. and Obed & Alexander, Wm. L.	Washington
4,155	Cate, Jacob R.	Washington
10,855	Cate, Obed and Henry T. & Alexander, Wm. L.	Washington
1,898	Cate, Obed C.	Washington
18,744	Catham, Richard H.	Drew
1,136	Caughman, Wm. H.	Washington
15,275	Cave, James F.	Washington
13,646	Cavender, James M., Estate of	Pulaski
19,313	Cavin, Ananias	Washington
18,080	Chambers, James	Polk
22,039	Chambers, Ransom, Estate of	Woodruff
17,189	Chambers, William	Pulaski
9,342	Chambliss, William W.	Ouachita
4,264	Champ, Robert	St. Francis
4,157	Chandlier, Jacob	Washington
4,156	Chandlier, Preston	Washington
22,044	Chapman, A.J.	Crawford
20,318	Chapman, Henry	Crawford
12,612	Chapman, Levi	Crawford
816	Chapman, Wilson	Washington
8,831	Chastain, Edward B.	Crawford
21,870	Chastain, Elizabeth M. & Wm. F.	Saline
19,250	Chastain, James	Franklin
19,182	Chastain, Joseph C.	Franklin
21,783	Chastain, Lucinda	Franklin
11,618	Chaupe, Hemis, Estate of	St. Francis
10,002	Cheairs, David B., Estate of	Desha
9,255	Cheek, James	Johnson
13,184	Chenault, Nancy	Sabine
9,350	Chenault, Rebecca A.	Calhoun
6,402	Childers, Green V.	Dallas
20,038	Chism, Louisa	Monroe
8,832	Chitwood, Daniel	Franklin
19,654	Chitwood, Joseph	Scott
11,549	Chitwood, Russel P.	Sarber
17,970	Church, C.B.	Sebastian
5,583	Church, Pine Bluff Baptist	Jefferson

18,812	Claiborne, John B.	White
10,845	Clanton, Alfred	Washington
11,727	Clark, Asa	Sebastian
13,682	Clark, James W.	Benton
1,175	Clegg, Thomas W., Jr.	Jefferson
3,380	Cleghorn, Sarah J.	Independence
11,161	Clement, Samuel, Estate of	Woodruff
9,609	Clement, Stephen R.	Benton
10,044	Clift, Harvey	Hot Springs
4,890	Cline, George M.	Washington
18,919	Cline, Thomas A.	Washington
10,788	Clinton, Choctaw	Jackson
13,135	Cloyes, N.A.	Hot Springs
14,507	Cobb, Bayliss E.	Jefferson
4,875	Cochran, Ned	Crittendon
17,817	Cody, William	Perry
5,227	Coffield, W.B.	Arkansas
3,018	Coffin, Wm. G.	Washington
1,474	Cohee, Gilbert	Washington
14,813	Cohen, Isaac	Ashley
2,709	Colclasure, Margaret	Washington
14,034	Coleman, Hawes H.	Clark
9,724	Coleman, Zill	Crawford
4,390: 4,391: 4,392:	Collier, Eli G.	Yell
9,215	Collins, Mitchell	Washington
5,716	Collins, Wilson W.	Franklin
21,551	Colvert, Robert	Franklin
9,790	Colville, Ann	Benton
3,785	Combs, Joel A.	Washington
1,320	Combs, Nathan	Washington
4,288	Conditt, James B.	Independence
17,632	Conley, Wm. L.	Boone
5,127	Connelly, Chas. W.	Crawford
21,276	Conner, Isaac S.	Washington
13,778	Conner, Jacob J.	Saline
4,286	Cook, Daniel	Pulaski
815	Cook, Jacob	Washington
14,030	Cook, Peter	Pulaski
18,111	Coolege, Henry P., Estate of	Phillips
20,373	Cooper, Ephraim	Phillips
13,643	Cooper, Maria	Saline
16,607	Cooper, Samuel	Sebastian
9,794	Coonfield, Isaac	Benton
19,253	Copeland, Daniel	Franklin
5,320	Cord, Charlotte W.	Johnson
10,050	Core, Elias R.	Pulaski
10,046	Core, Hugh	Pulaski
20,319	Corey, Chester	Crawford
11,022	Corley, Christopher C.	Sarber
16,101	Cornwell, George	Washington
19,183	Cosby, Charles	Washington
1,373	Cosby, Wiley	Washington
15,795	Cothran, Ella	Prairie
19,194	Cotner, Morrison	Sarber
13,452	Cotton, John C.	Franklin
16,960	Couch, Mary A.	Crawford
2,874	Covington, Franklin	Pulaski
9,801	Cowan, Catharine	Benton
21,091	Cowan, Robert	Johnson
14,420	Cowan, Stephen	Johnson
13,113	Cowan, Wm.	Sebastian
9,026	Cowdren, Alfred L.	Sebastian
18,056	Cowley, Elizabeth A.	Phillips
17,881	Cox, A.Y.	Washington
9,928	Cox, Catharine E.	Sebastian
19,310: 4,125:	Cox, Elizabeth	Washington
6,950	Cox, Holden	White
16,825	Cox, Holden W.	Crawford
1,475	Cox, John	Washington
10,186	Cox, Nash L, Estate of	Lawrence
5,731	Cox, Sarah	Saline
18,139	Cox, Theressa	Madison
21,660	Crabtree, Bryant M.	Arkansas
19,309	Crawford, Andrew B.P.	Washington
13,999	Crawford, Arthur	Washington
13,779	Crawford, Cunningham A., Estate of	Sebastian

1,167	Crawford, Wm. M.	Yell
10,063	Crease, John H.	Saline
15,749	Creekmore, Hannah	Crawford
14,174	Crenshaw, John W., Heirs of	Phillips
9,286	Cribbins, Thomas P.	Johnson
14,292	Crisp, James W.	Monroe
14,202	Croft, Samuel W.	Pulaski
2,409	Cromwell, John B.	Saline
10,145	Crosby, Wm. M.	White
14,763	Crow, Mary	Jefferson
18,478	Crowder, Masten C.	Benton
1,298	Crowell, Charles	Crawford
5,940	Crutchfield, Elizabeth A.	Crawford
13,101	Cunningham, Jacob	Washington
19,959	Cunningham, Susan	Crawford
1,092	Curtis, F.F.	Washington
13,512	Curtis, John	Monroe
17,271	Curtis, John N.	Benton
5,776	Curtis, John N. & Thomas Austin	Benton
13,684	Curtis, Robert	Benton
22,007	Dabbs, Thos. R.	Crawford
22,007	Dabbs, Thomas R.	Franklin
11,664	Dailey, Wm. M.	Crawford
15,973	Dallas, Robert	Washington
8,815	Dalton, Carson R.	Phillips
18,753	Damm, Elizabeth	Benton
10,148	Danelly, Geo. A.	White
9,271	Daniel, John	Benton
22,163	Daniels, Charlotte	Sebastian
9,923	Darby, Jesse	Phillips
2,410	Dardenne, John	Jefferson
22,081	Darnell, Milton	Washington
11,217	Daughterty, James	St. Francis
13,920	Daughterty, Naomi	Washington
21,063	Daugherty, Samuel D.	Crawford
18,579	Davenport, Mary A.	Benton
10,844	Davidson, Elizabeth	Benton
21,990	Davidson, Samuel F.	Phillips
15,666	Davis, Abraham E.	Ashley
18,261	Davis, Alexander	Conway
13,954	Davis, Catharine	Washington
12,352	Davis, Cornelius, Estate of	St. Francis
16,382	Davis, Dorothy	Crawford
13,644	Davis, Edmond M.	Pulaski
22,036	Davis, George W.	Sebastian
16,773	Davis, Hamilton R., Mrs.	Arkansas
17,113	Davis, Isabella C.	Phillips
5,568	Davis, Isham J.	Newton
1,096	Davis, Thornsbury	Washington
4,287	Davis, William	Independence
5,782	Dawson, George	Benton
5,387	Dawson, John	Clark
13,685	Dean, Alfred	Benton
6,569	Dean, Jackson	Marion
9,771	Deane, Reuben	Benton
9,610	Deans, Andrew	Arkansas
1,091	Dearing, John M.	Washington
9,611	De Armond, Monarky	Benton
13,900	Decker, Josephine	Phillips
16,508	Degan, Herman, Estate of	Sebastian
20,339	Deihl, Augusta W.	Pulaski
20,341	Deihl, John	Pulaski
19,918	Dell, Valentine	Sebastian
13,052	Dement, Margaret A.	Grant
18,147	Deputy, Mark A. and Quintine M. & Lucy J. Penny	Phillips
9,796	Derreberry, Samuel B.	Benton
9,797	Derreberry, Wm. C.	Benton
15,150	Derrick, Alexander	Phillips
10,871	Derring, C.C.	Washington
12,655	Deuell, Edward V.	Pulaski
12,654: 21,304:	Deuell, Ethan A.	Pulaski
2,929	Dial, Samuel	Newton
12,287	Diamond, Eli T.	Phillips
5,955	Dibrell, James A.	Crawford
5,388	Dickerson, David	Clark
20,153	Dickey, Susan	Benton
9,025	Dickinson, Harriet	Crawford

18,083	Dickson, Alanson E.	Montgomery
17,102	Dicus, Jason H.	Prairie
20,341	Diehl, John	Pulaski
16,213	Dikes, Nancy B.	Drew
14,889	Dill, Louisa F.	Washington
22,180	Dismukes, Elisha E.	Prairie
18,480	Dobkins, Hugh	Benton
11,873	Dobson, Isaiah	Crawford
5,578	Dodd, David	Saline
9,547	Dodd, Orrin L.	Marion
2,993	Dodson, R.T.	Prairie
19,121	Dodson, Wesley	Washington
13,284	Dodge, Roderic L.	Pulaski
5,855	Doline, Robert	Pulaski
3,444	Donham, John	Drew
21,188	Dorman, Lina Anne	Sebastian
11,617	Dorris, Otnello S.	Madison
9,346	Dortch, Alexander	Ouachita
15,838	Dotson, Clarissa	Johnson
2,411	Doty, George B.	Crawford
9,028	Dougherty, John, Estate of	Sebastian
3,100	Douthit, Wm. A.	Washington
9,612	Drake, Celia	Washington
20,249	Drake, Elijah, Sr.	Madison
10,866	Drake, Margaret	Washington
10,047	Drake, Warren	Pulaski
14,000	Drake, Wesley	Washington
6,268	Drennen, John, Estate of	Pulaski
698	Dreyer, Henry	Pulaski
12,062	Dudley, W.M.	Crawford
21,506	Duff, John D. & Mary E.	Pulaski
21,506	Duff, Mary E. & John D.	Pulaski
4,484	Dugan, Andrew J.	Franklin
12,581	Dugger, Wm. M.	Boone
12,019	Duke, S.A.	Drew
22,030	Duncan, James H.	Desha
18,138	Duncan, Sarah	Madison
1,080	Dunham, Jane	Benton
12,901	Dunlap, Absalom H.	Benton
12,902	Bunlap, Daniel G.	Benton
13,969	Dunlap, Eli	Carroll
19.096	Dunlap, Francis	Washington
9,689	Dunlap, John F.	Ouachita
9,690	Dunlap, Samuel M.	Ouachita
21,375	Durham, H.F.	Calhoun
819	Dutton, Seborn	Washington
16,383	Dye, Reuben T.	Lincoln
20,214	Dye, Richard	Washington
16,112	Dye, Wm. R.	Washington
9,355	Earle, Kate P.	Ouachita
9,792	Easley, Rebecca	Benton
1,299	Echols, Hiram M.	Crawford
9,613	Eden, Jonathan	Benton
2,202	Edens, L.E. & Landon C.	Washington & Benton
3,102	Edminston, H.H.	Washington
19,750	Edminston, Moses A., Heirs of	Washington
11,159	Edmonds, Wm. W., Estate of	Woodruff
6,419	Edmondson, Ann	Sebastian
14,586	Edmondson, James	Sebastian
7,028	Edmons, Stephen	Clark
13,995	Edmonson, Thomas	Washington
5,368	Edwards, John A.	Washington
10,782	Egner, Joseph H.	Independence
20,370	Eidson, Wm. H.	Washington
5,774	Elder, Mary	Clark
11,964	Ellick, John G.	Sebastian
22,096	Ellison, David W.	Phillips
9,347	Elliot, Lusius Q.C.	Ouachita
903	Elms, Jonathon	Washington
10,055	Elrod, Abraham	Saline
13,137	Elrod, George	Saline
10,068	Elrod, Joel	Saline
14,354	Elston, James	Pulaski
9,802	England, Edward	Benton
13,356	England, Mary A.	Crawford
1,476	Engles, W.H.	Washington
10,860	English, Valentine	Washington
5,540	Enloe, Thomas E.	Hemstead

5,090	Eppler, Isaac T.	Sebastian
3,178	Epps, James H.	White
294	Erwin, Georgia M.	Mississippi
4,469	Esix, Issac	Washington
15,493	Estes, Elisha	Crawford
2,704	Estes, John	Marion
18,371	Estes, Nancy W.	Crawford
2,111	Etherdige, Caleb	Monroe
4,265	Evans, Hiram	St. Francis
4,252	Evans, James S.	Jefferson
11,377: 23,186:	Evans, Samuel	Franklin
21,537	Evans, William	Benton
13,645	Ewell, George W.	Prairie
5,324	Ewing, Young	Washington
4,495	Factor, Martha	Franklin
20,057	Fain, Wm. G.	Washington
9,919	Fair, Nancy H.	Benton
5,325	Fallin, R.R.	Washington
9,614	Fanning, Abram	Carroll
18,136	Fanning, Taylor, Estate of	Madison
18,135	Fanning, Wm. M.	Carroll
17,810	Farish, Stephen	Conway
10,862	Farmer, Jasper	Washington
1,895	Farmer, Margaret C.	Johnson
11,808	Farnum, John R.	Sarber
18,507	Farrer, Junius H.	Benton
3,580	Ferguson, Alfred H.	Pulaski
21,806	Ferguson, John C., Estate of	Washington
17,069	Ferguson, William L.	Sarber
11,247	Fetherston, B.W.	Benton
13,134	Feverstein, Jacob	Sebastian
21,538	Fields, Mahaley	Benton
18,079: 19,520:	Filpot, Jackson	Polk
18,078: 19,522:	Filpot, John	Polk
19,251	Filpot, Martha	Polk
18,077	Filpot, William	Polk
22,083	Fincher, Wm. L.	Washington
2,710	Fine, Thomas J.	Washington
12,821	Fine, Wm. B.	Washington
13,796	Finiker, John	Washington
9,032	Finton, Wm. F.	Sebastian
	Fish (See Gess)	
20,257	Fish, Nathaniel H.	Jefferson
1,820	Fisher, Davis M.	Woodruff
1,477	Fisher, Jacob	Washington
19,668	Fitz, John W.	Washington
12,037	Fitzgerald, Edward	Pulaski
14,541	Fitzgerald, Isaac S.	Washington
1,807: 1,808:	Fitzgerald, Lucinda	Washington
19,803	Fitzhugh, Elizabeth	Izard
18,853	Fitzhugh, Saml. H.	Monore
17,454	Fitzhugh, Sarah L., and Edward L. & Wm. St. John Hubbard	Phillips
16,096	Flanagan, William, Estate of	Pulaski
16,212	Flemming, Mark M.	Drew
13,511	Flener, Abraham	Monroe
2,204	Fletcher, Jesse L.	Washington
2,151: 2,270:	Fletcher, Richard	Pulaski
20,157	Flinn, Hugh	Crawford
11,264	Ford, Elizabeth	Crawford
10,188	Ford, Iven S. & Jackson	Benton
4,289	Ford, Moses	Independence
22,290	Ford, Sallie G.	Phillips
5,933	Foster, Elizabeth	Benton
19,669	Foster, John C. & Josiah	Crawford
13,736	Foster, John W.	Benton
19,669	Foster, Josiah & John C.	Crawford
5,785	Foster, Robert C.	Benton
12,718	Foster, Thomas	Phillips
20,343	Foust, Samuel E.	Pulaski
6,417	Fowler, Elizabeth	Hot Springs
2,203	Franklin, Joshua	Washington
21,781	Frazier, Gillie	Franklin
9,336	Frazier, Wm. W.	Ouachita

12,923	Freeman, Elmira	Phillips
4,743	Freeman, John G.	Arkansas
18,693	French, Henry	Crawford
19,653	French, Samuel S.	Scott
13,955	Froshon, Jane R.	Washington
3,778	Furlong, James	Arkansas
10,432	Furr, Delemand	Pulaski
6,079	Gaery, Thomas	Crawford
7,372	Gaines, William H.	Hot Springs
11,181	Gallagher, Anthony	Sebastian
1,490	Gallaher, Henry	Washington
6,407	Gallian, Jonas	Bradley
5,934	Gallian, Shadrick	Benton
1,621	Galloway, Edwin C., Estate of	Pulaski
14,712	Galusha, Thomas B.	Pulaski
9,269	Gambell, Benj. E.	Benton
3,786	Gambell, George W.	Benton
11,023	Garner, James L.	Sarber
2,840	Garner, William	Hot Springs
16,388	Garner, William, Sr.	Hot Springs
21,190	Garrison, Allen S.	Sarber
9,615	Garrison, James C.	Carroll
6,658	Garrison, Moses Z.	Yell
15,663	Garrison, Wm. R.	Arkansas
13,647	Gates, Elizabeth	Pulaski
17,808	Gay, Thomas	Conway
22,158	Geiger, Jesse J.	Yell
12,618	George, Alexander	Pulaski
12,756	George, Andrew J.	Phillips
19,525	Gess (Fish), Margaret C.	Polk
6,580	Geyer, John C.	Conway
4,179	Gibson, Henry J.	Searcy
6,993	Gibson, John	Nevada
10,869	Gibson, John (Boonsboro)	Washington
16,468	Gibson, John (Greenville)	Washington
12,715	Gibson, Moses	Madison
9,260	Gibson, William	Benton
12,925	Gilbert, Marinda	Phillips
19,954	Gilbreath, Cyrus G.	Washington
4,569	Gilbreath, Henderson W.	Washington
19,650	Gill, Thomas W.	Scott
9,224	Gillenwater, Tivis	Washington
6,626	Gillespie, John	Crawford
19,574	Gilliland, Wm. J.	Washington
13,011	Gillstrap, John	Sebastian
15,225	Gilstrap, Wesley H.	Washington
8,109	Givens, Martha R.	Crawford
9,616	Glascox, George W.	Benton
21,874	Glenn, Cynthia	Saline
10,059	Glenn, John	Saline
10,042	Glenn, William	Saline
5,957	Glenn, William W.	Independence
2,841	Godbehere, William	Hot Springs
15,483	Goddard, King R.	Benton
4,158	Goddard, T.M.	Washington
6,319	Goddard, Wesley	Washington
14,678	Golden, Isaac	Clark
14,685	Golden, Richard	Clark
17,327	Goliher, Drewry W.	Sebastian
11,618	Goodner, Sardis S.	Madison
12,828	Goodwin, Sanford E.	Phillips
9,617	Gorden, Thomas J.	Benton
6,965	Gordon, Francis R.	White
15,996	Gordon, Noah	Madison
10,787	Gosscatt, Richard L.	Jackson
9,348	Gossett, Martin C.	Ouachita
7,668	Gossett, Wm.	Boone
17,753	Gouger, Henry A.	Sebastian
14,336	Govan, John J.	Phillips
8,883	Graham, Alexander	Crawford
2,446	Graham, Emeline	Washington
10,854: 20,058:	Graham, W.C.	Washington
14,001	Graham, Wilson	Washington
9,030	Grangeene, Oliver	Crawford
21,494	Grape, Michael	Sebastian
11,062	Grattan, Albert G.	Pulaski
11,408	Graves, Martha J.	Arkansas
699	Graves, Richard B.	Pulaski

11,414	Graves, William	Arkansas
2,205	Gray, Sanford F.	Washington
17,117	Green, Demaques L.	Phillips
3,445	Green, Francis N.	Drew
12,245	Green, Isaac L.	Phillips
12,927	Green, James C.	Phillips
21,872	Green, John L.	Saline
4,513	Green, Jerry J.	Johnson
17,991	Greenwood, Beverly S.	Pulaski
4,618	Greer, Elijah M.	Pulaski
10,856	Gregg, Maston F., Estate of	Washington
20,089	Gregory, M.S.	Washington
10,785	Grier, Samuel	Independence
12,815	Griffeth, Jesse	Pulaski
20,209	Griffin, Isaac	Sarber
19,524	Griffith, Sarah	Polk
3,630	Grigory, Philip	Washington
12,905	Grinder, John J.	Sebastian
14,593	Guinn, James F.	Prairie
18,482	Guinn, James S.	Yell
14,525	Guinn, Joseph H.	Johnson
6,414	Gullett, Benjamin F.	Hot Springs
5,706	Gum, Louisa	Benton
12,615	Gwynn, Andrew B.	Pulaski
17,274	Haddox, Isaac	Pope
20,211	Hague, John M.	Carroll
11,586	Haigh, A.V.	Arkansas
11,582	Haigh, Geo. B.	Arkansas
11,559	Haigh, Jacob	Arkansas
15,818	Hale, Benjamin F.	Crawford
22,072	Hale, D.C.	Washington
7,031	Hale, Henry B.	Clark
9,150	Hale, Henry N.	Clark
10,009	Hale, John A.	Pike
10,009	Hale, John A.	Pulaski
7,030	Hale, Nancy	Clark
7,029	Hale, Reuben	Clark
22,090	Hale, Robert E.	Phillips
5,935	Hall, Armize P.	Benton
14,281	Hall, D.D.	Johnson
13,510	Hall, Sarah B.	Monroe
18,086	Hall, Thomas	Carroll
14,814	Hallaway, Imogine	Ashley
9,340	Halloway, Major C.	Calhoun
14,306	Halton, E.W.	Drew
8,450	Hamilton, David	Clark
8,710	Hamilton, Henry	Conway
1,798	Hamilton, John H.A.	Conway
1,068: 6,620:	Hamilton, Theophilus M.	Cross
19,166	Hamlin, W.T., Estate of	Washington
16,330	Hamm, Joseph	Franklin
11,261	Hammon, Daniel	Woodruff
14,035	Hammon, Richard	Pulaski
8,174	Hammond, Samuel E.	Monroe
5,581	Hammonds, Delila	Hot Springs
5,586	Hampton, Elizabeth J.	Pulaski
20,210	Haney, Samuel	Madison
22,052	Hank, Lorrenze	Sebastian
22,051	Hank, Valentine, Estate of	Sebastian
5,370	Hanks, Nathan	Washington
2,413	Hanks, Thomas A.	Yell
21,486	Hanna, Andrew J.	Sebastian
14,602	Hanna, George W., Estate of	Prairie
9,618	Hanna, Jeremiah C.	Washington
5,762	Happy, James H.	Sebastian
9,868	Harbison, Matilda A.	Pulaski
17,412	Hardage, Joseph A.	Clark
11,371	Hardin, Tarlton	Pulaski
14,002	Hardin, William	Crawford
6,409	Hardy, Jos. D.	Hot Springs
22,060	Hare, Margaret E.	Cross
4,377	Harkreider, Samuel	Johnson
9,773	Harper, John	Benton
14,036	Harper, Mary A.C.	Calhoun
9,620	Harral, Isaac	Benton
9,621	Harral, Leaman	Benton
15,484	Harrel, Elizabeth	Washington
19,548	Harrell, Josiah	Crawford
20,327	Harrington, Ann	Sebastian

827	Harrington, Hezekiah	Conway
20,328	Harrington, John, Estate of	Sebastian
10,064	Harris, Adison R.	Saline
18,033	Harris, Charles	Crawford
17,816	Harris, Jefferson	Perry
14,411	Harris, Jeremiah H.	Phillips
18,085	Harris, Margaret M.	Carroll
11,160	Harris, Richard	Woodruff
3,446	Harris, Sarah J.	Drew
12,926	Harris, Thomas R.	St. Francis
18,137	Harrison, Geo.	Madison
11,219	Harrison, Jonathan	Woodruff
10,056	Harrison, Martha, and Oliver P. Lister	Hot Springs
14,862	Harrison, William	Independence
1,083	Harston, James D.	Benton
10,521	Harston, Robert	Benton
12,204	Hart, Calvin D.	Pulaski
9,619	Hart, Edmond L.	Benton
15,852	Harton, William D.	Madison
1,321	Hash, A.C.	Washington
5,958	Hassell, Wm. J., Estate of	Independence
9,282	Hastings, Henry C.	Benton
9,798	Hastings, Louisa	Benton
1,625	Hastings, William	Benton
18,050	Haughton, Jeffrey A.	Cross
15,839	Hawkins, Benj. C.	Madison
3,396	Hawkins, Henry L.	Independence
21,193	Hawkins, James M.	Madison
13,648	Hawkins, Julia A.	Clark
9,798	Hawkins, Louisa	Benton
17,618	Hawkins, Wm.	Monroe
7,624	Hayes, Elias	Crawford
10,794	Hayman, Henry C.	Crawford
22,160	Haynes, John L., Estate of	Scott
15,485	Haynie, Benj. K.	Washington
15,840	Hays, John, Sr.	Madison
9,238	Hays, John N.	Benton
9,799	Hays, William	Benton
20,204	Hayter, Daniel S.	Carroll
1,171	Heard, Emily F.	Pulaski
21,488	Heckler, George	Sebastian
11,728	Henderson, John H.	Crawford
9,622	Henderson, M.C.	Benton
6,076	Henderson, Matthew	Crawford
20,418	Hendrick, Wm. J.	Monroe
17,167	Hendricks, Isaac	Franklin
17,187	Hennessey, Margaret	Sebastian
18,133	Hennessey, Patrick	Sebastian
20,504	Henry, James	Washington
9,277	Henry, Thos. P.	Benton
11,204	Hensley, George W.	Sarber
6,582	Hensley, J.W.	Searcy
14,203	Hensley, Jacob	Pulaski
15,316	Heppel, Martha	Pulaski
15,317	Heppel, William	Pulaski
11,955	Herman, John H.	Washington
4,290	Hess, Thomas M.	Independence
818	Hester, Ransom	Washington
20,311	Hewitt, Lorenzo D., Estate of	Arkansas
6,420	Hiatt, Henry	Franklin
2,930	Hickey, James	Johnson
13,181	Hicks, Allen W.	Pulaski
12,611	Hicks, Isaac	Franklin
20,156	Higgins, Nancy A.	Crawford
21,769	High, Lorenzo D., Estate of	Carroll
11,672	Hignight, Chester A.	Clark
12,753	Hill, Charles H.	Phillips
18,745	Hill, James	Ashley
4,117	Hill, John C.	St. Francis
17,968	Hill, John W.	Sebastian
11,674	Hill, Margret	Clark
13,567	Hillian, Caleb	Clark
11,985	Hilyer, Catharine	White
8,195	Hinds, Albert	Crawford
15,841	Hinds, William	Madison
16,107	Hinkle, Joseph B.	Crawford
21,664	Hinnant, Hobbs H.	Arkansas
14,865	Hinton, Edwin, Estate of	Prairie

21,258	Hison, Alexander	Sarber
8,834	Hobbs, Solomon M.	Franklin
21,810	Hodges, Anson, Estate of	Washington
22,038	Hodges, Caloway	Sebastian
20,368	Hodges, Edward	Washington
19,332	Hodges, H.	Scott
10,847	Hodges, Roland E.	Washington
4,472	Hodges, Wm.	Washington
3,797	Hodges, Wm. F.	Johnson
19,966	Hogan, Charles, Estate of	Crawford
13,182	Hogue, Powell E.	Pulaski
9,335	Hogue, William J.	Ouachita
13,649	Holder, Leanna	Clark
13,650	Holiman, Warren	Grant
9,696	Holleman, James G., Estate of	Ouachita
13,686	Holleman, John B.R.	Sebastian
9,695	Holleman, Richard T.	Ouachita
18,724	Hollingshed, Julia	Benton
20,248	Holman, Frances	Carroll
1,170	Holman, Stephen L.	Pulaski
16,839	Holmes, Mary E.	Chicot
1,095	Holt, Alfred P.	Washington
9,623	Holt, De Kalb	Washington
1,495	Holt, Eli F.	Washington
20,366	Holt, John W.	Crawford
19,451	Holt, Leonidas	Washington
4,407: 15,790:	Holthoff, Frank	Ashley
17,118	Holtzclaw, Elijah	Phillips
15,804	Homesley, Sidney E.	Washington
13,651	Hooker, Zadock	Conway
18,400	Hopkins, John W.	Pulaski
9,624	Hopkins, Lucretia	Washington
12,244	Horn, John A.	Phillips
19,099	Horn, Matthew	Crawford
20,320	Horton, Willis	Crawford
11,332	Hough, Thomas	Woodruff
10,870	House, Merrill	Washington
21,992	Housted, Robert	Phillips
14,658	Houston, John S.	Johnson
5,569	Houston, William	Newton
5,126	Howard, Charles J.	Crawford
1,173	Howard, Edward	Jefferson
21,548	Howard, Joseph N.	Carroll
13,129	Howard, Lemuel B.	Sebastian
683	Howard, Samuel A.	Benton
9,334	Howard, William B.	Ouachita
1,073	Howard, William F.G.	St. Francis
18,145	Howell, John Bright, Sr.	Yell
17,454	Hubbard, Edward L. & William St. John & Sarah L. Fitzhugh	Phillips
22,068	Huff, James A.	White
13,140	Hugens, Rachel	Pulaski
5,091	Hughes, Andrew J.	White
6,581	Hughes, George W.	Crawford
9,263	Hughey, Henry M.	Pope
9,033: 9,034:	Hukill, James S.	Sebastian
8,110	Hulsey, Jordan M.	Crawford
12,755	Humphreys, James M.	Phillips
18,798	Hunt, John	Scott
9,211	Hunt, John	Washington
19,155	Hunt, John and Reed, Geo. Wm.	Washington
18,808	Hunt, Wm.	Scott
9,219	Hunt, Wm.	Washington
21,202	Hunter, Burnes	Franklin
14,316	Hunter, Sarah	Pulaski
21,550	Hunter, Sherrod	Franklin
550	Hurd, Columbus	Cross
4,291	Hurt, Charles	Pulaski
12,944	Hurtzig, Ann	Sebastian
1,097	Hutcheson, John J.	Washington
1,135	Hutcheson, Wm. H.	Washington
9,151	Hutson, Solomon	Clark
5,695	Hyde, Charles T.	Monroe
13,505	Ingram, Henry	Monroe
20,152	Ingram, Sandy	Benton
1,134	Isaac, Wm. C.	Washington
3,447	Isaacs, Harriet F.	Drew
14,854	Ivey, James	Franklin

22,159	Ivey, Turner	Yell
15,222	Ivey, William R.	Franklin
4,473	Jack, Henry	Washington
7,623	Jackson, Abram W.	Crawford
13,653	Jackson, Alfred	Pulaski
13,714	Jackson, James	Benton
20,344	Jackson, James	Pulaski
9,018	Jackson, Jane	Arkansas
8,111	Jackson, John F.	Crawford
14,643	Jackson, Margaret	Sebastian
5,075	Jackson, Montgomery	Crawford
14,352	Jackson, Sarah E.	Monroe
13,300	Jackson, Shadrack	Madison
9,625	Jackson, Thomas	Benton
18,747	Jackson, Thomas A.	Ashley
16,214	Jackson, Wiley S.	Ashley
21,507: 21,877:	Jacobi, Henry	Pulaski
1,843	Jacobs, Stokly	Johnson
14,307	James, Edward C.	Chicot
12,283	James, Manning R.	Phillips
1,478	James, Nancy	Washington
17,815	Jamison, Charity	Conway
15,842	Janeway, Looney	Madison
7,032	Jasper, Alford	Clark
4,941	Jeanes, Phoebe A.	Jackson
6,571	Jefferson, Thomas	Marion
5,787	Jeffries, Obedience	Benton
2,447	Jenkins, Floyd	Washington
10,628	Jenkins, Jackson	Crawford
20,293	Jenkins, Leander	Pulaski
14,551	Jobe, Daniel B.	Washington
16,327	Johnson, Andrew J.	Washington
4,865	Johnson, C.C.	Crawford
13,654	Johnson, Christopher	Pulaski
11,158	Johnson, D.H.	Woodruff
4,958	Johnson, E.M.	St. Francis
11,416	Johnson, Edward	Arkansas
9,273	Johnson, Elizabeth	Benton
18,782	Johnson, Francis M.	Washington
2,875	Johnson, Gustavens	Pulaski
17,619	Johnson, Henrietta M.	Monroe
4,292	Johnson, Henry	Pulaski
9,262	Johnson, Hugh	Johnson
18,920	Johnson, Jacob Q.	Washington
9,626	Johnson, Jane L.	Benton
1,493	Johnson, John	Washington
15,224	Johnson, John J.	Arkansas
18,386	Johnson, Lycurgus L.	Chicot
15,843	Johnson, Martin	Madison
11,769	Johnson, Mary	Cross
4,405	Johnson, Melinda	Crawford
2,207	Johnson, Micager	Washington
15,844	Johnson, Noah	Madison
13,655	Johnson, Peterson	Pulaski
18,267	Johnson, Robert	Madison
13,655	Johnson, Peterson	Pulaski
18,267	Johnson, Robert	Madison
6,320	Johnson, Robert	Washington
1,289	Johnson, Robert B.	Johnson
21,512	Johnson, Thos.	Pulaski
18,140	Johnson, Thomas M.	Madison
13,956	Johnson, Wm.	Washington
8,196	Johnson, Wm. M.	Crawford
4,621	Johnston, Gregory	Randolph
16,211	Johnston, Martin	Ashley
18,332	Jolly, Peter	Monroe
2,206	Jones, A.J.	Washington
13,951	Jones, Barney, Heirs of	Washington
11,948	Jones, Bryan W.	Jackson
22,032	Jones, Charles L.	Phillips
14,418	Jones, Eliza J.	Johnson
13,951	Jones, Gilbert, Estate of	Washington
13,656	Jones, Hardy	Pulaski
21,779	Jones, Isham	Franklin
19,409	Jones, James F.	Washington
15,689	Jones, James J.	Pulaski
21,973	Jones, James T.	Arkansas
11,178	Jones, John T.	Phillips
21,659	Jones, Nancy A.	Arkansas
9,244	Jones, Nancy D.	Benton
17,168	Jones, Narcissa	Sebastian
12,285	Jones, Phillip R.	St. Francis
9,232	Jones, Riley	Washington
11,823	Jones, Simon	Newton
15,229	Jordan, James	Washington
16,775	Jordan, Jesse	Washington
16,538	Jordan, John	Pulaski
13,652	Joy, Henry M.	Pulaski
139	Joyce, Oliver C.	Phillips
10,646	Jugo, Wm. H.	Jackson
10,041	Julian, Margaret A.	Saline
12,616	Kadel, George	Pulaski
15,845	Kane, James	Madison
14,647	Kane, Patrick O.	Pulaski
1,099	Karnes, Oliver L.	Washington
9,627	Karnes, Wm.	Washington
14,969	Keaton, John B.	Arkansas
19,519	Keatss, Henry, Estate of	Pulaski
4,269	Keatts, James B.	Pulaski
4,276	Keatts, Robert	Pulaski
9,280	Keele, John	Benton
4,474	Keeler, George G.	Jefferson
18,726	Keith, William	Benton
2,444	Keller, Mary A.	Washington
9,300	Kellogg, Ralph	Jackson
10,685: 13,957:	Kelly, James F.	Washington
20,055	Kelly, Wm. B.	Washington
9,274	Keltner, Andrew J.	Benton
6,601	Keltner, Wm. C.	Saline
21,991	Kendall, James	Phillips
15,486	Kennedy, Daniel F.	Saline
11,407	Kennedy, Jerome B.	Arkansas
4,926	Kennedy, Moses A.	Hot Springs
14,293	Kerr, A.C.	Franklin
8,425	Kerr, Nancy	Sebastian
11,679	Kerr, Tallefero	Clark
9,037: 8,184:	Kersey, Thomas	Sebastian
8,920	Kibler, John B.	Crawford
20,367	Kidd, T.K., Estate of	Washington
21,873	Kilgore, Wilson	Saline
1,176	Killain, Miles, Estate of	Pulaski
11,415	Kimbrough, William A.	Arkansas
17,241	Kindley, Cyrus	Benton
9,035	King, Dixon P.	Sebastian
17,657	King, Eveline	Washington
13,715	King, George C.	Sebastian
6,979	King, James	White
12,682	King, Wiley	Fulton
11,368	Kingcade, Rebecca J.	Washington
4,860	Kinman, Riley	Jackson
6,412	Kirkman, Lemuel	Hot Springs
15,792	Kirkpatrick, James W.M.	Ashley
20,338	Kirwin, John	Pulaski
482	Klaine, Peter	Franklin
3,018: 20,831:	Knaggs, Alexander H.	Pulaski
12,900	Kneutsen, John S.	Washington
10,790	Knowles, Wesley	Independence
17,222	Knox, Eudora E.	Crawford
19,275	Krickel, Edward F.	Phillips
21,514	Kurtz, John	Conway
15,690	Kurtz, Peter	Pulaski
7,373	Kyle, Gayle H., Estate of	Clark
10,049	Labelle, Charles	Pulaski
13,276	Lacefield, Wm. P.	Phillips
12,284	Lackey, Henry	Phillips
21,667	Lacott, John	Arkansas
3,641	Lacy, Mary E.	Washington
11,025	Ladd, Thomas, Estate of	Johnson
21,515	Laferre, Mary	Pulaski
15,264	Lain, John, Estate of	Desha
18,986	Lamb, Caroline, Iram M. & Rich.	Phillips
6,081	Lamb, Matilda	Crawford
12,701	Lamb, Micajah	Arkansas
16,160	Lambeth, Alson G.	Benton
15,353	Landers, Jacob	Arkansas

16,289	Landers, Michael	Pulaski
19,526	Langley, Moses	Polk
17,888	Langley, Nancy J.	Pulaski
22,064	Lanier, Samuel, Estate of	Mississippi
14,176	Larkin, William M.	Phillips
3,454	Larremore, Geo. W.	Washington
11,020	Lasater, Burrel	Sarber
9,239	Lasater, H.T.	Benton
6,602	Lasiter, Bryant	Saline
6,603	Lasiter, Tabitha	Saline
11,539	Latham, Thomas	Benton
684	Latty, Matilda	Benton
9,698	Lavender, Jacob	Nevada
5,128	Lawless, Augustine	Crawford
21,922	Lawrence, Levi J.	Pulaski
9,226	Layne, Andrew J.	Benton
4,253	Lea, Pryor N.	Sebastian
4,499: 16,772:	Leach, Ambrose	Washington
9,628	Leach, James	Benton
13,515	Leach, Richard	Washington
8,449	Leatherman, Peter	Clark
8,448	Leatherman, T.S.	Clark
15,846	Lear, Nancy	Madison
21,086	Ledbetter, Eli	Madison
20,203	Ledbetter, Harvy C.	Madison
13,115	Ledford, Noah	Sarber
14,836	Lee, James H.	Sarber
9,351	Lee, Thomas H.	Ouachita
10,058	Lee, William S.	Saline
10,065	Leech, Wm.	Saline
9,631	Lefors, John	Benton
13,359	Leftwick, Wm. J.	Sarber
4,924	Lemley, Moses C.	Crawford
13,453	Leverett, Joseph W.	Franklin
14,707	Lew, James H.	Sarber
1,899	Lewis, Brackin	Pulaski
7,033	Lewis, Charles	Clark
20,603	Lewis, Francis C.	Sebastian
1,297	Lewis, Geo.	Washington
19,964	Lewis, George W.	Washington
9,687	Lewis, Hugh	Ouachita
9,629	Lewis, Jane	Washington
21,084	Lewis, John S.	Johnson
22,078	Lewis, Joseph	Washington
20,561	Lewis, Joseph, Estate of	Sebastian
11,057: 11,058: 11,260:	Lewis, Margaret	Sebastian
1,296	Lewis, Rebecca	Washington
15,266	Lewis, Violet	Independence
20,222	Lewis, Wesley	Washington
21,633	Lewis, William, Estate of	Pulaski
21,275	Lewis, Wm. P.	Washington
22,162	Lewis, Wilson J., Estate of	Scott
21,510	Lindsay, John Y.	Saline
13,138	Lindsey, Jane	Saline
10,073	Linzy, William, Estate of	Johnson
18,594	Lipscomb, James C.	Sebastian
7,665	Lipscomb, Monroe	Crawford
10,056	Lister, Oliver P. & Martha Harrison	Hot Springs
18,809	Liston, Andrew J.	Scott
1,137	Little, Perry F.	Washington
4,293	Little, Thomas	Independence
4,293	Little, Thomas	Pulaski
6,052	Locke, Nancy H.	Clark
1,169	Lockhart, Samuel A.	Jefferson
19,407	Loftin, Meredith	Washington
967	Loftis, Morris	Craighead
1,093	Lofton, Giles	Washington
1,322	Lofton, Matilda	Washington
22,095	London, Lula Ingle	Sebastian
16,623	Long, Fannie B.	Independence
17,981	Long, John C.	Franklin
14,655	Long, Minor	Pulaski
2,711	Long, Moses B.	Washington
12,065	Losson, Lonesey Ann	Crawford
6,408	Low, Matthew	Hot Springs
20,994	Lowe, Mary	Arkansas

14,419	Lozan, Isaac	Crawford
9,302	Lucas, Richard S.	St. Francis
21,662	Luckado, Peter P.	Jefferson
1,970	Lumpkins, Geo. H., Estate of	Conway
3,327	Luper, Gilbert	Washington
9,630	Luttrel, Shelton	Washington
9,726	Lytal, George C.	Crawford
3,101	Maberry, David, Jr.	Washington
20,215	Maberry, David, Sr.	Washington
20,221	Maberry, Jacob D.	Washington
9,354	Mack, William	Lafayette
11,729	Macklin, Barney	Sebastian
14,204	Magee, Benjamin H.	Saline
1,810	Magness, Maridaye	Washington
4,296	Magness, Perry G.	Franklin
22,071	Mahaney, Paul A.	Washington
8,167	Mahurin, Samuel	Benton
18,971	Main, John H.T.	Sebastian
17,143	Mainard, E.L.	Pulaski
13,960	Malacote, Deadman	Washington
12,945	Maledon, Jacob	Sebastian
13,961	Malicote, James	Washington
2,433	Mallett, Francis M.	Conway
13,997	Malone, Josephy	Washington
15,173	Mankins, Peter, Sr.	Washington
5,790	Mann, Cynthia C.	Benton
22,289	Mann, James R.	Pulaski
10,947	Manus, William	Fulton
11,730	Markham, Reuben T.	Conway
17,048	Marlott, James	Desha
15,920	Marr, Sarah	Pulaski
2,210	Marrs, Aaron A.	Washington
2,211	Marrs, Alexander	Washington
5,326	Marrs, Arrey	Washington
2,209	Marrs, Isaac N.	Washington
1,323	Marrs, M.W.	Washington
9,416	Marrs, Matthew L.	Madison
15,390	Marrs, Samuel P.	Washington
21,942	Marshall, Felix	Phillips
4,216	Marshall, Henry S.	Washington
10,868	Marshall, Joseph E.	Washington
9,632	Marshall, Thomas R.	Benton
10,857	Martin, Abner	Benton
1,324	Martin, Caleb B.	Washington
10,861	Martin, Elizabeth A.	Washington
10,849	Martin, Galatine	Benton
3,067	Martin, George W.	Conway
6,985	Martin, Henry	White
11,325	Martin, Henry C.	Washington
7,670	Martin, Jared C.	Pulaski
11,156	Martin, Jesse	Woodruff
5,943	Martin, John L.	Benton
9,247	Martin, John L.	Johnson
5,791	Martin, Mary	Benton
1,733	Martin, Mary E.	Washington
2,208	Martin, V. L.	Washington
11,326	Martin, Wm. J.	Washington
5,789	Martin, William N.	Benton
8,882	Marzoll, John	Crawford
9,633	Mason, David B.	Washington
9,634	Mason, John J.	Benton
9,243	Mason, Littleberry E.	Benton
2,432	Mason, Salathial	Conway
3,381	Mason, Thomas R.	Jackson
9,635	Mason, William H., Sen.	Benton
8,113	Matlock, Geo. W.	Crawford
2,932	Mattock, John L.	Johnson
20,321	Matlock, Wm. A.	Crawford
6,082	Maxey, Rabe	Crawford
16,328	Maxey, Ran	Crawford
17,131	Maxwell, Elenor	Arkansas
9,245	Maxwell, James W.	Benton
686	Maxwell, Michael B.	Benton
685	Maxwell, Ozios D.	Benton
69	Mayers, Michael	Sebastian
12,603	Mayberry, Cordelia	Hot Springs
11,262	Mayberry, Geo. W.	Woodruff
9,636	Mayes, John	Washington
19,575	Mayes, Saml.	Washington
14,837	Mayes, Wm. H.	Washington

18,285	Mayes, Wm. Z.	Washington
9,921	Mayfield, S. H.	Benton
16,393	Mays, Alexander	Montgomery
14,415	McAllister, Andrew	Saline
21,491	McCabe, Patrick	Sebastian
14,031	McCallum, Edward	Clark
9,039	McCaslen, Ira	Saline
9,040	McCaslin, Webster	Saline
7,929	McCeiver, Nancy	Clark
14,861	McClellan, Thomas T.	Independence
10,852	McClendon, J.J.	Polk
15,794	McCombs, Wm. F.	Ashley
10,780	McCord, Christopher C.	Independence
21,946	McCord, Moses S., Estate of	Jefferson
9,638	McCormick, Peter	Washington
22,084	McConnell, Lewis	Washington
15,847	McCracken, John	Madison
5,582	McCrary, Olivia	Saline
9,637	McCraw, George W.	Sebastian
10,060	McCray, Henry M.	Saline
4,879	McCreaner, Chas.	Prairie
17,889	McCrew, Rebecca	Pulaski
5,657	McCullough, William	Independence
5,747	McCurdy, James K. P.	Crawford
8,112	McCurdy, Samuel	Crawford
11,409	McCurly, Susan	Arkansas
2,770	McDaniel, John	Greene
20,602	McDaniel, John E.	Sebastian
9,261	McEver, Andrew	Pope
9,222	McGarrah, Mathew	Washington
4,294	McGee, Edward	Pulaski
21,296	McGee, Mary A.	Crawford
9,640	McGee, Telitha, Mrs.	Washington
5,888: 17,811:	McGihee, John	Conway
14,646	McGill, William	Pike
14,848	McGuire, Easter	Grant
4,295	McGuire, Thomas	Pulaski
13,658	McHenry, Mary E.	Pulaski
19,097	McIlroy, Wm.	Washington
9,037	McInterf, Thomas	Saline
12,521	McIntyre, James	Crawford
9,639	McKeen, Elizabeth	Benton
11,109	McKeil, J.S., Estate of	Phillips
11,643	McKenney, Jonathan	Washington
11,412	McKewen, John W.	Arkansas
12,514	McLaren, Andrew J.	Conway
11,681	McLaughlin, Thomas	Clark
9,153	McLelland, Carroll	Clark
18,860	McMillen, Andrew J.	Madison
1,236	McMillen, Cynthia A.	Conway
13,358	McMinn, James P.	Yell
4,267	McMurray, Hugh	St. Francis
17,952	McMurray, James C.	Franklin
21,487	McNally, Michael	Sebastian
11,443: 21,770:	McNair, Elizabeth	Searcy
14,360	McNealy, John B.	Pulaski
11,340	McNew, John	Pulaski
20,154	McPhail, John, Estate of	Benton
14,505	McPherson, Lewis A.	Johnson
13,717	McRoy, Allen	Washington
12,684	McRussell, Garner	Hot Springs
2,771	McVey, John	Marion
14,037	McWhaley, Elijah	Conway
18,169	Meaders, George W.B.	Crawford
10,793	Meadors, Elisha B.	Crawford
9,234	Mecklin, Wesley	Washington
9,264	Medling, Martha C.	Benton
13,139	Medlock, John A.	Saline
964	Meek, Jacob A.	Carroll
20,150	Meek, John	Benton
22,045	Meek, Louisa	Benton
11,246	Meek, Samuel S.	Carroll
21,974	Menitt, James H.	Arkansas
5,633	Meredith, Louisa B.	Hempstead
15,796	Meriweather, Robt. D.	Chicot
16,402	Merrill, Joseph	Jefferson
14,507	Merriweather, Joseph, Estate of	Bradley

4,297	Merriwether, William D.	Independence
13,457	Metcalf, Isaac F.	Franklin
18,284	Metzgor, Fannie & Mary E. Whitehead	Phillips
14,985	Mews, Stephen	Montgomery
6,572	Meyers, Margaret	Marion
13,921	Mhoon, Jesse T.	Washington
22,010	Mhoon, Stark	Washington
9,176	Mickle, Harmon	Sebastian
9,642	Middleton, James R.	Johnson
9,041	Mildham, John A.	Franklin
1,635	Miles, John	Benton
22,288	Miller, Daniel	Pulaski
12,820	Miller, E. R.	Washington
3,448: 3,449:	Miller, Eliza	Drew
19,312	Miller, George D.	Washington
17,814	Miller, John W.	Conway
10,240: 10,241:	Miller, John W.	Crawford
21,194	Miller, Joseph D.	Washington
8,114	Miller, Mary A.	Crawford
1,327	Miller, Syrenah M.	Washington
21,809	Miller, Thomas, Heirs of	Washington
9,643	Mills, B. F.	Washington
21,780	Mills, H. M.	Franklin
13,718	Milor, Volney V.	Sebastian
5,584	Minor, Major	Jefferson
20,878	Minor, Mary S., Heirs of	Washington
11,682	Minyard, James	Clark
9,787	Miser, Elizabeth	Benton
9,281	Miser, John	Benton
9,644	Mitchell, Elizabeth	Washington
13,659	Mitchell, Felix, Estate of	Pulaski
13,719	Mitchell, Geo. W.	Benton
21,517	Mitchell, Joshua	Saline
8,880	Monds, John C.	Crawford
8,879	Monds, Lorenzo D.	Crawford
13,065	Monks, Francis M.	Sebastian
18,041	Montgomery, A.H.	Monroe
**	Montgomery, George	Lawrence
10,187	Montgomery, George	Johnson
19,311	Montgomery, James M.	Washington
20,053	Montgomery, Thomas R.	Washington
22,178	Moody, Francis H.	Pulaski
15,848	Moody, Jonathan	Madison
11,001: 11,508:	Moody, Leroy	Madison
20,562	Moody, Martha	Sebastian
3,039	Mooney, William	Crawford
19,659	Mooney, Wm. M.	Scott
5,585	Moore, Amanda	Hot Springs
12,816	Moore?, Andrew J.	Pulaski
9,038	Moore, Benjamin F.	Sebastian
20,094	Moore, David A.	Crawford
21,295	Moore, Emily H.	Crawford
14,253	Moore, Frederick J.	Sarber
10,147	Moore, Hannah	Pulaski
1,328	Moore, John D.	Washington
20,469	Moore, John P.	Phillips
12,819	Moore, John R.	Washington
4,298	Moore, John W.	Independence
21,772	Moore, Lewis	Sebastian
28	Moore, Lewis B.	Pulaski
11,807	Moore, Lovet	Sarber
4,787	Moore, Sampson	Prairie
12,601	Moore, Thomas	Phillips
17,251	Moores, Wm. C.	Yell
15,798	Morgan, John G.	Chicot
20,563	Morgan, Phebe	Sarber
17,669	Morrow, Geo.	Washington
5,136	Morrill, Ann V.	Prairie
13,183	Morris, George W.	Hot Springs
4,867	Morris, Hiram	Independence
22,219	Morris, James L.	Pulaski
16,238	Morris, James T.	Pulaski
19,527	Morris, John W.	Polk

** Montgomery is listed in index, with no number provided.

14,178	Morrison, Sarah A. E.	Phillips
6,077	Morrow, Robert P.	Crawford
13,660	Morton, J.S.	Grant
3,103	Morton, Wm.	Washington
8,873	Moseley, Peter	Bradley
9,223	Moulden, Mary J.	Washington
4,035	Moulder, Lewis E.	Woodruff
14,003	Mules, James A.	Washington
15,097	Mullen, Joseph S.	Crawford
14,740	Murphrey, William C.	Pulaski
3,634	Murphy, J. W. M.	Jefferson
22,042	Murphy, John L.	Woodruff
4,547	Murphy, Justus L.	Randolph
4,614	Murphy, Vincent, W.	Crawford
9,257	Murray, John L.	Johnson
17,620	Murrell, J. S.	Monroe
20,207	Muse, James	Carroll
11,017	Mustain, Ann B.	Benton
12,918	Mustain, Avery S.	Pulaski
20,063	Muzick, Joab	Prairie
15,927	Myree, William F.	Pulaski
4,266	Myrick, James M.	St. Francis
3,784	Nail, James K.	Benton
13,133	Naish, John W.	Shelby
1,595	Neal, Elizabeth	Washington
13,782	Neal, George W.	Crawford
17,223	Neal, William I.	Crawford
13,508	Neely, Elizabeth J.	Monroe
12,068: 12,069: 12,070:	Neely, Esther A. B., Lizzie E., and Mary E.	Independence
2,839	Neighbors, Levin S.	Hot Springs
16,386	Neighbors, Levin S.	Saline
2,838: 16,389:	Neighbors, William J.	Hot Springs
7,666	Nelson, Martin	Crawford
13,516	Nelson, Samuel	Washington
9,152	Nelson, Wm. M.	Clark
20,744	Nevil, Sarah W.	Phillips
15,717	Nevils, John	Pulaski
21,871	Newkirk, James H.	Saline
10,885	Newland, Mary H.	Independece
21,916	Newman, Reuben	Madison
20,949	Newman, Wm.	Marion
9,789	Nicholds, Geo. W.	Benton
13,871	Nichols, Francis and Philip	Pulaski
14,335	Nichols, John R.	Arkansas
13,871	Nichols, Philip and Francis	Pulaski
1,636	Nichols, Thomas	Benton
18,748	Nichols, William	Drew
9,645	Nicum, Nancy	Washington
18,754	Nidifer, Jacob	Benton
22,006	Nidifer, John and Nancy	Crawford
22,066	Nidifer, Nancy and John	Crawford
7,487	Noe, Wm. M.	Marion
9,230	Nolan, Samuel	Washington
13,158	Nolen, Eliza M.	Washington
5,273	Nolen, Green B.	Washington
9,221	Nolen, Wm. L.	Washington
4,406	Nordan, Elizabeth	Crawford
16,387	Norman, Evaline	Hot Springs
1,376	Norris, A. J.	Washington
2,417	Norris, John	Benton
19,528	Norris, Moses M.	Polk
19,656	Norris, Nelson	Sebastian
8,115	Norwood, Robert	Crawford
14,989	Nowlin, James S.	Pulaski
4,159	Nunley, Wm. A.	Washington
10,434	Nunn, Admiral N.	Dallas
12,290	Nunnally, Brighberry B.	Phillips
5,792	Oakes, William	Benton
9,646	Oakley, James W.	Benton
13,743	Oates, John T.	Monroe
1,239	O'Broyn, Arnold	Crawford
11,339	O'Connell, Mary	Pulaski
19,379	O'Connor, Laura E.	Phillips
14,647	O'Kane, Patrick	Pulaski
14,200	Old, W.A., Estate of	White
11,548	Oliver, Percilla	Sarber
11,962	Oliver, Willoughby N.	Sarber

10,053	O'Neal, Henry H.	Jefferson
5,079	Orme, Walter	Crawford
8,116	Orrick, Wm. J.	Crawford
5,174	Otey, Walter L.	Phillips
5,858	Outlaw, Harriet B.	Pulaski
9,341	Overstreet, John W.	Calhoun
2,418	Overstreet, William	Pulaski
20,342	Overton, Jesse	Clark
18,810	Owen, Charles M.	Sarber
13,661	Owen, Cynthia M.	Pulaski
13,662	Owen, Robert	Pulaski
14,526	Owens, W.B.	Johnson
9,276	Pace, Wm. R.	Benton
15,487	Packard, Amanda	Benton
9,212	Paddock, S.F.	Washington
2,975	Page, John	Sebastian
10,440	Page, Susan D.	Sebastian
14,684	Paine, Gabriel W., Estate of	Johnson
8,825	Paine, Thomas B.	Johnson
11,852	Pardue, Elizabeth	Crawford
19,399	Park, Andrew, St.	Monroe
20,567	Parke, Wm.	Scott
9,275	Parker, Wm.	Benton
14,004	Parks, Wm. B.	Washington
17,070	Parker, Wm. C.	Sebastian
9,254	Parks, William J.	Johnson
8,045	Parrott, Julius C.	Bradley
12,829	Paschal, Jeremiah	Phillips
18,832	Patrick, Geo. W.	Washington
19,242	Patrick, Wiley	Madison
11,002	Patrick, William	Madison
22,256	Patte, Wm. C.	White
4,187	Patterson, Elisha	Searcy
5,372	Patterson, James R.	Woodruff
20,536	Patterson, Philip	Sebastian
20,564	Patton, Thomas, Estate of	Sebastian
19,314	Patton, Thomas C.	Washington
14,689	Payne, Dorastus & Mary E.	Crawford
12,063	Payne, Margaret Jane	Washington
14,689	Payne, Mary E. and Dorastus	Crawford
13,114	Payne, Samuel H.	Sebastian
17,809	Payne, Thomas	Conway
17,533	Pearce, Francis M.	Sebastian
18,481	Pearce, John	Washington
22,080	Pearson, Esther	Washington
19,316	Pearson, John	Washington
9,647	Pearson, Mahala A.	Benton
20,501	Pearson, Wm. C.	Washington
21,796	Peer, Edward	Washington
22,009	Peer, Jacob	Washington
4,570	Peerson, Daniel L.	Washington
18,704	Peerson, John	Washington
9,474	Peete, Sallie M.	Monroe
12,938	Peil, George, Estate of	Pulaski
15,926	Pence, William	Crawford
3,698	Pendergrass, Thomas J.	Woodruff
22,041	Penn, Thomas H., Estate of	Woodruff
13,663	Pennington, Jacob W.	Clark
20,560	Pennington, Roseda	Scott
18,147	Penny, Lucy J. and Mark A. & Quintine M. Deputy	Phillips
4,255	Perkins, Dempsey	Benton
6,078	Perkins, Richard P.	Crawford
16,392	Perry, Clayborn	Hot Springs
16,390	Perry, Mary A.	Hot Springs
9,353	Perry, Joseph W.	Ouachita
15,849	Perry, William	Madison
5,750	Peters, Andrew J.	Crawford
5,742	Peters, Arrena	Crawford
20,155	Petty, Thomas H.	Sebastian
10,859	Phelan, Abijah F.	Washington
13,922	Phelan, Abijah T.	Washington
13,923	Phelan, Wm., Estate of	Washington
5,138	Phelps, Calvin	Crawford
691	Philips, Wilson	Washington
672	Phillips, Alexander	Washington
13,720	Phillipps, Geo. W.	Madison

21,189	Phillips, H.B.	Carroll
20,245	Phillips, James	Madison
20,246	Phillips, Mary	Madison
18,749	Phillips, Matthew A.	Ashley
10,647	Phillips, Theodore H.	Jackson
12,604	Phillips, Thomas	Hot Springs
3,330	Phipps, James	Washington
3,328	Phipps, Thomas J.	Washington
968	Pierce, John	Craighead
17,376	Pike, Dedrick	Monroe
9,337	Pile, Parilee	Ouachita
14,038	Pillow, Wm. A.	Clark
5,583	Pine Bluff Baptist Chruch	Jefferson
6,990	Pinegar, Clarissa	White
11,874	Pinkerton, Joseph	Crawford
19,200	Pirtle, John W.	Polk
13,063	Pistole, John	Sebastian
12,579	Pitman, Jane	Boone
9,258	Pitts, Benjamin	Johnson
13,721	Pitts, John W.	Benton
11,896	Platt, Obadiah H.	Prairie
17,083	Pledger, Isaac	Franklin
16,096	Poe, Elizabeth E.	Pulaski
18,084	Pointer, Margaret M.	Carroll
12,246	Polk, Burns	Phillips
1,900	Polk, John S.	Madison
9,648	Pollard, Sarah S.	Benton
2,212	Pool, Augustin C.	Washington
5,746	Pope, Nancy A.	Crawford
2,334	Pope, Peter	Dallas
19,620	Pope, Rebecca	Crawford
21,943	Porter, William	Phillips
17,019	Porter, William	Pulaski
19,529	Posey, Seburn	Polk
7,667	Potts, David	Crawford
9,241	Potts, Polly	Benton
9,922	Pounds, Lavinia	Benton
20,201	Powell, James	Madison
16,216	Powell, John	Ashley
21,490	Powell, John	Sebastian
10,048	Power, Jemima M.	Hot Springs
15,480	Powers, Henry A.	Pulaski
18,040	Poynter, Judith B., Estate of	Monroe
11,417	Prater, Elijah	Madison
9,649	Pratt, Lewis	Benton
1,638	Preddy, Chas. W.	Drew
91	Price, John H.	Benton
6,418	Price, John H.	Hot Springs
1,896	Price, John S.	Johnson
21,971	Price, Mathis	Benton
6,400	Price, Morgan	Hot Springs
11,673	Price, W. R.	Clark
15,277	Price, William A., Estate of	Arkansas
2,844	Prichard, James E.	Hot Springs
18,037	Pride, William, Estate of	Monroe
21,518	Prilliman, Mrs. E.N.	Saline
21,509	Prilliman, J.G.	Saline
1,494	Privett, J.H.	Washington
20,498	Privett, Wm. S.	Washington
9,345	Proctor, Thomas A.	Ouachita
10,786	Pugh, Edwin	Izard
11,680	Pullen, John P.	Clark
11,683	Pullen, Lucinda	Clark
11,454	Puryear, William	Craighead
21,785	Putnam, B.B.	Franklin
19,201	Putnam, Elizabeth	Sebastian
13,617	Pyeatt, Jesse H.	Washington
10,853	Pyeatt, Martha J.	Washington
13,962	Pyeatt, Wm. S.	Washington
21,547	Qualls, Jasper N.	Madison
3,769	Quattlebaum, Henry M.	Jefferson
17,982	Queener, Jacob	Franklin
19,408	Quinton, Alfred R.	Washington
18,708: 13,998:	Quinton, Jefferson	Washington
21,993	Rabb, Harriet A.	Phillips
12,717	Ragan, John	Lawrence
4,893	Ragsdale, Rhoda	Johnson
19,755	Rainwater, Benjamin F.	Washington

21,805	Rainwater, James	Washington
4,768	Rainwater, John	Washington
5,137	Rainwater, John S.	Crawford
3,631	Rainwater, Matthew	Washington
16,106	Rainey, Saml. B.	Washington
687	Ramsey, Saml.	Benton
11,871	Raney, Nancy	Crawford
21,920	Rather, John M.	Washington
12,289	Ray, Lucy C.	St. Francis
14,378	Ray, Stephen	Pulaski
16,375	Read, Edwin O.	Phillips
9,650	Reddick, Jane	Benton
1,255	Redman, Aaron W.	Jackson
10,789	Redman, P.H.	Jackson
22,027	Redman, William A.	Desha
1,329: 20,061:	Reed, Adam J.	Washington
9,213	Reed, A.W.	Washington
21,795	Reed, Elizabeth	Washington
19,955	Reed, George Wm. and Hunt, John	Washington
10,848	Reed, Geo. W.C.	Crawford
1,597: 19,164:	Reed, George Wm.	Washington
20,347	Reed, Harriet	Pulaski
2,214	Reed, J.G.	Washington
2,215	Reed, James H.	Washington
1,491: 20,223:	Reed, John	Washington
2,213	Reed, Keziah	Washington
1,596	Reed, Martha	Washington
20,371	Reed, Martha B.	Washington
9,651	Reed, Minter	Benton
13,664	Reed, Richard	Pulaski
20,224	Reed, Richard, Heirs of	Washington
18,593	Reeder, Agnes, Estate of	Sebastian
14,542	Reese, John	Washington
10,846	Reese, Wm. W.	Washington
11,476	Reeves, James R.	Madison
11,963	Reichert, Julius	Sebastian
14,939	Reiff, John H.	Washington
5,575	Reynolds, A.W.	Newton
18,132	Reynolds, John S.	Benton
20,218	Reynolds, T.A.	Washington
12,752	Rhodes, Frank	Phillips
9,653	Rice, Absalom	Washington
8,185	Rice, Charles W.	Benton
22,034	Rice, F.H.	Phillips
18,306	Rice, W.D.	Phillips
5,299	Richards, Geo. W.	Clark
12,818	Richardson, David	Washington
9,339	Richardson, Henry W.	Ouachita
11,747	Richardson, Rebecca	Clark
19,252	Richardson, Susan	Franklin
6,578	Richmond, Asa	Pulaski
5,793	Riddle, James, Estate of	Benton
20,364	Riddle, Lewis F.	Crawford
6,668	Riddle, Nancy	Clark
8,117	Riddle, Nathan	Crawford
10,873	Rinehart, Michael	Washington
5,586	Ripetoe, Sophia M.	Hot Springs
9,654	Ritter, Aaron	Benton
18,508	Ritter, Joel	Benton
4,769	Ritter, Wm. R.	Washington
3,450	Rives, Geo. W.	Drew
2,217	Rizley, Wilson	Washington
10,872	Roach, Wm. F.	Washington
13,455	Roark, John	Franklin
12,606	Robbins, David	Hot Springs
9,045	Robbins, John G.	Sebastian
19,611	Robbins, Joseph	Madison
14,522	Roberts, Mary	Washington
12,589	Robertson, James	Phillips
13,180	Robertson, Stephen F.	Pulaski
6,411	Roberts, Thomas J.	Jefferson
12,754	Robertson, Wm. N.	Phillips
19,794	Robertson, Reuben	Jefferson
20,168	Robins, John, Heirs of	Pulaski
19,965	Robins, Lucinda	Madison
18,705	Robinson, Alexander C.	Washington

1,374	Robinson, David E.	Washington
9,228	Robinson, Elisha B.	Washington
1,190	Robinson, Jacob	Johnson
13,332	Robinson, James	Desha
11,538	Robinson, James	Prairie
14,524	Robinson, Michael, Estate of	Madison
2,218	Robinson, Sherrod	Washington
13,730	Robinson, Wiley S.	Saline
18,909	Rockwell, Simeon B., Estate of	Randolph
4,616	Rodgers, John	Benton
20,340: 15,971:	Roesch, Christian	Pulaski
5,587	Rogers, Archibald	Lincoln
12,288	Rogers, Ezekiel	Phillips
11,330	Rogers, Green W.	Crawford
1,788	Rogers, James	Crawford
8,840	Rogers, James C.C.	Crawford
19,398	Rogers, Jesse G.	Monroe
1,897	Rogers, John M.	Johnson
14,254	Rogers, John	Sarber
8,118	Rogers, Jonathan	Crawford
9,044	Rogers, John C.	Crawford
20,310	Rogers, Mary, Estate of	Arkansas
18,797	Rogers, Mary E.	Scott
15,392	Rogers, S.E.	Washington
9,655	Rogers, S.G.	Washington
3,104	Rogers, Wm.	Washington
22,082	Rogers, W.D.	Washington
2,216	Roggers, Wm. L.	Washington
1,152	Roller, Geo. W.	Benton
17,114	Rollins, James, Estate of	Phillips
9,352	Rooks, Wm. R.	Ouachita
18,813	Rose, Henry	White
1,479	Rose, James	Washington
13,665	Rose, Jane	Pulaski
8,881	Ross, Wesley W.	Crawford
11,677	Ross, Wm. D.	Clark
21,666	Rosson, Virginia, Estate of	Arkansas
9,270	Rotramell, Mary	Benton
19,655	Rowe, Josephine and Woodard, Amos	Sebastian
13,731	Rowland, Elijah	Saline
13,687	Rudd, Wm. M.	Carroll
19,828	Rudel, Edward	Sebastian
8,929	Rumph, John B.	Ouachita
9,046	Rupe, David P.	Sebastian
9,652	Rupe, George W.	Sebastian
16,192	Push, Martin, V.	Sebastian
15,925	Rush, Nancy	Crawford
5,588	Russell, Alfred	Grant
18,362	Russell, Jarber	Crawford
12,924	Russell, Mary Ann	Phillips
2,419	Russell, William M.	Pulaski
20,497	Rutherford, John A.	Washington
1,806	Rutherford, John W.	Washington
20,225	Rutherford, Wm. B.	Washington
13,959	Sanders, Anderson	Washington
12,432	Sanders, Milton	White
9,656	Sanders, Stephen	Washington
9,251	Sanders, Walter B.	Johnson
21,634	Sanders, William	Pulaski
17,353	Sagely, John	Crawford
13,064	Sagely, John C.	Crawford
9,267	Sager, Christian C.	Benton
3,258	St. Clair, George W.	Franklin
5,389	Sanders, David	Clark
19,413	Sanger, Stephen S.	Pulaski
10,534	Sangster, James W.	Crawford
16,339	Satterfield, Carter	Pulaski
9,657	Saurey, Washington R.	Benton
20,056	Sawyers, Henry A.	Washington
10,864	Sawyers, James M.	Washington
16,103	Sawyers, John M.	Washington
5,794	Sawyers, Robert A.	Benton
5,744	Scantlen, Geo. W.	Crawford
8,119	Scarberry, Thomas	Sebastian
20,198	Schaad, Fanny	Pulaski
10,066	Scott, Anne	Saline

12,469: 20,346:	Scott, Armistead	Pulaski
6,625	Scott, Benjamin	Crawford
5,859	Scott, Charles G.	Pulaski
5,212	Scott, James D.	Clark
3,455	Scott, James W.	Washington
10,067	Scott, Robert I.	Saline
17,243	Scott, Thomas H.	Sebastian
10,629	Scott, William	Crawford
1,480	Scott, William P.	Benton
13,073	Scroggins, Wilborn	Saline
10,981	Scull, James, Estate of	Jefferson
11,186	Seagraves, Michael	Crawford
11,155	Seamans, Benjamin F.	Woodruff
21,670	Seamons, Mesheak	Arkansas
18,752	Seay, Calvin	Benton
19,973	Sechler, Danl. M. & Prter, W.H.	Crawford
16,034	Seigrist, Chas. H.	Crittendon
11,961	Selig, August	Sebastian
11,960	Selig, Julius	Sebastian
10,648	Selvey, Garlin	Jackson
4,965	Sembler, John R.	St. Francis
18,479	Setser, John	Benton
7,622	Sewell, Humphrey	Crawford
21,549	Shaefer, Vincent	Sebastian
22,087	Shannon, Jefferson, Heirs of	Washington
12,066	Shannon, John L.	Washington
4,206	Sharp, Wm. S.	Washington
18,859	Shastid, Samuel	Madison
2,420	Shaw, John N., Estate of	Pulaski
18,081: 19,530:	Shed, Lorenzo D.	Polk
4,490	Sheffield, John A.	Izard
6,413	Shelby, H. G.	Jefferson
3,382	Shelton, Daniel B.	Jackson
11,154	Shelton, Edward N.	Woodruff
12,085	Shelton, Margret	Clark
20,219	Shepard, John	Crawford
11,465	Shepley, Benjamin	Franklin
9,049	Sheppe, Barnhard	Sebastian
21,354	Shepperd, James, Estate of	Jefferson
19,756	Sherrod, Arthur W.	Washington
20,372	Sherrod, Wm.	Washington
20,499	Sherrod, Wm. H.	Washington
19,274	Shinkle, Margaret	Phillips
7,930	Shope, William	Clark
10,061	Shoppack, Mrs. Sibby	Saline
13,963	Shores, William D.	Franklin
11,410	Shurlock, Drury F.	Arkansas
21,798	Simco, Thomas, Estate of	Crawford
11,218	Simons, Simon, Estate of	Woodruff
16,210	Simpson, Benj. F.	Ashley
9,138	Simpson, Harriet T.	Washington
7,741	Simpson, John B.	Crawford
21,875	Simpson, Louisa	Saline
11,448	Sims, David Q.	Craighead
14,838	Singleton, Andrew J.	Franklin
14,447	Sivley, James M.	Sarber
2,956	Sively, John D.	Johnson
14,448	Sivley, Wm. R.	Sarber
9,252	Skaggs, William, Estate of	Johnson
5,364	Skillern, James V.	Clark
20,199	Skillian, Isaac C.A.	Pulaski
5,300	Skinner, Geo. W.	Clark
21,090	Skinner, Thomas	Madison
16,391	Slaight, James	Hot Springs
14,182	Slate, Sarah	Phillips
7,931	Sloane, Caroline	Clark
9,481	Sloan, Ranklin	Hot Springs
16,761	Slone, Eliza	Crawford
7,842	Slosson, John N.	Sebastian
12,613	Smart, Wm. J.	Sebastian
14,017	Smith, A.G.	Washington
10,045	Smith, Anna	Woodruff
906	Smith, Boling	Washington
13,688	Smith, David	Washington
9,279	Smith, Edward W.	Benton
11,245	Smith, Elizabeth	Carroll

12,286	Smith, George F.	Phillips
20,202	Smith, G.W.R.	Madison
13,327	Smith, Geo. R.	Washington
13,908	Smith, Geo. W.	Washington
18,923	Smith, James	Washington
5,727	Smith, James S.	Jackson
16,708	Smith, John	Conway
13,328	Smith, John A.	Washington
14,599	Smith, J.G.	Washington
14,184	Smith, Jonathan	Washington
20,601	Smith, Mary	Sebastian
19,738	Smith, Morocco D.	Phillips
9,658	Smith, Mortimer D.	Benton
3,451	Smith, Peyton R.	Drew
6,075	Smith, Philip	Crawford
15,267	Smith, Robert	Independence
18,811	Smith, Robert J.	Scott
12,064	Smith, Robert N.	Sarber
14,509	Smith, Sarah J.	Jefferson
14,644	Smith, Wm. M.	Sebastian
2,219	Smodley, G.E.	Washington
9,727	Snead, Benjamin E.	Crawford
12,593	Snider, Jacob	Sebastian
18,069	Snodgrass, Joseph, Estate of	Franklin
15,206	Snodgrass, Robert	Franklin
11,249	Sommers, Robt.	Carroll
22,164	Sorrels, Washington F.	Scott
12,602	Sorter, Nancy Ann	Hot Springs
18,082	Southern, John	Polk
17,467	Spake, Minerva J.	Pulaski
11,615	Sparks, Martha	St. Francis
13,301	Spencer, Elijah	Crawford
13,666	Spiva, Jonas B.	Montgomery
22,040	Spivy, Wm. J., Estate of	Woodruff
22,043	Spring, Lucinda	Benton
4,217	Springston, Wm.	Washington
21,536	Spurgeon, Greenberry J. and Butler, Israel S.	Sebastian
5,765	Stacey, Elizabeth	Jefferson
15,098	Stafford, Margaret	Crawford
6,415	Staggs, Zachariah	Hot Springs
8,502	Stahle, George	White
13,722	Stanton, Simon	Sebastian
2,445	Stapp, August J.	Ouachita
15,750	Stapps, Jesse L.	Sevier
2,843	Staton, William A.	Hot Springs
10,057	Stedham, Wilson	Hot Springs
5,327	Steel, M.D.	Washington
19,967	Steinberg, Mary E.	Crawford
9,772	Stephens, James B.	Sebastian
18,963	Stevens, Wilkins	Randolph
834	Stevenson, Joseph	Dallas
22,076	Stevenson, Samuel, Estate of	Washington
15,218	Stewart, Jesse	Crawford
17,068	Stewart, Minerva	Sarber
6,150	Stewart, Thomas	Phillips
9,338	Stewart, William	Nevada
15,667	Stewart, William H.	Crawford
9,795	Stidham, David W.	Benton
13,565	Stiles, Henry P.	Franklin
21,495	Stiles, John	Franklin
21,642	Stone, Henry H.	White
814	Stone, L. D.	Washington
1,375	Stone, Lucinda E.	Washington
9,692	Stone, Mary E.	Ouachita
1,094	Stone, Melissa J.	Washington
3,452	Stone, Thomas P.	Drew
9,686	Stone, Wm. F.	Ouachita
4,861	Stout, James	Independence
21,642	Stone, James B., Estate of	Jefferson
9,250	Storms, John	Johnson
9,047	Stoppleman, Henry	Sebastian
15,850	Stotts, William	Madison
15,323: 2,438:	Stout, James M.	Conway
6,421	Stribling, Sabra	Hot Springs
9,569	Strickler, Jacob	Washington
12,899	Strickler, W. B.	Washington
9,048	Stromberg, William	Sebastian
9,343	Stroud, James	Calhoun

9,412	Sturdivant, Wm. C.	Columbia
1,166	Stutts, Henry B.	Pulaski
6,619	Sullivan, J.H.	Crawford
13,509	Sullivan, Louisa C.	Monroe
1,177	Sumner, Catharine E.	Pulaski
2,980	Sutherland, Geo. W.	Franklin
12,751	Sutton, Joseph G.	Phillips
4,895	Sutton, Samuel J.	Phillips
2,842	Surratt, James	Hot Springs
21,277	Sutton, Martha A.	Washington
1,741	Swillain, Berry T.	Woodruff
11,675	Swink, Amanda I.	Clark
14,970	Tackett, Edmund P. G.	Arkansas
14,860	Talmsher, Theodore	Fulton
22,029	Tapp, Vincent	Phillips
14,039	Tarver, Mahala	Clark
18,800	Tate, Jacob P.	Scott
18,799	Tate, Jeremiah J.	Scott
9,031	Tault, Patrick	Sebastian
20,216	Taylor, Aaron S.	Washington
14,421	Taylor, James H.	Johnson
5,032	Taylor, John	Jefferson
1,995	Taylor, John Q.	Phillips
22,161	Taylor, Nathaniel B., Estate of	Sebastian
1,809	Taylor, Stewart	Washington
2,587	Taylor, Wm. A.	Washington
4,930	Taylor, Wm. H.	Searcy
21,307	Taylor, Zachariah, Estate of	Sebastian
15,997	Teague, Lorenzo D.	Crawford
13,142	Temple, William, Estate of	Pulaski
2,588	Templeton, Thomas	Madison
4,160	Tenant, T. H.	Washington
18,831	Terry, James	Scott
19,518	Thibault, Maria E., Esate of	Pulaski
18,355	Thomas, Irena	Washington
14,355	Thompson, James H.	Pulaski
9,660	Thompson, Josiah	Washington
21,808	Thompson, Leonard M.	Washington
14,723	Thurston, Mary	Sebastian
19,196	Thurston, Thomas W.	Sebastian
905: 1,598:	Thurman, John (Fayetteville)	Washington
15,175	Thurman, John (Rheas Mills)	Washington
7,034	Thomas, Henrietta E.	Clark
18,555	Thomas, Irena	Washington
12,086	Thomas, James N.	Clark
5,301	Thomas, Lewis	Clark
7,932	Thomas, Mary A.	Clark
11,676	Thomas, Nelson G.	Clark
16,639	Thomason, Pleasant A.	Prairie
19,389	Thompason, James S.	Newton
12,247	Thompson, Joseph S.	Phillips
4,149	Thompson, Pleasant H.	St. Francis
5,391	Thompson, Ransom	Saline
9,800	Threet, Harmens	Benton
20,743	Threlkeld, David H.	Phillips
21,876	Tillery, Hugh	Saline
14,527	Timberlake, James S.	Johnson
1,235	Tiner, Elias	Conway
21,541	Titsworth, Lorenzo, Estate of	Scott
18,034	Tobin, Patrick, Estate of	Crawford
12,549: 18,461:	Tobin, Sarah Ann	Crawford
19,193	Todd, Ale	Franklin
17,880	Todd, James C.	Washington
5,371	Tollet, Henry	Washington
5,328	Tollet, Rebecca	Washington
19,752	Tollet, Rowland C.	Washington
4,770	Tollet, Wm. J.	Washington
9,344	Toney, Elijah Y.	Ouachita
5,898	Townsend, Robt. B.	Conway
5,795	Trammell, Thomas R.	Benton
18,784	Trammell, Winney	Sebastian
1,787	Trask, Edmund F.	Crawford
21,067	Trice, Matthew A., Estate of	Arkansas
11,153	Trice, Taxwell W.	Woodruff
15,227	Tragdon, Wm.	Washington
5,796	Trolinger, James N.	Benton
13,751	Trotten, Benjamin Y.	Monroe

9,661	True, Wallis	Benton
9,242	Truesdell, John P.	Benton
6,318	Tuck, Wm. D.	Washington
7,010	Tucker, Luke	Pulaski
18,268	Tucker, Thos. J.	Madison
15,851	Tucker, William W.	Madison
1,072	Turnage, Joseph	Mississippi
13,277	Turner, Annie M.	St. Francis
11,418	Turner, Elizabeth	Arkansas
5,759	Turner, Jane H.	Izard
15,788	Turner, John, Estate of	Ashley
11,851	Turner, John P.	Crawford
1,646	Turner, Paskel	Benton
17,188	Turner, Sterling M.	Sebastian
19,270	Turner, Wm. S. and Annie	Phillips
2,773	Tutt, Nancy A.	Marion
13,136	Tyler, Benjamin C.	Hot Springs
17,328	Tyler, Redrick	Sebastian
13,744	Tyler, William	Monroe
11,152	Tyree, Christopher C.	Woodruff
20,141	Tyus, Ellen M., James H., & Martha A.	Hempstead
21,372	Underwood, Q. K.	Phillips
10,867	Vandever, Angeline	Washington
1,330	Vandever, Wm.	Washington
17,813	Vann, Sarah	Conway
12,605	Vansickle, Miles W.	Hot Springs
6,080	Vassan, Charles W.	Crawford
15,043	Vaughan, Joseph T.	Crawford
1,901	Vaughn, Elizabeth B.	Madison
9,723	Vaught, Sarah Ann	Crawford
837	Venon, Lucinda A.	Washington
22,188	Vernon, Samuel	Washington
13,506	Vernon, Joseph M.	Monroe
14,005	Vines, Wm. E.	Washington
17,116	Vinyard, Wm. James	Phillips
2,878	Wade, Abraham	Pulaski
18,851	Wade, Henry G., Estate of	Drew
2,377	Wade, James	Pulaski
21,191	Wade, James J.	Carroll
9,296	Wafford, Isaac, Estate of	Hot Springs
22,035	Wagner, C., Estate of	Sebastian
14,294	Walker, Andrew J.	Monroe
13,667	Walker, George	Pulaski
14,179	Walker, Green B.	Monroe
13,454	Walker, James M.	Franklin
14,180	Walker, John	Monroe
16,425	Walker, Susan	Washington
12,621	Walker, Thomas	Washington
9,662	Walker, Thomas H.	Benton
4,571	Walker, Wm.	Washington
4,492	Wall, Emma	Jackson
14,181	Wallace, Benj. F.	Phillips
18,918	Wallace, Bryant	Washington
11,367	Wallace, Jackson	Washington
5,761	Walker, Hartwell B.	Izard
19,127	Wallace, Cyrus	Pope
5,322	Wallace, Ruth C.	Johnson
1,168	Wallis, John A.	Jefferson
5,797	Walls, Charles	Benton
19,801	Walter, John A.	Yell
21,665	Walton, John R.	Arkansas
9,788	Wammack, Wm.	Benton
2,943	Ward, Anna	Phillips
17,184	Ward, Carleton	Sebastian
17,185	Ward, F. M.	Sebastian
17,186	Ward, Joseph	Sebastian
6,410	Ward, Frances A.	Hot Springs
15,075	Ward, Hiram	Benton
21,544	Ward, Louisa	Benton
5,592	Ward, Martha	Grant
19,098	Ward, Preston	Polk
22,075	Ward, Squire, Estate of	Washington
21,668	Ware, Robt. P.	Arkansas
9,259	Warren, Harden	Johnson
9,285	Warren, Hugh	Johnson
9,253	Warren, James	Johnson
9,248	Warren, Margaret	Johnson
11,019	Warren, Michael	Johnson
9,284	Warren, William	Johnson

4,278	Washington, Beaver	Pulaski
8,187: 9,051:	Waters, Wm. A.	Sebastian
15,811	Watkins, Green B.	Crawford
2,267	Watkins, James	Madison
21,643	Watkins, Margaret E.	White
22,287	Watkins, Thomas	White
9,237	Watson, Isom	Benton
2,933	Watson, John W.	Johnson
14,040	Watson, Orrin	Pulaski
11,018	Watts, Malicka	Johnson
9,052: 9,053:	Watts, Marion J.	Sebastian
15,805	Watts, Samuel	Washington
22,077	Watts, Wm.	Washington
7,035	Wazoner, Samuel	Clark
19,531	Wear, John	Polk
7,723	Weather, Henry J.	Johnson
4,485	Weaver, Alfred G.	Franklin
5,798	Weaver, Ephraim	Benton
14,205	Weaver, George	Perry
8,874	Webb, Andrew J.	Bradley
13,458	Webb, Hampton N.	Sarber
12,721	Webb, Thomas	Benton
9,663	Webb, William	Benton
4,299	Weber, Hannah M.	Independence
10,851	Weber, Nicholas	Washington
1,996	Weekes, Mary	Conway
18,578	Weir, John H.	Sebastian
7,036	Welch, Moses	Clark
4,285	Welch, Thomas	Independence
3,329	Weldon, Thomas F.	Washington
8,884	Wells, Dolphius	Franklin
4,257	Wells, Elizabeth	Jefferson
12,939	Wells, Elizabeth A.	Pulaski
19,427	Welter, Nicholas	Polk
11,248	West, James S.	Washington
3,040	West, John Q.	Crawford
13,966	West, Lucinda	Randolph
9,664	West, Thomas M.	Washington
12,683	West, William M.	Jefferson
17,531	West, Wm.	Sebastian
15,995	Westmoreland, Wilber	Madison
13,507	Wetherford, Nancy C.	Monroe
14,206	Wheat, T. J.	Nevada
5,748	Wheelan, Thomas	Crawford
19,753	Wheeler, H. B.	Washington
2,221	Whinery, Abraham J., Estate of	Washington
8,501	Whisenant, Nancy	White
22,033	White, C. M., Estate of	Sebastian
19,430	White, John C.	Washington
4,478	White, David C.	Jefferson
4,258	White, Eliza	Jefferson
9,272	White, James	Benton
9,665	White, James	Boone
12,702	White, John	Arkansas
8,121	White, Luther C.	Crawford
18,284	Whitehead, Mary E. & Fanny Metzgor	Phillips
13,360	Whitfield, William	Crawford
10,535	Whitfield, William V.	Crawford
2,974	Whitford, Isaac S.	Woodruff
11,671	Whitten, Thomas	Clark
20,212	Whorton, R. C.	Madison
2,774	Wickersham, Elizabeth A.	Marion
1,079	Wight, James H.	Benton
10,522	Wight, Simeon	Benton
1,472	Wilbank, Wm.	Washington
18,964	Wilburn, Felix G.	Boone
19,191	Wilcox, M. J.	Franklin
9,050: 11,263:	Willhof, Mary	Crawford
10,853	Willhite, Mary	Washington
3,699	Williams, Alexander	Woodruff
11,191	Williams, Allen C.	Pulaski
9,265	Williams, Cynthia C.	Benton
21,669	Williams, Emery	Arkansas
22,286	Williams, Henry	Pulaski
19,808	Williams, Henry	Monroe

4,161	Williams, Ira	Washington
19,165	Williams, John C.	Washington
20,742	Williams, John R.	Phillips
21,784	Williams, Nancy	Franklin
8,506	Williams, Parker	Desha
10,054	Williams, Robert	Jefferson
20,206	Williams, S. B.	Madison
3,648	Williams, Samuel T.	Johnson
9,561	Williams, William	Dallas
10,577	Williamson, Jack	Crawford
17,969	Williamson, John	Sebastian
16,290	Williamson, Wm. W.	Montgomery
19,452	Williford, Henry	Washington
11,244	Willis, John T.	Crawford
3,649	Willis, John W.	Johnson
17,242	Willmuth, Albert R.	Sebastian
9,054	Willsie, Micha	Sebastian
5,726	Wilmans, James E.	Jackson
8,120	Wilson, Andrew L.	Crawford
5,775	Wilson, Elizabeth	Clark
1,902	Wilson, James F.	Washington
5,329	Wilson, John	Washington
8,023	Wilson, John M.	Clark
10,784	Wilson, Jonathan	Saline
10,784	Wilson, Jonathan J.	Sharp Co.
13,668	Wilson, Lazarus	Pulaski
17,416	Wilson, Martha, Estate of	Dallas
16,367	Wilson, Mary A.	Sebastian
13,928	Wilson, Matilda	Washington
16,547	Wilson, Robert	Woodruff
14,528	Wilson, Simon	Johnson
19,395	Wilson, Thomas	Washington
11,097	Wilson, Wm. F.	Washington
18,042	Windly, Susan E.	Monroe
5,323	Wines, Geo. W.	Crawford
4,300	Winfrey, Solomon	Pulaski
2,220	Winkler, Samuel	Washington
19,120	Winn, Eliza H.	Washington
20,054	Winn, James, Estate of	Washington
13,669	Winsett, Alfred	Pulaski
13,964	Wisenor, Mary A.	Washington
21,337	Withers, Albert G.	Arkansas
17,460	Wolf, Levicy	Benton
16,583	Womack, John A.	St. Francis
9,564	Womack, John P., Estate of	Ashley
9,666	Wood, Catharine	Washington
11,157	Wood, Daniel, Estate of	Woodruff
8,421	Wood, Elizabeth	Sebastian
20,208	Wood, Geo. W.	Carroll
9,055	Wood, James M.	Crawford
18,921	Wood, Nelson	Washington
21,192	Wood, Martha	Carroll
14,539	Wood, Mary	Washington
12,243	Wood, Pinckney C.	Phillips
20,502	Wood, Sarah	Washington
20,247	Wood, Thomas	Carroll
22,079	Wood, Wm., Estate of	Washington
19,655	Woodard, Amos and Rowe, Josephine	Sebastian
8,422	Woodard, Lewis, Estate of	Sebastian
21,511	Woodruff, A. M.	Pulaski
22,073	Woodruff, Wyatt F.	Washington
9,791	Woods, David C.	Benton
6,401	Woods, Eliza	Hot Springs
9,793	Woods, Elizabeth K.	Benton
688	Woods, Robert S.	Benton
17,771	Woods, Samuel P.	Benton
689	Woods, William H.	Benton
2,792	Woodson, J. Alexander	Jefferson
8,822	Woolley, Allen	Woodruff
9,691	Word, Amerial L.	Ouachita
17,605	Word, James C.	Phillips
11,355	Word, Wm., Estate of	Arkansas
16,731	Works, Martha A.	Dallas
11,564	Worsham, Wm. B.	Phillips
20,349	Wortham, Louisa B.	Pulaski
20,365	Wright, Delha A.	Crawford
10,062	Wright, Nelson	Saline
14,256	Wright, N. F.	Sarber
1,071	Wylds, Mary	St. Francis
13,116	Yaden, Thomas H.	Sebastian
14,974	Yandell, David	Saline
19,251	Yandell, Samuel	Scott
12,242	Yarbrough, Wm. H.	Phillips
19,375	Yell, James, Estate of	Jefferson
7,375	Yerby, Henry, Heirs of	Phillips
8,500	Yingling, Christina	White
11,164	York, Wm., Estate of	Woodruff
19,100	Young, Elisha	Polk
17,942	Young, Jones, Estate of	Arkansas
21,663	Young, Narcissa	Arkansas
10,850	Young, Nathan M.	Washington
11,242	Young, Oliver M.	Benton
19,576	Zillah, Joseph C.	Washington

FLORIDA

15,045	Albrilton, Thomas H.	Manatee
5,108	Austin, Emond	Franklin
8,860	Bagwell, Berry E.	Hernando
13,477	Bailey, John	Escambia
17,170	Balsam, Henry von	St. John
3,794	Balsam, J. von	St. John
12,740	Bangs, Isaac S., Jr.; Brownell, Charles A., and Corson, Joseph B.	Escambia
12,804	Bates, John M.	Manatee
13,903	Bennett, Wm. R., Dewey, Wm. G. and Elridge, John	Monroe
13,476	Babe, Francis	Escambia
13,525	Braddock, Sarah	Nassau
20,987	Bronnum, Lars F.	Santa Rosa
9,904	Brooker, Joseph	Clay
13,740	Brownell, Charles A.; Corson, Joseph B.; and Banks, Isaac S., Jr.	Escambia
12,206	Burney, James	Clay
11,222	Bush, Warren S.	Columbia
14,912	Carr, Wm. W.	Escambia
20,713	Collins, Alexander S.	Marion
13,740	Corson, Joseph B.; Bangs, Isaac S., Jr.; and Brownell, Charles A.	Escambia
706	Curry, William; Filor, James, Estate of; and Pinckney, Wm.	Monroe
14,686	Davison, Yeoman	Santa Rosa
13,903	Dewey, Wm. G.; Elridge, John; and Bennett, Wm. R.	Monroe
12,010	Douglas, Alexander	Walton
15,718	Ells, Thomas S.	Duval
13,903	Elridge, John; Bennett, Wm. R.; and Dewey, Sm. G.	Monroe
3,795	Ferriera, F. P.	Duval
17,911	Fillingain, John	Escambia
706	Filor, James, Estate of; Pinckney, William; and Curry, Wm.	Monroe
4,550	Finlayson, Martha E.	Jackson
16,416	Flynn, John	Escambia
16,162	Forrister, Lewis C.	Clay
12,000	Franklin, Frank	Duval
15,046	Gaines, Wm. B.	Santa Rosa
2,619	Garrett, Robert	Walton
18,354	Germond, Richard M.	Nassau
21,306	Gianople, George	St. John
16,287	Gilbert, Washington, Estate of	Washington
11,087	Gillen, James	Duval
11,429	Green, James D.	Manatee
17,917	Henderson, Wm. D.	Escambia
8,675	Hendricks, Martha L.	Clay
10,216	Holden, Wm. H.	Orange
10,768	Hull, W. W.	Clay
219	Huot, Cleophas H.	Nassau
18,338	Hurlbert, Ann, Estate of	St. John

18,339	Hurlbert, James, Estate of	St. John
4,489	Jackson, Wiley	Escambia
8,861	Johnson, James	Hernando
18,340	Keogh, Eliza	St. John
11,090	Knowles, Bird K.	Clay
11,091	Knowles, L. Jackson	Clay
2,626	Lastinger, Annie	Hamilton
1,107	Lee, Jacob	St. John
9,548	Lee, James R.	Escambia
21,151	Martin, James	Volusia
3,796	Mattaire, Samuel	Duval
20,852	Matthews, Annie Paul	Escambia
8,148	Mattox, Bethel	Holmes
11,201	McCullom, Sanday	Volusia
8,147	McDonald, Daniel K., Estate of	Volusia
8,146	McDonald, Wm.	Volusia
11,210	McGovern, John	Clay
17,926	McVoy, Wm.	Escambia
19,124	Miller, John	Franklin
10,217	Mizell, David	Orange
13,781	Mooney, Patrick	Escambia
8,136	Parish, Owen T.	Holmes
12,007	Pearce, Wm.	Holmes
17,173	Pellicer, Andrew J.	St. John
17,174	Pellicer, John A.	St. John
14,735	Pepino, George	St. John
8,240	Petry, Christian	Franklin
17,931	Pfeiffer, George	Escambia
706	Pinckney, William; Curry, William; and Filor, James, Estate of	Monroe
12,009	Pitman, Anderson A.	Holmes
12,008	Pitman, George W.	Holmes
13,695	Platt, Joshua A.	Manatee
13,925	Potter, Wm. W.	Santa Rosa
307	Powell, J. S.	Duval
10,215	Powers, Alex C.	St. John
2,327	Powers, Charles	Escambia

10,127	Prescott, Moses	Clay
17,765	Rioles, Daniel C.	Hernando
11,831	Roberts, Wm. A. D.	Clay
18,149	Rogers, Jesse, Sr.	Santa Rosa
22,167	Rogers, John	Santa Rosa
16,161	Russ, Robert S.	Volusia
9,902	Russ, Samuel T.	Washington
16,153: 21,901:	Sammis, John S.	Duval
16,286	Sheffield, Henry	Washington
16,285	Sheffield, Nancy	Washington
3,030	Shemwell, Poindexter	Alachua
17,172	Simms, Henry W.	St. John
17,169	Simms, John	St. John
1,431	Sinclair, George	Franklin
16,178	Southwick, Emily	St. John
15,207	Springer, Stephen S., Estate of	Duval
5,031	Strong, Eliza J.	Escambia
11,089	Taylor, James	Clay
9,905	Taylor, Tilmon	Clay
4,551	Thomas, Basheba	Jackson
22,292	Townsend, Jesse	Duval
17,170	Von Balsam, Henry	St. John
3,794	Von Balsam, J.	St. John
17,171	Walker, Wm. A.	St. John
14,736	Walton, George W.	St. John
13,475	Waters, Susan	Escambia
17,940	Waters, Travis	Escambia
15,939	Watts, Robert H.	Escambia
1,697	Weaver, Wm. T.	Escambia
12,906	Whidder, Eleanor	Manatee
8,149	Wilcox, Mark	Holmes
11,088	Wilkinson, Joseph	Duval
13,478	Williams, Mary J.	Escambia
18,787	Williams, Wm.	Jackson
20,169	Yates, Wm. T.	Orange
15,573	Yearty, Wm.	Levy

GEORGIA

17,088	Abbott, Goodwin W., Estate of	Effingham
9,552	Abbott, Prudence	Cherokee
9,553	Abbott, Thomas D.	Cherokee
21,279	Adair, Jour L.	Coweta
16,636	Adams, Camelus C.	Chattooga
20,515	Adams, Curtis R.	Cherokee
6,185	Adams, Hiram S.	Clayton
13,385	Adams, J. B. N.	Whitfield
6,734	Adams, Julia A.	Jasper
3,928	Adams, Toby	Chatham
17,406	Adams, Wm. B.	Chatham
9,437	Adamson, Wm. L.	Carroll
18,655	Addington, Henry	Bartow
4,971	Addington, John	Bartow
2,097	Addington, Nancy E.	Cherokee
11,442	Aderhold, Frederic	Douglas
11,421	Aderhold, Frederick	Campbell
11,440	Aderhold, Wm.	Campbell
12,803	African Methodist Church	Cobb
5,946	Akeridge, Jno. T.	Fulton
2,806	Akin, Samuel	Gordon
7,273	Akins, Thomas J.	DeKalb
14,603	Alexander, Wm. S.	Carroll
12,308	Allen, Alfred	Floyd
7,561	Allen, Elizabeth O., Estate of	Clayton
3,282	Allen, Hannah	Clayton
7,766	Allen, Jane M.	Carroll
3,268	Allen, Matilda W. & Waggoner, Levi S.	Clayton
7,459	Allen, Robert	Chattooga
718	Allen, Young W.	Carroll
17,571	Allison, Wm. P.	Walker
5,462	Allmond, Matthew	Emanuel
11,376	Allred, Samuel J.	Pickens
5,121	Alston, Jos. E.	Monroe

20,635	Alvin, Titus	Liberty
14,747	Ambos, Henry	Chatham
17,746	Ambos, Lewis, Estate of	Chatham
7,458	Anders, Wm.	Chattooga
21,412	Anderson, Ben.	Liberty
8,268	Anderson, David B.	Fulton
5,109	Anderson, David M.	Baldwin
17,461	Anderson, Edward	Chatham
21,803	Anderson, Elizabeth A.	Bibb
1,051	Anderson, Francis M.	Whitfield
18,546: 21,414:	Anderson, James	Liberty
20,634	Anderson, July	Liberty
915	Anderson, Manda	Bartow
10,975	Anderson, Nancy A.	Fulton
16,022	Anderson, Richard	Catoosa
5,440	Anderson, Robert	Walker
13,596	Anderson, Samuel	Floyd
7,391	Anderson, Sarah J.	DeKalb
5,176	Anderson, Thomas E.	Dade
18,215	Anderson, Wm.	Chatham
16,347	Anderson, Wm.	Murray
5,461	Andrews, Eliza	Emanuel
6,051	Andrews, Ezra	Fulton
6,597	Andrews, Henry G.	Henry
5,117	Andrews, Sarah A.	Upson
18,276	Angier, Nedom L.	Fulton
15,111	Anthony, Alston V.	Floyd
9,157	Arendall, Susan	DeKalb
7,767	Armor, Frances	Carroll
12,260	Armrous, Mary M.	Chatham
4,059	Armstrong, James F.	Cherokee
1,008	Arnold, A. H.	Henry
17,177	Arnold, Francis M.	Walton
151	Arnold, Obadiah	Baldwin
1,007	Arnold, Susan	Henry
12,205	Arnold, Wm.	Walker

15,819	Arnett, Edmund G.	Heard
2,469	Ashworth, Linsey	Whitfield
16,478	Atkins, Bayless G.	Walker
6,860	Atkins, Charles B.	Walker
16,806	Atkins, Wm. J.	Walker
13,363	Atkinson, Henry	Chatham
4,870	Atkinson, Mary	Chattooga
18,006	Audouin, Alphonso, Estate of	Bibb
341	Ault, Wiley J.	Whitfield
6,323	Austell, Alfred	Fulton
13,601	Austin, Clarissa H.	Floyd
7,390	Austin, Jno. C.	DeKalb
18,639	Austin, Joseph B.	Paulding
20,636	Austin, Sandy	Liberty
6,161	Austin, Wm. H.	Paulding
6,527	Autrey, Elizabeth Y.	Clayton
13,619	Avary, Mary	Floyd
1,705	Awtery, Margaret	Haralson
21,456	Axon, Thomas	Liberty
21,472	Axon, Tony	Liberty
13,597	Aycock, Burwell P.	Floyd
7,170	Aycock, Jno. M.	Wilkinson
15,106	Aycock, Nancy	Floyd
7,274	Aycock, Reddick	Rockdale
18,543	Bacon, Edmund	Liberty
21,436	Bacon, Jno., Jr.	Liberty
21,434	Bacon, Jno., Sr.	Liberty
21,431	Bacon, Jos., Jr.	Liberty
21,447	Bacon, Jos., Sr.	Liberty
21,406	Bacon, Nancy	Liberty
2,406	Bacon, Nicholas H.	Fulton
21,464	Bacon, Pompey	Bryan
18,542	Bacon, Richard	Liberty
22,129	Bacon, Samson	Liberty
9,328	Bagg, Mary E.	Liberty
9,711	Baggs, David S.	Liberty
12,024	Baggs, Jno.	Troup
7,772	Bagnell, Willis	Carroll
4,942	Bagwell, Eliza Ann	Gwinnett
7,198	Bagwell, Littleberry	Floyd
15,755	Bailey, Calvin B.	Chattooga
8,356	Bailey, Curtis	Floyd
6,861	Bailey, Eli	Polk
2,809	Bailey, Ferdinand	Murray
2,805	Bailey, George	Walker
16,717	Bailey, Jno.	Walker
2,807	Bailey, Jno. C.	Murray
15,756	Bailey, Wm., Estate of	Walker
13,681	Bailey, Winford H.	Wilkinson
12,696	Baker, Alexander	Gwinnett
6,529	Baker, Arcada	Fulton
1,309	Baker, Clarrissa	Whitfield
20,717	Baker, Daniel N.	Rockdale
4,398	Baker, Henry H.	Floyd
12,570	Baker, Joel C.	Floyd
13,580	Baker, Jno.	Floyd
18,609	Baker, Jno.	Paulding
18,272	Baker, Jno. W.	Fulton
21,405	Baker, Louisa	Liberty
21,415	Baker, Lydia	Liberty
5,947	Baker, Oliver	Fulton
120	Baker, Pleasant	Bartow
21,446	Baker, Pulaski	Liberty
6,202	Baker, Riley S.	Campbell
7,768	Baker, Robert F.	Campbell
21,451	Baker, Silvy	Liberty
403	Baker, W. W.	Whitfield
3,000	Baker, Wm. A.	Bartow
6,528	Baker, Wm. C.	Campbell
7,275	Baker, Zadock C.	DeKalb
12,538	Baldwin, Sarah S.	Cobb
8,622	Baldwin, Wm. L.	Fulton
6,443	Ball, James	Milton
19,633	Ball, Peter	Fulton
921	Ballew, Thomas	Murray
4,169	Banks, Andrew J.	Baldwin
9,531	Banks, Henry	Fulton
1,060	Bankston, Wm. H.	Monroe
14,910	Barber, Geo. W.	Butts
5,691	Barber, W. C.	Polk

3,556	Barbour, Thomas	Chattooga
6,575	Bard, Wm. D.	Whitfield
7,770	Barge, Aaron	Haralson
14,240	Barge, Alison W.	Campbell
7,771	Barge, Jacob	Campbell
7,769	Barge, Margaret, Estate of	Campbell
8,626	Barker, Obadiah	Floyd
20,793	Barker, Rufus	Floyd
1,610	Barker, Thomas G.	Chattooga
20,092	Barnard, Alfred	Chatham
13,402	Barnes, Henry	Butts
13,400	Barnes, Jno.	Butts
920	Barnett, James R.	Gordon
9,873	Barnett, Larkin, Estate of	Floyd
16,471	Barnett, Wm. J.	Floyd
7,680	Barret, Martha A.	DeKalb
18,452	Barrett, Thomas J. & Goette, Bridgett	Chatham
12,518: 13,399:	Barron, Cary A.	Butts
12,533	Barrow, Augustine C.	Upson
10,179	Barton, Wells	Glascock
3,270	Barton, Wm. M.	Clayton
3,052	Barwick, Jno.	Washington
2,098	Bass, Redding	Cherokee
2,623	Baswell, Harrison	Cobb
3,429	Bates, Isaac	Gordon
5,655	Bates, Mathias	Cherokee
6,576	Batey, Robert	Whitfield
6,579	Batey, Robert and Hill, Jno.	Whitfield
4,170	Batson, Tabitha	Baldwin
4,579	Battle, Wm. C.	Monroe
7,394	Baugh, Elizabeth	Gwinnett
20,838	Baxter, Nathaniel	Paulding
8,279	Bayless, Jno. P.	Walker
925	Beal, Richard	Gordon
18,273	Bealey, W. H.	Campbell
5,566	Bean, Mary	Fulton
15,115	Beard, Lucinda	Floyd
18,648	Bearden, Wm. C.	Whitfield
3,471	Beasley, James	Fulton
7,299	Beatenbaugh, Adam	Campbell
3,559	Beatty, Robert	Chattooga
8,705	Beaver, Jefferson J.	Towns
10,988	Beavers, Margaret	Fulton
5,989	Beckworth, Anna	Glascock
11,909	Bedingfield, Eli P.	Jefferson
11,913	Bedingfield, John	Jefferson
15,314	Beedles, Henry and Polly	Fulton
15,314	Beedles, Polly and Henry	Fulton
1,027	Belcher, Joseph N.	Clayton
13,462	Belcher, Obediah R.	Jasper
13,100	Bell, Elizabeth A.	Paulding
6,530	Bell, Ellender	Clayton
17,444	Bell, Mary A.	Emanuel
7,985	Bell, Matthew R.	Baldwin
740	Bell, Silas	Bartow
10,791	Bell, Wm. L.	Carroll
5,398	Belote, John L.	Chattooga
2,305	Belt, Elizabeth T.	Bullock
16,020	Bence, Fannie	Catoosa
331	Bender, Lewis	Whitfield
3,176	Bennett, Freeman	Cherokee
6,446	Bennett, Henry K.	Dade
10,500	Bennett, James R.	Henry
7,656	Bennett, Julia L. and Kent, E. H. & A.	Chatham
21,473	Bennett, Scipio	Liberty
1,241	Bentley, Milton M.	Rockdale
3,925	Bently, Catharine	Chatham
3,558	Berrein, Albert	Floyd
3,557	Barrett, Nancy	Milton
4,327	Berry, Jno.	Henry
1,035	Berry, Joshua	Clayton
20,588	Berry, M. R.	Fulton
4,945	Berry, Miles D.	Pickens
6,068	Berry, Tamer	Murray
2,161	Berry, Wm.	Chattooga
13,589	Berryhill, Jno.	Floyd
19,345	Best, Hezekiah	Bartow

20,820	Best, Pheraby	Scriven
13,160	Betts, Elizabeth	Gwinnett
1,039	Betts, Wm. O.	Clayton
21,745	Biddenback, Joshua	Effingham
21,774	Biddenback, Saml.	Effingham
795	Biee, David	Milton
7,565	Biffle, Leander	DeKalb
4,091	Biggers, Robert	Paulding
3,561	Binion, Abram D.	DeKalb
2,239	Binion, Ann B.	Cobb
7,661	Binion, Isaac S.	Gordon
2,237	Binion, Job, Estate of	Milton
2,238	Bird, Charles C.	Dawson
13,876	Bird, Mary H.	Liberty
16,021	Bird, Philip H.	Walker
801	Bird, Thomas, Sr.	Gordon
931	Bishop, Alexander	Gordon
15,107	Bishop, Franklin	Floyd
9,506	Bishop, Joseph, Estate of	Campbell
7,395	Bishop, Joshua I.	DeKalb
16,482	Black, Allen	Catoosa
11,910	Black, Joshua L.	Jefferson
18,222	Black, Sarah Ann	Chatham
15,113	Black, Wm. G.	Floyd
12,320	Blackman, Augustus Y.	Polk
4,315	Blackman, Jno.	Henry
4,089	Blackstock, Jas. C.	Forsyth
10,884	Blackwelder, Wilson	Floyd
17,826	Blackwell, Samuel B.	Chatham
4,088	Blackwood, Robert N.	Forsyth
16,267	Blair, Joseph W.	Whitfield
8,402	Blair, Samuel M.	Chatham
1,497	Blakeman, Levi R.	Floyd
4,011	Blalock, Reuben W.	Upson
6,166	Blankenship, Thomas B.	Paulding
7,460	Blanks, Allen	Chattooga
20,513	Blanton, Daniel	Cherokee
10,221	Blatz, Ann, *et al*	Chatham
16,480	Blaylock, D. C.	Catoosa
20,984	Blitch, Laura M.	Bullock
18,322	Blitch, Moore	Chatham
18,219	Blitch, Thomas, Estate of	Effingham
7,396	Bloodworth, Margaret	Wilkinson
327	Blount, Anesworth E., Estate of	Whitfield
6,531	Boartfield, Saml.	Fulton
16,737	Boatwright, J. S.	Wilkinson
15,993	Boatwright, James M.	Whitfield
5,465	Boatwright, Jno.	Emanuel
5,464	Boatwright, Reuben, Sr.	Emanuel
8,898	Boggs, Zenus L.	Liberty
18,780	Bogle, Wm. J.	Pickens
15,741	Bohannon, Elizabeth	Whitfield
3,751	Boisfillet, Celia	Chatham
20,333	Bolding, B. M.	Gordon
790	Bolton, Matthew M.	Gwinnett
2,470	Bolton, Peter	Catoosa
3,287	Bonner, Bennett W.	Clayton
8,830	Boone, Jno. M.	Wilkinson
6,862	Bostick, James B.	Walker
3,269	Boutwright, Lucinda	Clayton
6,693	Bouchillon, Lemuel D.	Floyd
12,256	Bourquin, Benedict	Chatham
15,641	Bowen, Samuel	Chatham
12,248	Bowers, James W.	Union
702	Bowker, Charles L.	Newton
1,614	Bowles, Wm. P.	Chattooga
4,097	Boyce, Meshack	DeKalb
4,323	Boyd, Mary	DeKalb
938	Boyle, Christopher C.	Chattooga
6,674	Boyles, Andrew J.	Walker
1,088	Bracewell, James R.	Gwinnett
16,804	Bradley, Austin H.	Walker
15,965	Bradley, Felix	Whitfield
15,966	Bradley, Jno.	Whitfield
4,943	Bradly, Ann	Pickens
13,598	Bradshaw, Wm.	Floyd
5,017	Bradwell, Asa	DeKalb
15,735	Bramblett, Elisha M.	Whitfield
7,681	Bramlette, Newton	Gwinnett

15,070	Brand, Eliza	Cobb
7,682	Brand, Elizabeth	Gwinnett
7,392	Brand, Isaiah C.	Walton
13,833	Brand, J. S.	Walker
14,327	Brandbacker, Frederick, Estate	Chatham
6,736	Brandon, Elizabeth	Jasper
8,892	Brandon, James L.	Upson
7,322	Brannen, James M.	Bryan
17,349	Brannen, Nancy E.	Liberty
7,018	Brannen, Wm. A.	Bullock
2,162	Branner, Benj.	Chattooga
2,471	Brantley, Matthew A., Mrs.	Whitfield
4,165	Brasher, Henry W.	Carroll
5,144	Bray, Cynthia, Estate of	Clayton
933	Bray, Jno. H.	Gordon
13,386	Bray, Wm. A.	Gordon
5,932	Brewer, Daniel, Sr.	Wilkinson
7,683	Brewer, Edmund	DeKalb
804	Bridewell, Jno.	Fulton
9,299	Bridges, Simeon	Carroll
7,536	Brightwell, Martha	Cobb
17,822	Brigman, Linsey	Walker
5,463	Brinson, Jesse A.	Emanuel
1,611	Brison, Macon H.	Chattooga
6,451	Broadwell, Mary J.	Milton
4,944	Broadwell, Needham	Milton
971	Broadwell, Wm.	Cherokee
2,808	Brock, James	Walker
4,588	Brock, Lucinda	Walker
975	Brock, Mary	Cherokee
18,218	Brogden, Mary	Effingham
2,894	Brooks, J. E.	Bartow
16,105	Brooks, Levi W.	Walker
7,684	Brooks, Lloyd	Gwinnett
7,684	Brooks, Lloyd	Walton
6,600	Brooks, Jno.	Spalding
7,745	Brooks, Royal	Walker
11,391	Broom, Leroy	Carroll
10,275	Brown, Arnold O.	Rockdale
18,776	Brown, Arnold O. & Owen, George A.	Paulding
22,183	Brown, Charles	Chatham
20,961	Brown, Coffee	Chatham
7,773	Brown, Debby M.	Cobb
20,637	Brown, Doddy	Liberty
20,638	Brown, Francis	Liberty
5,467	Brown, Henry S.	Emanuel
974	Brown, Isaac	Cherokee
9,203	Brown, James F.	Bullock
20,086	Brown, Jerry	Chatham
8,280	Brown, Jno.	Walker
3,279	Brown, Jno. H.	Clayton
3,564	Brown, Lovie P.	Milton
34: 8,270:	Brown, Martin	Clayton
5,466	Brown, Saml.	Emanuel
18,225	Brown, Sid	Chatham
18,090	Brown, Stephen	Chatham
7,171	Brown, Susan	Cobb
3,016	Brown, Wm. F.	Fulton
18,873	Browne, Danton	Chattooga
13,361	Brownfield, Rachel	Chatham
7,397	Browning, Ann H.	DeKalb
1,811	Brownlow, Geo. W.	Gordon
13,620	Brownlow, James	Floyd
4,343	Bryan, George H.	Muscogee
7,393	Bryan, Jesse	Gwinnett
14,018	Bryan, Michael	Chatham
18,547	Bryant, Daniel	Liberty
5,177	Bryant, Hugh, Estate of	Pickens
16,076	Bryant, James S.	Chattooga
21,242	Bryant, Julia	Floyd
12,559	Bryant, Muse T.	Floyd
712	Bryons, Wm. H.	Newton
15,604	Bryson, Thomas M.	Gwinnett
16,015	Buchanan, Moses	Catoosa
1,245	Buck, Seaborn W.	Washington
16,345	Buffington, J. B.	Cobb
7,172	Bullard, Jno.	Cobb

7,173	Bullard, Mary	Cobb
15,757	Bullard, Wm.	Chattooga
2,592	Burch, Able	Gordon
2,985	Burch, James H.	Gordon
4,060: 16,870: 17,846:	Burdett, Gideon T.	Chatham
15,761	Burge, Mary H.	Floyd
11,403	Burge, Thomas, Estate of	Newton
21,705	Burgstiner, Jno. R.	Effingham
4,316	Burks, Elizabeth	Henry
507	Burnett, Geo. P.	Floyd
13,591	Burney, Sarah A.	Floyd
13,387	Burns, Cornelius	Gordon
17,141	Burns, George	Effingham
6,154	Burson, Joseph H.	Campbell
8,362	Burtz, L. W.	Fulton
6,532	Busbee, John M.	Campbell
9,847	Bush, Brooks	Fulton
12,736	Bush, Cynthia A.	Newton
4,014	Bush, Jackson	Monroe
5,145	Bush, Jane E.	Clayton
17,563	Butler, Binah and Stikes, Moses	Chatham
21,462	Butler, Charlotte	Liberty
21,470	Butler, Elcy	Liberty
3,565	Butler, Daniel	Milton
3,566	Butler, Jno.	Milton
16,766	Butler, Josiah E.	Liberty
18,089	Butler, Leah Bowen	Chatham
8,223	Butler, Richard	Chatham
6,053	Butler, Thomas	Chatham
7,997	Byers, Joseph	Cherokee
21,363	Byrne, Thomas	Clayton
1,791	Cagle, Rebecca	Cherokee
21,264	Cagle, Wm.	Fulton
6,194	Cain, Jno.	Paulding
10,981	Calahan, Wm. A.	Fulton
4,749	Calder, Elizabeth	Chatham
4,748	Calder, Susan	Chatham
5,990	Calhoun, Louisa	Glascock
1,022	Callaway, Francis A.	Henry
3,568	Camp, Arthur T., Estate of	Milton
18,631	Camp, Bisha J.	Paulding
8,670	Camp, Bob	Polk
18,642	Camp, Burrell M.	Paulding
8,671	Camp, Elias A.	Polk
580	Camp, Harry, Jr., Richard, Sarah A. and Sarah J.	Newton
15,325	Camp, Hosea M.	Floyd
18,643	Camp, Ira	Paulding
580	Camp, Richard, Sarah A., Sarah J., and Harry, Jr.	Newton
11,512	Camp, Robert A.	Milton
580	Camp, Sarah A., Sarah J., Harry, Jr., and Richard	Newton
7,685	Campbell, George A.	Gwinnett
19,228	Campbell, James	Walker
3,331	Campbell, Joseph	Gordon
2,598	Campbell, Joseph P.	Gordon
8,631	Campbell, Lucy F.	DeKalb
6,197	Campbell, Mary E.	Fulton
3,736	Campbell, Nancy	Chatham
21,475	Campbell, Patsy	Liberty
7,400	Campbell, Shelton H.	DeKalb
6,865	Campbell, Thomas P.	Polk
7,376	Campbell, Wm. L.	Clayton
5,875	Campmire, Geo. W.	Pickens
18,637	Cane, Michael, Estate of	Paulding
5,468	Cannedy, Wm. E.	Emanuel
18,652	Cannon, Jno. F., Estate of	Gordon
4,590	Cannon, John M.	Walker
180	Cantrel, Aaron	Whitfield
20,519	Cantrell, Thos. A.	Pickens
15,807: 330:	Carden, James A.	Whitfield
18,629	Carlton, Henry S.	Paulding
10,976	Carlton, J. K. P.	Fulton
3,404	Carlton, Sicily M.	Campbell
10,694	Carmichael, Jno. T.	Cobb
36: 8,211:	Carnes, Jno. O.	Clayton
14,915	Carnes, Shem	Bartow
7,775	Carney, Elizabeth	Carroll
17,561	Carney, Mary Griffin	Chatham
2,240	Carpenter, Jno.	Milton
15,678	Carpenter, Mary W.	Whitfield
6,691	Carr, Jesse G.	Floyd
16,077	Carrell, Elias	Chattooga
1,615	Carrell, Peter T.	Chattooga
6,608	Carrier, Susan	Chatham
13,444	Carroll, Edmond E.	Fayette
1,240	Carroll, Jesse W.	Rockdale
11,406	Carroll, John W.	Carroll
14,423	Carson, Joseph	Walker
3,386	Carter, Austin D.	Bartow
18,946	Carter, Ezekiel M.	Paulding
2,257	Carter, John A.	Chatham
20,089	Carter, Stephen	Liberty
21,895	Carter, Pinson M.	Paulding
20,088	Carter, Pulaski	Chatham
20,088	Carter, Pulaski	Liberty
18,600	Carter, Shadrack	Fulton
20,089	Carter, Stephen	Chatham
20,506	Carter, Susan W.	Brooks
10,968	Cartwright, Mary A., Estate of	Carroll
10,967	Cartwright, Wilson, Estate of	Carroll
6,164	Casey, Ausbun J.	Campbell
387	Casey, Ellison	Cherokee
9,488	Casey, Hiram	Fulton
7,277	Casey, Isaac E.	Whitfield
9,404	Casey, Jno. A.	Fulton
7,399	Cash, Geo. W.	DeKalb
8,618	Cash, Nancy	Fulton
7,398	Cash, Rufus	DeKalb
21,481	Cassels, Cephus	Liberty
21,438	Cassels, Wm.	Liberty
18,046	Cassin, Cornelius P.	Fulton
16,791	Castleberry, Odian	Walker
2,031	Cates, Ira W.	DeKalb
16,149	Catlett, Jno. M.	Walker
7,174	Causey, Eliza A.	Cobb
6,227	Causey, Israel	Cobb
3,567	Chaffin, Jno.	Milton
5,110	Chaffinch, Hiram	Baldwin
20,019	Chambers, Caroline L.	Chatham
2,427	Chambers, Ira	Washington
3,400	Chambers, Josiah	Carroll
3,314	Chandler, Mary	Chattooga
7,686	Chandler, Sarah A.	Rockdale
4,494	Chapman, Charles W.	Muscogee
1,234	Chapman, James	Bartow
1,936	Chapman, John	Chatham
468	Chappel, Thos.	Gordon
12,038	Chasteen, Wm.	Carroll
7,776	Cheeves, Allison	Carroll
12,529	Cheney, Andrew J.	Cobb
22,013	Cheney, Jno. L.	Muscogee
12,211	Chesser, Rebecca	Floyd
7,566	Chewning, Ambrose	DeKalb
3,761	Chewning, Lorenzo W.	DeKalb
12,315	Childers, James	Floyd
8,601	Childress, David	Walker
1,796	Chitwood, James	Bartow
121	Chitwood, Richard	Bartow
12,450	Christian, Cephas A.	Rockdale
4,251	Christian, Charles W.	Hart Co.
15,758	Christopher, David M.	Chattooga
12,803	Church, African Methodist	Cobb
15,031	Church, Pleasant Grove	Catoosa
22,021	Clark, Benk.	Hall
4,747	Clark, George S.	Chatham
4,346	Clark, Joe	Muscogee
4,439	Clark, Larkin	Hart
17,348	Clark, Susan	Liberty
18,647	Clark, Wm. H., Estate of	DeKalb
13,834	Clarkson, James H.	Walker
5,725	Clarody, Eliot	Gordon
143	Clay, David	Bibb

7,276	Clay, Green B.	DeKalb	2,242	Copeland, A. J.	Milton
6,212	Clay, Robert K.	Cobb	2,243	Copeland, Elijah	Milton
2,644	Clay, Russell W.	Paulding	5,992	Coplin, John M.	Glascock
6,170	Clay, Wm. J.	Cobb	3,996	Corbin, Laura, Estate of	Bartow
7,774	Clayton, Richard G.	Fulton	16,094	Cordell, Jeremiah	Walker
9,720	Cleaveland, Early	Monroe	2,847	Costen, Nancy	Bartow
944	Cleckler, Jacob	Catoosa	5,149	Couch, Gilla A.	Clayton
15,099	Cleghorn, Rebecca S.	Chatham	6,732	Couch, Nathan H.	Jasper
5,118	Clements, Thomas C.	Monroe	20,991	Couche, Thomas R.	Bartow
16,853	Clemmons, Henry A.	Gordon	3,673	Coughlin, Jno.	Fulton
1,648	Clemmons, Mary Jane	Chattooga	3,679	Coughlin, Selana	Fulton
12,347	Cleveland, Benj. F.	Polk	16,796	Coulter, Charles, Estate of	Walker
14,548	Clifton, Ann	Chatham	6,225	Coursey, Charles P.	Fulton
16,098	Clifton, George W.	Chatham	10,982	Coursey, Danl.	Fulton
16,271	Clifton, Levin, Estate of	Scriven	7,779	Coursey, Harrison	Douglas
15,118	Climer, Bennett	Gordon	10,698	Coursey, Loyd	Fulton
15,829	Cline, Danl. L.	Whitfield	5,284	Courter, Tabitha	Chatham
2,099	Cline, Wm. M.	Cherokee	16,476	Covington, Elias	Gordon
9,540	Cloud, Jason	Walker	12,319	Cowan, Elizabeth	Floyd
6,687	Clowdis, S. C., Mrs.	Chattooga	5,763	Cowan, James J.	DeKalb
236	Cobb, James N. B.	Whitfield	12,304	Cowan, Reuben A.	Floyd
16,351	Coburn, Francis M.	Chattooga	10,977	Cox, Car	Fulton
2,524	Cochran, Elisha	Cobb	18,645	Cox, Charnick L.	Murray
15,187	Cochran, Thomas M., Estate of	Chattooga	2,599	Cox, Jacob	Gordon
			16,854	Cox, Jacob R.	Gordon
21,147	Cockine, Wm.	Cobb	3,570	Cox, Jno.	Floyd
10,532	Cockrell, Mary Ann	Carroll	3,257	Cox, Jno.	Whitfield
3,349	Coffee, Elijah	Whitfield	2,966	Cox, Robert D.	Whitfield
15,605	Cohen, Jacob	Chatham	3,348	Cox, Samuel W.	Whitfield
14,600	Cohen, Raphael	Chatham	3,654	Cox, Young A.	Washington
6,210	Cole, Caswell M.	Campbell	14,819	Craft, Carl, Estate of	Chatham
15,021	Cole, Elizabeth	Floyd	8,706	Crane, Andrew J.	Towns
13,312	Cole, Henry G.	Cobb	17,686	Crane, Eliza	Chatham
7,145	Cole, Irbane C.	Gwinnett	907	Cranston, Uriah	Chatham
13,394	Cole, Jno. B.	Butts	14,261	Craven, Thomas W.	Floyd
16,003	Cole, Wm.	Whitfield	21,453	Crawford, Jno.	Liberty
20,639	Coleman, Cyrus and Isaac	Liberty	17,564: 4,061:	Crawford, John S. E. J.	Chatham
3,335	Coleman, David L.	Henry			
5,469	Coleman, Elias	Emanuel	13,390	Crawford, R. L., Estate of	Butts
20,639	Coleman, Isaac and Cyrus	Liberty	7,461	Crawford, Thaddeus C.	Chattooga
3,940	Coleman, John	Chatham	18,796	Creekmore, Edward	Whitfield
909	Collier, Robert M.	Upson	5,146	Creel, Geo.	Clayton
4,019	Collier, Wm. M.	Monroe	5,148	Creel, Wm.	Clayton
2,472	Collins, Moses G.	Whitfield	1,432	Crisler, Abel	Milton
14,941	Collins, Sarah A.	Butts	13,810	Croft, James	Chattooga
18,152	Collins, Thomas R.	Cherokee	4,176	Croom, Francis H.	Baldwin
1,233	Collins, Wiley	Bartow	4,175	Croom, Jesse	Baldwin
1,671	Collins, Wm.	Bartow	12,210	Crossley, Noah S.	Floyd
15,020	Colquitt, Hudson	Walker	2,473	Crow, James	Whitfield
3,334	Colston, Elizabeth A.	Floyd	18,635	Crow, Levi	Paulding
6,673	Comer, Nancy C.	Floyd	14,917	Crow, Sarah	Bartow
14,916	Conaway, Aaron	Bartow	7,401	Crumbley, Jesse	Wilkinson
6,694	Cone, Gilbert	Floyd	15,125	Crumley, Louisa M.	Chattooga
7,463	Coney, Andrew	Chattooga	15,122	Crumly, Salena	Chattooga
7,462	Coney, Henry L.	Chattooga	655	Crussell, Thomas G. W.	Fulton
12,334	Coney, Wm. Y., Estate of	Floyd	6,065	Cudd, Elizabeth	Walker
6,533	Conine, Nancy O.	Clayton	21,410	Cumming, Prince	Liberty
7,933	Conine, Wm. Y.	Clayton	21,439	Cumming, Richard	Liberty
10,499	Connelly, Marble F.	Meriweather	18,091	Cummings, Diana	Chatham
16,812	Conner, Isaac, Estate of	Scriven	17,681	Cunningham, H. T.	Talbot
12,146	Connolly, Wm. L.	Walker	15,033	Cupp, Wm.	Catoosa
8,272	Coogler, Jesse	Clayton	1,108	Curtis, James M.	Gordon
3,059	Cook, Benjamin	Baldwin	21,485	Cusbert, James	Liberty
6,188	Cook, Burton W.	Clayton	16,978	Custard, James	Chatham
6,195	Cook, Charles G.	Clayton	13,362	Cuthbert, Amy	Chatham
17,298	Cook, Edmund S.	Bartow	18,096	Cuthbert, John	Chatham
473	Cook, George	Cherokee	20,640	Cuthbert, Marshall	Liberty
4,325	Cook, Geo. Henry	Henry	1,734	Cutter, Marsh N.	Floyd
16,869	Cook, Henry K.	Chatham	13,607	Dabbs, Malita J.	Floyd
7,300	Cook, Isaac	Campbell	15,213	Dallas, Harriet	Chatham
6,156	Cook, Jesse	Campbell	14,696	Daly, Jno.	Chatham
7,301	Cook, John W.	Campbell	20,777	Dancer, Madison	Muscogee
2,100	Cook, Nathaniel J.	Cherokee	1,831	Dangaix, Joseph	Glynn
7,777	Cook, Rachel D. M.	Campbell	11,388	Daniel, Henry	Fulton
7,612	Cooley, Mark	Clayton	6,214	Daniel, Richard	Clayton
725	Coolidge, Wm.	Chatham	5,470	Daniell, Damilton G.	Emanuel
7,778	Cooper, Benj.	Douglas	2,764	Daniels, Jno. S.	Chatham
12,310	Cooper, James S.	Floyd	21,450	Daniels, Steven	Liberty
7,279	Cooper, Jno. N.	Cobb	9,557	Darnel, Thos. A.	Cherokee
12,261	Cooper, Wm.	Liberty	20,956	Dasher, Jno.	Effingham

3,206	Davidson, Jno. P.	Floyd
8,281	Davis, Adam A.	Walker
2,058	Davis, Amanda	Washington
15,124	Davis, Archibald	Floyd
15,919	Davis, Clara R.	Chatham
15,762	Davis, E., Major	Floyd
6,191	Davis, Eliza A.	Cobb
1,217	Davis, Gary	Cobb
6,489	Davis, James L.	Haralson
4,491	Davis, Jno. L.	Fayette
828	Davis, Larkin	Bartow
3,391	Davis, Larkin H.	Fulton
15,76	Davis, Major E.	Floyd
3,416	Davis, Mary Ann	Fulton
17,576	Davis, Monroe	Catoosa
18,583	Davis, Reuben	Polk
11,171	Davis, Susan	Lumpkin
1,735	Davis, Thos. J.	Floyd
13,093	Davison, Samuel T.	Chattooga
6,754	Daws, Joel	Jasper
20,023	Dawson, Margaret	Chatham
4,408	Day, Frank	Fulton
10,697	Dean, Lemuel	Fulton
10,696	Dean, Thomas W.	Fulton
12,610	Deans, James A.	Wilkinson
1,616	Dees, Mary	Chattooga
11,914	Deese, James Ira	Wilkinson
16,217	Defoor, James N.	Fulton
2,590	Defoor, Sidney	Gordon
6,659	Deihl, Kate	Fulton
12,312	De Journette, Jno.	Floyd
17,840	Delannoy, Sarah O.	Chatham
21,443	De Legal, Hamlet	Liberty
21,413	De Legal, LaFayette	Liberty
15,832	De Lettre, Maximillian	Chatham
3,939	Delions, David	Chatham
2,241	De Long, Wm.	Milton
6,324	Delpey, Amans	Fulton
16,081	De Lyons, Sandy	Chatham
6,158	Demoney, Samuel	Campbell
7,176	Demong, Geo.	Douglas
7,210	Dempsey, B. S.	Floyd
12,336	Dempsey, Duke	Floyd
11,112	Denison, James	Chatham
3,488	Dennis, Wm.	Henry
16,242	Denslow, Amos	Chatham
348	Denton, Bartholomew	Whitfield
5,220	Derden, A. J.	Fulton
9,856	Deasusure, July	Baldwin
16,079	Desvergess, Ella C.	Chatham
8,275	Devaughn, Eliza B.	Clayton
8,274	Devaughn, M. B.	Clayton
13,463	Dicken, Marion M.	Butts
4,552: 15,927:	Dickenson, Naomi V.	Upson
734	Dickerson, Anna	Chatham
21,924	Dickert, Wm. S.	Catoosa
8,145	Dickey, Jno.	Henry
7,567	Dickinson, Michael	DeKalb
5,994	Dickman, Clarkey, Mrs.	Glascock
16,539	Dickson, Eli H.	Chattooga
6,435	Dickson, Henry J.	Bibb
5,995	Dickson, Hickman	Glascock
16,350	Dickson, Thomas	Chattooga
5,996	Dickson, Thomas	Glascock
16,532	Dickson, Wm.	Wilkinson
5,993	Dickson, Wm. B.	Glascock
144	Dickson, Wm. N.	Bibb
16,801	Dillard, Robert	Gordon
5,235: 7,451:	Dillion, David R.	Chatham
1,828	Dillion, Robert	Chatham
1,243	Dimock, Wm.	Rockdale
22,014	Dimon, Joseph K.	Muscogee
11,383	Dimpsey, Lazarus	Cobb
20,821	Dixon, James C.	Scriven
3,297	Dixon, Warren N.	Clayton
8,000	Dobbs, Clarissa	Cherokee
2,367	Dobbs, Jno.	Milton
4,107	Dobbs, Joseph D.	Forsyth

4,106	Dobbs, Martin W.	Forsyth
6,585	Dobson, Starritt N.	Whitfield
5,129	Dodd, Jno. J.	Gordon
1,687	Dodds, James M.	Milton
9,675	Dodson, Constantine M.	Campbell
14,318	Dodson, Elijah	Campbell
7,780	Dodson, Hamilton C.	Campbell
7,464	Dodson, Samuel, Estate of	Chattooga
6,172	Dodson, Stephen	Clayton
6,201	Dodson, Wm.	Clayton
10,901	Dollar, Ambrose	Floyd
10,900	Dollar, Lucinda	Floyd
7,782	Donahoo, C. M.	Fulton
2,999	Donald, John H.	Barton
2,035	Donaldson, Abner B.	Fulton
7,403	Donaldson, Reuben	Gwinnett
19,904	Donovan, Wm.	Jefferson
10,689	Donsey, Macks	Fulton
14,818	Dooley, Timothy	Chatham
3,574	Dorris, James	Milton
2,703	Dorsey, Stephen G.	Clayton
21,953	Doughtry, Augustus	Scriven
16,147	Douglas, Edward	Chatham
16,099	Douglas, Franklin	Chatham
16,080	Douglas, Henry	Chatham
1,439	Douthit, N. C. W.	Bartow
20,516	Dowdy, Benjamin	Cherokee
16,205	Dowman, Charles	Fulton
17,261	Downs, Alexander	Floyd
17,845	Drake, Ann	Emanuel
1,672	Drake, Emilie	Bartow
6,867	Drummond, Henry	Polk
8,672	Drummond, Sarah	Polk
20,685	Dryer, Jacob	Liberty
369	Duckett, J. Thomas	Bartow
18,610	Duddley, Joab	Paulding
3,949	Dudley, Fanny	Chatham
1,029	Duffey, David L.	Clayton
4,249	Duffy, Jno.	Chattooga
13,837	Duggan, Emildred	Chattooga
16,754	Dugger, Chesley	Chatham
17,347	Duke, Albert M.	Liberty
8,001	Duke, Emery	Cherokee
15,114	Duke, Sally S.	Walker
7,781	Dunahoo, Elizabeth	Fulton
10,990	Dunaway, Adaline	Fulton
7,688	Dunbar, Joseph	DeKalb
17,637	Duncan, John	Gwinnett
7,402	Duncan, Peyton	Wilkinson
8,360	Dunlop, Tebitha	Campbell
16,151	Dunn, Jno. C.	Walker
12,212	Dunn, Larkin	Floyd
21,315	Dunn, Mary	Chatham
12,302	Dunnahoo, Jno. W.	Floyd
7,330	Durden, Matthew	Baldwin
1,268	Durham, Lavina	Gordon
18,632	Durham, Young M. A. H.	Paulding
9,489	Dye, Sarah	Fulton
11,392	Dyer, Joel H.	Bartow
18,828	Dyer, Micajah, Estate of	Catoosa
2,984	Dyer, Narcis, Mrs.	Gordon
6,678	Dykes, Geo. J.	Floyd
9,671	Eady, Rebecca	Chatham
13,838	Earp, Matthew	Chattooga
17,057	Earp, Matthew	Floyd
346	Easeby, G. M.	Whitfield
14,319	Easom, James	Campbell
18,323	East, Henry	Chatham
10,218	Ebbs, Wm.	Chatham
5,020	Echols, Mayson P.	DeKalb
17,542	Echols, Phillip W. J.	DeKalb
1,440	Eddleman, Elijah	Bartow
6,664	Eddleman, Francis M.	Fulton
17,153	Edge, Jane	Walker
11,439	Edge, John M.	Campbell
11,401	Edge, Joseph	Carroll
13,442	Edge, Newton N.	Butts
6,050	Edwards, Geo.	Fulton
22,131	Edwards, Mahetable	Effingahm
18,161	Edwards, Wm. A.	Cherokee

7,404	Elam, James E.	De Kalb
7,689	Elam, John F.	De Kalb
1,105	Elden, Sarah	Chatham
16,755	Elkins, Maria P.	Effingham
17,823	Ellenburgh, Hezekiah	Walker
3,285	Elliot, Augustus C.	Clayton
8,888	Elliot, Lydia	Pike
21,448	Elliot, Saml.	Liberty
7,302	Elliot, Swannah	Fulton
21,441	Elliot, Toney	Liberty
8,886	Elliot, Zach H.	Pike
3,275	Ellis, Francis M.	Henry
475	Ellison, Elijah G.	Cherokee
1,226	Ellison, Hannah	Cherokee
340	Ellison, Mary J.	Whitfield
1,619	Ellison, Thompson	Chattooga
16,663	Elrod, Thomas	Whitfield
18,624	Elsberry, James P.	Paulding
10,972	Embry, Christopher C.	Paulding
20,735	England, Perry M.	Whitfield
11,203	Enwright, Catharine M.	Fulton
21,080	Epping, Carl	McIntosh
21,081	Epping, Isaure	McIntosh
10,219	Eppstein, Jno. B.	Chatham
344	Eslinger, James S.	Whitfield
3,286	Estes, Allen T.	Clayton
7,783	Estes, Joel	Clayton
833	Ethridge, James	Newton
10,974	Evans, Emeline	Fulton
6,209	Evans, James J.	Fulton
6,868	Evans, John	Pickens
10,693	Evans, Jno. W.	Fulton
16,531	Evans, Julius W.	Wilkinson
20,511	Evans, Larkin M.	Cherokee
7,147	Evans, Reuben D.	De Kalb
1,433	Evans, Wilson	Forsyth
19,672	Evatt, James H.	Walker
7,265	Everett, T. P.	Floyd
9,490	Fain, John J.	Fulton
2,869	Faith, John	Whitfield
5,739	Fambro, Wm. L.	Monroe
4,577	Farley, Matthew T.	Monroe
3,278	Farmer, Lindley M.	Clayton
15,711	Farrar, Wm. B.	Whitfield
20,642	Farris, Joseph	Chatham
4,326	Faulkner, Wm. W.	Henry
9,719	Fears, Elizabeth E.	Morgan
9,718	Fears, Jesse W.	Bibb
5,448	Ferguson, Wm. H., Estate of	Fulton
14,161	Ficken, Jno.	Fulton
10,986	Fickett, Susan	Fulton
7,405	Fields, Bartley	Gwinnett
15,354	Fields, Henry	Chatham
15,447	Fields, Henry & Shellman, Alfred	Chatham
10,983	Fincher, Nancy E.	Fulton
1,257	Findly, James	Henry
7,465	Finley, Samuel	Chattooga
15,799	Finely, Samuel C.	Chattooga
16,756	Finsterer, Leonhard	Chatham
1,019	Fisher, Charles C. P.	Henry
16,250	Fisher, Eliza	Chatham
16,802	Fite, Isaac M.	Gordon
1,967	Fite, Jacob A.	Gordon
5,879	Fite, Peter	Gordon
20,020	Flatley, Andrew	Chatham
5,471	Fleetwood, Wm. N.	Telfair
19,445	Fleming, Mahala	Fulton
20,644	Flemming, James C.	Liberty
20,646	Flemming, Lazarus	Liberty
14,169	Fletcher, Dix	Cobb
20,643	Flowers, Raymond	Chatham
8,445	Floyd, Andrew J.	Burke
927	Floyd, David	Gordon
11,687	Floyd, Edward	Gordon
3,577	Floyd, Jason	Liberty
16,472	Floyd, Leonard	Floyd
13,104	Floyd, Lewis B.	Floyd
16,684	Floyd, London	Chatham
2,597	Floyd, Miles A.	Gordon
3,946	Floyd, Rena	Chatham
7,406	Floyd, Richard	DeKalb
18,950	Flynn, Eliza	Fulton
9,676	Flynn, Thomas	Campbell
7,784	Ford, Cyntha	Clayton
1,020	Ford, James Y.	Henry
1,013	Ford, Mark D.	Henry
1,736	Ford, Simeon	Floyd
20,995	Foreman, Joshua T.	Floyd
6,211	Foresyth, Maria	Campbell
13,614	Formby, Obadiah	Floyd
1,310	Forsyth, James	Whitfield
18,633	Forsyth, Lamarcus L.	Paulding
21,286	Forsyth, Wm. G.	Fulton
10,984	Foster, James M.	Cobb
6,870	Foster, Jno.	Chattooga
7,796	Foster, Moses, Sr., Estate of	Campbell
1,620	Foster, Robert S.	Chattooga
4,004	Foster, Stephen	Monroe
18,155	Fountain, Artemissea	Cherokee
16,072	Fountain, Beheathiland	Wilkinson
7,280	Fowler, Alfred S.	DeKalb
1,485	Fowler, Edward	Catoosa
2,810	Fowler, Indiana P.	Gordon
8,426	Fowler, James S.	Warren
16,807	Fowler, Joel A.	Walker
3,579	Fowler, Nicey	Milton
14,918	Fowler, Thomas M.	Bartow
13,092	Fox, Jno. B.	Chattooga
12,142	Fraliex, Lucretia	Walker
20,990	Frank, Jane and Moses	Fulton
20,990	Frank, Moses and Jane	Fulton
19,908	Frankenstein, Leah	Chatham
21,458	Fraser, Nedger	Liberty
17,402	Frazer, Allen and Mary	Fulton
20,647	Frazer, Jno.	Liberty
17,402	Frazer, Mary and Allen	Fulton
20,645	Frazer, Plimoth, Jr.	Liberty
20,648	Frazer, Plimoth, Sr.	Liberty
5,056	Frazer, Quives	Chatham
22,154	Freeman, Albert, and Henderson, James M.	Chatham
8,217	Freeman, Alexander	Monroe
16,475	Freeman, Benton	Gordon
15,679	Freeman, Elizabeth	Wilkinson
21,241	Freeman, Francis M.	Floyd
4,001	Freeman, Henry	Upson
361	Freeman, James	Fulton
2,783	Freeman, James C.	Spalding
15,680	Freeman, James G.	Wilkinson
15,682	Freeman, Jno., Estate of	Wilkinson
15,681	Freeman, Jno. H.	Wilkinson
18,638	Freeman, Thos. F.	Paulding
16,075	Freeman, Thos. M.	Wilkinson
8,282	Fricks, La Fayette	Walker
1,005	Frix, Joel	Gordon
9,408	Fry, Drury	Chattooga
20,641	Fry, Stephen, Estate of	Bryan
18,088	Fudge, Rodah	Effingham
6,536	Fuller, Lackey	Clayton
1,966	Fuller, W. G.	Bartow
7,636	Fuller, W. J.	Calhoun
5,285	Fulton, Edward S., Estate of	Chatham
12,564	Funderburk, Isaac C.	Floyd
11,397	Furcron, Wm. C., Estate of	Fulton
7,281	Furguson, Marshall	Gwinnett
13,588	Gaddis, Thomas J.	Floyd
17,250	Gaines, Pleasant	Chatham
7,149	Gainey, Elizabeth	Wilkinson
926	Gains, Margaret	Gordon
7,148	Ganey, Sarah A.	Wilkinson
7,785	Ganns, Malinda	Clayton
6,537	Ganns, Melissa	Clayton
5,715	Garcia, Bernardo	Fulton
3,954	Gardner, George	Chatham
4,750	Gardner, Mary	Chatham
8,887	Gardner, Robert B., Estate of	Pike
16,399	Gardner, Sarah M.	Walker
14,154	Gardner, Solomon	Chatham
4,003	Garland, Reuben H. J.	Upson

8,891	Garland, Sarah A.	Upson
16,104	Garmany, Wm. N.	Walker
823	Garner, Geo. H.	Henry
7,150	Garner, Thomas	Gwinnett
1,290	Garnett, Thomas S.	Chatham
7,407	Garret, Jno. M.	Wilkinson
16,361	Garrett, Absalom	Jefferson
9,710	Garrison, Margaret	Fulton
19,319	Gates, Henry	Chatham
10,323	Gates, James M.	Bibb
16,032	Gatewood, Sarah	Whitfield
18,119	Gaulden, Saml., Sr.	Liberty
18,118	Gaulden, Saml., Jr.	Liberty
21,313	Gaylord, Jno. A.	Effingham
3,937	Geary, Elizabeth	Chatham
934	Geber, S. C., Mrs.	Gordon
15,943	Geil, Jacob, Estate of	Chatham
13,992	Geil, Nicholas	Chatham
2,474	Gentry, Eliza V.	Murray
6,538	Gentry, Harvey A.	Clayton
16,852	George, Rachel	Gordon
14,155: 14,815:	Gerstmann, Simon	Chatham
57	Gibson, Sterling, Estate of	Warren
7,568	Gibson, Wm.	DeKalb
11,472	Gideon, Berry W.	Gordon
15,992	Giebelhouse, Philip	Chatham
4,862	Gilbert, Eliza	Upson
6,540	Gilbert, Louisa	Clayton
4,936	Gilbert, Rody	Upson
16,024	Gilbert, Wm. W.	Catoosa
7,466	Gilbreath, Geo. H.	Chattooga
15,759	Gilbreath, Hiram H.	Chattooga
7,467	Gilbreath, James H.	Chattooga
16,016	Gilbreath, Margaret	Catoosa
15,035	Gilbreath, Wm. C.	Catoosa
7,468	Gilbreath, Wm. H.	Chattooga
20,083	Gildersleeve, Stephen	Chatham
14,241	Giles, John H.	Douglas
6,697	Gilleland, Francis	Floyd
15,758	Gillespie, Jane A.	Carroll
2,005	Gilliam, Jno. W.	Floyd
21,480	Gillmore, Wm.	Liberty
10,987	Gillthrop, John J.	Fulton
10,618	Gilmore, Humphrey J.	Butts
10,620	Gilmore, Margaret	Butts
20,652	Girardeau, Andrew	Liberty
7,127	Glass, Wm. R.	Murray
2,329	Glaze, Moses	Whitfield
21,376	Glenn, James H.	Green
10,177	Glover, Seaborn	Glascock
351	Glover, Wm. M.	Murray
20,916	Gochel, Andrew	Chatham
2,064	Godard, Daniel	Monroe
6,183	Godbee, Albert	Campbell
7,787	Godby, Henry B.	Clayton
15,126	Goddard, Elias	Floyd
10,619	Goddard, Lucius	Butts
7,569	Goddard, Wm.	DeKalb
22,016	Godwin, Eliza	Muscogee
18,452	Goette, Bridgett & Barret, Thomas J.	Chatham
20,653	Golden, Mark	Liberty
601	Golden, Pleasant A.	Fulton
20,654	Golding, Jacob	Liberty
21,422	Golding, Major	Liberty
20,651	Golding, Wm.	Liberty
16,618	Golphin, Richard	Chatham
4,517	Goodman, Robert M.	Cobb
19,842	Goodwin, John C.	Fulton
19,841	Goodwin, Mary A.	Fulton
362	Goodwin, Merrill P.	Bartow
602	Goodwin, Starling	Fulton
363	Goodwin, Wm. L.	Bartow
6,751	Goolsby, Cardin	Jasper
6,752	Goolsby, Wm.	Jasper
7,789	Gordon, Alexander	Cobb
16,379	Gordon, Daniel L.	Fulton
8,089	Gordon, Harriet Y.	Chattooga
4,751	Gordon, John	Chatham
8,225	Gordon, June R.	McIntosh
16,148	Gordon, Mary	Walker
16,269	Gordon, Scipio	Chatham
20,091	Gordon, Wooster	Chatham
11,856	Gore, Henry	Chattooga
16,322	Gorner, Thomas	Henry
7,690	Goss, James	DeKalb
18,217	Gould, Baccus	Chatham
21,408	Gould, George	Liberty
18,129	Goulding, Wm. A.	Liberty
7,570	Goza, Harriet	DeKalb
7,282	Graham, Joseph	Rockdale
8,002	Graham, Martha A.	Cherokee
6,049	Graham, Wm. M.	Baldwin
17,462	Grant, Elsie	Chatham
1,011	Grant, Isaac W.	Henry
14,192	Grant, Josiah	Chatham
7,788	Graves, Martha	Fayette
10,971	Gravitt, Winney W.	Fulton
5,692	Gravley, Ballenger	Polk
6,535	Gray, A. F.	Clayton
16,349	Gray, James	Murray
13,398	Gray, James R.	Butts
12,517	Gray, James R.	Henry
1,912	Gray, Sarah C.	Fayette
943	Gray, Wm.	Catoosa
15,683	Green, Andrew J.	Whitfield
7,786	Green, Ann	Carroll
20,649	Green, Daphney	Chatham
19,082	Green, Elizabeth	Fulton
6,189	Green, J. M.	Clayton
2,814	Green, Lucinda	Gordon
18,651	Green, Meshack	Gordon
20,301	Green, Robert	Clayton
20,300	Green, Robert H.	Clayton
1,244	Green, Samuel	Hancock
10,501	Greene, Chas. H.	Upson
8,234	Greene, Thomas B.	Upson
17,260	Greenwood, John P.	Polk
18,875	Greer, Andrew E.	Chattooga
2,594	Greeson, Abraham	Gordon
16,800	Greeson, Mount	Gordon
1,267	Gregory, Thomas Y.	Newton
233	Grier, James V.	Bibb
13,101	Griffin, Eugenia A.	Floyd
4,586	Griffin, Jerusha	Walker
15,763	Griffin, Rosannah	Floyd
6,872	Griffin, Thomas	Walker
4,178	Griffin, Wm.	Hancock
22,248	Griggs, Jesse R.	Towns
14,820	Grimm, Franz	Chatham
21,248	Grindle, Daniel	Hall
7,303	Grizzard, Andrew J.	Campbell
6,737	Grubb, Jno. W.	Jasper
10,979	Grubbs, E. W.	Fulton
20,534	Gue, Mary E.	Chatham
13,395	Guyn, Jno. L.	Butts
18,584	Guyton, Benjamin	Polk
18,656	Guyton, Philip J.	Bartow
365	Hackett, Taylor	Bartow
342	Hackney, Wm. P.	Whitfield
10,973	Hadaway, Wm.	Cobb
7,994	Hagerty, James	Cherokee
18,620	Hagin, Edward	Paulding
18,634	Hagin, Henry N.	Paulding
7,285	Hairston, Albert M.	DeKalb
544	Hale, Churchwell O.	Catoosa
17,515	Hall, David	Walker
14,823	Hall, Fenton	Floyd
15,746	Hall, Louisa	Chatham
7,284	Hall, Nancy B.	DeKalb
5,112	Hall, Wm. H.	Washington
7,151	Hambrick, Carrie E.	DeKalb
7,692	Hambrick, Jno. M.	DeKalb
654	Hambright, John S.	Catoosa
18,157	Hamer, Presley	Cherokee
1,078	Hames, Thomas	Whitfield
8,233	Hamil, Elizabeth	Pike
2,443: 2,475:	Hamilton, Benj.	Whitfield

8,283	Hamilton, J. W.	Walker	21,925	Hawkins, John	Walker
10,165	Hamilton, Rachel C.	Floyd	10,621	Hay, Washington	Butts
1,907	Hammond, Miles R.	Chattooga	8,236	Haygood, Benj.	Monroe
4,929	Hammond, Peter	Bartow	8,893	Haygood, Thomas M.	Upson
17,638	Hammons, Jno. J.	Walton	16,109	Haym, Harry	Chatham
6,873	Hampton, David N.	Polk	16,168	Haynes, George J.	Carroll
15,116	Hampton, Penny	Floyd	1,017	Haynes, Isaac A.	Henry
1,400	Hamrick, J. M.	Carroll	10,992	Haynes, Nancy	Fulton
1,030	Hamrick, John W.	Clayton	13,586	Haynes, Thos.	Polk
735	Hancock, Charity	Chatham	5,999	Hays, Nancy	Glascock
7,562	Hancock, Harner F.	Clayton	14,671	Hays, R. Luther	Newton
15,071	Haney, Hezekiah	Cobb	2,988	Hays, Sarah	Gordon
7,152	Haney, Robert E.	Gwinnett	9,204	Hayward, Matthew	Chatham
4,791	Haney, Thomas	Fulton	15,315	Haywood, Stephen	Fulton
1,624	Hannon, Warren W.	Bartow	17,718	Hazel, Wm. M.	Chatham
6,824	Hanson, Francis E.	Floyd	13,083	Hazelton, Mary	Floyd
324: 329:	Harben, Nathaniel P.	Whitfield	5,122	Head, B. A., Mrs.	Pike
			7,410	Head, Jane A.	Gwinnett
13,618	Harbin, James R.	Polk	2,476	Head, Jeptha	Whitfield
13,617	Harbin, Richard G., Estate of	Cobb	15,478	Head, Martha F.	Butts
			2,468	Head, Wm.	Whitfield
2,467	Harcastle, Wm.	Whitfield	18,692	Healey, Thos. G.	Fulton
20,835	Hardaway, Mary E.	Muscogee	22,017	Heard, Elizabeth	Muscogee
21,463	Harden, June	Liberty	6,617	Heard, Hugh H.	Butts
345	Harden, Morle	Whitfield	18,654	Heath, Benjamin	Bartow
21,407	Harden, Richard	Liberty	6,874	Heaton, Jno. R.	Polk
7,304	Harden, Sarah S. A.	Clayton	2,987	Hefner, John	Walker
4,705	Hardin, Benjamin J.	Morgan	18,649	Hell, Jno. W.	Cobb
830	Hardin, Jno. F.	Newton	16,798	Helton, Richard	Gordon
831	Hardin, Thos. H.	Newton	18,402	Hembre, Elihu M.	Milton
4,609	Hardin, Wm. P.	Monroe	3,315	Hemphill, David, Estate of	Chattooga
22,155	Hardwick, Redding C.	Chatham	20,022	Hemphill, Joseph L.	Clarke
15,937	Hardy, Thomas	Floyd	3,313	Hemphill, Wm.	Chattooga
20,655	Hargraves, Prime	Liberty	4,951	Henderson, Elizabeth	Pickens
15,130	Harkins, James M.	Floyd	22,154	Henderson, James M. & Freeman, Albert	Chatham
12,699	Harlow, James	Chattooga			
2,765	Harmon, Harriet	Bartow	2,477	Henderson, John P.	Whitfield
2,589	Harmon, Jennet	Walker	582	Henderson, Jno. W.	Henry
3,316	Harpe, Wm.	Chattooga	20,607	Henderson, S.	Fayette
7,385	Harper, Ecloe A.	Chattooga	16,680	Henderson, Stephen	Chatham
15,625	Harper, Edward	Chatham	15,891	Henderson, Thomas P.	Whitfield
7,384	Harper, Samuel	Chattooga	326	Henderson, Thomas R.	Whitfield
7,383	Harper, Wm.	Chattooga	15,684	Henderson, Wm.	Whitfield
1,443	Harris, A. B.	Bartow	16,018	Henderson, Wm. H., Estate of	Catoosa
20,532	Harris, Andrew T.	Murray	973	Hendon, Elmira O.	Cherokee
545	Harris, Ezekial	Catoosa	37	Hendon, George N.	Clayton
21,430	Harris, Henry	Liberty	20,363	Hendrick, Caroline V.	Bartow
16,395	Harris, James M.	Chatham	3,414	Hendrick, Jacob B.	Walker
18,953	Harris, James O.	Fulton	16,822	Hendrick, Jno. J.	Heard
2,969	Harris, Jno.	Fulton	6,458	Hendricks, James H.	Cherokee
7,691	Harris, Jno.	Gwinnett	5,150	Hendrix, Robert W.	Coweta
7,571	Harris, Jno. C.	DeKalb	13,609	Henley, Elihue	Chattooga
6,057	Harris, Loudon	Bryan	17,471	Henly, Hartford	Chattooga
16,797	Harris, Mahala	Whitfield	16,348	Henry, James C.	Murray
13,391	Harris, Mathew L.	Butts	12,560	Henry, James M.	Floyd
18,123	Harris, Saml.	Liberty	7,153	Henry, Jno. W.	Gwinnett
12,255	Harris, Sarah A.	Henry	6,542	Henry, Mary A.	Clayton
21,483	Harris, Simon	Liberty	14,170	Henry, Wm.	Catoosa
12,288	Harris, Susannah	Chatham	13,091	Hens, Peter	Chattooga
6,192	Harris, Thos. M.	Fulton	16,244	Herb, Straffon	Chatham
8,224	Harris, Wm.	Chatham	2,478	Herndon, Isabella	Whitfield
2,799	Harris, Wm. A.	Polk	8,621	Herod, Dred	Campbell
6,541	Harrison, Asa R.	Clayton	15,744	Herron, Andrew J.	Chattooga
14,729	Harrison, Nancy	Bartow	20,021	Herschback, Clara	Chatham
21,362	Hart, Augustus F.	Fulton	6,560	Hesterly, P. H.	Carroll
22,135	Hart, Harriet A.	Liberty	15,256	Hetzel, Wm.	Fulton
15,391	Hart, John, Estate of	Chatham	13,581	Hickey, Wm. H.	Floyd
6,180	Hart, John J.	Clayton	6,822	Hickman, Wm.	Polk
3,290	Hartesfield, Charlotte	Clayton	13,365	Hicks, Jacob, and Moric, Ed	Chatham
15,092	Harvey, Willis	Chatham	15,685	Hicks, Mary	Wilkinson
2,986	Harwood, Andrew S.	Gordon	4,017	Hickson, Seaborn	Pike
13,081	Haskins, Joseph	Pulaski	3,650	Higginbotham, Wm. B.	Floyd
7,409	Hatcher, Caroline	Wilkinson	4,952	Hightower, Alfred	Pickens
13,613	Hatchett, Josiah	Floyd	6,062	Hightower, James M., Estate of	Pike
18,827	Hatfield, John	Catoosa			
6,153	Hathcock, Arminda	Fulton	2,970	Hilburn, Samuel	Newton
7,177	Hathcock, Sophronia	Campbell	7,934	Hildebrand, Annie	Douglas
15,712	Hawkins, Bennett	Cobb	1,269	Hill, Alexander	Gordon
7,469	Hawkins, James T.	Chattooga	14,162	Hill, Ann P.	Bibb
1,622	Hawkins, Jasper N.	Chattooga	7,790	Hill, J. B.	Carroll

713	Hill, James	Fulton
16,855	Hill, James W.	Gordon
13,602	Hill, James W.	Newton
6,574	Hill, Jno.	Whitfield
6,579	Hill, Jno. and Batey, Robert	Whitfield
21,681	Hill, Joshua	Morgan
3,763	Hill, Samuel K.	Fulton
14,242	Hinton, H. B.	Fulton
3,231: 17,005:	Hinton, Martin J.	Fulton
5,286	Hitchcock, Catharine J.	Chatham
6,876	Hitchcock, J. C.	Polk
10,970	Hitchens, Amey	Fulton
6,618	Hoard, Wm.	Butts
1,225	Hodgens, Jacob B.	Cherokee
14,816	Hodges, Asbury	Bullock
20,285	Hodges, Flourenoy G.	Bullock
16,883	Hodges, Joel	Liberty
2,978	Hogan, Elvira	Gordon
20,779	Hogan, Thomas M.	Muscogee
8,007	Hogan, Wm.	Cherokee
7,178	Holaway, Levi	Douglas
3,790	Holbrook, Wm.	Fulton
17,201	Holcomb, James M.	Chattooga
16,004	Holcomb, John	Whitfield
16,523	Holcomb, Joseph	Gordon
8,629	Holcomb, Sarah G.	DeKalb
5,883	Holcombe, Harmon	Murray
20,066	Holcombe, Henry C.	Fulton
8,836	Holder, Benj.	Wilkinson
19,187	Holder, Charles M.	Walker
18,618	Holland, Archibald, Estate of	Paulding
15,810	Holland, Benj. F.	Whitfield
2,448	Holland, Chesley	Bartow
15,967	Holland, James	Whitfield
10,951	Holland, Joseph	Fulton
11,395	Holland, Rhoda	Fulton
18,626	Holland, Samuel D.	Paulding
10,692	Holland, Thomas	Fulton
19,447	Holland, Wm.	Fulton
3,581	Holliday, Andrew	Chatham
1,018	Hollingsworth, Isaiah	Henry
145	Hollingsworth, Walter T.	Bibb
6,821	Hollis, Thomas	Floyd
5,123	Holloway, Martha W.	Upson
11,393	Holmes, Daniel A.	Fulton
21,479	Holmes, David	Liberty
20,656	Holmes, Jane	Liberty
20,642	Holmes, Patty, Estate of	Chatham
12,565	Holmes, Sandiford	Floyd
929	Holmes, Washington	Gordon
16,638	Holt, Alfred, Estate of	Chattooga
7,286	Holt, Mahala	Gwinnett
6,173	Holtzclaw, H. J.	Fulton
7,539	Holtzclaw, Jno. W.	Cobb
1,628	Honecker, Christian	Fulton
7,412	Honeycutt, Faithey C.	Wilkinson
7,472	Hood, Delia	Chattooga
12,323	Hood, Rebecca D.	Floyd
2,845	Hood, Rebecca P.	Bartow
17,224	Hooke, Samuel A. B.	Dade
14,326	Hoot, Rudolph	Chatham
6,157	Hope, Albert	Hall
4,954	Hopkins, Hosea	Pickens
7,287	Hopper, Charles	Whitfield
7,411	Horn, Britain	Wilkinson
7,474	Horn, Elisha	Chattooga
7,475	Horn, John	Chattooga
7,473	Horn, Nancy L.	Chattooga
31	Hornsby, Edward	Chatham
1,961	Hornsby, Joseph	Campbell
7,305	Hornsby, Thos.	Fulton
2,596	Horton, Elizabeth	Gordon
21,001	Hoskins, John A.	Whitfield
802	Houk, Berry	Gordon
15,022	House, Memory	Floyd
20,657	Houston, Booby	Liberty
16,976	Houston, Charles	Chatham
6,055	Houston, Richard	Chatham

10,502	Howard, Asa W.	DeKalb
5,113	Howard, Harriet	Baldwin
4,024	Howard, Joseph, Estate of	Pike
8,894	Howe, Hiram	Pike
14,694	Howe, Wm. D.	Chatham
11,511	Howell, James	Pickens
17,296	Howell, Pinckney F.	Murray
2,850	Hubbard, Margaret and Thomas W.	Cherokee
2,850	Hubbard, Thomas W. and Margaret	Cherokee
7,154	Hudgens, Hamlen,	DeKalb
15,066	Hudgins, Cora A.	Chattooga
3,608	Hudgins, Floyd S.	Chattooga
11,405	Hudgins, Wm. W.	DeKalb
11,386	Hudson, Wm. J.	Fulton
5,660	Huey, Jno. T.	Cherokee
12,328	Huffman, Sinclair	Floyd
14,657	Huge, Peter	Fulton
5,181	Hughes, Wm. T.	Dade
6,543	Hughey, E. G. C.	Clayton
923	Hughey, James M.	Gordon
16,987	Huguley, Mason J.	Monroe
6,178	Huie, David	Clayton
15,120	Hume, Jno.	Floyd
15,139	Humphries, Benjamin	Baldwin
7,179	Humphries, Jno. W.	Douglas
15,140	Humphries, Robert C.	Baldwin
16,168	Hunnicutt, Joseph M.	Fulton
15,036	Hunsucker, James	Catoosa
21,362	Hunt, Augustus F.	Fulton
6,433	Hunt, Elisha	Cobb
12,345	Hunt, Jno. M.	Floyd
16,014	Hunt, Lydia	Catoosa
9,874	Hunt, Saml., Estate of	Floyd
18,125	Hunter, Ephraim	Effingham
10,178	Hunter, W. R.	Glascock
16,272	Hurst, Felix, Estate of	Scriven
4,955	Hutchins, Adaline M.	Forsyth
3,585	Hutchins, Harris	Cobb
13,311	Hutchins, J. H.	Chattooga
4,119	Hutchins, Jonathan W.	Lumpkin
5,151	Hutchinson, Mary N.	Clayton
7,307	Hutchinson, Nancy	Clayton
7,306	Hutson, Mill C.	Fulton
8,459	Hyatt, Jno.	Fannin
15,808	Inman, William	Whitfield
21,477	Irving, Thomas	Liberty
7,693	Irwin, Willis	Walton
12,349	Isbell, Milton J.	Polk
12,348	Isbell, Pendleton	Polk
10,512	Isdol, Leviticus	Upson
19,416	Ivey, H. G.	Muscogee
4,956	Ivy, Benjamin	Pickens
8,628	Jackson, Alson	Walker
3,943	Jackson, Cato	Chatham
7,574	Jackson, Dicey	DeKalb
398	Jackson, Fannie A.	Gordon
16,073	Jackson, James	Wilkinson
4,021	Jackson, Jno. S.	Upson
794	Jackson, L. B.	Gwinnett
3,933	Jackson, Paul	Chatham
3,994	Jackson, Robert, Sr.	Campbell
4,020	Jackson, Robert M.	Upson
13,070	Jackson, Tyler, and Mann, Young	Gordon
4,580	Jackson, Wilkins W.	Monroe
11,380	Jacobs, Allen T.	Gwinnett
18,213	James, Benjamin	Chatham
21,427	James, Eliza	Liberty
18,548	James, Frank	Liberty
20,664	James, Joseph	Liberty
20,661	James, Jupiter	Liberty
20,081	James, Paris	Chatham
21,459	James, Wm. (Midway Church)	Liberty
20,659	James, Wm. (Reedeon Plantation)	Liberty
16,150	James, Wm. M.	Walker
18,160	Jarvis, Samuel	Cherokee
2,101	Jefferson, Geo. O.	Cherokee

2,262	Jefferson, James A.	Bartow
17,020	Jefferson, Sambo	Chatham
7,572	Jenkins, Bartlett M.	Gwinnett
20,665	Jenkins, Isaac	Liberty
12,566	Jenkins, Mary	Floyd
15,123	Jenkins, Silas W.	Chattooga
7,015	Jenkins, Wm., Estate of	Polk
6,385	Jennings, Ira	Bibb
932	Jennings, James	Gordon
930	Jennings, Patrick	Bartow
3,947	Jess, Mary	Chatham
7,413	Jett, Jno.	DeKalb
8,739	Jett, T. R.	Milton
15,129	Jett, Wm.	Floyd
16,704	Jetzen, Jno. H. & Oelrich, Peter H.	Fulton
16,023	Jobe, Isaac R.	Catoosa
11,389	Johns, Elizabeth	Fulton
7,573	Johns, John B.	DeKalb
7,694	Johns, Robert S.	DeKalb
2,449	Johnsey, Hastings A.	Bartow
3,930	Johnson, Abraham	Chatham
21,763	Johnson, Araam, Mrs.	DeKalb
16,017	Johnson, Abijah	Catoosa
3,586	Johnson, Adarine	Chattooga
15,505	Johnson, Bason	Liberty
15,268	Johnson, Caesar	Chatham
1,629	Johnson, Catharine	Chattooga
17,387	Johnson, Edwin	Gwinnett
7,986	Johnson, Elizabeth	Floyd
5,475	Johnson, Emanuel B.	Emanuel
7,695	Johnson, Frank	DeKalb
12,491	Johnson, Geo. W.	Towns
1,270	Johnson, Isaac, Estate of	Gordon
6,464	Johnson, James A.	Newton
10,531	Johnson, James H.	Liberty
14,821	Johnson, Jerry R.	Chatham
4,957	Johnson, John S.	Pickens
16,352	Johnson, Jno. W.	Chattooga
12,516	Johnson, John W.	Monroe
17,463	Johnson, Louisa	Scriven
14,940	Johnson, Martha R.	Chattooga
20,822	Johnson, Mary A.	Scriven
1,832	Johnson, Monemia	Cobb
8,630	Johnson, Naomi	Fulton
15,269	Johnson, Peter	Chatham
12,572	Johnson, Pleasant	Gordon
6,208	Johnson, Pleasant P.	Clayton
3,587	Johnson, R. H. C.	Chattooga
21,311	Johnson, Riley J., Estate of	Floyd
16,078	Johnson, Robt. A.	Fulton
6,466	Johnson, Samuel	Newton
7,288	Johnson, Thomas	DeKalb
13,603	Johnson, Wm. H.	Floyd
12,331	Johnston, Carrie J.	Floyd
6,637	Johnston, E. A. (Mrs.)	McIntosh
14,333	Johnston, Elizabeth A.	Liberty
1,631	Johnston, James	Chattooga
7,476	Johnston, James P.	Chattooga
7,477	Johnston, John	Chattooga
1,632	Johnston, Joshua	Chattooga
6,750	Johnston, Martha	Jasper
1,630	Johnston, Wyatt	Chattooga
7,180	Joiner, Celia A. E.	Douglas
7,835	Joiner, Nancy	Clayton
18,947	Jolly, Artelissia	Bartow
15,044	Jolly, Asa, Estate of	Macon
13,404	Jolly, Jesse	Butts
19,411	Jolly, Martha J.	DeKalb
234	Jolly, Zilley	Bartow
6,607	Jones, Adam	Chatham
7,598	Jones, Adam, Sr.	Warren
9,085	Jones, Alfred E.	Chatham
11,398	Jones, Ann B.	DeKalb
20,662	Jones, Caesar and Linda	Liberty
3,277	Jones, Edward L.	Fulton
7,696	Jones, Elizabeth	DeKalb
15,400	Jones, Elizabeth	Whitfield
5,152	Jones, Enoch G.	Fayette

15,119	Jones, Francis S.	Floyd
14,691	Jones, Green	Jefferson
5,154	Jones, Hartwell	Clayton
20,658	Jones, Ingraham	Chatham
5,156	Jones, James S.	Clayton
2,414	Jones, James V.	Burke
10,170	Jones, Jno.	Gwinnett
14,993	Jones, John C.	Pickens
2,102	Jones, Jno. J.	Cherokee
5,155	Jones, John S.	Clayton
21,424	Jones, Joseph	Liberty
20,662	Jones, Linda and Caesar	Liberty
17,511	Jones, M. Maria	Richmond
20,660	Jones, Marlborough	Liberty
11,375	Jones, Martha A. H.	DeKalb
3,234	Jones, Mary A.	Catoosa
8,625	Jones, Mary H.	Floyd
4,318	Jones, Mila	Henry
3,136	Jones, Nancy	Paulding
2,815	Jones, P. C., Mrs.	Gordon
20,087	Jones, Rosanna	Chatham
604	Jones, Samuel	Fulton
20,959	Jones, Sanders	Chatham
10,980	Jones, Sarah E.	Fulton
20,663	Jones, Saul	Liberty
2,811	Jones, Wm.	Gordon
10,770	Jones, Wm. D.	Floyd
5,153	Jones, Wm. G. C.	Clayton
22,020	Jordan, G. W.	Talbot
20,608	Jordan, James B. H.	Fulton
5,764	Jordán, Patrick	Fulton
18,274	Jordan, Thos. W.	Fulton
12,312	Journette, Jno. De	Floyd
7,599	Jowers, Sarah A.	Burke
12,333	Judkins, Robertson B.	Polk
1,833	Julian, Elizabeth	Cobb
350	Justus, James D.	Whitfield
4,062	Kagle, James	Cherokee
3,633	Kahn, Valentine	Bibb
4,752	Kaiser, John	Chatham
18,158	Karr, Toliver M.	Cherokee
14,552	Kautz, Christian	Fulton
7,662	Kay, Fielden	Gordon
2,812	Kay, James	Gordon
7,663	Kay, M. G.	Gordon
5,458	Kay, R. W.	Bartow
4,002	Keadle, Joshua J.	Monroe
20,689	Keating, Cato	Chatham
16,975	Keaton, Francis J.	Chatham
16,763	Keaton, Keader L.	Liberty
1,973	Keen, James M.	Gordon
7,791	Keese, Wm. S.	Fulton
916	Keever, James	Bartow
2,662	Keith, Phillip	Cherokee
15,877	Keller, Stephen F.	Effingham
7,697	Kelly, Benj. O.	Gwinnett
21,923	Kelly, Elisha, Sr.	Catoosa
15,586	Kelly, Georgiana	Chatham
12,305	Kelly, Thomas P.	Floyd
5,474	Kemp, Phady	Emanuel
15,698	Kendy, Prince	Chatham
20,716	Kennedy, James A.	Rockdale
12,216	Kennedy, James L.	Dade
7,793	Kennedy, Jno. J.	Douglas
803	Kennedy, Joseph B.	Bartow
5,472	Kennedy, Sarah	Emanuel
6,181	Kennedy, Seleta A.	Fulton
12,215	Kennedy, Thomas L.	Dade
7,656	Kent, A. & E. H., and Bennett, Julia L.	Chatham
7,656	Kent, E. H., and A., and Bennett, Julia L.	Chatham
18,976	Keown, Nathan L.	Walker
13,590	Kerce, Hugh H.	Floyd
13,595	Kerce, Richard H.	Floyd
13,584	Kerr, Daniel R.	Floyd
12,330	Kerr, James H.	Floyd
13,082	Kerr, Nancy	Floyd
10,516	Kersey, Sarah	Upson
18,275	Kesley, David M.	Fulton

15,072	Key, James L.	Fulton
16,915	Key, Wm.	Walker
3,952	Keyfer, Nelly	Chatham
7,992	Keykendall, Jno.	Cherokee
5,222	Keys, Jno. B.	DeKalb
152	Keys, Sarah	Bartow
14,580	Kieffer, Allen N.	Effingham
13,388	Kiker, Amelia	Gordon
12,692	Kiker, Milley	Gordon
6,198	Kile, Robert M.	Clayton
3,640	Kiley, Jno.	Fulton
10,691	Killan, Elizabeth M.	Fulton
6,444	Killion, Serug	Dade
16,270	Kimball, Amelia	Chatham
7,936	Kimberly, Elizabeth	Campbell
6,223	Kimberly, James M.	Clayton
6,463	Kimble, John W., Estate of	Newton
7,478	Kimble, Sarah	Chattooga
7,698	Kimbrell, Jackson H.	DeKalb
3,180	King, Alfred C.	Cherokee
5,411	King, Berry	Paulding
4,064	King, Cynthia C.	Cherokee
4,063	King, Green	Cherokee
19,661	King, Horace	Troup
6,586	King, Isam C.	Gordon
13,612	King, Jane A.	Polk
2,103	King, Jno. T.	Cherokee
3,350	King, Mary Ann	Whitfield
13,592	King, Mary J.	Floyd
21,429	King, Scipio	Liberty
5,696	King, Stephen	Polk
3,272	Kinkland, Mary	Clayton
12,568	Kinnebrew, Newton	Floyd
5,157	Kinsey, Caroline M.	Clayton
19,446	Kirkham, Mary	Fulton
7,600	Kirkland, Abraham L.	Emanuel
7,601	Kirkland, Elizabeth	Emanuel
1,913	Kitby, Elijah	Whitfield
2,479	Kittle, Jeremiah	Whitfield
16,019	Kittles, Francis M.	Catoosa
7,792	Kitton, Catharine	Fulton
22,156	Kline, Samuel F.	Chatham
3,938	Knight, Catherine	Chatham
2,734	Knight, Chas. G.	Polk
2,491	Knight, James C.	Catoosa
7,699	Knight, Jno.	Gwinnett
20,954	Knight, Prince	Chatham
5,077	Knight, Rufus, Estate of	Emanuel
7,414	Knight, Ruthey	Gwinnett
18,453	Knight, Sam	Chatham
13,099	Knowles, Charles	Gordon
1,633	Knowles, Jno. B.	Chattooga
7,289	Knox, Robert S.	Whitfield
6,325	Kreis, Michael	Fulton
15,736	Kreishure, Peter	Whitfield
1,014	Kugler, Lewis A.	Henry
22,004	Ladd, Danl. B.	Fulton
2,044	Lamar, James M.	Fulton
9,134	Lambert, John	Baldwin
18,605	Lambert, Jno.	Liberty
16,660	Lambert, Joseph	Fulton
3,594	Land, Gideon	Milton
2,628	Landers, Mathew	Cobb
9,494	Landrum, James	Fulton
1,230	Langmade, Edward S.	Washington
5,476	Lane, Benj. L.	Emanuel
928	Lanear, Timan	Gordon
5,714	Lang, Thomas M.	Coweta
22,046	Langford, Sarah B.	DeKalb
6,733	Langston, David M.	Jasper
367	Lankford, Abraham B.	Bartow
13,339	Lankston, E. B.	Clayton
13,594	Larey, James	Floyd
5,596: 15,365:	Larkin, James	Liberty
14,949	La Roche, Adrian V.	Chatham
20,985	La Roche, Isaac Do.	Chatham
15,708	La Roche, James A.	Chatham
20,718	Lasiter, Joel	Rockdale
3,294	Lassiter, Elijah M.	Clayton

13,604	Latimer, Geo.	Chattooga
15,747	Lattimore, Wm. and Lovell, Nathl.	Chatham
14,348	Lavender, George W.	Chatham
16,074	Lavender, Nancy	Wilkinson
16,520	Law, Andrew	Chatham
20,085	Law, Charles	Chatham
18,097	Law, July	Chatham
20,671	Law, Wm.	Liberty
17,825	Law, Wm. D.	Bartow
15,564	Lawrence, Allen, Sr.	Putnam
3,926	Lawrence, John A.	Chatham
16,792	Lawrence, John M.	Walker
3,164	Lawrence, Martin	Chattooga
7,377	Lawrence, Wm. A. C.	Clayton
2,784	Lawson, Nancy	Butts
13,405	Lawson, Robert, Estate of	Butts
917	Layton, Joshua D.	Bartow
4,612	Lazenby, Vandella I.	Warren
13,392	Leach, Benj.	Butts
17,853	Leak, Moses A.	Gordon
21,266	Leake, John Fletcher	Bartow
20,585	Leake, John W.	Bartow
20,586	Leake, Sally, Estate of	Bartow
14,690	Leaptrott, James	Jefferson
9,875	Leazer, Rachel	Floyd
8,363	Lebetter, Martha	Dawson
20,669	Leconte, Aberdeen	Liberty
20,668	Leconte, Henry	Liberty
20,667	Leconte, Hercules	Liberty
21,449	Leconte, John	Liberty
20,675	Leconte, Joshua	Liberty
20,674	Leconte, Paul	Liberty
20,670	Leconte, Primus	Liberty
20,672	Leconte, Richard	Liberty
20,676	Leconte, Wm.	Liberty
18,545	Le Count, Adam	Liberty
18,117	Le Count, July	Liberty
10,991	Lee, Elizabeth B.	Fulton
7,700	Lee, Emily H.	Gwinnett
18,619	Lee, Hartwell, Estate of	Paulding
4,026	Lee, James M.	Walker
8,465	Lee, John C.	Walker
11,470	Lee, Mary Jane	Upson
7,794	Lee, Nancy I.	Fulton
1,026	Lee, Samuel, Estate of	Henry
11,666	Lee, Thomas	Gwinnett
20,082	Lee, Thos. B.	Liberty
1,037	Lee, Wm. C.	Clayton
15,236	Leffler, Abraham	Chatham
13,403	Lemon, John	Butts
3,064	Leonard, Joseph	Baldwin
3,065	Leonard, Joseph S.	Baldwin
4,583	Le Sueur, Cary L.	Monroe
13,460	Letson, Robert	Jasper
7,290	Leverett, Talitha	DeKalb
20,715	Levi, Louis	Chatham
22,153	Lewis, Antonio, Estate of	Chatham
10,268	Lewis, George R.	Henry
5,457	Lewis, Harriet M.	Bartow
15,820	Lewis, Harriet M.	Heard
2,450	Lewis, Jno.	Paulding
2,451	Lewis, Nathaniel D.	Paulding
5,477	Lewis, Wm.	Emanuel
3,280	Lewis, Wm. A.	Henry
6,070	Liles, Ephraim	Walker
17,369	Lilienthal, Levi	Chatham
7,416: 17,270:	Lindsey, Chaney M.	Wilkinson
16,288	Lindsey, Dolphin	Butts
4,012	Lindsey, Jno. C. W.	Upson
14,349	Lineberger, John T.	Chatham
3,596	Lippman, Joseph	Chatham
20,673	Livingstone, Richard	Liberty
3,935	Lloyd, Frank	Chatham
10,769	Lloyd, Geo. W.	Floyd
20,666	Lloyd, Richard, Estate of	Chatham
7,480	Loden, Thomas	Chattooga
16,030	Long, Caroline E.	Chatham
1,036	Long, George T.	Henry

22,130	Long, Henry	Liberty
6,878	Long, Jonathan	Polk
4,082	Long, Malitta	Clayton
7,417	Long, Richard A.	Walton
332	Long, Wm. R.	Whitfield
238	Longley, John Campbell	Whitfield
15,686	Lord, Geo. W., Sr.	Wilkinson
8,837	Lord, James	Wilkinson
16,664	Lord, Sarah A.	Wilkinson
4,960	Lott, John G.	Forsyth
2,348	Louis, Caroline	Haralson
9,207	Love, Andrew M.	Whitfield
5,094	Love, Charles B.	Fulton
17,299	Love, Hugh R.	Catoosa
4,587	Love, Wm. J.	Walker
7,418	Loveless, Levi	Gwinnett
6,879	Lovell, Madison	Polk
15,747	Lovell, Nathl. & Lattimore, Wm.	Chatham
4,065	Lovinggood, Eli	Cherokee
3,182	Lovinggood, Samuel	Cherokee
5,459	Lowe, Isaac	Bartow
13,096	Lowry, Daniel, Sr.	Bartow
13,606	Lowry, David	Bartow
7,843	Lowry, James	Fulton
17,648	Lufburrow, Matthew, Estate of	Chatham
12,562	Lumpkin, Edmund	Floyd
10,008	Lumpkin, Elijah	Bartow
15,541	Lumpkin, Geo. W. F.	Floyd
6,684	Lumpkin, John C.	Walker
12,326	Lumpkin, Pitman	Polk
12,573	Lumpkin, Thomas	Floyd
6,332	Lumsden, Elizabeth	Clayton
1,050	Lundy, Sarah D.	Baldwin
3,047	Lutes, David and D. F.	Gordon
12,700	Lyday, Jno.	Chattooga
6,193	Lyle, Dilmus	Cobb
3,283	Lyle, Robert S.	Clayton
6,730	Lynch, Grief	Jasper
6,326	Lynch, Michel	Fulton
15,677	Lynch, Patrick, Estate of	Fulton
4,518	Lynch, Peter	Fulton
18,053	Lynes, Timothy D.	Fulton
5,740	Lyon, James P.	Upson
11,370	Lyons, F. R.	Liberty
4,016	Lyons, Jordan	Upson
8,010	Maberry, Ephrain M.	Cherokee
19,167	Machod, Francis, Estate of	Cobb
336	Mack, Henry	Whitfield
16,977	Mack, Prince	Chatham
15,103	Maddox, Caleb J.	Floyd
7,577	Maddox, Fielden	DeKalb
7,578	Maddox, Jno. P.	DeKalb
7,156	Maddox, Wm. C.	DeKalb
13,393	Maddux, David	Butts
14,942	Maddux, Lutitia S.	Butts
14,943	Maddux, Malinda L.	Butts
7,938	Mahoffy, Jno.	Cobb
12,325	Madry, Mary	Floyd
474	Maeger, Richard	Cherokee
18,952	Magnus, Rebecca A. & minor children	Floyd
16,805	Mahan, Robert H.	Walker
13,812	Mallet, Sarah	Chattooga
20,424	Mallette, Lewis	Effingham
20,606	Mallory, George H.	Campbell
13,610	Maloney, Adam B.	Chattooga
8,378	Man, John A.	Clayton
20,600	Mangum, Lavinia	Fulton
35	Mann, Claiborne S.	Clayton
7,798	Mann, Elizabeth	Clayton
11,766	Mann, Jno. E.	Liberty
14,871	Mann, Richard P.	Butts
13,070	Mann, Young & Jackson, Tyler	Gordon
3,274	Mann, Zachariah	Clayton
4,066	Manswell, Samuel	Cherokee
18,653	Mansfield, Patrick	Bartow
2,029	Marchman, Wiley G.	Carroll
18,223	Marell, John R.	Chatham
14,581	Margraf, Margaret	Chatham
4,868	Marion, Wm. J.	Chattooga
4,344	Markham, Timothy	Muscogee
20,503	Markham, Wm.	Fulton
7,937	Marlow, Anna	Paulding
20,682	Marshall, Andrew & Way, Linden	Liberty
20,677	Marshall, Morris	Chatham
2,245	Martin, Ambry	Milton
368	Martin, Anderson	Cass
9,872	Martin, Catharine	Floyd
3,336	Martin, Cornelius G.	Henry
7,702	Martin, Elisah	Gwinnett
20,067	Martin, Geo. A.	Fulton
5,460	Martin, Nancy C.	Floyd
388	Martin, Robert	Floyd
3,563	Martin, Robert	Milton
2,937	Martin, Sarah	DeKalb
6,074	Martin, Stanwix H.	Murray
8,599	Mason, Austin	Union
8,847	Mason, Martha	DeKalb
5,021	Massey, Nathan	Fulton
2,817	Massingill, Aaron G.	Gordon
2,868	Master, James	Whitfield
14,019	Mastick, Henry	Chatham
6,200	Mathews, Hester A.	Campbell
2,896	Mathis, Frank P.	Gordon
4,010	Matthews, Fielding F.	Upson
6,665	Matthews, Geo. W.	DeKalb
7,291	Matthews, James	Whitfield
2,263: 17,514:	Mattox, James	Walker
18,646	Mauldin, Andrew	Murray
7,157	Mauldin, Drury	DeKalb
15,073	Mauldin, Miller D.	Fulton
547	Maxwell, Emberson	Catoosa
2,848	Maxwell, J. P.	Bartow
21,404	Maxwell, James	Liberty
20,680	Maxwell, Prince	Liberty
20,678	Maxwell, Samuel	Liberty
6,002	May, Joseph B.	Glascock
10,191	May, Pryor	Union
15,764	May, Thos.	Floyd
10,995	May, Wm. H.	Chatham
4,000	Mays, James M.	Pike
11,204	Mays, Richard	Fulton
7,227	McAbee, Barnett G.	Floyd
5,478	McBride, Thos.	Emanuel
22,018	McBryde, Jno. T.	Talbot
7,576	McCalpin, Elizabeth	DeKalb
7,575	McCalpin, Floyd T.	DeKalb
325	McCarson, Wm. G.	Whitfield
12,309	McCarter, Rebecca	Floyd
12,264	McCarttey, Michael D.	Chatham
322: 338:	McCauley, Chelsea	Whitfield
14,022	McCay, James	Bartow
18,650	McClain, C. P.	Cobb
7,419	McClain, James W.	DeKalb
7,183	McClarty, Alexander	Cobb
10,969	McClellan, Wm.	Fulton
21,148	McCleod, Mary A.	Cobb
7,109	McClung, Thornton M.	Paulding
1,224	McClure, Robert	Cherokee
7,308	McCluskey, Hugh	Clayton
6,445	McCollum, Joab	Dade
15,077	McCollum, Joseph	Rockdale
500	McCombs, Wm. S.	Baldwin
20,681	McConnell, Geo.	Liberty
18,874	McConnell, Jno. M.	Chattooga
7,378	McConnell, Joseph A.	Clayton
1,227	McConnell, Peter	Cherokee
11,665	McConnell, Tilford	Gwinnett
8,276	McConnell, Wm. N.	Clayton
6,196	McCool, Andrew P.	Fulton
14,822	McCormick, Wm.	Chatham
4,185	McCoy, Daniel	Baldwin
7,481	McCoy, Julia M.	Chattooga
4,184	McCoy, Wm.	Baldwin
8,427	McCrary, Ezra	Warren

7,795	McCrary, Martha	Clayton	125	Meldrim, Ralph	Chatham
14,864	McCrory, Leroy B.	Talbot	6,475	Meloney, Robert	DeKalb
14,863	McCrory, W. H.	Talbot	18,949	Merchant, John R.	Fulton
7,420	McCullar, Jno. W.	Wilkinson	7,423	Meredith, Celia	Wilkinson
7,854	McCullough, Ruth P.	Henry	10,617	Meredith, James	Butts
2,481	McCurdy, George T.	Whitfield	8,838	Merkerson, Epsey	Whitfield
405	McCurdy, John N.	Whitfield	7,482	Meroney, Wm.	Chattooga
12,318	McCurry, Elizabeth C.	Floyd	5,383	Merriwether, David, Estate of	Jasper
17,300	McCutchen, Benj.	Whitfield	7,894	Metcalf, Wm. F.	DeKalb
19,838	McCutchen, Robert B.	Pickens	12,803	Methodist Church, African	Cobb
10,624	McDaniel, Lucy A.	Carroll	14,582	Metzger, Geo. L.	Effingham
4,502	McDaniel, Sarah B.	Spalding	14,817	Metzger, Moses	Effingham
6,545	McDonald, Alexander	Clayton	502	Middlebrook, Hiram	Muscogee
18,970	McDonald, Daniel	McIntosh	4,018	Middlebrook, James M.	Upson
2,846	McDonald, Jane M.	Bartow	6,624	Middlebrook, Levi N.	Upson
1,232	McDonald, Mary	Bartow	6,877	Middleton, Hollis	Chattooga
119	McDonald, Rachel M.	Bartow	18,454	Middleton, Major	Chatham
7,797	McDonald, Sarah E.	Fulton	20,084	Middleton, Simon	Chatham
14,919	McDow, Samuel	Bartow	21,437	Miflin, James	Liberty
14,920	McDow, Wm.	Bartow	5,161	Miles, Henry	Clayton
14,921	McDurment, John W.	Bartow	7,484	Milican, Andrew	Chattooga
18,214	McElpin, Aaron	Chatham	541	Miller, Ambrose E.	Catoosa
2,816	McElrath, Joseph P.	Gordon	3,430	Miller, Clayton	Gordon
7,155	McElroy, Arch'd	DeKalb	3,332	Miller, E. A., Mrs.	Gordon
8,273	McElroy, Martha, Estate of	Clayton	7,426	Miller, Henry G. H.	DeKalb
14,320	McElroy, Sarah	Campbell	18,455	Miller, James	Chatham
7,292	McElroy, Margaret M.	DeKalb	20,679	Miller, James	Liberty
9,303	McFarlane, Thomas	Chatham	20,834	Miller, James P.	Talbot
6,431	McGaff, Edward L.	Fulton	18,092	Miller, Jane	Chatham
15,102	McGee, Hugh B.	Floyd	3,068	Miller, Jonathan	Baldwin
1,155	McGee, James	Bartow	15,271	Miller, Lewis	Chatham
20,952	McGert, Hector	Bryan	7,425	Miller, Mark	Gwinnett
404	McGill, Hugh M.	Whitfield	16,366	Miller, Martin	Chatham
4,487	McGinnis, Barbara	Gordon	6,735	Miller, Mary S.	Jasper
11,378	McGority, Solomon S.	Paulding	18,094	Miller, Peter	Chatham
16,533	McGowin, E. A.	Laurens	3,923	Miller, Sally	Chatham
7,701	McGuffey, Charles	Gwinnett	1,311	Miller, Samuel	Whitfield
13,436	McGuire, Green M.	Carroll	7,428	Miller, Sarah	Whitfield
15,270	McGuire, Rosanna	Chatham	2,482	Miller, Thomas R.	Whitfield
3,597	McHan, Alanson	Pickens	2,591	Miller, Wm.	Gordon
339	McHan, T. M. I.	Whitfield	7,427	Miller, Wm. W.	Wilkinson
3,765	McIntire, Philip	Fulton	2,872	Millerous, Rebecca	Whitfield
114	McIntire, Robert	Chatham	4,254	Millholland, Jas.	DeKalb
18,121	McIntosh, Matilda	Liberty	12,339	Millicen, Charles F.	Floyd
21,418	McIver, Lucy	Liberty	18,220	Mills, Baccus	Liberty
15,642	McIver, Samuel	Chatham	3,598	Mills, H. M.	Chattooga
6,609	McIver, Saml.	Liberty	2,920	Milner, J. P.	Spalding
18,113	McIver, Wm. M.	Liberty	3,393	Milwee, John, Heirs of	Bartow
20,794	McKay, Jno. B.	Hall	11,804	Mims, Azariah	Campbell
7,421	McKay, Sina	Wilkinson	3,276	Mims, Wm. D.	Clayton
4,322	McKee, Martin Copel	DeKalb	7,159	Minor, Andrew J.	Gwinnett
9,411	McKeehan, Job	Chattooga	7,424	Minor, George W.	Gwinnett
4,501	McKensie, Samuel	Polk	7,895	Minor, Jno. R.	DeKalb
4,501	McKenzie, Samuel	Floyd	7,158	Minor, Mark H.	DeKalb
7,602	McKinne, John	Emanuel	19,085	Minton, Eliza J.	Cherokee
16,678	McLoud, Samuel	Chatham	19,723	Minton, John P.	Cherokee
13,873	McMahan, Robert	Butts	14,207	Mira, Anthony F.	Chatham
2,452	McMahan, Thomas	Bartow	21,009	Mitchell, Henry M, Estate of	Decatur
16,200	McMaster, Isabella	Fulton	323	Mitchell, James C.	Whitfield
7,563	McMillen, James	Clayton	7,429	Mitchell, Louisa	DeKalb
730	McMurray, Margaret J.	Bartow	8,284	Mitchell, Mary	Walker
2,480	McNair, Price	Catoosa	7,799	Mitchell, Mary A.	Douglas
1,028	McPeck, Aley	Clayton	7,184	Mitchell, Mary G.	Douglas
11,202	McTier, Amanda	Bartow	7,639	Mitchell, Samuel, Estate of	Pike
5,158	McVicker, James	Clayton	3,298	Mitchell, Thomas	Clayton
9,508	McWilliams, Alexander,		15,892	Mitchell, Thomas B.	Whitfield
	Estate of	Campbell	707	Mitchell, Thomas W.	Bryan
9,709	McWilliams, Catharine	Clayton	17,218	Mitchell, Warren	Chatham
6,222	McWilliams, David	Campbell	21,265	Mitchell, Wm. A.	Fulton
6,190	McWilliams, John	Campbell	6,160	Moates, Hillery F.	Campbell
6,221:	McWilliams, Robert	Campbell	12,537	Mobley, Fleming	Spalding
6,228:			13,616	Mobley, Saml.	Floyd
6,215	McWilliams, Wm.	Campbell	21,741	Monroe, Crawford	Fulton
11,390	Means, Wm. H.	Cobb	3,953	Monroe, John	Chatham
15,572	Meddlebrooks, Alfred	Monroe	3,945	Monroe, Murray	Chatham
6,638	Meeker, N. C.	McIntosh	13,599	Montgomery, Barkley	Floyd
12,214	Meeks, Nancy J.	Floyd	6,666	Montgomery, Ransom	Fulton
16,401	Mehrtens, Henry C.	Chatham	2,895	Montgomery, Robert S.	Bartow
15,859	Mehrtens, Jno. R.	Chatham	5,184	Moody, Jno. S.	Paulding
18,739	Mehrtens, Ludu, Estate of	Chatham	7,703	Moon, Joseph	Walton

4,396	Mooney, Horace G.	Floyd
7,485	Moore, Andrew J.	Chattooga
8,011	Moore, Ann	Cherokee
16,005	Moore, Charles, Estate of	Whitfield
918	Moore, Churchwell T.	Gordon
9,385	Moore, Elizabeth B. D.	Cherokee
7,800	Moore, Ezekiel P.	Clayton
3,273	Moore, Hilliard I.	Clayton
16,793	Moore, John	Walker
6,175	Moore, Richard	Campbell
5,160	Moore, Sanford	Coweta
15,109	Moore, Sarah	Floyd
2,163	Moore, Thomas	Clayton
4,221	Moore, Wm. C.	Fulton
16,794	Moore, William D.	Walker
16,479	Moorland, James S.	Catoosa
4,546	Mooty, Alexander	Heard
5,159	Moran, Nancy	Clayton
13,365	Mordic, Ed & Hicks, Jacob	Chatham
16,767	Morehead, Eugene	Chatham
16,025	Morgan, Andrew J.	Catoosa
7,339	Morgan, Ephraim H.	Bartow
7,340	Morgan, Henry	Cherokee
6,880	Morgan, Joseph D.	Polk
7,386	Morgan, P. N.	Chattooga
12,640	Morgan, R. A.	Dade
17,844	Morrell, Ann Ellen	Chatham
2,483	Morris, Catharine	Murray
12,026	Morris, Christopher C.	Douglas
3,333	Morris, Elizabeth	Whitfield
3,337	Morris, Francis A.	Henry
12,340	Morris, Gad	Floyd
4,067	Morris, Isaac	Cherokee
7,642	Morris, J. M., Estate of	Pike
6,456	Morris, James B.	Clayton
7,309	Morris, Joseph T., Estate of	Fulton
15,104	Morris, Margaret	Floyd
1,032	Morris, Richard	Henry
15,108	Morris, Thaddeus	Floyd
2,370	Morris, Wm.	Milton
5,890	Morrison, James	Pickens
7,486	Morrison, Reuben	Chattooga
5,377	Morrow, Isaac	Bartow
16,365	Morton, Silas, Estate of	Scriven
15,882	Morton, Simeon L.	Scriven
15,448	Moses, David	Chatham
20,776	Moshell, Jacob H.	Muscogee
18,972	Moss, Christopher C.	Newton
13,605	Moss, Flemmon	Chattooga
3,651	Moss, J. L.	Gordon
6,457	Moss, Joshua	Pickens
16,637	Mosteller, Andrew	Chattooga
3,600	Mosteller, Jeremiah	Milton
6,067	Mostelly, George	Walker
10,445	Moxley, Benj. A.	Emanuel
5,479	Moxley, Martha R.	Emanuel
5,597	Moxley, Miriah	Emanuel
6,218	Mozeley, Miles S.	Douglas
3,599	Mozley, I. J.	Douglas
11,432	Mulkey, Mary I.	Floyd
10,288	Muller, Jno. N.	Chatham
3,674	Mullin, James	Fulton
4,961	Mullinax, Isaac	Pickens
3,106	Munday, E. W.	Fulton
14,952	Mundorf, Frederick	Chatham
21,432	Munroe, Jacob	Liberty
21,428	Munroe, Saml.	Liberty
7,387	Murdock, David	Chattooga
7,422	Murkison, Mary A.	Wilkinson
11,966	Murphey, Elizabeth	Fayette
11,967	Murphey, Jane	Fayette
16,029	Murphy, James L.	Chatham
1,033	Murphy, Lemuel M.	Clayton
19,905	Murphy, Millege	Jefferson
18,216	Murray, Charles	Chatham
19,941	Murray, Henry	Muscogee
328	Murray, John N.	Whitfield
19,766	Murray, Limerick	Effingham
12,539	Muselwhite, Luzana P.	Cobb
5,663	Myers, Henry	Scriven

375	Nace, Jno. M.	Fulton
5,550	Nailor, Thomas	Whitfield
7,295	Nash, Abraham T.	Gwinnett
7,430	Nash, Joseph A.	Gwinnett
7,293	Nash, Larkin	DeKalb
7,283	Nash, Lewis	Gwinnett
7,855	Nash, Thompson E.	Clayton
5,384	Nasworthy, James, Estate of	Upson
12,561	Nations, Leah	Floyd
3,312	Neal, Adam	Chattooga
10,124	Neal, David, Eddie, Ernest, George B. & Julius	Warren
719	Neal, Wm.	Whitfield
4,512	Ned, Gabriel	Chatham
5,224	Needham, Whitley	DeKalb
7,704	Neely, Emil	Newton
20,958	Neidlinger, Charles W.	Effingham
20,957	Neidlinger, Samuel, Estate of	Effingham
14,350	Nelson, Andrew	Chatham
7,488	Nelson, Lydia C.	Chattooga
4,218	Nesbit, Mary K.	Gwinnett
14,922	Nevil, James B.	Bartow
10,892	Newmark, Meyer	Chatham
5,480	Newton, John L.	Emanuel
4,500	Newton, Lucinda	Bartow
6,755	Niblett, James H.	Jasper
6,753	Niblett, Tilman	Jasper
7,705	Nichols, Sarah	Gwinnett
6,547	Niles, Silvester	Campbell
17,574	Nichols, Charles W. & Mahala E.	Cobb
2,484	Nichols, F. H.	Forsyth
2,484	Nichols, Frank H.	Floyd
17,574	Nichols, Mahala E. & Charles W.	Cobb
7,978	Nicholson, Nathan'l	DeKalb
3,601	Nix, Jno.	Milton
7,160	Nix, Joseph T. O.	Rockdale
20,996	Noble, James, John, Samuel & Wm.	Floyd
13,583	Nobles, David	Floyd
14,171	Noblett, Isaac	Whitfield
7,706	Nolan, Isaac N.	DeKalb
13,397	Nolen, Edward G.	Butts
14,968	Nolen, James, Estate of	Newton
21,416	Norman, Rachel	Liberty
18,740	North, Margaret	Fulton
17,338	Northrop, Claudian, Estate of	Chatham
4,996	Norton, W. E.	Clayton
16,649	Nugent, Terence	Chatham
4,753	Nunny, Elizabeth	Chatham
15,174	Nuton, Ann	Chatham
15,687	O'Bannon, Bryant	Wilkinson
6,681	Obannon, Jno. B.	Chattooga
1,737	O'Barr, Robert, Sr.	Floyd
1,312	O'Dell, Wm.	Whitfield
5,481	Oglesby, John	Emanuel
16,704	Oelrich, Peter H. & Jetzen, Jno. H.	Fulton
14,328	Ohl, Joseph	Chatham
7,939	Oliver, James	Fulton
6,182	Oliver, Pleny R.	Fulton
7,802	Oliver, Sanford C.	Campbell
16,619	Olmstead, Susan C.	Chatham
17,624	Opie, Wm. F.	Scriven
2,485	Orr, David	Catoosa
4,186	Osborn, James	Hancock
21,435	Osgood, Saml.	Liberty
17,687	O'Steen, Mary	Chatham
13,079	Oswalt, Rhoda Ann	Floyd
13,877	Ott, George	Chatham
7,801	Otto, Rebecca M.	Fulton
10,274	Owen, George A.	Paulding
18,776	Owen, George A. & Brown, Arnold O.	Paulding
1,061	Owen, Glen	Monroe
1,062	Owen, Newton	Monroe
18,095	Owens, Anthony	Chatham
7,489	Owings, Matthew	Chattooga
16,986	Oxforn, Jonathan	Monroe

3,271	Ozburn, John M.	Clayton
4,516	Pace, Drewry W.	Henry
20,065	Pace, Hardry, Estate of	Cobb
5,023	Paden, James W.	DeKalb
6,467	Padgett, Wiley J.	Douglas
7,707	Palmer, Elijah	Walton
14,392	Pannal, E. J.	Jefferson
7,134	Parker, David	DeKalb
8,713	Parker, James	Fulton
11,467	Parker, John H.	Chatham
7,432	Parker, Jno. T.	Wilkinson
18,641	Parker, Lemuel M.	Paulding
7,161	Parker, Maria	DeKalb
6,224	Parker, Martha S.	Campbell
18,922	Parker, Mary A.	Fulton
7,940	Parker, Mary K.	Clayton
6,243	Parker, Sally	Wilkinson
5,447	Parker, Wm. C.	Fulton
1,937	Parker, Wm. H.	Chatham
4,009	Parker, Wm. H.	Pike
7,490	Parks, Elizabeth	Chattooga
8,896	Parks, Gabriel	Monroe
6,425	Parmelee, Perry S.	Spalding
4,476	Parris, Peter	Fannin
8,714	Parsons, Richard	Fulton
4,133	Partin, Berry W.	Paulding
13,615	Partin, Mary Ann	Floyd
15,128	Partlow, Jno.	Gordon
10,513	Partridge, Robert F.	Upson
1,261	Pass, Jno. J.	Gordon
3,603	Pass, Romulus	Floyd
7,431	Passmore, Pheriba	Wilkinson
18,401	Pate, Charles R.	Milton
5,162	Pate, James M.	Clayton
1,016	Patillo, Benj. F.	Henry
1,009	Patillo, James E. F.	Henry
1,025	Patillo, Jno. R. J.	Henry
1,360	Paxson, James A.	Whitfield
1,359	Paxson, John F.	Whitfield
12,332	Payne, Obadiah E.	Floyd
15,110	Payne, Wm.	Floyd
15,479	Payne, Wm. H.	Butts
480	Payne, Silas K.	Cherokee
7,433	Payton, Randolph	DeKalb
6,213	Peacock, Lewis P.	Fulton
6,186	Peacock, Merit J.	Campbell
13,087	Peal, Josiah	Floyd
10,882	Pearce, Elizabeth B.	Floyd
13,982	Pearson, Elisha	Chatham
4,584	Pearson, Malinda A.	Monroe
5,024	Pekerson, Dempsy	DeKalb
6,207	Perkerson, George W.	Cobb
7,185	Perkerson, Martha F.	Cobb
15,866	Perkins, Wm. H.	Chatham
7,491	Perry, Oscar F.	Chattooga
832	Persall, Jno.	Newton
5,736	Persons, Pinkney	Monroe
5,826	Petty, Susan J.	Paulding
18,876	Pharr, Samuel	Chattooga
13,097	Phelps, Aquilla, Estate of	Floyd
12,338	Phelps, Thos. H.	Floyd
334	Philips, E. Caney	Walker
626	Philips, George W.	Baldwin
17,639	Philips, James, Estate of	DeKalb
17,640	Philips, Jno. W.	DeKalb
17,641	Philips, Paschal C.	DeKalb
9,086	Phillips, Elmira	Bullock
17,517	Phillips, John	Walker
12,373	Phillips, Jno. L.	Spalding
7,916	Phillips, Jno. W.	Butts
11,382	Phillips, Sarah	Fulton
13,389	Phillips, Wm.	Butts
7,917	Phillips, Wm. P.	Spalding
15,127	Phillips, Wm. W.	Floyd
1,721	Phillips, Wineford	Washington
7,708	Pierce, Geo. W.	DeKalb
7,434	Pierce, James	DeKalb
1,263	Pierson, Wm.	Gordon
1,939	Pike, Jesse P.	Walker
5,025	Pinnell, Richard	DeKalb
15,121	Pinson, Elijah	Bartow
18,973	Piper, Gabriel M.	Newton
12,691: 13,382:	Pittman, Nancy E.	Gordon
6,731	Pitts, Carrington	Jasper
22,136	Pitts, Elizabeth A.	Effingham
2,104	Pitts, Jesse L.	Cherokee
7,826	Pitts, Jno. W.	Newton
14,674	Pitts, Nestor	Newton
20,512	Pitts, Wm.	Cherokee
15,031	Pleasant Grove Church	Catoosa
7,492	Pledger, Elizabeth T.	Chattooga
7,494	Plowman, Matilda	Chattooga
6,882	Poe, S. J.	Walker
19,906	Polhill, F. A.	Jefferson
20,684	Polite, Boston	Liberty
20,953	Polite, Harry	Chatham
20,955	Polite, James B.	Chatham
4,039: 13,930:	Ponder, Geo. F.	Morgan
2,486	Ponder, John	Whitfield
18,601	Ponder, Prince	Fulton
5,026	Pool, Benj. J.	Fulton
6,611	Pooler, Dora	Chatham
7,995	Pope, Daniel	Cherokee
17,804	Pope, John R.	Carroll
7,803	Pope, Martha I.	Carroll
10,978	Pope, Thos. T.	Fulton
18,286	Poppell, Susan	McIntosh
8,895	Porch, Elizabeth A.	Monroe
20,650	Porter, Abraham	Chatham
21,804	Porter, Amanda	Effingham
22,133	Porter, Benj. C.	Effingham
18,544	Porter, Clarinda	Liberty
22,134	Porter, Edward B.	Effingham
20,683: 21,417:	Porter, Harry	Liberty
21,433	Porter, Plenty	Liberty
6,455	Potts, Francis S.	Pickens
5,573	Pound, Jno. G.	Fulton
7,435	Pounds, Richard D.	Gwinnett
10,005	Pounds, Wm. N.	DeKalb
16,999	Powell, Daniel H.	Chatham
18,602	Powell, George	Liberty
17,572	Powell, Gree O.	Walker
3,768	Powell, Jno. A.	DeKalb
6,005	Powell, Levina	Glascock
17,570	Powell, Sevier	Walker
15,833	Power, Edward	Chatham
4,962	Presley, Jacob M.	Pickens
18,621	Presett, Guilford	Paulding
18,644	Prewett, James W., Estate of	Paulding
18,617	Prewett, Joel R.	Paulding
8,709	Prewett, Jno. R.	Towns
18,549	Price, Martha	Burke
16,477	Prichard, Henry	Whitfield
13,383	Prichett, William	Whitfield
6,162	Prickett, George W.	Cobb
1,023	Prickett, Martha	Henry
12,218	Prime, Sanford	Dade
9,498	Prince, Mary M.	Fulton
4,608	Pringle, Patience	Monroe
3,511	Prosser, Mary	Baldwin
16,028	Prudden, Sidney C.	Putnam
15,078	Puckett, Green	Newton
5,482	Pugsley, Robert J.	Emanuel
3,070	Pulley, James H.	Baldwin
3,606	Purdy, Clark J.	Dawson
8,013	Pursell, Benk.	Cherokee
4,869	Pursley, James M.	Chattooga
12,317	Quarles, Geo. B.	Floyd
21,409	Quarterman, Charlotte	Liberty
21,426	Quarterman, Edward	Liberty
21,420	Quarterman, Gus	Liberty
21,465	Quarterman, Jacob	Liberty
20,686: 21,471:	Quarterman, Malbro	Liberty
20,687	Quarterman, Mingo	Liberty
21,421	Quarterman, Moses	Liberty
21,461	Quarterman, Ned	Liberty

20,008	Quarterman, Thomas W.	Liberty
7,805	Quick, Martha	Fulton
1,738	Quinn, Wm.	Floyd
11,469	Ragland, Eve, Estate of	Upson
7,495	Ragland, Sarah	Chattooga
9,502	Ragsdale, Wm. P.	Troup
3,948	Rhan, Thomas	Chatham
11,911	Raiford, Hamilton	Jefferson
3,608	Rainwater, Jno. M.	Milton
3,607	Rainwater, Lacy D.	Milton
8,890	Ralls, Jno. R.	Monroe
7,641	Ralls, Wm. O.	Monroe
6,066	Ramsey, David R.	Chattooga
16,035	Ramsey, Jno. C. B. & Mahaley	Fulton
16,035	Ramsey, Mahaley & Jno. C. B.	Fulton
8,735	Randall, Lucy A.	Jefferson
11,744	Ranis, Webster M.	Bibb
7,436	Rannals, Jno.	Gwinnett
6,072	Ranney, Wm. P.	Walker
16,716	Ransom, Washington	Walker
14,422	Rawlings, Elenor	Walker
2,006	Rawlins, Nicholas	Floyd
7,709	Rawlins, Peter	Gwinnett
9,501	Ray, Arabella C.	Fulton
1,262	Ray, Elisha, Estate of	Gordon
2,630	Ray, Emanuel	Cobb
7,806	Read, Frederick	Clayton
14,384	Read, Geo. W.	Walker
14,283	Reardon, Dennis	Chatham
4,015	Reaves, Benj. F.	Monroe
1,049	Reaves, Wm. L.	Hancock
17,301	Rede, Mitchell	Whitfield
2,965	Redwine, Mary A.	Whitfield
5,574	Reedy, Wm.	Talbot
9,503	Reese, John W.	Carroll
5,772	Reese, Tabitha W., Estate of	Jasper
3,340	Reeves, Aquilla	Carroll
13,112	Reeves, Frank	DeKalb
15,401	Reid, Mary W.	Whitfield
17,120	Reid, Thomas W.	Cobb
2,813	Rell, Jno. M.	Gordon
21,402	Repley, Harry	Liberty
5,147	Reynolds, Edward W.	Campbell
6,069	Reynolds, James M. C.	Walker
11,433	Reynolds, Jane G.	Floyd
546	Rhodes, Wesley	Catoosa
4,068	Rhyme, Jacob S.	Cherokee
17,140	Rials, Skip	Effingham
12,571	Rice, Fleming	Floyd
608	Rice, Wiley	Fulton
656	Rice, Wm. H.	Fulton
5,487	Rich, Andrew J.	Emanuel
15,831	Rich, Augustus and Christina C.	Floyd
5,485	Rich, Danl. E.	Emanuel
5,488	Rich, Joseph A.	Emanuel
5,486	Rich, Stephen E.	Emanuel
11,394	Richards, Angeline M.	Carroll
347	Richards, Joshua	Whitfield
101	Richards, Reuben	Gordon
5,697	Richardson, E. H.	Polk
5,483	Richardson, Elizabeth	Emanuel
6,073	Richardson, Frances	Walker
5,555	Richardson, John M.	Whitfield
5,554	Richardson, Lewis	Whitfield
6,071	Richardson, Robert J.	Walker
13,587	Richardson, Robert W.	Floyd
17,562	Richardson, Samuel C.	Chatham
5,556	Richardson, Wm., Estate of	Whitfield
5,484	Richardson, Viney	Emanuel
2,246	Ridling, Anna A.	DeKalb
17,142	Rielley, James	Effingham
15,214	Riesser, Christopher F.	Effingham
4,321	Riley, Susan M.	Henry
12,697	Riley, Thomas G.	Richmond
15,188	Rinehart, Lewis	Chattooga
18,130	Ring, Peter	Camden
12,486	Rivers, Benj.	Jasper
16,230	Rivers, Joseph	Floyd
5,124	Rivers, Thos. R.	Pike

5,163	Rivers, Wm. J.	Clayton
581	Rivers, Wm. M.	Henry
4,006	Riviere, H. S.	Pike
16,738	Roach, Peter	Wilkinson
17,651	Roachford, Henry	Chatham
6,006	Robbins, Mary	Glascock
15,745	Robbs, James	Chattooga
17,652	Roberts, Adela	Chatham
20,688	Roberts, Amy	Liberty
4,844	Roberts, Asa	Paulding
21,467	Roberts, Caesar, Estate of	Liberty
5,601	Robert, Eli	Emanuel
5,028	Roberts, Green B.	Fulton
2,870	Roberts, James	Whitfield
4,397	Roberts, Jno. H.	Floyd
13,406	Roberts, Michael A.	Butts
13,524	Roberts, S. D.	Walker
17,807	Roberts, Thos. N.	Carroll
20,690	Roberts, Wm.	Liberty
18,607	Roberts, Wm. (Riceboro), col'd.	Liberty
2,801	Robertson, Bennett	Gordon
5,724	Robertson, Eliza	Gordon
20,915	Robider, Beatrix	Chatham
16,026	Robinson, Eli	Catoosa
8,915	Robinson, J. M.	Carroll
17,175	Robinson, James C.	Walton
7,896	Robinson, Joseph	DeKalb
12,694	Robinson, Levinah	DeKalb
4,409	Robinson, Morrill M.	Fulton
10,934	Robinson, Moses	Cherokee
8,232	Robson, Elizabeth W.	Monroe
2,629	Robson, Richard	Cobb
5,027	Rodgers, Andrew	DeKalb
939	Roe, Jno.	Chattooga
3,609	Roger, Benj. P.	Campbell
7,437	Rogers, Elizabeth	Wilkinson
16,095	Rogers, James H.	Walker
5,557	Rogers, Jno. L.	Whitfield
12,213	Rogers, Joseph J. B. W.	Floyd
12,569	Rogers, Mary	Floyd
10,225	Romback, Kate *et al*	Chatham
16,006	Rose, Charles E.	Chatham
15,867	Rose, Judy	Chatham
7,135	Rose, Sarah F.	Fulton
3,999	Rose, Thomas E.	Upson
10,702	Ross, Currell	Baldwin
9,136	Ross, John	Baldwin
7,496	Rounsavall, Gracy	Chattooga
6,332	Rountree, Elizabeth	Clayton
78	Rowan, Geo. W.	Henry
21,746	Rowland, Ida F.	Morgan
3,611	Rucker, Wm. D.	Milton
18,098	Runnels, Wm.	Chatham
12,346	Rush, Jno.	Floyd
5,002	Rushin, James	Bladwin
17,139	Russel, Allen	Chatham
15,766	Russell, Andrew R.	Floyd
15,090	Russell, David R.	Talbot
16,484	Russell, Jacob B.	Catoosa
15,091	Russell, Jno. R.	Talbot
6,058	Russell, Nancy	Bartow
542	Russell, Thomas	Catoosa
17,824	Rutherford, Hugh J.	Walker
16,808	Rutherford, Wm.	Chatham
7,710	Rutledge, Alexander W.	Gwinnett
3,251	Rutledge, Benjamin E.	Bartow
7,296	Rutledge, Joseph S.	DeKalb
7,498	Rutledge, Mary	Chattooga
15,878	Rutledge, Phebe	Chatham
20,962	Rutledge, Washington	Chatham
17,871	Ryan, Michael	Chatham
7,162	Ryle, Matilda C.	Wilkinson
19,844	Rynehart, Wm.	Muscogee
2,867	Sailors, Jeremiah	Whitfield
15,112	Sale, Smith B.	Floyd
3,614: 15,499:	Salte, Wm.	Chatham
4,963	Samples, Phebe	Forsyth
4,144	Samples, Thomas C.	Forsyth

2,489	Sams, Parnesia	Whitfield
5,944	Sanders, King	Wilkinson
153	Sanders, Reuben	Bartow
6,453	Sandow, Jno.	Cherokee
3,612	Sarratt, Ellender	Milton
18,557	Saunders, Saml. F.	Bullock
13,461	Saunders, Thomas J.	Butts
6,476	Saunders, Thomas M.	DeKalb
14,163	Savage, Thos., Estate of	Fulton
9,574	Sawyer, Wm.	Pickens
9,558	Say, Mary A.	Cherokee
5,164	Scales, Edney	Fayette
17,297	Scales, Wm. F. I.	Whitfield
1,024	Scarborough, Thomas	Henry
11,174	Sconyen, Jane B.	Chatham
5,492	Scott, Brettain	Emanuel
10,883	Scott, Jno.	Floyd
935	Scott, M. M.	Gordon
10,985	Scott, Mary A.	Cobb
2,295	Scott, Sarah F.	Bartow
2,949	Scott, Wm. H.	Milton
6,550	Scroggans, Nancy	Cobb
14,760	Seale, Richard J.	Milton
6,001	Seals, John D.	Glascock
21,508	Seay, John	Jackson
835	Sebastion, Edward	Gordon
1,498	Seibly, Peter M.	Floyd
5,029	Sells, Holmes	Fulton
7,310	Sewell, Asa	Campbell
12,540	Sewell, Isaac	Cobb
12,541	Sewell, Isaac P.	Cobb
7,809	Sewell, James P.	Fulton
7,311	Sewell, Mary	Campbell
4,250	Sewell, Susan C.	Chattooga
7,564	Shadrick, Nancy, Estate of	Clayton
5,165	Shadrick, Wm.	Clayton
4,591	Shahan, Ann M.	Walker
16,998	Sharger, Samuel	Walker
12,582	Sharman, Owen C.	Upson
7,438	Sharp, Jno. D.	DeKalb
6,333	Sharp, Wm. H., Estate of	Clayton
12,314	Sharpe, Joseph	Floyd
2,453	Shaw, Edmund J.	Bartow
1,814: 18,661:	Sheffield, Isham	Paulding
1,801	Sheffield, Josiah	Meriweather
14,284	Sheftall, Abraham	Chatham
6,610	Sheftall, Adam, Estate of	Chatham
3,924	Sheftall, J. B.	Chatham
16,701	Sheftall, Mordecai	Chatham
14,285	Sheftall, Solomon	Chatham
7,711	Shell, Daniel L.	Gwinnett
15,447	Shellman, Alfred & Fields, Henry	Chatham
20,022	Shelman, Albert	Chatham
3,950	Shelman, Simon	Chatham
20,015	Shepard, Chas. J.	Cobb
16,473	Shepherd, James R.	Whitfield
7,440	Sheppard, David M.	DeKalb
7,439	Sheppard, Wm.	DeKalb
16,790	Shields, James M.	Walker
548	Shields, Mary E.	Catoosa
15,402	Shira, Jacob P.	Whitfield
12,316	Shirley, Geo.	Floyd
15,598	Shockley, Jeptha J.	Floyd
12,341	Shoemaker, Mary E.	Floyd
3,163	Shropshire, Wesley	Chattooga
16,851	Shugart, Alfred	Gordon
7,442	Shumate, Benj. F.	DeKalb
16,194	Shumate, Berryman D.	Polk
7,443	Shumate, Francis F.	DeKalb
13,459	Shy, Carry F.	Jasper
1,940	Siler, Jesse P.	Walker
20,064	Silvey, Drewry H., Estate of	Fulton
20,587	Silvey, Jno.	Fulton
4,966	Simmons, A. A.	Walker
2,437	Simmons, Allen S.	Monroe
12,337	Simmons, Benj. R.	Floyd
6,841	Simmons, Elenor	Floyd
2,871	Simmons, Geo. W.	Whitfield
18,159	Simmons, Jno.	Cherokee
11,510	Simmons, Thomas G.	Liberty
9,294	Simmons, Thos. J.	Whitfield
9,298	Simms. Allen D.	Carroll
11,381	Simons, Jefferson	Fulton
3,944	Simons, Peter	Chatham
10,006	Simons, Stephen F.	DeKalb
21,401	Simpson, Isaac	Liberty
20,791	Simpson, Moses H.	Hall
7,712	Simpson, Wm. K.	Walton
6,883	Simpson, Wm. W.	Polk
1,642	Sims, Henry A.	Chattooga
8,376	Sims, Jesse G.	Chattooga
4,589	Sims, Louisa	Walker
3,289	Sims, Robert M.	Henry
792	Singleton, Luke E.	Gwinnett
2,487	Sinor, Geo.	Whitfield
13,015	Skelly, Thomas W., Estate of	Gordon
21,263	Skinner, Julius, Estate of	Bartow
14,243	Skipper, Edmond	Fulton
12,530	Slade, D. A.	Washington
924	Slaton, Zebudee	Gordon
14,944	Slaughter, Matilda	Butts
16,679	Slee, David	Chatham
16,346	Sloan, Ellis	Whitfield
3,942	Small, Guy	Chatham
3,931	Small, Sandy	Chatham
6,918	Smets, S. C. N.	Chatham
18,612	Smith, Abram, Estate of	Paulding
18,627	Smith, Allen	Paulding
6,152	Smith, Archibald M.	Clayton
4,498	Smith, Archibald M.	Wilkinson
12,209	Smith, Asahel R.	Floyd
21,457	Smith, Augustus	Liberty
16,799	Smith, Barclay M.	Whitfield
14,321	Smith, David	Campbell
20,693	Smith, Dennis	Bryan
18,603	Smith, Dennis	Chatham
1,988	Smith, Elijah	Bartow
5,166	Smith, Eliza	Clayton
5,738	Smith, Elizabeth	Monroe
6,206	Smith, Francis O.	Campbell
14,322	Smith, George	Campbell
1,690	Smith, Hampton	Milton
7,022	Smith, Hilliard J.	Newton
13,831	Smith, Isaac S.	Chattooga
9,766	Smith, J. H.	Walker
16,355	Smith, James	Liberty
335	Smith, James	Whitfield
7,164	Smith, James J. M.	DeKalb
20,533	Smith, James L.	Murray
4,710	Smith, James M.	Fulton
7,500	Smith, John	Chattooga
1,436	Smith, Jno. H.	Forsyth
77	Smith, John J.	Bartow
1,941	Smith, John M.	Walker
20,599	Smith, John N.	Campbell
7,441	Smith, Jno. N.	DeKalb
3,415	Smith, Jno. P.	Whitfield
5,223	Smith, Jno. S.	Fulton
6,236	Smith, Joseph	Dade
16,850	Smith, Jos.	Gordon
6,236	Smith, Joseph	Jackson
7,810	Smith, Joseph M.	Carroll
6,884	Smith, Julia A.	Walker
4,576	Smith, Lawrence	Pike
4,005	Smith, Levi	Pike
5,116	Smith, Levin J.	Baldwin
16,400	Smith, Madison	Chatham
1,385	Smith, Margaret	Carroll
4,486	Smith, Martha	Bartow
2,488	Smith, Melvin J.	Whitfield
1,015	Smith, Miles G.	Henry
3,295	Smith, Nathan W., Sen.	Clayton
16,774	Smith, Nath'l, Estate of	DeKalb
12,672	Smith, Patsey T.	Baldwin
2,950	Smith, Robert W.	Milton
20,692	Smith, Samuel	Chatham
3,284	Smith, Seaborn	Clayton
7,388	Smith, Thomas S.	Chattooga

5,120	Smith, Wesley F.	Monroe
5,490	Smith, White R.	Emanuel
6,465	Smith, Wm. J.	Newton
18,636	Smith, Wm. W.	Paulding
16,764	Smylie, James	Tatnall
3,927	Sneed, Joseph	Chatham
14,583	Snider, Christopher	Chatham
10,514	Snipes, Jno. T.	Upson
22,132	Snook, Rebecca S.	Effingham
7,165	Solomon, David	Wilkinson
11,399	Sorrells, Russel B.	Cobb
19,768	Soula, Caesar	Effingham
1,010	South, Jno.	Henry
11,913	Spann, James O.	Jefferson
8,600	Sparger, Elizabeth	Walker
14,020	Spears, Wm.	Chatham
10,515	Speer, Guilford	Upson
1,223	Speights, Emily	Baldwin
14,954	Spieldock, Leopold	Chatham
1,034	Spence, James	Clayton
5,489	Spence, Jno. A.	Emanuel
18,115: 21,440:	Spencer, Jno.	Liberty
16,268	Spencer, Lydia	Chatham
21,484	Spencer, Stephen	Liberty
16,136	Spinks, Susannah	Whitfield
21,442	Stacy, Andrew	Liberty
18,604	Stacy, James	Liberty
2,456	Stafford, Alvis	Pike
4,023	Stafford, Anderton W.	Pike
21,962	Stafford, Robert	Camden
16,757	Staley, Jno. A.	Chatham
8,885	Stallings, Jno. W., Estate of	Monroe
3,338	Stallings, Simeon N.	Newton
13,993	Stamm, A. Bernard	Chatham
2,989	Stancel, Jane	Gordon
4,069	Stancil, Cader B.	Cherokee
17,345	Standfield, Paul J.	Liberty
8,827	Standley, Rickels S.	Fannin
1,254	Stansell, Jason W.	Whitfield
1,265	Stanton, Robert S.	Rockdale
4,345	Stapler, Equilla	Muscogee
6,548	Starnes, Joel	Fulton
3,385	Steadman, Wm.	Bartow
18,126	Steckenger, Thomas E.	Effingham
16,979	Steel, Wm.	Chatham
229	Steele, Alexander	Chatham
3,212	Steelman, Nathan M.	Haralson
3,618	Steen, George	Cobb
7,163	Stell, James D.	Rockdale
21,419	Stencil, Stephen	Liberty
13,098	Stephens, Absalom	Floyd
7,188	Stephens, Curren P.	Clayton
14,424	Stephens, Hezekiah D.	Dade
20,027	Stephens, Jesse, Estate of	Walker
3,773	Stephens, Lewis	DeKalb
16,175	Stephens, Nancy	Jefferson
7,312	Stephens, Simeon	Clayton
7,808	Stephens, Uriah	Fulton
4,709	Stephens, Wm. H.	Fulton
6,462	Stephenson, Martha	DeKalb
3,261	Stevens, Charles, Estate of	Chatham
16,176	Stevens, David	Haralson
21,476	Stevens, David	Liberty
17,573	Stevens, Gallatin	Dade
8,619	Stevens, H. J.	Fulton
20,694	Stevens, Hagar	Liberty
21,468	Stevens, Henry (Midway Church)	Liberty
20,695	Stevens, Henry (New Hope)	Liberty
9,551	Stevens, James (Gordon)	Wilkinson
13,689	Stevens, James (Irwinton)	Wilkinson
15,288	Stevens, James (Toomsboro)	Wilkinson
12,542	Stevens, Jos. G.	Liberty
18,221	Stevens, Prince	Chatham
20,696	Stevens, Prince	Liberty
21,403	Stevens, Robt.	Liberty
2,803	Stevens, Simeon	Gordon
21,445	Stevens, Solomon	Liberty
21,411	Stevens, Windsor	Liberty
21,423	Stevens, York	Liberty
2,849	Stevenson, John R.	Bartow
8,613	Stewart, Abram	Chatham
237	Stewart, Edward A.	Whitfield
4,312	Stewart, George, Estate of	Spalding
922	Stewart, Henry, Estate of	Gordon
2,802	Stewart, Jno.	Gordon
10,498	Stewart, John F.	Henry
3,683	Stewart, Joseph	DeKalb
18,114	Stewart, Moses	Liberty
7,189	Stewart, Nancy	Douglas
20,697	Stewart, Prince	Liberty
18,630	Stewart, Samuel N.	Paulding
20,691	Stewart, Somerset	Liberty
3,951	Stewart, Thomas	Chatham
7,499	Stewart, Wm.	Chattooga
21,314	Stibbs, Agnes J.	Chatham
17,563	Stikes, Moses, and Butler, Binah	Chatham
13,401	Stodghill, Justina A.	Butts
950	Stokes, Amelia	Chatham
32	Stone, Amherst W.	Chatham
738	Stone, Thomas L.	Bartow
8,285	Stout, Daniel	Walker
7,501	Stout, Martha Jo.	Chattooga
6,454	Stover, James	Pickens
3,431	Strain, Wm. L.	Gordon
15,182	Strange, Amos. A.	Chattooga
1,640	Strange, Little Berry	Chattooga
15,748	Strange, Lorenzo L.	Effingham
8,215	Strauss, Berry	Chatham
14,971	Strauss, Peter	Chatham
3,288	Strickland, Caney	Clayton
3,281	Strickland, Charles P.	Clayton
4,146	Strickland, Gincey	Forsyth
14,607	Strickland, Jno. M.	Carroll
7,811	Strickland, Roswell	Douglas
7,190	Strickland, Wm. C.	Cobb
21,786	Strong, Charles, Estate of	Newton
5,491	Stroud, Thomas	Emanuel
366	Sugton, John W.	Bartow
364	Sugton, Nathaniel F.	Bartow
2,454	Sugton, Philip J.	Bartow
19,444	Sullivan, Christopher	Fulton
7,941	Sullivan, Julia	Clayton
19,632	Sullivan, David B.	Cobb
5,493	Summer, Alexander	Johnson
13,080	Summerhill, Sanford	Floyd
19,087	Summerlin, Jacob	Liberty
12,303	Summers, Solomon	Floyd
18,122	Summersall, Elizabeth	Liberty
4,928	Summerville, Sarah	Bartow
5,494	Sumner, Richard	Emanuel
9,991	Supple, Wm. C.	Baldwin
6,846	Sutherland, Matthew H.	Floyd
6,216	Suttle, Wiley	Fulton
6,551	Suttles, Nancy C.	Campbell
5,495	Sutton, Abner	Emanuel
8,105	Swanton, Benj. Franklin	DeKalb
10,503	Swift, Jno. N.	DeKalb
14,950	Swindle, Henry A.	Liberty
6,007	Swint, Mary	Glascock
21,400	Sykes, Harriet	Liberty
12,698	Taliaferro, Richard	Fulton
349	Tally, Sally W.	Whitfield
7,713	Talton, Matilda	DeKalb
1,906	Tanner, Archibald W.	Butts
13,917	Tanner, Jno. C.	Monroe
6,552	Tanner, Joseph J. M.	Clayton
6,553	Tanner, Thomas J.	Clayton
6,554	Tanner, Wm. G.	Clayton
15,713	Tapp, Wm. F.	Chattooga
15,809	Tate, George F.	Whitfield
4,147	Tate, Miles G.	Forsyth
16,474	Tate, Wm. J.	Whitfield
13,916	Taylor, Cicero H.	Pickens
15,749	Taylor, Edward	Chatham
377	Taylor, Henderson	Morgan
6,167	Taylor, James R.	Campbell

5,005	Taylor, John	Baldwin
16,526	Taylor, Jno.	Gordon
11,377	Taylor, Lucinda	Fulton
1,242	Taylor, Malinda N.	Rockdale
19,681	Taylor, Mary S.	Burke
22,019	Taylor, Moses	Muscogee
18,124	Taylor, Solomon	Effingham
19,840	Taylor, Solomon, Estate of	Pickens
21,964	Taylor, Toby	Chatham
1,434	Teasley, Isham	Milton
4,456	Teasley, James A.	Murray
13,085	Teat, Nancy	Floyd
9,805	Temples, Henry	Baldwin
12,306	Terrell, Frances E.	Floyd
402	Terrell, Garret	Whitfield
1,429	Terrell, Richmond J.	Newton
10,004	Terry, Mary J.	DeKalb
5,234	Terry, Noah	Cobb
7,993	Thacker, Andrew B.	Cherokee
10,993	Thackstan, Emily	Fulton
9,405	Thames, James T.	Clayton
1,643	Thames, Wm.	Clayton
15,034	Thedford, Allen	Catoosa
16,485	Thedford, John H.	Catoosa
16,650	Thieme, August	Chatham
6,008	Thigpen, Montclaben	Glascock
4,871	Thomas, Elizabeth	Chattooga
1,802	Thomas, John F.	Bartow
17,024	Thomas, Mahala	Polk
13,593	Thomas, Sarah	Floyd
15,105	Thomas, Wm. H.	Floyd
6,885	Thomas, Wm. N.	Walker
10,792	Thomason, James R.	Carroll
10,950	Thompson, Bartley	Fulton
2,595	Thompson, Bayliss	Cherokee
3,929	Thompson, C., Mrs.	Chatham
14,945	Thompson, Eliza J.	Butts
7,446	Thompson, Elizabeth A.	DeKalb
4,853	Thompson, Frederick	Paulding
17,948	Thompson, Gideon B.	Walker
7,013	Thompson, James A., Estate of	Polk
3,031	Thompson, James D.	Polk
7,445	Thompson, James R.	Wilkinson
2,804	Thompson, John	Murray
17,176	Thompson, Jno. W.	Walton
16,758	Thompson, Levi J.	Chatham
3,620	Thompson, Morton	DeKalb
20,823	Thompson, Mary A.	Scriven
7,502	Thompson, Narcissa	Chattooga
16,534	Thompson, S. P.	Wilkinson
7,014	Thompson, Thomas J.	Polk
7,444	Thompson, Thurza A.	DeKalb
16,247	Thompson, Wm.	Chatham
21,469	Thomson, E. D.	Liberty
21,455	Thomson, Morris	Liberty
7,604	Thorne, Stephen	Bullock
9,297	Thornton, Blanton F.	Carroll
8,286	Thornton, F. W.	Walker
15,691	Thornton, Francis A.	Floyd
540	Thrailkill, Joseph	Catoosa
1,645	Thurman, Benj.	Fulton
10,989	Thurman, David	Fulton
17,015	Thurman, Elizabeth	Walker
11,011	Thurman, James M.	Butts
6,598	Tidwell, Seaborn M.	Henry
13,585	Tillery, Sarah A.	Floyd
337	Tillman, Eliza	Whitfield
979	Tillman, Francis	Chatham
708	Tillman, Rebecca	Chatham
12,324	Tilly, Robert A.	Floyd
6,848	Timos, Wm. A.	Floyd
21,981	Tinley, James	Bibb
374	Tippin, David	Cherokee
343	Tipton, E. L.	Whitfield
16,481	Tipton, Thomas J.	Walker
8,828	Tipton, Wiley	Fannin
18,606	Todd, Moke	Liberty
12,563	Tolbert, Ransom	Floyd
3,621	Tolleson, Burrell M.	Fulton

18,709	Tompkins, Caleb	Cass
6,174	Toney, John F.	Clayton
7,714	Towers, Mary	DeKalb
12,322	Towns, Edmund J.	Floyd
18,109	Towns, Sarah W.	Coweta
7,294	Townsend, Jno.	Whitfield
9,209	Townsend, Margaret	Dade
426	Travis, Joe	Baldwin
739	Trawick, Frederick	Hancock
5,119	Trayler, Jno.	Upson
6,622	Trice, James	Upson
6,623	Trice, Wm. B., Estate of	Upson
3,791	Trimble, John M.	Campbell
7,812	Trimble, Moses	Campbell
6,203	Trimble, Moses H.	Campbell
10,695	Tripp, Henry	Fulton
15,974: 21,963:	Trowell, Martha E.	Chatham
7,814	Tucker, Burdine	Douglas
2,490	Tucker, Edward	Whitfield
6,165	Tuckr, Eliza	Douglas
6,219	Tucker, Jno. C.	Fulton
1,031	Tucker, Thomas T.	Clayton
15,615	Tuggle, Thos. S.	Muscogee
7,816	Tumlin, Reuben	Fulton
20,312	Turnby, Prior L.	Floyd
9,167	Turner, A. A.	Rockdale
7,813	Turner, Aaron	Douglas
2,077	Turner, Aaron	Haralson
9,900	Turner, Absalom	Meriweather
13,396	Turner, Andrew J.	Butts
15,181	Turner, Case	DeKalb
50	Turner, Clark	Walker
2,078	Turner, James R.	Haralson
20,017	Turner, Jane R.	Chatham
20,018	Turner, Jane R. and Williams, Maria	Chatham
7,313	Turner, John	Clayton
3,291	Turner, Jno. A., & Estate of Rebecca	Henry
3,685	Turner, Jno. B.	Fulton
7,715	Turner, John W.	DeKalb
20,914	Turner, Lawrence T.	Chatham
7,314	Turner, Martha A.	Fulton
3,291	Turner, Rebecca, Estate of & John A.	Henry
7,815	Turner, Wm. A.	Carroll
6,204	Turnipseed, Redrick W.	Fulton
4,967	Tweedell, Hiram	DeKalb
10,220	Ubele, Christian	Chatham
20,913	Ulmer, John C.	Chatham
8,620	Umphreys, Allen	Paulding
9,507	Umphreys, Jesse	Paulding
16,810	Vance, David G.	Fulton
17,429	Vandiver, James C.	Floyd
5,699	Vason, J. M.	Fulton
4,582	Vaughan, Littleton R.	Monroe
15,565	Vaughan, Wm. M.	Putnam
7,447	Vaughn, Alexander	DeKalb
118	Vaughn, Grandison F.	Bartow
18,623	Vaughn, Jonathan	Paulding
19,083	Vaughn, Virginia A.	Fulton
7,579	Veal, Alen J.	Gwinnett
18,625	Veal, Alexander	Paulding
9,786	Veal, Benj. F.	DeKalb
7,580	Veal, Francis	DeKalb
7,581	Veal, James	DeKalb
7,716	Veal, Millard F.	DeKalb
7,583	Veal, Wm. J.	DeKalb
7,582	Veal, Wm. W.	DeKalb
8,226	Verdere, Daniel	Chatham
8,222: 14,972:	Verdery, Joseph	Chatham
13,364	Verene, Charles	Chatham
8,235	Virdin, Thos. G.	Upson
12,143	Voils, Anthony	Walker
14,953	Volaski, Jacob	Chatham
18,128	Von Glahu, Henry	Chatham
14,351	Von Waldner, George	Chatham
16,009	Vornberg, Frank	Murray

15,902	Wacaser, Daniel C.	Whitfield
16,770	Wacaster, Jno.	Floyd
7,818	Waddell, S. H.	Carroll
603	Wade, David	Fulton
7,943	Wade, James A.	Cobb
7,717	Wade, Thompson	DeKalb
3,624	Wadsworth, Walter	DeKalb
3,268	Waggoner, Levi S. & Allen, Matilda W.	Clayton
6,220	Waits, David S.	Campbell
6,009	Walden, Henry	Glascock
6,159	Waldrep, Simeon N. J.	Clayton
7,379	Waldrop, James L. H.	Clayton
3,296	Waldrop, Nancy J.	Clayton
9,769	Waldrup, Eli	Cherokee
7,556	Waldrup, Ira	Cherokee
5,496	Wales, Elijah	Emanuel
16,007	Walford, April	Chatham
6,177	Walker, Bartlett J.	Campbell
18,613	Walker, David	Paulding
15,504	Walker, Jack	Liberty
7,448	Walker, Joseph	DeKalb
433	Walker, Levi	Baldwin
18,951	Walker, Louisa	Fulton
16,490	Walker, Nathaniel F.	Sumter
6,187	Walker, Wiley A.	Campbell
11,010	Wall, Margaret	Henry
18,224	Wallace, Collins	Chatham
7,817	Wallace, Rebecca	Fulton
4,190	Wallace, Samuel	Fulton
7,942	Wallace, Sarah	Fulton
10,517	Wallace, Wm.	Upson
16,871	Waller, George	Chatham
16,131	Waller, Samuel J.	Chatham
16,152	Wallin, Jessie	Walker
16,718	Walling, Elisha	Walker
33	Wallis, Reuben	Clayton
7,853	Wallis, Richard	Clayton
4,314	Wallis, Zaphnathpaaneat	Newton
919	Wallraven, Wm.	Gordon
16,769	Walraven, Martha C.	Floyd
20,535	Walsh, Thomas J.	Chatham
3,623	Walters, Luther	Floyd
21,474	Walthorn, Abraham	Liberty
21,452	Walthorn, Brister	Liberty
18,127	Walthour, Silva	Chatham
16,100	Walthour, Simeon	Chatham
9,484	Walton, Isaac L., Estate of	Morgan
15,074	Warbington, Ellemander	DeKalb
6,584	Ward, Eber	Whitfield
2,003	Ward, Geo. R.	Floyd
7,140	Ward, Jno.	Henry
16,535	Ward, Patrick	Wilkinson
15,936	Wardlow, Joseph M.	Floyd
21,460	Warner, Charles	Liberty
7,166	Warren, Rebecca	DeKalb
15,474	Washington, Mary A.	Bibb
3,922	Waters, David	Chatham
18,924	Waters, James	Henry
3,293	Waters, Richmond H.	Clayton
15,688	Watkins, Celia	Wilkinson
8,841	Watkins, Franklin M.	Wilkinson
13,600	Watkins, Hezekiah	Floyd
11,843	Watson, I. P.	Douglas
3,934	Watson, James	Chatham
17,602	Watson, Sarah Ann	Liberty
20,698	Watts, Robert	Chatham
20,706	Way, John	Liberty
20,682	Way, Linden, & Marshall, Andrew	Liberty
21,482	Way, Peter	Liberty
63	Wayne, Mary J.	Chatham
12,558	Weathers, Isaac	Floyd
6,064	Weaver, Abraham M.	Monroe
7,168	Weaver, Henry H.	DeKalb
7,504	Weaver, Lucy	Chattooga
20,068	Weaver, Parthena	Cherokee
12,614	Webb, Alfred	Dawson
7,297	Webb, Elijah	DeKalb
7,298	Webb, George	DeKalb

7,718	Webb, James W.	Walton
8,606	Webb, Jno. H.	Fulton
2,306	Webb, Wm. H.	Floyd
1,427: 3,932:	Webster, Robert	Fulton
14,951	Weiland, Carl	Chatham
1,266	Weiper, Jacob N.	Newton
14,730: 18,657:	Weitenger, John	Bartow
16,795	Welborn, James M.	Walker
583	Welch, Geo. W.	Henry
631	Welch, Wesley C.	Henry
18,093	Welcome, Jeffrey	Chatham
9,414	Wellborn, Wm. R.	Morgan
5,737	Wellmaker, Mary	Pike
6,169	Wells, Andrew J.	Clayton
6,184	Wells, Jeremiah	Clayton
49	Wells, Jno.	Whitfield
17,346	Wells, Nancy	Liberty
7,584	Wells, Wm. R.	DeKalb
5,712	Wendelken, Martin	Chatham
14,329	Werm, Larence	Chatham
7,167	Wesley, Marvin H.	DeKalb
21,478	West, Benj.	Liberty
18,116	West, Betsey	Liberty
16,177	West, Isam	Campbell
20,707	West, Tony	Liberty
15,737	West, Wm. W.	Whitfield
778	Wheeler, Wm.	Polk
370	Wheeler, Wm. D.	Bartow
10,994	Whitaker, Louisa M.	Campbell
7,505	White, Amanda	Chattooga
13,994	White, Christopher	Chatham
19,839	White, Ebenezer T.	Douglas
7,720	White, Edward H.	Gwinnett
16,326	White, Elizabeth	Floyd
14,587	White, Elizabeth	Fulton
10,169	White, Francis A.	Fulton
4,319	White, James	Henry
972	White, James M.	Cherokee
1,499	White, Jane S.	Floyd
10,990	White, Jno. C.	Fulton
16,662	White, Joseph	Chatham
4,313	White, Mary A.	Henry
18,977	White, Newton	Walker
12,307	White, Seaborn	Floyd
4,324	White, Thomas	DeKalb
13,090	White, Wm.	Chattooga
4,317	White, Wm.	Henry
11,379	Whitehead, Hester A.	Fulton
1,500	Whitehead, Jno. C.	Floyd
8,899	Whitehead, Mary L., Estate of	Butts
13,836	Whitely, Nancy	Walker
3,078	Whitfield, Bryant	Washington
18,616	Whitfield, Thomas	Paulding
17,538	Whitley, Evan R.	Douglas
17,512	Whitley, Francis L.	Walker
7,719	Whitlow, Wm. D.	Rockdale
15,403	Whitten, Wm.	Whitfield
2,048	Whitton, Jane	Haralson
6,852	Whorton, Green M.	Polk
5,497	Wiggins, Jno.	Emanuel
11,667	Wiggins, Lewis	DeKalb
5,498	Wiggins, Michael	Emanuel
16,362: 18,378:	Wiggins, Michael	Jasper
5,499	Wiggins, Sarah	Emanuel
18,640	Wigley, Jno.	Paulding
9,770	Wilber, Rebecca A.	Cherokee
6,010	Wilcher, Larkin	Glascock
6,738	Wilkes, Reuben	Jasper
18,781	Wilkie, Jessie	Pickens
11,396	Wilkins, Ellen	DeKalb
1,021	Wilkinson, James W.	Henry
4,320	Willaford, David	Henry
4,713	Willborn, Nancy	Morgan
16,325	Williams, Alexander	Floyd
2,873	Williams, Artemesia R. S.	Whitfield
20,701	Williams, Augustus	Liberty
539	Williams, Britani	Catoosa

16,008	Williams, Charlotte	Chatham
20,699	Williams, Edwin	Liberty
3,941	Williams, Eliza	Chatham
8,627	Williams, Harney M.	Walker
20,702	Williams, Isaac	Liberty
20,704	Williams, Jackson	Liberty
18,622	Williams, James, Estate of	Paulding
10,176	Williams, James M.	Glascock
11,444	Williams, Jno. H.	Chatham
6,163	Williams, Jno. H.	Paulding
3,955	Williams, Judy	Chatham
14,157	Williams, Larry	Chatham
16,486	Williams, Lewis J.	Walker
7,380	Williams, Lowry	Chattooga
20,018	Williams, Maria & Turner, Jane R.	Chatham
6,452	Williams, Mary	Milton
12,543	Williams, Matthew J.	Cobb
15,477	Williams, Patrick	Chatham
20,090	Williams, Rebecca	Chatham
17,516	Williams, S. A.	Walker
13,120	Williams, Thomas	Gwinnett
16,483	Williams, Thomas A.	Catoosa
543	Williams, Thomas H.	Catoosa
9,562	Williams, Wm. W.	Henry
6,456	Williams, Zebulon	Cherokee
1,260	Williamson, Benj. T.	Gordon
15,404	Williamson, Robert M.	Whitfield
18,153	Williamson, Wm. R.	Cherokee
1,012	Willingham, Darius S.	Henry
7,721	Willingham, Rolly S.	Walton
20,016	Willink, Henry F., Jr.	Chatham
4,022	Willis, Aaron	Upson
5,766	Willis, Abel	Bartow
11,402	Willis, Thomas	Carroll
6,063	Willis, Wm. H.	Pike
4,013	Willis, Wm. J.	Upson
18,614	Wills, Harvey J.	Paulding
18,615	Wills, Jno. W.	Paulding
394	Wilmoth, Mary	Cobb
21,425	Wilson, Albert	Liberty
17,000	Wilson, Delia	Chatham
16,108	Wilson, Frances Ann	Effingham
15,215	Wilson, Furgos, Sr.	Camden
8,269	Wilson, J. H.	Fulton
20,703	Wilson, Jack	Liberty
12,099	Wilson, Jacob	Chatham
6,054	Wilson, Jno.	Liberty
6,886	Wilson, Jno.	Walker
8,990	Wilson, Jno. W.	Chatham
17,653	Wilson, Louisa	Chatham
6,555	Wilson, Mary A.	Campbell
16,803	Wilson, Mary Jane	Catoosa
8,680	Wilson, Micajah C.	Polk
12,695	Wilson, Milly	DeKalb
6,155	Wilson, Nancy E.	Fulton
16,033	Wilson, Oliver	Whitfield
21,444	Wilson, Paul	Liberty
20,708	Wilson, Primus, Sr.	Liberty
5,010	Wilson, R. R.	Bartow
20,700	Wilson, Wm.	Liberty
13,102	Wimpee, J. N. and M. A.	Floyd
13,102	Wimpee, M. A. and J. N.	Floyd
12,567	Wimpee, Jno. N.	Floyd
793	Windsor, Anderson	Gwinnett
18,120	Wing, Rachel	Liberty
12,447	Wingard, Derrill L.	Bartow
7,194	Winn, Drucilla	Douglas
9,014	Winn, Lorenzo D.	Cobb
7,820	Winn, Mahala	Douglas
21,454	Winn, Peter	Liberty
20,705	Winn, Saml.	Liberty
8,216	Wise, Creed T.	Butts
11,384	Wise, Jno. S.	Fulton
18,611	Wisener, Allen	Paulding
17,094	Witcher, Allen	Floyd
15,183	Withers, Jacob P.	Chattooga
20,790	Withers, Walter S.	Fulton
11,478	Withrow, Joseph M.	Fannin
10,221	Wolfe, Frank, Lizzie *et al*	Chatham
4,262	Womack, Francis S.	Newton
4,191	Wood, Collin	Baldwin
6,432	Wood, Elias	Fulton
18,628	Wood, Jeremiah	Paulding
6,226	Wood, John M.	Campbell
10,952	Wood, Thomas	Cobb
1,192	Wood, Wm.	Baldwin
7,315	Woodall, Martha A.	Campbell
7,350	Woods, Jno.	Whitfield
7,503	Woods, Samuel P.	Chattooga
13,582	Woods, Wm. H.	Floyd
10,511	Woodson, Hiram H.	Upson
4,607	Woodward, Abner L.	Monroe
4,578	Woodward, Orrin S.	Monroe
6,176	Wootan, Nancy K.	Clayton
6,556	Wootan, Wm. S.	Clayton
6,199	Wootan, Willis	Clayton
4,008	Wooter, Richard W.	Pike
20,514	Worley, E. G.	Cherokee
18,154	Worley, Wm.	Cherokee
6,171	Wortham, Duncan	Paulding
6,685	Worthy, Abner	Chattooga
333	Worthy, Wm.	Whitfield
382	Wright, Austin	Fulton
7,449	Wright, Elizabeth L.	DeKalb
1,038	Wright, James	Clayton
3,292	Wright, James R.	Clayton
1,017	Wright, John	Clayton
3,932	Wright, Jubiter	Chatham
9,139	Wright, Mitchell	Baldwin
17,056	Wright, R. M.	Chattooga
13,776	Wright, Samuel M.	Haralson
15,923	Wright, Thomas	Cobb
6,179	Wright, Wm.	Clayton
7,169	Wright, Wm.	DeKalb
4,007	Wright, Wm. A.	Pike
18,156	Wright, Wm. W.	Cherokee
701	Wrinkle, Andrew N.	Whitfield
15,738	Wrinkle, David	Whitfield
10,497	Wyatt, Joshua	Henry
2,593	Wylie, Mowining, Mrs.	Gordon
68	Wylly, Frederick R.	Chatham
12,327	Wynn, Robert C.	Polk
7,819	Wynn, Solomon	Carroll
7,821	Wynn, Solomon R.	Carroll
14,238	Wynn, Wm., Estate of	Wilkinson
18,045	Yaeger, Henry	Whitfield
7,822	Yancey, D. S.	Fulton
11,387	Yarborough, Harriet O.	Fulton
5,167	Yarborough, Mary E.	Clayton
7,897	Yarbrough, Wm. T.	Gwinnett
15,037	Yates, Benj. C.	Catoosa
7,823	Yates, Joel P.	Carroll
15,038	Yates, Presley	Catoosa
13,621	York, Josiah	Polk
19,765	Young, Alfred	Effingham
3,035	Young, David	Clayton
21,262	Young, Dillard M.	Cobb
20,960	Young, Frederick	Effingham
3,956	Young, John	Chatham
6,887	Young, Joseph C.	Polk
17,025	Young, Wm. M.	Floyd
15,676	Young, Willis	Scriven
12,335	Youngblood, Peter	Floyd
20,423	Zittrouer, Esther	Effingham
8,984	Zellner, Andrew	Monroe
16,765	Zorn, Wm. F.	Liberty
12,321	Zuber, Daniel, Estate of	Floyd
392	Zuber, Williamson	Gordon

LOUISIANA

3,474	Abadie, Julia E.	Lafourche
21,718	Akers, Wm.	Tangipahoa

18,065	Alford, Clarissa P.	Morehouse
18,066	Alford, Warren	Morehouse
17,649	Allain, Aspasie	W. Baton Rouge
15,093	Allain, Julian, Estate of	Iberville
22,139	Allain, Levi	Pointe Coupee
22,138	Allain, St. Luke	Pointe Coupee
429	Allen, Richard H.	Lafourche
17,455	Amacker, Elizabeth J.	Ste. Helena
18,067	Andrews, Thomas	Morehouse
20,729	Angamar, Zulime	Orleans
2,137	Archinaud, E.	Rapides
7,741	Aubre, Eugene	Pointe Coupee
17,900	Austin, Elisha S.	Ouachita
10,933	Austin, William A.	E. Feliciana
14,680	Auzenne, Felix	St. Landry
20,746	Avery, Henry	E. Baton Rouge
17,672: 20,322:	Axley, John S.	Natchitoches
4,041	Bacon, Thomas S., Rev.	Rapides
961	Badeaux, Ulgere	Lafourche
15,362	Badley, Henry	E. Baton Rouge
412	Bagaley, Wm. & Rhodes, Joshua, Assingees	Ouachita
980	Bailey, Wm	Rapides
9,329	Baillio, Landry	Rapides
18,329	Baird, John; Berthoud, Wm. B.; Kellar, Wm.; and Rolffs, George	Jefferson
2,747	Baker, Anna M.	Ouachita
16,195	Baker, Monroe	St. Martin
8,377	Baker, Wesley J. Q.: Strother, Eliza L.; and Warfield, Eliza W.	Ouachita
19,882	Ballard, Rice C., Estate of	Madison
14,681	Balquais, Joseph	St. Landry
19,088	Banister, Aaron	Washington
10,598	Banks, Frank	Pointe Coupee
6,936	Banks, Matilda	Madison
10,588	Baptiste, Antoine	Pointe Coupee
20,259	Barlow, James H. C.	Ouachita
12,400	Barnes, Seth	Washington
10,608	Barra, Francois	Pointe Coupee
13,975	Barrow, Mary I.	Ouachita
5,371	Baudreaux, Alcide	Lafourche
1,193	Baudreaux, Gustave	Lafourche
17,269	Bauers, Henrietta	Madison
15,488	Beauchamp, Daniel S.	Morehouse
3,467	Beauchamp, Stephen E.	E. Feliciana
21,334	Beaulieu, Antoine	W. Baton Rouge
21,331	Beaulieu, Philip	W. Baton Rouge
6,937	Bedat, Francois	Ascension
1,686	Belden, James K.	Ouachita
15,544	Beenel, Pierre Aime	St. John the Baptist
22,026	Beers, Elias	St. Mary
7,316	Bemiss, John, Estate of	Pointe Coupee
3,242	Benit, Harriet E. H. & Follen, Harriet H.	Ouachita
19,077	Benjamin, H. B.	E. Baton Rouge
9,201	Benjamin, Wm., Estate of	Carroll
18,510	Benoist, Marie Suzette, Estate of	Natchitoches
14,713	Bento, Thank W.	Ouachita
3,179	Benton, Warren M.	Carroll
9,359	Bergmann, Theodora	Rapides
11,267	Berry, James M.	Richland
1,100	Berthin, Dominique	Ouachita
1,927	Berthin, Jean	Ouachita
18,329	Berthoud, Wm. B.; Kellar, Wm.; Rolffs, George; & Baird, John	Jefferson
10,602	Bertrand, Pierre	Pointe Coupee
10,932	Bickel, Michael	E. Feliciana
14,264	Biggs, Susan A.	Madison
4,412	Bills, Nancy	Ouachita
20,441	Birney, Robert W., Estate of	Madison
16,208	Bishop, Clarissa	Ouachita
18,385	Blackburn, David F., Estate	Carroll
921	Blanchard, C. H., Estate	Rapides
18,511	Blanchard, Cornelia C. & Cornelia F.; Payne, Marie Eliza; and Sudduth, Edwina C.	Natchitoches
18,518	Blanchard, Emma, Estate of	Grant
1,194	Blanchard, Octave L.	Lafourche
12,185	Blunt, James R. & Wm. Blunt, heirs of	Ouachita
9,555	Bogan, John, Jr.	Rapides
562	Bokenfohr, Wm.	Ouachita
14,265	Boney, Green L.	Madison
21,338	Bonner, Amanda	Rapides
14,804	Boudreau, Ozenie	St. Martin
10,613	Bouligny, Francois	Pointe Coupee
4,070	Boullt, David H.	Winn
19,135	Bour, Louisa	Ouachita
10,593	Bourgeois, Pierre F.	Pointe Coupee
6,863	Boutelon, Jean V.	Ouachita
6,864	Bouvillain, Loweski	Terrebonne
3,562	Bowman, Jane B.	Ouachita
9,356	Boyce, Charles W.	Rapides
13,164	Boyce, Henry	Rapides
13,976	Boyle, Lucey J.	W. Feliciana
21,944	Bradford, Foster, Sr.	E. Baton Rouge
7,621	Bradford, William	Catahoula
17,368	Brewer, Owen H.	Carroll
10,615	Britto, Alfred	Pointe Coupee
1,150	Broadway, Wm. V.	E. Feliciana
17,386	Brooks, James M.	Ouachita
18,567	Brooks, Evins	Concordia
2,013	Broussard, Zenon J.	Lafayette
14,682	Brown, A. I.	De Soto
9,331	Brown, Clair L.	Rapides
9,332	Brown, Irma	Pointe Coupee
12,359	Brown, John M., Estate of	Ascension
20,109	Brown, Mary Kay	E. Baton Rouge
22,140	Brown, Peter	Pointe Coupee
12,249	Brown, Sophia	E. Feliciana
19,387	Brown, Wm. R.	E. Baton Rouge
17,654	Brownell, Edward R.	Natchitoches
15,787	Bruner, Mary S. and Wm. J.	Caddo
15,787	Bruner, Wm. J. and Mary S.	Caddo
10,927	Bry, Nancy, Estate of	Ouachita
17,285	Buffington, Wm. C.	Ouachita
21,626	Burges, Halcot T.	Ouachita
21,177	Burgess, Fannie	Rapides
7,123	Burr, Freeman	St. Landry
9,435	Burrows, John M.	Ouachita
15,258	Bush, Louis	Tensas
10,590	Bush, Philip	Pointe Coupee
207	Butman, Benj.	Tangipahoa
12,674	Byrne, Henrietta W.	Ouachita
13,162	Byrne, John L.	Ouachita
16,957	Caffery, Jefferson I.	Lafayette
5,500	Caillouet, Lucien J.	Lafourche
20,105	Cain, Geo. L.	Ouachita
19,385	Cain, James C.	Pointe Coupee
19,980	Callaham, James	Avoyelles
15,381	Calleham, David M.	Rapides

7,317	Camp, Robert C.	Iberville
3,569	Campbell, Addie A.	E. Feliciana
425	Canto, Francisco	Ouachita
8,608	Carb, David	Ouachita
8,875	Carlin, Celestin F.	St. Mary
18,408	Carlin, Euphrazee	St. Mary
17,631	Carlin, Hilaric, Estate of	Terrebonne
15,489	Carlin, Mary	Ouachita
20,745	Carmena, John	E. Baton Rouge
18,512	Carnaham, Mrs. Marcia	Rapides
9,702	Carr, Carter	Rapides
6,262	Carradin, Eliza A.	Ouachita
18,347	Carter, Albert G.	E. Feliciana
22,142	Carter, Gabrielle	Pointe Coupee
6,945	Case, Margaret	Madison
6,946	Case, Rufus, Heirs of	Madison
9,357	Casson, Adelia E.	Rapides
1,102	Castille, Alexander Estate	St. Landry
5,533	Castille, Michael	St. Landry
5,175	Cavalier, Louis, Jr.	Jefferson
2,014	Chambers, W. A., Estate of	Tangipahoa
14,412	Chemier, Hilaire	St. Landry
4,413	Chew, Sylvia	W. Feliciana
18,367	Chivers, James T.	Lafourche
7,125	Chotard, Stephania M.	Concordia
14,812	Chretien, Hypolite	Ouachita
1,109	Christie, John	Ouachita
14,714	Clark, Maria P., Estate of	W. Baton Rouge
5,386	Clark, Samuel	Ouachita
18	Cochran, Asa F.	Ouachita
13,146	Cochran, Elizabeth	St. Mary
6,583	Coco, Lucien Dominique	Avoyelles
15,695	Coco, Valery	Avoyelles
20,108	Cole, Robert	St. Helena
1,821	Collins, Maria	Lafourche
18,513	Compere, Irma	Natchitoches
21,176: 21,621:	Compton, John, Estate of	Rapides
21,869	Compton, J. Martin	Rapides
20,888	Conant, Jean	Natchitoches
20,073	Condley, Charles	St. Martin
7,454	Cook, John M.	St. Mary
8,616	Cook, W. H.	St. Mary
21,253	Cordill, Joseph	Franklin
13,145	Cooper, Mary D. & Guzman, Mary C.	Ouachita
17,259	Cosgrove, James	Orleans
14,715	Cotten, James & Heirs of Rosanna	Pointe Coupee
3,694	Courrege, Simon	Ouachita
10,113	Crawford, Lariene	St. Mary
16,841	Crisp, Eliza & William H.	Iberia
16,841	Crisp, William H.	Iberia
16,842	Crisp, William H.	Iberia
22,141	Croizat, Adrien	Pointe Coupee
15,945	Cross, Benj. F., Estate of	Lafourche
6,558	Cross, Edward, Estate of	Terrebonne
13,053	Cunningham, Cornelius T.	Tangipahoa
11,086	Cunningham, James; Johnson, Benj,; and Weaver, B. J.	Rapides
12,107	Currie, Wm. C.	Carroll
17,001	Curtis, Asahel	Morehouse
21,683	Daigle, Isadore & Woodruff, Rose Daigle	W. Baton Rouge
9,906	Daigle, Mathurin	Lafourche
21,359	Daigre, Mary C.	E. Baton Rouge
16,898	Danel, Victor	St. Landry
15,257	Danenman, John	Tensas
12,394	Daniel, Robert	Washington
5,353	Daniels, Ellen	Washington
373: 12,597:	Darby, James	Ouachita
20,235	Dauterive, Celestine	Iberia
22,031	Davidson, Pleasant W. & Wm. H.; and Taylor, Rosa M.	Rapides

21,326	Davis, Ezra, Estate of	Orleans
16,040	Decoux, Martin	Pointe Coupee
16,185	Decuir, Arnaud, Estate of	Pointe Coupee
10,604	Decuir, Babey	Pointe Coupee
10,603	Decuir, Divine	Pointe Coupee
7,729	De France, Laura L.	Carroll
16,882	Dejean, George	Assumption
19,026	Dejean, Honore, Estate of	Ouachita
21,801	Delacroix, Francois T.	Iberia
8,673	Delahoussaye, Laura	Iberia
5,611	Delahoussaye, Sidonie	St. Mary
10,243	Delano, Charles	Madison
2,244	Delcazal, Ludovic	Ouachita
12,686	De Lee, Charles P.	E. Feliciana
14,024	Dellucky, Francis	St. Mary
16,204	Demy, Jacob	St. James
2,738	Deshotes, Raymond	St. Landry
18,519	Dietrich, Emily; Hickman, Mary T. & Lemee, Ernestine	Grant
13,622	Dilts, Wesley	Madison
13,345	Domingue, Louis	W. Baton Rouge
11,738	Dopf, Philip	Ouachita
8,065	Dorris, Jeremiah F.	Carroll
13,337	Douglas, Daniel B.	Morehouse
65	Downes, Lavinia J.	Iberville
16,323	Doucett, Pierre Z., Estate of	Lafourche
8,951	Downing, Wm. D. V.	Pointe Coupee
21,333	Dubardeau, Agricole	W. Baton Rouge
10,155	Dubroc, Louis	Ouachita
15,387	Duckworth, Elnathan D.	Morehouse
18,334	Ducournan, John A.	Natchitoches
4,310	Duffard, Guillaume	Lafourche
15,237	Dunn, Charles T.	Morehouse
9,436	Duperrier, Alfred	Iberia
20,740	Duplantier, Alfred	E. Baton Rouge
10,536	Dupree, Eufrasie	Rapides
13,723	Dupuy, Faustin	Iberia
1,804	Durand, Victor, Estate of	Natchitoches
19,293	Duvall, A. P. H., Estate of & Harrison, Thomas P.	Morehouse
609	Earnest, R. G.	Terrebonne
3,576	East, John	E. Feliciana
1,220	Eastwood, Elisha	Assumption
15,696	Edwards, Fielding	Avoyelles
17,130	Elliot, Claudius, Estate of	Tensas
5,019	Elliot, Robert J.	E. Baton Rouge
10,592	Escot, Azelie	Pointe Coupee
3,095	Esnault, Virginie	Pointe Coupee
3,107	Evans, Marie P.	Ouachita
16,725	Evans, William	Ouachita
432	Ewing, Fayette C.	Lafourche
12,472	Farrel, John M., Estate of	Ouachita
2,155	Fassman, Henry	Ouachita
21,344	Felps, Catharine N.	E. Feliciana
226	Ferre, Auguste, & Lapene, Jules	Ouachita
1,362	Ferriday, Wm. C.	Concordia
11,208: 21,175:	Fields, A. L., Estate of	St. Mary
17,626	Filhiol, Hypolite	Ouachita
10,365	Fitzgerald, Julia Agnes	Ouachita
9,870	Flower, Clara H.	Rapides
21,345	Fluker, Owen W.	E. Feliciana
2,442	Foley, Henry B.	Ouachita
3,242	Follin, Harriet H. S. & Benit, Harriet E. H.	Ouachita
21,145	Follette, J. F. & Huges, John and Morgan R.	Ouachita
10,597	Fontenau, Simond	Pointe Coupee

18,514	Fontenot, Gervais	Natchitoches
6,312	Foreman, Asa	Iberia
16,897	Foreman, Colbert W.	St. Landry
12,383	Fornea, Cleopatra	Washington
3,754	Fort, Wm. J., Estate of	W. Feliciana
15,697	Fortunee, Delphine	Pointe Coupee
14,983	Fournier, Alexander	St. Landry
3,753	Gall, Jasper	Iberia
5,014: 8,950:	Gant, Elbert	St. Landry
14,396	Gardiner, John J.	St. Landry
1,824	Gardiner, Mary	St. Landry
5,015	Garrett, Wm.	St. Mary
13,094	Gates, Alfred	St. Mary
16,324	Gaude, Charles F.	Lafourche
3,401	Gaudin, Francois	Assumption
5,593	Gay, Jean	St. Landry
790	Gentilly, Adelaide Caroline	Ouachita
3,549: 3,550:	Gibbens, James H.	E. Baton Rouge
11,005	Gibbs, Martha A.	Madison
10,412	Gilfoil, Patrick	Madison
20,965	Gillett, Thomas J.	St. Mary
21,255	Gillis, Marcellen	Ouachita
5,693	Gillis, Priscilla	Lafourche
17,673	Givanovich, Marco	Natchitoches
11,068	Gleeson, Ann	E. Feliciana
10,144	Glover, Emily V.	Ouachita
8,734: 15,096:	Godwin, David R.	Ouachita
13,737	Goffe, Charles H.	Carroll
13,243	Graves, Richard W., Estate of	Madison
18,148	Gray, Jackson	Madison
20,808	Green, Alexander C.	Ouachita
5,400	Greenwood, John J.	St. Mary
862	Gregory, Paul	De Soto
20,792	Gregg, Elizabeth H.	W. Feliciana
17,023	Grevenberg, Euphemie	St. Mary
15,238	Griffith, Ann Minor	Madison
3,457	Griffith, Francis Ann	Madison
3,169	Grove, Celia A.	St. Tammany
18,608	Guichard, Leopold	St. Bernard
14,339	Guidry, Augustin	Lafayette
16,958	Guidry, Hypolite	St. Landry
18,515	Gunney, George, Estate of	Natchitoches
13,145	Guzman, Mary C. & Cooper, Mary D.	Ouachita
1,124	Hanford, Wm. H., Jr.	Pointe Coupee
14,716	Hanraham, Richard	W. Baton Rouge
15,895	Hardesty, Ophelia E.	E. Feliciana
21,385	Hardy, Mary F., Estate of	St. Landry
21,356	Harris, George	E. Feliciana
19,731	Harris, Thomas B.	Ouachita
19,293	Harrison, Thomas P. & Duvall, A. P. H., Estate	Morehouse
12,108	Harris, Wm. H.	Carroll
12,395	Harvey, Nehemiah, R. D., Sarah Ann, & Willis W.	Washington
9,410	Hasley, Daniel	Ouachita
18,517	Haurut, Marie L. Rachal Cloutier	Natchitoches
8,948	Hawkins, Austin Ross	St. Landry
13,440	Hawthorn, Albert	Grant
20,964	Hayden, Wm.	Madison
8,383	Hayes, Barry, Estate of	Ouachita
782	Haynes, Dennis E.	Winn
1,238	Hays, Rosella	Avoyelles
18,912	Hebert, Eliza E.	Ouachita
14,383	Heinn, Mary	Ouachita
9,701	Henderson, Eleanora L.	Rapides
11,774	Henderson. Louisa	Carroll
3,682	Hennessey, Wm.	Ouachita
12,036	Hertzog, Amire R., Mrs.	Natchitoches
7,924	Hewitt, Clariece	Ouachita
18,519	Hickman, Mary T.; Lemee, Ernestine; & Dietrich, Emily	Grant

16,959	Higginbotham, James	Lafayette
19,733	Hill, Alexander	Ouachita
1,156	Hills, Horace C.	E. Feliciana
3,792	Hine, B. S., Estate of	Madison
7,129	Hobgood, Wm. B.	E. Feliciana
7,455	Hoffman, August & Holmes, D. H.	Ouachita
11,004	Hoggart, Anthony, Heirs of	Madison
7,455	Holmes, D. H. & Hoffman, August	Ouachita
10,606	Honore, Omer	Pointe Coupee
10,611	Honore, Zacharie	Pointe Coupee
18,075	Hopkins, Jane H.	Iberia
18,520	Howerton, Eliza	Natchitoches
21,347	Hudson, Hulda	Tensas
21,145	Hughes, John and Morgan R., and Follette, J. F.	Ouachita
21,146	Hughes, Morgan R.	Ouachita
21,145	Hughes, Morgan R. and John, and Follette, John	Ouachita
16,041	Humphrey, Abner	Pointe Coupee
17,891	Hutchinson, Elizabeth	Morehouse
15,853	Hymel, Octave	St. John the Baptist
5,236	Ingraham, Alfred & Elizabeth M.	Ouachita
21,691	Iron Company, Mount Savage	Rapides
18,718	Irwin, W. H.	St. Bernard
20,809	Jackson, George	Lafourche
15,473	Jacob, Ursin	St. John the Baptist
20,316	James, A. J.; Nixon, Mrs. A. C., Henry K., James R., R. L. M., and Wm. R.; & Warfield, Mrs. M.	Ouachita
431	James, Louisa	Ouachita
15,896	Jay, Wm. Estate of	Ouachita
12,477	Jeffrey, Rosa V. *et al*	
9,146: 11,234:	Jenkins, Nathaniel	Ouachita
11,086	Johnson, Benj.; Weaver, B. J.; and Cunningham, James	Rapides
15,100: 15,101:	Johnson, S. K.	Rapides
19,081	Jones, A. W. & E. G., heirs	Morehouse
18,516	Jones, Carroll	Natchitoches
20,891	Jones, Catharine	Natchitoches
19,081	Jones, E. G. & A. W., heirs	Morehouse
20,889	Jones, Florentine, and Metoyer, Annie	Natchitoches
12,436	Joseph, Lucy M. and Mark	Ouachita
12,436	Joseph, Mark and Lucy M.	Ouachita
12,399	Keaton, Benj.	Washington
14,601	Keene, A. C., Heirs of, & Morgan, Julia A.	Carroll
729	Kehoe, Ellen	Carroll
18,329	Kellar, Wm.; Rolffs, George, Baird, John; and Berthoud, Wm. B.	Jefferson
2,733	Keller, Victorin	Ascension
18,717	Kelley, Jacob	Concordia
7,620	Kelly, Thomas N.	Ouachita
9,704	Kelso, Wm.	Rapides
3,590	Kennedy, Clementina B.	E. Feliciana
9,703	Kennedy, Jefferson	Rapides
3,591	Kennedy, Leonora J.	E. Feliciana
16,167	Kimpe, Jules Edward	St. James
10,596	King, John	Pointe Coupee
18,521	Kirkland, Emilie	Natchitoches
3,592	Kleinpeter, George, Jr.	E. Baton Rouge
3,593	Kleinpeter, Sarah A.	E. Baton Rouge
4,043	Knight, Michael	Ouachita
9,765	Labatt, Carline H.	Ouachita
9,674	Labranche, Euphemie	Ouachita

20,892	Lacase, Ceraphin	Natchitoches
21,332	Lacour, Colin and Rosamond	W. Baton Rouge
21,332	Lacour, Rosamond and Colin	W. Baton Rouge
261	Lacroix, Edward	Ouachita
10,605	Ladmirault, L. J.	Pointe Coupee
13,084	Laforest, Antoine A.	Leforche
1,164	Lahey, Patrick, Estate of	E. Feliciana
17,129	Lambert, Harriet	E. Feliciana
22,242	Landry, Dorville A. & Dorville J., Estate of	W. Baton Rouge
3,413	Lapene, Jules	Ouachita
226	Lapene, Jules & Ferre, Auguste	Ouachita
16,413	Lastrapes, Charles, Estate of	St. Martin
16,414	Lastrapes, Charles, Jr.	St. Martin
16,905	Lawhead, John	Morehouse
14,717	Le Blanc, Villeneuve	W. Baton Rouge
1,066	Ledet, Henry E.	Lefourche
10,607	Leduf, Alexis	Pointe Coupee
3,645	Legarde, Mrs. Adrien	Lefourche
16,899	Lejeune, Alex	St. Landry
18,519	Lemee, Ernestine; Dietrich, Emily; & Hickman, Mary T.	Grant
20,893	Lemee, Eugenie	Natchitoches
11,565	Lester, Charles	Ouachita
3,595	Levi, A.	Ouachita
1,101	Levois, Joseph *alias* Jules Caesar	St. Charles
19,129	Levy, Emanuel	Ouachita
1,264	Lilley, Thomas	E. Baton Rouge
2,139	Lirette, Alexander	Terrebonne
11,626	Lobdel, Charles S.	W. Baton Rouge
19,597	Locke, Charity M.	Ouachita
9,330	Lockhart, Sylvia	Rapides
14,258	Loeb, Henry & Louis	Ouachita
14,258	Loeb, Louis and Henry	Ouachita
9,992	Loeb, Michael W. & Munzenheimer, Frederick	Ouachita
1,251	Lonsdales, Ida B., and Thompson, Annie B.	Carroll
1,487	Lorio, Rosemond	Ouachita
3,096	Luquet, Francois	Ouachita
22,143	Lynch, John	Pointe Coupee
16,893	Lyons, Jacob	St. Landry
17,354	Lyons, Lewis W., Estate of	Ouachita
8,241	Mackie, Thomas G.	Ouachita
3,171	Madden, Luke	St. Tammany
3,172	Madden. Patrick	Madison
18,522	Maddox, Laura P.	Rapides
21,335	Mahier, Theophile	W. Baton Rouge
10,430	Mahoney, John	Ouachita
3,214	Mahoudeau, Amy L.	Pointe Coupee
1,057	Maliot, E. E.	Assumption
1,586	Manning, Ann C., and Neal, Francis H.	Rapides
12,348	Manning, Elizabeth	Washington
1,154	Mansker, Juliet	E. Feliciana
20,741	Mansur, Hiram	E. Baton Rouge
16,884	Markham, Wm.	E. Baton Rouge
12,675	Markle, Johanna	E. Feliciana
14,973	Marks, Francois, Estate of	St. Landry
16,648	Marsh, John B. & Robert H.	St. Martin
16,648	Marsh, Robert H. & John B.	St. Martin
21,800	Marshall, Levin R., Estate of	Madison
19,317	Martin, Edmund H.	St. Landry

10,185: 10,266:	Martin, John M.	Ouachita
20,324	Martin, Joseph	Natchitoches
14,718	Martin, Louisa B.	Tensas
16,207	Martin, Octave, Estate of	St. Mary
10,928	Masich, Francis	Ouachita
5,981	Mathews, Harriet	W. Feliciana
9,013	Mathieu, Jean C.	Ascension
208	Mayronne, Alfred & Estate of Fergus and Gustave	St. Charles
18,378	McAdams, Joseph	Ouachita
5,385	McAdams, Wm.	Ouachita
16,956	McBride, Romulus L.	Lafayette
16,985	McCleland, A. B., Estate of	St. Landry
18,730	McConnell, Alexander & Samuel	Ouachita
22,192	McCullough, Hamilton	Tensas
22,105	McIntosh, Janet F.	Richland
16,823	McFarland, Mary A.	Madison
1,447	McNamara, Patrick	Ouachita
22,144	McWaters, Margaret A.	W. Feliciana
20,894	Merity, Richard	Natchitoches
12,596	Merrill, Perry	Ouachita
21,144	Mestayer, Francis, Estate of	St. Martin
20,889	Metoyer, Annie & Jones, Florentine	Natchitoches
18,523	Metoyer, F. Azenor	Natchitoches
20,895	Metoyer, Gassion	Natchitoches
20,896	Meziere, Joseph C.	Natchitoches
13,315	Miller, Arthur	Madison
14,720	Miller, Catharine S. A.	Tensas
15,894	Mills, Elizabeth S.	E. Feliciana
13,335	Minor, Rebecca A.	Terrebonne
7,132	Molyneax, Peter	Ouachita
5,534	Moreau, Ann	Avoyelles
16,163	Morgan, Charles, Estate of	Pointe Coupee
14,811	Morgan, James A.	Pointe Coupee
20,897	Morin, Suzette A., Estate of	Natchitoches
21,945	Morgan, Daniel	E. Baton Rouge
14,601	Morgan, Julia H. & Keene, A. C., Heirs of	Carroll
379	Morris, Benjamin F.	E. Feliciana
14,577	Mossy, Clara	Ouachita
21,691	Mount Savage Iron Company	Rapides
9,992	Munzenheimer, Frederick & Loeb, Michael W.	Ouachita
17,133	Murphy, Nutter	Tensas
1,586	Neal, Francis H., and Manning, Ann C.	Rapides
1,337: 1,938:	Nelson, John	Lafourches
14,432	Nimich, James	Ouachita
20,316	Nixon, Mrs. A. C., Henry K., James R., R. L. M., and Wm. R.; Warfield, Mrs. M.; and James, A. H.	Ouachita
19,572	Noland, Ann Victoria	Madison
7,677	Noulen, J. A.	Madison
18,967	Oglesby, R. C.	Ouachita
19,763	Oliver, Dubriel, Estate of	St. Landry
14,867	O'Neal, Samuel	Rapides
15,699	O'Rourk, James	Ouachita
9,360	Osborne, John	Rapides
7,741	Oubre, Eugene	Pointe Coupee
10,589	Oubre, Marcelin	Pointe Coupee
7,124	Owen, Andrew, Dr., Estate of	Carroll
15,502	Owen, Jane M. & John J.	Richland
7,133	Packer, Rebecca V.	E. Feliciana
20,104	Palmer, Archibald D., Estate	E. Feliciana
18,794	Palmer, Wm. L. & Stanton, Joseph W.	Ouachita
10,536	Parham, Henry, Mrs. (Eufrasie Dupree)	Rapides
10,419	Parker, John M. G.	Ouachita
16,221	Parlange, Virginia	Pointe Coupee

11,168	Parrot, Eliza M.	St. Landry
148	Patrick, Dr. J. C.	W. Baton Rouge
14,165	Payne, Isaac B.	Winn
18,524	Payne, Marie Eliza	Natchitoches
18,511	Payne, Marie Eliza; Sudduth, Edwina C.; and Blanchard, Cornelia F. & Cornelia C.	Natchitoches
1,826	Pedesclaux, Ernest	Ascension
14,578	Pellerin, Celeste	Iberia
9,700	Penny, Albert G.	Rapides
17,408	Perkins, John F.	Ouachita
6,321	Perret, Corinne, Mrs.	St. Mary
5,647	Perret, F. P., Mrs.	St. Mary
17,973	Perret, Frank	Ouachita
1,151	Perry, Isaac	E. Feliciana
1,999: 2,000:	Petetin, Eugene	St. Landry
1,292	Pierson, Alfred	Ouachita
10,609	Pollard, Antoine	Pointe Coupee
1,216	Pollingue, Jean Baptiste	Ouachita
10,612	Porche, Aglaee	Pointe Coupee
22,145	Porche, Hermina	Pointe Coupee
10,610	Porche, John A.	Pointe Coupee
17,403	Porche, L. V.	Pointe Coupee
11,731	Porter, Anna & Mary W.	St. Mary
11,731	Porter, Mary W. & Anna	St. Mary
22,146	Powell, Polyte	Pointe Coupee
3,605	Powell, Sarah A.	E. Feliciana
5,893	Plauche, V. T. B.	Natchitoches
5,022	Pratt, James	E. Feliciana
20,323	Prothro, James E.	Natchitoches
21,388	Prudhomme, Achille, Heirs of	Natchitoches
20,899	Prudhomme, Clara	Natchitoches
18,526	Prudhomme, John E.	Natchitoches
18,525	Prudhomme, Lestan	Natchitoches
20,898	Prudhomme, Marie Aglae	Natchitoches
18,527	Prudhomme, Narcisse	Natchitoches
18,528	Prudhomme, Theophile	Natchitoches
3,470	Pryor, John, Estate of	E. Feliciana
12,208	Pugh, David	Lafourche
1,332	Pugh, Joseph H.	Laforuche
18,529	Rachal, Louis B.	Natchitoches
18,530	Rachal, Victor	Natchitoches
26	Radovich, Marco N.	Ouachita
10,441	Railey, James, Estate of	Carroll
406	Randolph, George W., Estate	Ouachita
17,506	Reeder, Charles T.	Ouachita
17,366	Register, Aaron	Tensas
1,249	Reynolds, John B.	Iberia
17,355	Reynolds, L. E.	Ouachita
21,324	Rhodes, John	St. Mary
412	Rhodes, Joshua & Bagaley, Wm., Assignees	Ouachita
16,894	Richard, Eliza	St. Landry
4,449: 5,698:	Richard, Jean B. V.	St. Landry
4,548	Richer, Fanny	Pointe Coupee
22,147	Rickard, Antoine	Pointe Coupee
1,623	Rickart, John, Estate of	E. Feliciana
244	Riggs, Wm. A.	Iberia
1,829	Rixner, Adele	Ouachita
19,972	Roberts, James T., Estate of	Rapides
20,164	Roberts, James W.	Tensas
3,610	Roberts, Mary M.	E. Feliciana
21,336	Roberts, Stephen, Estate of	E. Baton Rouge
14,923	Robertson, Frozine, Heirs of	Rapides
15,240	Robertson, Wm.	Iberia
10,594	Robillard, Aurelie	Pointe Coupee
10,600	Robillard, Jules	Pointe Coupee
6,564	Rogers, Lizzie	St. Mary
18,329	Rolffs, George; Baird, John; Berthaud, Wm. B.; and Kellar, Wm.	Jefferson
17,427	Rollins, Amariah	Tensas
5,080	Rooker, Alonzo P.	St. Mary
5,016	Rose, Wm.	Iberia
18,531	Rost, Emile	Natchitoches
15,023	Roy, John B.	St. Landry
9,015	Rubi, Michael	Ascension
10,601	Rue, Nicholas	Pointe Coupee
1,639	Sadler, Wm.	E. Feliciana
18,532	St. Andre, St. Ville	Natchitoches
10,614	St. Armand, Alphonse	Pointe Coupee
10,587	St. Cye, Joseph	Pointe Coupee
7,009	Saizan, Pierre	Pointe Coupee
18,533	Sampite, Alphonse	Natchitoches
20,900	Sarpy, Jerome	Natchitoches
680	Sasser, Wittey M.	Rapides
7,136	Scarborough, Jno. W.	Ouachita
12,687	Schnurr, Martin	E. Feliciana
9,705	Schrader, Louisa	Rapides
7,012	Schreiber, Gaspard I.	Ouachita
10,599	Scott, Joseph	Pointe Coupee
18,534	Scruggs, Samuel O., Dr.	Natchitoches
5,030	Seals, Lucius I.	E. Feliciana
9,930	Segura, Joseph Ozeme	St. Martin
17,838	Sellers, Matthew Bacon	Carroll
19,386	Selser, Mary E.	E. Baton Rouge
2,140: 8,733:	Senette, Eugene	St. Mary
17,339	Shaw, Thomas	Madison
1,641	Shelton, John	E. Feliciana
20,747	Shelvin, Clark	E. Baton Rouge
16,224	Shelton, Julia Ann	Concordia
8,308	Shirk, Milton S.	Caddo
5,250	Short, Nancy	Carroll
17,474	Sigur, Edward	St. Mary
17,475	Sigur, Louise E.	St. Mary
16,155	Silverstone, Wolf	Tangipahoa
10,537	Simmons, Samuel S.	Natchitoches
5,354	Singeltary, Benj.	Livingston
11,978	Singer, John V.	Jefferson
20,070	Skaggs, Ewing M.	Ouachita
15,873	Smith, Armalie H.	Plaquemines
15,700	Smith, Caroline	Jefferson
16,904	Smith, Daniel	Morehouse
310: 2,736:	Smith, John N.	Iberia
8,946	Smith, Mary Ann	Ouachita
11,073	Smith, Thomas K.	Grant
22,993	Smizer, Geo.	E. Baton Rouge
13,163	Sneed, Jane B. & Richardson W.	Pointe Coupee
18,070	Soulie, Norbert, Estate of	Ouachita
9,358	Southwick, Adelphia F.	Rapides
797	Spearing, Henry E.	Ouachita
21,620	Speigle, Jacob	Rapides
18,535	Sprigg, Frances	Rapides
15,364	Spyker, Sarah M.	Ouachita
18,794	Stanton, Joseph W., and Palmer, Wm. L.	Ouachita
4,256	Starn, Levi	E. Feliciana
19,770	Stockley, Joseph H.	Ouachita
20,417	Stonaker, David	Ouachita
67	Stone, Adolphus A.	Ouachita
16,711	Stone, Amanda S.	Madison
9,202	Strauss, Leon	Caddo
8,377	Strother, Eliza L.; Warfield, Eliza W.; and Baker, Wesley J. Q.	Ouachita
7,137	Strother, Robert C.	Ouachita

18,511	Sudduth, Edwina C.; Blanchard, Cornelia C. & Cornelia F.; and Payne, Marie Eliza	Natchitoches
10,010	Sullivan, Dennis	Rapides
250	Sullivan, James B., Dr.	Rapides
15,576	Swain, John W., Estate of	Pointe Couptee
12,265	Tarkington, J.S.	Ouachita
22,031	Taylor, Rosa M.; Davidson, Pleasant W. & Wm. H.	Rapides
20,071	Taylor, Wm.	Ouachita
3,086	Tebbets, Hiram B.	Carroll
703	Tebbets, Horace B. & John C.	Carroll
17,002	Temple, Benjamin	Morehouse
4,620	Temple, John R.	Morehouse
19,022	Terry, Thomas L.	De Soto
11,739	Terry, Wm.	Jefferson
18,536	Tessier, Henry V.	Natchitoches
21,058	Tessier, John M.	Natchitoches
10,818	Theriot, Etienne	St. Martin
19,598	Thomas, Emily A.	St. Martin
15,388	Thomas, John H.	Morehouse
1,251	Thompson, Annie B., & Lonsdale, Ida B.	Carroll
1,065	Thompson, James F.	Lafourche
16,417	Thompson, Wm. C.	Rapides
5,102	Tircuit, Alexander	Pointe Coupee
5,101	Tircuit, Eugene	Pointe Coupee
12,396	Thompson, Robert	Washington
10,595	Tonnoir, Celina	Pointe Coupee
22,148	Tonnoir, Celanie	Pointe Coupee
10,616	Tonnoir, Heluter	Pointe Coupee
10,591	Tonnoir, Joseph F.	Pointe Coupee
10,682: 20,440:	Town, Ezra B.	Madison
9,839	Tregre, Louis	St. John the Baptist
20,901	Turner, Wm. H.	Natchitoches
17,892	Turpin, Baynard	Morehouse
18,134	Tynes, Tyra J.	Tangipahoa
21,983	Utz, Gabriel	Madison
1,647	Vallean, Sarah J.	E. Feliciana
16,762	Van Fossen, Thomas L.	Carroll
22,220	Van Hofen, Henry	Jefferson
12,676: 12,475:	Van Wickle, Jacob Chas.	Ouachita
378	Vaughan, Robert S.	E. Feliciana
4,311	Verneiul, Adrien	Pointe Coupee
9,194	Verret, Adolph	Terrebonne
246	Vest, George	Iberia
5,870	Viator, Andrew	Iberia
4,152	Vidal, Ellen	Tangipahoa

20,354	Wagner, Wm. W.	Iberia
18,537	Walker, Emily	Rapides
3,034	Walker, Marcus	St. Mary
14,721	Wallace, Sarah A.	Richland
21,802	Ward, John	St. Landry
19,294	Ward, Robert H.	Morehouse
8,377	Warfield, Eliza W.; Baker, Wesley, J. Q.; and Strother, Eliza L.	Ouachita
20,316	Warfield, M., Mrs.; Nixon, Mrs. A. C., Henry K., James R., R. L. M. & Wm. R.; and James, A. J.	Ouachita
12,385	Warren, Sarah	Washington
12,393	Warren, Wm. C.	Washington
10,131	Waterman, Jedediah	Ouachita
13,739	Watson, Wm. W.	Tensas
11,211	Watt, George	Madison
14,911	Weakley, Anthony	Concordia
11,086	Weaver, B. J.; Cunningham, James; Johnson, Benj.	Rapides
13,016	Webb, Frank	Assumption
864	Webre, John	Lafourche
18,538	Wells, Fannie M. & Ida F.	Rapides
19,675	Wells, J. Madison	Rapides
21,353	Wells, Michael B., Estate of	Rapides
18,539	Wells, M. L., Mrs., Estate of	Rapides
10,238	Wentzell, Rebecca P.	Ouachita
1,250	Whalen, James A.	St. Charles
14,766	Whaley, Lee	Madison
21,357	White, John C., Estate of	E. Feliciana
17,689	White, Samuel N.	W. Feliciana
20,442	White, Zachary, Estate of	Madison
10,126	Wieser, Louis	Jefferson
12,266	Will, Margaret	Jefferson
9,485	Williams, Alfred A., Estate of	Ouachita
17,615	Williams, Benj. C.	Richland
14,605	Williams, George G.	Caldwell
22,190	Williams, Narcissa P.	Carroll
13,161	Winder, Martha G.	Terrebonne
17,022	Winn, Hattie E.	Carroll
8,921	Winn, Mary E.	Rapides
18,540	Withers, Gustavus	Rapides
235	Witkowski, Julius	Carroll
10,443	Witkowski, Simon	Carroll
21,342	Wolf, Daniel	E. Feliciana
560	Wood, James	Ouachita
936	Wood, Vincent J.	Ouachita
18,541	Woodard, Thomas	Rapides
9,467	Woodruff, C. V., Estate of	Ouachita
21,683	Woodruff, Rosa Daigle, and Daigle, Isadore	W. Baton Rouge
20,439	Wolly, Elizabeth M., Heirs of	Madison
22,103	Woodward, Margaret E., Estate	E. Feliciana
17,674	Wright, James C., Estate	Morehouse
19,662	Yoes, Nathan C., Heirs of	E. Baton Rouge

MISSISSIPPI

17,821	Abernathy, Taylor	De Soto
15,441	Abney, Mary T.	Lafayette
6,934	Acuff, Mary E.	Warren
3,732	Adair, Elisha G.	Alcorn
6,273	Adair, Wm. F.	Alcorn
3,709	Adams, Barnette, Estate of	Alcorn
3,165	Adams, Isaac	Warren
8,540: 22,243:	Adams, Sylvanus, Estate of	Lafayette
22,243	Adams, Sylvanus, Estate of	Marshall
17,670	Addington, Isaax	Lafayette
17,496	Addington, Jesse	Lafayette
15,355	Aikin, Wm. B.	Oktibbeha
9,951	Alderson, Wm. M.	Lafayette
12,259	Aldrich, Bettie M.	Washington
7,653	Aldrich, L. D.	Adams
3,852	Aldridge, N. M.	Alcorn

16,550	Alexander, Alex	Warren
16,840	Alexander, Jane B., Estate of	Panola
12,360	Alexander, V. P. F.	Washington
7,047	Allbritton, Richard	Lincoln
8,761	Allen, Benj. D.	Lafayette
15,692	Allen, James H.	Prentiss
774	Allen, Joseph H.	Tishomingo
3,347: 4,336: 8,355:	Allen, Lewis D.	Adams
14,213	Allen, Margaret	Tishomingo
16,436	Allen, Wyatt, M., Estate of	De Soto
11,867	Alston, Nancy	Hinds
2,457	Alsworth, Benj. C.	Madison
5,390	Alverson, John	Warren
4,668	Alvis, Gabriel M.	Lafayette
12,278	Ambrogio, Mary D.	Hinds

9,939	Anderson, Andrew	Lafayette
5,767	Anderson, Bettie D. & Dougherty, Eliza J.	De Soto
1,942	Anderson, Ellen	Warren
14,172	Anderson, Elvira	Warren
3,838	Anderson, Frank	Prentiss
17,480	Anderson, Henry	Adams
2,105	Anderson, James	Newton
14,368	Anderson, John	Madison
6,935	Anderson, Matilda	Warren
16,164	Anderson, Wm.	Alcorn
21,501	Andrews, E., Estate of	Lafayette
14,807	Andrews, Newton F.	Tunica
1,470	Anthony, Minerva O.	Marshall
8,287	Appleton, Thomas M.	Panola
9,943	Archer, Peter F.	Lafayette
3,810	Armor, M. B.	Alcorn
8,762	Arnold, Mary M., Estate of	Lafayette
2,617	Asbury, Wm.	Warren
20,457	Ashby, Nelson	Warren
191	Ashby, Preston	Tishomingo
7,989	Askew, Bryan	Hinds
15,330	Atkins, Alexander	De Soto
15,331	Atkins, John H.	De Soto
6,764	Atkins, Peyton	Alcorn
7,633	Austin, Elizabeth	Adams
3,729	Austin, John W.	Alcorn
12,363	Austin, Mark	Hinds
2,107	Auzborne, Penelope	Newton
5,690	Ayres, Martin	Alcorn
2,222	Babb, M. J.	Alcorn
19,104	Bacon, Mary A.	Chickasaw
3,054	Badon, Henry	Pike
9,434	Bagnell, Mary P., Estate of	Claiborne
15,138	Bailey, John C.	Marshall
19,199	Bailey, Joseph A.	Adams
13,438	Bailey, Richard E.	De Soto
16,217	Bailey, Wm. A.	Wilkinson
6,278	Baily, Mayhina	Alcorn
3,848	Baker, Charlotte	Alcorn
16,203	Baker, Grafton	Washington
2,600	Baker, Henry	Warren
12,279	Baker, Lewis	Warren
15,332	Baker, Nannie E.	Panola
17,200	Ballaon, Thomas C.	Madison
21,757	Ballard, Sidney	Adams
7,086	Banks, Alice C. S.	Lowndes
14,443	Banks, Henry	Warren
5,681	Banks, Thomas R.	Marshall
20,782	Barber, George M.	Warren
5,752	Barber, Littleton	Adams
12,780	Barkley, Benj.	Tippah
5,064	Barlow, Alonzo D.	Madison
3,884	Barnes, Elijah	Prentiss
18,688	Barnes, Louisa	Warren
3,832	Barnes, Martha A.	Prentiss
13,937	Barnes, Toney	Hinds
10,560	Barnett, Ephraim	Alcorn
3,849	Barnett, J. W. B.	Tishomingo
3,727	Barnett, James H.	Alcorn
3,831	Barnett, Jefferson	Alcorn
3,750	Barnett, John W., Estate of	Tishomingo
20,940	Barnett, Matthew	Tishomingo
2,737: 20,941:	Barnett, Michael	Tishomingo
12,719	Barrett, Mary	Hinds
5,047	Barry, Andrew M.	Alcorn
9,944	Barry, Wm. H.	Lafayette
9,406	Batchelor, Eliza K.	Jefferson
7,143	Batchlor, Ellen D.	Warren
7,048	Bates, Elceba	Amite
1,483	Batte, Wm. H.	Rankin
4,388	Battle, Wm. B.	De Soto
18,755	Baum, John D.	Marshall
17,426	Baumgart, Ann	Claiborne
12,807	Bazinsky, Abraham	Warren
3,423	Beale, Jesse W.	Warren
14,765	Beard, H. H., Estate of	Coahoma
17,443	Beardsley, M. W.	Tishomingo
4,384	Bearfield, Susan	Warren
9,114	Beasly, Julian	Calhoun
22,245	Beatie, Samuel P.	Alcorn
22,245	Beatty, Sam. P.	Prentiss
21,762	Beekman, Aaron	Adams
4,514	Beker, Jacob	Adams
3,858	Bell, David	Alcorn
5,035	Bell, John T.	Panola
14,831	Bell, Nelson	Oktibbeha
514	Belue, N. H.	Tishomingo
3,817	Belue, Reaney	Tishomingo
512	Belue, Zachariah	Tishomingo
20,049	Bennett, Margaret S.	Yazoo
16,278	Benson, Lafayette W.	Marshall
14,784	Berry, Joseph B.	Yalobusha
6,938	Berry, Martha	Warren
13,293	Berry, Thomas, Estate of	Claiborne
19,568	Berry, Thomas Y.	Claiborne
19,569	Berry, Wm. S., Estate of	Claiborne
154	Bertinatti, Eugenia	Warren
17,213	Bibb, Maria E.	Monroe
73	Bickart, Leopold	Adams
20,945	Bickerstaff, Henry	Tishomingo
16,181	Bigby, Emely	Warren
8,511	Bigger, Joseph W.	Lafayette
3,909	Biggers, A. J.	Alcorn
14,215	Billings, George	Tishomingo
10,827	Billingsled, Sarah	Warren
15,274	Billingsled, Walter R.	Warren
9,532	Billingsley, Cyrus	De Soto
19,271	Bingham, Caroline	Warren
17,249	Bird, Samuel	De Soto
11,990	Birdsong, Jefferson J.	Hinds
11,988	Birdsong, Joseph M.	Hinds
4,233	Bishop, David	Panola
17,367	Bishop, Emily	Pike
4,234	Bishop, Wm.	Panola
14,869	Bizzell, Frederick	Adams
10,361	Black, Andrew	Warren
14,792	Black, Katie E.	Yalobusha
8,541	Black, Sarah A.	Lafayette
16,453	Blackburn, Alexander	De Soto
4,670	Blackburn, Elizabeth	Marshall
13,271	Blackburn, Robert E.	Yalobusha
3,819	Blackney, Frederick	Tishomingo
17,409	Blackwell, John L.	Yalobusha
3,813	Blagg, Mary	Alcorn
2,601	Blake, Mary	Warren
20,112	Blake, Mary B.	Warren
17,253	Blakely, R. D.	Lafayette
3,820	Blakney, Thomas	Alcorn
17,676	Blanton, Martha R.	Washington
134	Blount, Wiley E.	Marshall
6,890	Bloxom, H. C.	Rankin
11,958	Blum, Jacob C.	Warren
18,432	Blunt, Elijah	Madison
1,144	Blunt, Wm. J.	Tishomingo
5,872	Bobbitt, Turner	Scott
16,709	Bobo, Barham	Panola
11,775	Bobo, Louisa S., Estate of	Coahoma
16,710	Bobo, Mary M., Estate of	Panola
14,859	Boger, Elizabeth	Adams
8,690	Bohannon, Sarah	Warren
4,974	Bolander, Joseph	Claiborne
10,837	Bolling, Rebecca L.	Warren
9,869	Bolling, Sarah	De Soto
14,273	Bolls, John H., Estate of	Hinds
19,725	Bolls, Martha	Hinds
14,271	Bolls, Martha, Estate of	Hinds
14,445	Bolls, Matthew, Estate of	Hinds
16,063	Bolls, Wm. E.	Jefferson
21,051	Boner, Barbara	Adams
15,786	Bonner, Charles	Marshall
11,827	Bontura, Joseph	Adams
14,216	Booker, Mercer M.	Tishomingo
18,277	Booth, Ann E.	Warren
2,407	Booth, Emily W.	Jefferson
20,988	Booth, Martha A.	Madison
13,274	Boothe, Henry	Tallahatchie
13,258	Boothe, Wm. R.	Tallahatchie
2,880	Borlance, Wm. A.	Marshall

6,941	Borman, Frederick	Warren
10,565	Boshears, Millie	Alcorn
19,279	Boston, Abraham	Adams
12,451	Boston, James	Hinds
8,644	Boudreau, Severin	Jackson
16,633	Bourg, Lennon, Estate of	Yazoo
10,504	Bourgeois, Maximillian	Hancock
3,918	Bowdry, Jane, Estate of	Prentiss
3,918	Bowdry, Jane, Estate of	Tishomingo
7,049	Bowen, John B.	Jefferson
16,625	Bowen, Reese, Estate of	De Soto
2,602	Bowie, Aquilla	Warren
17,459	Bowles, Elisha	Lafayette
6,984	Bowles, Green, Estate of	Warren
14,795	Bowles, Mary E.	Grenada
4,235	Bowles, Paulina A.	Panola
19,346	Bowles, Wm. M.	Lafayette
14,272	Bowls, Samuel R., Estate of	Hinds
3,706	Box, James, Sr., Estate of	Alcorn
12,183	Box, James B.	Newton
1,237	Boyd, Carolinus	Newton
2,852	Boyd, Elijah	Adams
20,046	Boyd, James L.	Oktibbeha
5,036	Boyd, Lavinia	Panola
6,942	Boyd, Minerva	Warren
16,291	Boyd, Reuben	Warren
6,940	Boyer, Gabriel	Warren
13,272	Boyles, Felix J.	Panola
14,832	Boyls, Wm. F.	Oktibbeha
19,826	Braboy, Tenor	Claiborne
21,163	Brabston, Ara Ann	Warren
19,881	Brabston, John B.	Warren
19,172	Brabston, Roche H.	Warren
15,291	Bradford, Nace	Claiborne
11,363	Bradshaw, Thomas	Warren
12,390	Brakefield, Helen M.	Marion
5,756	Branch, Charlotte	Adams
799	Branch, James	Chickasaw
11,828	Brandon, Charlotte L.	Adams
21,055	Branigan, Peter, Estate of	Madison
5,037	Brasell, Catharine E.	Panola
22,012	Brasell, David, Estate of	Panola
8,763	Bratton, Jemima	Yalobusha
15,333	Breckinridge, David, Estate of	Panola
10,563	Bridges, Martha	Prentiss
14,610	Bridges, Wiley C.	Choctaw
17,181	Bridgforth, Thomas H. & W. D.	De Soto
10,825	Brien, A. W.	Warren
19,199	Briley, Joseph A.	Adams
16,408	Briscoe, Eli C.	Claiborne
16,631	Brister, John	Yazoo
12,659	Brock, Francis M.	Hinds
2,141	Broder, D. A.	Panola
16,293	Brooke, Stephen	Warren
18,433	Brooker, Alex	Madison
1,888	Brooks, Ambrose D.	Washington
8,267	Brooks, Bettie & Lucie	Washington
16,665	Brooks, Geo.	Madison
15,334	Brooks, Joseph H.	Marshall
8,267	Brooks, Lucie & Bettie	Washington
10,826	Brooks, O. C., Estate of	Warren
16,994	Broome, Matthew	Hinds
17,886	Brown, Alanzine D.	Hinds
21,950	Brown, Alexander	Adams
2,258	Brown, Andrew	Adams
4,972	Brown, Ann M.	Claiborne
1,599	Brown, Daniel	Tishomingo
3,807	Brown, E. H., Mrs.	Prentiss
16,811	Brown, Frederick	Choctaw
8,783	Brown, James	Adams
9,942	Brown, James K.	Yalobusha
12,207	Brown, L. L.	Prentiss
7,050	Brown, Latham	Jefferson
11,971	Brown, Lawrence L.	Alcorn
19,741	Brown, Noah	Adams
9,556	Brown, Randolph	Newton
5,911	Brown, Sam	Madison
18,419	Brown, Seaborn J.	Wayne

5,910	Brown, Valentine	Madison
8,173	Brown, Wm. A.	Alcorn
10,272	Browning, Albert G.	Lafayette
4,671	Browning, John A.	Lafayette
8,580	Browning, Jones, Heirs of	Lafayette
8,543	Browning, Robert S.	Lafayette
8,900	Browning, Wm. H.	Pontotoc
17,038	Brunson, E. J.	Marshall
3,718	Bruton, Benj.	Alcorn
18,777	Bryan, Dorcas	Wilkinson
12,015	Bryan, L. E.	Warren
9,945	Bryson, Robert M.	Lafayette
8,578	Buchanan, Eli	Marshall
2,331	Buck, Poleman	De Soto
19,023	Buckingham, Frank, Estate of	Warren
16,502	Buell, Kilbourn A.	Adams
18,000	Buford, Albert G.	Yalobusha
8,290	Bugg, Squire	Warren
7,052	Buie, Maria C.	Jefferson
7,051	Buie, Mary	Lincoln
5,131	Bullen, Albert	Warren
18,473	Bullitt, A. C., Estate of	Washington
8,536	Bunch, Wm. S.	Lafayette
8,288	Buntin, Christopher T.	Tallahatchie
9,974	Bunyan, Robert & Meador, A.	Scott
14,789	Burdeshaw, Wm. M.	Tallahatchie
9,482	Burford, W. H.	Yalobusha
4,674	Burgess, Eliza	Marshall
3,905	Burgess, Wm.	Alcorn
14,688	Burlison, David	Choctaw
19,116	Burnett, Daniel	Monroe
13,268	Burnett, John H.	Panola
10,931	Burnham, Doctor J.	Scott
13,725	Burns, John	Hinds
3,809	Burress, Thomas	Prentiss
4,673	Burrows, Isham C.	Marshall
10,303	Buet, Joseph J.	Tishomingo
3,738	Burt, Reddin	Tishomingo
12,607	Burton, Sarah	Warren
111	Burwell, Armistead	Warren
2,789	Bush, Mary H.	Hinds
7,326	Bustin, R. H.	Scott
10,072	Butler, Branch	Lafayette
18,278	Butler, Charles G., Estate of	Lafayette
9,955	Butler, Margaret J.	Lafayette
7,044	Butler, Mary	Amite
18,350	Butler, Mary A.	Leflore
4,600	Butler, Nathan	Adams
4,025	Byers, Amzi W.	Panola
10,894	Byers, H. J.	Panola
3,805	Bym, W. H., Estate of	Alcorn
3,911	Bynum, Joseph, Estate of	Alcorn
11,743	Cabaniss, Edwin W.	Hinds
11,471	Cabaniss, Ellen B.	Hinds
16,936	Cage, Eliza C.	Madison
1,928	Cagle, Sarah	Rankin
18,177	Cain, Edward	Tishomingo
12,221	Caker, Martha C.	Jones
18,434	Caldwell, Henry	Madison
18,690	Caldwell, James L.	Lafayette
3,711	Caldwell, Samuel S., Estate of	Alcorn
8,488	Cameron, Catharine	Warren
12,106	Cameron, Daniel A.	Warren
11,584	Cameron, S. Virginia	Warren
12,079	Campbell, Cornelius	De Soto
2,618: 11,335:	Campbell, Geo. W.	Alcorn
10,313	Campbell, Jacob H.	Hinds
10,582	Campbell, John	Alcorn
2,959	Campbell, John G.	De Soto
9,956	Campbell, Lewis H.	Lafayette
11,840	Campbell, Mattie A., et al	Warren
21,164	Campbell, Trionce	Warren
16,657	Campbell, Wm. R., Estate of	Washington
7,846	Canady, James	Scott
21,165	Canon, Alfred O.	Marshall
20,828	Cantwell, Elijah	Lafayette
16,455	Caradine, Andrew	De Soto
20,167	Cardwell, Geo. W.	Lafayette

12,758	Carey, Harriet J.	Hinds	3,921	Clausel, R. W.	Prentiss
12,381	Carley, Lyman	Marion	284	Clayton, W. W.	Marshall
10,895	Carlisle, James &		5,178	Clemmer, Eli	Benton
	Tindall, John L.	Monroe	4,676	Clopton, Sarah E.	Monroe
13,263	Carlton, Martha J.	Panola	2,297	Cloud, Mariah J.	Marshall
19,857	Carnes, James A., Estate of		5,876	Coates, W. B.	Scott
	(of Shelby Co., TN) &		6,949	Cobb, Henry	Warren
	Terry, James C.	Coahoma	21,341	Cochran, Eliza A.	Adams
15,030	Carpenter, Churchill	Oktibbeha	7,740	Cocke, Hopsie	Copiah
18,304	Carr, Benjamin H., Jr.	Yalobusha	228	Cofer, Jane	Marshall
8,903	Carr, Elizabeth	Adams	21,119	Coffey, Larkin B.	Lincoln
6,947	Carraway, Jackson	Warren	21,343	Cogan, Cicero & Wm. H.	Jefferson
15,924	Carroll, James	Yazoo	21,343	Cogan, Wm. H. & Cicero	Jefferson
18,435	Carson, Austin	Madison	14,927:		
21,053	Carter, Armistead, Estate of	Adams	20,103:	Coker, George M.	Hinds
16,460	Carter, Ebenezer, Estate of	De Soto	14,531	Colbert, Antonio, Estate of	Harrison
21,761	Carter, Geo. W.	Adams	16,558	Cole, John	Warren
19,102	Carter, James C., Estate of	Monroe	2,712	Cole, John Monroe	Jasper
11,986	Carter, Maria	Hinds	10,680	Coleman, James M.	Copiah
8,497	Carter, Mary E.	Lafayette	15,335	Coleman, John Scott	Marshall
1,258	Carter, Willis	Adams	10,833	Collier, Winneford	Warren
8,499	Casebott, Job	Warren	12,045	Collins, Agnes	Adams
12,014	Cash, Alex	Warren	17,660	Collins, Burrell H.	Yalobusha
1,048	Castleberry, Elizabeth	Tishomingo	16,432	Collins, Caroline	Yalobusha
8,530	Castleman, Joseph	Warren	17,662	Collins, Emily F.	Yalobusha
14,197	Cathel, James Estate of	Warren	21,648	Collins, Isaac W.	Franklin
6,592	Cathey, Andrew	Tishomingo	17,324	Collins, James	Leake
8,553	Cathey, John W.	Lafayette	8,591	Collins, James D.	Lafayette
8,062	Cathey, Mahulda	Tishomingo	17,688	Collins, Margaret A.	Rankin
8,542	Cathey, Robert F., Estate of	Lafayette	18,051	Collins, Reuben	Hinds
3,322	Cato, John D.	Warren	8,144	Collum, Clayton	Prentiss
7,055	Cato, Lewis	Jefferson	14,219	Colquit, James	Tishomingo
7,054	Cato, Sterling	Jefferson	18,349	Coman, James M.	Tishomingo
2,224	Causey, J. W.	Alcorn	20,299	Combs, David	Adams
14,780	Cauthen, Ludy	Panola	20,443	Compton, Eliza	Warren
14,217	Cayce, Joseph	Tishomingo	10,276	Compton, Richard	Jefferson
1,600	Cayce, Newman	Tishomingo	6,590	Conn, Samuel	Alcorn
16,937	Cessna, Elizabeth	Hinds	5,012	Conne, Thomas	Warren
16,620	Chamberlain, Mary	De Soto	18,315	Conrad, Andrew	Marshall
17,585	Chamberlain, Pauline and		2,790	Cook, Ann S.	Warren
	T. Jeff	Jefferson	8,535	Cook, Barbara P.	Lafayette
22,149	Chambers, Albert G.	Warren	12,104	Cook, David	Warren
9,996	Chambers, Robert P.	Scott	8,547	Cook, Elizabeth	Lafayette
19,094	Chambers, Royal	Yazoo	2,954	Cook, Elizabeth Jane	Marshall
16,061	Chambliss, Matilda E.	Jefferson	19,185	Cook, James F.	Lafayette
8,434	Champion, E. S.	Scott	17,419	Cook, Jared R.	Warren
3,318	Chandler, Marshall M.	Warren	10,371	Cook, John	Warren
22,065	Chandler, Mary F.	Yazoo	16,995	Cook, John S., Estate of	Hinds
7,053	Chandler, Samuel H.	Lincoln	21,499	Cook, Milas J.	Lafayette
10,189	Chappell, Eliza M.	Hinds	17,841	Cook, Nat	Lafayette
16,552	Chappel, Geo. A.	Warren	17,208	Coop, Pleasant H.	Warren
17,180	Charlton, James C.	Tishomingo	21,867	Cooper, Amos	Yazoo
10,835	Chase, Samuel	Warren	13,261	Cooper, Emily D.	Lafayette
6,943	Chavis, Jordan	Warren	15,149	Cooper, Silas	Oktibbeha
6,944	Chavis, Preston	Warren	4,675	Coopwood, W. I.	Marshall
1,308	Chavis, Thomas D., Estate of	Marshall	12,121	Copeland, Thomas E.	Issaquena
13,750	Cheatham, M. C.	Yazoo	11,832	Cora, Louisa C.	Hinds
3,701	Cheeves, Moses	Prentiss	18,743	Corbin, G. Lane	Lafayette
3,090	Chester, Hannah W.	Rankin	15,336	Corbishley, Marha A.	Marshall
3,860	Cheves, Calvin	Alcorn	16,209	Cordell, Alexander C.	Hinds
6,270	Cheves, James	Alcorn	20,783	Cordell, Lucy, Estate of	Hinds
3,816	Cheves, Thomas N.	Alcorn	11,826	Cory, Lewis H.	Adams
6,289	Childers, Ana	Tippah	11,813	Cotton, Willis	Hinds
6,271	Childers, W. H.	Alcorn	19,347	Couch, Drury	Lafayette
10,583	Childress, Wm. H.	Alcorn	9,432	Couch, James	Claiborne
227	Chism, Peter	Marshall	3,842	Coudry, Lewis	Tishomingo
7,126	Chotard, Henry, Estate of	Adams	16,658	Courtney, John T.	Washington
17,677	Chotard, Mary A.	Washington	13,126	Covington, Mary J.	Amite
13,270	Church, Moses, Estate of	Panola	21,172	Covington, Susan C., Estate	Warren
8,527	Clark, Albert T.	Warren	14,266	Cowan, John, Estate of	Warren
10,683	Clark, Debby E.	Warren	14,444	Cowan, Sarah, Estate of	Warren
2,603	Clark, Drucilla W.	Warren	10,832	Cowan, Wm. J.	Warren
4,389	Clark, J. M.	De Soto	4,605	Cowen, Wm. H.	De Soto
6,284	Clark, James J.	Tippah	8,245	Cowley, A. B.	Marshall
3,821	Clark, Jane P.	Alcorn	8,554	Cox, Eliza	Marshall
6,296	Clark, Joseph	Tippah	4,813	Cox, Elizabeth	Alcorn
3,168	Clark, Thomas C., Estate of	Warren	17,607:		
20,050	Clarke, John W.	Warren	17,608:	Coxe, Matthew J.	Marshall
8,552	Clarke, Kenith	Lafayette	21,358	Cozart, Wm. M.	Monroe
1,110	Clarke, Rowena	Warren	2,853	Cozzens, Brown	Adams

13,266	Craig, Alfred C.	Tallahatchie
9,952	Craig, Ellen	Lafayette
8,517	Craig, Wm. B.	Warren
8,313	Crane, Martha	Claiborne
8,312	Crane, Robert F., Estate of	Claiborne
4,414	Crawford, A. C.	Benton
15,262	Crawford, Nancy	Claiborne
20,486	Crizer, Jacob, Estate	Adams
6,294	Crook, John A.	Tippah
16,180	Crosby, Peter	Warren
6,948	Crosby, Sarah A.	Warren
10,829	Crouch, Mary J.	Warren
16,225	Crouch, Solomon, Estate of	Marshall
7,327	Crow, Eveline	Claiborne
7,652	Culhane, Catharine	Adams
3,422	Culkin, Thomas	Warren
11,270	Cully, Devando V.	Madison
3,874	Cumly, M. G.	Alcorn
10,834	Cummings, Phoebe	Warren
4,874	Cunningham, Alex, Henry, James, Robert & Spicer	Marshall
5,231	Cunningham, James & Gorman, Logan	Marshall
18,068	Cunningham, Jeremiah E.	Monroe
12,406	Cupstid, Absalom	Pike
8,433	Curday, Thomas M.	Scott
4,385	Curran, Michael	Warren
1,141	Curtis, Moses	Tishomingo
4,678	Dagg, James, Estate of	Marshall
5,366	Daily, Josiah	De Soto
9,200	Dalton, Terry	Alcorn
8,520	Dana, Charles	Warren
875	Daniel, Alex	Marshall
5,355	Daniel, Asa B.	Monroe
4,415	Daniel, G. C.	Marshall
6,951	Daniel, R. D. & Roberts, H.C.	Monroe
8,291	Daniel, Wm. H.	Tunica
5,751	Danneman, Catharine	Adams
8,436	Danniels, Henry	Claiborne
13,273	Darby, Levi, Estate of	Panola
10,285	Darden, Jess H.	Jefferson
12,273	Darden, Mary S.	Hinds
11,184	Davenport, Moses	Claiborne
3,746	Davenport, Robert	Prentiss
21,502	Davidson, Abraham W.	Lafayette
4,976	Davidson, Chatman	Newton
13,259	Davidson, Geo. W. S.	Yalobusha
6,952	Davidson, Margaret	Warren
4,677	Davidson, Wm.	Benton
9,827	Davis, Alfred W.	Tishomingo
4,597	Davis, Ann E.	Adams
6,953	Davis, Benj. M.	Warren
876	Davis, George	Marshall
16,415	Davis, George M.	Adams
16,549	Davis, J. H., Heirs of	Hinds
15,201	Davis, John	Leake
16,279	Davis, John B., Estate of	Lafayette
4,788	Davis, Kye	Hinds
10,580	Davis, Lewis P.	Alcorn
9,831	Davis, Littleton	Tishomingo
798	Davis, Phil	Chickasaw
2,604	Davis, Presly	Jefferson
18,707	Davis, Samuel	Jackson
5,713	Davis, Samuel	Marshall
8,505	Davis, Thomas O.	Hinds
8,764	Davis, Waller	Lafayette
2,110	Davison, John	Newton
12,177	Day, Charles W.	Newton
15,337	Day, Henry, Estate of	De Soto
2,458	Dean, David	Madison
5,111	Dean, Mary	Bolivar
15,203	Dean, Willis	De Soto
20,043	Deanes, Daniel	Oktibbeha
13,028	Dees, Calvin E., Estate of	Jackson
12,039	De France, Caroline M.	Adams
16,628	Dement, David H.	Yazoo
3,036	Denevans, Anna	Claiborne
18,573	Denhard, Adam	De Soto
21,978	Dent, Geo. R., Estate of	Jefferson

6,616	Dent, Jane	Adams
20,336	Dent, Warren R.	Jefferson
16,438	Deshago, David, Estate of	De Soto
12,270	Deterly, John L.	Hinds
6,954	Deval, Albert	Warren
5,618	Devaney, Hugh	Smith
9,828	Dexter, Daniel	Tishomingo
21,064	Dickens, Catharine E.	Panola
20,487	Dickens, Edward V.	Panola
21,323	Dickson, Joseph C.	Union
10,140	Dickson, Sam	Panola
16,449	Dilleshaw, James D.	Panola
11,364	Dillon, Squire	Warren
18,036	Dillon, Wm.	Alcorn
6,955	Dillon, Wilson F.	Hinds
3,881	Dilworth, Eveline J.	Alcorn
3,866	Dilworth, Richard C.	Alcorn
3,841	Dilworth, Susan F.	Alcorn
3,899	Dilworth, Thomas W.	Alcorn
20,795	Dixon, Ludie Martha	Hinds
19,443	Dobson, George	Monroe
15,405	Dodson, Wm. H.	Alcorn
5,340	Dodson, Wm. S., Sr.	Jackson
18,756	Dogan, Wm.	Marshall
3,808	Dogget, G. T.	Alcorn
3,837	Donaldson, Joseph	Prentiss
6,956	Donelson, Ann C.	Monroe
21,497	Donham, Benj. F.	Calhoun & Yal.
1,346	Donoho, Francis D.	Jefferson
17,103	Donoho, James	Pike
15,372	Dooley, Edward Joseph & Elizabeth	Adams
4,337: 20,298:	Dorsey, Richard	Adams
5,767	Dougherty, Eliza J. & Anderson, Bettie D.	De Soto
9,829	Douthit, Absalom	Tishomingo
21,952	Dowk, A. M., Estate of	Lafayette
12,823	Downer, J. C.	Tippah
12,103: 12,105:	Downs, Andrew	Warren
12,476	Downs, Frank	Warren
21,325	Downs, Mary J.	Warren
4,599	Doxey, Wm.	Adams
17,997	Drane, Amos	Madison
17,665	Drane, Wesley	Clark
4,416	Dressler, Theoph.	Marshall
5,048	Driver, Andrew H.	Alcorn
5,049	Driver, Wm. J.	Alcorn
19,405	Dromgoole, James I.	Hinds
16,294	Drummond, Thomas C.	Warren
4,330	Duck, John	Adams
13,188	Duke, Mary, Estate of	Yalobusha
70	Dumm, A. G.	Marshall
16,059	Dunbar, Celeste	Jefferson
19,810	Dunbar, Martha W., Estate of	Adams
12,452	Dunbar, Peter	Hinds
8,440	Duncan, J. M.	Scott
164	Dunn, E. A. (Mrs.), Estate of	Washington
5,335	Dunn, Mary J.	Lee
20,943	Dunn, Rachel	Tishomingo
21,166	Durden, Henry V.	Warren
14,785	Durden, Penelope W.	Yalobusha
3,885	Dyer, Alva G.	Alcorn
3,715	Dyer, J. L., Estate of	Alcorn
16,604	Earnest, John	Madison
16,434	Eason, Lucy A.	De Soto
8,403	Eastman, Bettie H.	Hinds
11,269	Eastman, Richard	Warren
11,268	Eastman, Wm.	Warren
15,693	Eaton, Rolen	Prentiss
16,456	Eaverson, Thomas, Estate of	De Soto
15,913	Edington, Philis	Oktibbeha
6,957	Edward, Benj.	Warren
12,806	Edwards, Charlotte M.	Calhoun
14,779	Edwards, Wm. W.	Panola
12,281	Ehs, John	Hinds
3,912	Elliot, Louisa	Prentiss

4,328	Elliott, Loyd	Adams
4,335	Ellis, Ann M.	Adams
10,561	Ellis, Geo. M.	Prentiss
3,877	Ellis, Wm. E.	Alcorn
3,712	Ellis, Wm. R.	Prentiss
520	Epps, Prince	Marshall
15,555	Eubank, Mary C.	Rankin
3,036	Evans, Anna Den.	Claiborne
16,843	Evans, John, Estate of	De Soto
6,272	Evans, John W.	Alcorn
13,904	Evans, Louisa	Hinds
16,445	Evans, Nathaniel	De Soto
14,008	Evans, Wm.	Hinds
11,825	Ewing, Ann	Hinds
14,700	Ewing, John J. & Sarah J.	Madison
14,700	Ewing, Sarah J. & John J.	Madison
8,588	Fake, Martha Jane	Warren
16,459	Farmer, Eliza L.	De Soto
19,402	Farr, George W.	Hinds
15,694	Faulkner, Marcus	Alcorn
2,935	Fawn, Charles E.	Yazoo
7,056	Felder, Charles F.	Amite
7,057	Felder, James W.	Amite
12,388	Fenn, Elizabeth	Marion
13,938	Ferguson, James G.	Warren
19,692	Ferguson, Jesse B.	Hinds
11,840	Ferrell, Mack & W. L., et al	Warren
14,773	Ferrell, Warren, Estate of	Yalobusha
1,361	Ferriday, Joseph C.	Adams
8,220	Field, Levi B.	Adams
14,732	Field, Virginia H. & Leicht, A. C.	Adams
3,725	Fielder, Eliza A.	Tishomingo
20,947	Fielder, Richard D.	Tishomingo
10,559	Fields, Levi	Alcorn
13,246	File, Anderson	Panola
14,267	Finley, Ann B.	Washington
16,219	Finley, Nelson	Wilkinson
6,959	Fisher, Geo. W.	Hinds
4,978	Fisher, Hiram	Claiborne
7,746	Fitler, Theodore	Issaquena
10,510	Fitz, Robert J., Estate of	Issaquena
14,782	Fitzgerald, Benj. J.	Panola
4,876	Fitzgerald, Burks	Adams
2,142	Fitzgerald, Francis F.	Panola
21,167	Fitzhugh, Francis M.	Warren
877	Fletcher, Randall	Marshall
12,002	Flowers, Ignatius D.	Claiborne
6,960	Flowers, Oliver B.	Warren
17,341	Flowers, W. G.	Warren
8,569	Floyd, Angeline	Benton
16,433	Flynt, Martin	De Soto
9,407	Foley, Burrell	Adams
14,929	Foley, James	Warren
8,581	Fondren, Urcilla	Lafayette
9,486	Foote, Hayward	Hinds
20,975	Forbes, Spooner	Claiborne
6,615	Forbes, Wm.	Jefferson
12,387	Ford, Eliza L.	Marion
2,855	Ford, Washington	Adams
4,219	Fore, Charles J., Estate of	Issaquena
6,958	Forgnerons, Mary, Estate of	Warren
19,401	Fort, L. A.	Oktibbeha
3,403	Fort, Robert D.	De Soto
12,379	Fortinberry, Ivin M.	Marion
8,528	Fortiner, Wm. L.	Warren
8,529	Fortner, Martin	Warren
21,503	Foster, John	Lafayette
7,332	Foster, Rebecca	Claiborne
8,597	Foster, Samuel	Lafayette
12,102	Foster, Wm. J.	Warren
981	Fouche, Isaac J.	Yazoo
10,282	Fowler, Naomi J.	Jefferson
16,064	Fowler, Olivia A.	Jefferson
5,038	Fowler, Sarah	Panola
10,142	Fox, A. J.	Panola
12,016	Fox, Elisha	Warren
14,268	Fox, Elizabeth	Warren
2,883: 2,884:	Fox, Geo. W.	Adams
10,663	Fox, James A.	Warren
10,335	Fox, Sophia A.	Warren
16,056	Foxworth, John	Marion
6,460: 21,149:	Franklin, John	Coahoma
6,283	Frazier, Clara	Tippah
10,071	Frazure, John I.	Lafayette
17,047	French, Jackson	Claiborne
10,578	French, Mary	Prentiss
10,369	Friend, Berry	Warren
17,254	Frierson, Jennett	Lafayette
18,436	Frost, E. C.	Madison
10,539	Fudge, James P.	Lafayette
10,538	Fudge, S. M.	Lafayette
16,562	Fugate, Vincent H.	Yazoo
18,416	Furguson, John, Estate of	Warren
3,046	Fussell, Wm. M.	Tishomingo
10,305	Gable, Henry	Tishomingo
8,292	Gage, Caroline	Panola
9,409	Gaither, Varina B.	Adams
8,766	Gallegly, Wm. T.	Lafayette
873	Gammel, John	Union
8,765	Gant, John J.	Yalobusha
18,580	Gardner, A. H.	Pike
2,260	Gardner, Geo. W.	Lee
7,640	Gardner, John	Prince (sic)
20,630	Garret, Elender	Tippah
5,915	Garrett, Isom	Madison
22,093	Garrett, Oliver	Warren
4,679	Garrett, Thomas L.	Lafayette
6,315	Garrett, Tom	Madison
21,168	Garvin, Samuel	Warren
16,182	Gary, Morris	Warren
19,112	Gathings, Geo. W.	Monroe
20,946	Geary, Thomas J.	Tishomingo
18,179	Gee, John P., Estate of	Warren
6,311	Gentry, C. C.	Alcorn
3,716	Gerhart, J. A.	Alcorn
9,544	Gibbon, Emily & Samuel	Marshall
14,764	Gibbs, Martha A.	Warren
20,458	Gibson, Francis E., Estate	Warren
1,058	Gibson, J. J.	Alcorn
17,456	Gibson, James M.	Warren
3,740	Gibson, John	Alcorn
3,857	Gibson, R. H.	Tippah
19,384	Gibson, Rachel E., Heirs of	Warren
5,104	Gibson, Thomas	Monroe
14,725	Gibson, Thomas J.	Warren
5,074	Gibson, Wm. W.	Madison
6,964	Gibson, York	Warren
18,404	Gilbert, Evan S.	Newton
12,961	Giles, Patrick	Hinds
11,583	Giles, Russell	Warren
7,058	Gill, Uriah	Lincoln
16,206	Gillespie, James A.	Adams
4,979	Gilmer, C. G.	Scott
10,579	Gilmer, Robert	Prentiss
913	Gilreath, Wilson R.	Adams
12,402	Ginn, Sarah	Pike
14,269	Glass, Juliet	Warren
6,705: 15,204:	Glenn, Wm. H.	Oktibbeha
1,692	Glover, James, Estate of	Marshall
1,693	Glover, R. M.	Marshall
8,767	Godfrey, Mary E.	Lafayette
17,617	Goff, John	Adams
14,930	Gold, James J.	Hinds
10,354	Golden, Patrick, Estate of	Warren
14,220	Gonde, Huldah L.	Tishomingo
8,512	Gooch, John M.	Lafayette
503	Gooch, Mary Ann	Noxubee
8,519	Goodrun, Eugene & Mary C. Estate of	Warren
21,504	Goodwin, Isaiah	Lafayette
4,682	Goodwin, Jospeh H.	Lafayette
7,335	Gooshorn, Sarah	Claiborne
3,394	Goran, Cato	Marshall
3,880	Gordon, John	Alcorn
7,059	Gordon, John	Copiah
17,361	Gordon, Wm. L.	Lauderdale

14,776	Gorin, H. H.	Yalobusha
21,322	Gorman, Henry	Marshall
5,231	Gorman, Logan & Cunningham, James	Marshall
1,818	Gorman, Wm.	Adams
19,067	Gormon, Ben	Benton
15,292	Gossin, Andrew	Claiborne
6,285	Goudy, Wm.	Tippah
6,301	Graham, Alfred	Tippah
16,057	Graham, Flora E.	Marion
20,358	Graham, Jacob	Bolivar
12,778	Graham, Nancy Jane	Hinds
3,458	Grant, Absalom	Warren
20,631	Grant, Lorenzo	Pontotoc
6,961	Grant, Virginia	Warren
8,579	Gray, Benj. S.	Lafayette
1,305	Gray, Charles H.	Lafayette
10,773	Gray, Isaac	Tishomingo
10,802	Gray, Lewis	Adams
16,220	Gray, Wm. B.	De Soto
16,630	Grayson, W. S., Estate of	Yazoo
6,963	Green, Dick	Warren
2,412	Green, Eliza	Warren
20,488	Green, George W.	Adams
15,027	Green, Hal W., Heirs of	Warren
3,855	Green, J. E.	Alcorn
13,728	Green, John F.	Yazoo
6,962	Green, Wm.	Warren
6,871	Green, Willis	Alcorn
8,949	Green, George	Claiborne
2,143	Greer, Georgia C.	Panola
2,144	Greere, Sallie G.	Panola
14,270	Gregory, Priscilla W.	Washington
5,228	Grier, James A.	Marshall
13,564	Grier, Samuel L., Estate of	Adams
10,838	Griffin, Henry	Warren
16,062	Griffing, Harriet M.	Jefferson
14,791	Griffis, Jesse	Yalobusha
12,809	Griffith, Nancy	Warren
13,906	Grimme, Theresa	Yazoo
8,587	Groce, John J.	Lafayette
18,368	Guion, F. A., Mrs.	Harrison
8,293	Gupton, James	Tallahatchie
1,472	Gwim, John A.	Marshall
13,570	Hackelton, James H.	Lincoln
13,267	Haile, Leeman	Yalobusha
15,789	Haills, John R. L.	Hinds
3,461	Haire, Milton S.	Hinds
9,954	Hale, Elijah	Lafayette
874	Hall, Constantine A.	Alcorn
1,943	Hall, Henderson	Warren
6,967	Hall, Lucinda	Warren
20,048	Hall, Nannie	Yazoo
1,944	Hall, Newton J.	Warren
4,307: 14,361:	Hall, Warren	Washington
8,487	Hall, Wm. C., Estate of	Warren
3,903	Hall, Wm. F.	Alcorn
2,298	Hall, Wm. McK.	Marshall
12,911	Hallum, Benj. S., Estate of	Warren
5,097	Halsey, Ann Dunn	Washington
20,419	Hamblen, James K.	Madison
7,956	Hamilton, Charles D., Estate	Claiborne
5,040	Hamilton, James	Lafayette
10,562	Hamilton, John	Prentiss
18,564	Hammet, Evelina M., Estate	Washington
16,183	Hammett, Mary A.	Warren
22,271	Hammock, Paschal D.	Newton
22,175	Hammond, Enos	Adams
10,278	Hanks, Lemuel R., Sr.	Amite
3,815	Hanley, Martin	Alcorn
22,028	Hanna, John W.	Bolivar
9,210	Harbin, Thomas M.	Lincoln
3,851	Harbour, Thomas J.	Alcorn
2,882	Hardaway, John P., Estate of	Marshall
14,276	Hardaway, Susan L., Estate of	Warren
12,275	Hardeman, Wm.	Hinds
21,364	Hardenstein, A. O. H.	Warren
19,537	Hardin, William	Adams
8,583	Harding, Amanda M. F.	Lafayette
4,982	Harding, Richard, Estate of	Claiborne
19,926	Hardwick, Johnson V.	Tishomingo
14,793	Hardy, Richard H.	Grenada
16,130	Hare, James, Sr.	Marshall
15,338	Hargis, James	Marshall
3,803	Hargrave, Wm.	Alcorn
3,823	Harlow, Joseph	Prentiss
15,938	Harmon, Eliza, and Lloyd, S.	Adams
8,592	Harmon, Sarah A.	Lafayette
18,001	Harper, Geo. C.	Scott
1,229	Harper, Joel B.	Copiah
17,356	Harrill, Geo. W.	Yalobusha
17,322	Harrington, Martha J.	Yazoo
16,557	Harris, Allen	Warren
4,399	Harris, Charles	Adams
21,056	Harris, Hardin	Madison
12,118	Harris, Hop T.	Tishomingo
8,577	Harris, James D.	Marshall
16,845	Harris, Judith W.	De Soto
3,818	Harris, Laura C.	Alcorn
3,720	Harris, M. A.	Tishomingo
4,801	Harris, Mary A.	Tallahatchie
6,966	Harris, Mary A. E.	Warren
19,008	Harris, Matilda	Warren
2,459	Harris, Samuel B.	Madison
17,465	Harris, Sarah, Estate of	Warren
15,339	Harris, Thomas	Panola
2,147	Harris, Wiley	Panola
19,291	Harris, Wm. H.	Hinds
3,721	Harris, Williamson	Tishomingo
8,568	Harris, Winnafred	Marshall
14,337	Harrison, Wm. M.	De Soto
1,945	Hart, Philip	Warren
10,368	Hartman, Margaret	Warren
17,273	Harton, Judith W.	Madison
3,681	Harvey, George	Tishomingo
19,249	Harvey, Mercy C.	Copiah
3,702	Harwood, Rhoda	Prentiss
19,107	Hatch, Benj. L., Sr.	Monroe
11,777	Hatcher, Rhesa	Hinds
12,277	Haverstraw, Martin	Hinds
16,458	Hawk, John	Marshall
5,768	Hawkins, George	Warren
18,437	Hawkins, Jacob	Madison
19,762	Hawkins, Thomas S.	Claiborne
18,035	Hawkins, Wm. B.	Alcorn
16,442	Hawkins, Wm. L.	De Soto
14,724	Hays, Issac	Warren
4,383	Hays, John S.	Warren
17,420	Hays, John W.	Panola
10,363	Hays, M. B.	Hinds
17,054	Hays, Wm.	Simpson
5,722	Hazlep, Cecilia	Adams
11,533	Heard, Samuel, Estate of	Hinds
14,187	Hearne, Joel A.	Union
22,168	Heatham, B., Estate of	Sunflower
15,490	Hebron, Adeline L.	Warren
10,291	Hebron, John, Estate of	Warren
5,594	Hedd, James	Monroe
15,067	Helm, Thomas E.	Hinds
16,996	Hemphill, Wm. L.	Hinds
15,340	Henderson, Elisha W.	Panola
8,531	Henderson, Felix C.	Warren
5,043	Henderson, James W.	Yalobusha
5,723	Henderson, Mary	Adams
5,041	Henderson, Mary A.	Yalobusha
5,042	Henderson, Sallie A.	Yalobusha
16,451	Hendrick, Anderson, Estate of	Chickasaw
18,983	Hendrick, Julia	Warren
12,913	Hendricks, Henderson W.	Hinds
21,958	Hendricks, James O.	Yalobusha
16,629	Hendricks, W. W., Estate of	Yazoo
10,566	Hendrix, Noah	Alcorn
17,894	Henington, Henry, Estate of	Copiah
9,193	Henry, John	Alcorn
10,585	Henson, John	Alcorn
17,182	Henson, Philip	Alcorn

4,115	Herd, Samuel	Newton	17,442	Hubbard, Nancy	Tishomingo
16,280	Herod, Sarah D.	Lafayette	9,940	Hudgins, Jesse E.	Lafayette
8,769	Herrin, Wm. A.	Yalobusha	13,255	Hudson, James, Estate of	Tallahatchie
9,948	Hewlett, Tamer	Lafayette	13,749	Hudson, Orange	Yazoo
8,760	Hickey, Joseph	Lafayette	10,929	Hudwell, Joseph	Rankin
12,941	Hicks, Belfield	Warren	4,332	Hughes, Isaac	Adams
836	Hicks, Wm. C. V.	Hinds	3,833	Hughes, S. W.	Alcorn
21,959	Higdon, Isaac	Adams	22,058	Hughey, Jacob, Estate of	De Soto
9,836	Higdon, Robert D.	Tishomingo	11,811	Hullum, Joel, Estate of	Warren
8,514	Higginbotham, Edmond	Lafayette	11,959	Hullum, Leroy	Warren
4,684	Higginbotham, J. G.	Lafayette	2,461	Hulme, Geo. J.	Madison
4,683	Higginbotham, Wm. G.	Lafayette	18,691	Humphreys, Jesse	Lafayette
8,768	Higginbotham, Wm. W.	Lafayette	18,689	Humphries, John W.	Lafayette
8,525	Hildebrand, Jacob, Heirs of	Warren	21,170	Hunt, Geo. F., Estate of	Issaquena
8,156	Hildebrand, Margaret	De Soto	20,438	Hunt, Geo. F., Estate of	Jefferson
10,830	Hill, Ann M.	Warren	19,423	Hunt, Geo. R.	Panola
12,419	Hill, Edward	Hinds	10,840	Hunt, Henry	Warren
4,718	Hill, George	Marshall	13,281	Hunt, Margaret M.	Amite
16,529	Hill, Henry W.	Grenada	19,009	Hunt, Nelson	Marshall
9,804	Hill, James M.	Tishomingo	14,835	Hunt, Robert	Benton
14,175: 17,421:	Hill, Jeptha	Panola	6,281	Hunt, Thomas	Tippah
			14,277	Hunt, Wm., Estate of	Bolibar
1,145	Hill, Lewis	Tishomingo	19,544	Hunter, Rebecca C.	Adams
4,685	Hill, Mack	Marshall	771	Hutchins, Abingdon V.	Tishomingo
8,560	Hill, Monroe	Marshall	21,169	Hutchinson, Alexander	Claiborne
4,417	Hill, Nathan	Marshall	8,314	Hutchinson, James A.	Claiborne
17,422	Hill, Wm. R.	Panola	13,264	Hutson, Joseph L.	Tallahatchie
10,428	Hillman, Horace H.	De Soto	10,289	Hyland, Francis, Estate of	Warren
16,634	Hilman, Addison L.	Yazoo	18,403	Hyland, Henry	Copiah
3,915	Hinkle, J. H.	Alcorn	19,956	Hyland, Jack	Warren
22,092	Hitch, Wm.	Warren	15,914	Hyland, W. S.	Warren
14,788	Hobbs, Mary E.	Tallahatchie	4,939: 21,758:	Hyman, James K.	Adams
5,105	Hobson, T. D.	Monroe			
19,693	Hodges, Caroline C.	Hinds	3,726	Hynemon, Susan	Alcorn
16,248	Hodges, Fleming	Chickasaw	15,281	Ingram, Hugh, Heirs of	Montgomery
1,602	Hodges, Robert, Estate of	Tishomingo	8,067	Irby, Thomas	Lafayette
1,601	Hodges, Robert S.	Tishomingo	6,776	Irish, H. T., Estate of	Washington
21,327	Hoggatt, Sandefur J.	Jefferson	3,091	Jack, Edward	Rankin
18,502	Holcomb, Hosea N.	Lafayette	4,236	Jackson, Edney, Estate of	Panola
8,490	Holcombe, John B.	Lafayette	15,791	Jackson, Jane H. T. & Wilford, Elizabeth H. (of Tennessee)	Marshall
11,146	Holden, Ebenezer	Lauderdale			
19,278	Holdman, John	Adams			
5,171	Holiman, John	Montgomery	14,295	Jackson, Peter	Warren
17,304	Holladay, Robinson M.	Kemper	10,279	Jackson, Rebecca E.	Amite
15,466	Holland, C. M.	Choctaw	6,972	Jackson, Wesley	Warren
15,465	Holland, J. W. & W. R.	Choctaw	21,759	James, Ann	Jefferson
15,465	Holland, W. R. & J. W.	Choctaw	3,916	James, Burgess J.	Alcorn
13,123	Holleman, James C.	Tishomingo	16,447	Jamison, Robert	De Soto
18,962	Holliday, Allen J.	De Soto	17,239	Jamison, Wiley J.	Hinds
17,762	Holloway, Joseph	Choctaw	19,859	Jaquess, Charlotte	Claiborne
17,762	Holloway, Joseph	Clark	16,143	Jarman, Elizabeth A.	Monroe
7,128	Hollowsay, Lewis B.	Hinds	10,343	Jarnagin, Mattie H.	Bolivar
19,117	Holloway, Samuel, Estate of	De Soto	17,256	Jarratt, Fortunatus	Marshall
4,483	Hollowell, Silas	Marshall	8,439	Jarrell, Thomas	Scott
6,971	Holmes, Ambrose	Warren	6,973	Jefferson, Joseph	Warren
10,568	Holmes, Bryant	Prentiss	2,606	Jefferson, Wm.	Warren
21,760	Holmes, Frank	Adams	20,159	Jeffries, Amaziah	Marshall
3,806	Holmes, Sarah C.	Prentiss	4,420	Jeffries, Miller	Marshall
6,968	Holmon, S. M. (Mrs.)	Marshall	9,106	Jeffries, Susan J.	De Soto
6,561	Holt, R. E.	Alcorn	10,284	Jenkins, Wm.	Amite
3,707	Honnell, Moses	Alcorn	7,613	Jenkins, Wm. M., Estate of	Warren
3,919	Honnel, Wm.	Alcorn	3,421	Jeter, John T.	Warren
19,131	Hooker, Calvin M.	Grenada	9,182	Jett, Thomas H.	Warren
12,453	Hooker, Eliza	Hinds	3,723	Jobe, J. T.	Alcorn
17,893	Hope, Levi	Lafayette	6,287	Johnsey, Jesse	Alcorn
10,685	Hopper, David	Warren	3,900	Johnsey, Leander	Alcorn
2,460	Horn, Preston A.	Madison	6,976	Johnson, Albert	Warren
14,796	Horton, David H.	Yalobusha	19,534	Johnson, Benj.	Adams
14,223	Hough, John	Tishomingo	9,973	Johnson, Charles Henry	Scott
10,306	Hough, Pleasant J.	Tishomingo	2,605	Johnson, Elisha R.	Warren
3,835	Houston, A. H.	Alcorn	20,047	Johnson, Frank	Sunflower
14,786	Houston, James A.	Tallahatchie	20,160	Johnson, George	Marshall
9,941	Houston, Martha	Lafayette	16,551	Johnson, George	Warren
3,346	Howard, George	Adams	22,056	Johnson, J. C.	Warren
839	Howard, Joseph	Marshall	6,977	Johnson, John	Warren
21,066	Howard, Mary A.	Lafayette	18,061	Johnson, John M. & Wm. B.	Warren
21,098	Howard, Mary E.	Yalobusha	10,684	Johnson, Lewis	Warren
15,094	Howard, Merryman	Jefferson	11,556	Johnson, Louisa H. M.	Hinds
840	Howell, Jane, Estate of	Marshall	17,340	Johnson, Margaret	Warren
19,292	Howry, James M.	Lafayette	21,505	Johnson, Peter	Yalobusha

5,753	Johnson, Robert	Adams
2,953	Johnson, Samuel	Marshall
18,071	Johnson, Sandy	Alcorn
14,872	Johnson, Thomas	Alcorn
10,003	Johnson, Vincent	Yalobusha
11,266	Johnson, Wm.	Warren
18,061	Johnson, Wm. B. & John M.	Warren
11,455	Johnson, Wm. C.	Scott
13,729	Johnston, Thomas	Attala
3,827	Johnston, Mary E.	Alcorn
8,582	Jolly, Wm. G.	Lafayette
11,185	Jonas, Sarah Ann	Warren
19,850	Jones, Amanda	Adams
3,459	Jones, Daniel W.	Warren
5,595	Jones, Harriet M.	Monroe
14,334	Jones, Jack	Madison
19,743	Jones, Jane	Adams
6,275: 11,972: 12,301:	Jones, John	Alcorn
8,563	Jones, John W.	Lafayette
6,975	Jones, Joshua C.	Warren
13,321	Jones, Lewis	Hinds
3,733	Jones, Mary E.	Alcorn
4,334	Jones, Miles	Adams
6,974	Jones, Minerva	Warren
16,440	Jones, Nancy J.	De Soto
3,743	Jones, Peyton G.	Alcorn
19,281	Jones, Richardson D.	Marshall
2,291	Jones, Thomas J., Estate of	Warren
11,338	Jones, Wm. H.	Warren
2,786	Jones, Wm. S., Estate of	Hinds
11,585: 16,556:	Jones, Zachariah	Warren
6,763	Jordan, Benj. B.	Alcorn
6,292	Jordan, E. F.	Tippah
19,118	Jordan, Fanny B.	Monroe
19,108	Jordan, Jesse G.	Monroe
19,095	Joshua, Robert, Estate of	Warren
13,249	Joslin, John C.	Panola
282	Julian, J. C.	Marshall
9,198	Jumper, James A.	Alcorn
16,603	Karpe, A.	Madison
7,672	Katzenmeyer, John G.	Warren
21,365	Keistler, Samuel, Heirs of	Warren
6,980	Kellam, Sam R.	Monroe
14,774	Kelley, James G.	Yalobusha
12,660	Kelly, E. J., Mrs.	Warren
14,611	Kelly, James, Estate of	Union
21,297	Kelly, Peter	Adams
3,745	Kelton, Wm. H.	Alcorn
19,280	Kenneday, David J.	Lafayette
17,986	Kennedy, Michael	Madison
2,885	Kenney, Nelson	Adams
3,902	Kerr, B. B.	Alcorn
10,799	Kerr, Henry M., Estate of	Yalobusha
3,914	Kerr, M. W.	Alcorn
15,975	Kershaw, Thos.	Washington
14,797	Kibber, Henry	Yalobusha
14,665	Kidd, Thomas	Hinds
5,106	Kile, Martin S.	Monroe
17,610	Kimmons, Hugh H.	Lafayette
2,290	Kincaid, Andrew J.	Alcorn
8,515	King, Benj. F.	Lafayette
16,906	King, John W., Estate of	Warren
21,933	King, K. W., Estate of	Marshall
146	King, Lou, Mrs.	Marshall
8,492	King, Peyton	Lafayette
17,476	Kinney, Francis	Tunica
18,141	Kinright, E. J.	Lafayette
10,280	Kirchner, John	Pike
9,834	Kirk, Columbus S.	Tishomingo
2,743	Kirk, John C.	Bolivar
14,224	Kirk, Lewis B.	Tishomingo
7,106	Kirkpatrick, John	Chickasaw
12,434	Kirkpatrick, W. M.	Hinds
10,374	Kizer, Frederick C.	Warren
4,419	Knable, Martin	Marshall
6,978: 15,916:	Knowland, Thomas K.	Warren
13,334	Knox, Allison	Franklin
2,296	Knox, Ambrose	Washington
18,387	Kramer, Charles	Clark
12,276	Kreamer, Christopher	Hinds
3,875	Kremer, Andrew	Prentiss
13,250	Kuykendall, Isaac, Estate of	Yalobusha
8,298	Kuykendall, Jacob	Panola
15,065	Kyle, Claro O., Lizzie H., and Warren S.	Madison
9,995	Lack, Moses H.	Scott
2,879	Lacy, Matthew M.	Marshall
19,103	Lake, David	Monroe
2,145	Lamb, Burneta	Panola
15,507	Lamb, Green B.	Choctaw
15,508	Lamb, Joshua	Choctaw
8,513	Lamb, Wm. T.	Lafayette
10,574	Lambert, F.	Tishomingo
19,403	Lambuth, J. R., Estate of	Madison
18,487	Lanagan, Thomas, Estate of	Madison
12,119	Lancaster, Amanda	Tishomingo
513	Lancaster, M. B.	Tishomingo
15,282	Lancaster, Sarah	Montgomery
7,364	Landrum, Thomas	Wayne
18,966	Lane, Edward M., Heirs of	Warren
8,510	Lane, Martha G.	Lafayette
306	Lane, Mary C.	Warren
15,793	Lane, Sarah C.	Warren
12,382	Lane, Wm. H. B.	Marion
3,427	Langford, Geo. N.	Rankin
14,126	Langham, Mary	Yalobusha
12,361	Langley, Aaron	Hinds
21,930	Langston, E. W.	De Soto
14,613	Langston, Harriet	Union
15,341	Langston, John M.	Lafayette
7,061	Lard, Joseph	Amite
7,060	Lard, Thomas M.	Amite
16,646	Larson, Barth & Wahlen, La Adoph, Estate of	Harrison
17,663	Lasley, Wm., Estate of	Issaquena
21,370	Latham, Ann L.	Madison
21,171	Latham, H. D.	Madison
10,424	Latham, John W., and Lawhorn, Harriet	Scott
13,941	Lathers, Catharine	Yazoo
15,356	Latimer, Anderson J.	Winston
3,843	Laughlin, R. M.	Alcorn
4,237	Lavender, James Fletcher	Panola
3,388	Lavender, Ruth	De Soto
4,238	Lavender, Wm. B.	Panola
10,424	Lawhorn, Harriet & Latham, John W.	Scott
20,243	Lawrence, Zebulon M.	Warren
16,443	Lea, Alfred M.	De Soto
8,518	Lea, Ellen D.	Warren
7,062	Lea, Hampton M.	Amite
11,006	Leake, Mary T.	Warren
1,364	Leckey, Wm. D.	Tishomingo
283	Ledbetter, Madison	Marshall
14,225	Ledbetter, Thomas C.	Tishomingo
12,488	Lee, Clarissa	Claiborne
10,040	Lee, John Barnett	Oktibbeha
16,990	Lee, Lucy	Hinds
10,664	Lee, Olive	Warren
14,772	Lee, Robert E., Estate of	Tallahatchie
14,732	Leicht, A. C. & Field, Virg. H.	Adams
2,146	Leigh, James H.	Panola
2,148	Leigh, Mrs. L. W.	Panola
18,572	Lemser, John	De Soto
16,409	Leonard, Alexander R.	Claiborne
17,987	Leonard, James F.	Madison
9,809	Leslie, Anna J.	Tishomingo
14,800	Lester, James D., Estate of	Yalobusha
21,182	Levy, Estelle	Claiborne
21,240	Levy, Mayer	Claiborne
3,870	Lewallen, Daniel	Alcorn
15,293	Lewis, Anthony	Claiborne
21,247	Lewis, Emma S.	Rankin

19,535	Lewis, Henry	Adams
5,378	Lewis, Hugh	Madison
6,981	Lewis, Isham	Warren
9,959	Lewis, James M.	Lafayette
13,125	Lewis, Nancy	Hinds
13,874	Lewis, Ozias, Estate of	Attala
5,295	Lilly, Lucie D. M.	Tallahatchie
11,531	Lindenmeyer, Gotlieb	Wilkinson
8,526	Lindigrin, Joseph	Warren
11,145	Lindley, Martha	Lauderdale
14,768	Lindsay, Elizabeth T.	Grenada
14,317	Lindsey, John Thomas, Estate	Lafayette
13,283	Lindsey, Samuel	Jasper
7,374	Lindsley, Nancy L.	Coahoma
8,550	Livermore, John B.	Lafayette
19,543	Livingston, John	Lafayette
15,938	Lloyd, S., & Harmon, Eliza	Adams
8,068	Lockard, Moses A.	Marshall
6,928	Locke, John	Tishomingo
14,363	Logan, Tyler	Lafayette
10,930	Loggings, Tilman	Rankin
17,370	Long, Henry W.	Tishomingo
19,114	Love, Columbus	Monroe
17,423	Love, Elizabeth E.	De Soto
9,190	Lowe, Adaline J.	Hinds
8,302	Lowe, Jesse	Panola
5,887	Lowe, Virginia	Claiborne
12,392	Lowe, Willis	Marion
3,397	Lowenberg, Isaac	Adams
11,259	Lowenberg, Levi M.	Warren
15,342	Lowry, Calvin	De Soto
18,459	Loyd, Washington	Adams
11,257	Lubinsky, Simon	Warren
16,373	Lucas, Gideon, Estate of	Adams
4,706	Lucas, John L., Estate of	Marshall
18,570	Luckett, Samuel, Heirs of	Warren
4,986	Lum, Edwin O.	Claiborne
20,781	Lum, William S.	Warren
880	Lunsford, Eliza	Alcorn
6,982	Lusha, Melvina	Warren
784	Lusher, Joseph O.	De Soto
3,747	Lusk, James	Alcorn
15,343	Lyon, Martha S.	De Soto
15,998	Lyons, Willie	Madison
10,359	Mack, John	Warren
16,060	Mackey, Anne E.	Claiborne
8,916	Mackin, Elizabeth	Adams
8,315	Maddox, Ida	Claiborne
3,210	Maddox, Thomas	Tippah
15,347	Maddux, John E.	Panola
12,262	Magruder, Benj.	Madison
17,527	Magruder, Thomas B.	Claiborne
9,838	Mahan, James A.	Tishomingo
3,704	Majors, Wm.	Prentiss
17,132	Mallory, Casey	Adams
20,881	Marion, John Henry	De Soto
8,596	Market, James E.	Lafayette
18,968	Markham, George	Warren
14,870	Marks, M. D.	Adams
3,719	Marlar, George W.	Tishomingo
14,275	Marley, Samuel	Warren
15,716	Marr, Wm. T.	Marshall
4,925	Marsh, Cyrus	Adams
18,240	Marshall, Thomas A.	Warren
9,907	Martin, Andrew	Alcorn
13,269	Martin, David	Panola
10,836	Martin, Emily R.	Warren
3,826	Martin, James M.	Alcorn
21,792	Martin, John M. H.	Lincoln
11,840	Martin, Lizzie, et al.	Warren
14,799	Martin, Martha L.	Yalobusha
16,281	Martin, Rebecca H.	Marshall
1,259	Martin, Richard	Marshall
3,742	Martin, Wm.	Alcorn
5,044	Martin, Wm. F.	Panola
15,704	Martin, Wm. S.	Prentiss
10,938: 12,378:	Mason, Benj., M. D.	Rankin
4,422	Massier, Jacob	Marshall
3,846	Mathis, Sallie C.	Prentiss

18,333	Matthews, Albert T.	Tishomingo
8,509	Matthews, Eliza	Lafayette
8,551	Matthews, Lucy	Lafayette
21,328	Maury, Caroline L.	Adams
16,781	Maury, James H.	Claiborne
4,127	Mavinovich, Antonio	Jackson
16,462	Maxville, Martha	De Soto
18,438	Maxwell, Alfred	Madison
15,658	Maxwell, James A.	Claiborne
18,030	Maxwell, Wm. P.	Tishomingo
15,283	May, Hampton, Estate of	Montgomery
14,274	Maybin, Joseph W.	Yazoo
8,567	McAlexander, D. F.	Marshall
6,927	McAlexander, Wm. C.	Marshall
13,279	McAlister, Saml.	Tippah
19,115	McAllister, James D.	Monroe
21,868	McAlpine, Claborne H.	Yazoo
9,433	McAlpine, John R.	Claiborne
3,893	McAnulty, Michael A.	Alcorn
13,698	McArdle, Peter	Hinds
11,792	McArthur, John J., Estate of	Claiborne
8,947	McAuthor, Laura	Claiborne
14,866	McBride, Joseph	Choctaw
5,683	McBride, R. R.	Union
13,322	McBride, Wm.	Madison
4,686	McCain, Mary A.	Lafayette
20,325	McCalla, J. M.	Alcorn
20,326	McCalla, J. M. & Saunders, M. L.	Alcorn
6,297: 12,786:	McCarly, Samuel	Tippah
13,260	McCarter, John C.	Panola
12,808	McCarty, Ellen	Warren
1,946	McCaskell, Julia Ann	Warren
11,265	McCauless, Joseph	Warren
14,987	McCay, Eliza	Pike
3,802	McClamrock, A.	Alcorn
14,775	McClendon, Charles	Yalobusha
7,272	McClenachan, Wm.	Scott
10,360	McClernand, Robert	Warren
5,050	McClure, Asa W.	Alcorn
4,338	McClure, Robert E.	Adams
13,244	McComb, Samuel	Claiborne
519	McCorkle, Hagan	Marshall
8,546	McCorkle, Samuel E.	Lafayette
17,630	McCosker, Bernard	Madison
15,357	McCoy, Edmond	Winston
3,387	McCrackin, D. J.	De Soto
18,778	McCready, Robert	Wilkinson
13,262	McCullar, James	Panola
19,827	McCullar, James	Yalobusha
20,784	McCutchen, John H.	Yazoo
15,153	McDaniel, Robert	Oktibbeha
4,421	McDermott, Patrick	Marshall
7,362	McDonald, John M.	De Soto
7,268	McDougal, Daniel	Alcorn
15,509	McDowell, John	Choctaw
8,770	McEachin, Malcom	Lafayette
8,504	McElroy, Ellen	Warren
2,415	McElwee, Wesley G.	Amite
19,163	McEwee, Jane	Copiah
60	McEwin, Cyrus	Lafayette
9,761	McGaughey, John H. (also 4617?)	Warren
2,292	McGee, Wm.	Warren
19,113	McGehee, Edmund, Estate of	Panola
16,276	McGehee, Susannah	Lafayette
15,442	McGhee, John C.	De Soto
16,277	McGowan, Catharine Q.	Marshall
3,170	McGregor, Mary T. M.	Warren
8,771	McGuire, Michael J.	Lafayette
2,607	McIver, Wm.	Warren
6,983	McKee, Eliza	Yazoo
17,611	McKee, James, Estate of	Lafayette
4,687	McKee, Mary W.	Lafayette
15,344	McKenney, Alfred, Estate of	Panola
3,636	McKenzie, Azarell	Marion
11,431	McKenzie, Daniel W.	Benton
1,603	McKinney, Judy	Tishomingo

587	McKnight, Wm.	Tishomingo
4,604	McLanahan, Michael	De Soto
3,689	McLean, Margaret I.	Carroll
12,404	McLenden, Marinda	Lincoln
19,397	McLeod, Norman, Estate of	Greene
19,397	McLeod, Norman, Estate of	Sunflower
9,993	McMullen, Eli	Madison
19,188: 21,007:	McNairy, B. Y., Estate of	Monroe
13,745	McNear, Joseph	Hinds
3,869	McPeters, Harriet F.	Alcorn
15,345	McRae, Catharine	Marshall
4,988	McRae, John	Tishomingo
1,146	McRae, Thomas J.	Tishomingo
11,143	McShann, Burrell	Lauderdale
21,351	McSwiggin, (Sister) Mary Thomas	Adams
15,346	McVey, Martin V. B.	Marshall
22,255	Meachem, Elizabeth C.	Warren
1,153	Mead, Fabius I.	Adams
9,974	Meador, A. & Bunyan, Robert	Scott
8,556	Meador, Pleasant	Marshall
16,446	Meador, Wm. H.	Grenada
5,045	Means, Charles T.	Yalobusha
9,957	Medders, Jane	Lafayette
9,833	Medley, John Pettis	Tishomingo
2,264	Melson, Henry A.	Lee
5,334	Merrill, Susan	Lee
15,547	Messenger, George, Estate of	Warren
18,563	Metcalf, Frederick A.	Washington
8,297: 8,299:	Metcalf, Josiah	Tallahatchie
21,054	Metcalfe, Wm. L.	Adams
11,869	Miazza, Angelo	Hinds
6,986	Miffleton, Geo. W.	Monroe
10,192	Miles, Ansel	Lafayette
8,576	Milham, Henry	Marshall
16,275	Miller, Ethelred H.	Marshall
15,133	Miller, Harvey, Estate of	Washington
16,374	Miller, Henry	Adams
11,494	Miller, J. M. D.	Tishomingo
15,239	Miller, John A.	Washington
14,228	Miller, Martha A.	Tishomingo
3,873	Miller, Mary	Prentiss
4,401	Miller, Ralph P.	Adams
8,772	Miller, Sam H.	Yalobusha
12,120	Miller, Samuel	Issaquena
14,794	Miller, Wm. T.	Lafayette
18,142	Miller, Wm. T.	Yalobusha
16,407	Milligan, Samuel, Estate of	Claiborne
15,176	Millikan, Samuel, Estate of	Claiborne
10,584	Mincy, Abel	Alcorn
3,830	Mink, Icy	Issaquena
16,205	Minor, Jane H.	Marshall
7,960	Minor, Catharine S., Mrs.	Adams
15,047	Minor, Lydia Ann	Warren
20,489	Minor, Rebecca Ann	Adams
15,348	Mitchell, Andrew T., Estate	De Soto
21,368	Mitchell, Grace A.	Coahoma
3,862	Mitchell, Mary D.	Alcorn
7,063: 21,257:	Mitchell, Nancy	Copiah
1,909	Mitchell, W. W.	Panola
5,754	Mock, Theodore	Adams
13,280	Mohundro, T. D., Estate of	Tippah
6,713	Montgomery, David	Oktibbeha
4,993	Montgomery, Henry S.	Claiborne
15,151	Montgomery, J. C., Estate of	Oktibbeha
2,462	Montgomery, John	Madison
3,223	Montgomery, Olivia F.	Hinds
16,292	Montgomery, Rebecca	Oktibbeha
17,612	Montgomery, Robert D.	Lafayette
15,015	Montgomery, Wm. P.	Washington
19,132	Mooney, Jacob, Estate of	Lafayette
21,351	Moore, Charlotte, Estate of	Adams
3,713	Moore, E. J.	Alcorn
13,265	Moore, Green D.	Yalobusha
4,992	Moore, Henderson	Claiborne
5,572	Moore, James	Lauderdale
19,696	Moore, James A.	Hinds
3,913	Moore, John D.	Alcorn

20,976	Moore, John Taylor	Claiborne
20,044	Moore, Jordan	Oktibeeha
12,182	Moore, Jordan	Scott
2,881	Moore, Lambert	Marshall
2,115	Moore, Lemuel D.	Newton
8,922	Moore, Mary H.	Tishomingo
3,811	Moore, Nancy C.	Prentiss
4,598	Moore, Pruda	Adams
8,548	Moore, Wm. H.	Lafayette
2,787	Moore, Wright A.	Scott
17,257	Mooring, James, Estate of	Marshall
16,528	Moorman, Benj.	Carroll
5,598	Moran, Pierre, Estate of	Hancock
15,797	Morehead, Franklin C.	Washington
5,107	Morehead, Richard J.	Benton
10,425	Morgan, John W.	Scott
5,039	Morgan, Joseph D.	Panola
21,089	Moring, Wm. M.	Yalobusha
8,142	Morris, Henry	Warren
6,146	Morris, James W.	De Soto
12,391: 18,146:	Morris, Mary	Marion
3,845	Morris, Mary J.	Alcorn
12,123	Morrison, Archibald	Tishomingo
10,362	Morrison, George	Hinds
4,688	Morrison, James	Lafayette
15,664	Morrison, James C.	Marshall
19,981	Morrow, Eli	Lafayette
7,673	Morrow, Wm. H. B.	Copiah
16,431	Morse, Bowry	Yalobusha
17,537	Mortimer, George B.	Copiah
3,850	Morton, Charles C.	Prentiss
10,564	Morton, James H.	Tishomingo
10,570	Morton, John W.	Alcorn
20,107	Mosby, Sarah J.	Warren
8,559	Mosely, Charles H.	Marshall
16,441	Mosely, Fleming	De Soto
3,839	Moses, Lucinda	Alcorn
1,910	Moses, Samuel	Marshall
13,942	Mosley, Peter J., Estate of	Yazoo
3,324	Moss, Robert	Hinds
16,992	Muh, George	Hinds
9,958	Mullins, Martin	Lafayette
9,926	Murchison, Catharine	Hinds
18,062	Murfee, Daniel	Warren
3,917	Murphy, Henry	Alcorn
7,858	Murray, Robert	Yalobusha
19,007	Musgrave, Jackson	Warren
10,193	Myers, Benj. F.	Yalobusha
4,991	Myers, Mary	Hinds
21,960	Nabors, Sina D.	Lafayette
10,370	Nailor, Hart	Warren
6,291	Nance, J. H.	Tippah
4,994	Nance, James J.	Claiborne
15,349	Nance, Sallie	De Soto
6,280	Nance, Wm. A.	Prentiss
4,239	Neel, Anthony	Panola
3,703	Neeley, Mary F.	Prentiss
21,321	Neely, Geo. H.	Marshall
3,173	Neely, Hester	Warren
6,302: 12,781:	Neely, Susan	Tippah
515	Nelms, Thede	Marshall
11,456	Nelson, John	Hinds
21,498	Nerres, Benj.	Lafayette
16,165	Nesbit, Wm. D.	De Soto
8,598	Newell, David H.	Lafayette
15,028	Newman, Alex, Estate of	Warren
10,358	Newman, Caudis	Warren
10,581	Newman, J. C.	Tishomingo
13,077	Newman, John H.	Warren
14,188	Newman, Laura C.	Warren
6,105	Newman, Minerva	Hinds
11,868	Newman, Samuel	Hinds
2,293	Newman, Shelby	Alcorn
4,995	Newsom, Rosetta L.	Claiborne
13,872	Newson, Sowell	De Soto
9,133	Nichols, Andrew	Marshall
16,461	Nichols, Harvey	Marshall
5,132	Nichols, Henry C.	Marshall
2,463	Nicholson, J. J.	Madison

6,279	Nicholson, Nancy	Alcorn
10,571	Nicholson, Sam A.	Prentiss
6,708	Noblin, Malinda	Oktibbeha
13,537	Noland, Henry P.	Warren
10,421	Noland, Pearce	Warren
21,077	Norfleet, Elizabeth O.	Marshall
11,996	Norris, Charles F.	Hinds
4,689	Nunalry, Thomas	Lafayette
8,779	Nunally, Eldred	Lafayette
21,093	Nunnally, D. Y., Estate of	Yalobusha
9,950	Nunnally, John V.	Lafayette
12,824	Nutt, J. J.	Union
994	Nutt, Julia A.	Adams
14,666	Oats, Jacob, Estate of	Warren
2,634	O'Beirn, Patrick	Warren
1,698	O'Briant, Randolph	Attala
8,073	O'Brien, James	Coahoma
3,767	O'Ferral, John	Adams
6,299	O'Neal, Wythal D.	Alcorn
11,142	Ormsby, Henry	Marshall
1,604	Orr, James	Tishomingo
14,612	Orr, Jefferson	Union
4,690	Orr, Mary Ann	Lafayette
7,991	Osborne, Stephen Watkis	Hinds
3,420	Oslin, Mary Ann	Warren
1,252	Oswald, John	Marshall
549	Owen, Francis A.	Tunica
7,341	Owen, J. G.	Scott
8,435	Owen, James H.	Scott
20,317	Owen, Wm., Estate of	Lafayette
4,998	Owens, Rebecca, Estate of	Claiborne
9,830	Ozbirn, G. W. L.	Tishomingo
3,836	Packit, Isham	Prentiss
1,142	Paden, Elizabeth, Estate of	Tishomingo
7,353	Page, James	Claiborne
17,417	Page, William	Adams
19,068	Paine, George	Benton
6,926	Palmer, Sylvester B.	Union
3,868	Pannell, W. B.	Alcorn
5,394	Parham, Emmet Y.	Benton
360	Parham, Richard H.	Benton
12,274	Parish, Consider	Hinds
3,731	Parish, Noel	Alcorn
9,177	Park, Nancy	Prentiss
9,175	Park, Robert	Prentiss
5,684	Parker, A.	Union
12,710	Parker, Lewis	Warren
22,067	Parker, Mary J.	Claiborne
6,274	Parker, Wiley	Alcorn
20,974	Parker, William St. John Elliot	Claiborne
15,263	Parkinson, Emily J.	Claiborne
18,143	Parks, Mahaley J., Mrs.	Lafayette
2,608	Parks, Samuel J.	Issaquena
3,652	Parks, Willis S.	Winston
16,448	Parnel, James M.	Panola
4,387	Parrish, Rowland H.	Warren
16,439	Partee, Squire Boon, Estate	De Soto
16,452	Patmon, Hawkins B.	De Soto
3,739	Patrick, James M.	Tishomingo
3,814	Patterson, Hardin	Tishomingo
3,714	Patterson, Mary A.	Alcorn
12,280	Patterson, Turner	Hinds
16,720	Patton, Martha	Hinds
5,283	Patton, Robert C.	Alcorn
9,837	Paulk, Newton C.	Tishomingo
3,865	Payne, Armstead	Tishomingo
3,895	Payne, Elizabeth A.	Alcorn
16,435	Payne, Simpson	Marshall
18,063	Peavy, Elizabeth	Lauderdale
17,362	Peavy, L. D.	Lauderdale
6,988	Peck, Walter W.	Jefferson
7,654	Peebles, Jacob	Adams
3,741	Peel, Daniel	Tishomingo
6,933	Pender, Daniel H.	Warren
12,405	Perkins, John R.	Lincoln
19,829	Perkins, Judith N.	Yazoo
20,884	Perry, Geo. W.	Marshall
18,181	Person, Alfred G.	Alcorn
14,771	Person, Presley C.	Yalobusha
19,105	Peters, Mary A. F.	Monroe
2,149	Petrea, Daniel	Panola
17,128	Petrie, Alice, Eva, & Herbert	Hinds
18,571	Pettit, Rachel F.	Warren
8,295	Petty, Martha B.	Panola
9,509	Phelps, Mary B.	Washington
4,432	Phillips, Eliza	De Soto
15,350	Phillips, James L.	Marshall
18,793	Phillips, J. R.	Lauderdale
3,806	Phillips, L. N.	Alcorn
13,343	Phillips, Mary	Alcorn
878	Phillips, Terrill	Alcorn
3,847	Phillpot, John	Prentiss
13,536	Phipps, Mary F.	Yazoo
20,942	Pickens, Elizabeth A.	Tishomingo
5,685	Pickens, Jackson A.	Union
13,697	Pickett, R. K., Estate of	Yazoo
13,253	Pickle, Francis, Estate of	Tallahatchie
22,176	Pierce, Abner	Adams
17,230	Pigford, Aurelia	Lauderdale
15,294	Pinn, Wm.	Claiborne
8,294	Pipkin, Francis M., Estate	Panola
12,912	Pittard, Samuel	Hinds
17,539	Platt, Norman, Heirs of	Hinds
19,433	Podesta, Joseph	Warren
2,116	Pointer, Philip	Newton
12,897	Poitevent, Wm. J.	Hancock
17,411	Pol, Miguel	Jackson
8,420	Ponder, John	Marion
12,681	Pons, Peter A.	Jackson
16,548	Pope, Phillip B.	Yazoo
12,044	Pope, Wiley	Adams
20,785	Porter, Wm. J.	Yazoo
8,570	Porter, Wm. W.	Marshall
16,231	Porterfield, Julia	Warren
11,094	Potter, Nelson	Hinds
15,467	Potts, Rosannah	Madison
10,139	Potts, Wm. W.	Panola
18,405	Powell, Ben	Marshall
3,876	Powell, Benj.	Alcorn
8,773	Powell, Bluford	Lafayette
3,317	Powell, Catharine	Warren
18,885	Powell, Jack	Marshall
7,678	Powell, Jesse S.	Lafayette
7,352	Powell, Mark	Scott
9,577	Powell, Mary	Warren
9,413	Powell, W. T., Estate of	Madison
7,603	Powers, Henry G. J.	Claiborne
5,000	Powers, John R.	Claiborne
3,844	Prather, Brice	Alcorn
5,140	Prayer, John	Adams
20,490	Price, Bem.	Lafayette
9,947	Price, John	Lafayette
8,521	Price, Lewellyn	Warren
2,153	Prince, Jane R.	Panola
6,300	Prince, Jordan	Tippah
6,276	Prince, Nancy	Alcorn
14,767	Prince, Wm.	Tallahatchie
11,812	Proctor, Sam J.	Rankin
12,784	Pryor, Henderson	Tippah
20,491	Pryor, John B.	Adams
1,856	Pugh, James	Warren
12,178	Pullen, Wiley N.	Newton
12,904	Purnell, Mary	Tippah
14,379	Putnam, Waldo W., Estate of	Hinds
14,790	Quarles, Richard O.	Tallahatchie
10,069	Quick, Nathan	Lafayette
8,498	Quine, Julia	Warren
4,691: 15,289:	Quinn, James	Marshall
12,092	Quinn, W. Monroe, Estate of	Pike
3,920	Ragan, G. W.	Prentiss
13,245	Ragsdale, Francis B., Estate	Claiborne
551	Rainey, Brazilla G.	Tunica
800	Ranaldson, Emma K.	Hinds
19,109	Randle, Emily F.	Monroe
20,162	Randle, Martha P.	Lafayette
3,320	Raney, David	Hinds

8,987	Raney, W. B.	Hinds
12,386	Rankin, Martha	Marion
20,951	Rapier, Henry	Tishomingo
20,830	Rawlings, John T., Estate of	Adams
8,589	Rawls, Claudius	Warren
8,534	Rawls, Elizabeth P.	Warren
11,453	Raymor, Thomas W.	Bolivar
11,333	Read, John	Montgomery
17,678	Redd, Thos. S.	Washington
3,825	Redus, Luther W.	Prentiss
8,774	Redwine, James A.	Lafayette
6,991	Reed, Lewis	Warren
12,043	Reed, Robert	Adams
869	Reeve, Lizzie C. & Walt, Robert H.	Warren
10,577	Reeves, Marget.	Tishomingo
4,488	Reeves, Wm.	Rankin
21,500	Reeves, Wm., Estate of	Lafayette
5,755	Regan, John A.	Adams
12,380	Regan, Wm. S., Sr.	Marion
5,600	Reid, James R.	Marshall
14,232	Reid, Matilda H.	Tishomingo
773	Reno, Emmett H.	Tishomingo
15,154	Rentfrow, Ellen	Oktibbeha
10,281	Revil, Catharine	Pike
4,423	Reynolds, E. L.	Marshall
8,432	Rhodes, Catharine	Scott
4,240	Rhodes, J. C. H.	Panola
14,028	Rice, Wm. H.	Warren
9,903	Richardson, Isaac	Alcorn
13,727	Richardson, Lucy A.	Warren
9,197	Richardson, M.	Tishomingo
16,181	Rigby, Emily	Warren
12,557	Rigley, Helen, Estate of	Hinds
8,441	Rigsby, M. A., Mrs.	Scott
17,536	Riley, Sarah	Marshall
3,812	Rineharte, Elias	Alcorn
12,598	Rist, John	Pike
5,895	Ritch, James J.	Scott
16,561	Ritter, Wm.	Warren
7,344	Rivers, Tennessee	Scott
20,045	Rives, J. M., Estate of	Winston
14,778	Roach, John	Yalobusha
16,201	Robb, Ann L.	Washington
13,320	Robb, Robert B.	Hinds
6,951	Roberts, H. C. & Daniels, R. D.	Monroe
6,993	Roberts, H. C. & H. M.	Monroe
6,995	Roberts, H. M.	Monroe
6,994	Roberts, Henry C.	Monroe
17,990	Roberts, Isaac	Hinds
11,271	Roberts, John M.	Hinds
16,993	Roberts, Wm.	Hinds
15,056	Roberts, Wm. L.	Hinds
12,959	Robertson, Charlotte G.	Hinds
18,750	Robertson, Drury	Lafayette
17,606	Robertson, L., Mrs., Estate	Issaquena
20,161	Robertson, Wm.	Marshall
21,088	Robinson, Basha	Yalobusha
3,424	Robinson, Charles	Yazoo
12,122	Robinson, Cynthia S.	Tishomingo
6,992	Robinson, George	Warren
21,087	Robinson, Geo. W.	Yalobusha
5,083	Robinson, John	Madison
4,692	Robinson, Josiah	Lafayette
11,093	Robinson, Payton	Hinds
12,269	Rochester, Lord	Hinds
16,866	Rogan, James	Tippa
3,736	Rogers, Ann	Alcorn
3,853	Rogers, Frances E.	Alcorn
19,776	Rogers, James M.	Marshall
19,694	Rogers, Wm. H.	De Soto
3,854	Rone, Susan H.	Prentiss
12,734	Rosenbaum, David	Lauderdale
17,601	Rosenbaum, Isaac	Lauderdale
18,279	Ross, Charles B. & Neil K.	Warren
879	Ross, James Wm.	Alcorn
18,279	Ross, Neil K. & Charles B.	Warren
6,277	Ross, Wm. F.	Alcorn
3,398	Rountree, Thomas	Marshall

3,864	Rowsey, Isabella	Alcorn
2,609	Royall, Joseph P.	Warren
1,694	Royston, Aaron	Marshall
20,973	Ruck, Henry, Estate of	Washington
4,877: 4,880:	Rucker, Jonathan	Adams
7,345	Rundell, J. F.	Claiborne
8,522	Russell, James	Warren
8,533	Russell, John	Warren
4,693	Russon, Margaret	Marshall
16,450	Russwurm, Martha W.	De Soto
10,141	Rutherford, Catharine J.	Panola
12,785	Rutherford, Thomas	Tippah
772	Rutledge, Richmond T.	Tishomingo
13,078	Ryan, J. D. and Co.	Lauderdale
2,981	Ryan, Thomas	Claiborne
17,441	Salyers, Wm. W.	Tishomingo
2,464	Sanders, Charles G.	Madison
8,318	Sanders, Geo. W.	Claiborne
7,674	Sanders, Julia	Warren
9,953	Sanders, Permelia A. F.	Lafayette
2,465	Sanders, Richard C.	Madison
8,317	Sanders, Wm.	Claiborne
133	Sanderson, David D.	Marshall
16,530	Sandidge, James M.	De Soto
20,456	Sarrett, Harmon J.	Hinds
17,613	Saunders, James W.	Lafayette
20,326	Saunders, M. L. & McCalla, J. M.	Alcorn
1,059	Saunders, Sarah Jane	Monroe
3,883	Savage, Granville	Alcorn
11,092	Savoy, Eliza A. & George	Warren
11,092	Savoy, George & Eliza A.	Warren
4,242	Scallon, Wm.	Panola
6,996	Scarborough, James R.	Yazoo
16,997	Schmidt, Charles	Rankin
17,357	Schrimsher, Lewis J.	Marshall
8,296	Schuiler, Louis	Adams
8,561: 8,562:	Schultz, Kate	Marshall
13,317	Schwab, Joseph M.	Warren
910	Schwartz, Christian	Adams
2,854	Schwartz, John C.	Adams
3,236	Scofield, Abraham	Adams
3,898	Scoggin, Smith	Alcorn
10,935	Scott, Athens F.	Jefferson
17,584	Scott, Charles D.	Franklin
7,000	Scott, David	Warren
3,908	Scott, Peter S.	Alcorn
7,001	Scott, Wm.	Warren
517	Seals, Alex	Marshall
2,150	Seigles, S. V.	Panola
18,767	Selden, Burr	Adams
5,004	Sessions, Franklin	Newton
8,507	Sessions, James	Warren
19,764	Sessions, Richard W., Estate	Claiborne
8,532	Sessions, Russell S.	Warren
3,734	Settle, Marcus, Estate of	Alcorn
17,464	Sexton, Rebecca E.	Warren
4,241	Shankle, Mary E.	Panola
2,636	Sharky, Wm. L.	Hinds
17,021	Sharp, Clarissa	Adams
3,890	Shaw, Caroline W.	Alcorn
17,365	Shaw, Elizabeth A.	Warren
12,435	Shaw, Jacob M.	Hinds
4,386	Sheehan, Patrick	Warren
17,679	Shelby, Thos.	Washington
386	Shelton, Henry F.	Rankin
3,897	Shelton, Taleaferro	Alcorn
11,995	Shepard, Frank	Hinds
14,029	Sheppard, P. R.	Chickasaw
8,304	Sherman, Ruth H.	Tallahatchie
3,863	Shields, Margaret	Alcorn
3,824	Shields, P. N.	Alcorn
8,777	Shipp, Felix G.	Lafayette
9,949	Shive, Allen	Lafayette
5,051	Shope, Margaret A.	Alcorn
7,065	Short, Monroe (also 15,351)	Panola
9,826	Shuffield, Wm.	Tishomingo

10,586	Shull, Philip	Tishomingo
3,705	Shull, Thomas P.	Tishomingo
108	Shultz, Samuel	Lafayette
10,681	Shy, Thomas	Warren
19,442	Sigmin, Wm. T.	Marshall
8,438	Simmons, James	Scott
13,944	Simmons, John	Yazoo
13,945	Simmons, John & Nancy	Yazoo
8,538	Simmons, Robert E.	Lafayette
8,491	Simmons, Wm. E.	Lafayette
6,295	Simpson, Jane	Tippah
14,798	Sims, Mary A.	Tallahatchie
8,595	Sims, Wm. B.	Lafayette
10,070	Singleton, Adams	Lafayette
4,400	Singleton, David	Adams
9,188	Singleton, Julia A.	Hinds
4,696	Sisk, Jesse	Lafayette
3,834	Skillman, John C.	Alcorn
6,293	Skinner, John W.	Tippah
20,093	Slack, W. H.	Tishomingo
5,084	Slaughter, James M.	Madison
3,892	Slaughter, Thomas S.	Alcorn
5,238	Sledge, F. M.	Alcorn
4,697	Sloan, Sarah Ann	Lafayette
2,746	Sloan, Wm.	De Soto
232	Small, Mary Ann	Panola
16,624	Smith, Aaron	Choctaw
21,366	Smith, Andrew	De Soto
3,345	Smith, Anna E.	Adams
5,757	Smith, Charles	Adams
14,868	Smith, Deborah	Adams
17,255	Smith, E. W., Estate of	Lafayette
17,727	Smith, Ebenezer	Alcorn
13,075	Smith, Elizabeth	Warren
19,006	Smith, Fisher	Warren
17,680	Smith, George	Washington
5,686	Smith, Gray W.	Marshall
10,576	Smith, Hardy	Alcorn
10,676	Smith, Harvey	Warren
3,882	Smith, Harvey N.	Alcorn
18,472	Smith, Irene	Washington
6,997	Smith, James M.	Monroe
21,278	Smith, James P., Estate of	Hinds
10,801	Smith, John	Adams
11,991	Smith, John	Warren
10,557	Smith, John D.	Alcorn
3,889	Smith, Joseph	Alcorn
18,316	Smith, Lourena	Warren
6,998	Smith, Maria	Warren
16,991	Smith, Mary	Hinds
6,288	Smith, P. D.	Tippah
5,125	Smith, Richard	Adams
3,867	Smith, Richard B.	Prentiss
17,258	Smith, Robert H.	Hinds
8,776	Smith, Semiramis M.	Lafayette
20,963	Smith, Sidney R. & Co.	Washington
21,057	Smith, Thomas I.	Madison
21,719	Smith, Wm.	Amite
16,058	Smith, Wm.	Pike
8,584	Smith, Wm. A.	Lafayette
15,491	Smith, Wm. C.	Clark
3,428	Smith, Wm. D. & Yeiser, Charles R.	Hinds
13,076	Smith, Wm. H.	Warren
8,594	Smith, Wm. L.	Lafayette
17,410	Smither, Wm. H.	Lafayette
13,747	Smithson, Jerry	Yazoo
8,493	Snipes, Elbert	Lafayette
8,316	Snodgrass, Margaret	Claiborne
3,735	Sorrelle, E. F.	Alcorn
9,832	Southard, Thomas	Tishomingo
8,593	Spairs, Sidney W.	Lafayette
11,493	Sparks, Lewis	Tishomingo
8,544	Spears, Benj. F.	Lafayette
16,202	Spears, Charlotte	Warren
8,545	Spears, James M.	Lafayette
4,695	Spears, Jane	Lafayette
15,295	Speed, Mack	Claiborne
12,590	Speed, Matilda	Warren
8,736	Spencer, Harriet S.	Pontotoc

624	Spencer, Horatio N.	Claiborne
9,199	Spight, Joseph C.	Tippah
3,174	Spratley, John W.	Warren
7,064	Sprich, Albert H.	Amite
10,558	Springer, Aaron	Alcorn
17,645	Springer, Dennis	Kemper
16,406	Sprott, Walter D.	Claiborne
10,423	Sprouse, Ira A.	Scott
2,299	Stafford, James H.	Warren
12,398	Stallings, James	Pike
16,055	Stampley, Mabella A.	Jefferson
17,528	Stamps, Jane	Claiborne
11,987	Stamps, Milton	Hinds
5,003	Stamps, Richard	Claiborne
17,523	Standifer, Archibald C.	De Soto
4,613	Standley, Lavinia	Union
20,492	Stanton, Elizabeth B. & Hulda M.	Adams
21,360	Stanton, Robert, Estate of	Adams
3,710	Steel, John N.	Alcorn
3,904	Steger, James H.	Alcorn
5,348	Stephens, Henry	Monroe
17,457	Stephens, Levi, Estate of	Warren
8,524	Stephens, Mary L.	Warren
16,444	Stephens, Thomas, Estate of	Marshall
14,787	Stephens, Wiley, Estate of	Tallahatchie
16,457	Stephens, Wm.	Marshall
19,441	Stephenson, Adams	Marshall
3,425	Stephenson, Madison	Warren
19,111	Stephenson, Wm. J.	Monroe
15,587	Stern, Jacob	Lincoln
16,454	Stevens, Caleb H.	Marshall
354	Stevens, John W., Jr.	Alcorn
2,884	Steward, Evaline	Adams
865	Stewart, Annie	Coahoma
12,179	Stewart, J. W.	Scott
10,283	Stewart, Marth J.	Jefferson
4,572	Stiles, D. M.	Adams
13,251	Stinson, Seaborn A.	Yalobusha
6,999	Stinyard, Benj.	Warren
12,271: 17,232:	Stites, Gerard	Warren
19,186	Stockard, Mary E.	Lafayette
9,178	Stokes, Littleton	Tippah
3,728	Stone, Jeremiah	Tishomingo
18,887	Stone, Melinda	Marshall
18,886	Stone, Melinda M.	Marshall
19,858	Stone, Saml. W., Estate of	Claiborne
4,698	Stone, Wm.	Marshall
1,143	Storment, Wm.	Tishomingo
5,602	Story, Elias W.	Yazoo
3,749	Stout, Joseph, Estate of	Alcorn
20,165	Strawhan, Nancy E.	Lafayette
6,282: 11,973:	Street, Donald	Alcorn
15,915	Strong, Augustus	Warren
3,460	Strong, C. W. & S. R.	Warren
5,687	Strong, David	Monroe
17,664	Strong, Nelson	Lafayette
7,002	Strong, Robert	Warren
3,460	Strong, S. R. & C. W.	Warren
5,333: 5,590:	Stubbs, Francis H.	Tippah
5,589	Stubbs, Thomas B.	Lee
8,775	Sugg, Andrew M.	Lafayette
3,822	Suitor, Emily	Alcorn
3,744	Suitor, Mary	Alcorn
13,275	Sullivan, Burcilla, Estate of	Panola
12,556	Sullivan, Daniel O.	Hinds
16,601	Sulm, George	Madison
7,347	Summers, Jonathan	Scott
3,840	Surratt, Jacob	Tippah
12,801	Surratt, Wm.	Alcorn
12,478	Sutherland, Job	Madison
18,182	Sutton, Roland D.	Alcorn
4,694	Swain, John	Union
21,352	Swain, John	Wilkinson
19,804	Swearingin, Alfred, Estate	Tunica
14,745	Swett, Daniel, Sr.	Warren

14,446	Switzer, Nannette	Washington
5,296	Sykes, Sarah	Panola
1,792	Tabb, Wm. L.	Choctaw
8,778: 17,671:	Tabor, Aquilla	Lafayette
8,503	Take, Emeline	Warren
14,770	Talbert, Mary D.	Yalobusha
8,780	Talliafero, Wm.	Lafayette
13,248	Tanner, Meredith, Estate	Panola
11,778	Tapley, M. C.	Hinds
11,209	Tarpley, Eliza	Hinds
14,608	Tarver, John	Yalobusha
13,870	Tarver, Robert	Yalobusha
7,066	Tate, Nancy L.	Amite
4,699	Tatum, Caroline	Lafayette
11,148	Tatum, E. W. & James	Monroe
11,148	Tatum, James & E. W.	Monroe
15,941	Tatum, John R.	De Soto
13,124	Taylor, James	Hinds
12,720	Taylor, John W.	Hinds
19,396	Taylor, John W.	Warren
3,319	Taylor, Richard	Warren
9,189	Tedar, W. B.	Hinds
10,277	Tegarden, Geo. W.	Pike
1,605	Telfair, James R.	Tishomingo
11,187	Tenney, Daniel K.	Warren
19,857	Terry, James C. & Carnes, James A., Estate of (from Shelby Co., Tenn.)	Coahoma
8,590	Thacker, Richard B.	Lafayette
10,166: 10,167:	Tharp, C. P.	Marshall
12,233	Thomas, Benj. R. & Mason, Thomas, M. of North Carolina	Warren
22,272	Thomas, John C.	Scott
11,829	Thomas, Sarah M.	Hinds
17,851	Thomas, Wm.	Warren
2,610	Thompson, Benj. B.	Warren
3,426	Thompson, Emma	Warren
8,305	Thompson, Grandison	Panola
4,938	Thompson, Lewis	Adams
8,508	Thompson, Robert	Warren
4,482	Thompson, Wm.	Marshall
10,307	Thorn, Joseph W.	Tishomingo
7,085	Thrash, Wilbourn	Scott
12,813	Threefoot, Abraham	Lauderdale
17,884	Thrift, Emily	Warren
4,700	Thurston, Wm.	Marshall
14,781	Tidwell, Berry R.	Panola
10,771	Tierney, John P.	Adams
17,683	Timleck, Matthew N.	Alcorn
10,895	Tindall, John L. & Carlisle, James	Monroe
8,319	Tinsley, Wm. R.	Claiborne
17,755	Tipton, Wiley W.	Attala
3,887	Tolar, Matthias H.	Alcorn
8,489	Tompkins, F. B., Estate of	Warren
4,220	Townsend, John	Warren
11,258: 14,278:	Townsend, Samuel	Warren
8,289	Trammel, Elisha, Estate of	Panola
13,247	Trapp, Julia	Lafayette
11,147	Truett, Melinda A.	Kemper
16,736	Tucker, Daniel	Adams
10,831	Tucker, Oteria E.	Warren
1,307	Turnage, Thomas T.	Marshall
13,972	Turnbull, Robert J., Estate	Issaquena
8,586	Turner, Elizabeth	Lafayette
10,803	Turner, Jane H.	Independence
12,403	Turner, Lucinda S.	Lincoln
4,329	Turner, Thomas	Adams
20,166	Turner, Wm.	Lafayette
14,777	Turner, Wm. H.	Yalobusha
13,254	Turner, Wm. J. F.	Tallahatchie
3,074	Tynes, Walter E.	Pike
11,989	Underhill, Geo. T.	Hinds
22,094	Underwood, A.	Bolivar
10,357	Unger, Elias	Claiborne
11,892	Vactor, Samuel Van	Madison
6,712	Valentine, James A.	Oktibbeha

7,348	Vance, David	Lauderdale
2,118	Vance, James I.	Newton
11,144	Vance, Robert	Lauderdale
872	Vanderford, Barzillia	Alcorn
7,003	Vanderford, John	Alcorn
11,892	Van Vactor, Samuel	Madison
8,516	Varner, Rufus M.	Lafayette
16,184	Verkins, Sarah	Warren
14,279	Vick, John W.	Warren
19,922	Viser, James H.	Lafayette
15,492	Volkening, Frederick W.	Clark
12,910	Von Seutter, Elisaues	Hinds
3,377	Wade, Alpheus	Alcorn
13,746	Wade, Waller	Yazoo
16,646	Wahlen, Adolph (La.), Estate of, and Larson, Barth	Harrison
21,173	Wailes, Levin	Warren
21,174	Wailes, Rebecca S. M.	Warren
8,539	Waldrick, Caroline	Lafayette
14,189	Waldrop, Harmon	Union
12,903	Waldrop, Penelope	Union
4,243	Waldrup, Mary M.	Panola
11,810	Walker, Abel	Tishomingo
7,068	Walker, Calvin	Pike
7,069	Walker, Hester	Pike
3,708	Walker, Jacob	Alcorn
1,839	Walker, James B.	Tishomingo
8,781	Walker, John	Lafayette
3,788	Walker, John	Monroe
9,835	Walker, John B.	Tishomingo
3,894	Walker, Josiah	Alcorn
13,726	Walker, Marietta	Yazoo
838	Walker, Sandy	Marshall
3,896	Walker, Thomas W.	Alcorn
22,259	Walker, W. R.	Tishomingo
13,206	Walker, Wm.	Alcorn
10,364	Walker, Wm. D.	Warren
16,437	Wall, John H.	Marshall
16,846	Wall, Wm.	Marshall
7,067	Wallace, James M.	Panola
3,888	Wallace, Wm. F.	Alcorn
16,779	Walsh, Antonet	Warren
19,538	Walton, Allen B.	Lafayette
5,331	Walton, Josiah N.	Monroe
19,106	Walton, Washington L.	Monroe
10,356	Ward, Adam J. & Martha S.	Hinds
15,029	Ward, Cyrus	Oktibbeha
16,554	Ward, David	Warren
2,266	Ward, E. P.	Marshall
7,004	Ward, Malinda	Warren
10,356	Ward, Martha S. & Adam J.	Hinds
4,896	Warner, James	Warren
2,466	Warren, Jackson	Madison
3,871	Warren, W. S.	Alcorn
695	Warren, Wm. C.	Marshall
8,219	Washington, Geo.	Adams
13,910	Washington, Geo.	Warren
19,805	Washington, Mack & Simon	Wilkinson
16,555	Watson, Henry	Warren
3,092	Watson, James M.	Rankin
17,890	Watson, Lewis C.	Issaquena
15,296	Watt, Robert, Sr.	Claiborne
869	Watt, Robert H. & Reeve, Lizzie C.	Warren
7,675	Watts, Dickerson	Warren
7,005	Watts, James C.	Warren
3,804	Wear, Robert B.	Alcorn
8,585	Weatherby, Joseph A.	Lafayette
21,934	Webb, A.	Marshall
16,179	Webb, W. M. C.	Winston
6,310	Webber, Jane	Tippah
3,321	Webster, Jacob	Warren
391	Weill, Charles	Rankin
3,722	Welch, Catharine	Tishomingo
279	Welch, Edmund L.	Tishomingo
4,333	Wells, Anderson	Adams
12,779	West, Elias	Warren
2,955	West, Wm. B.	Marshall
866	Wells, Nancy	Hinds
12,811	Wells, Nancy W.	Hinds

4,701	West, Holeman F.	Lafayette
278	West, J. L.	Tishomingo
13,748	West, J. R., Estate of	Holmes
5,046	West, Sarah A. R.	Lafayette
13,319	Weyer, Seraphin	Hinds
5,139	Whaley, Hamilton	Adams
911	Wharton, Mary Jane	Adams
21,965	Wheeler, Drummond	Lafayette
19,539	Wheeler, James E.	Lafayette
19,134	Wheeler, Thomas W.	Lafayette
3,730	Wheeler, Wm.	Alcorn
1,606	Wheelock, Josephus	Tishomingo
289	Whitaker, Wm.	Warren
12,267	White, Alex	Warren
14,876	White, John	Chickasaw
4,702	White, John H.	Lafayette
3,872	White, Jonathan	Prentiss
5,009	White, Martha	Claiborne
14,783	White, Matilda C.	Yalobusha
12,272	White, Wm.	Warren
5,680	White, Wm. T.	Monroe
12,817	Whitehurst, B. B. L.	Alcorn
10,573	Whitehurst, Eser H.	Tishomingo
3,748	Whiteside, Elizabeth C.	Prentiss
3,801	Whiteside, H. S.	Prentiss
3,828	Whiteside, Isaac N.	Alcorn
3,859	Whiteside, John F.	Alcorn
3,724	Whitfield, Nancy	Tishomingo
10,198	Whitney, Franklin S.	Claiborne
18,660	Whittaker, Eli	Marshall
2,300	Whittaker, Sam	Warren
18,569	Whittington, Susan	Warren
15,297	Wicklip, Henry	Claiborne
15,352	Wilbourne, Wm. R., Estate	Panola
384	Wilbunn, Julia M.	Benton
17,614	Wilcox, Joseph D.	Lafayette
3,910	Wilder, Geo. E.	Lee
3,886	Wildman, Benj.	Prentiss
16,632	Wilkins, Maria L.	Yazoo
10,575	Willet, Richard	Tishomingo
20,163	Williams, A., Judge	Lafayette
11,776	Williams, Bovina	Warren
19,924	Williams, Butler	Adams
21,052	Williams, Byron	Adams
17,616	Williams, Charles H.	Lafayette
14,769	Williams, G. W., Estate of	Yalobusha
7,006	Williams, Henry G.	Tishomingo
12,397	Williams, Jane	Amite
10,839	Williams, Jesse	Warren
7,070	Williams, Joseph R.	Amite
20,163	Williams, Judge A.	Lafayette
19,272	Williams, Lamb, Estate of	Warren
10,304	Williams, Levi	Tishomingo
12,362	Williams, Lewis	Hinds
19,843	Williams, Malinda	Bolivar
8,081	Williams, Mary Ann	De Soto
8,549	Williams, Roderick, Estate	Lafayette
19,695	Williams, Samuel	Lafayette
22,069	Williams, Silas H.	Claiborne
10,372	Williams, Susan	Warren
4,714	Williams, W. J.	Marshall
8,303	Williams, Wm. H., Estate	Panola
12,401	Williams, Winney	Pike
7,614	Williamson, Cisilie M. J.	Warren
10,567	Williamson, L. E.	Alcorn
19,883	Willis, Joel H., Estate	Warren
2,119	Willis, John	Newton
12,389	Willoughby, Catharine	Marion
12,257	Wilson, Annie, Bettie & Mary	Washington
11,968	Wilson, David L.	Rankin
21,079	Wilson, Harvey D.	Benton
8,537	Wilson, Jason C.	Lafayette
13,256	Wilson, Josephine	Tallahatchie
9,938	Wilson, Judith	Lafayette
13,696	Wilson, Louis H.	Warren
12,257	Wilson, Mary, Annie & Bettie	Washington
12,591	Wilson, Millis	Warren
20,264	Wilson, Tillissee, W., Heirs of	Tishomingo
9,946	Wimberly, Lewis	Lafayette
16,553	Winfield, Harrison	Warren
2,851	Winston, James A. G.	Adams
16,780	Winston, Nicholas	Benton
18,415	Winter, George	Madison
13,252	Winter, Henry W.	Yalobusha
1,947	Wixon, Oliver H. P.	Warren
16,602	Wohner, Michael	Madison
22,070	Womble, Wm. H.	Yalobusha
5,976	Wood, Abram	Madison
8,300	Wood, James S.	Panola
19,884	Wood, Robert Y.	Jefferson
16,627	Wood, Wm. W.	Yazoo
17,992	Woodbury, George W., & Robt. S.	Yazoo
12,960	Woodcock, Harrison	Hinds
3,737	Woodruff, John H.	Prentiss
10,290	Woodry, John A.	Warren
7,318	Woods, John	Tishomingo
5,603	Woods, Lewis	Monroe
4,703	Woods, M. F.	Marshall
17,037	Woodson, R. O.	Marshall
3,879	Woodward, Hester Ann	Alcorn
9,565	Wooley, James F.	Pike
15,290	Wooten, Wm.	Marshall
8,301	Wootton, Wm. R.	Panola
15,016	Worthington, Ann	Washington
8,523	Wright, James B.	Warren
12,735: 3,077:	Wright, John, Estate of	Tippah
4,244	Wright, Joseph J.	Panola
3,891	Wright, Mary E.	Alcorn
17,843	Wright, Mary G.	Warren
7,605	Wright, Martha M.	Claiborne
16,989	Wright, Rebecca L.	Issaquena
21,966	Wright, Wm.	Lafayette
4,331	Yager, Peter	Adams
8,143	Yates, Napoleon B.	Hinds
3,901	Yeats, Wm.	Prentiss
14,897	Yeiser, A. L.	Hinds
3,428	Yeiser, A. L. & Smith, Wm. D.	Hinds
6,298: 12,782:	Young, Amanda	Tippah
7,007: 9,187:	Young, Amanda H.	Hinds
3,878	Young, B. F.	Alcorn
8,320	Young, Clarissa	Claiborne
10,828	Young, Elizabeth D.	Warren
8,782	Young, Henry S.	Lafayette
3,829	Young, Isaac R.	Prentiss
10,800: 17,497:	Young, John	Yalobusha
4,897	Young, Marvel W.	Benton
6,290	Young, Milton	Tippah
14,734	Young, T. J., Estate of	Tishomingo
13,074	Youngs, James W., Estate	Warren
8,566	Yowell, Lewis	Marshall
11,824	Zanders, Evaline	Warren

NORTH CAROLINA

21,029	Aaron, Lipman	Warren
8,404	Abbott, James D.	Cherokee
17,750	Abernathy, Coleman	Gaston
9,156	Adams, Alford	Wake
10,404	Adams, Allen	Watauga
5,719	Adams, John Q.	Cumberland
13,194	Adams, John Q., Sr.	Wake
13,193	Adams, Quinton	Johnston
8,171	Albertson, Edward C.	Perquimans
18,043	Albright, Wm. R.	Alamance
10,168	Aldridge, Lemuel H.	Lenoir
14,758	Aldridge, Robert	Wayne

4,163	Allen, Wm. H.	Franklin
6,388	Allison, Mary	Transyl-vania
11,935	Allman, Jacob	Buncombe
4,092	Allred, Jacob C.	Yadkin
20,520	Allred, Mary	Yadkin
4,225	Altman, Alfred	Johnston
21,250	Ambrose, Wilson G.	Tyrrell
18,311	Anders, John C.	Buncombe
3,552	Anderson, Caswell	Wake
17,735	Anderson, John A., Estate	Hertford
18,309	Anderson, Robert	Madison
16,301	Anderson, Wm.	Madison
16,307	Andress, Abram	Madison
14,556	Andrews, G. W.	Stokes
2,187	Andrews, Ivey	Jones
3,553	Andrews, John G.	Wake
1,222	Andrews, Joseph G.	Wake
2,188	Andrews, Peter	Jones
3,551	Andrews, Wm. N.	Wake
20,804	Arendell, Mary B. & Willey L.	Carteret
20,804	Arendell, Willey L. & Mary B.	Carteret
19,178	Armstrong, Arthur	Gaston
3,479	Armstrong, James A.	Yadkin
18,841	Armstrong, John L.	Gaston
17,747	Armstrong, John M.	Gaston
9,418	Arnold, Abel D.	Harnett
10,948	Arnold, Elizabeth	Harnett
9,417	Arnold, Wm.	Harnett
11,945	Arrington, Robert W.	Madison
20,411	Asher, Isaac Heirs of	Pasquotank
9,889	Atkins, Josiah, Jr.	Orange
8,126	Atkinson, G. W.	Wake
10,820	Atkinson, Wm. F.	Wayne
19,990	Atwater, Joseph W.	Chatham
21,789	Atwater, Matthew	Orange
6,343	Atwater, Wesley	Orange
6,342	Atwater, Wilson	Orange
4,623	Avent, John F.	Wake
7,627	Avera, Catharine	Harnett
17,390	Austin, Thos. J.	Caldwell
13,195	Babcock, Palmer	Wake
11,116	Bagley, Russell	Cumberland
1,860	Bagwell, Berry	Wake
1,862	Bagwell, Granberry R.	Wake
1,861	Bagwell, Green B.	Wake
1,863	Bagwell, Needham	Wake
1,864	Bagwell, Wm. S.	Wake
8,689	Bailey, Benj. E.	Washington
18,979	Bailey, James	Mitchell
14,695	Bailey, John C. & Hart, Levi	New Hanover
2,611	Bailey, Mary	Wake
1,859	Bailey, Sarah A.	Wake
2,054	Baird, Mary A. P.	Person
2,055	Baird, Nathaniel H.	Person
10,407	Baird, Rittenhouse	Watauga
14,356	Baity, Henry	Davie
15,461	Baker, David, Estate of	Davie
5,931	Baker, Rebecca	Cherokee
4,045	Baker, Wm.	Wake
19,925	Baldwin, Benj.	Cumberland
20,200	Baldwin, Joseph J.	Chatham
21,303	Baldwin, Melville T.	Chatham
12,788	Ball, Marcus	Orange
2,304	Ball, Philip	Davidson
17,501	Ballance, James C.	Hyde
11,734	Ballew, John R.	Cherokee
11,206	Banks, Davis	Richmond
11,623	Banks, Joseph Ballard	Jones
6,478	Banks, Lynn	Wake
6,766	Banks, Susan A.	Wake
15,706	Banks, W. Gaston	Johnston
18,937	Barbee, Fletcher	Orange
4,090	Barber, Bilson B.	Yadkin
4,457	Barber, Simeon	Johnston
5,732	Barefoot, Handy	Harnett
5,733	Barefoot, John	Harnett
11,581	Barnes, Manley	Caldwell

18,357	Barnes, Sarah	Dare
17,715	Barnes, Solomon D.	Wilkes
21,204	Barnum, Charles H., Heirs	Onslow
14,296	Barr, James	Stokes
677	Barrentine, Charles A.	Richmond
678	Barrentine, Philip J.	Richmond
676	Barrentine, Stephen T.	Richmond
11,936	Barrett, John E.	Buncombe
5,718	Barrow, Wiley	Greene
5,065	Bashford, James	Wake
9,803	Bass, Wm.	Wayne
13,234	Basswood, Gideon	Currituck
6,344	Batchalor, Bennett	Chatham
18,982	Baum, Samuel	Dare
13,229	Baxter, James F.	Currituck
755	Beaird, Dorcas S.	Gaston
12,915	Beamon, R. C. D.	Greene
3,481	Beamon, Thos. W.	Yadkin
5,302	Beasley, Kembrick M. C.	Johnston
10,021	Beckham, Edward	Alexander
18,226	Becton, Thos., Estate of	Lenoir
7,324	Beel, Christopher	Lincoln
8,127	Bell, Burrell	Wake
9,762	Bell, Cornelius	Carteret
1,669	Bell, Dan	Carteret
15,875	Bell, David W.	Carteret
21,246	Bell, Durant H. L.	Carteret
20,026	Bell, Elijah S.	Carteret
12,048	Bell, G. W.	Pasquotank
8,668	Bell, Gideon C.	Carteret
1,950	Bell, James M.	Clay
9,764	Bell, Josiah	Carteret
19,073	Bell, Rufus W.	Carteret
7,909	Bell, Sam N.	Clay
1,437	Benfield, Joseph	Burke
3,480	Benham, Bilson Bilza	Yadkin
8,785	Bennett, Charles	Orance
18,945	Bennett, James	Orange
4,625	Bennett, John	Wake
6,060	Bennett, Risten H.	Anson
3,057	Bennick, David R.	Lincoln
3,058	Benton, David	Gates
786	Berry, Wm. A.	New Hanover
3,056	Bess, Lawson	Lincoln
3,055	Bess, Peter	Lincoln
5,907	Beth, Dicey	Harnett
6,621	Bethune, Luachlin	Cumberland
16,240	Biggs, Philip H.	Cumberland
10,399	Bishop, Sam J.	Watauga
8,038	Bizzell, Samuel	Sampson
9,708	Black, Daniel	Cumberland
5,777	Black, Joseph	Cherokee
3,053	Black, Vincent	Gaston
10,242	Blackburn, Wm.	Lincoln
1,849	Blake, Craty	Wake
1,844	Blake, Marinda	Wake
15,450	Blackwelder, Allen M.	Davie
1,948	Blackwell, Elisha C.	Cherokee
1,949	Blackwell, James W.	Cherokee
8,787	Blackwood, Alex	Orange
8,768	Blackwood, Robert	Orange
9,578	Blalock, Wm.	Mitchell
1,865	Bledsoe, Jacob	Wake
4,171	Bliven, Geo. B.	Dare
20,186	Blount, Benj.	Bladen
3,759	Blue, Christian	Robeson
10,450	Blue, Duncan, Estate of	Cumberland
19,962	Blythe, James	Cherokee
11,915	Blythe, James	Henderson
17,027	Bobbitt, John J.	Wake
14,382	Bodenhamer, Jacob B.	Davidson
10,728	Bodenhamer, Wm.	Davidson
7,617	Boggan, Alex M.	Anson
17,306	Boils, Harrison	Iredell
2,108	Bolger, Abel V.	Craven
1,707	Bolick, Matthias	Alexander
5,429	Bolton, Peter, Sr.	Cumberland
5,909	Bolton, Woodson	Wake
20,623	Bond, Geo.	Chowan
18,406	Bond, Henry A., Sr.	Chowan

2,030	Bond, James F.	Gates
15,999	Boner, Jonathan	Davidson
15,451	Booe, Nancy C.	Davie
13,196	Booker, Dilly	Wake
1,708	Boon, Wm.	Gates
20,591	Boothe, Alfred, Estate of	Orange
4,078	Boothe, J. W.	Wake
18,892	Boswood, Gideon C.	Currituck
9,680	Bottoms, John	Camden
20,009	Bovey, Harriet	Catawba
13,341	Bowditch, Joseph H.	Yancey
9,427	Bowdon, Mary A., and Hare, Susan L.	Cumberland
3,758	Bowen, Bryan	Robeson
8,039	Bowen, Lewis	Cumberland
6,345	Bowers, Cannon	Orange
8,784	Bowers, W. G.	Orange
13,638	Bradbury, Ephraim	Wayne
13,639	Bradbury, Mary H.	Wayne
17,333	Bradley, Wm.	McDowell
2,029	Brady, John	Gates
18,582	Bragg, Sam D.	Hyde
1,846	Branham, Needham	Wake
13,062	Bratcher, Lewis	Craven
5,067	Brendel, Elizabeth	Catawba
5,778	Brendle, Wm. N.	Cherokee
11,545	Brewer, Nancy	Orange
12,200	Bridges, Thomas S.	Cleveland
13,232	Bright, Elizabeth A.	Carrituck
5,908	Bright, Oren	Wake
4,626	Bright, Wm.	Wake
15,452	Brineger, Thomas H.	Davie
9,745	Brinkley, Martin L.	Chowan
11,553	Brinn, Joseph C.	Perquimans
15,068	Brinson, Ida	Wayne
3,194	Briscoe, Mary E.	Gates
3,042	Bristow, G. W.	Richmond
1,867	Britt, Hardy	Wake
7,749	Britt, J. Pinkney	Wayne
15,830	Britt, Joseph L.	Wake
6,307	Britt, Kinchen	Wayne
1,866	Britt, Marion D.	Wake
15,560	Britton, Charles	Northampton
18,409	Britton, W. P., Estate of	Hertford
4,627	Broadwell, Josiah	Wake
17,847	Brockett, John A.	Camden
20,388	Brockwell, Anderson	Orange
6,346	Brockwell, Elizabeth	Orange
6,347	Brockwell, Thos.	Orange
7,072	Brockwell, Wm.	Orange
20,624	Brothers, James C.	Pasquotank
13,814	Brothers, Richard	Pasquotank
3,690	Broughton, Matilda	Wake
18,227	Brown, Burton	Buncombe
6,316	Brown, James	Haywood
14,877	Brown, James H.	Wilkes
9,444	Brown, John	Cherokee
13,228: 21,724:	Brown, Joseph, Estate of	Currituck
17,307	Brown, Mary	Surrey
11,459	Brown, Murdock	Richmond
17,581	Brown, Nicholas	Cumberland
22,184	Brown, Sarah P. C.	Rowan
4,946	Brown, Solomon	Wake
9,898: 9,901:	Brown, W. W.	Pasquotank
10,879	Brown, Wm.	Brunswick
21,288	Brown, Wm. C.	Buncombe
6,573	Brown, Wm. M.	Wake
3,482	Brummell, H. W.	Davidson
11,312	Bryan, Austin & Wm.	Chatham
12,928	Bryan, Benj. L.	Jones
8,853	Bryan, Harrison	Northampton
9,181	Bryan, Lewis	Craven
8,747	Bryan, Moses	Craven
1,709	Bryant, Dan. A.	Cumberland
17,582	Bryant, Wm. S.	Cumberland
7,920	Bryson, Wm.	Cherokee
6,447	Buchanan, Elbert	Chatham
1,868	Buck, James W.	Wake
1,668	Bucklin, Wm. H.	Craven
11,943	Buckner, Jeremiah	Buncombe
8,461	Buckner, Manley	Chatham
17,520	Buie, Gilbert E.	Cumberland
6,438	Buie, Rebecca	Cumberland
760	Bulcken, John G.	New Hanover
4,466	Bullard, Thomas	Sampson
18,729	Bullock, Thomas	Cumberland
3,760	Bunn, Frederick	Caldwell
7,073	Burges, Wm.	Orange
508	Burgess, Green Y.	Cherokee
5,567	Burgess, Hezakiah	Camden
19,542	Burgess, John S.	Pasquotank
1,392	Burgess, Thomas	Burke
9,580	Burleson, Jonathan	Mitchell
9,581	Burleson, Wilson	Mitchell
6,599	Burnes, Silas	Chatham
20,389	Burnett, Atlas A.	Chatham
6,348	Burroughs, Louisa	Orange
4,628	Burt, Jesse	Wake
17,904	Burton, Dempsey	Currituck
10,734	Burton, Eli G.	Davidson
757	Butler, Thos.	Richmond
16,000	Butner, John	Forsyth
1,813	Butts, Elias H.	Pitt
13,677	Byers, Francis C.	Henderson
14,357	Cain, Richmond F.	Davie
9,583	Calaway, Benj.	Mitchell
19,244	Caldwell, Andrew J.	Catawba
8,430	Caldwell, Hannah P. R.	Burke
1,158	Cameron, A. McF.	Greene
8,205	Cameron, Hugh A.	Harnett
11,504	Campbell, Angus	Richmond
11,977	Campbell, Dan W.	Richmond
7,628	Campbell, Flora A.	Harnett
11,932	Candler, James M.	Madison
5,949	Cannon, Henry	Lenoir
16,259	Cantrell, John	Henderson
12,802	Capps, John B.	Wayne
825	Carigan, James A.	Alexander
11,540	Carlton, A. M.	Orange
10,387	Carlton, Wyatt	Watauga
1,795	Carpenter, Joseph	Gaston
4,174	Carpenter, Mary	Lincoln
5,068: 20,967:	Carr, John W.	Orange
17,275	Carrell, John L.	Rockingham
9,159	Carroll, Piety	Wake
11,427	Carron, Sam T.	Wake
3,483	Carson, John	Rowan
20,185	Carson, John M.	Alexander
3,484	Carson, Wm. L.	Rowan
3,195	Carter, Henry	Gates
20,605	Carter, Henry, Sr.	Cumberland
15,561	Carter, Jeremiah	Northampton
6,264	Carver, James B.	Cumberland
9,333	Carver, Mary E.	Cumberland
4,878	Case, Enos	Greene
11,931: 16,256:	Case, Wm.	Transylvania
12,503	Castle, Wm. H.	Orange
1,280	Cemetary Co., Pine Forest	New Hanover
10,739: 14,297:	Chadwick, John	Davidson
21,742	Chaffin, Nathan S. A.	Davie
606	Chambers, Jessie	Person
2,057	Chandler, Dan S.	Person
4,921	Chapel, Ann	Cumberland
4,543: 4,544:	Chapin, Ansel B.	Chatham
1,681	Chapman, Geo.	Alexander
13,571	Chappell, Edward	Wake
12,495	Chappel, Sam	Wake
10,710	Charles, Elisha	Guilford
9,291: 10,715:	Charles, Elisha, Jr.	Guilford
10,957	Charles, Jacob	Forsyth
15,453	Charles, John T.	Davie
11,312	Chatham, Wm. and Austin	Chatham
17,736	Chavers, John	Richmond

19,225	Chavers, John A.	Wilkes
679	Chavis, James	Richmond
6,349	Cheek, James M.	Orange
8,633	Copeland, Henry	Northampton
9,066	Copeland, John	Northampton
3,485	Copeland, John H.	Burke
10,391	Cordel, John	Surrey
12,531	Corn, Jesse M.	Henderson
12,528	Corn, Nolen P.	Henderson
4,792	Costen, Joseph B.	Gates
17,749	Costner, Simon P., Sr.	Gaston
12,553	Cottrell, James M.	Caldwell
7,074	Couch, Dicey	Orange
9,884	Couch, John	Orange
7,075	Couch, Wm.	Orange
2,776	Councill, Jesse	Watauga
10,384	Councill, Sally L.	Watauga
10,416: 11,165:	Covert, Henry	Craven
660	Covington, Elizabeth	Richmond
11,460	Covington, James D., Estate	Richmond
17,739	Covington, James P.	Richmond
2,032	Cowper, Wills	Gates
7,765	Cox, Isaac H.	Wayne
9,754	Cox, James W.	Wayne
13,122	Cox, John W.	Wayne
8,756	Cox, Lydia P.	Wayne
7,752	Cox, Nathan B.	Wayne
7,750	Cox, Wm.	Wayne
4,103	Cox, Wm. S.	Hyde
7,751	Cox, Wm. T.	Wayne
15,169	Craig, Wm. M. & Elisha	Cherokee
8,788	Craige, Elizabeth	Orange
17,909	Crain, Julia	Currituck
21,940	Crawford, Sylvia	Craven
2,372	Crawford, Wm. G.	Wayne
9,180	Creech, James H.	Wake
10,718	Crews, Charles E.	Forsyth
10,719	Crews, Joseph L.	Forsyth
9,003	Crisp, John A.	Cherokee
8,833	Crisp, John M.	Cherokee
5,912	Crowder, Lewis H.	Wake
8,128	Crowder, Thos. A.	Wake
5,979	Crowley, Elijah	Cherokee
3,671	Crumpler, Wm., Wiley (also 3,668)	Wayne
7,479	Culpepper, Henry, Estate of	Pasquotank
9,115	Currie, Dan	Richmond
1,812	Dail, T. T.	Greene
3,343	Dailey, Daniel	Pasquotank
3,344	Dailey, Edmund	Pasquotank
11,575	Dala, John	Caldwell
11,628	Cherry, Blount	Carteret
20,118	Cherry, Jacob	Beaufort
11,449	Cherry, Nancy	Martin
12,199	Chesson, John B.	Washington
17,498	Chester, Wm.	Hyde
6,472	Chinard, Andrew	Davidson
720	Clapp, Elisha B. & Heap, John G.	Mitchell
5,735	Clark, D. & Archibald	Harnett
2,708	Clark, George	Davidson
11,558	Clark, Wm. R.	Cumberland
299	Clarke, Henry	Richmond
14,298	Clayton, H. F.	Forsyth
19,130	Clayton, Richard	Chowan
20,592	Clayton, Sam S.	Orange
17,521	Clements, Clavin	Harnett
1,682	Cline, Elijah	Alexander
22,296	Cloninger, Michael	Gaston
19,949	Coats, John R.	Johnston
9,056	Goates, Thos. H.	Wake
5,088	Coffey, James	Clay
17,308	Coffin, Elwood	Iredell
17,374	Cohen, Esidore	Edgecombe
14,549	Colbert, Elisha	Beaufort
9,057	Colclough, John T.	Wake
20,390	Cole, Elijah	Chatham
19,432	Cole, G. W.	Buncombe
300	Cole, Geo.	Richmond
12,688	Cole, Hugh	Pasquotank
8,789	Cole, Isaiah	Orange
21,289	Cole, Jeremiah	Buncombe
12,789	Cole, John	Orange
17,740	Cole, John M.	Richmond
12,790	Cole, Sam	Orange
8,791	Cole, Stephen E.	Chatham
8,790	Cole, Wesley	Orange
11,895	Cole, Willis	Wayne
1,084	Coleman, A.	Cherokee
3,572	Coley, H. D.	Wake
15,454	Collette, Charles	Davie
9,160	Collins, Eaton	Wake
17,097	Colton, Richard C.	Chatham
16,319	Colwell, Andy C.	Haywood
6,317	Colwell, David M.	Haywood
6,102	Conley, Albert	McDowell
10,029	Copeland, Edwin G.	Wayne
22,177	Copeland, Eli C.	Northampton
18,866	Copeland, Elizabeth	Wake
7,146	Dale, Elizabeth & Mahala	Cherokee
21,702	Dale, James	Duplin
7,146	Dale, Mahala & Elizabeth	Cherokee
3,487	Dalton, Sarah	Yadkin
19,217	Dancey, Rachel	Wilkes
5,877	Daniel, Alex	Alexander
11,661	Daniel, Ferry	Orange
2,373	Daniel, Wm.	Wayne
8,041	Darrock, Daniel	Cumberland
17,216	Daugherty, Daniel	Craven
4,105	David, Andrew	Alexander
13,236	Davis, Andrew J.	Currituck
9,859: 14,908:	Davis, Anthony	Lenoir
2,612	Davis, Benj. H.	Wake
6,350	Davis, Charles	Orange
11,919	Davis, D. F.	Madison
18,131	Davis, Dorcas E.	Gaston
6,351	Davis, Duncan C.	Orange
16,669	Davis, Horace C.	Yadkin
1,851	Davis, Israel S.	Carterel
14,909	Davis, James, Estate of	Lenoir
2,374	Davis, John, Jr.	Wayne
4,468	Davis, John, Sr.	Wayne
15,455	Davis, Jones	Davie
10,740	Davis, L. Franklin	Guilford
18,410	Davis, Levi S.	Hertford
14,936	Davis, Robert W.	Brunswick
16,320	Davis, Wilburn R.	Haywood
6,352	Davis, Wyatt	Orange
422	Dawkins, Benj. C.	Richmond
17,309	Day, Triplet	Yadkin
18,596	Day, Wm. P.	Person
1,683	Deal, Aaron	Alexander
20,267	Deal, Hosea	Catawba
3,659	Deal, John E.	Alexander
1,684	Deal, Silas	Alexander
1,281	Deal, Susan	Halifax
5,072	Deanes, Dan T.	Rockingham
2,375	Deanes, George	Wayne
2,724	Deanes, James	Wayne
6,308	Deanes, Thos. A.	Wayne
9,004	Deaver, T. S.	Cherokee
9,005	Deaver, Wm. H.	Cherokee
5,954	Deile, Elbert	Greene
21,101	Delen, Phineas, Estate	Pasquotank
8,634	Deloatch, Dorsey S.	Northampton
16,315	Dempsey, Luke M.	Haywood
3,060	Detherow, Geo.	Lincoln
13,235	Dey, J. S., Estate	Currituck
12,929	Dibble, James H.'	Lenoir
11,314	Dickens, Nehemiah	Moore
12,743	Dickenson, Dan, Estate of	Carteret
13,817	Dickenson, Wm. H.	Carteret
4,717	Dickinson, John: Walker, Wilson; and Whedber, James S.	Currituck
17,742	Dickson, Wm. S., Estate of	Gaston
16,304	Dillinger, Matthias	Mitchell
19,950	Dishman, Joshua	Wake

12,791	Dixon, Abner A.	Orange
11,477	Dixon, James S.	Greene
18,916	Dockery, Fannie S.	Richmond
7,910	Dockery, John	Cherokee
7,076	Dodd, Frances	Orange
8,792	Dollar, Jesse	Chatham
6,353	Dollar, Sidney	Orange
1,951	Donaldson, Wm.	Cherokee
9,756	Dougherty, Aley	Sampson
10,403	Dougherty, Louisa	Watauga
3,489	Douthit, Jacob	Davie
14,140	Dowdy, Samuel	Currituck
19,125	Downs, James	Caldwell
17,504	Doxey, John; Halstead, Tully; and Sears, C. T.	Currituck
15,806	Drake, Elsie	Cumberland
3,399	Drake, James, Estate of	Henderson
5,913	Dudley, James	Harnett
13,239	Dudley, Wm.	Currituck
10,821	Duffy, Margaret	Wayne
8,793	Duke, Eliza A.	Orange
12,144	Dula, James	Watauga
11,579	Dula, Wm. S.	Caldwell
2,249	Duncan, James H.	McDowell
12,532	Duncan, John G.	Henderson
12,073	Duncan, Jonathan	Pasquotank
17,583	Dunn, Lewis	Cumberland
13,237	Dunton, Spence	Currituck
1,869	Dupree, Alvin	Wake
4,948	Dupree, John G.	Wake
4,630	Dupree, L. H.	Wake
13,192	Dupree, Louis	Wake
4,632	Dupree, Nancy	Wake
9,161	Dupree, Sarah A.	Wake
3,575	Duprey, S. G.	Wake
17,277	Durham, Harry	Johnston
16,199	Dwinn, Columbus	Henderson
14,557	Eades, Winston	Stokes
21,199	Eason, Jesse	Gates
4,226	Eason, John	Johnston
6,534	Eason, Robert W.	Gates
3,490	Eaton, Ebenezer	Yadkin
4,633	Eddins, Matthew	Wake
4,634	Eddins, S. W.	Wake
18,483	Edgerton, John Henry	Wayne
14,006	Edgerton, Richard W.	Wayne
2,725	Edwards, John	Wayne
12,184	Edwards, Marcellus J.	Wilson
1,618	Edwards, Robert	Greene
15,079	Edwards, Solomon T.	Stokes
1,617	Edwards, Wm. L.	Greene
4,227	Eldridge, Abigail	Johnston
4,229	Eldridge, Elizabeth	Johnston
4,228	Eldridge, John	Johnston
4,230	Eldridge, Susannah	Johnston
16,782	Elliot, Elias	Northampton
2,250	Elliot, Mary A.	McDowell
10,007: 19,865:	Elliot, Mordecai M.	Pasquotank
1,797	Elliot, Thos.	Perquimons
9,067	Elliot, Thos. P.	Northampton
19,127	Ellis, Allen	Chatham
203	Ellis, Daniel	Cumberland
14,739	Ellis, Elijah W.	Craven
204	Ellis, Flora	Cumberland
2,112	Ellis, Hamson	Gates
5,430	Elmore, John H.	Samspon
5,914	Emery, A. B.	Wake
3,762	Epps, Elizabeth	McDowell
10,943	Ernest, Elizabeth E.	Caldwell
20,725	Etheridge, Josiah H.	Bertie
20,024	Etheridge, Wm. D.	Bertie
7,331	Eubank, L. L.	Jones
8,129	Evans, Enoch	Wake
14,158	Evans, Evan	Lenoir
9,072	Evans, Sam	Henderson
2,376	Evans, Warren	Wayne
20,115	Evington, James	Beaufort
14,878	Fairchild, Wilson	Wilkes
12,916	Faircloth, James B.	Greene
18,842	Falls, Nancy S.	Gaston
13,227: 21,725:	Fanshaw, John & Snowden, Barbara	Currituck
18,314	Farmer, Andrew	Madison
5,784	Farmer, John H.	Cherokee
9,885	Farrar, Thos. B.	Chatham
18,893	Farrow, Tilmon	Hyde
18,382	Farthing, Reuben	Watauga
18,944	Farthing, Thos. H.	Orange
4,933	Faucett, Henry	Harnett
6,354	Fawcett, W. R.	Orange
20,190	Fearington, Batheina, Estate	Chatham
8,794	Fearrington, Edward P.	Chatham
9,893	Fearrington, John J.	Chatham
12,745: 19,071:	Felton, Wm.	Carteret
16,670	Felts, Harrison C.	Wilkes
4,109	Felts, Harrison C.	Yadkin
7,955	Fennell, Sarah	Northampton
13,231: 19,158:	Ferebe, James M.	Currituck
1,160	Fields, Bennett	Greene
18,559	Finger, Solomon, Estate of	Lincoln
10,651	Fink, John	Cabarrus
13,443	Fisher, Elijah	Duplin
471	Fisher, Joseph	Rowan
15,710	Fisher, Squire	Buncombe
4,110	Fisher, Timothy M.	Hyde
8,852	Flanner, Alex	New Hanover
10,406	Fletcher, Enoch	Watauga
21,340	Fletcher, Philip C.	Pasquotank
15,719	Flint, Wm. H.	Stokes
11,067	Flippin, Sam M.	Stokes
17,848	Flora, Susan	Camden
1,713	Flowers, Adam	Alexander
7,753	Flowers, Joel	Sampson
260	Floyd, Hugh H.	Gaston
18,383	Floyd, John W.	Watauga
13,226: 22,193:	Forbes, Joseph B.	Currituck
3,579	Ford, C. M.	Wake
9,752	Forehard, Elizabeth	Sampson
20,995	Foreman, Joshua T.	Carteret
5,263	Forrest, Wm. P.	Wake
17,712	Forsyth, Mary, Estate of	Granville
17,977	Foster, Charles M.	Dare
21,982	Foster, Flavel W.	New Hanover
15,456	Foster, Ransom	Davie
747	Foster, Thos. J.	Rowan
11,576	Foster, Wilson	Caldwell
17,524	Fowler, Hillmon	Granville
16,261	Fowler, Nathan	Henderson
2,861	Fowler, Sam R.	Beaufort
1,149	Fox, Solomon	Alexander
19,155	Foy, Mary A.	New Hanover
10,205	Franck, Maria	Onslow
3,493	Franklin, Biddie	Burke
3,492	Franklin, Ferlina	Burke
4,635	Franklin, G. B.	Wake
8,679	Franklin, Joe R.	Carteret
18,307	Franklin, John	Madison
7,020	Frederick, Martha	Duplin
7,019	Frederick, Norris	New Hanover
9,882	Freeland, Geo. S.	Orange
19,092	Freeman, G. W.	Madison
2,037	Freeman, James	Gates
7,557	Freeman, James	Lenoir
21,094	French, Henry E.	Craven
756	Friday, Elizabeth C.	Gaston
22,249	Fulcher, C.	Dare
13,818: 19,070:	Fulcher, Jesse	Farteret
13,819	Fulcher, Reuben	Carteret
9,860	Fulcher, Wm. T.	Carteret
15,080	Fulk, Wm.	Forsyth
11,169	Fuller, Evander	Richmond
18,839	Furguson, Mary	Gaston
14,879	Furguson, Wm. T.	Wilkes
10,518	Futrell, Ira & Morris; and Revell, James	Northampton

17,849	Gallop, Elihu	Camden
2,113	Gamble, John Gaston	Guilford
5,435	Garden, Rebecca	McDowell
4,636	Gardner, David H.	Wake
10,541	Gardner, Benj.	Harnett
16,698	Garmon, Isaac	Buncombe
9,196	Garner, Elijah M.	Carteret
10,128	Garner, Francis M.	Carteret
18,895	Garner, Siloam Jane; and Morton, David W.	Craven
16,312	Garrett, W. G. B.	Haywood
11,916	Garrison, Isaac	Buncombe
11,834	Gaskins, Arthur	Craven
6,436	Gaskins, Seth	Pitt
3,196	Gatling, Elizabeth	Gates
2,038	Gatling, Joseph	Gates
20,391	Gattes, Thos. W.	Chatham
7,077	Gattis, James B.	Wake
18,934	Geer, Frederick C.	Orange
18,936	Geer, Jesse B.	Orange
18,933	George, Henderson	Orange
19,065	Gibbs, Susan M.	Wilkes
17,914	Gibson, Abner	Currituck
672	Gibson, Caroline J.	Richmond
4,637	Gill, Turrell	Wake
11,313	Gilmore, John A.	Chatham
19,221	Glass, John	Wilkes
3,494	Glen, Tyre	Yadkin
3,580	Glenn, Anderson	Wake
12,737	Glidewell, Zachariah	Stokes
17,499	Glover, Andrew J.	Hyde
16,777	Godfrey, Thos. N.	Yadkin
418	Godwin, Henry D.	Hertford
2,344	Godwin, Joshua	Sampson
8,757	Godwin, Wm. C.	Sampson
9,861	Golding, Martin	Carteret
4,638	Gooch, Dan	Wake
1,847	Gooch, Duncan, Estate of	Wake
12,241	Gooch, Roldan	Wake
12,494	Goodin, Frederick	Wake
10,449	Goodman, Elizabeth	Cumberland
1,870	Coodwin, Anderson T.	Wake
4,245	Goodwin, Calvin	Chatham
5,438	Goodwin, Edwin	Cumberland
778	Goodwin, Jefferson	Wake
17,897	Goodwin, Kenney	Northampton
1,871	Goodwin, Kindrick	Wake
13,197	Goodwin, Simon P.	Wake
11,927	Googe, Wiley C.	Mitchell
8,130	Gower, James	Wake
20,075	Gragg, Wm. M.	Watauga
661	Graham, Angus D.	Richmond
9,419	Graham, Frances	Cumberland
4,073	Graham, M. N.	Cherokee
20,270	Graham, Stephen	Catawba
9,753	Grantham, Needham	Sampson
14,289	Grantham, Uriah	Wayne
1,926	Gray, Alfred	Cherokee
19,051	Gray, John	Henderson
21,096	Gray, Joseph, Estate of	Craven
17,310	Green, James, Estate of	Yadkin
15,457	Green, Jesse	Davie
19,044	Green, Joseph W.	Rutherford
18,942	Green, Mager	Orange
7,911	Green, Silas M.	Cherokee
15,276	Green, Smith P.	Watauga
10,386	Gregg, Nelson	Watauga
479	Gregory, Joseph	Perquimans
21,339	Gregory, Silas S.	Camden
7,558	Grey, Wm.	Lenoir
10,954	Grice, Jacob	Cumberland
15,081	Griffin, Charles	Forsyth
20,625	Griffin, Isaac	Pasquotank
671	Grim, Anderson	Richmond
3,527	Grimes, Jacob	Craven
579	Grimsley, W. P.	Greene
10,878	Grissom, Nancy	New Hanover
10,877	Grissom, Wm.	New Hanover
498	Groner, Austin	Gaston
15,559	Grubb, John, Estate of	Hertford

11,934: 16,302:	Gudger, Adolphus M.	Buncombe
19,091	Gudger, Joseph J.	Madison
12,501	Guess, Wm. W.	Orange
21,095	Guion, Frank	Craven
17,502	Guirkin, Eli H.	Hyde
19,919	Guirkin, R. R.	Camden
17,647	Gulley, John G.	Johnston
9,162	Gulley, Needham G.	Johnston
12,497	Gunter, A. B.	Wake
11,316	Gunter, John	Chatham
11,568	Gurner, Wealthy	Carteret
124	Guthrie, Hugh B.	Orange
11,543	Guthrie, Jane C.	Orange
15,076	Haddock, John H.	Craven
8,207	Hair, Flora A.	Harnett
8,204	Hair, Hugh L. & M. B.	Harnett
8,209	Hair, Isaac	Harnett
20,604	Haithcock, Wm. H.	Cumberland
13,886	Hall, Nathan	Cumberland
16,814	Hall, Raford	Cumberland
12,263	Hall, Thos. L.	Wilson
17,504	Halstead, Tully; Sears, C. T.; and Doxey, John	Currituck
3,664	Ham, Penelope	Wayne
14,880	Hamby, Wesley	Wilkes
16,666	Hamilton, Betty A.	Henderson
15,170	Hamilton, Elizabeth Ann	Cherokee
16,429	Hamilton, V. C. V.	Henderson
6,587	Hampton, G. W.	Cherokee
11,173	Hancock, Robert, Sr.	Craven
8,676: 12,744:	Hardesty, John, Estate of	Carteret
13,820: 19,069:	Hardesty, Micajah	Carteret
15,082	Hardgrove, James	Stokes
1,971	Hardison, Elijah, Estate of	Craven
7,618	Hardison, Gabriel	Craven
10,314	Hardison, Henry C.	Martin
13,191	Hardle, Richard	Gates
5,881	Hardy, Allen W.	Greene
9,427	Hare, Susan L. & Bowdon, Mary A.	Cumberland
6,355	Hargrave, Nelson	Orange
21,201	Harmon, Malden C.	Watauga
10,956	Harmon, Rebecca	Forsyth
3,198	Harrell, Elijah	Gates
3,197	Harrell, Noah	Gates
9,492	Harrell, Reddick	Bertie
20,977	Harrill, Housen	Rutherford
17,217	Harrington, Eliza G.	Craven
7,619	Harrington, W. D.	Craven
9,894	Harris, Eli	Chatham
18,504	Harris, Jesse R.	Sampson
1,872	Harris, O. E.	Chatham
17,766	Harris, Thos. D.	Hyde
21,284	Harris, W. L., Heirs of	Cherokee
8,131	Harrison, Berry	Wake
9,493	Harrison, Harmon	Washington
22,165	Harrison, Hester P.	Washington
10,949	Harrison, Isaac	Washington
2,190	Harrison, James L.	Jones
3,692: 5,916:	Harrison, John	Wake
4,950	Harrison, Mahulda	Wake
16,186	Harshaw, Joshua	Cherokee
19,050	Hart, Andrew J.	Henderson
14,695	Hart, Levi A., & Bailey, John C.	New Hanover
2,189	Hart, Titus	Jones
15,171	Hartness, Hiram	Cherokee
1,952	Hartness, Marion	Cherokee
18,803	Hartness, Marion	Cherokee
1,444	Hartness, Silas	Alexander
13,344	Harvey, Henry L.	Beaufort
18,940	Harward, Lewis M.	Orange
14,212	Haskins, Wm.	Jones
22,166	Hassell, Thos. S.	Washington
5,432	Hastell, Siddia	Gates
10,721	Hasten, Moses M.	Forsyth

4,231	Hathaway, Jacob R.	Gates
3,583	Hathcock, Francis W.	Wake
17,627	Hauser, John R.	Forsyth
3,497	Hauser, Margaret E.	Yadkin
17,828	Hawkins, Jesse D.	Caldwell
5,431	Hawley, John	Sampson
1,930	Hay, James	Johnston
7,336	Hay, James E.	Jones
1,221	Hayes, Joseph D.	Wake
3,663	Hays, Everett	Wayne
14,388	Haywood, Frank P.	Franklin
15,942	Haywood, Frank P., Jr. & Minnie M.	Franklin
10,727	Hayworth, Alfred	Davidson
10,731	Hayworth, John	Davidson
720	Heap, John G. & Clapp, Elisha B.	Mitchell
18,044	Heartsfield, Wesley	Wake
10,730: 14,400:	Hedgcock, Barnett	Davidson
13,835	Hefner, Michael	Caldwell
3,495	Hege, Edward L.	Forsyth
10,963	Hege, Geo. F.	Forsyth
10,961	Hege, Sam	Forsyth
1,445	Helton, Andrew J.	Catawba
18,312	Henderson, Lee	Madison
6,356	Henderson, Willie	Orange
18,313	Henderson, Zackariah	Madison
11,192	Hendrix, Joseph A.	Davie
19,046	Henry, Joseph	Henderson
2,377	Herring, James	Wayne
11,519	Herring, John, Sr.	Wayne
16,856	Hersey, Ira	Cumberland
4,180	Hevner, Stephen	Lincoln
3,496	Hickerson, Charles	Yadkin
1,649	Hicks, James Y.	McDowell
2,497	Hill, Arthur J.	New Hanover
12,133	Hill, Hatch B.	Carteret
9,767	Hill, Isaac S.	Carteret
1,954	Hill, Joshua	Cherokee
109	Hines, Elijah	Alexander
2,191	Hines, Freeman	Jones
8,322	Hinnant, G. W.	Johnston
2,039	Hinton, Gordon R.	Gates
10,398	Hix, Adam	Watauga
3,584	Hobby, Reuben	Wake
18,503	Hockaday, Gray W.	Cumberland
8,132	Hodge, Madison	Wake
10,411	Hodges, Hollan	Watauga
7,625	Hodges, James	Harnett
10,388	Hodges, Louisa	Watauga
12,193	Hoffman, Jonas	Gaston
18,843	Hoffman, Levi	Gaston
21,200	Hofler, John W.	Gates
6,358	Hogan, Alex	Orange
11,544	Hogan, Daniel Reid	Orange
8,796	Hogan, John R.	Orange
7,078	Hogan, Joseph C.	Orange
20,968	Hogan, Thos.	Orange
6,360	Hogan, Wm. J.	Orange
19,276	Hoggard, Calvin	Bertie
17,389	Hoke, Laban	Caldwell
248	Holden, Marsden	New Hanover
6,359	Holder, Henry	Orange
10,401	Holesclaw, Willey	Watauga
4,640	Holland, Bennett	Wake
16,581	Holland, Exum	Johnston
4,641	Holland, Mary A.	Wake
4,953	Holland, Merrit	Wake
4,643	Holland, Rebecca	Wake
4,642	Holland, Wm.	Wake
4,644	Holleman, J. A.	Wake
8,310	Holleman, W. J.	Wake
4,797	Holley, Susan A.	Gates
16,861	Hollis, Jeremiah	Washington
7,754	Hollowell, Jesse	Wayne
8,324	Hollowell, John	Wayne
8,325	Hollowell, Levi	Wayne
8,323	Hollowell, Thos. L., Estate of	Wayne

6,442	Holt, Geo. A.	Chatham
8,133	Holt, Richard J.	Chatham
12,071	Honeycutt, Samuel	Yancey
16,284	Hood, J. L.	Henderson
16,929	Hood, James H.	Transylvania
5,303	Hood, John C.	Johnston
8,795	Hooper, Jerry	Orange
2,251	Hoover, Moses G.	McDowell
9,891	Hopson, Wm.	Wake
18,353	Horn, Dan	Sampson
7,615	Horn, James E.	Anson
4,410	Horn, Patrick C.	Anson
10,735	Horney, Stephen G.	Guilford
5,917	Horton, Annie	Wake
20,392	Horton, Candace	Chatham
10,944	Horton, Dan L.	Caldwell
6,357	Horton, John	Orange
10,393	Horton, John	Watauga
16,626	Horton, Rufus D.	Wilkes
18,742	Horton, Rufus H.	Wake
10,945	House, Mary	Sampson
17,745	Houser, James F.	Gaston
19,245	Howard, Abner B.	Hyde
11,577	Howard, Joseph	Caldwell
3,498	Howard, Marmaduke D.	Yadkin
745	Howard, Wm.	Rowan
18,411	Howard, Wm. B.	Hertford
3,666	Howell, Henry A.	Craven
2,728: 10,028:	Howell, John, Estate	Wayne
11,821	Howell, John D., Estate of	Haywood
2,726	Howell, Major	Wayne
1,931	Howell, Martha A. S.	Wayne
1,932	Howell, Maurice	Wayne
5,433	Howell, Miles W.	Gates
2,727	Howell, Stanton	Wayne
7,755	Howell, Stephen	Wayne
893	Howle, Malinda	Wake
3,063	Hoyle, Lightfoot W.	Lincoln
2,040	Hudgins, Warner R.	Gates
5,884	Hudson, Joel	Sampson
1,972	Hudson, Pharaoh	Sampson
281	Huffsteller, John	Gaston
19,053	Huggins, Sarah N.	Henderson
15,551	Huggins, Wm. F.	Wake
9,586	Hughes, Evan	Mitchell
20,188	Huneycutt, Blackman	Bladen
5,788	Hunsucker, A. G.	Cherokee
11,525	Hunsucker, David	Catawba
3,499	Hunt, Pleasant	Yadkin
11,818	Hunter, John L., Estate of	Perquimans
14,706	Hurdle, Henry B.	Perquimans
2,041	Hurdle, Joseph	Gates
17,311	Hutchens, Alex	Yadkin
900	Hutchins, John T.	Wake
12,792	Hutchins, Rebecca	Orange
17,112	Hyatt, James H.	Perquimans
8,835	Hyde, John	Cherokee
1,685	Icenhour, A. C.	Alexander
9,292: 10,712:	Idol, Andrew S.	Guilford
10,717	Idol, Caleb	Forsyth
1,106	Ingram, Dixon	Anson
12,018	Ipock, Morgan	Craven
8,797	Ivey, Joseph	Orange
1,714	Jackson, Alex, Sr.	Cumberland
5,899	Jackson, Bennett, Estate of	Sampson
6,266	Jackson, Dan	Sampson
2,378	Jackson, Eppsie	Wayne
6,562	Jackson, Geo.	Lenoir
15,935	Jackson, Geo. Estate of	Pasquotank
2,347	Jackson, Henry T.	Sampson
12,072	Jackson, Robertson	Pasquotank
11,183	Jackson, Sarah	Wake
6,130	Jackson, Travis	Sampson
4,794	Jacobi, Nathaniel	New Hanover
744	Jacobs, Lewis	Rowan
301	Jacobs, Wm.	Richmond
5,937	James, Elizabeth C.	Cherokee
10,737	Jeans, Mary E.	Guilford

499	Jenkins, Aaron	Gaston
19,176	Jenkins, Nicholas	Caldwell
7,756	Jennett, Charity	Wayne
7,757	Jennett, Joab	Wayne
7,630	Jernigan, Wm.	Johnston
9,516	Jessup, Jesse	Perquimans
7,655	Jimison, James	Henderson
5,918	Jinks, R. H.	Wake
17,026	Jinks, Wm.	Wake
7,758	Jinnett, Barney C.	Wayne
20,437	Jinnings, Elijah	Wilkes
19,223	Jinnings, Wm.	Wilkes
4,920	Johnson, David	Cumberland
13,676	Johnson, Hugh	Henderson
4,123	Johnson, Levi	Yadkin
13,198	Johnson, Matthew	Wake
19,218	Johnson, Moses C.	Wilkes
4,959	Johnson, Polly	Wake
13,933	Johnson, Richard M.	Wayne
11,858	Johnson, Richard W.	Cumberland
1,086	Johnson, Sam H.	Cherokee
9,931	Johnson, Stephen	Wilkes
5,938	Johnson, W. G. W.	Cherokee
8,908	Johnson, Willis	Harnett
9,445	Johnston, John D.	Rowan
9,896	Johnston, Lydia	Orange
824	Jolly, Elizabeth	Alexander
12,047	Jones, A. E.	Pasquotank
11,580	Jones, Charles P.	Caldwell
4,181	Jones, E. D.	Craven
4,122	Jones, Edward, Estate of	Hyde
10,962	Jones, Eliza	Forsyth
4,083	Jones, Enoch	Chowan
21,902	Jones, Frederick J.	Craven
5,920	Jones, Friday	Wake
2,797	Jones, Jackson M.	Davidson
10,408	Jones, John	Watauga
19,177	Jones, John H.	Caldwell
17,401	Jones, Kinsey	Duplin
5,919	Jones, Martha A.	Wake
8,635	Jones, Mason	Martin
8,326	Jones, Matthew M.	Wayne
18,867	Jones, Nancy	Wake
18,894	Jones, Newton E.	Pasquotank
13,441	Jones, Owen W.	Greene
8,134	Jones, Reddin	Wake
4,038	Jones, Sarah	Henderson
9,428	Jones, Wiley	Hertford
3,500	Jordan, Abner Fields	Yadkin
2,404	Jordan, Alfred	Martin
3,764	Jordan, Joseph J.	Hertford
20,724	Jordan, Willis	Chowan
14,559	Joyce, Letty	Stokes
9,576	Joyner, John H.	Hertford
19,331	Judd, Henderson, Estate of	Moore
2,114	Julian, John	Rowan
18,978	Jump, Thomas	Buncombe
4,645	Justice, R. R.	Wake
16,922	Justus, Wesley M.	Henderson
11,922	Justus, Wm. D.	Henderson
3,589	Keaton, F. B.	Pasquotank
20,812	Keaton, Joshua	Burke
3,588	Keaton, Wm. F.	Pasquotank
9,430	Keen, Jesse	Hertford
20,258	Keith, Caleb N., Estate of	Madison
10,711	Keith, Francis M.	Guilford
15,552	Keith, Mariah H.	Wake
2,916	Keller, Martha	Burke
19,222	Kelley, James	Wilkes
16,671	Kelly, Leonard D.	Yadkin
8,123	Kendall, John W.	Wilkes
8,135	Kendall, Thos.	Wilkes
9,534	Kenedy, Patsy	Lenoir
8,647	Kephart, A. T.	Cherokee
10,402	Kernels, Mary	Watauga
748	Kester, Wm. Henry	Rowan
6,386	Kilpatrick, Robert P.	Transy-lvania
6,364	King, Andrew J.	Orange
17,388	King, Calvin S.	Caldwell
2,780	King, Elbert	Wake
5,547	King, Elizabeth	Lenoir
19,424	King, Hiram	Henderson
7,747	King, Isaiah	Wake
11,520	King, James	Wayne
16,134	King, Jeremiah	Henderson
7,669	King, Richard W.	Lenoir
4,459	King, Susan	Wake
6,366	King, Turner	Orange
4,458	King, Willis J.	Wake
13,167	Kinyan, John H., Estate of	Pasquotank
6,362	Kirkland, James	Orange
6,361	Kirkland, John	Orange
6,363	Kirkland, Lucy T.	Orange
8,798	Kirkland, Mary Jane	Orange
14,299	Kiser, Tandy	Forsyth
2,613	Knester, Charles	Wake
140	Knox, Penelope	Johnston
15,476	Laboyteaux, Sarah	Pasquotank
2,252	Lackey, James D.	McDowell
11,064	Lackey, Squire	Stokes
7,559	Laftin, Henderson	Lenoir
7,321	Lamb, Edmund	Pasquotank
11,552	Lamb, Elish	Perquimans
11,554	Lamb, Townsend	Perquimans
14,857	Lamb, Uriah	Guilford
18,308	Lamberth, Edward	Madison
9,886	Lambeth, Benj. G.	Chatham
7,908	Lambert, Hugh	Cherokee
302	Lampley, Wm. P.	Richmond
12,689	Land, Eliza Ann	Caldwell
11,819	Lane, Chas.	Perquimans
12,342	Lane, James	New Hanover
12,748: 19,072:	Langdale, Jehu N.	Carteret
10,964	Langworth, Reuben	Forsyth
10,898	Lankford, Braxton	Stokes
19,057	Lanning, John, Estate of	Buncombe
3,501	Lash, Thos. B.	Forsyth
4,646	Lashlee, Henry C.	Wake
19,867	Lassiter, Henry E.	Pasquotank
17,734	Lassiter, John	Hertford
9,074	Lassiter, Wm. A.	Lenoir
18,939	Latta, Fanny F.	Orange
2,416	Laverty, Sarah, Estate of	Pasquotank
13,178	Lawrence, Joseph	Pasquotank
184	Lawton, Matthew, Estate of	New Hanover
5,434	Layton, John A.	Sampson
1,715	Leary, Matthew N.	Cumberland
5,939	Leatherwood, Abel J.	Cherokee
16,310	Leatherwood, Jason	Haywood
16,260	Ledbetter, Ephraim	Henderson
10,394	Ledbetter, Henry	Guilford
4,182	Ledford, Joseph W.	Rutherford
12,101	Lee, Erasmus B.	Sampson
5,886	Lee, Ivy	Sampson
2,455	Lee, James R.	Cumberland
5,305	Lee, John, 1st.	Johnston
8,033	Lee, Larry, Estate of	Wake
7,338	Lee, Pharaoh	Sampson
5,304	Lee, Thos.	Johnston
9,677	Lee, Timothy F.	Wake
3,691	Lee, Wm. E.	Wake
17,924	Lee, Wilson	Currituck
9,743	Leflin, Thos. C.	Davidson
15,083	Lehman, Wm. H.	Forsyth
7,131	Leigh, Eleanor	Pasquotank
1,239	Leigh, Richard L.	Orange
1,975	Leonard, Joseph B.	Davidson
4,183	Leonhardt, Ann E.	Lincoln
4,594	Leslie, Dan & Hugh	Harnett
17,738	Leviner, Marshall	Richmond
135	Levy, Jonas P.	New Hanover
16,083	Levy, Lewis W., Sr.	Cumberland
12,680	Lewis, Anna	Guilford
10,385	Lewis, David	Watauga
2,045	Lewis, Exum	Gates
12,365	Lewis, Isaac W.	Craven
11,536	Lewis, Willis M.	Craven
6,897	Liggon, Addison	Wake

9,083	Lindsay, Eliza Jane	Davidson
10,730	Lindsay, James M.	Davidson
6,365	Lindsey, Sheffey T.	Orange
6,672	Lindsey, Wade	Yadkin
3,066	Linhardt, John W.	Lincoln
21,029	Lippman, Aaron	Duplin
12,046	Lister, Nancy L.	Pasquotank
53	Little, John R.	Cumberland
14,667	Livengood, John H.	Forsyth
6,367	Lloyd, Orren	Orange
6,368	Lloyd, Stephen	Orange
8,799	Lloyd, Wm.	Orange
6,369	Lloyd, Wm. H.	Orange
7,080	Lloyd, Wm. R.	Orange
5,921	Lockhart, Fletcher	Wake
19,417	Locklayer, Wyatt	Wake
19,049	Loftis, Andrew J.	Transy-lvania
255	London, Pricy, Estate of	New Hanover
2,707	Long, Charles	Davidson
20,593	Long, Charles	Orange
419	Long, E. T.	Richmond
4,247	Long, James B.	Chatham
20,268	Long, John W.	Catawba
423	Long, Mial T.	Richmond
14,984	Long, Richmond T.	Richmond
4,764	Long, Sally F. C.	Washington
20,269	Long, Thos. S.	Catawba
11,551	Long, Wm. W.	Yadkin
8,043	Love, Wm. R.	Cumberland
963	Lowry, W. C.	Perquimans
11,503	Lytch, Niel	Richmond
10,896	Mabe, Edward, Jr.	Stokes
21,243	Macomber, James N.	New Hanover
10,726	Macy, John S.	Forsyth
6,371	Maddry, Abel	Orange
2,194	Mallard, W. H.	Jones
12,750	Malloby, Henry	Wayne
4,126	Malone, Andrew J.	Alexander
13,199	Mangum, Priestly M.	Wake
16,719	Mann, Daniel	Wake
9,195	Mann, J. B.	Carteret
22,252	Mann, Lewis S.	Dare
20,969	Mann, Martha E.	Chatham
17,098	Mann, Zachariah	Chatham
5,535	Mannel, Daniel	Cumberland
5,942	Mannering, Christian	Stokes
1,666	Manson, Caesar	Carteret
18,938	Marcom, Nancy	Orange
9,892	Marcom, Thos.	Wake
19,726	Marion, Abraham	Surrey
6,372	Markham, Wm. A.	Orange
18,073	Marley, Abner S.	Wilkes
14,881	Marley, Henry	Wilkes
16,783	Marsh, James H.	Lincoln
1,716	Marshall, A. G.	Alexander
10,724	Marshall, Tandy	Forsyth
12,746: 19,156:	Marshall, Thomas, Estate of	Carteret
11,066	Martin, James G.	Stokes
17,276	Martin, John W.	Rockingham
8,989	Martin, Silas N.	New Hanover
3,502	Martin, Thos. S.	Yadkin
17,767: 20,239:	Martin, Wm.	Craven
20,238	Martin, Wm. & Moore, Silas	Craven
6,103	Mashburn, Hodge	McDowell
5,891	Mashburn, Matthew E.	Cherokee
9,897	Mason, Elizabeth	Chatham
13,887	Mason, Foster	Cumberland
17,040	Mason, James B.	Orange
11,663	Mason, James Pleasant	Orange
8,800	Mason, Jesse	Chatham
17,768	Mason, Jesse S.	Hyde
8,801	Mason, John E.	Chatham
5,226	Mason, Luke	Craven
12,233	Mason, Thomas W. (of NC) and Thomas, Benj. R. (of MS)	Northampton
9,888	Mason, Wm. C.	Orange
6,370	Massey, John	Orange

1,231	Massy, Hardy	Orange
14,839	Mastin, Darius, Estate of	Forsyth
14,727	Mastin, Robert L.	Forsyth
9,421	Mathis, Frederick	Sampson
9,422	Mathis, Joel	Cumberland
15,553	Matthews, Reuben	Harnett
1,667	Matthewson, Henry & Pendar, John	Carteret
4,647	May, W. B.	Wake
21,031	Mayers, Max	Duplin
14,381	Maynard, Jacob	Guilford
19,329	Maynard, Jacob	Wake
17,505	McAllister, Todd	Richmond
16,499	McArthur, Alex	Cumberland
8,206	McArthur, Malcolm	Cumberland
1,634	McBee, Mary	McDowell
19,175	McCall, John	Caldwell
16,667	McCall, John A.	Transylvania
19,425	McCall, S. B. O.	Henderson
11,063	McCauless, W. W.	Stokes
7,082	McCauley, Benj.	Orange
7,083	McCauley, Matt J. W.	Orange
7,081	McCauley, Matthew	Orange
20,013	McClamrock, Robert R.	Davie
4,593	McCormic, Duncan	Cumberland
2,253	McCormic, James	McDowell
4,592	McCormick, Harriet E.	Harnett
14,604	McCoy, John S.	Camden
5,711	McCoy, Wm. F.	Lenoir
4,080	McCullen, Bryan	Lenoir
15,458	McCulloh, James	Davie
8,652	McDonald, Alex	Richmond
12,196	McDonald, Archibald B.	Richmond
9,116	McDonald, John A.	Richmond
19,911	McDonald, Lovedy	Bladen
8,454	McDonald, Randolph	Richmond
107	McDougald, Alex	Cumberland
13,885	McDougald, Allen	Cumberland
18,054	McDowell, Charles G.	Henderson
11,917	McDowell, Geo. M.	Madison
205	McGill, Dan K.	Cumberland
9,707	McGill, Mary B.	Cumberland
13,888	McGill, Neil	Cumberland
12,690	McGlaughn, Luke A.	Hertford
17,769	McGowan, Sylvester	Hyde
3,044	McGraedy, James F., Estate	Guilford
19,515	McGuire, James H.	Watauga
1,955	McGuire, Michael	Cherokee
6,437	McKay, James, Sr.	Cumberland
17,219	McKenzie, Wm. P.	Sampson
662	McKinnon, L. L.	Richmond
5,294	McKown, L. & Millspaugh, Albert	Edgecombe
4,596	McLam, Thos.	Harnett
10,939	McLauchlin, Sarah	Robeson
4,766	McLean, Arch.	Robeson
17,179	McLean, Hector	Robeson
19,048	McLean, Sidney S.	Madison
10,946	McLemore, Amos	Cumberland
9,420	McLemore, Mary Jane	Cumberland
7,912	McLemore, Wm.	Cherokee
2,354	McMillan, Hector	Cumberland
14,364	McMillan, Malcom	Cumberland
10,092	McMinn, G. W.	Henderson
5,571	McMinn, James M.	Henderson
10,091	McMinn, John L. J.	Henderson
16,318	McNab, M. H.	Haywood
2,919	McNeely, J. C.	Burke
11,642	McNeil, Archibald	Richmond
9,423	McPhail, Alex	Sampson
21,005	McPhail, Margaret	Cumberland
12,198	McPherson, Duncan	Richmond
420	McPherson, James	Richmond
11,976	McPherson, John	Richmond
104	McQueen, Neil	Cumberland
8,653	McRae, John O.	Richmond
8,907	McRae, Margaret & Mary A.	Harnett
9,541	McTerry, Wm.	Wake
15,095	Mebane, Robert L.	Alamance
6,104	Melarkey, John	New Hanover

12,181	Mercer, Furney	Jones
12,180	Mercer, John	Jones
14,719	Mercer, Malachi	Camden
14,358	Merony, Philip F.	Davie
11,624	Merrett, Francis	Jones
12,253	Merrick, Wm.	Wayne
12,741	Merrill, Aaron	Carteret
16,065	Merrill, Alex, Estate of	Henderson
6,389	Merrill, John	Transy-lvania
18,560	Merrill, M. S.	Gaston
11,662	Merrit, Eli	Orange
4,128: 20,521:	Messick, Henry P.	Yadkin
10,686	Michael, Philip	Davidson
17,503	Midgett, John	Hyde
10,955	Millender, Willie	Cumberland
10,926	Miller, Caroline & Mary A.	Rutherford
2,120	Miller, John	Catawba
16,001	Miller, John	Davidson
14,882	Miller, John B.	Wilkes
3,504	Miller, John Wesley	Forsyth
15,084	Miller, Jonathan	Forsyth
8,623	Miller, Mathias	Davie
10,926	Miller, Mary A. & Caroline	Rutherford
14,359	Miller, Philip A.	Yadkin
17,737	Millikin, Isaiah	Richmond
5,294	Millspaugh, Albert & McKown, L.	Edgecombe
16,527	Misenheimer, Geo. M.	Cabarrus
1,873	Mitchell, Kelley	Chatham
20,626	Mitchell, Robert G.	Chowan
8,80	Mitchell, Wm. R.	Chatham
4,232	Mitchum, Aaron	Lincoln
10,129	Mizell, Jonathan T.	Carteret
4,763	Mobley, James	Washington
14,300	Mock, A. L.	Davidson
11,735	Mock, Aquilla J.	Rowan
3,505	Mock, John Anderson	Yadkin
15,720	Mock, Philip	Forsyth
15,184	Modlin, Harmon, Sr.	Martin
16,673	Money, Henry E.	Yadkin
102	Monroe, Dan C.	Cumberland
11,232	Monroe, Peter	Robeson
16,311	Moody, Wm. L.	Haywood
20,117	Moore, Alex F.	Beaufort
20,393	Moore, Caesar	Orange
16,093	Moore, Charles	Buncombe
7,759	Moore, Curtis P.	Wayne
10,392	Moore, Huldah	Guilford
3,662	Moore, Lancaster J.	Wayne
1,956	Moore, Levi	Cherokee
4,411	Moore, Lucy	Anson
9,517	Moore, Lucy Ann	Perquimans
18,356	Moore, Richard M.	Polk
20,238	Moore, Silas & Martin, Wm.	Craven
11,940	Moore, Wm. H.	Buncombe
969	Mooring, Lemuel B.	Greene
14,532	Morgan, Elwood	Guilford
3,342	Morgan, Miles	Pasquotank
18,397	Morgan, Rebecca	McDowell
504	Morgan, Thos.	Johnston
10,123	Morgan, Thos. A.	Perquimans
467	Morgan, Timothy	Perquimans
10,409	Morphew, Silas	Watauga
9,895	Morphus, Sam	Orange
10,722	Morris, Frederick	Forsyth
9,495	Morris, Jacob	Gates
19,054	Morris, Richard	Henderson
21,049	Morrisett, Wm. J.	Camden
16,309	Morrow, A. C.	Haywood
14,558	Mortin, R. A.	Stokes
829	Morton, C. D.	Onslow
12,670	Morton, David W.	Carteret
18,895	Morton, David W. & Garner, Siloam Jane	Craven
11,627	Morton, Francis and Mary F. & Oglesby, Martha J.	Carteret
10,880	Morse, Caroline	Brunswick
10,732	Motsinger, Henry	Davidson
663	Mudd, Henry E.	Richmond
4,937	Murchison, Isaac	Harnett
18,361	Murden, Thos. J.	Pasquotank
18,844	Murdock, Hugh	Carteret
6,480	Murphy, John R.	Davidson
7,760	Musgrave, Eliza	Wayne
15,898	Myers, Wm.	Forsyth
3,509	Nading, Sanford Harrison	Yadkin
106	Nance, Washington J.	Cumberland
4,277	Neal, Rebecca	McDowell
4,884	Neale, Julia	Craven
1,874: 9,164:	Nelson, Alex M.	Wake
10,899	Nelson, Leander	Stokes
20,394	Nevill, Alfred	Orange
8,804	Nevill, Charles	Orange
8,803	Nevill, Elizabeth	Orange
7,084	Nevill, John	Orange
6,373	Nevill, Nancy	Orange
10,133	Newbern, Ellerton	Chowan
9,496	Newberry, J. P.	Washington
13,165	Newbold, James	Perquimans
13,166	Newbold, Wm., Estate of	Pasquotank
13,934	Newell, Dempsey	Wayne
3,507	Newman, Avery	Yadkin
18,981	Newman, Jonathan	Henderson
10,874	Newton, James S.	Brunswick
421	Newton, Mary	Richmond
18,412	Nichols, Lemuel	Hertford
17,104	Nicholson, Thomas W.	Halifax
20,522	Nicks, Rachel S.	Yadkin
4,245	Nixon, Elizabeth A.	Wake
1,448	Nixon, Francis	Perquimans
3,602	Nixon, Reuben	Gates
9,744	Nixon, Wm.	Gates
1,637	Noblett, Ann	McDowell
8,839	Noggle, Jacob	Cherokee
18,969	Norcom, James	Chowan
3,508	Norman, Rebecca	Yadkin
10,410	Norris, David	Watauga
4,648	Norris, Robert T.	Wake
17,703	Norris, Sam	Wake
277	Northam, George & Lucinda	Richmond
276	Northam, John T.	Richmond
277	Northam, Lucinda & George	Richmond
8,453	Norton, Eli	Richmond
666	Norton, Elijah	Richmond
664	Norton, Godfrey	Richmond
665	Norton, Handy T.	Richmond
3,766	Norton, Nehemiah	McDowell
667	Norton, Reuben	Richmond
21,790	Norwood, Wm.	Chatham
8,099	Nowell, Alvin & Wm.	Wake
1,875	Nowell, Berry	Wake
8,099	Nowell, Wm. & Alvin	Wake
3,087	Nowell, Willis W.	Wake
9,887	Nutt, Erasmus D.	Wake
605	O'Briant, Tabitha	Granville
17,741	O'Brien, Drucilla	Gaston
12,668	Oglesby, Contentna	Carteret
19,157	Oglesby, Levi T.	Carteret
11,627	Oglesby, Martha J. & Morton, Francis & Mary F.	Carteret
5,967	Oldham, Alex	New Hanover
11,541	Oldham, Allen	Chatham
6,374	Oldham, Wesley	Chatham
4,650	Olive, Ira	Wake
4,649	Olive, Merrill	Wake
6,375	Olive, Monroe C.	Orange
6,387	Orr, Azra	Transylvania
19,058	Orr, Joseph N.	Henderson
16,786	Orrell, Robert M.	Cumberland
16,536	Osteen, Elijah	Henderson
19,052	Osteen, Edward	Henderson
16,086	Outland, Cornelius	Northampton
16,087	Outland, Elijah	Northampton
16,088	Outland, Josiah	Northampton
1,718	Overbaugh, Ambrose	Cumberland
8,137	Overby, Parker	Wake
7,761	Overmans, Jesse	Wayne

17,896	Overton, Amon, Estate of	Hertford
17,770	Owens, Pembrook	Hyde
21,330	Oxendine, Hugh	Robeson
21,329	Oxendine, Solomon	Robeson
9,075	Oxley, A. W.	Pitt
5,551	Oxly, Elbert H.	Pitt
898	Pace, James M.	Wake
21,006	Page, Elizabeth	Cumberland
20,386	Pain, James	Madison
1,957	Palmer, Philip	Cherokee
10,451	Parker, Elijah	Cumberland
3,200	Parker, Elisha	Gates
21,197	Parker, Elmer	Gates
12,367	Parker, Joel, Estate of	Sampson
10,452	Parker, Simon	Cumberland
17,522	Parker, Warren J.	Harnett
8,210: 9,424:	Parker, Wm.	Harnett
4,460	Parish, Berry	Wake
5,992	Parrish, Mordecai	Johnston
11,215	Parrott, Benj. F.	Lenoir
8,805	Parten, Bennett, Estate of	Orange
1,848	Partin, Drury	Wake
3,667	Pate, Clarissa	Wayne
668	Pate, Elijah S.	Richmond
3,670	Pate, Elizabeth	Wayne
1,933	Pate, Geo. D.	Wayne
10,030	Pate, Hymon	Wayne
10,173	Pate, Lewis, Estate of	Richmond
10,027	Pate, Shadrack	Wayne
7,762	Pate, Willoughby	Wayne
8,212	Patrick, Edward, Estate	Greene
1,163	Patrick, Joel	Pitt
1,159	Patrick, John M.	Greene
20,970	Patterson, Robert D.	Orange
6,106	Patton, Reuben E.	McDowell
16,082: 21,972:	Payditt, Nancy J.	Martin
21,703	Payne, Abel, Sr.	Cumberland
17,933	Payner, Nathan, Estate of	Currituck
6,376	Peace, Wm.	Orange
5,306	Peacock, Nancy	Johnston
10,297	Pearson, Ichabod	Wayne
10,026	Pearson, Jonathan	Wayne
8,327	Pearson, Lazarus	Wayne
12,793	Pearson, Nancy	Orange
4,651	Peebles, Joseph A.	Wake
1,667	Pendar, John & Matthewson, Henry	Carteret
18,265	Pendleton, John F.	Pasquotank
17,751	Pendleton, Ken R.	Perquimans
12,554	Pennell, Larkin	Caldwell
8,758	Pennington, Kinchen	Wayne
1,720	Peppers, Wilson	Cumberland
11,311	Perkins, James	Chatham
7,763	Perkins, Sally W.	Wayne
8,328	Perkins, Wm. R.	Wayne
8,646	Perkinson, B. J.	Wake
18,868	Perkinson, John M.	Wake
19,951	Perry, Allen R.	Wake
2,193	Perry, Calvin	Craven
3,780: 17,930:	Perry, Josiah N., Estate of	Tyrrell
6,450	Perry, R. S.	Wake
14,249	Perry, Seborn	Guilford
940	Perry, Wiley R.	Wake
13,200	Perry, Wm.	Wake
15,869	Petree, Riley F.	Stokes
9,499	Pettiford, Alfred	Washington
9,500	Pettiford, Judy	Washington
8,748: 11,625:	Pettipher, Israel	Craven
11,420	Pettipher, Wm.	Craven
4,135: 16,674:	Pettyjohn, Wiliam	Yadkin
4,615	Phifer, John F.	Lincoln
16,668	Phillips, A. E.	Henderson
9,587	Phillips, Blake	Mitchell
8,213	Phillips, J. A. D.	Greene
12,749: 19,179:	Phillips, Solomon C.	Carteret

3,510	Phillips, Wm.	Yadkin
9,169	Phinney, Robert	New Hanover
8,848	Phinney, Wm.	New Hanover
10,716	Phipps, Ransom	Forsyth
8,807	Pickett, Charlotte	Orange
9,084	Pickett, David W.	Davidson
12,794	Pickett, John	Orange
12,506	Pickett, Mary	Orange
12,499	Pickett, Wm.	Orange
14,748	Pierce, Arthur	Johnston
8,677	Piggott, Eliza	Carteret
12,747	Piggott, Jane	Carteret
10,301	Pike, James E.	Wayne
10,302	Pike, Matthew	Wayne
10,300	Pike, Micajah	Wayne
3,665	Pike, Wm.	Wayne
1,280	Pine Forest Cemetary Co.	New Hanover
10,032: 10,937:	Piner, G. W.	Pasquotank
15,876	Piver, Asa	Carteret
262	Plonk, Jacob F.	Gaston
16,313	Plot, D.	Haywood
5,439	Plummer, Zachariah	Cumberland
14,301	Poindexter, John F.	Forsyth
12,914	Pool, Chas., E.	Pasquotank
1,876	Pool, Henry	Wake
8,101	Poole, Wm. J.	Wake
1,157	Pope, Sam D.	Greene
11,118	Pope, Stephen, Estate of	Cumberland
10,454	Porter, Archibald	Cumberland
11,559	Porter, Wiley	Cumberland
19,159	Porter, Wm. J.	Perquimans
8,100	Potter, Sarah	Wake
8,806	Potts, Nancy M.	Orange
1,877	Powell, Cabot	Wake
1,878	Powell, Caswell	Wake
20,187	Powell, Douglas	Bladen
8,405	Powell, James	Cherokee
1,845	Powers, Elizabeth	Wake
10,383	Presnell, Solomon	Watauga
18,055	Price, Anthony	Wayne
5,095	Price, G. W., Sr.	New Hanover
1,722	Price, Jehu	Alexander
1,723	Price, Manering	Alexander
8,808	Pritchard, John W.	Orange
9,588	Pritchard, Thos. O.	Mitchell
20,010	Proctor, F. S.	Pasquotank
12,795	Proctor, Mary A.	Orange
12,504	Proctor, Starling	Orange
12,796	Proctor, Wm.	Orange
12,678	Prophet, Wm.	Wilkes
18,913	Pullen, Willis	Wake
5,237	Pulley, Turner	Wake
4,079	Purdy, Aluri, Estate of	Pasquotank
6,377	Purefoy, G. W.	Orange
11,765	Purify, Arrington	Craven
12,574	Quinn, David S., Sr.	Carteret
22,024	Rains, Henry	Johnston
2,294	Ramsey, Baldy	Person
19,578	Ramsey, Garret	Madison
11,942	Ramsey, J. D.	Madison
11,941	Ramsey, James	Madison
20,387	Ramsey, Job, Jr.	Madison
19,047	Ramsey, John W.	Madison
1,800	Ramsour, Andrew L.	Catawba
18,413	Rawles, Dempsey	Hertford
202	Ray, John	Cumberland
206	Ray, John (Puppy Creek)	Cumberland
11,944	Ray, Sonny	Buncombe
16,308	Rector, Franklin	Madison
19,226	Redding, Enos M.	Wilkes
13,526	Redding, John, Estate of	Wilkes
7,342	Reep, John	Lincoln
10,822	Reeves, Robert	Duplin
4,303	Reid, Asbury	Gates
2,729	Reid, Percy	Wayne
9,589	Renfro, Wm.	Mitchell
10,518	Revell, James & Futrell, Ira & Morris	Northampton
20,191	Revels, Ann	Cumberland

17,899	Reynolds, Arthur	Hertford
17,895	Reynolds, James	Hertford
17,898	Reynolds, Manuel	Hertford
18,943	Rheu, Strudwick	Orange
16,820	Rhodes, Alex	Jones
4,654	Rhodes, James A.	Wake
15,234	Rhodes, Joannah	Stokes
14,749	Rhodes, Joseph E.	Wayne
5,082	Rhoney, John G.	Catawba
8,636	Rhoney, Wm.	Catawba
496	Rhyne, James	Gaston
1,958	Rice, Isaac	Cherokee
1,450	Rice, James	Gates
19,075	Rice, James E.	Madison
11,930	Rice, Job	Madison
18,310	Rice, Reuben	Madison
4,304	Riddick, Lassiter	Gates
16,049	Riggs, Wiley	Surrey
6,378	Riggsbee, Andrew J.	Orange
7,079	Riggsbee, Asa S.	Chatham
8,809	Riggsbee, Atlas J.	Chatham
6,379	Riggsbee, James J.	Orange
15,562	Roberson, Benj. L.	Carteret
20,806	Roberts, James	Carteret
12,135	Roberts, James B.	Carteret
18,932	Roberts, Lorenzo D.	Orange
11,925	Roberts, Moses W.	Madison
18,414	Roberts, Watkins	Northampton
11,822	Robinson, A. R.	Haywood
1,451	Robinson, Alfred N.	Catawba
296	Robinson, Elhanan W.	Gaston
1,452	Robinson, Henry W.	Catawba
17,748	Robinson, James A.	Gaston
1,934	Robinson, John	Wayne
263	Robinson, Nancy S.	Gaston
12,797	Robson, James W.	Orange
13,201	Rogers, Benj. Y.	Wake
19,045	Rogers, C. T.	Macon
8,309	Rogers, Calvin J.	Wake
18,802	Rogers, Wm. H.	Cherokee
14,895	Rominger, Martin, Estate of	Forsyth
11,290	Rooks, Wm.	Gates
8,446	Roper, Wm.	Burke
3,514	Rose, Benj.	Wilkes
14,750	Rose, John	Wayne
3,513	Rose, Sterling	Yadkin
10,819	Rose, Wm.	Wayne
8,239	Rose, Wm. N.	Wayne
1,195	Rosemond, John	Wake
3,072	Rountree, Deborah	Gates
4,655	Rowland, A. E.	Wake
5,307	Royals, Jane	Sampson
4,653	Royster, Mariah P.	Wake
10,875	Ruark, Hanson R.	Brunswick
21,977	Ruck, Naaman, Estate of	Forsyth
16,612	Rudisill, John	Lincoln
20,114	Ruff, Warren W.	Beaufort
18,805	Runions, Thos.	Cherokee
21,198	Russell, Elvery	Gates
21,196	Russell, F. H.	Gates
14,302	Ryons, Daniel	Forsyth
19,216	Sale, Robert	Wilkes
3,770	Sampson, Henry	Robeson
4,656	Sanderford, Elisha	Wake
3,613	Sanderford, Geo. A.	Wake
12,496	Sanders, Edwin T.	Wake
15,874	Sanders, Eli W.	Carteret
4,304	Satterfield, Jeremiah	Person
11,315	Saul, Joseph H.	Chatham
13,935	Sauls, Fennel	Wayne
4,143	Saunderson, Erasmus H.	Hyde
2,117	Savage, Wm. H.	Gates
18,865	Sawyer, Miles, Estate of	Pasquotank
3,672	Scott, Annie	Wayne
3,669	Scott, Bryant A.	Wayne
16,821: 18,869:	Scott, Jacob F.	Jones
10,453	Seaberry, Raleigh	Cumberland
290	Seaman's Friend Society	New Hanover
17,504	Sears, Caleb T.; Doxey, John; and Halstead, Tully	Currituck
8,810: 21,030:	Sears, Robert T. D.	Chatham
8,753	Sellers, Richard L.	New Hanover
17,743	Selvey, James M.	Gaston
18,840	Selvey, Wm.	Gaston
16,257	Sentell, J. B.	Henderson
16,258	Sentell, Richard	Henderson
8,910	Senter, D. D.	Harnett
7,334	Setzer, G. W.	Catawba
8,909	Sexton, Willie	Harnett
17,728	Shannon, Nathan	Dare
11,706	Sharp, Sam	Brunswick
9,165	Shaw, Francis	Johnston
10,936	Shaw, Joseph B.	Pasquotank
8,203	Shaw, Neil	Harnett
17,041	Sheek, Jacob	Davie
10,774	Sheek, Richard Gilpin	Davie
11,937	Shelton, John	Madison
13,202	Shepard, Richard	Wake
16,254	Shepherd, Jesse M.	Henderson
15,459	Shermer, James	Yadkin
11,933: 16,255:	Shipman, M. P.	Henderson
746	Shoaf, Alex	Rowàn
10,965	Shoaf, David	Forsyth
4,260	Shope, Jacob	Cherokee
15,460	Shores, John	Yadkin
3,518	Shores, Martin	Wilkes
743	Shuping, Michael	Rowan
17,650	Sides, John G.	Forsyth
17,028	Sikes, Almus W.	Wake
12,254	Simmons, Bryant	Wayne
14,883	Simmons, Edmond	Wilkes
13,233	Simmons, Edmond B.	Currituck
13,240: 21,723:	Simmons, Edmund	Currituck
6,131	Simmons, Geo. D.	Cumberland
12,136	Simmons, Green	Wayne
13,238	Simmons, H. H.	Currituck
10,953	Simmons, Isaiah	Cumberland
9,560	Simmons, Josiah	Pasquotank
15,069	Simmons, Sarah	Wayne
11,205	Simpson, Clifford F., Estate	Craven
1,665	Simpson, Rossiter	Carteret
16,300	Sircy, M. W.	Madison
8,641	Skipper, Zachariah P.	Richmond
18,870	Slade, Robert	Jones
10,687	Sledge, Moses S.	Davidson
7,040	Sloan, W. R.	Alex
4,189	Sloop, Caleb	Alexander
9,505	Smallwood, Louisa	Washington
675	Smith, Alex	Richmond
669	Smith, Anderson	Richmond
15,899	Smith, Anderson	Stokes
3,771	Smith, Anne	Robeson
4,595	Smith, Calvin	Harnett
1,990	Smith, Cannon	Craven
12,197	Smith, Christian	Richmond
8,046	Smith, Daniel L.	Cumberland
670	Smith, Duncan	Richmond
2,196	Smith, Eli	Richmond
19,349	Smith, Freeman	Lenoir
5,974	Smith, James J.	Greene
10,172	Smith, James M.	Richmond
12,082	Smith, Jane	Richmond
6,133	Smith, John	Sampson
11,065	Smith, John	Stokes
1,991	Smith, John A.	Craven
674	Smith, John H.	Richmond
3,772	Smith, Joseph	Gates
2,197	Smith, Joseph K.	Jones
10,405	Smith, Josiah	Watauga
10,413	Smith, Levi G.	Davis
4,932	Smith, Mary	Anson
8,811	Smith, Mary	Orange
16,900	Smith, Matthew	Wake

2,380	Smith, Needham	Wayne
3,516	Smith, Phoebe Ann	Davidson
13,203	Smith, Rachel	Wake
1,989	Smith, Sam	Sampson
4,660	Smith, Talbot B.	Wake
5,923	Smith, Wm.	Wake
11,921	Smith, Wm. D.	Buncombe
15,900	Smith, Wm. H.	Stokes
6,132	Smith, Wm. J.	Cumberland
899	Snead, Alford	Wake
1,850	Snead, Charles G. & Jacob J.	Wake
1,850	Sneed, Jacob J. & Charles G.	Wake
8,648	Sneed, M. M.	Cherokee
2,614	Snelling, Wm. M.	Wake
4,661	Snellins, Robert	Wake
13,204	Snellins, Wm.	Wake
10,960	Snider, Benj. J.	Forsyth
15,233	Snider, Ester	Stokes
12,583	Snipers, Bridgers	Johnston
20,189	Snipes, Alvis	Chatham
21,791	Snipes, Benj. F.	Chatham
12,584	Snipes, David	Johnston
21,302	Snipes, Wm.	Chatham
13,230	Snowder, Wm., Estate of	Currituck
13,227: 21,725:	Snowdon, Barbara & Fanshaw, J.	Currituck
290	Society, Seaman's Friend	New Hanover
17,029	Sorrell, Jacob	Wake
16,303	Sorrells, Jackson F.	Madison
6,549	Sparkman, James R.	Gates
8,458	Sparks, James	Cherokee
16,305	Sparks, Whitfield M.	Mitchell
9,927	Sparrow, Charity	Washington
20,595	Sparrow, John Barker	Orange
20,971	Sparrow, Wm. H.	Orange
14,840	Speace, John	Forsyth
2,047	Speight, Henry	Gates
7,736	Spence, Franklin	Camden
8,208	Spence, Neil A.	Harnett
7,626	Spencer, John	Harnett
5,536	Spikes, Suton	Gates
3,515	Spilman, Ruth B.	Yadkin
3,517	Spilamn, Wm.	Yadkin
1,992	Spurgeon, Wm. B.	Davidson
4,549	Spurlin, Matthew	Rutherford
17,850	Squires, Dan B.	Camden
19,440	Staley, Adam	Wilkes
19,224	Staley, Alfred	Wilkes
19,220	Staley, Joseph	Wilkes
13,189	Stallings, Henry E.	Perquimans
19,174	Stallings, Sidney	Caldwell
10,101	Stanley, James G.	Lenoir
3,653	Stanley, Mary	Guilford
14,533	Stanley, Sarah	Guilford
12,742	Stanton, Cecelia	Carteret
10,296	Stanton, G. W.	Wilson
19,161	Stanton, James	Carteret
19,868	Stanton, John	Pasquotank
4,659	Stedman, D. P.	Wake
5,291	Steelman, Sam	Wilkes
3,260	Steger, Wm.	Pasquotank
8,138	Stephens, Crawford	Chatham
4,658	Stephenson, Alfred	Johnston
4,964	Stevens, Candis	Wake
14,759	Stevens, Ezekiel	Wayne
1,853	Steward, Julia	Carteret
10,714	Stewart, Erasmus J.	Guilford
7,631	Stewart, G. W.	Harnett
6,061	Stewart, Jesse	Harnett
1,986	Stewart, John	Craven
7,632	Stewart, Lazarus	Harnett
6,380	Stewart, Manson	Orange
195	Stewart, N. C., Miss	Madison
11,835	Stilley, John W.	Craven
15,085	Stoltz, Sam	Forsyth
14,728	Stolta, Thomas S.	Forsyth
5,924	Stone, M. P.	Wake
8,813	Strain, Wm.	Orange
758	Strauss, John W.	New Hanover
13,884	Strickland, Richardson	Cumberland

497	Stroup, Moses, Sr.	Gaston
298	Stroup, Solomon, Estate of	Gaston
20,594	Strowd, Wm. F.	Chatham
8,812	Strowes, Manly D.	Orange
15,721	Strupe, Wm. A.	Forsyth
5,925	Stuart, Thos.	Wake
5,972	Stunly, John B.	Lenoir
8,034	Sturdevant, Benj.	Wake
19,128	Sturdivant, Robert E.	Chatham
5,800	Styles, Louisa	Cherokee
6,439	Suggs, John B.	Wake
12,195	Suggs, Mary S.	Gaston
19,227	Sullivan, Geo. L.	Caldwell
21,701	Sullivan, Sam	Duplin
2,730	Summerline, Hardy	Wayne
5,734	Surles, James C.	Harnett
7,892	Sutton, John A.	Lenoir
7,891	Sutton, Mary C.	Lenoir
7,893	Sutton, Nancy	Lenoir
17,730	Sutton, Wilson R.	Dare
7,890	Sutton, Wm.	Lenoir
10,736	Swain, Ashley	Guilford
10,876	Swain, John C.	Brunswick
1,162	Swann, Aquilla	McDowell
2,254	Swann, Emily S.	McDowell
2,195	Sween, Sarah M.	Richmond
11,309	Sweezy, Alpha	Rutherford
16,360	Swinson, Andrew J.	Brunswick
2,405	Swinson, John	Martin
21,050	Sykes, Percival D.	Pasquotank
15,462	Tackett, Samuel	Davie
9,757	Tadlock, James	Sampson
9,755	Tadlock, Joshua	Sampson
5,783	Tanner, Wm. P.	Cherokee
7,629	Tart, Furney	Harnett
8,035	Tatham, J. W.	Cherokee
7,138	Tatum, John, Heirs of	Pasquotank
11,419	Taylor, Alex	Craven
9,117	Taylor, Eliza	Richmond
6,441	Taylor, Hicksy	Wake
11,117	Taylor, John R.	Cumberland
2,198	Taylor, Moses, Estate of	Jones
9,425	Taylor, Wm. S.	Cumberland
10,733	Teague, Abram O. P.	Davidson
16,306	Teague, Solomon	Madison
10,022	Teague, Wm.	Alexander
6,381	Temple, M. D.	Orange
6,382	Tenny, Jane B.	Orange
3,619	Terrell, Rufus K.	Wake
10,958	Test, Emanuel	Forsyth
8,047	Tew, Holly J.	Cumberland
8,227	Thayard, Susan	Cumberland
2,381	Thigpen, Wm.	Wayne
8,048	Thomas, Aaron	Harnett
12,194: 19,330:	Thomas, Anderson	Moore
12,233	Thomas, Benj. R. (of MS) & Mason, Thomas of (of NC)	Northampton
1,644	Thomas, Franklin	Greene
4,968	Thomas, J. W.	Wake
17,101	Thomas, Joseph	Chatham
10,414	Thomason, G. W.	Rowan
472	Thomason, Mary E.	Rowan
1,454	Thompson, Amy	Alexander
1,455	Thompson, Elizabeth	Alexander
19,133	Thompson, John	Chowan
16,249	Thompson, John R.	Wayne
1,935	Thompson, Maria	Wayne
7,271	Thompson, Nelson T.	Wake
6,309	Thompson, Thos. A.	Wilson
18,941	Thompson, Wm. H.	Orange
10,299	Thornton, Nathaniel K.	Sampson
10,298	Thornton, Sam L.	Sampson
21,287	Tillery, Thos.	Madison
10,390	Tillery, John	Surrey
13,875	Tilley, Minerva	Orange
5,945	Tilly, Reuben G.	Stokes
18,331	Tilton, John R.	Wayne
15,614	Tise, Jacob	Surrey
15,722	Tise, Solomon	Forsyth

18,359	Tolson, Cornelius C.	Carteret
19,160	Tolson, Kilby	Carteret
12,669	Tolson, Wm. N.	Carteret
17,500	Tooly, Nancy T. M. & Wm. B.	Hyde
17,500	Tooly, Wm. B. & Nancy T. M.	Hyde
297	Torrence, Mary W.	Gaston
17,744	Torrence, Sam A.	Gaston
11,820	Towe, Joseph B.	Perquimans
477	Towlson, Isaac, Estate of	Perquimans
16,655	Townsend, John T.	Cumberland
15,928	Transon, Joseph	Forsyth
9,890	Trice, Pleasant	Orange
17,716	Triplett, Rebecca	Wilkes
10,942	Triplett, Thos.	Caldwell
9,746	Trotman, John C.	Gates
18,804	Truett, Mary	Cherokee
10,540	Trulove, John C.	Harnett
4,663	Tucker, Ann H.	Wake
10,897	Tucker, Gabriel W.	Stokes
3,088	Tucker, McLenden	Wake
15,865	Tugman, James F.	Wilkes
383	Turner, Richard	New Hanover
8,321	Tutrell, Benj. J.	Wayne
15,929	Tuttle, Alex	Stokes
15,930	Tuttle, Wm.	Stokes
11,923	Tweed, Albert S.	Madison
13,190	Twine, Alfred	Gates
14,353	Twine, James W.	Perquimans
6,265	Underwood, Uriah	Cumberland
4,664	Upchurch, John	Wake
4,665	Upchurch, Kearney	Wake
3,622	Upchurch, Williford	Wake
6,383	Utley, Foster	Orange
17,100	Utley, Merrell	Chatham
13,333	Uttley, Jacob	Carteret
7,139	Valentine, Daniel	Hertford
11,918	Vance, Hutsell	Buncombe
10,400	Vandike, Wm.	Watauga
17,731	Varser, Wm. H.	Dare
5,926	Vaughn, James	Greene
105	Vaughn, James C.	Cumberland
103	Vaughn, Ruffin	Cumberland
17,358	Vernoy, Silas	Dare
1,929	Vest, Calvin C.	Wayne
12,798	Vickers, David	Orange
12,799	Vickers, Martha F.	Orange
17,733	Vinson, Lawrence	Hertford
3,693	Vorheef, Louis	Wake
6,134	Wade, Wm. H.	Cumberland
10,723	Waggoner, Spencer	Forsyth
8,037	Wakefield, Thomas	Cherokee
5,565	Waldrop, James L.	Guilford
4,969	Walker, Dicey	Yadkin
13,329	Walker, E. H.	Currituck
2,079	Walker, Jesse D.	Person
6,393	Walker, John H., Estate of	Currituck
17,525	Walker, John T.	Wake
17,526	Walker, Richard	Granville
16,903	Walker, Wilson	Wilkes
4,717	Walker, Wilson; Whedber, James S.; and Dickinson, John	Currituck
14,303	Wall, John W.	Stokes
15,623	Walls, Nelson	Randolph
14,884	Walsh, Sam	Wilkes
5,537	Walters, Caroline	Gates
11,924	Ward, A. B.	Henderson
11,566	Ward, Andrew	Carteret
1,835	Ward, Andrew J.	Polk
19,043	Ward, B. K.	Henderson
11,487	Ward, Barker	Perquimans
10,397	Ward, James	Watauga
12,134	Ward, Leah	Carteret
5,901	Ward, Mary	Sampson
5,900	Ward, Robinson	Sampson
10,396	Ward, Simon	Watauga
3,202	Ward, Timothy	Chowan
15,723	Warner, Jacob, Sr.	Forsyth
15,931	Warren, Reuben	Stokes
17,746	Warren, Wm.	Gaston
19,612	Warters, James	Lenoir
14,304	Waterson, Robert	Forsyth
10,725: 14,668:	Watkins, Abel C.	Forsyth
264	Watkins, Jacob	Richmond
15,232	Watkins, Peter D.	Stokes
10,389	Watson, G. W.	Watauga
9,397	Watson, James	Rowan
759	Watson, John	Richmond
20,966	Watson, John H.	Orange
10,023	Watts, James	Alexander
17,302	Weatherford, Ira G. S., Estate	Rockingham
5,927	Weathers, Eliza A.	Wake
20,396	Weaver, John H.	Orange
11,546	Weaver, Jordan	Orange
8,906	Weaver, Theophilus	Harnett
11,542	Weaver, Thos. S.	Orange
5,008	Webb, Mary G.	Rutherford
22,185	Webb, Robert B.	Beaufort
5,456	Webber, Sam	Greene
1,960	Weeks, Drury	Cherokee
13,527	Welborn, John	Wilkes
19,064	Welborn, Mary M.	Wilkes
13,528	Welborn, Thos. V.	Wilkes
16,314	Welch, Elbert	Haywood
17,312	Wells, Hulda	Yadkin
2,328	Wells, Isaac	Johnston
17,732	Wescott, Geo. W.	Dare
17,729	Wescott, John	Dare
12,822	Wescott, Lewis W.	Brunswick
16,299	West, Benj. F.	Madison
4,934	West, Jacob	Harnett
15,554	West, James H.	Wake
5,902	West, Wiley	Sampson
15,724	Westmoreland, Nathaniel G.	Stokes
4,717	Whedber, James S.; Dickinson, John; and Walker, Wilson	Currituck
9,426	Wheeler, G. W.	Cumberland
12,498	Whitaker, David	Orange
8,353	Whitaker, James	Cherokee
705	White, Benj. J.	New Hanover
12,030	White, Elijah	Craven
11,926	White, H. Allen	Madison
8,036	White, Jesse	Cherokee
6,384	White, John	Orange
15,932	White, John H.	Forsyth
18,047	White, L. D.	Dare
295	White, Mary	Gaston
18,935	White, Nancy	Orange
844	Whitehead, Susan Virginia	Greene
1,664	Whitehurst, Joseph B.	Carteret
12,577	Whitfield, Wm. J.	Bladen
14,751	Whitsitt, Wm. C.	Wayne
19,056	Whitted, Wm. B.	Henderson
10,395	Whittington, L. D.	Watauga
11,567	Whittington, Parker	Carteret
12,438	Wiggins, Jacob	Craven
9,076	Wiggins, Thos. M., Estate	Pitt
11,939	Wilbar, John T. O.	Buncombe
11,938	Wild, Jacob R.	Madison
11,216	Wiley, Reding	Craven
12,500	Wilkerson, Harris	Orange
3,774	Wilkins, Carey	Robeson
11,894	Williams, Bryant	Johnston
896	Williams, Burchett	Wake
895	Williams, Clinton W.	Wake
673	Williams, G. W.	Richmond
2,049	Williams, Henry G.	Gates
12,004	Williams, James	Wayne
20,116	Williams, Jarvis M.	Beaufort
8,125	Williams, Jesse F.	Yadkin
17,941	Williams, John	Currituck
7,764	Williams, John A.	Wayne
19,180	Williams, John W.	Craven
4,970	Williams, M. M.	Wake
20,171	Williams, Margaret	Burke
14,995	Williams, Margaret M.	Wayne
19,063	Williams, Michael	Wilkes

897	Williams, Napolean B.	Wake
17,872	Williams, Nosa S.	Dare
16,537	Williams, Olive	Wayne
3,627	Williams, P. P.	Wake
19,181	Williams, Sam	Burke
19,055	Williams, Walter	Henderson
20,170	Williams, Wm.	Burke
9,429	Williamson, Ely	Hertford
10,720	Williamson, James A.	Forsyth
66,135	Williford, Henry J.	Cumberland
9,068	Willis, A. J.	Guilford
7,349	Willis, Major	Craven
17,976	Willis, Thos. G.	Dare
1,803	Wilson, David	Burke
5,905	Wilson, Jesse	Sampson
1,997	Wilson, Joseph	Sampson
3,076	Wilson, Maxwell	Lincoln
3,521	Wilson, Peter Adams	Forsyth
6,392	Wilson, Samuel	Transyl-vania
9,883	Wilson, Willis C.	Chatham
16,778	Windsor, Elisha A.	Yadkin
13,148	Winebarger, Silas	Catawba
9,563	Winkler, Abraham	Burke
19,219	Winkler, Anderson	Wilkes
14,305	Winkler, C. A.	Forsyth
20,074	Winkler, Joshua	Watauga
13,936	Winn, Levi	Wayne
14,906	Winn, Washington	Wayne
3,201	Winslow, John S.	Chowan
14,709	Winslow, Kedar	Gates
9,518	Winslow, Nathan	Perquimans
11,555	Winslow, Thos. E.	Perquimans
14,417	Wiswall, Howard	Beaufort
1,724	Wittenburg, David	Alexander
1,663	Wolf, John B.	Carteret
4,667	Womble, Thos.	Wake
10,447	Wood, Henry H.	Cumberland
10,448	Wood, John	Cumberland
19,017	Woodard, James A.	Chowan
8,141	Woodell, Mark	Chatham
1,456	Woodered, John W.	Burke
2,081	Woodey, Thos.	Person
3,522	Woodruff, Wm. B.	Surrey
12,505	Woods, Harris	Orange
12,502	Woods, Henry	Orange
18,741	Woody, James R.	Person
5,906	Wooten, Crawford	Sampson
11,207	Worley, Levi	Johnston
2,382	Worrell, John	Wayne
1,998	Worthington, Solomon	Craven
4,790	Wright, Basil H.	Lincoln
10,713	Wright, Micajah	Guilford
17,099	Wyndham, Robert	Chatham
8,098	Wynn, Caroline	Wake
13,307	Wynn, Charles	Wayne
4,463	Yates, Calvin	Wake
7,616	Yates, James C.	Anson
10,729	Yokley, Andrew	Davidson
10,959	Yokely, Sam D.	Forsyth
185	Young, Armand D.	New Hanover
15,988	Young, Lewis	Buncombe
4,553	Young, Ruth	Wake
9,168	Young, Wm.	Wake

SOUTH CAROLINA

19,619	Agerton, Alfred	Chesterfield
20,547	Agerton, John	Chesterfield
9,364	Airs, Elizabeth	Beaufort
4,084	Allman, Jacob	Marlborough
16,927	Alston, Edward H.	Georgetown
6,889	Amick, John D.	Lexington
21,251	Anderson, Martha H.	Georgetown
7,596	Anderson, Thomas	Fairfield
19,622	Andrews, Alfred	Lancaster
13,353	Armstrong, Wm.	Charleston
22,225	Arthur, John H.	Lexington
19,137	Ashford, Thomas W.	Richland
20,727	Bacot, Joseph	Darlington
19,624	Bailey, Lucy	Lancaster
16,740	Baker, John	Charleston
22,210	Ballentine, John A.	Lexington
5,654	Barnes, Wm. R.	Beaufort
8,637	Barrentine, Peter	Chester
414	Bass, Nancy	Marlborough
13,500	Baxley, Esther	Barnwell
13,026	Beckham, Mary	Lancaster
12,641	Bell, Ella W.	Lancaster
1,207	Bell, March	Marlborough
12,644	Belt, Hugh L.	Lancaster
9,366	Belton, C. B., Mrs.	Beaufort
4,094	Bennett, Margaret	Marlborough
13,027	Bennett, Philemon W.	Lancaster
13,028	Bennett, S. L.	Lancaster
3,661	Bethea, Jacob	Marlborough
275	Beverly, James	Marlborough
9,367	Bing, Hezekiah	Beaufort
16,729	Black, Thos.	Charleston
4,222	Blake, Arthur M.	Charleston
22,240	Blume, Darling Pinckney	Orangeburg
22,205	Boozer, Jacob N.	Richland
3,205	Boozer, Lemuel	Lexington
7,267	Bouknight, Geo.	Lexington
7,266	Bouknight, Robert A.	Lexington
4,096	Bowen, Reese	Pickens
13,029	Bowers, Anderson	Lancaster
22,224	Bowers, Eli W.	Lexington
13,030	Bowers, James W.	Kershaw
14,153	Bowers, Robt. C.	Beaufort
6,651	Bowers, Susan A.	Beaufort
12,647	Bowers, Susannah	Lancaster
19,811	Bowman, Peyton B.	Darlington
1,283	Bowyer, Peter W.	Marlborough
11,194	Bradham, John	Beaufort
18,456	Brady, Patrick	Charleston
7,998	Brant, Charles	Barnwell
4,087	Brantley, Wm.	Chesterfield
20,761	Breazeale, Nancy, Estate of	Anderson
495	Breeden, Lucy	Markham
4,093	Brewington, Wm. R.	Marlborough
628	Brigman, Thos.	Marlborough
494	Bristow, Oliver P.	Marlborough
8,638	Britt, Thos. P.	Chesterfield
884	Broaddy, Edward	Marlborough
22,200	Brooker, Henry	Lexington
21,768	Brown, Edward	Beaufort
14,662	Brown, James, Estate of	Richland
15,643	Brownfield, Abram	Charleston
590	Bruce, Anderson	Marlborough
13,031	Bruce, James	Lancaster
271	Brutus, James	Malborough
10,081	Bryant, Robert	Beaufort
17,031	Bucro, Angelo	Charleston
7,597	Busby, Lewis	Lexington
488	Butler, Elijah	Marlborough
19,355	Campbell, Alex	Anderson
490	Cannon, Henry	Marlborough
14,362	Carlisle, Mary E.	Chester
15,410	Caulfield, Martin	Charleston
3,099	Caulk, Gincey	Marlborough
13,033	Cauthen, Agnes	Lancaster
13,034	Cauthen, John C.	Lancaster
13,035	Cauthen, John M.	Lancaster
13,036	Cauthen, Mary	Lancaster
13,037	Cauthen, Nancy M.	Lancaster
7,996	Chassereau, Abraham	Barnwell
20,757	Chastain, John B.	Anderson
1,286	Chaves, James	Marlborough
415	Chaves, John	Marlborough
12,652	Clark, Joseph	Lancaster
4,100	Coates, John	Anderson
9,368	Cochran, John	Beaufort

9,369	Cochran, Thos.	Beaufort	22,197	Gartman, Timothy	Lexington
9,370	Cohen, Sheldon	Beaufort	22,228	Garven, Robert	Lexington
9,371	Condon, Argan	Beaufort	1,462	Gay, Josiah	Darlington
20,335	Coney, C. J.	Darlington	8,876	Geiger, Jacob	Richland
589	Conner, Lucy	Marlborough	1,591	Geraty, Christopher	Charleston
5,773	Coogler, John W.	Lexington	13,039	Gibson, J. C.	Kershaw
6,116	Coogler, Joseph	Lexington	10,076	Ginn, Abner	Beaufort
4,102	Cook, Silas	Marlborough	6,653	Goettee, Anne	Beaufort
9,372	Cook, Wm.	Beaufort	9,378	Goettee, Eliza	Beaufort
591	Cook, Wm.	Marlborough	6,654	Goettee, Rose	Beaufort
17,256	Corder, Benj.	Fairfield	17,323	Goldfinch, Dan	Georgetown
17,267	Cork, David H.	Fairfield	20,773	Goodwin, John H.	Greenville
22,211	Corley, Barbara L.	Lexington	13,758	Gradick, Nathan	Richland
8,816	Corley, Jacob S.	Lexington	2,330	Grant, James B.	Charleston
416	Cottingham, Jonathan	Marlborough	4,112	Grant, Jeremiah	Marlborough
5,069	Covington, A. B.	Marlborough	4,111	Grant, John G.	Marlborough
4,101	Covington, James C.	Marlborough	1,463	Grant, Peter	Marlborough
749	Covington, Thos. S.	Marlborough	659	Grant, Wm.	Charleston
10,083	Cradock, John	Barnwell	9,377	Green, Plenty	Beaufort
10,082	Crapse, Nathaniel	Beaufort	17,661	Green, Wm. H.	Charleston
9,373	Creeves, Harriet	Beaufort	11,199	Guarvin, Andrew	Beaufort
20,302	Creighton, Sam M.	Chester	22,203	Gunter, Wm.	Lexington
3,412	Crews, Sam F.	Beaufort	17,352	Hagood, Adaline	Pickens
12,643	Croxton, Thomas	Lancaster	12,649	Haile, John	Lancaster
22,236	Culclasure, Sarah A.	Orangeburg	20,759	Hall, Aaron	Anderson
19,145	Culler, Wesley W.	Orangeburg	9,380	Hall, Henry	Beaufort
6,652	Dais, Caesar	Beaufort	1,464	Hall, Joel	Marlborough
6,118	Daniels, Wm.	Richland	15,645	Hallon, Geo.	Georgetown
887	Dargan, Essex	Marlborough	750	Hamer, Robert C.	Marion
20,726	Dargan, Peter	Darlington	9,379	Hamilton, Cupid	Beaufort
886	David, Daniel	Marlborough	15,311	Harris, Hartwell	Chesterfield
18,321	David, Raphael L.	Charleston	10,090	Harrison, Prince	Beaufort
156	David, Thomas	Marlborough	5,659	Harter, Henry J.	Beaufort
19,140	Davis, Dan D.	Orangeburg	8,003	Harvey, David	Beaufort
13,355	Day, Michael C.	Charleston	17,990	Harvey, Milo A., Estate of	Spartanburgh
20,011	Deal, Joseph C.	Georgetown	6,655	Harvey, Sarah Ann	Beaufort
19,354	Dean, B. D.	Anderson	6,797	Harvey, Wm. V.	Beaufort
889	Deese, Betty	Marlborough	22,198	Harward, Charles P.	Lexington
1,208	Deese, Israel	Marlborough	3,799	Haskew, Thomas	Marlborough
13,968	Delvach, Jacob C.	Beaufort	22,223	Hayes, Boliver I.	Lexington
6,896	Derrick, Jacob J.	Lexington	8,639	Haywood, Anderson	Marlborough
8,746	Derrick, James D.	Lexington	6,656	Heap, Mary H.	Beaufort
8,745	Derrick, Jesse	Lexington	6,263	Heise, John H.	Richland
5,657	Dowling, James T.	Beaufort	19,352	Hembrel, Mary J.	Anderson
6,800	Dowling, Susan	Beaufort	22,199	Hendrix, Wm.	Lexington
7,999	Dowling, Wm. M.	Beaufort	267	Herndon, John P.	Marlborough
10,096	Drayton, Wm.	Beaufort	4,116	Higgins, G. W.	Pickens
1,854	Driggars, Matthews	Marlborough	21,065	Hilton, Thomas	Richland
5,688	Duane, Timothy	Richland	5,381	Hitt, Wiley	Greenville
20,756	Duckworth, Wilborn	Anderson	14,156	Hoffman, George	Marion
355	Dudley, Alex	Marlborough	1,731	Hogan, Patrick	Charleston
155	Dudley, C. W.	Marlborough	491	Hollens, Henry	Marlborough
15,117	Duncan, Parmelia A.	Union	19,136	Holmes, Mary A.	Richland
17,842	Dunlap, Emily S., Estate of	Lancaster	6,643	Holtiwanger, David	Lexington
270	Dunn, John	Marlborough	8,005	Hoover, Jackson M.	Barnwell
486	Easterling, Crawford	Marlborough	4,118	Hopkins, Asa	Marlborough
485	Easterling, David	Marlborough	20,507	Horn, Ellender	Chesterfield
484	Easterling, G. W.	Marlborough	16,354	Horton, Charity A.	Beaufort
4,108	Easterling, Joel L.	Marlborough	8,006	Horton, Ellender	Beaufort
417	Easterling, Sam	Marlborough	9,381	Horton, James	Beaufort
439	Ebaugh, David C.	Charleston	19,630	Horton, Lavinia E.	Lancaster
6,641	Edwards, Nathan E.	Richland	12,083	Howard, James B.	Charleston
8,817	Eleazer, Mary R.	Lexington	22,227	Huckabaa, James	Lexington
22,209	Elleson, Jesse	Lexington	9,382	Hutson, Joseph	Beaufort
9,375	Ellis, N. W.	Beaufort	22,212	Hutto, Britton E.	Lexington
424	Epstein, Philip	Richland	22,196	Hutto, Charles	Lexington
6,642	Epting, Geo.	Lexington	22,224	Hutto, Martin V.	Lexington
8,457	Epting, Jacob, Jr.	Lexington	22,213	Hutto, W. H. D.	Lexington
3,475	Estabrook, Benj. R.	Charleston	5,661	Ihly, Samuel R.	Beaufort
21,542	Ferrill, Jemima	Colleton	9,383	Jackson, Agnes	Beaufort
5,454	Flanigan, Patrick H.	Fairfield	11,198	Jackson, Andrew, Sr.	Beaufort
13,038	Floyd, A.	Lancaster	22,147	Jackson, Arch.	Beaufort
1,253	Flynn, John and Meehan, John	Charleston	19,147	Jackson, Elizabeth M.	Orangeburg
19,146	Fogle, Jacob	Orangeburg	15,646	Jackson, F. Alonzo	Georgetown
15,644	Ford, Frederick W.	Georgetown	18,002	Jackson, Josiah	Beaufort
16,928	Frazer, Sidney S.	Georgetown	2,403	Jackson, Marion	Charleston
22,195	Freshley, Joseph	Fairfield	9,384	Jackson, Thos.	Beaufort
19,353	Fretwell, Joseph T.	Anderson	1,336	Jacobs, Freidaig A.	Richland
888	Fuller, Sam	Marlborough	22,229	Jacobs, Laban P.	Lexington
22,241	Funderburk, Joseph	Orangeburg	2,248	Jacobs, Wm.	Marlborough

8,238	James, Isaac K.	Oconee
17,030	Jancovish, Sylvester, Estate	Charleston
17,036	Jefferson, Geo.	Charleston
19,150	Jennings, Isaac S.	Colleton
4,124	Joe, Frank	Marlborough
17,228	Johnson, Ferriby, Mrs.	Chesterfield
19,623	Johnson, James T.	Lancaster
10,085	Jones, Binckey	Colleton
4,121	Jones, John	Marlborough
487	Jones, Lisbon	Marlborough
17,351	Jones, Nancy B.	Pickens
19,943	Jordan, Madison	Chesterfield
11,329	Jordan, Richard	Horry
15,647	Joy, Henry	Georgetown
13,040	Joyner, Hiram	Lancaster
19,148	Joyner, Wm.	Orangeburg
19,138	Kaigler, Catharine	Lexington
10,089	Keese, Isaac	Beaufort
14,661	Kennedy, A. W.	Richland
6,084	Kennerty, John	Charleston
8,456	Kessler, John G.	Lexington
3,800	Kinney, Fereba	Marlborough
13,437	Klipstein, Louis F.	Charleston
20,750	Knowls, Martha	Beaufort
6,122	Koon, Solomon D.	Lexington
15,648	La Bruce, John	Georgetown
16,282	Lance, M. H., Rev.	Georgetown
1,284	Langley, Isaac	Marlborough
753	Lawson, Richard	Marlborough
22,206	Leaird, Jacob	Lexington
22,214	Lee, Catharine	Lexington
1,855	Leggett, James S.	Marlborough
2,621	Lester, Asenith	Marlborough
12,422	Lever, Kiziah	Lexington
2,793	Leviner, Thomas	Marlborough
358	Lewis, John C.	Marlborough
882	Lewis, Pompey	Marlborough
10,080	Lipsey, Rivan, Mrs.	Barnwell
19,144	Livingston, Henry	Orangeburg
19,142	Livingston, Maxamillian	Orangeburg
10,075	Loadholst, Mary A.	Beaufort
6,657	Long, Wm.	Beaufort
16,321	Lorenz, August D.	Charleston
21,382	Low, Kate	Richland
1,081	Lowman, Jacob W.	Lexington
10,156	Lowry, Leonidas	Chesterfield
22,218	Lybrand, Barnet C.	Lexington
22,217	Lybrand, Emanuel J.	Lexington
22,216	Lybrand, Simeon R.	Lexington
15,313	Macmillian, Claudia C.	Barnwell
20,242	Magill, John D., Estate of	Georgetown
1,393	Manly, Jeremiah	Greenville
6,644	May, Simon	Richland
14,846	Mayo, Joshua C., and Weld, G. W.	Beaufort
1,087	Mayzck, Job	Georgetown
3,469	McAteer, Alex S.	Lancaster
788	McCall, Dugal	Marlborough
15,650	McConnell, John H.	Georgetown
3,248	McCullough, John A.	Williamsburg
266	McDaniel, Ira W.	Marlborough
157	McFarland, Wm.	Marlborough
2,620	McIntire, Martha J.	Marlborough
11,197	McKenzie, Charels J.	Beaufort
11,196	McKenzie, Lawrence	Beaufort
4,125	McLean, Sandy	Marlborough
19,356	McLesky, James	Anderson
13,042	McManus, Hugh L.	Lancaster
13,738	McMichael, Cephas M.	Orangeburg
15,366	McNamara, Michael	Charleston
1,465	McPherson, Ducan	Marlborough
1,209	McQueen, James	Marlborough
356	McQueen, Oscar	Marlborough
17,035	McSwiney, David	Charleston
1,253	Meehan, John, and Flynn, John	Charleston
8,604	Meetze, Jacob	Lexington
17,111	Melton, Mary Jane	Chesterfield
10,293	Metz, E. Sherod	Lexington
6,659	Mew, Ann	Beaufort
6,799	Mew, J. P.	Beaufort
10,351	Middleton, Edward	Charleston
15,651	Middleton, Henry A.	Charleston
22,201	Miller, John A.	Lexington
12,471	Mitchell, Wm. L.	Lexington
13,043	Mobley, F.	Lancaster
19,629	Mobley, Sarah L.	Kershaw
7,611	Moran, John	Charleston
18,457	Moran, Wm.	Charleston
10,433	Morgan, Mary	Georgetown
6,881	Morree, John	Beaufort
751	Morris, Benj.	Marlborough
9,079	Mullikin, James	Anderson
15,652	Munnerlyn, Wm. C.	Georgertown
22,204	Neese, Edward P.	Lexington
9,386	Newton, Henry	Beaufort
1,466	Newton, Wm. W.	Marlborough
20,758	Norris, Catharine D.	Anderson
22,225	O'Cain, Mary, Estate of	Orangeburg
1,703	O'Dell, Calvin	Pickens
510	O'Dell, Perrin	Pickens
4,130	Odorn, James W.	Marlborough
594	Odorn, Thomas	Marlborough
11,195	Orr, Mary	Beaufort
11,193	Overstreet, Nancy	Beaufort
4,131	Parham, Dan	Marlborough
4,132	Parish, Alfred	Marlborough
10,074	Patrick, G. Y.	Barnwell
15,653	Pauley, Thos. D.	Georgetown
19,627	Peach, George	Kershaw
4,134	Pearce, Wm. H.	Marlborough
359	Pearson, Handy	Marlborough
158	Pearson, John	Marlborough
1,467	Peavy, James	Marlborough
1,313	Peavy, Simon	Marlborough
5,666	Peeples, Isham	Beaufort
9,387	Peeples, Mary P.	Beaufort
5,668	Peeples, Pierson	Beaufort
5,665	Peeples, Rigdon	Beaufort
5,667	Peeples, Wm. J.	Beaufort
4,163	Pickerel, Jonathan	Anderson
10,365	Pigg, Ransom P.	Chesterfield
10,088	Platts, Benj.	Beaufort
5,664	Platts, Elizabeth	Barnwell
308	Pledger, Cato	Marlborough
1,338: 22,238:	Pollard, Edward	Richland
22,202	Popwell, Elijah	Lexington
8,603	Porter, Wylie, Jr.	Richland
1,594	Powell, Mary Ann	Marlborough
4,497	Power, James	Charleston
159	Powers, John W.	Marlborough
5,669	Preacher, Wm.	Beaufort
9,389	Price, Toby	Beaufort
8,012	Priester, Geo.	Barnwell
1,210	Prince, Napoleon	Marlborough
268	Prince, Priscilla	Marlborough
4,137	Quick, Abel	Marlborough
160	Quick, Allan	Marlborough
1,314	Quick, Anderson	Marlborough
2,795	Quick, Elenor	Marlborough
2,794	Quick, Evander McIver	Marlborough
1,315	Quick, Gamewell	Marlborough
4,138	Quick, Harry	Marlborough
3,660	Quick, Lewis	Marlborough
890	Quick, Malachi	Marlborough
1,316	Quick, Martin	Marlborough
1,285	Quick, Moses	Marlborough
1,317	Quick, Murdoc	Marlborough
2,622	Quick, Sarah	Marlborough
16,002	Redding, Julia D.	Sumter
15,654	Reed, E. Jane	Georgetown
13,044	Reeves, Gethina	Lancaster
8,640	Reese, John A.	Marlborough
6,660	Reid, Philip	Beaufort
13,354	Reynolds, Edward	Charleston
12,017	Reynolds, Mark	Sumter
18,319	Richardson, Fanny	Georgetown
15,655	Richardson, Richard	Georgetown
6,661	Riley, Andrew	Beaufort

8,014	Riley, Wm. H.	Beaufort
22,230	Rirter, John A.	Lexington
11,844	Risley, Joseph H.	Georgetown
13,352	Ristig, Wm.	Charleston
5,070	Rivers, Susan A.	Beaufort
14,663	Roane, James L.	Richland
19,152	Robertson, David G.	Richland
19,153	Robertson, John	Fairfield
12,651	Robertson, Lucenia	Lancaster
20,760	Rogers, Elizabeth	Anderson
787	Rogers, Wm. A.	Marlborough
22,232	Roland, Ellen	Lexington
5,671	Rosier, Joseph	Beaufort
4,142	Rowe, Joseph J.	Marlborough
10,650	Rucker, Hiram C.	Lexington
10,649	Rucker, Mathias J.	Lexington
20,748	Russell, David	Beaufort
20,749	Russell, Wm.	Beaufort
8,016	Ruth, James	Beaufort
10,079	Sandifer, Nancy	Barnwell
1,985: 5,455:	Schwartze, Philip B.	Fairfield
13,971	Scott, Eldred	Beaufort
5,673	Searson, Z. Z.	Beaufort
17,032	Seel, Louis	Charles
6,910	Seigler, Wm.	Lexington
6,716	Sessions, Thos.	Kershaw
12,299	Shannon, Wm. M.	Kershaw
22,222	Sharp, Francis	Lexington
22,233	Sharp, James	Lexington
22,231	Sharp, Reuben	Lexington
22,215	Shealy, Andrew	Lexington
6,905	Shealy, John A.	Lexington
18,719	Sheridan, John	Charleston
22,207	Shull, Adam	Lexington
15,413	Shumpert, Joseph	Lexington
15,412	Shumpert, Noah	Lexington
5,769	Simmons, G. A. C., Mrs.	Beaufort
7,737	Simon, Alex	Edgefield
19,628	Sims, M. A., Mrs.	Lancaster
1,372	Sinclair, Geo.	Lancaster
5,674	Sinclair, Mooney	Beaufort
17,350	Singleton, Elizabeth	Pickens
7,660	Slattery, John	Charleston
2,421	Slawson, Hamilton, Jr.	Charleston
12,646	Small, Joel B.	Lancaster
593	Smith, Abner	Marlborough
881	Smith, Charlotte A.	Marlborough
592	Smith, Edward D.	Marlborough
1,699	Smith, H. G.	Pickens
10,086	Smith, Harriet	Beaufort
5,186	Smith, Herbert	Marlborough
8,017	Smith, James	Beaufort
833	Smith, Martha E.	Marlborough
161	Smith, Peter T.	Marlborough
1,318	Smith, Philip	Marlborough
8,018	Smith, Pompey	Beaufort
10,078	Smith, Rebecca	Beaufort
19,149	Smoak, David	Orangeburg
19,151	Smoak, Henry L.	Orangeburg
22,239	Smoke, Jacob	Orangeburg
5,672	Speakes, Julia R.	Beaufort
22,228	Spires, Eliza	Lexington
17,752	Sprigg, Ross	Spartanburgh
20,012	Springs, Catharine	Georgetown
10,084	Stafford, Benj.	Beaufort
595	Stancil, John	Marlborough
10,077	Stanley, James	Beaufort
489	Stanton, Eliza	Marlborough
892	Stanton, Peter	Marlborough
5,380	Steen, Henry	Greenville
492	Stephens, Henry	Marlborough
483	Stephens, Mary	Marlborough
5,379	Stokein, Diedrich	Charleston
6,662	Stokes, Ezekiel	Beaufort
272	Stubbs, James	Marlborough
269	Stubbs, John W.	Marlborough
265	Stubbs, Paul W.	Marlborough
2,938	Stubbs, T. P.	Marlborough
629	Stubbs, Thos. A.	Marlborough
12,645	Sullivan, Wm.	Lancaster
8,455	Summer, Polly	Lexington
10,292	Summer, Wm.	Newberry
885	Swinney, John	Marlborough
20,546	Tadlock, Wiley Ingram	Chesterfield
22,237	Taylor, Amelia B.	Richland
6,645	Taylor, Andrew	Lexington
5,689	Taylor, Caroline	Lexington
6,646	Taylor, Edwin	Lexington
6,795	Taylor, R. A.	Beaufort
13,045	Terrell, Richmond R.	Lancaster
1,282	Thomas, John T.	Marlborough
4,150	Thomas, Joseph S.	Marlborough
311	Thomas, Nathan S.	Marlborough
162	Thomas, Sam R.	Marlborough
9,170	Thomson, John	Charleston
13,757	Tilton, Henry W.	Georgetown
8,019	Tison, Benj.	Beaufort
20,714	Tison, R. H.	Beaufort
13,046	Todd, Wm.	Lancaster
274	Townsend, Frank	Marlborough
789	Townsend, Jabish N.	Marlborough
8,020	Trowell, Benj. F.	Beaufort
10,087	Trowell, Mary P.	Beaufort
752	Turnage, Crawford	Marlborough
21,740	Turner, Reuben H.	Beaufort
5,675	Tuten, Felix W.	Beaufort
9,390	Tuten, Mary B.	Beaufort
5,676	Tuten, Wm. R.	Beaufort
754	Usher, James	Marlborough
12,650	Ussery, D. M.	Lancaster
17,229	Vann, Harriet	Darlington
6,129	Vansant, Isaac	Lexington
805	Venning, Mortimer W.	Charleston
19,617	Vick, Wm.	Chesterfield
13,047	Vincent, Mary J.	Lancaster
4,151	Vining, Thomas A.	Marlborough
19,942	Wadsworth, Martin H.	Chesterfield
438	Wakfer, Charles S.	Charleston
9,391	Wallace, Francis	Beaufort
273	Wallace, Prince	Marlborough
8,021	Washington, Moses M.	Beaufort
630	Watson, James D.	Marlborough
627	Watson, Julia C.	Marlborough
19,618	Watts, Thos. H.	Chesterfield
891	Weatherly, Cornelius A.	Marlborough
5,677	Weekly, Wm., Rev.	Beaufort
493	Welch, Mary	Marlborough
14,846	Weld, Geo. W. & Mayo, Joshua C.	Beaufort
19,625	West, Eli	Kershaw
19,626	West, Henry C.	Kershaw
17,034	Weston, Anthony	Charleston
19,141	Whissenhunt, Lewis	Orangeburg
1,206	Wilkes, Solomon T.	Chesterfield
357	Williams, Cornelius	Marlborough
12,648	Williams, David	Lancaster
22,208	Williams, Elizabeth	Lexington
20,753	Williams, M. B.	Anderson
13,048	Williams, M. M.	Lancaster
17,033	Williams, Mack Duff	Charleston
5,678	Williams, Nero	Beaufort
8,642	Williams, Sam L.	Marlborough
9,392	Williamson, Charles J.	Beaufort
9,394	Williamson, John D.	Beaufort
19,143	Wilson, G. W.	Orangeburg
1,911	Winstock, Moses	Abbeville
19,139	Wirick, Joseph	Fairfield
11,594	Wolf, Simon	Richland
309	Woodel, Henry	Marlborough
9,393	Youmans, Elizabeth	Beaufort
11,102	Young, Hugh	Kershaw
11,103	Young, John	Kershaw
15,657	Young, Wm.	Georgetown
15,411	Zanoquera, Sebastian	Charleston

196: 20,059:	Abbay, Anthony S.	Davidson
196	Abbay, Anthony S.	Shelby
10,336	Abbott, Emer G.	Shelby
20,277	Abbott, Roger H.	Roane
17,220	Abbott, S. W.	Roane
11,026	Abel, Geo. F.	Loudon
2,631	Abernathy, James P.	Giles
18,038	Abington, James B.	Shelby
10,226	Abington, James B. & Joseph H.	Shelby
10,226	Abington, Joseph H.	Fayette
10,226	Abington, Joseph H. & James B.	Shelby
19,415	Acres, David	Scott
10,119	Acuff, Rebecca	Grainger
17,053	Adair, James M.	Humphreys
18,458	Adams, David	Hardin
15,060	Adams, Edward	Rutherford
11,699	Adams, G. W.	Weakley
12,588	Adams, George W.	Haywood
12,733	Adams, James	Dickson
4,520	Adams, Jasper	Henderson
17,556	Adams, Joseph	Marshall
8,495	Adamson, Greenberry	Madison
10,554	Adcock, John	Sevier
5,506	Akin, George A.	Gibson
16,171	Akord, Jacob D.	Washington
11,849	Albright, J. E. R.	Shelby
11,848	Albright, W. A.	Shelby
15,087	Alderson, J. B.	Maury
10,476	Alderson, Jane	Hamblen
8,159	Alexander, Elias	Jefferson
12,053	Alexander, Geo. A.	Loudon
20,416	Alexander, Hiram K.	Shelby
1,502	Alexander, John H.	Carroll
19,833	Alexander, Joseph M.	Loudon
12,760	Alexander, Madison H.	Rutherford
12,766	Alexander, Pleasant	Rutherford
15,956	Alexander, Richard	Sumner
7,507	Alexander, S. R.	Weakley
19,712	Alexander, Stephen H.	Bledsoe
18,255	Alexander, Wm. C.	Bedford
18,960	Alford, John	Hamilton
20,531	Alford, Wm. C.	Bradley
12,940	Allen, A. J.	Dickson
9,317	Allen, Andrew	Loudon
10,270	Allen, Mary E.	Carroll
20,376	Allen, Matt	Davidson
9,119	Allen, W. H.	Carroll
14,193	Allen, Wm. J.	McNairy
732	Allen, Wm. W.	Davidson
1,501	Allen, Young W.	Carroll
17,206	Allison, Robert	Bedford
16,597	Allison, Thos. C.	Bedford
10,375	Allison, Wm.	Madison
10,376	Allison, Wm. A.	Gibson
11,696	Allmond, Aaron G.	Weakley
16,235	Almarode, David	Sullivan
14,842	Alred, John	Warren
14,290	Alsobrook, James C.	Lauderdale
17,468	Alsobrook, Nathan	Shelby
18,235	Ambrister, Joseph	Blount
11,614	Ament, Sam P.	Davidson
12,861	Amis, James A.	Hawkins
12,848	Amis, Thos. J.	Hawkins
21,928	Anderson, Alex L.	Sequatchie
3,997	Anderson, Geo.	Sullivan
19,894	Anderson, Isaac G.	Blount
1,783	Anderson, James	Wayne
1,782	Anderson, James & Warfield, Thos., Estate of	Wayne
14,130	Anderson, Jesse	Madison
853	Anderson, John F.	Franklin
5,344	Anderson, John M.	McMinn
10,480	Anderson, Malvina	Hamblin
17,379	Anderson, Martin D.	McMinn
21,985	Anderson, Matilda J.	Shelby

15,156	Anderson, Matilda W., Est.	Haywood
17,144	Anderson, Sarah	Rutherford
8,158	Anderson, Thomas	Hamblin
12,169	Andes, Lorenzo D.	Jefferson
10,037	Andrews, Elbert	Gibson
13,761	Andrews, John M.	Hardin
11,150	Andrews, Mark L.	Williamson
8,919	Angell, Richard	Loudon
5,218	App, Matthias	Shelby
14,538	Applewhite, Jesse	Shelby
14,590	Arbuckle, Sam T.	Henry
15,376	Archer, Michael	Rutherford
13,533	Argo, Josiah B.	Warren
10,267	Armstead, Henry	Davidson
10,229	Armstrong, Abel	Franklin
14,041	Armstrong, Edward	Washington
12,841	Armstrong, F. B.	Knox
10,228	Armstrong, John	Franklin
12,635	Armstrong, Mary B.	Shelby
19,011	Armstrong, Sally	Bradley
12,139	Armstrong, Wm. C.	Franklin
2,713	Arnold, Frank A.	Greene
6,614	Arnold, Wm.	Sullivan
9,073	Arnold, Willis N.	Henderson
13,539	Arrowood, Thos.	Greene
2,616	Arthur, Wm.	Henry
6,704: 18,103:	Arwood, L. P.	McMinn
6,780	Ash, James W.	McNairy
20,826	Ashford, Jackson J.	Giles
8,681	Ashmore, David	Jefferson
15,048	Atchley, Benj. M.	Sevier
15,049	Atchley, Joshua F.	Sevier
10,550	Atchley, Joshua H.	Sevier
18,281	Atchley, Welcome	Bradley
20,527	Atchley, Wm.	Sevier
11,369	Atkinson, Ben. H.	Shelby
20,710	Atkinson, Frank M.	Rutherford
21,628	Atkinson, Richard	Davidson
17,377	Atlee, E. A., Estate of	McMinn
18,336	Austell, Littleberry	Coffee
14,873	Austell, Sam	Coffee
5,501	Austin, John C.	McNairy
2,928	Austin, Wm. T.	Hamblen
8,749	Avans, Isam	Monroe
10,125	Avett, Wm. H.	Tipton
19,541	Aymett, Wm.	Giles
6,424	Ayres, Treadwell S.	Shelby
5,527	Azbill, Allen	Henderson
14,057	Babb, Catharine	Greene
2,788	Bachman, Sam	Sullivan
14,991	Bacon, Dana A.	Loudon
15,200	Badger, E. Carolina	Shelby
16,970	Baer, Henry H.	Cocke
7,847: 18,505:	Bailes, Jesse	Jefferson
5,240	Bailey, Charles A.	Williamson
12,156	Bailey, Charles M.	Jefferson
3,417	Bailey, Clinton	Gibson
10,551	Bailey, Jesse	Sevier
12,172	Bailey, John C.	Jefferson
15,778	Bain, Abner, Estate of	Bradley
11,496	Bain, James	Madison
13,630	Bain, John K.	Hardin
15,782	Bain, Joseph	Bradley
15,777	Bain, Wm.	Bradley
13,439	Baird, James P.	Maury
14,198	Baird, John	Rutherford
19,705	Baird, Louisa	Shelby
11,130	Baker, Elizabeth B.	Knox
16,694	Baker, Isaac	Knox
16,863	Baker, James	Sevier
19,556	Baker, John C.	Union
13,071	Baker, Joseph D.	Davidson
21,318	Baker, Mary A., Heirs of	Sumner
12,832	Baker, Toliver	Knox
19,394	Baker, Wm.	Davidson
22,244	Bales, John	Jefferson

10,555	Bales, Noah	Knox
19,643	Baley, Wm.	Monroe
6,930	Ballard, Andrew J.	Fayette
11,524	Ballard, Charles	Knox
13,882	Ballard, Elizabeth E.	Loudon
8,926	Ballenger, Aaron	Jefferson
19,821	Ballinger, Silas R.	Humphreys
11,537	Banks, Elizabeth	Robertson
2,286	Baque, Louis	Shelby
14,385	Barbour, A. M.	Sumner
8,737	Barger, James J.	Henderson
18,914	Barger, John P.	Knox
14,141	Barker, J. M. & W. G.	Sullivan
16,496	Barker, Joel W.	Hamilton
16,515	Barker, John H.	Hamilton
14,141	Barker, W. G. & J. M.	Sullivan
11,107: 14,042:	Barkley, Ebenezer	Washington
17,966	Barkley, Lucinda	Bradley
14,058	Barkley, Wm. S., Estate of	Washington
8,682	Barnard, Joseph A.	Grainger
13,631	Barnes, Alex B.	Hardin
15,725	Barnes, Jacob	Hamilton
15,869	Barnes, James	Giles
16,172	Barnes, James H.	Washington
17,599	Barness, Henry C.	McNairy
10,841	Barr, Benj.	Madison
8,060	Barrett, Richard S.	Tipton
19,349	Barrett, Simeon S.	Bradley
16,968	Barry, Peter L.	Washington
21,270	Barry, Thos.	Sumner
17,705	Bartlett, Seacil B.	Bedford
14,631	Bartley, Phebe A.	Greene
2,083	Barton, Henry M. L.	Gibson
17,245	Barton, Robert	Rutherford
7,732	Barton, Robert A.	Gibson
14,937	Bashor, Christian, Estate of	Washington
14,043	Bashor, Lucy E.	Washington
14,060	Bashor, Peter	Washington
21,748	Basket, John	Washington
15,828	Bass, John	Putnam
19,773	Bass, Reuben B.	Hardeman
19,466	Bates, Abraham	Bradley
19,467	Bates, Benj.	Bradley
19,635	Bates, James P.	Bradley
12,716	Bates, Mary E.	Shelby
12,162	Bates, Parnell	Jefferson
6,406	Bates, Wm. B.	De Kalb
11,343: 11,352:	Batey, Benj.	Rutherford
7,733	Baucum, Wyatt	Benton
5,308	Baugh, S. E., Mrs.	Williamson
20,230	Baxter, Squire B.	Franklin
17,706	Baxter, Wm. H.H.	Bedford
5,530	Beachman, Elijah	Henderson
16,187	Beals, Isaac H.	Grainger
2,763	Bean, Andrew	Knox
18,283	Bean, Hazard	Bradley
18,715	Bean, John A.	Bradley
21,747	Beard, J. Samuel	Washington
20,291	Beard, James S.	Washington
9,171	Bearden, Flora A. C. & Matthew G.	Knox
10,745	Beasley, Wm. M.	Giles
8,417	Beatty, Susan	Fentress
15,177	Beaumond, Milly	Dickson
11,969	Beazley, Charles G.	Davidson
21,696	Beck, Joshua	Hamilton
7,365	Beckham, Jeremiah	Fayette
11,287	Beckley, Jane	Franklin
11,220	Beckner, Abraham	Hamblen
10,481	Beckner, Perry	Hamblen
14,762	Bedford, Julian	Shelby
11,241	Beeber, Max	Davidson
16,372: 16,567:	Beech, Matt	Williamson
1,471	Beehn, Chas. A.	Shelby
20,172	Beene, John	Bradley
12,763	Beesley, Christopher	Rutherford
7,864	Beets, G. W.	Grainger

1,508	Belew, Giles	Gibson
6,427	Belew, John G.	Carroll
9,120	Belew, Thos.	Carroll
8,354: 16,744:	Bell, Andrew, Estate of	Jefferson
11,901	Bell, John B.	Madison
12,550	Bell, Robert F.	Davidson
1,541	Bell, S. W.	Carroll
5,529	Bell, Valentine	Gibson
19,308	Belote, Jeremiah	Sumner
17,697	Belote, John L.	Sumner
9,121	Bennett, A. D.	Carroll
14,560	Bennett, F. M.	Franklin
13,623	Bennett, James W.	Hardin
1,887	Bennett, John D.	Maury
5,142	Bennett, John M.	Frank
1,509	Bennett, Sam H.	Carroll
16,584	Benson, Wilkin	Giles
2,672	Benton, J. M.	Carroll
2,741	Benton, Martha A.	Shelby
7,898	Berrong, H. N.	Monroe
1,248	Berry, Wm. T.	Davidson
13,435	Best, Andrew J.	Blount
17,178	Best, Elias L.	Franklin
21,290	Bettis, Aaron P. C.	Jefferson
10,492	Bewley, John W.	Hamblen
13,545	Bible, Christian	Greene
4,424	Biggs, Henry	Fayette
8,744	Bills, John H.	Hardeman
11,957	Billus, Robert B.	Monroe
807	Binkley, Patterson	Davidson
9,535	Binkley, Wm. B.	Davidson
8,925	Bird, John	Grainger
7,876	Bird, Wm. J.	Grainger
19,090	Bishop, Charles H.	Roane
6,724	Bishop, Richard, Estate of	Grainger
19,298	Bivens, Henry	Sumner
16,827	Bivens, James	Monroe
13,762	Bivens, Wm. S.	Hardin
19,684	Bivins, L.	Rutherford
9,963	Black, Leah	Shelby
5,502	Black, Thos.	Henderson
17,856	Black, Wm. A.	Bedford
8,178	Blackburn, Benj. A.	Jefferson
21,102	Blackburn, John	Bradley
11,346	Blackman, Alfred	Rutherford
9,468	Blackstone, Hudson	Shelby
5,948	Blair, David	Monroe
5,168	Blair, David B.	Shelby
14,924	Blair, Hugh E. F., Laura I., and Wm. W.	Loudon
18,792	Blair, James, Estate of	Loudon
14,924	Blair, Laura I., Wm. W. & Hugh, E. F.	Loudon
10,795	Blair, Wm., Estate of	Loudon
14,924	Blair, Wm. W., Hugh E. F. & Laura I.	Loudon
21,519	Blake, George W.	Lincoln
9,470	Blakemore, James L.	Gibson
9,470	Blakemore, James L.	Shelby
17,642	Blakemore, John A.	Bedford
6,423	Blakemore, Wm. B.	Weakley
13,408	Blankenship, Blackburn H.	Blount
21,647	Blankenship, F. D., Heirs of	Monroe
3,254	Blankenship, Peyton	Loudon
13,219	Blanton, Burrell	Monroe
13,529	Blanton, Meredith	Bedford
12,769	Blanton, N. C.	Rutherford
1,507	Bledsoe, L. Y. & Sims, Wm.	Haywood
10,444	Blevins, Isaac	Scott
9,469	Bogan, Margaret	Shelby
16,705	Boiling Fork Baptist Church	Franklin
7,366	Boland, Martin	Shelby
16,039	Bolton, Rosanna	Maury
14,547	Bolton, Sam	Washington
11,954	Bolton, Sam A.	Davidson
11,423	Bolton, Wm. T.	Humphreys
17,550	Bomar, Bibby B.	Bedford
19,890	Bond, Thos.	Haywood

18,072	Bone, Martha H.	Franklin
11,139	Booker, Wm. B.	Haywood
4,973	Boon, Anderson	Obion
18,713	Boone, Daniel	Bradley
21,721	Boone, Israel	Bradley
20,444	Boone, John	Bradley
2,673	Boren, Susan	Henderson
13,490	Boring, Hartsell	Blount
12,219	Bostick, Mary T.	Williamson
15,039	Boudurant, E. C., Mrs. Est.	Davidson
15,600	Boudurant, E. P.	Davidson
3,252	Bounds, John W.	Knox
19,697	Bower, Francis	Rhea
13,422	Bowerman, G. W.	Blount
16,608	Bowers, Abraham	Franklin
11,463	Bowers, Bradford	Davidson
18,327	Bowers, Hezekiah, Estate of	De Kalb
7,865	Bowers, James C.	Hamblen
8,992	Bowling, Henry G.	Rutherford
9,140	Bowling, James A.	Haywood
16,749	Bowman, Chas.	Knox
14,061	Bowman, Dan B.	Washington
13,493	Bowman, Geo., Estate of	Loudon
15,952	Bowman, James A.	Sumner
9,320	Bowman, James B.	Loudon
15,219	Boyd, Abraham B.	Warren
20,737	Boyd, S. B. & Thos. J.	Bradley
20,734	Boyd, Spencer B.	Bradley
8,330	Boyd, Thos.	Knox
20,737	Boyd, Thos. J. & S. B.	Bradley
9,714	Brabson, Henry	Sevier
14,044	Brabson, Oscar M.	Washington
4,208	Bradford, Virginia A.	Davidson
11,530	Bradford, Wall C., Estate of	Shelby
21,947	Bradley, Geo. C.	Hawkins
3,093	Bardley, John	Montgomery
13,223	Bardley, John L.	Monroe
315	Bradley, Martha W.	Shelby
12,831	Bradley, Robert	Knox
12,834	Bradley, Wm.	Knox
18,174	Bradley, Wm. M.	Hardin
4,434	Bradshaw, Joseph C.	Loudon
10,110	Bradshaw, Thos.	Grainger
10,109	Bradshaw, Wm. H.	Grainger
1,358	Brady, Michael	Davidson
12,825	Bramlett, Lunsford, Heirs of	Giles
8,172	Branch, Benj. L.	Shelby
3,162	Branch, Neeham	Haywood
1,794	Branch, Wm. M.	Maury
1,503	Brandon, H. S.	Carroll
1,504	Brandon, James M.	Carroll
1,505	Brannock, Amos W.	Carroll
1,506	Brannock, Mary	Carroll
6,390	Brannon, Joseph J.	Fentress
19,304	Brannon, Wm.	Sumner
11,054	Branson, Ben	Grainger
5,653	Branson, Sam	Grainger
13,072	Brantley, James H.	Davidson
14,194	Branum, Alex	Hardin
13,049	Brasel, Jesse	Morgan
17,690	Brassell, Wiley	Sumner
17,698	Brassell, Wm.	Sumner
5,141	Bratton, Argalus	Frank
4,521	Bray, John	Henderson
8,369	Brazelton, Dan	Frank
4,263: 17,555:	Brazelton, Green	Franklin
8,842	Brazelton, Lanty A.	Jefferson
16,251	Brazelton, Mary	Franklin
12,882	Brazelton, Wm., 2d	Jefferson
18,258	Brecheen, John H.	Marshall
11,723	Breeden, John	Monroe
3,639	Breedlove, Cloey	Morgan
19,970	Brewer, Eliza V.	Shelby
10,341	Brewer, Nathaniel	Carroll
1,706	Brester, Wm. M.	Claiborne
11,351	Bridge, Nancy M. B.	Rutherford
19,110	Bridges, Geo. R.	Shelby
19,552	Bridges, John	Union
12,052	Bright, Bartlett	Loudon

19,255	Bright, James E.	Loudon
16,864	Brimer, Thos. J.	Loudon
16,742	Brimer, Vineyard	Jefferson
1,516	Britt, Hiram	Henderson
11,098	Britt, W. Y.	Carroll
19,902	Broady, Joseph	Blount
14,670	Brock, Isaac	Rutherford
5,361	Brockman, Sam; and Porter, P.H.	Montgomery
15,422	Bromley, David	James
11,754	Brooks, A. N. B.	Williamson
17,998	Brooks, Aaron T., Estate of	Shelby
10,379	Brooks, Benj. F.	Madison
17,265	Brooks, Cannon L.	Shelby
8,061	Brooks, James M.	Shelby
21,629	Brooks, John	Madison
20,275	Brouder, John	Loudon
1,613	Brown, Aaron V., Mrs.	Davidson
15,989	Brown, Alfred F.	Washington
10,919	Brown, Benj. H.	Hamblen
6,461	Brown, Charley	Rutherford
4,464	Brown, David	Knox
16,568	Brown, Eli	Loudon
17,221	Brown, Elizabeth	Roane
18,902	Brown, Henry	Bedford
12,244	Brown, James	Greene
4,873	Brown, James C.	Loudon
11,560	Brown, James W.	Carroll
6,891	Brown, Jefferson	Rutherford
8,475	Brown, Jesse A.	Henry
21,111	Brown, John	Hamilton
11,138	Brown, John	Haywood
12,525	Brown, John	Knox
16,570	Brown, John F.	Bedford
20,080	Brown, John P.	Bedford
22,246	Brown, Margaret	Greene
20,738	Brown, Peter	Polk
2,775	Brown, Randall	Davidson
10,222	Brown, Robert	Madison
17,965	Brown, Robert H.	Bradley
15,189	Brown, Robert H.	Knox
16,622	Brown, Thos. H.	Greene
13,851	Brown, Thos. H. & Wm.	Greene
13,850	Brown, Wm.	Greene
18,379	Brown, Wm.	Loudon
1,744	Brown, Wm. A.	Haywood
14,975	Brown, Wm. H.	Maury
13,851	Brown, Wm. & Thos. H.	Greene
563	Brown, Wm. N., Estate of & Jones, Martin B. and Reuben	Shelby
11,347	Brown, Willie	Rutherford
13,559	Brown, Woodson F.	Greene
1,517	Browning, John	Carroll
14,062	Broyles, Isaac	Washington
14,063	Broyles, Jacob	Greene
20,572	Broyles, Nile M.	Rhea
14,064	Brumley, A. J.	Greene
14,065	Brumley, Alfred	Greene
21,910	Bryan, Ahas W.	Sevier
21,898	Bryan, Peter L.	Bradley
10,036	Bryan, Wm. H.	Gibson
17,717	Bryant, Eddy M., Mrs.	Davidson
11,899	Bryant, James E.	Maury
17,873	Bryant, McDonald	Hamilton
11,853	Bryant, N. A. D.	Hardeman
1,510	Bryant, Zach	Gibson
9,863	Buchanan, Alex & Estate of Lucinda	Davidson
21,534	Buchanan, James B., Estate	Rutherford
5,847	Ruchanan, John K., Mrs. Estate of	Davidson
9,863	Buchanan, Lucinda, Estate of, & Alex	Davidson
859	Buchanan, Moses R.	Rutherford
21,894	Buchanan, Thos. W. & Hughey, Robert	Bedford
21,894	Buchanan, Thos. W. & Hughey, Robert	Lincoln
4,425	Buchanan, Wm. R.	Fayette

21,520	Buckner, Melinda L.	Franklin
10,382	Buckner, Wm. P.	Union
17,694	Buford, Wesley	Sumner
10,925	Bull, Elijah	Sevier
17,792	Bulliner, Geo.	McNairy
3,700	Bullock, John, Estate of	Montgomery
15,968	Bullock, Sarah S.	Shelby
16,522	Bunch, Charles	Maury
14,199	Buntyn, Geraldus, Estate of	Shelby
806	Burch, Lemuel	Davidson
16,691	Burchfiel, James H.	Jefferson
13,295	Burchfiel, Joseph R.	Monroe
16,714	Burchfiel, Robert	Jefferson
19,641	Burchfiel, Robert	Monroe
17,999	Burem, Margaret S.	Hawkins
13,852	Burgner, Henry	Greene
5,436	Burk, David	Claiborne
15,226	Burk, Herod	Rutherford
7,743	Burk, Nancy	Hamilton
17,380	Burk, Wm.	McMinn
19,600	Burnett, Chesley J.	Hamblen
15,506	Burns, Jeremiah	Maury
22,186	Burt, John	Coffee
14,427	Burt, Susan	Bedford
10,674	Burton, J. G.	Madison
15,190	Burton, Wm. P.	Loudon
16,547	Burwick, John M.	Rhea
5,362	Busby, Mr., et al	Montgomery
12,872	Bussell, Mary	Hawkins
19,257	Bussull, Wm.	Loudon
4,522	Butler, A. J.	Carroll
16,587	Butler, James A.	Giles
20,254	Butler, James P.	Madison
2,674	Butler, P. T.	Carroll
5,345	Butler, P. T.	Monroe
6,779	Butler, Wm. B.	McNairy
21,632	Butler, Wm. E.	Madison
19,368	Butt, Martin	Hamblen
14,585	Buttram, Wm.	Scott
15,379	Butts, Thos. P., Estate of	Maury
21,656	Byars, Henry	Rutherford
18,955	Byerley, Jacob	Rhea
10,114	Byerly, James	Knox
18,230	Byers, Nimrod	Blount
18,008	Byrd, Robert K.	Roane
6,634	Cage, John O.	Sumner
19,030	Cage, S. S., Mrs.	Shelby
14,856	Cagle, Henry	Monroe
13,224	Cagle, Martin	Monroe
7,866	Cain, John W.	Hamblen
14,510	Caldwell, Andrew	Jefferson
14,512	Caldwell, James A.	Jefferson
17,864	Caldwell, John C., Estate of	Bedford
14,513	Caldwell, John H.	Jefferson
14,066	Caldwell, Reuben	Greene
12,889	Caldwell, Robert (Newmarket)	Jefferson
14,514	Caldwell, Robert (Strawberry Plains)	Jefferson
12,888	Caldwell, Sam M.	Jefferson
17,857	Caldwell, Thos. H.	Bedford
13,498	Calfee, Jeremiah	Monroe
19,377	Calhoon, James F.	Bedford
11,200: 19,369:	Calhoun Presbyterian Church	McMinn
20,069	Callahan, Sam M.	Monroe
9,966	Callann, Thos.	Gibson
10,670	Callaway, Wm. S.	Madison
22,248	Calvin, Michael, Estate of	Davidson
16,126	Calzy, Mary	Sumner
18,771: 20,382:	Cameron, James	Grainger
17,391	Cameron, James	James
7,508	Campbell, Alex	Weakley
22,280	Campbell, Alex, Estate of	Giles
20,581	Campbell, Eli	Rhea
22,278	Campbell, David C.	Giles
22,279	Campbell, James Ross	Giles
13,350	Campbell, Jennie	Maury
13,853	Campbell, John	Greene
9,968	Campbell, John M.	Gibson
12,294	Campbell, Mary E.	Franklin
20,530	Campbell, Robert	Bradley
1,710	Campbell, Robert	Claiborne
14,511	Campbell, Sarah M., Estate of	Jefferson
2,675	Campbell, Thos.	Henderson
181	Campbell, Washington G.	Shelby
17,960	Campbell, Wm. W.	Meigs
7,846	Canady, James	Scott
4,098	Cannon, Jane W.	Jefferson
6,773	Cannon, Joseph	Obion
15,702: 21,890:	Cannon, Lee	Sevier
17,704	Cannon, Robert	Marshall
13,384	Carden, Rufus M.	Loudon
15,423	Cardin, Robert H.	James
2,033	Cardwell, Wm.	Claiborne
11,081	Cardwell, Wm. S.	Giles
19,024	Carey, Chris C.	Jefferson
5,052	Carlton, Obadiah	Weakley
12,849	Carmichael, Hamilton	Hawkins
6,630	Carnes, Andrew W.	Monroe
19,857	Carnes, James A., Estate of and Terry, James C. (of Coahoma Co., MS)	Shelby
9,569	Carney, Alfred	Polk
16,759	Carney, Wm. J.	Rutherford
17,209	Carothers, James	Bedford
13,060	Carothers, John	Bedford
17,693	Carothers, Joseph	Sumner
3,017	Carpenter, James M.	Claiborne
10,763	Carpenter, Richard	Giles
20,287	Carr, David J.	Washington
13,407	Carr, James M.	Blount
14,160	Carr, Wm. M.	Claiborne
15,619	Carrier, Thos.	Sullivan
17,787	Carroll, Clemuel C.	McNairy
15,601	Carroll, Peter	Davidson
13,840	Carson, Alvin B.	Monroe
4,071	Carson, Caroline B.	Monroe
13,409	Carson, E. M.	Blount
4,072	Carson, J. L.	Monroe
12,150	Carson, James H.	Jefferson
5,346	Carson, John	Monroe
21,979	Carson, Wm. C.	Jefferson
6,557	Carter, Allen E.	Humphreys
1,219	Carter, Bellfield N.	Houston
13,121	Carter, Felix	Davidson
5,309	Carter, Fountain B.	Williamson
1,773	Carter, Henry N.	Carroll
20,375	Carter, James M.	Knox
16,693	Carter, Peyton	Knox
2,677	Carter, R. H.	Carroll
8,406	Carter, Robert	Rutherford
11,272	Carter, Stephen	Madison
14,257	Cary, Alex, Estate of	Obion
18,358	Casada, Wm. H.	Loudon
11,920	Case, Joshua F.	Cocke
15,141	Casey, Sam, Sr.	Davidson
4,765	Cash, Elizabeth	Coffee
17,807	Cason, Peter	McNairy
20,578	Cass, Benj. E.	McMinn
19,419	Cass, James M.	McMinn
8,160	Cate, Anderson	Jefferson
20,329	Cate, Andrew J.	Bradley
18,848	Cate, Green Berry	Bradley
12,176	Cate, Joseph	Sevier
12,174	Cate, Nancy	Sevier
15,774: 20,732:	Cate, Wm.	Bradley
17,343	Cate, Wm. C.	Jefferson
9,573	Cathcart, J. G.	Monroe
6,775	Catron, Hugh A.	Obion
5,096	Cavenaugh, Michael	Davidson
11,600	Cawood, Alex	Sullivan
20,427	Cawthon, Jame L.	Cannon
2,676	Cawthon, John B., Estate of	Henderson
5,437	Chadwick, John Y.	Claiborne
15,086	Chaffin, James B.	Maury
12,061	Chafin, Thornton & Webster, Cyrus	Maury

21,062	Chambers, C. L.	McNairy
14,291	Chambers, Jemima	Fayette
11,702	Chambers, John	Scott
1,519	Chambers, Robert P.	Carroll
4,268	Chambers, Thomas, Estate of	Scott
18,598	Chambers, Wm. A.	Scott
9,122	Chambless, Seth H.	Carroll
21,016	Chandler, H. R. & Johnson, Anthony W., Jr.	Davidson
18,711	Chandler, Handy	Blount
8,655	Chaney, Fleming W.	Haywood
22,247	Chaney, Henry	Jefferson
12,153	Chaney, Wm., Sr.	Jefferson
18,251	Chapman, John	Bedford
6,143	Chappell, Joel R.	Madison
14,067	Chase, Walter J.	Washington
17,947	Chatata Christ Church	Bradley
14,127	Cheatham, John	Maury
9,994	Cheek, Isaac	Wilson
13,624	Cherry, John	Hardin
17,782	Cheshier, Pitser M.	McNairy
10,911	Chesnult, Rodham	Hawkins
16,169	Chesnutt, Sam, Estate of	Hawkins
16,046	Childers, Isaac	Rutherford
17,110	Childers, James	James
704	Childress, Armand, Estate of	Davidson
1,119	Childress, Mitchell J.	Knox
6,768	Chilton, Thos. W.	Davidson
10,234	Chitwood, John	Franklin
15,255	Choate, James	Dickson
16,705	Church, Boiling Fork Baptist	Franklin
11,200: 19,369:	Church, Calhoun Presbyterian	McMinn
17,947	Church, Chatata Christ	Bradley
8,381	Claiborn, James H.	Shelby
20,029	Claman, Jacob L.	Hawkins
18,774	Clapp, Boston	Claiborne
13,378	Clark, Eli S.	Loudon
18,834	Clark, George	Bradley
14,669	Clark, Harvey	Knox
4,975	Clark, Hiram K.	Obion
9,008	Clark, Jacob F.	Haywood
19,891	Clark, James W.	Haywood
1,520	Clark, John K.	Carroll
13,059	Clark, Robert S.	Bedford
5,532	Clark, Sam P.	Gibson
21,153	Clark, Thos. N., Estate of	Roane
1,204	Clarke, Edwards E.	Shelby
21,043	Clarke, Job	Sevier
18,249	Claxton, John	Bedford
17,875	Clayton, Jesse	McNairy
21,638	Cleage, David	McMinn
9,325	Cleaveland, Sidney G.	Loudon
12,448	Cleaver, Alfred, Estate of	Carroll
1,069	Cleer, Robert H.	Shelby
8,856	Clement, Ann Henry	Tipton
3,462	Clement, Caleb R.	Gibson
15,424	Cleveland, Eli M.	James
20,032	Cleveland, Eliza A.	Claiborne
8,843	Clevenger, Elizabeth	Jefferson
11,569	Clevenger, Thomas S.	Jefferson
15,157	Click, Wm.	Monore
15,580	Clift, Robert B.	Hamilton
15,608	Clift, Wm.	Hamilton
14,218	Clifton, James W.	Hardin
10,553	Cline, Joseph H.	Jefferson
8,656	Clinton, John	Haywood
10,120	Cloner, Andrew	Grainger
10,902	Coatney, Martha	Hamblen
5,503	Cobb, Dan W.	McNairy
21,649	Cobb, Elbert S.	Loudon
2,891	Cobb, Jessie B.	Giles
13,556	Cobble, McKindric	Greene
13,296: 13,558:	Cobble, Sylvanus	Greene
5,953	Cochran, John	Monroe
5,952	Cochran, Robert L.	Monroe
13,575	Cochran, Wm. J.	Maury
21,709	Cochran, Wm.	Grainger
6,596	Cocke, Thos. R.	Fayette

17,204	Coe, Adam	Davidson
18,108	Coffey, Dan	McMinn
13,225: 13,448:	Coffin, T. T.	London
20,034	Coffman, Sterling	Grainger
20,295	Cogswell, Anna M.	Shelby
12,217	Cohen, W. D.	Marion
7,867	Coil, James C.	Jefferson
7,868	Coil, John L.	Jefferson
5,950	Cole, James E.	Monroe
7,259	Cole, John R.	Monroe
10,488	Cole, Martin	Hamblen
5,951	Cole, S. G.	Monroe
13,709	Cole, Wm. F.	Giles
14,737	Coleman, W. F. T.	Rutherford
18,372	Collet, John E.	Greene
12,772	Collier, E. L.	Rutherford
20,451	Collier, Thos. T.	Bradley
22,284	Collier, Wm.	Bedford
17,469	Collier, Wm. R.	Madison
10,429	Collins, D. M.	Polk
18,714	Collins, H. M.	Bradley
8,978	Collins, James	Grainger
18,396	Collins, James E.	Meigs
20,576	Collins, James P.	Rhea
15,944	Collins, Pinkney	Rhea
14,259	Collins, Sarah G.	Franklin
17,760	Collins, Wm.	Franklin
12,006	Collins, Wm. L.	Franklin
11,660	Colman, Benj.	Shelby
16,980	Colquitt, Hutson	Hamilton
12,738	Colson, Elizabeth K.	Shelby
18,162	Colter, John	Blount
22,270	Colvin, Wm., Estate of	Union
14,738	Compton, Felix, Estate of	Davidson
15,901	Compton, Henry W.	Davidson
2,828	Compton, Mangum	Knox
21,951	Conatser, Amasa	Sevier
18,303	Condon, S. M., Mrs.	Davidson
9,546	Coner, James Z.	Davidson
1,652	Congill, Mary A.	Davidson
11,080	Conley, Calvin	Giles
5,219	Connelly, Peter	Shelby
17,579	Conner, Wesley P., Estate of	Hamilton
3,526	Conner, Wm.	Lauderdale
14,023	Cook, Geo. S.	Rutherford
10,417	Cook, James	Humphreys
5,053	Cook, James R.	Weakley
19,436	Cook, Mary M.	Shelby
7,142	Cook, S. M. N.	Wilson
7,509	Cooley, W. G.	Obion
17,955	Cooper, Bennett	Bradley
17,568	Cooper, Thos.	McMinn
5,452	Cope, Jennie	Hardeman
10,904	Cope, Jesse	Hawkins
6,894	Copeland, G. W. & Sam	Rutherford
6,894	Copeland, Sam & G. W.	Rutherford
20,447	Copeland, W. J.	Polk
7,328	Copinger, John	Monroe
1,779	Coppedge, Thos. C.	Haywood
10,381	Coppock, Wm. J.	Union
15,602	Corley, John J.	Davidson
19,259	Cormichael, Dan L. & James H.	Loudon
19,259	Cormichael, James H. & Dan L.	Loudon
10,237	Corn, G. W.	Franklin
19,383	Corn, John A.	Lincoln
2,958	Corns, John W.	Shelby
3,523	Corson, Alphonzo	Shelby
20,459	Cossitt, Frank D.	Fayette
13,428	Costner, Mary	Blount
14,068	Cotter, Hugh E.	Greene
13,768	Couch, Nancy	Hardin
19,702	Coulter, Thos. J.	Rhea
2,678	Council, Merrill	Henderson
15,609	Courtney, John, Estate of	Hamilton
7,141	Covert, Oliver C.	Davidson
2,832	Covington, Dan	Sevier

4,301	Cowan, A. J.	Lincoln
18,773	Cowan, Hiram, Estate of	Claiborne
21,984	Cowan, Varner, D., Estate of	Rutherford
17,332	Coward, Wm.	Tipton
995	Cowart, Cynthia	Hamilton
15,540	Cowen, Dorsey	Humphreys
19,771	Cox, Caleb	McNairy
14,069	Cox, Elbert S.	Washington
2,833	Cox, Geo.	Sevier
8,730	Cox, Leroy	Hamblen
11,701	Cox, Moses	Weakley
20,573	Cox, Rebecca	Rhea
12,866	Cox, Sarah	Hawkins
22,053	Cox, Sarah	Morgan
18,975	Cox, Wm.	Dickson
9,318	Cozart, Abram W.	Loudon
1,518	Cozart, David	Henderson
14,070	Crabtree, John	Greene
9,582	Crabtree, Rheas S.	Jackson
9,399	Crafton, Mary	Gibson
21,027	Craigmiles, Pleasant M.	Bradley
17,952	Craigmiles, Wm. H.	Bradley
16,385	Cram, Ezra, Estate of	Davidson
2,976	Cramer, Ferdinand	Shelby
8,211	Crandall, Asa H.	Loudon
18,064	Creekmore, Green B.	Scott
14,410	Crenshaw, Thos. B., Estate of	Shelby
1,521	Crenshaw, Wm. E.	Gibson
2,084	Crews, James M.	Gibson
16,831	Crick, Sam	Williamson
18,733	Crisp, James & Mahala	Loudon
18,732	Crisp, Joel	Loudon
18,733	Crisp, Mahala & James	Loudon
14,928	Crittenden, M. A.	Madison
6,895	Crockett, Calvin	Rutherford
13,823	Crockett, Catharine W.	Williamson
5,310	Crockett, James	Williamson
1,830	Crockett, James B.	Fentress
11,602	Crockett, James M.	Sullivan
5,054	Crockett, John	Obion
14,874	Crockett, John T.	Coffee
5,848	Crockett, Mary, Estate of	Williamson
12,661	Cross, Joel J.	Lawrence
4,611	Crow, Henry C.	Giles
1,522	Crow, Isaac S.	Carroll
20,402	Crowder, Robert P.	Monroe
10,545	Crowder, Terrill T.	Giles
20,401	Crowder, Thos., Estate of	Monroe
7,954	Crownover, Benj.	Franklin
16,707	Crox, Henry A.	Loudon
12,080	Crump, John	Shelby
18,558	Crunk, James J.	Marshall
321	Crutchfield, Wm.	Hamilton
1,523	Culp, Benj.	Carroll
13,411	Cummings, Joseph B.	Blount
20,041	Cunningham, Elizabeth F.	Shelby
19,714	Cunningham, Elvina	Rhea
12,730	Cunningham, John W.	Coffee
16,516	Cunningham, Leroy	Hamilton
12,520	Cunningham, Leroy T.	Davidson
13,625	Cunningham, Levi	Hardin
20,426	Cunningham, Matthew T.	Bedford
14,071	Cunningham, Samuel A.	Carter
17,238	Curl, Joshua D.	Grainger
1,781	Curlin, Lemuel	Obion
12,771	Currin, Adele	Rutherford
12,770	Currin, Amanda	Rutherford
4,451	Curry, James	Jefferson
20,829	Curry, James C.	Bradley
10,796	Curtis, Isham L.	Loudon
8,819	Curtis, John A.	Franklin
21,543: 21,878:	Curtin, Joshua	Loudon
13,433	Cuthbertson, David	Blount
2,890	Cuthbertson, Mary L.	Loudon
4,209	Cyrus, Virginia P.	Davidson
20,882	Dabbs, E. J., Mrs.	Fayette
6,725	Dailey, John	Grainger
6,762	Dailey, Sarah	Grainger
18,985	Daily, Wm. C.	Bradley
16,229	Daley, Henry	Grainger
681	Dallas, Henry C.	Shelby
8,179: 10,921:	Dalton, David T.	Jefferson
6,729	Dalton, M. B.	Grainger
12,117	Damron, Joseph	Lincoln
5,312	Danel, Connell O.	Davidson
8,161	Daniel, Isaac B.	Jefferson
10,916	Daniel, James H.	Jefferson
7,878	Daniel, Marcus L.	Grainger
15,964	Daniel, Ralph W.	Madison
21,272	Daniel, Rufus A.	Coffee
21,273	Daniel, Sam H.	Coffee
20,433	Daniel, Thomas, Estate of	Coffee
4,104: 10,923:	Daniel, Wm. F.	Jefferson
1,333	Daniels, R. W., Estate of	Montgomery
21,521	Dardis, James B.	Frank
18,903	Darnall, James	Bedford
14,429	Darwin, James M.	Franklin
20,614	Darwin, John, Estate of	Franklin
20,569	Darwin, Thos. C.	Rhea
14,683	Darwin, Wm., Estate of	Franklin
15,626	Daugherty, Matthew	McMinn
16,981	Daughtry, John	Hamilton
19,690	Davault, James M.	Sullivan
5,538	Davenport, Isaac N.	Henderson
22,063	Davidson, Aaron	Shelby
13,869	Davidson, James F.	Giles
1,191	Davidson, John W.	Coffee
20,431	Davidson, Mary A.	Coffee
182	Davie, Montgomery D.	Montgomery
18,807	Davis, Cain, Emmett & Jacob	Wilson
13,130	Davis, Caleb B.	Lawrence
715: 6,628:	Davis, Charles T. P.	Loudon
6,627	Davis, Charles T. P. & Nancy P.	Loudon
3,339	Davis, Dan	Knox
18,807	Davis, Emmett, Jacob & Cain	Wilson
17,398	Davis, Henry B.	Bradley
18,807	Davis, Jacob, Cain & Emmett	Wilson
15,426	Davis, James	Bradley
7,856	Davis, James	Grainger
15,425	Davis, James	James
7,887	Davis, Jane A. M.	Davidson
14,072	Davis, Jerry W.	Greene
13,557	Davis, John	Greene
13,051	Davis, John	Morgan
6,405	Davis, John, Sr.	DeKalb
6,629	Davis, Nancy P.	Loudon
6,627	Davis, Nancy P. & Charles T. P.	Loudon
13,430	Davis, Tarrence	Blount
13,540	Davis, Thos.	Greene
16,971	Davis, Thomas W.	Cocke
5,453	Davis, Wiley J.	Hardeman
693	Davis, Wm.	Monroe
12,005	Davis, Wm. A.	Davidson
10,442	Davis, Wm. A.	Williamson
7,918	Davis, Wm. G.	Jefferson
13,576	Davis, Zachariah	Marshall
9,301	Davy, Jacob	Montgomery
19,455	Davy, Jehu L.	Hardin
19,454	Davy, Jehu L. & White, Meady	Hardin
1,203	Dawson, Eliza M.	Shelby
20,271	Dawson, Joshua F.	Loudon
15,191	Dawson, Simeon A.	Knox
21,881	Dawson, Wm. H.	Monroe
10,478	Day, Mary C.	Hamblen
7,175	Day, Ransom	Grainger
996	Deady, John	Hamilton
7,260	Dean, Abijah	Monroe
18,057	De Armand, John	Roane
14,632	Dearston, Susan	Greene
11,523	DeBusk, James	Claiborne
16,577	Delk, Wm. R.	Bedford

8,063	DeLooch, Josiah	Shelby	13,298	Dunn, John R.	Rutherford
12,919	Demike, Wm.	Robertson	2,887	Dunn, Joseph W.	Loudon
19,363	Dennis, Robert	Bedford	2,332	Dunn, Nancy	Lauderdale
16,699	Denny, Jacob E.	Hawkins	16,923	Dunn, Thomas M.	Cheatham
11,725	Denton, Charles	Monroe	2,333	Dupuy, Nancy	Shelby
11,724	Denton, Dorcas	Monroe	2,742	Dyer, Elizabeth P.	Fayette
16,689	Denton, James P.	Jefferson	10,910	Dyer, John S.	Jefferson
13,342	Derieux, Jesse B.	Knox	10,102	Dyer, Pryor H.	Grainger
17,109	Derieux, Peter, Estate of	Knox	12,859	Dyer, Richard F.	Hawkins
19,599	Derrick, Calvin	Jefferson	18,907	Dysart, James P.	Marshall
17,382	Derrick, Erastus L.	McMinn	11,280	Dysart, R. C., Estate of	Marshall
2,679	Deshong, L. W.	Carroll	12,634	Earnest, Benj. F.	Greene
16,609	Deveney, Martin	Davidson	13,855	Earnest, Harvy W.	Greene
13,120	Dews, Pink	Davidson	14,079	Earnest, Isaac, Estate of	Greene
12,885	Dice, Geo. W.	Jefferson	13,856	Earnest, James O.	Greene
20,425	Dick, Lemuel M.	Jefferson	13,547	Earnest, Jesse R.	Greene
10,378	Dickens, Wm. T.	Gibson	21,271	Earthman, Isaac	Rutherford
20,525	Dickey, Steward O.	Sevier	11,741	Easley, Alfred	Grainger
10,652	Dickirman, Isaiah & M. J.	Davidson	20,037	Easley, John G.	Grainger
10,652	Dickirman, M. J. & Isaiah	Davidson	8,983	Easly, Allen	Grainger
18,178	Dill, Martin	Carroll	8,982	Easly, Henry	Grainger
17,830	Dill, Marvel M.	Rutherford	5,313	Eason, Sam S.	Davidson
10,025	Dillard, Wm. L.	Polk	14,080	Easterly, Jonathan H.	Greene
5,717	Dinker, Patrick	Giles	17,086	Eblen, Isaac N.	Roane
8,180	Dinwiddie, J. H.	Jefferson	5,579	Eastham, G. W.	DeKalb
4,524	Dinwiddie, Thos. H.	Carroll	19,468	Eastridge, Ephraim, Estate of	Claiborne
13,985	Dishner, Jacob	Sullivan			
19,378	Dixon, Robert A.	James	2,036	Eastridge, Hiram	Claiborne
5,539	Dixon, Thomas Y.	Decatur	10,039	Eaves, Dudley F.	Gibson
18,102	Dixon, Wm. M.	McMinn	5,089	Eberly, Hiram W.	Shelby
7,262	Dobbins, Archibald Monroe	Monroe	17,437	Edger, Wm. J. J.	Jefferson
20,031	Dobbins, Watt, Estate of	Hawkins	4,167	Edington, Sam	Monroe
14,073	Dobson, David M.	Greene	10,762	Edmondson, Sam	Lawrence
14,074	Dobson, Isaac C.	Greene	18,447	Edmonson, Wm.	Giles
14,075	Dobson, Mary A.	Greene	15,949	Edwards, Gincy	Sumner
1,357	Dodd, Benj. N.	Davidson	20,006	Edwards, Mary, Heirs of	Shelby
14,076	Dodd, Elizabeth	Greene	11,348	Edwards, Nancy A.	Rutherford
17,781	Dodds, Kindred M.	McNairy	11,099	Edwards, Nathan J.	Carroll
19,421	Dodson, Oliver	McMinn	3,680	Edwards, Redman G.	Shelby
13,577	Dodson, Whit	Giles	12,171	Elder, John H.	Sevier
19,420	Dodson, Wm. L.	McMinn	11,354	Elder, Joshua W.	Ruth
808	Doherty, Patrick	Davidson	19,013	Eldrige, I. E.	Bradley
4,523	Dolan, John D.	Davidson	19,261	Eldridge, John H.	London
19,005	Dollins, David B.	Giles	16,156	Elkins, James M.	Franklin
15,781	Donivan, Michael, Estate of	Bradley	15,172	Eller, John	Sullivan
588	Donkers, Henry	Shelby	9,016	Elliott, Alpha	Tipton
25	Donley, Owen	Shelby	15,951	Elliot, Elizabeth	Sumner
6,335	Donley, Wm.	Monroe	12,152	Elliot, Geo. M.	Jefferson
12,116	Donnaldson, Docia A.	Franklin	20,003	Elliot, N. D., Estate of	Shelby
1,339	Donnelly, John	Davidson	8,991	Elliott, Thos. A.	Rutherford
14,077	Donnelly, R. H. M.	Greene	17,190	Ellis, Dan	Carter
15,955	Donnell, Robert W.	Sumner	20,374	Ellis, Edward	Knox
22,057	Dooly, Mary J.	Shelby	17,979	Ellis, Edward, Sr.	Scott
20,227	Dortch, Willie Blount	Davidson	14,081	Ellis, Isaac	Greene
15,701	Dotsen, Geo. C.	Dickson	4,302	Ellis, John N.	Lincoln
12,624	Dotson, Cornelius	Greene	13,543	Ellis, John W.	Greene
14,515	Douglass, Alex	Jefferson	21,987	Ellis, Katharine	Shelby
4,426	Douglass, Asa	Shelby	13,552	Ellis, Margaret	Greene
8,064	Douglass, Mary L.	Tipton	4,427	Ellis, Robert L.	Shelby
18,395	Downey, Jackson H.	Meigs	21,032	Ellis, Wm. R.	Sevier
3,542	Doxey, John L.	Sumner	18,900	Ellis, Willie	Bedford
13,854	Doyle, Thos. J.	Greene	8,844	Elmore, Mary	Jefferson
14,078	Drake, Estell M.	Greene	15,727	Elsea, John, Sr.	Hamilton
16,428	Drake, H. D.	Claiborne	1,712	Ely, Elias	Claiborne
809	Drake, Henry C.	Davidson	12,060	Embry, Emily S.	Maury
18,440	Drake, Isaac E.	Sullivan	2,931	Emert, Dan M. J.	Grainger
10,418	Drake, Isaac W.	Humphreys	1,739	England, John	Fentress
10,315	Duff, James	Grainger	18,770	England, Valentine	Claiborne
17,777	Duke, Edmund F.	McNairy	15,409	Enoch, Benj. S.	Smith
5,956	Duncan, A. J.	Claiborne	6,336	Ervin, James	Monroe
19,903	Duncan, Andrew	Blount	10,546	Erwin, David P.	Maury
2,777	Duncan, Andrew J.	Davidson	17,862	Erwin, Henry B.	Marshall
1,129	Duncan, Craven	Morgan	11,077	Erwin, W. H.	Giles
12,161	Duncan, Isaac A.	Jefferson	17,580	Ervin, Wm.	Roane
12,160	Duncan, John H., Estate of	Jefferson	957	Eslick, Mary	Lincoln
19,707	Dungan, Charles L.	Rhea	15,862	Esselman, Rebecca	Giles
19,323	Dunlap, James D.	Blount	21,623	Essman, Wm.	Shelby
18,165	Dunlap, Matilda	Blount	4,210	Ester, Martha	Davidson
14,591	Dunlap, Ripley E.	Henry	16,715	Estes, James	Hamblen
12,729	Dunn, John	Coffee	11,509	Estes, Wm.	Hamblen

9,017	Etheridge, Mark	Shelby
17,858	Evans, Alex H.	Bedford
21,033	Evans, James M.	Sevier
4,977	Evans, John E.	Obion
7,510	Exum, Lucy Ann	Weakley
12,859	Fain, Alex	Hawkins
17,066	Fain, H. Crawford	Sullivan
5,130: 14,045:	Fain, Hugh C.	Washington
12,575	Fain, Thos. W.	Jefferson
12,578	Faison, P. B.	Hardeman
5,318	Fall, John T. S.	Davidson
13,632	Falls, Andrew	Hardin
4,428	Falls, John	Fayette
13,633	Falls, Robert K.	Hardin
22,100	Falps, John	Claiborne
21,298	Fancher, Francis	Sevier
19,699	Fann, James M.	Rhea
17,593	Fariss, Thos. J.	McNairy
14,167	Farley, John A.	Fayette
15,771	Farmer, Amos, Estate of	Meigs
14,801	Farmer, Sarah L.	Shelby
18,229	Farr, Absalom T.	Blount
1,524	Farr, Poleman	Gibson
7,511	Farron, Joseph J.	Haywood
4,376	Faucett, Frances	Hamblen
17,541	Faught, Moses M.	Obion
11,137	Faulk, Jacob C.	Obion
12,138	Faulkner, Margaret M.	Wilson
12,731	Featherstone, Clement A.	Franklin
15,057	Featherstone, Richard, Estate	Franklin
14,516	Felkner, Sam F.	Hamblen
14,083	Fellers, Sarah G.	Greene
13,857	Fellers, Susan E.	Greene
136	Fellis, Frances	Davidson
15,734	Felts, James, Estate of	Loudon
20,545	Feltz, Louisiana E.	Shelby
4,573	Fenton, Wm. M.	Shelby
5,849	Fergeson, J. R.	Giles
10,232	Ferris, John S.	Franklin
14,185	Fielding, Lieutitia	Jefferson
2,681	Fields, Alex	Henderson
12,962	Fields, Elijah & Rose Ann	Davidson
5,055	Fields, John G.	Obion
12,962	Fields, Rose Ann & Elijah	Davidson
4,523	Finch, Edward	Carroll
17,329	Finney, Washington	Rutherford
16,138	Fish, Etheldred D.	De Kalb
18,957	Fisher, Francis A.	Rhea
9,512	Fisher, Geo. M.	Gibson
18,956	Fisher, Henry, Estate of	Rhea
9,319	Fisher, Wm.	Loudon
15,414	Fitzgerald, Elijah	James
14,082	Fitzgerald, James B.	Greene
15,665	Fitzpatrick, Michael	Shelby
15,870	Flant, James	Giles
10,548	Fleming, Ruth A.	Maury
7,515	Fletcher, John L.	Obion
13,759	Flieman, G. W., Estate of	Giles
20,435	Floyd, James W.	Bedford
19,550	Floyd, John	Knox
18,344	Fly, Tipp	Rutherford
10,671	Fogg, Mary L.	Madison
10,809	Fogg, Sarah L.	Giles
10,744	Fogg, Thos. S.	Giles
785	Foley, Timothy	Shelby
19,302	Fonerill, Valerious E.	Sumner
19,233	Ford, Thos. S.	Rutherford
7,734	Forest, Baylus B.	Benton
12,837	Forest, Henry	Anderson
13,375	Forister, Mary	Loudon
9,668	Forkner, Dan Peter	Monroe
16,832	Forman, J. F.	Cocke
9,857	Forner, Cornelius	Polk
21,152	Forsythe, Darius, Estate of	James
11,612	Fortner, Anna	Polk
11,611	Fortner, Levi F.	Polk
2,682	Foster, D. W. C.	Carroll
10,655	Foster, Isaac C.	Obion

9,205	Foster, John	Polk
15,879	Foster, Wm.	McMinn
19,711	Foust, Philip F.	Rhea
14,834	Foust, Sam K.	Giles
20,579	Foust, Wm. P., Estate of	Rhea
20,273	Foute, John A. J.	Roane
14,633	Fowler, Wm. F.	Greene
13,858	Fox, James, Sr.	Greene
12,633: 14,084:	Fracker, G. W.	Greene
9,323	France, John	Loudon
7,514	Francis, Henry C.	Weakley
7,513	Francis, John M.	Weakley
9,570	Frank, Robertson	Monroe
10,767	Franklin, Benj. F.	Jefferson
21,028	Franklin, D. J., Heirs of	Jefferson
20,251	Franklin, David J.	McNairy
21,044	Franklin, Henry	Sevier
17,565	Franklin, J. H.	Sumner
5,392	Franklin, Mary Louisa	Shelby
17,701	Franklin, Ned	Sumner
17,268	Franks, Isaac	Davidson
21,045	Frazier, Martin	Sevier
19,813	Frazier, Thos. N.	Davidson
7,452	Freel, Rosetta	Shelby
13,634	Freeman, Benj. R.	Hardin
11,764	Freeman, Edward	Wilson
13,626	Freeman, James J.	Hardin
17,974	French, Henry S.	Davidson
12,165	French, Lucinda B.	Jefferson
19,154	French, Margaret	Bradley
12,157	French, Moses	Jefferson
21,046	Frey, Joseph	Knox
5,658	Friar, Thomas	Claiborne
12,519	Friend, Ellen C.	Maury
5,519	Friend, John O.	Maury
1,130	Fritts, David	Morgan
12,239	Fritts, Jacob S.	Morgan
12,240	Fry, James, Estate of	Madison
19,540	Fry, Jesse	Giles
20,615	Fryar, James	Hamilton
14,245	Fullen, Adam B.	Greene
11,274	Fuller, Turner J.	Madison
17,784	Fullwood, Sam M.	McNairy
8,981	Fulton, A. J.	Claiborne
21,076	Fulton, Hugh	Sevier
16,686	Furgusun, Elijah	Jefferson
5,194	Gaines, Albert M.	Giles
13,066	Gaines, Wm. N.	Montgomery
16,381	Gains, Nathan, Estate of	James
3,647	Galbrath, John H.	Davidson
14,085	Gallager, John	Washington
6,338	Galyan, J. P.	Loudon
16,743	Galyon, John	Jefferson
8,683	Galyon, Robert F.	Jefferson
15,415	Gamble, James	Polk
18,167	Gamble, John	Blount
19,325	Gamble, Josiah	Blount
18,164	Gamble, Moses	Blount
17,786	Gamble, Neill S. B.	McNairy
997: 17,399:	Gamble, Robert L.	Hamilton
10,705	Gamewell, Mary A.	Madison
7,560	Gammon, Isaac	Knox
16,889	Gann, Preston	Hamilton
5,169	Gans, Isaac M.	Shelby
12,170	Gant, G. W.	Jefferson
16,488	Gantz, John	Jefferson
17,073	Gardenhire, James T.	Hamilton
9,069	Gardner, James	Williamson
11,362	Gardner, Martha Ann	Madison
18,556	Gardner, Thos.	McMinn
17,758	Garner, Griffin	Franklin
17,759	Garner, John	Franklin
7,408	Garrett, Wm. G.	Rutherford
14,086	Garst, David	Washington
12,149	Gass, Sam G. M.	Jefferson
16,589	Gaunt, Elizabeth, Estate of	Bedford
21,040	Gautt, Judson	Maury
696	Gay, Louisa M.	Monore

850	Gee, James W.	Davidson
8,244	Gee, Robert J.	Tipton
6,144	George, Evan	Fayette
9,775	Gerber, G. Frederick	Hamilton
13,551	Gerstle, Abraham	Greene
17,451	Gettys, James	McMinn
11,224	Gholson, Aaron	Maury
11,223	Gholson, Anthony	Maury
10,656	Gibbs, C. H.	Obion
9,865	Gibbs, John	Knox
8,051	Gibson, Elizabeth J.	Cumberland
14,046	Gibson, Jeremiah D., Estate	Washington
4,393	Gibson, Joseph	Giles
7,676: 18,738:	Griffin, Bartley	Knox
20,096	Giffin, Jerusha H.	Knox
955	Gilbert, D. A.	Lincoln
21,695	Gilbert, Sam	Shelby
1,526	Giles, Cloe	Carroll
15,158	Giles, James M.	Monroe
1,527	Giles, Jesse, Estate of	Carroll
5,814	Giles, Thos. H.	Rutherford
13,905: 16,031:	Gill, James	Smith
9,401	Gill, John P.	Gibson
15,251	Gill, Sarah E.	Maury
17,557	Gill, Winston W.	Bedford
9,879: 22,182:	Gillespie, Geo. L. Estate of	Rhea
13,939	Gillespie, James H.	Shelby
22,181	Gillespie, John C.	Hamilton
15,061	Gillespie, John H.	Franklin
14,047	Gillespie, Robert L.	Washington
8,824	Gillilan, James E.	Dickson
13,769	Gillis, Dugald P.	Hardin
21,707	Gilmore, Sarah A.	Grainger
13,770	Ginn, James B.	Hardin
15,961	Givins, James, Estate of	Monroe
17,286	Glaleher, Michael	Grundy
3,267	Glancey, John, Estate of	Shelby
505	Glassie, D. W. & Minnie H., and Nash, Emma & Joseph C.	Davidson
17,067	Glaze, Wm. B.	Washington
4,429	Gloster, Arthur B.	Fayette
13,986	Glover, Sam	Sullivan
9,077	Godfrey, Thos.	Grainger
4,980	Godsey, Thos. H.	Hamilton
14,588	Goffin, Susan E.	Monroe
21,888	Goforth, John	Sevier
6,723	Goins, Edward	Claiborne
20,035	Goin, Wilson	Cocke
5,241	Gooch, Eliza A.	Rutherford
14,088	Good, Solomon	Greene
14,087	Good, Wm.	Greene
20,972	Goodall, Jane M.	Smith
18,074	Goodman, Solomon P.	Grundy
15,025	Goodrum, Nath'l E. E.	McNairy
11,337	Goodwin, Augustine B.	Madison
858	Goodwin, John B.	Rutherford
18,373	Goodwin, Lawson H. & Robert E.	Carter
8,030	Goostree, James W.	Davidson
17,247	Gordon, Wm.	Rutherford
20,544	Gordon, Wm. C.	Bedford
17,235	Gorrell, Joseph K.	Cocke
20,540	Gose, Stephen	Cocke
10,235	Gossage, Wm. W.	Franklin
16,890	Gothard, Wm. B.	Rhea
18,441	Gott, John G.	Sullivan
4,515	Gotthardt, Charles	Perry
998	Goucher, Harriet V.	Hamilton
999	Goucher, John W.	Hamilton
17,711	Gowdey, Thos., Estate of	Davidson
19,079	Gowing, James M.	Shelby
18,448	Gragg, Joseph	Marshall
8,347	Graham, David	Fentress
17,549	Graham, James H., Estate of	Bedford
20,430	Graham, James R.	Coffee
5,541: 10,204:	Graham, Sam R.	Carroll
8,905	Granger, Edward B.	Shelby
15,728	Grant, Lavinia	Hamilton
2,745	Graves, John O.	Fayette
13,710	Graves, Nathaniel	Giles
10,355	Graves, Thos. J.	Fayette
1,525	Graves, W. H.	Carroll
7,021	Gray, Boswell T.	Williamson
14,900	Gray, Geo. L.	Franklin
14,260	Gray, Geo. S.	Franklin
17,134	Gray, Hamilton	Roane
12,442	Gray, Isaac	Franklin
20,288	Gray, Matilda	Washington
16,972	Gray, Newton	Cocke
20,030	Gray, Wm.	Hawkins
15,726	Gray, Wm. B., Estate of	Hamilton
7,450	Gray, Wm. Slaughter	Davidson
19,673	Green, Augustus P.	Hamilton
12,637	Green, Fanny	Shelby
17,560	Green, Fielding	Loudon
12,774	Green, James H., Estate of	Rutherford
14,089	Green, Jane	Washington
9,881	Green, Lucy N.	Shelby
18,702	Green, Nathan	Sullivan
16,748: 19,708:	Green, Wm. A.	Rhea
22,055	Greene, B. Y.	Roane
4,113	Greenlee, Geo.	Grainger
7,869	Greenlee, John	Grainger
7,722	Greenlee, John Calvin	Grainger
3,021	Greener, John G., Estate of	Davidson
21,932	Greer, David S.	Shelby
18,246	Greer, G. W.	Bedford
8,050	Greer, John F.	Cumberland
5,542	Greer, Thos.	Gibson
8,980	Greer, Wm.	Grainger
13,771	Greeson, David	Hardin
5,259	Gregory, Andrew	Davidson
22,250	Grider, Frederick	Grainger
8,979	Griffen, John	Grainger
2,972	Griffin, Francis J., Mrs.	Knox
15,159	Griffin, Jefferson	Knox
4,802	Griffin, Joseph W.	Davidson
9,706	Griffiths, Geo.	Loudon
13,485	Griffiths, John	Loudon
17,278	Griffitts, Wm. S.	Blount
10,310	Grigsby, Wm.	Hamblen
18,242	Grimsley, Abraham	Hamilton
21,954	Grissom, Isaac	Fayette
20,517	Griswold, Wm. A.	Grundy
11,101	Groom, Wm. H.	Carroll
15,427: 16,918:	Gross, Jacob	James
17,944	Gross, Mary Jane	James
20,385	Grove, Geo. H.	Grainger
15,559	Grubb, John, Estate of	Smith
12,357: 13,424:	Gryder, Joseph	Loudon
20,723	Grundlach, Helmuth C.	Knox
18,789	Gunn, Simpson	Coffee
15,428	Guthrie, Geo. G. F., Estate	James
15,729	Guthrie, James A. P.	James
1,202	Guy, Ella M.	Shelby
18,884	Guy, Wilson E.	Williamson
14,592	Gwinn, Andrew I.	Madison
13,297	Hack, Wm.	Shelby
17,535	Hackney, Hiram W.	Knox
17,534	Hackney, Hiram W. & Heiskell, Frederick	Knox
14,049	Haga, Eliza	Washington
9,543	Hagen, Gideon M.	Knox
12,871	Hagood, Sarah A.	Hawkins
5,393	Hahn, Benj.	Fayette
13,058: 20,429:	Hailey, Sam R.	Bedford
1,000	Hale, Elijah M.	Hamilton
12,173	Hale, Henry	Jefferson
14,091	Hale, Hiram D.	Washington
1,528	Hale, John B.	Obion
16,173	Hale, Smith H.	Washington

7,889: 18,736:	Hale, Stephen P.	Monroe
1,529	Hale, Stephen S.	Gibson
21,749	Hale, Wm. K.	Washington
16,878	Haley, John	Rutherford
17,092	Haliburton, Gloster	Rutherford
4,505	Hall, Albert S.	Loudon
2,287	Hall, Ann	Knox
19,928	Hall, Caswell	Bradley
4,776	Hall, Hinton	Shelby
2,683	Hall, Jane	Henderson
4,506	Hall, Jerry	Loudon
11,532	Hall, Levicy	Knox
2,684	Hall, M. E.	Carroll
17,954	Hall, Mary	Bradley
1,530	Hall, Robert H.	Carroll
18,250	Hall, Robert T.	Bedford
14,595	Hall, Robert W.	Madison
15,834	Hall, Thos., Estate of	Knox
19,889	Hall, Wm. E.	Haywood
20,192	Hallum, Asbury, Heirs of	Shelby
17,096	Hambaugh, P. C. & Pettus, Thos. F.	Montgomery
3,220	Hamby, Joel M.	Scott
15,260	Hames, Andrew	Fayette
1,001	Hamill, David C.	Hamilton
9,471	Hamilton, David P.	Gibson
14,314	Hamilton, Emeline	Monroe
2,685	Hamilton, Joseph	Carroll
16,745	Hamilton, Joseph	Hamblen
13,987	Hamilton, Joshua	Sullivan
15,627	Hamilton, Robert N.	Loudon
20,195	Hamilton, Westley	Fayette
9,712	Hammond, Geo., Estate of	Maury
6,762	Hammond, M. M.	Madison
12,887	Hammond, Wm.	Jefferson
17,470	Hammonds, Jesse N.	Giles
13,492	Hammer, Thos. C.	Loudon
2,288	Hampton, John P.	Fayette
20,509	Hampton, Wm. H.	Grundy
20,355	Hanauer, Louis	Shelby
10,813	Hancock, Hull H.	Giles
18,838	Hancock, Nancy	Bradley
17,865	Handley, Henry	Rutherford
15,628	Haney, Wm.	McMinn
18,477	Hankins, Polly Ann O.	Lawrence
17,205	Hanlon, Ann, Sister	Davidson
8,372	Hanmer, Horace H.	Davidson
13,550	Hann, Lewis M.	Greene
10,812	Hannah, Andrew	Giles
19,060	Hannah, Sam B.	Shelby
16,967	Hans, James	Washington
21,957	Harden, Nancy & Headrick, Nancy A.	Sevier
10,749	Hardiman, Wm. J.	Giles
20,528	Hardin, Caffrey M.	Sevier
14,092	Hardin, Cornelius	Greene
13,217: 16,830:	Hardin, John C. R.	Monroe
6,317	Hardin, Peter	Marion
2,779	Harding, Buril	Davidson
15,558	Harding, Elizabeth W.	Davidson
8,820	Harding, G. W.	Davidson
20,455	Hardwick, F. E.	Bradley
1,593	Hargrondan, Elijah	Montgomery
14,914	Harlan, Benj.	Maury
733	Harlan, Joseph	Sumner
14,938	Harlan, Peter H.	Sumner
1,532	Harlon, Isaac	Carroll
13,562	Harmon, Harrison C.	Greene
13,561	Harmon, John	Greene
17,951	Harold, Elwood D. & Francis M.	Bradley
17,951	Harold, Francis M. & Elwood D.	Bradley
14,093	Harold, James W.	Greene
19,301	Harper, Green	Sumner
9,118	Harper, James	Knox
10,842	Harper, Jesse H.	Madison
5,402	Harrill, B. J.	Monroe

8,695	Harris, Crampton S.	Hamblen
6,604	Harris, G. K.	Montgomery
9,006	Harris, Henry	Bradley
17,774	Harris, Henry C.	McNairy
20,286	Harris, J. E. T.	Washington
55	Harris, Jeremiah G.	Davidson
17,596	Harris, Joel B.	McNairy
18,904	Harris, John N.	Bedford
11,212	Harris, John W.	Fayette
8,857	Harris, John W., Jr.	Tipton
13,691	Harris, Zeno T., Estate of	Shelby
17,236	Harrison, Aaron	Williamson
18,788	Harrison, Benj. T.	Loudon
20,577	Harrison, Henderson	Rhea
12,377	Harrison, James B.	Giles
19,254	Harrison, James F., Estate of	Loudon
6,771	Harrison, John B.	Obion
19,516	Harrison, John W., Estate	Roane
20,986	Harrison, Wm., Sr., Estate	Williamson
19,041	Harrison, Wm. C.	Rutherford
2,686	Hart, Henry C.	Henderson
8,474	Hart, James	Henderson
20,079	Hart, John	Bedford
10,639	Hart, Mary A.	Giles
17,553	Hart, Roland J.	Shelby
14,094	Hart, Solomon	Carter
14,095	Hartman, Joseph	Greene
21,926	Hartman, Thos. J.	Hamilton
1,533	Hartman, Wm. G.	Carroll
13,294	Hartsell, Charles R.	Monroe
3,232: 14,050:	Hartsell, Isaac W.	Washington
16,829	Hartsell, Wm. A.	Monroe
13,410	Harvey, Michael	Blount
16,961	Harvy, D. A.	Washington
10,633	Harwell, Hannah	Giles
18,449	Harwell, Logan D.	Giles
10,810	Harwell, Porthenia P.	Lincoln
10,632	Harwell, Thos.	Giles
5,232	Harwood, Wm. G.	Gibson
7,824	Hash, Charley	Rutherford
3,384	Haskins, Thos. S.	Loudon
4,496	Hass, E. D.	Knox
19,305	Hassel, Margaret	Sumner
19,364	Hastings, James	Bedford
10,260	Hastings, James P.	Henry
16,579	Hastings, Louarkh, Mrs.	Bedford
1,534	Hatch, John W.	Henderson
13,413	Hatcher, Elijah L.	Blount
17,381	Hatcher, John	McMinn
6,559	Hatcher, John L.	Humphreys
6,391	Hatfield, Ale	Scott
4,028	Hathaway, Ruth C.	DeKalb
5,056	Hatten, Gilbert H.	Weakley
10,470	Haun, Geo.	Hamblen
10,457	Haun, Isaac P.	Hamblen
10,490	Haun, Joel	Hamblen
1,075	Haupt, J. F.	Knox
12,709	Hauser, Augusta	Shelby
19,642	Hawkins, Gregory F.	Monroe
5,959	Hawthorn, H. T.	Claiborne
8,643	Hayes, Thos. H.	Rutherford
14,561	Haynes, E. M.	Grundy
21,535	Haynes, Everett B.	Rutherford
17,337	Haynes, James H.	Rutherford
15,588	Haynes, Josiah	Claiborne
2,635	Haynes, Wm. R.	Williamson
18,833	Hays, John F., Estate of	Bradley
13,883	Hays, Joshua O.	Loudon
20,529	Hays, Nathan W.	Bradley
19,822	Hays, Sam I., Estate of	Madison
19,799	Hays, Susan C.	Bradley
22,098	Hayse, Wm.	Claiborne
21,908	Hayworth, Isaac F.	Jefferson
8,731	Hayworth, Richard	Jefferson
14,096	Head, Amanda M.	Washington
17,692	Head, Green	Sumner
19,322	Headrick, John D.	Blount
21,955	Headrick, Minerva T.	Sevier

21,957	Headrick, Nancy A. & Harden, Nancy	Sevier	20,617	Hill, Louisa J.	Franklin
21,956	Headrick, Salina & Wm.	Sevier	17,988	Hill, Richard	Haywood
20,381	Heath, David N.	Grainger	17,799	Hill, Richard	McNairy
7,735	Heathcock, Newton J.	Gibson	14,391	Hinch, John C.	Bledsoe
6,398	Hedgcoth, Bazzel	Cumberland	18,363	Hines, Wiley J.	Franklin
6,316	Hefner, John P.	Marion	21,750	Hinkal, Abner L.	Washington
15,475	Heiskell, Dan	Monroe	5,543	Hinson, John W.	Henderson
17,534	Heiskell, Frederick & Hackney, Hiram W.	Knox	8,066	Hitch, Morris	Shelby
19,893	Heiskell, Frederick S.	Knox	8,707	Hittson, Thomas & Leger, Archibald	Hancock
17,547	Helton, Abraham	Bedford	19,366	Hix, Joshua M.	Bedford
17,543	Helton, Austin	Bedford	18,819	Hixson, Henry G.	Hamilton
10,012	Helton, Cynthia	Hamblen	7,870	Hixson, James K.	Grainger
7,879	Helton, James	Grainger	16,984	Hixson, Washington	Hamilton
17,691	Helton, Sylvester	Sumner	18,826	Hixson, Wilson	Hamilton
12,896	Henard, Wm. J.	Hawkins	17,863	Hobbs, James M. & Powell, Wm. J.	Bedford
9,785	Henderson, Albert G.	Rutherford	15,051	Hobbs, Jesse	Hamblen
18,343	Henderson, Clavin	Rutherford	14,195	Hobbs, Jesse B.	Hardin
6,770	Henderson, F. H.	Carroll	9,972	Hobson, Nicholas	Davidson
20,445	Henderson, John, Estate of	Bradley	6,429	Hodge, James	Maury
13,215	Henderson, Rachel A.	Monroe	5,242	Hodge, Jane C.	Williamson
15,220	Henderson, Samuel	Warren	12,880	Hodge, Logan S.	Jefferson
12,865	Henderson, Samuel L.	Hawkins	11,226	Hodge, Sarah A.	Maury
9,389	Henderson, Thos.	Knox	15,050	Hodges, Calvin M.	Sevier
10,482	Henderson, Wm.	Hamblen	11,707	Hodges, Ganum C.	Jefferson
18,823	Henderson, Wm. A.	Bradley	2,192	Hodges, Granville	Claiborne
9,141	Hendren, Hudson J.	Haywood	10,914	Hodges, Jacob E.	Grainger
7,360	Hendrix, Joshua	Giles	13,055	Hodges, James C.	Jefferson
7,357	Hendrix, Wm. C.	Giles	17,438	Hodges, John	Jefferson
6,404	Hendrixson, Joseph L.	DeKalb	19,940	Hodges, Lewis & Kelly, Mack	Claiborne
3,207	Heninger, Wm. W.	Union	19,937	Hodges, Preston	Claiborne
16,595	Henley, James H.	Bedford	20,290	Hodges, Roland	Washington
2,732	Henley, R. W.	Gibson	9,715	Hodges, Wm. R.	Knox
13,497	Henley, Thos. O.	Monroe	10,753	Hogan, Anderson	Giles
18,375: 19,713:	Henry, Calvin	Rhea	6,772	Hogan, W. R.	Obion
			19,636	Hoge, Ellen I. & Wallace N.	Bradley
1,535	Henry, James A.	Henderson	19,636	Hoge, Wallace N. & Ellen I.	Bradley
18,716	Henry, James M.	Bradley	18,381	Holahan, Eugene J.	Shelby
8,162	Henry, John	Jefferson	16,569	Holland, Martin	Shelby
20,272	Henry, John R.	Blount	14,901	Holland, Sam J., Estate of	Franklin
20,278	Henry, Sam H.	Loudon	11,850	Holliday, Geo. F.	Marshall
1,536	Henry, Wm.	Carroll	4,051	Holloway, James	Davidson
11,276	Henry, Wm. M.	Madison	13,050	Holloway, Joseph	Morgan
19,258	Henson, Henderson	Loudon	15,377	Hollowell, Joseph	Rutherford
20,241	Herrin, Thos. & Scott, Alfred	Davidson	20,040	Hollowell, Oliver	Shelby
5,356	Hessen, John	Shelby	5,221: 9,287:	Holly, Ezekiel	Knox
20,872	Hessey, John H.	Frank	1,537	Holmes, G. J.	Carroll
20,873	Hessey, Robert H.	Franklin	19,746	Holston, James E.	Hamblen
5,057	Hester, H. G.	Weakley	10,431	Holt, Henry	Williamson
12,636	Hewett, Jesse T.	Shelby	15,638	Holt, Isaac B.	Bedford
21,938	Hickey, David	Knox	15,358	Holt, John	Sullivan
17,959	Hickman, Bates	Bradley	8,237	Holt, John M.	Hamblen
16,888	Hickman, Henry	Rhea	2,086	Holt, Joseph B.	Gibson
15,062	Hickman, James	Davidson	5,850	Holt, Thos.	Williamson
16,695	Hickman, John	Hamilton	17,578	Hoodenpyle, Robert	Sequatchie
21,158	Hickman, Stephen	Sevier	21,880	Hooker, John	Loudon
18,821	Hickman, Wm. A.	Hamilton	10,320	Hoover, Frederick A.	Rutherford
20,824	Hickman, William T.	Sevier	9,585	Hoover, Harris B.	Jackson
14,594	Hicks, Geo.	Madison	18,443	Hoover, Noah	Sullivan
18,442	Hicks, Henry C.	Sullivan	5,508	Hopkins, John H.	Gibson
20,574	Hicks, Jane	Rhea	14,672	Horbell, Catharine	Rutherford
21,644	Hicks, Mary H.	Monroe	15,446	Hord, Coleman F.	Coffee
14,097	Hicks, Sam	Washington	9,396	Horn, David	McNairy
2,085	Hicks, W. J.	Haywood	17,788	Horn, James F.	McNairy
5,882	Higdon, Miles C.	Maury	7,025	Horn, James F., Estate of	Henderson
15,739	Higgins, F.	Davidson	17,785	Hornbuckle, Hiram	McNairy
5,311	Hightower, R. R.	Williamson	10,468	Horner, Pleasant	Hamblen
12,879	Hightower, Sarah E.	Jefferson	1,538	Horr, R. C.	Haywood
17,063	Hilbert, John H.	Washington	2,496	Horton, Elmore R.	Franklin
17,065	Hilbert, Wm.	Washington	13,984	Horton, Margaret	Williamson
9,515	Hildebrand, David H.	Shelby	12,892	Hoskins, Geo. C.	Jefferson
17,874	Hill, Andrew J.	McNairy	3,253	Hoss, Landon C.	Knox
17,595	Hill, Dan A.	McNairy	16,692	Houk, Henry	Sevier
5,545	Hill, Jacob	Madison	15,824	Houk, Hopkins L.	Sevier
17,780	Hill, James W.	McNairy	11,353	House, Julia A.	Rutherford
8,818	Hill, Jethrie	Jefferson	11,692	House, Mary I.	Weakley
9,967	Hill, John J.	Gibson	7,825	House, Nicholas	Rutherford
18,244	Hill, John W.	Hamblen	6,314	Houser, Finley A.	Lawrence

11,720	Houston, James H.	Monroe
18,245	Houston, Robert W.	Bedford
4,430	Houston, W. A.	Fayette
15,417	Howard, Allison	James
11,721	Howard, John	Monroe
17,567	Howard, John R.	McMinn
13,316	Howard, Sam	Henderson
18,150	Howard, Thos.	Lawrence
5,357	Howard, Wm. P.	Madison
19,809	Howell, James	Dickson
9,078	Howell, Jesse, Estate of	Hamblen
9,584	Howell, John B.	Jackson
10,107	Howell, John H.	Grainger
4,029	Howell, Sylvanus, Estate of	Knox
8,684	Howell, Wm. A.	Jefferson
5,314	Howington, James W.	Davidson
21,818	Howland, John F.	Rutherford
21,818	Howland, John F.	Shelby
1,189	Howry, Lewis	Hamblen
10,920	Hubbard, Mary Jane	Jefferson
16,868	Huddleston, Israel F.	McNairy
19,551	Huddleston, John F., Sr.	Union
10,104: 19,554:	Huddleston, Lafayette	Union
19,914	Hudgens, Hampton	White
17,558	Hudlow, Martha F.	Bedford
17,656: 17,989:	Hudson, Richard G.	Morgan
11,726	Huff, Joseph	Monroe
17,950	Huffaker, Christopher	Bradley
10,552	Huffaker, Geo.	Knox
19,465	Huffar, Pleasant A.	Coffee
19,256	Huffine, Benj.	Loudon
14,550	Huffine, Dan	Roane
15,416	Huffine, Ephraim D.	James
9,862	Huggins, Wm. S.	Coffee
12,054	Hughes, Enoch M.	Loudon
11,695	Hughes, Henry C.	Weakley
13,940	Hughes, Indiana E.	Shelby
14,098	Hughes, John	Carter
17,636	Hughes, Martha W.	Madison
17,798	Hughes, Wm. C.	McNairy
21,894	Hughey, Robert & Buchanan, Thos. W.	Bedford
21,894	Hughey, Robert & Buchanan, Thos. W.	Lincoln
6,606	Hukill, Richard	Shelby
5,180	Hull, Isaac	Hamblen
17,458: 5,180:	Hull, Isaac	Jefferson
15,953	Hullitt, John W.	Sumner
15,606	Humble, Benj. F.	Warren
1,540	Humble, G. W.	Carroll
1,542	Humble, Jacob	Carroll
12,893	Humbord, Wm. R.	Jefferson
12,877	Hume, David P.	Jefferson
2,494	Humes, Anthony	Knox
15,160	Humphreys, Alfred C.	Monroe
13,379	Humphreys, Sam A.	Blount
17,195	Humphreys, Jesse	Washington
15,429	Humphreys, John	James
4,272	Humphries, Richard	Washington
19,747	Humpston, John W.	Jefferson
20,616	Hunt, Elizabeth	Franklin
22,091	Hunt, Fannie T.	Shelby
1,446	Hunt, Francis M.	Maury
17,240	Hunt, Mary S.	Tipton
5,358	Hunt, Sarah	Shelby
11,059	Hunt, Smith H.	Hamblen
18,837	Hunt, Wm.	Bradley
15,430	Hunter, Addison P.	James
13,708	Hunter, H. H., Estate of	Giles
10,672	Hunter, James N.	Madison
18,330	Hunter, Robert N.	Rutherford
13,627	Hurst, Dan R.	Hardin
6,781	Hurst, Fielding	McNairy
19,361	Hurst, John L.	McMinn
13,628	Hurst, Lynna E.	Harding
8,418	Hurst, Robert	Fentress
13,427	Hurst, Wm.	Marion

5,172	Hurt, Berry F.	Shelby
8,494	Hurt, Fannie M.	Madison
3,022	Hurt, Mary A.	Davidson
2,739	Hurtt, Sarah	Morgan
17,971	Hutchinson, Geo. & Kerr, Alex	Dickson
15,629	Hutsell, Andrew	McMinn
13,417	Hutton, Josiah C.	Blount
7,042	Hude, Thos. J.	Davidson
5,544	Hyde, Wesley H.	Gibson
15,621	Hyder, Pleasant M.	Putnam
17,191	Hyder, W. F. M.	Carter
851	Hynes, Bernard	Davidson
18,849	Hysinger, Jacob	Bradley
13,447	Ingram, David J.	Loudon
13,446	Ingram, Sandford	Roane
13,450	Inman, Alex	Monroe
20,252	Inman, John B.	Madison
10,673	Irwin, John	Madison
8,696	Irwin, Mark W.	Jefferson
18,399	Irwin, Wm. B., Estate of	James
15,802	Isaacs, Solomon	Shelby
4,378	Isbell, Nicholas H.	Fayette
8,750	Isbell, Sarah A.	Monroe
13,220	Ivens, Wm. S.	Monroe
11,689	Ivie, Benj. W.	Weakley
4,404	Jacobs, Elizabeth	Monroe
21,645	Jacobs, John, Estate of	Monroe
16,914	Jackson, A. B.	Hamilton
1,074	Jackson, A. G., Sr.	Knox
16,491	Jackson, Francis A.	Hamilton
8,357	Jackson, German	Humphreys
29	Jackson, Henry C.	Davidson
3,023	Jackson, James A.	Davidson
16,492	Jackson, James J.	Hamilton
13,841	Jackson, John H.	Loudon
7,358	Jackson, John Y.	Giles
16,983	Jackson, Jonathan	Hamilton
17,831	Jackson, Thos. N.	Rutherford
20,880	James, Amos	Henry
15,603	James, John D.	Davidson
5,960	James, Joseph H.	Monroe
12,761	Jamison, Sarah W.	Rutherford
10,556	Janeway, Isaac B.	Knox
17,833	January, Sallie H., Estate of	Rutherford
9,060	Jarnagin, Nelson	Grainger
8,975	Jarnagin, Russell	Grainger
19,685	Jarrett, Thompson	Rutherford
12,830	Jefferson, Richard	Knox
16,784	Jenkins, Calvin E.	Bedford
19,637	Jenkins, David	Monroe
19,042	Jenkins, Hiram, Estate of	Rutherford
19,184	Jenkins, Jennie & Nannoma	Rutherford
13,372	Jenkins, John	Loudon
10,473	Jenkins, Joseph	Hawkins
19,184	Jenkins, Nannoma & Jennie	Rutherford
17,477	Jenkins, Wm.	Bedford
2,042	Jennings, D. F.	Claiborne
14,808	Jennings, Peter	Davidson
20,036	Jennings, Robert	Grainger
863	Jernigan, Mary E.	Davidson
17,789	Jeter, Wm. M.	McNairy
17,869	Jitton, Lafayette	Rutherford
17,957	John, Andrew	Bardley
21,016	Johnson, Anthony W. Jr., & Chandler, H. R.	Davidson
7,181	Johnson, Claiborn	Grainger
2,836	Johnson, Demey	Knox
6,588	Johnson, Dudley G.	Fayette
11,177	Johnson, Geo. M.	Williamson
16,174	Johnson, Henry	Washington
21,319	Johnson, Jacob	Sumner
9,173	Johnson, James	Williamson
22,169	Johnson, Joel	Jefferson
12,201	Johnson, John H.	Roane
15,162	Johnson, John L. & Looney, Absalom	Knox
9,962	Jones, John M.	Knox
16,544	Johnson, John O.	Rhea

11,344	Johnson, John R.	Rutherford
19,189	Johnson, Jonathan, Estate of	Sevier
12,846	Johnson, Joseph R.	Hawkins
13,494	Johnson, Lewis F.	Loudon
12,851	Johnson, Lilbourn	Hawkins
1,246	Johnson, Luther M.	Maury
4,443	Johnson, Major Willis	Lawrence
14,010	Johnson, Nancy	Roane
12,869	Johnson, Sanford	Hawkins
2,687	Johnson, Sarah	Henderson
4,909	Johnson, Thomas	Davidson
17,335	Johnson, Thomas	Jefferson
4,209	Johnson, Thos. J.	Haywood
20,575	Johnson, Uriel	McMinn
4,443	Johnson, Willis, Major	Lawrence
5,962	Johnston, E. K.	Monroe
5,961	Johnston, F. G.	Monroe
19,262	Johnston, Joseph A.	Loudon
19,929	Johnston, Josephine	Franklin
6,145	Johnston, Mary B.	Fayette
18,817	Johnston, Sam M.	Loudon
14,131	Johnston, Susan O.	Madison
4,435	Johnston, Wm. F.	Loudon
8,924	Jolly, Charles T.	Jefferson
8,711	Jolly, Elizabeth	Jefferson
11,069	Jolly, Wm.	Hamblen
16,697	Jones, Alex	Hamilton
20,072	Jones, Alfred, Estate of	Sumner
19,806	Jones, Caleb B.	Fayette
12,444	Jones, Charles L.	Frank
1,775	Jones, D. P.	Carroll
14,656	Jones, Dan	Claiborne
15,581	Jones, Dan S.	Hamilton
9,964	Jones, Edward	Shelby
7,608	Jones, Eli A.	Grainger
8,976	Jones. Elijah	Grainger
7,130	Jones, Emma J.	Madison
5,963	Jones, Furney D.	Claiborne
14,596	Jones. G. W.	Madison
14,609	Jones, Hannah	Roane
4,525	Jones, Henderson T.	Henderson
21,369	Jones, Henry J.	Shelby
14,099	Jones, Henry M.	Washington
7,607	Jones, J. B.	Grainger
17,943	Jones, James L.	Bradley
11,740	Jones, John	DeKalb
13,546	Jones, John	Greene
13,487	Jones, John D.	Loudon
10,519	Jones, John R.	Fayette
21,522	Jones, John W.	Franklin
13,488	Jones, Joseph	Loudon
12,056	Jones, Joseph D.	Loudon
20,730	Jones, M. V.	Bradley
7,516	Jones, Marion D.	Haywood
11,908	Jones, Marrell H.	Henderson
563	Jones, Martin B. & Reuben; and Brown, Wm. N., Estate of	Shelby
15,610	Jones, Mary	Hamilton
5,546	Jones, Matthew, Estate of	Henderson
10,668	Jones, Morgan	Madison
15,750	Jones, Nathaniel S.	Maury
16,862	Jones, Pleasant J.	Hamblen
12,238: 20,253:	Jones, Rebecca	Madsion
12,653	Jones, Redrick Yancy	Loudon
563	Jones, Reuben & Martin B.; and Wm. N. Brown, Estate of	Shelby
563	Jones, Reuben S. & Brown, Wm. A.	Shelby
21,630	Jones, Richard B.	Madison
17,832	Jones, Richard C.	Rutherford
8,912	Jones, Ross, Estate of	Monroe
18,790	Jones, Rufus	Loudon
21,523	Jones, Sam L.	Franklin
6,595	Jones, Thos. C.	Fayette
20,042	Jones, Wilie Baker	Fayette
10,014	Jones, Wm.	Grainger
21,935	Jones, Wm.	Hardeman
12,148	Jones, Wm.	Jefferson
10,136	Jones, Wm. H.	Obion

13,489	Jones, Wm. R.	Blount
3,233	Jordan, Edward L.	Rutherford
8,009	Jordan, Sam B.	Davidson
11,305	Jordan, Wm.	Davidson
10,823: 12,714:	Joyner, Giles D.	Morgan
8,416	Joyner, Hugh	Sumner
11,997	Joyner, Micajah	Henderson
17,394: 18,393:	Julian, Geo.	Bradley
20,330	Julian, Isom	Bradley
4,436: 4,437:	Julian, Solomon	Loudon
9,082	Julian, Wm. C.	Loudon
16,422	Kagley, Joseph	Blount
7,882	Karr, John H.	Grainger
8,053	Kearley, Wm.	Cumberland
1,543	Keaton, C. W.	Carroll
6,765	Keeble, Joseph	Rutherford
19,324	Keeble, Richard	Blount
1,111	Keebler, Joseph	Washington
14,100	Keebler, Sam	Washington
20,879	Keegan, Mary E.	Shelby
11,273	Keelen, Floridore A.	Madison
13,414	Keen, Gilbert P.	Blount
5,473	Keener, Leroy S.	Knox
10,422	Keesee, Thos. W.	Maury
10,157	Keeton, Harrison	Scott
20,095	Keith, Alex H.	McMinn
20,570	Keith, Chas M.	McMinn
12,713	Keith, Geo. W.	Morgan
20,874	Keith, James N.	Franklin
12,202	Keith, Moses M.	Franklin
16,892: 19,710:	Keith, Nicholas	Rhea
20,541	Kelley, Ann J.	Cocke
19,703	Kelley, Julia F.	Rhea
16,264	Kelley, Nathan	McMinn
14,697	Kelley, Wylie	Cocke
21,651	Kelly, Clarissa	Rutherford
19,700	Kelly, James J.	Rhea
19,940	Kelly, Mack; and Hodges, Lewis	Claiborne
7,595	Kelly, Peter	Madison
12,862	Kelly, Polly	Hawkins
4,872	Kelso, Nancy J.	Monroe
17,805	Kemp, Geo. R.	Hardin
15,024	Kendrick, Elihu E.	Maury
3,793	Kennedy, Alex	Blount
14,390	Kennedy, Marcus L.	Hamilton
19,406	Kennedy, Sam	Jefferson
12,728	Kennedy, Sam J.	Franklin
9,864	Kennedy, Susan	Williamson
9,961	Kennedy, Wm.	Knox
5,290	Kenner, W. D.	Hawkins
12,297	Kennerly, John P.	Franklin
8,657	Kenney, Benj.	Shelby
14,101	Kenney, Geo. E.	Greene
13,772	Kerby, Calvin A.	Hardin
21,936	Kerby, John	McNairy
17,598	Kerby, Wm. W.	McNairy
17,971	Kerr, Alex; and Hutchinson, Geo.	Dickson
1,799	Kerr, Andrew R.	Maury
5,367	Kerr, John	Shelby
16,232	Ketron, John W.	Sullivan
9,020	Key, James	Blount
21,752	Keys, Elizabeth	Washington
21,751	Keys, James M.	Washington
21,893	Keys, Wm.	Knox
14,414	Kibert, John	Claiborne
21,899	Kibler, Montgomery	Bradley
17,946	Kibler, Sam	Bradley
22,152	Kidwell, Henderson	Grainger
10,460	Kidwell, Rufus J.	Hamblen
11,308	Kiggins, Wm.	Loudon
4,504	Kile, W. W.	Loudon
14,562	Kilgore, Stephen	Grundy
20,848	Kilmartin, Rodger	Lincoln
18,561	Kimbro, Elizabeth V.	Davidson

7,415	Kimbro, John B.	Rutherford
5,347	Kimbrough, Elisha	Monroe
18,737	Kimbrough, Jacob C.	Monroe
17,885	Kimbrough, John C.	Shelby
13,842	Kimbrough, John M.	Monroe
18,257	Kimmons, Thos., Estate of	Bedford
9,472	Kincaid, John, Estate of	Fayette
20,250	Kincheloo, James, Estate of	Hawkins
4,431	King, Charles	Shelby
12,895	King, Elizabeth, Estate of	Hawkins
2,830	King, Geo.	Knox
15,026	King, Henry	McNairy
2,087	King, Henry A.	Gibson
12,842	King, Hiram	Hawkins
19,730	King, Ira W.	Smith
17,806	King, Jackson J.	McNairy
2,688	King, Jeremiah	Carroll
1,774	King, Ransom	Carroll
7,748	King, Robert	Hawkins
2,423	King, Sarah C.	Knox
13,373	King, Stephen	Loudon
21,034	King, Wm. H.	Sevier
20,231	Kinningham, Ira	Franklin
20,232	Kinningham, Wm. M., Estate of	Franklin
20,571	Kirby, Geo.	McMinn
21,722	Kirby, James L.	Bradley
13,554	Kirk, Abraham B.	Greene
2,689	Kirk, James	Carroll
13,560	Kirk, James, Estate of	Greene
13,555	Kirk, Rebecca E.	Greene
5,965	Kirkland, James M.	Monroe
7,261	Kirkland, Jesse R.	Monroe
22,137	Kirkpatrick, David	Hawkins
1,545	Kiser, Robert	Henderson
10,912	Kite, Martha	Hawkins
12,853	Kite, Pinckney	Hawkins
8,977	Kitts, Henry	Grainger
14,051	Klepper, John B.	Washington
9,713	Klepper, Joseph	Carter
8,850: 18,380:	Kline, James A.	Loudon
21,524	Knight, Matilda	Franklin
10,665	Knight, Rebecca	Madison
18,954	Knight, Thos., Estate of	Rhea
4,031	Knott, Andrew	Knox
1,546	Knowles, Edward	Henderson
12,356	Knox, James	Loudon
3,262	Kouns, John	Giles
4,168	Kreis, Deitrick	Morgan
9,439	Kries, John	Morgan
5,964	Kyes, John	Monroe
1,544	Kyle, E. J.	Carroll
11,280	Lacy, Demetrius	Madison
6,095	Lacy, Hugh R.	Madison
17,708	Lacy, John	Bedford
21,260	Lacy, John W.	Carter
20,449	Ladd, Amos	Polk
14,021	Ladd, D. L., Estate of	Roane
18,342	Ladd, Sam N.	Roane
10,703	Ladd, Thornton G.	Tipton
18,587	Lahay, John	Davidson
2,088	Lamb, S. D.	Carroll
16,540	Lamon, John	Hamilton
15,611	Lamon, John (Igones Ferry)	Hamilton
20,580	Landers, Rachel	McMinn
1,547	Landrum, Wm. H.	Carroll
13,495	Lane, Edward R.	Loudon
18,318	Lane, J. J., Estate of	Loudon
18,317	Lane, J. W.	Loudon
18,734	Lane, James P. & M. A.	Blount
10,458	Lane, John S.	Hamblen
18,734	Lane, M. A. & James P.	Blount
14,102	Lang, Jacob	Washington
10,214	Langan, Thos.	Humphreys
14,128	Langham, Ransom	Maury
1,740	Langley, Ephraim	Morgan
18,282	Langston, Martin	Bradley
11,922	Lanier, Hetty	Shelby
15,152	Lanier, John C.	Shelby

8,658	Lanier, Wm. B.	Haywood
3,213	Larkin, John	Shelby
11,752	Larkin, Sam	Davidson
12,445	Larkin, Wm.	Franklin
12,881	Larrance, Jonathan	Jefferson
7,039	La Rue, J. C.	Cocke
15,582	Lasley, Martin V.	Hamilton
1,777	Lassiter, Hance	Carroll
11,176	Laster, Robert E.	Coffee
15,889	Latture, Jacob	Sullivan
16,127	Lauderdale, James	Sumner
17,795	Laughlin, James	McNairy
9,326	Laughlin, Thos., Estate of	Loudon
17,794	Laughlin, Wm. W.	McNairy
14,563	Law, Wm. & Parson, S.	Grundy
4,526	Laws, G. L.	Henderson
1,548	Laws, John W.	Carroll
20,736	Lawson, Ardelia A.	Bradley
12,852	Lawson, Calaway H.	Hawkins
12,867	Lawson, Preston	Hawkins
17,883	Lay, Emeline	Hardeman
19,647	Lay, James	Claiborne
1,549	Laycook, John S.	Carroll
16,690	Layman, Geo.	Jefferson
16,713	Layman, James	Jefferson
12,732	Laymance, Isaac J.	Morgan
14,931	Lea, F. A., Mrs.	Madison
18,806	Lea, Harmon G.	Grainger
15,431	Lea, Isaac R.	Bradley
13,187	Lea, Lorenzo	Fayette
16,027	Leahy, James	Davidson
12,186	Leatherwood, Aquilla	Polk
11,132	Ledford, Wesley	Polk
13,218	Lee, Alex	Monroe
20,276	Lee, Augustin B.	Loudon
20,733	Lee, Charley, Estate of	Bradley
13,483	Lee, Ephraim	Blount
18,850	Lee, Isaac, Estate of	Bradley
21,636	Lee, James	Grainger
9,473	Lee, John	Gibson
4,211	Leek, Thomas	Davidson
13,496	Leeper, Saunders M.	Loudon
12,078	Leeper, Wm. K.	Knox
15,014: 17,985:	Leftwich, Wm. W.	Knox
19,198	Legard, John A. J.	Sullivan
8,707	Leger, Archibald & Hittson, T.	Hancock
11,498	Leinart, John	Anderson
20,539	Lement, Sam D.	Knox
13,222	Leming, John	Monroe
12,167	Lennon, Rebecca	Jefferson
21,226	Lenoir, Albert S., Estate of	Loudon
21,225	Lenoir, Catharine F.	Loudon
10,679	Lenton, Wm.	Lauderdale
17,207	Lentz, James, Estate of	Bedford
17,336	Leonard, L. B.	Haywood
18,439	Lesley, Andrew, Estate of	Sullivan
14,564	Levan, Thomps. T.	Grundy
16,498	Levi, Geo.	Hamilton
11,703	Lewallen, Anderson S.	Scott
122	Lewis, Abner D.	Fayette
15,630	Lewis, David, Estate of	Meigs
770	Lewis, Ezekiel, Estate of	Davidson
9,142	Lewis, John E.	Haywood
15,577	Lewis, Mary A.	Loudon
316: 14,858:	Lewis, Mary A.	Sumner
4,032	Lewis, Nichols	Knox
13,381	Lewis, Susan K.	Loudon
21,967	Lewis, W. R.	Wilson
18,374	Lewis, Wm.	Carter
10,653	Ligon, S. A., Mrs.	Obion
14,692	Lillard, Abraham F.	Marshall
259	Lillard, Albert	Sumner
7,730	Lillard, Benj., Estate of	Rutherford
17,870	Lillard, Wm.	Rutherford
15,161	Lindsey, David M.	Monroe
7,872	Line, Matterson	Hamblen

7,883	Linn, Amelia	Grainger
19,812	Linn, Robert	Jefferson
8,751	Linn, W. H.	Monroe
12,084	Lipscomb, Ann D., Estate of	Franklin
4,803	Lipscomb, Jane L.	Franklin
12,446	Lipscomb, Wm. C.	Franklin
10,755	Literal, Harriet	Giles
5,362	Little, Arthur et al	Montgomery
10,675	Littlepage, Mary J.	Madison
14,992	Littleton, Mary E.	Loudon
18,444	Litz, Joel & Lucinda	Sullivan
18,444	Litz, Lucinda & Joel	Sullivan
11,135	Livingston, Charles H.	Polk
15,784	Livingston, Ned	Knox
8,069	Locke, Benj. F.	Tipton
19,758	Locke, Franklin	Rhea
13,753	Locke, James W.	Lawrence
10,906	Lockhart, John N.	Jefferson
18,254	Logan, David M.	Marshall
9,059	Long, James	Grainger
10,309	Long, James	Hamblen
12,856	Long, James	Hawkins
9,061	Long, John	Grainger
10,312	Long, John	Hamblen
20,383	Long, John D.	Grainger
15,921	Long, John S.	James
7,849	Long, Levi	Grainger
11,060	Long, Philip	Jefferson
10,464	Long, Robert	Hamblen
15,380	Long, Sacharissa M.	Maura
10,493	Long, Wm. P.	Grainger
21,914	Longmire, John L.	Washington
15,162	Looney, Absalom; and Johnson, John L.	Knox
4,033	Looney, Wm.	Knox
14,430	Lopp, Lewis	Davidson
4,772	Lord, Easter	Knox
821	Lord, Sarah	Knox
17,802	Lott, John	McNairy
19,367	Love, Ebzan	Hamblen
17,106	Love, Mason M.	Washington
1,550	Love, Robert B.	Gibson
5,650	Love, Robert E.	Davidson
18,989	Lovegrove, Jordan	Washington
16,514	Lovelady, Geo.	Hamilton
17,430	Lovelady, Gideon	Hamilton
13,541	Low, Alfred B.	Greene
18,845	Low, Wm. H.	Bradley
17,993	Lowe, Alfred Prior	Rutherford
8,973	Lowe, Edward M.	Grainger
14,246	Lowe, Joseph	Loudon
17,994	Lowe, Wm., Estate of	Rutherford
13,881	Lowery, Dan, Estate of	Loudon
7,638	Lowery, Susan	Monroe
13,214	Lowry, A. M.	McMinn
14,196	Loyd, Ervin	Hardin
11,773	Lucas, Foster G. & John	Davidson
11,773	Locas, John & Foster G.	Davidson
15,542	Lucas, Nimrod F.	Humphreys
22,062	Luck, Silas M.	Shelby
2,781	Lusck, James	Grundy
17,392	Luttrell, Geo.	James
4,214	Luttrell, James C.	Knox
17,199	Lyle, John	Washington
1,889	Lyles, Hiram	Smith
16,237	Lynn, Charles, Heirs of	Sullivan
16,283	Lynn, John	Tipton
12,629: 13,859:	Lynch, Henderson	Greene
19,778	Lynch, James R.	Hardeman
15,864	Mabry, Wiley	Knox
10,700	Mack, Dan	Davidson
8,685	Maddox, Thos.	Jefferson
14,742	Madox, Silas	Putnam
10,743	Madry, Elizabeth	Giles
10,747	Madry, John P.	Giles
13,846	Magill, Nathaniel	Monroe
16,380	Mahan, Alex	James
15,730	Mahan, Wm.	Hamilton
586	Mahon, Theresa	Shelby

12,188	Major, John S.	Cheatham
20,832	Malatista, Nicolla	Shelby
8,175	Malloy, Ellen P.	Shelby
21,631	Malone, Benj. J.	Madison
12,527	Malone, Elias	Giles
2,892	Malone, John	Giles
10,797	Malone, Murdock M.	Giles
4,074	Malone, Nancy	Polk
9,019	Malone, Stephen M.	Tipton
14,106	Maltsbarger, Catharine	Greene
16,776	Maney, James	Rutherford
15,408	Maney, Silas	Rutherford
9,774	Mangum, Susan M.	Shelby
12,883	Manley, Wilson	Jefferson
10,115	Manly, Absalom	Grainger
20,077	Manly, Joseph	Davidson
8,971	Manly, Wilson	Grainger
10,918	Mann, Wm.	Hamblin
3,209	Manfield, John	Grainger
17,330	Many, Jack	Rutherford
15,779	Maples, Andrew J.	Bradley
21,035	Maples, Gideon M.	Sevier
12,081	Maples, James	Sevier
21,036	Maples, Malicia C.	Sevier
20,296	Maguire, Mary	Shelby
18,228	Maranville, Riley P.	Blount
1,551	Marcrum, Henry	Gibson
15,861	Marks, Carrol M.	Giles
18,450	Marks, Lewis B.	Giles
19,171	Markum, Frank	Lincoln
385	Marr, Duncan	Montgomery
20,886	Marsh, D. H., Estate of	Hardeman
17,956	Marsh, Henry	Bradley
16,963	Marsh, Henry	Washington
15,163	Marsh, Thos. E.	Blount
8,163	Marshall, Coleman	Jefferson
10,456	Marshall, Enoch	Hamblen
9,969	Marshall, Gilbert	Davidson
10,748	Marshall, John H.	Giles
15,767	Marshall, Nancy	Tipton
15,631	Marshall, Wm.	Meigs
16,610	Martin, Edward	Davidson
7,016	Martin, Elisha, Jr.	Roane
7,017	Martin, Elisah, Sr., Estate	Roane
20,875	Martin, Elizabeth	Franklin
6,999	Martin, Gus	Rutherford
21,753	Martin, Henry A.	Washington
10,741	Martin, Ira B.	Giles
16,891	Martin, Isaac A.	Rhea
18,391	Martin, James R.	Roane
11,149	Martin, John	Davidson
565	Martin, John D.	Shelby
4,379	Martin, John W.	Lincoln
5,526	Martin, Martha L.	Monroe
2,082	Martin, Martin B.	Gibson
3,240	Martin, Patrick M.	Davidson
3,026	Martin, Wm.	Rutherford
14,338	Martin, Wm. D.	Lauderdale
19,376	Martin, Zachariah	James
15,406	Mask, Jesse	Madison
20,978	Mason, Joseph, Estate of	Rutherford
3,463	Mason, Joseph T.	Shelby
16,771	Mason, Martha M.	Shelby
19,892: 21,227:	Mason, Thos. J.	Loudon
21,912	Massengill, Jane M.	Jefferson
16,273	Massey, Wm.	Carroll
7,518	Matheany, Asa	Weakley
8,380	Mathes, John P., Estate of	Jefferson
14,634	Mathis, John	Hamblen
18,101	Matlock, John W.	McMinn
16,901	Matthews, E. L.	Rutherford
8,373	Matthews, Jane	Franklin
12,237	Matthews, John J.	Madison
13,486	Matthews, Joseph	Loudon
13,491	Matthews, Stephen	Loudon
5,315	Matthias, Elizabeth	Davidson
8,597	Maultsby, Thos. A.	Giles
5,059	Maxey, E.	Weakley
9,327	Maxwell, Robert W.	McMinn

13,773	Maxweil, Thos. Hardin	Hardin
17,344	May, Frederick	Jefferson
17,709	Mayers, Jasper L.	Bledsoe
22,254	Mayes, John	Grainger
9,670	Mayes, Noble Irvin	Monroe
17,868	Mayfield, Dan	Rutherford
7,914: 13,919:	Mayfield, Robert C.	Williamson
11,841	Mayhan, James A.	Davidson
5,243	Maynor, Pleasant, Estate of	Davidson
694	Mayo, Blackmore H.	Loudon
697	Mayo, May C.	Monroe
19,938	Mayse, James D.	Claiborne
14,853	Mayse, Sam	Hawkins
19,939	Mayse, Sterling	Claiborne
18,253: 19,371:	McAdams, James	Bedford
18,252	McAdams, John	Bedford
14,386	McAdams, Thos. C.	Washington
9,513	McAfee, Wm. J.	Gibson
11,281	McAlexander, Sebert H.	Madison
21,704	McAlhany, Hugh	Grainger
21,282	McAllister, John	Bradley
17,963	McAndrew, Joseph	Bradley
16,274	McArthur, Wm. A.	Carroll
13,763	McBride, Morris	Hardin
2,690	McCall, Henry	Carroll
4,034	McCall, Henry	Knox
11,336	McCall, John	Henderson
1,552	McCall, Joseph W.	Carroll
15,946	McCampbell, Elizabeth	Knox
2,691	McCarter, J. J. P.	Carroll
9,571	McCaslin, Wm. H.	Monroe
5,720	McCauly, Thos., Estate of	Loudon
12,922	McClain, Charles D.	Shelby
11,466	McClanahan, Alex	Hamblen
15,776	McClary, Jacob L.	Polk
3,024	McClay, Robert	Davidson
13,844	McClung, John	Monroe
5,098	McClure, Elizabeth	Montgomery
3,629	McClure, Louisa	Montgomery
16,427	McCollum, Abner	Carroll
19,639	McConkey, James	Monroe
9,960	McConnell, Alex W.	Shelby
19,899	McConnell, Alford	Blount
11,898	McConnell, James	Maury
1,553	McConnell, John	Obion
19,901	McConnell, Moses	Blount
19,900	McConnell, Newton	Blount
19,014	McConnell, W. E.	Bradley
10,636	McCord, Wm. G.	Giles
2,424	McCormick, Martin	Shelby
8,659	McCoy, James	Dyer
20,538	McCroskey, John S.	Sevier
20,537	McCroskey, Mary M.	Sevier
16,860	McCroskey, Robert H.	Loudon
21,892	McCroskey, Wm. R.	Sevier
12,154	McCuistion, Sam	Jefferson
16,576	McCullough, Isaac	Marshall
21,371	McCullum, Malcolm, Estate of	Shelby
7,182	McDaniel, Eli	Grainger
4,204	McDaniel, John	Claiborne
10,922	McDaniel, Lewis	Jefferson
20,542	McDaniel, Wm. B.	Claiborne
6,727	McDaniel, Wm. G.	Grainger
14,855	McDermott, Albert	Monroe
12,767	McDermott, John	Rutherford
13,845	McDermott, Thos.	Monroe
15,439	McDonald, Alex	James
16,543	McDonald, Benj. J.	Hamilton
16,546	McDonald, Edward, Estate of	Hamilton
24	McDonald, Ellen	Shelby
10,637	McDonald, John M.	Giles
13,553	McDonald, Leah	Greene
18,462	McDonough, John P.	Rutherford
11,779	McDowell, John	Fayette
10,206	McElroy, Andrew M.	Rutherford
10,206	McElroy, Andrew M.	Rutherford
18,341	McElwee, Thos. B.	Rhea
3,025	McEwen, Clarissa	Davidson

5,319	McEwen, John J.	Davidson
12,773	McFadden, Hallie	Rutherford
17,859	McFarlin, Benj.	Bedford
9,549	McGavock, John	Davidson
21,915	McGaw, John P.	Maury
17,591	McGee, Marion J.	Henderson
19,303	McGee, Robert	Sumner
19,306	McGee, Sam	Sumner
21,223	McGhee, Barclay, Estate of	Monroe
19,517	McGhee, Charles	Monroe
18,471	McGhee, Richmond	Loudon
21,907	McGhee, Robert H.	Hamblen
1,554	McGill, Eli T.	Davidson
19,898	McGinley, John N.	Blount
7,517	McGough, Minerva J.	Obion
10,335	McGowan, Ann B.	Hardeman
16,722	McGreedy, D. A.	Davidson
8,072	McGregor, Isaac	Tipton
8,071	McGregor, Mary E. O.	Tipton
10,634	McGrew, G. W.	Giles
10,764	McIntosh, Neill M.	Giles
15,040	McKay, Felix J.	Davidson
14,103	McKeeham, Wm. A.	Greene
3,466	McKenna, Robert	Shelby
11,994	McKenna, Sam	Shelby
12,860	McKenney, Alfred	Hawkins
12,868	McKenney, Chas. J.	Hawkins
11,361	McKinna, Patrick	Gibson
5,548	McKinney, James P.	Henderson
22,023	McKinney, John F.	Shelby
10,311	McKinney, Margaret	Hamblen
1,890	McKinney, Temperance E.	Lincoln
5,359	McKnight, David M.	Gibson
13,635	McKnight, John K.	Hardin
14,850	McKnight, Wm.	Jefferson
12,765	McKnight, Wm. J.	Rutherford
12,884	McLean, Wm. M.	Jefferson
7,900	McLendon, Margaret J.	Monroe
13,860	McMahon, James	Greene
4,528	McMahon, Wm. V.	Haywood
11,365	McMannaman, Mary	Shelby
12,187	McMillan, Edward W.	Shelby
6,632	McMillan, James H.	Giles
10,756	McMillion, H. P.	Giles
19,234	McMurphy, Michael	Sumner
12,840	McMurray, B. R.	Blount
4,891	McMurray, Margaret	Sevier
5,058	McMurray, V. T.	Obion
21,900	McNabb, John	Blount
14,105	McNees, Elihu	Greene
14,104	McNees, Jacob	Greene
15,765	McNeil, Elcans H.	Humphreys
5,362	McNeily, Thos., et al	Montgomery
5,182	McNish, Wm.	Jefferson
19,698	McPherson, James A.	Rhea
17,393	McPherson, John	Bradley
4,910	McPherson, Wm. H.	Davidson
22,048	McQuiddy, John, Estate of	Bedford
15,583	McRee, Robert C.	Hamilton
16,887	McReynolds, Stephen	Hamilton
21,927	McRoy, Lively, Estate of	Hamilton
12,166	McSpadden, Marshall W.	Jefferson
12,147	McSpadden, Sam	Jefferson
10,118	McStone, Wm., Estate of	Grainger
13,764	McVey, Joseph P.	Hardin
13,426	McWilliams, David	Sequatchie
13,425	McWilliams, John	Sequatchie
9,590	Mead, Jared	Blount
4,529	Meals, Lewis M.	Carroll
20,883	Meath, Patrick G.	Shelby
17,867	Meddors, Amy	Rutherford
14,635	Medlin, Bainster	Hamblin
8,660	Medlin, Gray V.	Haywood
1,555	Medlin, Robert	Haywood
16,816	Meek, Frank M.	Hamilton
12,168	Meek, Marcus D.	Jefferson
12,222	Meguiar, Wm.	Robertson
17,592	Milton, Henry	Henderson
21,884	Melton, James H., Estate of	McMinn
21,882	Melton, John N.	McMinn

18,263	Melton, Joseph	Warren
22,059	Mendenhall, Francis M.	Shelby
5,183: 8,712:	Mendenhall, Joseph R.	Jefferson
8,923	Mendenhall, Wm. F.	Jefferson
12,631	Mercer, Joseph F.	Greene
6,591	Merrill, Barbara	Tipton
16,879	Merritt, James P.	Rutherford
7,988	Mesier, L. H.	Morgan
22,283	Metison, Levi	Bedford
11,668	Meyer, Isaac A.	Shelby
19,745	Michael, Elijah	Jefferson
766	Milam, A. J., Estate of	Davidson
12,175	Miles, Ashley	Sevier
13,752	Miles, Hosea	Lawrence
2,692	Milian, R. L.	Henderson
21,921	Millard, Elkhanah	Sullivan
15,617	Miller, Adam	Knox
15,612	Miller, Alex Y.	Hamilton
16,687	Miller, Christopher	Jefferson
7,530	Miller, Dan	Davidson
16,886	Miller, Francis M.	Knox
16,721	Miller, Isaac L.	Rutherford
8,054	Miller, James M.	Cumberland
7,884	Miller, John	Grainger
16,611	Miller, John I.	Franklin
15,632	Miller, Julius	McMinn
16,985	Miller, Moses D., Estate of	Hamilton
19,456	Miller, Napoleon	Madison
17,791	Miller, Robert S.	McNairy
16,353	Miller, Sam H.	Washington
14,111	Miller, Sarah	Greene
16,047	Miller, Solomon	Rutherford
12,800	Miller, Washington W.	Maury
16,615	Miller, Wesley	Knox
187: 189: 190:	Milliger, James	Davidson
21,897	Million, Joseph J.	Bradley
12,886	Mills, Branson	Jefferson
15,165	Mills, Richardson, Estate of	Monroe
18,163	Millsaps, Jesse	Blount
18,772	Miney, Sam	Grainger
10,494	Minich, Isaac	Hamblen
5,239	Mink, James E.	Claiborne
15,378	Minter, Levina	Rutherford
9,288	Minton, John	Loudon
19,212	Mires, Benj. T.	Sumner
22,101	Mitchell, Aquilla	Grainger
17,071	Mitchell, C. G.	Rutherford
17,342	Mitchell, David	Rutherford
10,117	Mitchell, G. B.	Grainger
11,279	Mitchell, G. G.	Gibson
10,380	Mitchell, Geo. T.	Gibson
17,675	Mitchell, Hansel	Rutherford
22,099	Mitchell, James H.	Grainger
8,972	Mitchell, John	Grainger
15,418	Mitchell, John B.	James
18,775	Mitchell, John W.	Warren
14,177	Mitchell, Joshua T.	Lauderdale
17,953	Mitchell, Martha, Estate of	Bradley
10,678	Mitchell, Moses C.	Gibson
15,432	Mitchell, Sam D.	James
13,931	Mitchell, Wm.	Rutherford
4,530	Mitchum, W. E.	Carroll
17,279	Mizer, Michael	Blount
3,545	Moffitt, James	Davidson
8,708	Moles, James	Hancock
1,473: 2,744:	Molitor, Francis	Shelby
17,197	Mongle, James H.	Washington
20,289	Mongold, Fred E.	Washington
21,526	Montgomery, Milton	Franklin
17,861	Montgomery, Robert S.	Bedford
15,359	Moody, Robert E.	Sullivan
7,873	Moody, Thos. B.	Grainger
15,890	Moody, Valentine	Sullivan
18,231	Mook, John T.	Blount
16,785	Moon, Pleasant B.	Bedford
10,340	Moon, R. G.	Carroll
4,212	Mooney, A. M., Mrs.	Davidson
14,753	Moore, Alex	Davidson
7,921	Moore, Charles	Loudon
15,633	Moore, David	Meigs
11,694	Moore, Edwin L.	Weakley
10,001	Moore, G. W.	Dickson
13,755	Moore, Geo. M.	McNairy
3,238	Moore, James	Hamblen
8,483	Moore, James G.	Shelby
19,336	Moore, Jane	Giles
14,673	Moore, Jane	Rutherford
15,768	Moore, John A.	Tipton
11,697	Moore, Joseph H.	Weakley
13,988	Moore, Levi	Sullivan
17,237	Moore, Manuel	Williamson
3,097	Moore, Robert G.	Carroll
10,455	Moore, Robert P.	Hamblen
10,466	Moore, Sam J.	Hamblen
8,484	Moore, Stativa	Shelby
5,851	Moore, Susannah A.	Wilson
6,631	Moore, Wiley	Maury
8,181	Moore, Wm.	Hamblen
12,431	Moore, Wm.	Robertson
21,155	Moore, Wm. F.	Maury
19,570	Moore, Wm. H.	Davidson
21,389	Moorman, Madison B.	Davidson
12,630: 14,112:	Morelock, Nathan	Greene
14,113	Morelock, Thos.	Greene
18,901	Morgan, Dan	Bedford
18,958	Morgan, Elias H.	Rhea
12,762	Morgan, Fannie	Rutherford
8,970	Morgan, J. M.	Grainger
11,083	Morgan, Jane S.	Davidson
21,078	Morgan, John B., Estate of	Shelby
9,063	Morgan, John K.	Grainger
9,206	Morgan, Lewis	Polk
18,959	Morgan, Louis	Rhea
17,962	Morgan, Rufus	James
16,594	Morgan, Thos.	Bedford
3,628	Morgan, W. H. T.	Davidson
20,028	Morgan, Washington	Rhea
11,790	Morphis, Wm. A.	Henry
9,403	Morphus, T. G.	Gibson
7,067	Morran, Morris J.	Davidson
1,891	Morris, Benj. Allen	Robertson
14,597	Morris, Benj. F.	Carroll
3,199	Morris, Nancy	Morgan
10,472	Morrisett, Richard M.	Hamblen
18,237	Morrison, James H. S.	Claiborne
7,368	Morrow, Sam R.	Fayette
12,343	Mort, John	Jefferson
6,327: 7,875:	Morton, Jane	Williamson
17,600	Morton, Thos.	McNairy
21,316	Moseley, Sam H.	Sumner
7,263	Moser, Jacob	Monroe
8,851	Moser, John	Monroe
5,966	Moser, Phillip	Monroe
10,805	Moses, Henry C.	Giles
4,567	Moss, Benj. A.	Hamilton
21,676	Moss, Edmond	Shelby
15,888	Moss, Griffin T.	Sullivan
16,263	Moss, Hardy	McMinn
14,517	Moulden, J. W.	Jefferson
14,518	Moulden, Wm.	Jefferson
12,833	Mount, Humphrey	Blount
2,889	Mowery, Adam	Loudon
14,660	Muirhead, Caroline R.	Rutherford
1,002	Muller, John P.	Hamilton
2,089	Mullins, Rebecca	Gibson
15,360	Mullins, Richard P.	Sullivan
10,463	Murdock, Wm. M.	Hamblen
14,159	Murfree, Edmund	Rutherford
16,588	Murfree, Martha A.	Rutherford
22,194	Murfree, W. L.	Rutherford
15,731	Murphrey, Wm.	James
11,866	Murphy, Patrick	Shelby
8,994	Murphy, Wm.	Davidson
18,988	Murr, David	Washington

1,776	Murray, W. W.	Carroll
10,917	Murrell, M. R.	Grainger
14,598	Muse, Dan C., Estate of	Madison
5,549	Myer, Myer B.	Davidson
14,110	Myers, Jacob	Greene
14,107	Myers, Jacob, James & John T.	Greene
14,108	Myers, James	Greene
16,545	Myres, Lesley	Rhea
5,060	Myrick, John	Weakley
17,121	Mysinger, Sam	Hamilton
18,965	Nail, Abraham H.	Bledsoe
8,661	Nail, John	Haywood
13,765	Nance, Hugh	Hardin
10,016	Nance, P.P.	Grainger
39	Nance, Wm. L.	Davidson
8,612	Napier, Wm. C.	Davidson
6,397	Narramore, Fielding M.	Cumberland
505	Nash, Emma & Joseph C. and Glassie, D. W. & Minnie	Davidson
9,009	Nash, John	Henry
505	Nash, Joseph C. & Emma and Glassie; Minnie & D. W.	Davidson
16,542	Nash, Wm.	Hamilton
17,405	Nave, John H.	Knox
18,328	Neal, Geo.	Wilson
9,010	Neal, Perry M.	Haywood
16,585	Neal, Wm., Estate of	Giles
6,719	Needham, Geo. B.	Grainger
6,720	Needham, Nancy	Grainger
22,061	Neel, Louisa	Shelby
10,533	Neeld, Wm. P.	Lincoln
8,624	Neeley, John J.	Rutherford
17,961	Neeley, Wm. Horton	Meigs
16,423	Neeper, Lee	Blount
10,459	Neil, John	Jefferson
10,495	Neil, John "colored"	Jefferson
10,475	Neil, Wm.	Jefferson
12,847	Neill, Sam	Hawkins
9,998	Neilson, Thos.	Jefferson
19,365	Nelson, Benj. A.	Bedford
15,164	Nelson, David	Knox
1,205	Nelson, Elisha	Gibson
3,028	Nelson, Geo. A.	Davidson
12,159	Nelson, John W.	Jefferson
14,114	Nelson, Nathan	Washington
11,350	Nelson, Sam B.	Rutherford
10,485	Nenney, Wm. B.	Jefferson
1,539	Nesbetts, B. H.	Carroll
18,898	Netherland, G. W., Estate of	Sullivan
19,691	Netherland, Robert G.	Hawkins
19,704	Newell, Jane, Estate of	Shelby
1,512	Newhouse, Thos. D., Heirs of	Gibson
19,824	Hewland, Wm. A.	Hardeman
15,947	Newman, Esquire	Sumner
15,770	Newman, Mary	Bradley
7,637	Newman, Alex A.	Monroe
5,185	Newman, David G.	Jefferson
9,716	Newman, Edward	Knox
21,038	Newman, James	Sevier
8,862	Newman, Jane K.	Jefferson
8,164	Newman, Jonathan	Jefferson
21,037	Newman, Vance	Sevier
12,190	Newsom, Ella K.	Shelby
11,277	Newsom, J. P.	Madison
15,055	Newsom, Joseph, Heirs of	Davidson
10,667	Newton, Lyttle	Madison
6,900	Nicholes, James	Rutherford
17,574	Nichols, Chas. W. & Mahala E.	Hamilton
17,574	Nichols, Mahala E. & Chas. W.	Hamilton
18,360	Nichols, Wyatt F.	Jefferson
12,600	Nickens, James	Cheatham
16,575	Niel, James H.	Bedford
8,194	Neil, Wm.	Jefferson
11,708	Noe, David S.	Hamblen
8,686	Noe, James C.	Grainger
7,369	Nolan, Z. C.	Haywood
20,731	Norman, C. A.	Bradley
1,556	Norman, John	Carroll

14,636	Northern, Alfred	Jefferson
12,891	Northern, Francis M.	Jefferson
10,469	Northern, James	Jefferson
21,527	Oakley, Eunice, Estate of	Franklin
14,902	Oakley, James S.	Franklin
8,407	Oakley, Stanford P.	Rutherford
11,307	O'Brien, B. M. G.	Carter
3,418	O'Brien, Marion M.	Davidson
1,306	O'Conner, Catharine	Shelby
8,687	Odell, Sam C.	Jefferson
15,089	Odell, Sarah E.	Maury
6,322	Oden, Thos. H.	Williamson
15,948	Odom, Wm.	Sumner
16,418	Oldham, Lucretia E.	Jefferson
8,858	Oldham, Sam, Estate of	Haywood
8,473	Olive, Howell	Henderson
10,758	Oliver, Henry	Giles
5,892	Oliver, John W.	Maury
14,389	Oliver, Richard	Washington
10,761	Oliver, Sam	Giles
8,952	Oliver, Skipworth M.	Fayette
1,557	Oliver, Thurston W.	Gibson
17,211	O'Neal, James M.	Bedford
14,282	O'Neal, John	Montgomery
3,089	O'Neill, Arthur	Shelby
8,074	O'Neill, James H.	Shelby
18,846	Onley, Wm. T.	McMinn
12,826	Ordway, Chas. N.	Davidson
8,055	Orme, Willen T.	Cumberland
21,986	Orne, Wm. P.	Shelby
18,836	Orr, W. F.	Polk
11,722	Orten, James	Monroe
18,801	Osment, Mary A.	Bradley
15,780	Osment, Pinckney	Bradley
5,446	Owens, Charles	Monroe
7,043	Owens, James C.	Williamson
16,193	Owens, Pleasant	Hamblen
12,599	Owen, Wm. C.	Davidson
16,265	Owen, Wm. C.	McMinn
16,902	Page, G. W.	Wilson
7,519	Page, James W.	Weakley
17,945	Pair, Andrew	Bradley
16,236	Palmer, Alex	Sullivan
21,259	Palmer, James L.	Gibson
6,987	Palmer, John	McNairy
10,489: 11,061:	Pangle, Mary A.	Hamblen
12,838	Pannel, Thos. A.	Jefferson
8,056	Parham, Elizabeth	Cumberland
5,244	Parham, Margaret F.	Lincoln
5,061	Parham, Ruth	Weakley
13,901	Park, Geo.	Carroll
14,637	Park, Geo. B.	Greene
14,115: 14,638:	Park, James	Greene
9,400	Park, Sam	Gibson
4,719	Park, Wm.	Maury
18,337	Parker, Allen	Hamilton
6,334	Parker, Elbert	Knox
2,893	Parker, Isaac T.	Giles
6,563	Parker, James C.	Carroll
2,090	Parker, Jane M.	Gibson
7,520	Parker, Jesse	Weakley
8,218	Parker, John C.	Knox
21,224	Parker, Mary K.	Loudon
2,091	Parker, Nathan	Gibson
1,558	Parker, Priestley E.	Henderson
6,717	Parker, Priestley E.	Carroll
1,719	Parker, Wm.	Claiborne
18,106	Parkison, Dan, Estate of	McMinn
18,107	Parkison, James	McMinn
21,000	Parks, Alex C.	Polk
10,640	Parks, Asberry	Giles
18,345	Parks, Lewis	Sullivan
20,452	Parks, Richard T.	Bradley
20,454	Parks, Susanna	Bradley
11,562	Parrott, Anderson	Hamblen
8,974	Parrott, Joseph H.	Grainger
7,957: 17,996:	Parrish, M. A.	Davidson

13,412	Parsons, J. Campbell	Blount	18,076	Phillips, Smith	Roane
19,418	Parsons, James	McMinn	10,465	Phillips, Wm. T.	Hamblin
14,563	Parsons, S. & Law, Wm.	Grundy	12,836	Pickens, Thos.	Blount
11,462	Pate, Wm., Estate of	Williamson	17,569	Picket, Edward D.	Sequatchie
11,999	Paton, Anthony	Davidson	17,517	Picket, Jesse	Sequatchie
8,165	Patrick, Marion	Jefferson	9,402	Pickler, James W.	Gibson
11,134	Patterson, Hence	Polk	12,890	Pierce, G. W.	Jefferson
21,710	Patterson, James	Grainger	16,493	Pierce, James	Rhea
18,451	Patterson, John Nelson	Giles	19,895	Pierce, John	Hamilton
5,968	Patterson, Levi T.	Roane	19,895	Pierce, John	Hamilton
8,969	Patterson, Sam	Grainger	3,340	Pilant, Susan	Knox
17,699	Patterson, Simon	Sumner	15,272	Pile, Brian	Sullivan
4,935	Patterson, Simpson A.	Giles	8,419	Pile, Wm., Sr.	Fentress
10,013	Patterson, Thos., Estate of	Grainger	13,879	Pillow, Elizabeth T.	Maury
21,765	Patterson, Wm. H.	Claiborne	1,561	Pinckley, Clark	Carroll
15,261	Patton, Benj.	Coffee	11,100	Pinckley, Wm. C.	Carroll
16,694	Patton, James C. B.	Washington	18,509	Pincky, Scott	Carroll
16,262	Patty, Raffail	McMinn	14,566	Pinion, M. C.	Grundy
4,075	Payne, A. T. W.	Monroe	22,221	Pittard, Grandison	Giles
14,387	Payne, Alex M.	Washington	8,482	Plischke, Augustine	Shelby
16,363	Payne, Charles, Estate of	Robertson	17,796	Plunk, Calvin	McNairy
14,565	Payne, G. W.	Grundy	17,797	Plunk, David	McNairy
4,044	Payne, G. W.	Monroe	17,575	Poe, Ansel	Hamilton
12,077	Payne, Jacob W.	Knox	15,436	Poe, John, Estate of	James
20,434	Payne, Joseph S.	Coffee	8,075	Poindexter, C. C., Estate of	Fayette
19,748	Payne, Thos.	Hamblen	7,370	Poindexter, Raleigh	Fayette
17,450	Pearce, David	McMinn	13,349	Pointer, Wm. H.	Maury
18,897	Pearce, Sam	Sullivan	21,041	Polk, Adam	Maury
7,922	Pearson, Mary J.	Monroe	14,664	Polk, Sarah	Davidson
2,680	Pearson, Peter	Henderson	14,851	Pollard, Wm.	Jefferson
4,531	Pearson, Shadrack	Carroll	17,594	Pool, Archibald P.	Hardin
7,521	Peck, Jospeh F.	Obion	2,355	Poor, Baxter M.	Claiborne
8,182	Peck, Lydia	Jefferson	22,102	Poor Farm	Grainger
1,559	Peek, Wm.	Gibson	11,282	Pope, Cordy, Estate of	Madison
10,138	Peeples, Sam	Weakley	20,887	Pope, John, Estate of	Shelby
18,445	Pence, Elizabeth	Sullivan	10,622	Porter, Harvey H.	Loudon
19,379	Pender, Thomas C.	James	5,404	Porter, Madison	Franklin
428	Pendleton, James M.	Rutherford	4,533	Porter, Mary L.	Carroll
7,024	Penix, John G.	Henderson	13,377	Porter, Melvin	Loudon
11,214	Penn, Lutisha B.	Shelby	16,525	Porter, Nimrod, Estate of	Maury
1,674	Penn, Wm.	Shelby	5,361	Porter, P. H. & Brockmon, Sam	Montgomery
15,584	Penney, G. W.	Hamilton	18,104	Porter, Wm. B.	McMinn
16,982	Penney, Isom	Hamilton	9,322	Porter, Wm. W.	Monroe
7,923	Pennington, John, Estate of	Monroe	13,943	Posey, Wm. P.	Lauderdale
17,395	Penny, Elizabeth	James	9,475	Postal, Wm. C.	Shelby
19,688	Penticord, Harvey	Sumner	12,189	Poston, B. F.	Montgomery
16,966	Peoples, D. W. F.	Washington	11,133	Poteet, Barnard M.	Polk
3,642	Peregoy, John P.	Washington	20,619	Powell, John	Franklin
17,518	Perkepile, Ralph	Blount	2,092	Powell, John	Gibson
4,164	Perkins, Elanor A.	Shelby	411	Powell, John M.	Shelby
6,796	Perkins, Geo. G.	Madison	17,863	Powell, Wm. J. & Hobbs, Jas. M.	Bedford
8,859	Perkins, Nicholas T., Jr.	Haywood			
10,342	Perritt, Johnson	Carroll	19,232	Powers, John W.	Hamilton
8,070	Perrit, W. P., Estate of	Tipton	20,375	Prater, James M., Estate of	Loudon
6,932	Perry, John S.	Fayette	14,701	Price, A., Major	Wilson
2,093	Perry, Wm. F.	Gibson	17,062	Price, Edmund	Washington
13,578	Perry, Willis	Maury	5,403	Price, Elizabeth	Franklin
15,434	Pesterfield, John	Bradley	1,132	Price, John	Morgan
17,246	Peters, Edd	Rutherford	14,701	Price, Major A.	Wilson
14,935	Peters, G. W.	Washington	17,378	Prichard, Reuben T.	McMinn
5,225	Peters, Geo. B.	Shelby	21,754	Prickett, Wm. T.	Washington
17,801	Pettigrew, John M.	McNairy	1,563	Priddy, James M.	Henderson
14,401	Pettit, Maria L.	Shelby	16,560	Priddy, John H.	Shelby
20,446	Pettitt, Jane	Bradley	11,497	Priddy, Piety	Shelby
17,095	Pettus, Thos. F.	Montgomery	8,694	Primm, Charles H.	Williamson
17,096	Pettus, Thos. F, & Hambaugh, P. C.	Montgomery	17,478	Primrose, John G.	Bedford
			17,696	Prince, Eliza	Sumner
10,467	Petty, G. W.	Hawkins	18,166	Pritchard, Barbara M.	Blount
20,825	Petty, Horatio	Sevier	1,562	Pritchard, John H.	Carroll
11,507	Peyton, Bailie	Sumner	17,383	Pryor, Andrew J.	Jefferson
10,337	Phagan, John P.	Jefferson	20,297	Pugh, James T.	Hardeman
1,560	Phelan, James G.	Gibson	8,845	Pullen, Eaton	Hamblen
4,507	Phifer, John P.	Loudon	5,109	Purseley, Mack	Wilson
4,532	Philips, Columbus P.	Henderson	10,137	Pursley, Catharine	Obion
9,840	Phillips, Andrew	Fayette	6,774	Pursley, Noel M.	Obion
19,689	Phillips, Chas. F.	Carroll	5,099	Pursley, Wm. B.	Wilson
20,233	Phillips, Elizabeth T.	Franklin	10,134	Pursley, Wilson Y.	Obion
10,477	Phillips, Isaac	Hamblen	3,239	Putnam, A. W.	Davidson
17,544	Phillips, John M.	Bedford	13,579	Putman, John R.	Maury
11,704	Phillips, Jonathan, Estate of	Scott	3,644	Putman, F. E. & M. W.	Davidson

3,644	Putnam, M. W. & F. E.	Davidson
14,379	Putnam, Waldo W., Heirs of	Coffee
8,846	Quarles, Mary	Jefferson
10,462	Quillen, Jackson L.	Hamblen
19,807	Quin, Robert	Fayette
16,703	Rackard, Michael	Knox
16,702	Rackard, Thos. E.	Knox
7,522	Radcliffe, Wm. S.	Obion
13,549	Rader, Reuben M.	Greene
10,373	Ragan, Bennett W.	Gibson
15,435	Ragon, Jesse S.	James
7,523	Ragsdale, Wm.	Obion
5,721	Raisin, James H.	Loudon
14,119	Rambo, Enos. R.	Greene
21,103	Ramsey, Edmund	Bradley
8,662	Ramsey, James H.	Shelby
20,436	Ramsey, John W.	Bradley
8,428	Ramsey, Richard W.	Shelby
10,625	Randles, Henry	Sevier
21,047	Randles, John B.	Sevier
2,829	Randles, Malissa	Sevier
717: 12,163:	Randles, Wm. M.	Jefferson
10,905	Rankin, Elizabeth	Jefferson
19,463	Rankin, James	Jefferson
17,876	Rankin, John D., Estate of	McNairy
8,688	Rankin, Josiah E.	Jefferson
10,484	Rankin, Patrick M.	Jefferson
12,576	Rankin, Wm., Estate of	Jefferson
13,548	Rankin, Wm. B.	Greene
21,020	Ransom, Benj. F.	Bedford
16,760	Ransom, Joseph	Rutherford
19,080	Rash, Eliza S.	Shelby
15,825	Rawlings, John A.	Sevier
10,230	Rawlins, John A.	Franklin
15,363	Rayl, Nancy H.	Hamblen
4,394	Rea, John T.	Giles
3,525	Read, Jane	Henderson
1,564	Read, Wm.	Henderson
5,553	Read, Wm. A.	Henderson
8,663	Read, Wm. B.	Haywood
15,634	Reagan, Malinda	McMinn
10,233	Reagin, M. P.	Franklin
11,691	Reavis, Elijah R.	Weakley
18,769	Rector, Wm. K.	Claiborne
13,843	Redman, John, Estate of	Monroe
5,852	Redman, John F.	Williamson
822	Redman, Martin F.	Morgan
18,815	Redman, Uriah, Estate of	Hamilton
20,620	Redmond, Andrew J.	Marion
10,913	Reed, Dan I.	Hamblen
15,419	Reed, Hugh J.	James
11,078	Reed, J. C. P.	Giles
11,629	Reed, Robert J.	Carroll
15,420	Reed, Robert W.	James
18,872	Reed, Wyatt	Jefferson
15,221	Reeder, Nathaniel B.	Warren
10,924	Reese, Geo. A.	Jefferson
12,628	Reeser, Isaac J.	Greene
13,861	Reeser, John	Greene
12,632: 13,862:	Reeser, W. F.	Greene
16,147	Reeves, Harry	Fayette
17,210	Reeves, Solomon G.	Bedford
15,994	Register, Arthur J.	Hickman
9,483	Reid, Wm.	Grundy
15,407	Reiney, Geo. S.	Gibson
6,722	Renfro, Sam S.	Grainger
17,203	Reno, Wm.	Loudon
7,186	Rentfro, H. J.	Grainger
9,062	Rentfro, James H.	Grainger
10,111	Rentfro, Jerusha A.	Grainger
19,269	Replogle, Frederick A.	Madison
16,048	Reynolds, Charles	DeKalb
16,614	Rhea, Matilda	Loudon
13,216	Rhea, Wm.	Monroe
19,971	Rhine, Solomon G.	Shelby
1,566	Rhodes, James P.	Henderson
1,565	Rhodes, John M.	Henderson
8,664	Rhodes, Richard V.	Haywood
18,259	Rhodes, Silas A.	Marshall
10,903	Rhoton, John F.	Jefferson
15,635	Rice, Austin, Jr.	Loudon
11,900	Rice, David	Madison
16,578	Rice, John H.	Bedford
5,321	Rich, G. W.	Grainger
4,894	Rich, Joseph	Grainger
7,046	Rich, Josiah N.	Grainger
15,962	Richards, S. H.	Monroe
19,547	Richardson, David A.	Marshall
3,697	Richardson, James	Claiborne
7,074	Richardson, Mary E.	Fayette
5,894	Richardson, Thos. T.	Maury
7,343	Richesin, J. W.	Loudon
6,426	Richesin, Jane	Monroe
15,803	Ricketts, Mary H.	Humphreys
19,086	Riddle, Linton	Franklin
10,549	Rieves, Thos. J.	Maury
567	Riley, John D.	Hawkins
21,299	Rimel, Geo., Estate of	Sevier
17,439	Rimmer, Wm.	Jefferson
13,863	Ripley, David S., Estate of	Greene
12,620: 13,864:	Ripley, Margaret	Greene
12,623: 14,116:	Ripley, Sylvester B.	Greene
9,011	Risner, Andrew J.	Decatur
21,917	Rivers, Braxton, Estate of	Giles
10,038	Rivers, Elizabeth	Gibson
13,419	Roach, Andrew	Knox
2,335	Roach, Eaton	Fayette
21,706	Roach, John	Grainger
8,968	Roach, Wm. S.	Grainger
16,969	Roadman, M. A.	Cocke
15,954	Robb, Harvey W.	Sumner
17,700	Robb, Mack	Sumner
14,439	Robbins, Milo	Grundy
5,114	Robbins, Wm.	Scott
5,135	Roberson, James	Loudon
10,669	Roberts, Catharine A.	Gibson
4,796	Roberts, John C.	Claiborne
1,659	Roberts, John D.	Williamson
21,911	Roberts, John W.	Knox
18,822	Roberts, Emerson	Hamilton
10,024	Roberts, Leathy	Polk
6,728	Roberts, Philip	Grainger
16,917	Roberts, Thos. B.	Hamilton
8,826	Robertson, Henry G.	Hardin
15,783	Robertson, James D.	Bradley
17,597	Robertson, James F.	McNairy
20,228	Robertson, Laura B.	Davidson
16,141	Robertson, W. D.; and Yarborough, James H.	Davidson
19,674	Robinett, John	Marion
17,804	Robins, Joseph L.	McNairy
6,929	Robinson, Drewsilla	Fayette
8,918	Robinson, Elisha D.	Loudon
6,148	Robinson, Geo. M.	Madison
5,134	Robinson, J. R.	Monroe
18,325	Robinson, John E.	DeKalb
5,133	Robinson, John W.	Loudon
13,847	Robinson, Louisa J.	Monroe
12,585	Robinson, Margaret	Stewart
17,707	Robinson, Michael	Bedford
6,589	Robinson, Monroe	Shelby
19,327	Robinson, Raburn	Blount
9,321	Robinson, Richard T.	Loudon
17,586	Robinson, Thos.	Henderson
15,166	Robinson, Titus	Knox
4,403	Robinson, Wm.	Monroe
18,326	Robinson, Wm. R.	DeKalb
10,426	Rockholt, James Henry	Shelby
13,416	Roddy, Wm.	Blount
19,299	Rodemer, Anna	Sumner
13,902	Rodes, Dangerfield	Giles
21,981	Rodes, J. E., Mrs.	Giles
10,757	Rodgers, John	Giles
5,316	Rodgers, Mary	Williamson
9,514	Roe, Benj. F.	Gibson
9,965	Roe, Jasper N.	Gibson

371	Roe, John A.	Gibson
13,306	Rogers, A. G., Estate of	Carroll
20,450	Rogers, Amanuel H.	Bradley
18,825	Rogers, Henry	Hamilton
4,223	Rogers, Henry R.	Montgomery
10,420	Rogers, James	Humphreys
2,265	Rogers, James W.	Hamilton
18,100	Rogers, John	McMinn
18,824	Rogers, John C.	Hamilton
5,970	Rogers, Thos.	Monroe
12,055	Rogers, Wm. H.	Blount
21,904	Rohr, Philip	Washington
6,341	Roland, Luke	Monroe
3,228	Roland, Mary, Estate of	Shelby
20,568	Roland, Rachel	McMinn
19,735	Roller, John, Estate of	Sullivan
12,268	Rosaman, John W.	Madison
5,173	Rose, Alex S. P.	Fayette
16,681	Rose, G. W.	Smith
12,074	Rose, Linesy	Knox
22,281	Rose, Manuel	Giles
13,449	Rose, Mitchell	Loudon
13,544	Rosenblatt, P. G.	Greene
9,504	Ross, Jabez L.	Knox
13,629	Ross, Kenneth M.	Hardin
14,117	Ross, Wm.	Greene
11,690	Ross, Wiley C.	Weakley
8,823	Rosson, David W.	Hardeman
2,247	Roth, G. A.	Montgomery
13,423	Roulston, Hugh L. W.	Marion
13,431	Roulston, James W.	Marion
3,029	Routh, Ellen	Grainger
12,132	Rowe, John M.	Carroll
10,271	Rowland, Amos	Carroll
10,201	Rowland, Ebin	Carroll
10,269	Rowland, Thos., Estate of	Carroll
11,349	Rowlett, James C.	Rutherford
15,960	Roy, Harrison	Monroe
12,626	Royston, Cyrus A.	Washington
14,118	Royston, Margaret F.	Greene
15,826	Rubel, James A.	Knox
17,331	Rucker, Jordan	Rutherford
14,934	Rucker, Susan	Rutherford
13,542	Rudder, John W.	Greene
15,550	Ruemekorf, Henry	Davidson
12,075	Rule, Geo. J.	Knox
13,432	Runion, G. W.	Blount
18,961	Runyan, Simeon P.	James
3,256	Runyon, Oliver P.	Knox
7,744	Ruohs, Joseph	Hamilton
6,565	Rushing, John R.	Humphreys
11,141	Russell, A. L.	Obion
19,501	Russell, Andrew H.	Lincoln
19,211	Russell, James	Marion
19,848	Russell, Priscilla, Heirs of	Marshall
4,402	Russell, Thos.	Loudon
16,541	Russell, Wm. M.	Rhea
21,528	Russey, Benj. F.	Franklin
11,289	Russey, J. M.	Franklin
17,775	Russom, John W.	McNairy
9,476	Rust, Alex H.	Gibson
5,332	Rust, Geo. B.	Gibson
4,767	Rust, Isaac	Grundy
1,778	Rust, O. R.	Carroll
8,076	Rutherford, Benj. F.	Tipton
18,899	Rutledge, Benj.	Sullivan
5,896	Rutledge, Wm. J.	Maury
15,740	Ryan, James	Davidson
20,060	Ryan, Patrick	Davidson
17,138	Ryon, W. S.	Morgan
1,131	Saffell, Chas. P.	Morgan
16,140	Saffell, Thos. F.	Sevier
138	St. Clair, Susan	Shelby
17,060	Salts, J. W.	Washington
17,949	Samples, Catharine & Wm. B.	Bradley
5,969	Sample, Wm.	Monroe
17,949	Samples, Wm. B. & Catharine	Bradley
11,601	Sampson, Charles N.	Sullivan
3,255	Sampson, Jonathan T.	Monroe

10,483	Samsel, Elizabeth	Grainger
5,504	Sanders, Byron L.	McNairy
18,260	Sanders, Loamma	Marshall
12,858	Sanders, Martha A.	Hawkins
5,853	Sanders, Patrick	Davidson
15,801	Sanders, Wm. C.	Giles
8,078	Sandford, Caroline E.	Tipton
21,970	Sandford, G. W., Estate of	Rutherford
12,777	Sandusky, James	Scott
12,366	Saulpaw, G. W.	McMinn
16,128	Saunders, Abraham	Sumner
17,334	Saunders, Hubbard H.	Sumner
61	Saylor, Abraham	Washington
18,256	Scales, James H. C.	Bedford
1,070	Scanlon, Elizabeth M.	Shelby
11,140	Scater, Wm. D.	Obion
5,062	Scates, Susan C.	Weakley
1,356	Schimmler, John	Davidson
9,324	Schooler, Ananias	Loudon
13,732	Schute, Philip C.	Davidson
11,084	Scobey, John B., Estate of	Wilson
6,594	Scott, Adam	Shelby
2,740	Scott, Albert	Knox
17,589	Scott, Albert	McNairy
20,241	Scott, Alfred & Herrin, Thos.	Davidson
20,033	Scott, Hamilton S.	Claiborne
3,465	Scott, Hubert P.	Fayette
19,896	Scott, James	Blount
17,590	Scott, James	McNairy
1,133: 19,089:	Scott, Julian F.	Morgan
13,338	Scott, Mitchell	Shelby
19,326	Scott, Wm. E.	Blount
1,660	Scrivener, Thos., Estate of	Davidson
13,848	Scruggs, John, Estate of	Monroe
10,224	Scurlock, G. W.	Shelby
21,887	Seaton, Philip	Sevier
4,433	Seawright, Nancy	Shelby
3,547	Seay, Eli A.	Rutherford
4,534	Segraves, Moses	Henderson
17,548	Sehorn, Alfred	Bedford
21,929	Seleer, Absalom	Hamilton
13,865	Self, Harrison	Greene
13,866	Self, Thos. F.	Greene
1,567	Sellers, Hardy S.	Carroll
18,871	Sellers, Sam	Jefferson
13,989	Seneker, James	Sullivan
1,275	Settle, Benj., Estate of	Fayette
8,079	Settle, Sarah P.	Fayette
18,896	Sevier, David	Sullivan
18,009	Sevier, Mary C.	Roane
21,764	Sewell, Gaston, Estate of	Claiborne
10,658	Sexton, Emanuel	Scott
3,524	Sexton, Richard	Shelby
10,657	Sexton, Robert	Scott
1,353	Seymour, H. C., Estate of	Davidson
21,886	Seymour, Margaret	Union
14,120	Shackleford, Jacob J.	Greene
10,907	Shadden, Alex M.	Jefferson
13,707	Shadden, Elisha M.	Giles
18,820	Shadrick, Rufus	Hamilton
17,434	Shadwick, Alex	Hamilton
16,592	Shaffner, Loton	Bedford
12,843	Shanks, Henry, Estate of	Hawkins
10,461	Shannon, H. P., Estate of	Hamblen
15,760	Shannon, James T.	Williamson
5,971	Shannon, Thos. S.	Monroe
19,555	Sharp, Francis	Union
16,574	Sharp, Graham B.	Bedford
12,151	Sharp, James B.	Jefferson
18,099	Sharp, Mary D.	McMinn
10,231	Sharp, Susan S.	Franklin
19,722	Shaver, John W.	Humphreys
21,797	Shaw, Ebenezer, Estate of	Maury
8,665	Shaw, Neal A.	Haywood
20,432	Shearin, Patrick	Bedford
16,489	Sheddan, Wm.	Jefferson
16,487	Sheddan, Wilson	Jefferson
17,194	Sheefey, Magdalene A.	Washington
553	Shell, Andrew	Sullivan

11,700	Shelton, Eli J.	Weakley
15,386	Shelton, Geo. P.	Fayette
8,466	Shelton, Isaac R.	Shelby
7,187	Shelton, Jacob	Grainger
15,636	Shelton, James T.	McMinn
19,907	Shelton, John	Giles
10,319	Shelton, Sam	Rutherford
15,957	Shepherd, Martha, Estate of	Sumner
13,351	Sheppard, Jesse	Maury
16,559	Sheppard, Reeder B.	Shelby
1,570	Sherman, Albert	Haywood
1,571	Sherman, John L.	Haywood
10,751	Sherrell, John S.	Giles
10,754	Sherrell, Sam	Giles
15,618	Sherretz, Alex A.	Knox
4,527	Sherrod, John H., Estate of	Henderson
17,440	Sherry, Patrick	Shelby
11,741	Sherwood, Rebecca C.	Hawkins
12,625	Shields, Carter	Greene
19,603	Shields, Sam	Grainger
18,446	Shipley, Sarah	Sullivan
16,430	Shipman, Alex	Greene
11,742	Shirley, Patrick A.	Grainger
12,513	Shivers, Jesse M.	Hardeman
9,669	Shoat, Jason	Monroe
17,452	Shoemaker, Calaway	McMinn
17,978	Shoemaker, Henry	Scott
22,257	Shropshire, James	Grainger
2,046	Shultz, Geo.	Claiborne
15,613	Shumate, Wm. J.	Williamson
15,445	Shute, Lee	Sumner
18,048	Siebert, Frederick	Shelby
19,040	Sikes, Jessie	Rutherford
20,007	Sills, Henry E.	Shelby
18,241	Simmerly, Jeremiah	Blount
3,684	Simmons, G. W.	Carroll
12,295	Simmons, Geo., Estate of	Franklin
4,777	Simmons, Jeremiah B.	Fayette
10,811	Simmons, Lavinia	Giles
20,876	Simmons, Susan	Franklin
1,488	Simms, P. L.	Lawrence
1,507	Simmsn, Wm. & Bledsoe, L.Y.	Haywood
13,760	Simonton, Wm.	Lawrence
4,037	Simpson, D. L.	Knox
14,121	Simpson, Geo. B.	Greene
3,341	Simpson, Jesse	Knox
14,675	Simpson, John	Rutherford
16,233	Simpson, Margaret W.	Sullivan
6,566	Simpson, Sam	Humphreys
13,445	Simpson, Sanford C.	Loudon
17,587	Simpson, Willis H.	McNairy
18,305	Sims, G. W.	Gibson
22,285	Sims, John G.	Bedford
11,958	Sims, Mary S.	Rutherford
5,523	Sinclair, Henry C.	Williamson
20,149	Sinnott, Della C. & Wooldridge, Adine	Shelby
20,622	Sisk, Dan J.	Franklin
8,447	Sivels, Jephta	McMinn
18,818	Sively, Thos. Jefferson, Estate of	Hamilton
4,224: 10,143:	Skeen, Moses	Jefferson
12,894	Skelton, Alex	Hawkins
15,827	Slagle, Wm.	Knox
12,158	Slaton, Thos.	Jefferson
20,805	Sloan, James	Dickson
960	Small, George	Lincoln
19,749	Smallman, David T.	Hamblin
13,221	Smallin, Jefferson	Monroe
17,196	Samlling, Duke W.	Washington
17,783	Smallwood, Churchwell B.	McNairy
4,535	Smith, A. H.	Carroll
16,513	Smith, Allen K., Estate of	Hamilton
6,434	Smith, Annie	Rutherford
5,115	Smith, Charles	White
10,116	Smith, Charles C.	Grainger
16,497	Smith, Dan C., Estate of	Hamilton
16,495	Smith, David	Hamilton
16,377	Smith, Francis J.	Maury

12,587	Smith, Frederick	Davidson
7,008	Smith, G. W.	Roane
18,364	Smith, G. W.	Rutherford
10,487	Smith, Geo.	Hamblen
18,816	Smith, Geo. F.	Marion
6,906	Smith, Green & Leanah	Rutherford
10,227	Smith, Hannah	Franklin
5,648	Smith, Henry	Sumner
2,834	Smith, Henry S.	Sevier
18,984	Smith, Isaac	Bradley
959	Smith, Isom	Lincoln
17,431	Smith, James A.	Hamilton
20,448	Smith, John	Bradley
2,695	Smith, John A.	Henderson
19,553	Smith, John A.	Union
17,964	Smith, John H. & Rebecca A.	Bradley
14,052	Smith, John T.	Washington
2,696	Smith, John W.	Carroll
17,087	Smith, John Y., Estate of	Roane
15,322	Smith, Joseph F.	Davidson
15,155	Smith, Joseph H.	Haywood
12,855	Smith, Joshua	Hawkins
6,906	Smith, Leanah & Green	Rutherford
2,782	Smith, Lucy	Davidson
2,888	Smith, Margaret E.	Loudon
14,053	Smith, Mary	Washington
10,808	Smith, Musadora A., Mrs.	Lincoln
17,264	Smith, Nathaniel	Greene
11,283	Smith, Neil A.	Madison
10,308	Smith, Peter	Hamblen
17,964	Smith, Rebecca A. & John H.	Bradley
10,706	Smith, Robert	Madison
17,551	Smith, Robert F.	Bedford
10,479	Smith, Sam	Hamblen
12,864	Smith, Thomas	Hawkins
16,252	Smith, Thos., Sr.	Marion
5,559	Smith, Thos. A.	Henderson
4,536	Smith, Thos. J.	Carroll
16,253	Smith, Thos. M.	Marion
12,854	Smith, Wade H.	Hawkins
11,897	Smith, Wm. M.	Maury
21,646	Smith, Wm. M.	Monroe
10,806	Smith, Wm. P.	Lincoln
11,256	Smith, Wm. T.	Knox
20,377	Smith, Zack	Giles
13,711	Smithson, John G., Sr.	Giles
17,803	Smithson, John S.	McNairy
16,962	Snapp, Wendell D.	Washington
12,739	Snead, Wm. H.	Shelby
2,694	Sneed, John	Carroll
5,973	Snider, Dan, Jr.	Monroe
19,646	Snider, James M.	Monroe
16,494	Sniteman, Christian	Hamilton
12,155	Snodgrass, Allen W.	Hamblen
21,980	Snodgrass, James	Jefferson
21,157	Snodgrass, Wm. H.	Jefferson
22,273	Snoffard, Aaron	Bledsoe
6,931	Somerville, Helen R.	Tipton
11,993	Somerville, Joseph B.	Haywood
3,464	Somerville, Thos. T.	Tipton
21,865	Soper, James	Sumner
19,969	Southern, Wm. F.	Shelby
10,750	Sovern, Susan	Giles
10,766	Spah, Fedel	Madison
13,990	Spahr, Aaron M.	Sullivan
17,972	Spain, Ann	Davidson
13,880	Sparks, A. L.	Loudon
2,693	Sparks, Isaac	Carroll
9,012	Speed, Joseph F.	Haywood
1,568	Spellings, J. M.	Carroll
1,569	Spellings, W. J. C.	Gibson
8,666	Spencer, C.	Haywood
13,766	Spencer, Wm.	Hardin
15,922	Spitzer, Henry H.	Knox
16,696	Spivey, Holloday	Hamilton
1,573	Springer, Hosea	Carroll
15,857	Sprolls, Elizabeth	Sullivan
15,273	Sprolls, Jonathan	Sullivan
13,867	Squibb, John	Greene
21,317	Staggs, James, Estate of	Sumner

19,300	Staggs, Thos.	Sumner
10,287	Stailey, Sarah Ann	Shelby
5,449	Stakeley, Abraham	Monroe
7,346	Stakeley, John C.	Monroe
8,239	Stamps, Asa L.	Bedford
12,137	Stamps, D. B.	Franklin
2,094	Stamps, Dan	Haywood
16,826	Standefer, Isaiah	Claiborne
19,936	Standefer, Joseph	Claiborne
12,712	Staples, B. F., Estate of	Morgan
17,055	Staples, Michael A.	Roane
8,022: 11,521: 22,054:	Staples, Millia	Morgan
17,373	Stakey, Frederick A.	Coffee
12,870	Starnes, John E.	Hawkins
10,843	Steed, Collier, A.	McNairy
19,546	Steele, Abner A.	Marshall
14,639	Steele, Sam	Greene
19,709	Steele, Wm. A.	Rhea
17,854	Stephen, David H.	Monroe
17,761	Stephens, Andrew	Franklin
5,348	Stephens, Henry	Monroe
11,705	Stephens, James G.	Scott
8,057	Stephens, John	Cumberland
14,996	Stephenson, A. W.	Gibson
21,961	Stephenson, Sarah A.	Maury
18,735	Sterling, Michael C.	Blount
18,004: 18,735:	Sterling, Michael C.	Knox
5,708	Stevens, Martha A.	Davidson
9,858	Stevens, Tarah H.	Polk
6,399	Stevens, Thos.	Cumberland
6,149	Stevenson, Wm. J.	Fayette
15,775	Stevenson, Wm. W.	Bradley
8,904	Stewart, Calvin E., Estate of	Fayette
1,572	Stewart, James	Gibson
1,276	Stewart, James	Shelby
6,127	Stewart, Joseph T.	Polk
8,350	Stewart, Robert	Fentress
10,377	Still, Wm. F.	Madison
12,031	Stine, Abraham	Sullivan
12,936	Stockbridge, Mary C.	Greene
5,395	Stockley, Lucy J.	Shelby
13,056	Stokes, John M.	Bedford
18,105	Stone, Benj. J., Estate of	McMinn
19,772	Stone, Hendley	Hardeman
956	Stone, Jeff M.	Lincoln
19,814	Stone, John L.	Sequatchie
21,720	Stone, Michael H.	Grainger
4,711	Stone, Oliver P.	Knox
7,192	Stone, Robert	Claiborne
7,907	Stones, W. E., Mrs.	Davidson
1,892	Stone, Wiley F.	Marshall
15,433	Stone, Wm., Estate of	James
19,774	Stone, Wm. H., Estate of	Hardeman
17,545	Story, Ann Bell	Bedford
1,574	Story, Catharine T.	Henderson
20,428	Story, Rebecca J.	Bedford
17,375	Stout, Josiah	Shelby
12,115	Stovall, Ancell M.	Franklin
7,525	Stovall, H. D.	Obion
7,524	Stowe, L. C.	Weakley
21,367	Strain, Thos. D.	Shelby
14,054	Strain, W. I.	Washington
16,965	Strain, Wm. S.	Washington
8,077	Strange, Edmund	Tipton
1,274	Street, Pork	Williamson
12,810	Streeter, James	Shelby
14,183	Stringfellow, Wm.	Hardeman
17,644	Strong, Francis M.	Bedford
20,380	Stroud, Thos.	Grainger
14,519	Stublefield, Wyatt	Hamblen & Jeff.
11,213	Stull, Geo. T.	Fayette
18,855	Sturm, Frederick	Sullivan
21,529	Sublett, John F.	Franklin
17,980	Sublett, Newton	Rutherford
10,547	Sullivan, John	Giles

10,824	Summner, Wm.	Morgan
12,492	Summers, B. P.	Houston
18,151	Summers, James P.	Grundy
20,051	Summers, Walter W.	Bedford
12,711	Summers, Wm.	Morgan
17,702	Summers, Wm. F.	Sumner
5,975	Summit, Joseph	Monroe
6,430	Sumner, Wm.	Davidson
18,847	Sutton, Calvin, Estate of	Bradley
21,891	Sutton, John W.	Sevier
15,639	Sutton, Wesley	Bedford
5,349	Sutton, Wm.	Monroe
16,973	Swagerty, Wm. R.	Cocke
17,779	Swain, Mary M. C.	McNairy
15,167	Swan, Andrew H. & D. P.	Knox
15,167	Swan, D. P. & Andrew H.	Knox
14,726	Swann, Edward D.	Franklin
14,907	Swann, John C.	Jefferson
9,550	Swanson, Richard, Sr.	Williamson
4,774	Sweat, Isaiah	McNairy
17,773	Sweat, Terrell	McNairy
6,767	Sweeney, Pyrene C.	Davidson
21,531	Sweeton, Mary E.	Franklin
20,008	Swift, Eliza A.	Fayette
17,860	Swing, G. W.	Bedford
18,905	Swing, Jacob H.	Bedford
4,380	Sykes, Henry O.	Fayette
18,175	Tacker, Thos. M.	McNairy
13,318	Taffe, Irwin H.	Shelby
16,817	Talbert, Wm. T.	Cannon
21,905	Talbott, John	Jefferson
21,906	Talbott, Ross, Estate of	Jefferson
13,434	Talen, Aaron P.	Knox
5,560	Talent, James	Blount
13,421	Tallent, John	Blount
15,437	Tallent, Wily B.	James
10,677	Talley, Benj. F.	Gibson
14,640	Talley, James	Hamblen
13,636	Talley, Nancy	Hardin
8,176	Talley, Robert	Shelby
16,746	Talley, Shadrack	Greene
19,849	Tally, Wm.	Hamilton
8,058	Tanner, James M.	Cumberland
2,357	Tapp, Isaac	Claiborne
10,213	Tarpy, Thomas	Humphreys
20,379	Tate, David N.	Grainger
22,187	Tate, James	Coffee
11,221	Tate, Mary I.	Jefferson
18,588	Tate, Washington	Coffee
11,336	Tatum, Sion	McNairy
10,225	Taylor, Abner, Estate of	Madison
19,307	Taylor, Allen	Sumner
13,830	Taylor, Benj. B.	Rutherford
19,645	Taylor, Cleveland B.	Monroe
14,122	Taylor, Caswell C.	Carter
12,844	Taylor, Geo. M.	Hawkins
4,381	Taylor, Henry L.	Lincoln
9,477	Taylor, Hugh B.	Gibson
11,079	Taylor, James H., Sr.	Giles
15,578	Taylor, James P.	Monroe
15,574	Taylor, James P.	Sumner
12,140	Taylor, John H.	Davidson
8,496	Taylor, John L.	Madison
11,693	Taylor, Jonathan	Weakley
16,635	Taylor, Martha W.	Tipton
21,261	Taylor, Wm. H.	Washington
5,561	Teague, Evan L.	Henderson
4,537	Teague, James A.	Henderson
2,697	Teague, Jasper N.	Henderson
2,698	Teague, Lander A.	Henderson
17,790	Tedford, James M.	McNairy
14,055	Telford, G. W.	Washington
13,535	Temple, Hartwell	Madison
19,328	Temple, Jordan	Blount
18,906	Temple, Leonard A., Estate of	Bedford
22,104	Templeton, John	Hawkins
15,863	Tenery, John E.	Giles
5,562	Terrill, A. T.	Henderson
16,097	Terry, James C.	Davidson

19,857	Terry, James C. (of Coahoma Co., MS) and Carnes, James A., Estate of	Shelby
10,807	Terry, James D.	Marshall
8,752	Terry, Wm.	McMinn
7,527	Test, Benj. F.	Haywood
19,263	Thacker, James L.	Loudon
13,774	Thacker, Shepherd	Hardin
12,839	Thomas, Aaron	Sevier
15,772	Thomas, Adam	Bradley
10,223	Thomas, Archibald R.	Madison
9,681	Thomas, Berkeley Reed	Shelby
18,814	Thomas, Bird	Hamilton
17,866	Thomas, Burton	Rutherford
17,568	Thomas, Cooper	McMinn
6,593	Thomas, Elam F.	Fayette
4,538	Thomas, Elizabeth	Carroll
17,778	Thompson, Ephraim	McNairy
21,039	Thomas, Henry M., Estate of	Sevier
16,688	Thomas, Jeremiah N.	Sevier
9,070	Thomas, John F.	Coffee
10,666	Thomas, John H.	Henderson
5,516	Thomas, Mary A. & Wm.	Maury
8,382	Thomas, Richard G.	Haywood
13,513	Thomas, Shadrack	Haywood
15,548	Thomas, Wilkin	Shelby
5,516	Thomas, Wm. & Mary A.	Maury
14,239	Thomas, Wm. S.	Carter
19,260	Thomason, Joel	Loudon
18,575	Thomason, John Scott	Loudon
4,261	Thomason, John W.	Monroe
13,420: 19,321:	Thompson, Amos	Blount
13,013	Thompson, Ann, Estate of	Rutherford
1,251	Thompson, Annie B.	Shelby
10,491	Thompson, Archibald	Hamblen
14,567	Thompson, Catharine	Grundy
15,088	Thompson, Frederick A.	Maury
15,773	Thompson, Gideon B.	Bradley
21,756	Thompson, Gideon D.	Roane
13,451	Thompson, Harvy	Loudon
16,598	Thompson, James A.	Bedford
18,007	Thompson, James P.	Warren
16,384	Thompson, John J. A.	Knox
18,005	Thompson, Joseph R.	Rutherford
13,054	Thompson, Mary	Jefferson
18,247	Thompson, Newcome, 2d	Bedford
18,712	Thompson, Robert L.	Blount
22,258	Thompson, Sarah E.	Washington
27	Thompson, Waddy	Shelby
15,053	Thornburgh, Ai (sic)	Jefferson
14,520	Thornburgh, Benj. C.	Jefferson
15,041	Thornburgh, O. A.	Jefferson
12,876	Thornburgh, Sam	Jefferson
10,508	Thurman, Calvin Y.	Polk
1,531	Thurman, E. C., Estate of	Carroll
5,563	Threadgill, Allen J.	Henderson
18,262	Thurman, Oliver M.	Warren
20,274	Thurston, Phineas	Loudon
11,076	Thweatt, Richard H.	Giles
10,352	Tilford, Ann T.	Rutherford
4,207	Tilghmon, Thos. O.	Wilson
18,394	Tillery, Thos. P., Estate of	Meigs
2,835	Tinsley, Brackin	Sevier
4,148	Tipton, A. J.	Carter
15,579	Tipton, Jacob J.	Monroe
21,879	Tipton, John B.	Loudon
8,080	Tisdale, Lewellen T.	Tipton
10,908	Tittsworth, Charlotte	Jefferson
10,474	Tittsworth, James O.	Jefferson
6,613	Tittsworth, John B.	Sullivan
7,453	Tompkins, James T., Estate of	Wilson
10,759	Tonget, T. R. C.	Giles
5,033	Toof, Elizabeth	Shelby
14,589	Torbert, Andrew W., Estate of	Monroe
1,575	Tosh, L. M.	Carroll

5,363	Townely, James B.	Monroe
20,148	Townsend, Peter	Shelby
7,356	Townson, Joseph	Giles
7,848	Travis, Ephraim	Jefferson
14,568	Travis, Mary A.	Grundy
12,768	Traylor, Hilas F.	Rutherford
21,864	Traynor, Richard	Davidson
15,575	Trent, E. A.	Davidson
7,193	Trent, Wm. G.	Grainger
7,526	Trevillian, Thos. C.	Weakley
18,144	Trew, Thos. H.	Loudon
14,133	Trice, Allie A.	Montgomery
12,449	Trigg, Joseph W.	Franklin
19,757	Trigg, L. A. T., Mrs.	Rutherford
17,958	Trim, Anderson	Bradley
12,282	Trotter, Isham A.	Shelby
13,348	Trotter, James T.	Sevier
13,346	Trotter, John A.	Sevier
13,347	Trotter, Wm. H.	Sevier
8,911	Tuck, Elizabeth	Loudon
6,151	Tucker, Edward J.	Fayette
7,371	Tucker, James	Fayette
15,135	Tucker, Lizzie F.	Fayette
17,546	Tucker, Needham C.	Bedford
19,012	Tucker, Wiley	Bradley
13,415	Tullock, John M.	Blount
20,196	Turner, Ann Eliza	Fayette
20,194	Turner, Henrietta Y.	Fayette
8,166	Turner, John	Jefferson
17,145	Turner, Madison	Rutherford
7,845	Turner, Ransom B. & Wilmarth E.	Wilson
17,776	Turner, Wm. M.	McNairy
1,003	Turner, Wm. P. H.	Lawrence
8,429	Twohig, Patrick	Shelby
3,249	Tyer, Mitchell	Montgomery
19,921	Underdown, Gilbert W.	Knox
21,048	Underwood, James	Sevier
18,392	Underwood, Nimrod	Roane
9,717	Underwood, Thos.	Sevier
10,752	Urban, Henry M.	Giles
9,478	Utlers, Alex	Gibson
17,244	Vallentine, Ellick	Rutherford
14,710	Van Buren, Martha O.	Shelby
5,103	Vance, E. R.	Wilson
10,015	Vance, James	Jefferson
16,234	Vance, James H.	Sullivan
14,521	Vance, John, Estate of	Jefferson
10,011	Vance, Sam, Estate of	Jefferson
5,564	Vancleave, Jasper N.	Carroll
2,261	Vandergriff, Joseph	Hamilton
19,231	Vandergriff, Mahala	Hamilton
6,721	Vandergriss, James	Grainger
12,224	Vandike, Henry	Jefferson
14,905	Vanhook, John R.	Dickson
14,641	Van Huss, Wm.	Hamblen
17,852	Van Pelt, John E.	Fayette
12,236	Vantreese, Wm.	Madison
12,164	Vanwhoser, Sam	Jefferson
15,054	Varnell, Josiah	Sevier
17,432	Varner, Allen	Hamilton
4,438	Varner, Dan	Loudon
17,433	Varner, Geo.	Hamilton
15,585	Varner, Madison	Hamilton
11,753	Vaughan, Adaline	Davidson
21,738	Vaughan, H. L.	Sumner
21,532	Vaughan, Sidney S. P.	Franklin
11,502: 14,380:	Vaughan, Turner	Wilson
18,829	Vaughn, John	Hamilton
15,637	Vaughn, Robert Y.	McMinn
14,569	Vaughn, Sarah	Grundy
18,176	Veal, Thos.	McNairy
12,850	Venerable, Dan	Hawkins
7,528	Verhine, E. H.	Obion
2,199	Vermillion, Isaac N.	Claiborne
14,123	Vestal, C. M.	Greene
21,919	Vester, James M.	Davidson
5,854	Vester, Wm.	Davidson

7,529	Vincent, J. E.	Weakley
10,106	Vineyard, G. B.	Grainger
10,112	Vineyard, Jacob	Grainger
13,878	Voorhies, Garrett D.	Maury
17,061	Waddell, David W.	Washington
2,158: 17,059:	Waddell, Sam D.	Washington
17,658	Wade, Levi	Ruth
2,095	Wade, Wm. E.	Gibson
1,354	Waggoner, Cornelius	Davidson
1,355	Waggoner, H. B.	Davidson
5,679	Waggoner, Wilkins W.	Benton
9,093	Wair, Wm. K.	Davidson
8,928	Waite, Thompson	Hardin
12,443	Wakefield, Joseph N.	Franklin
14,393	Wakefield, Thos. J.	Macon
9,667	Walker, C. E.	Monroe
2,837	Walker, Charles	Knox
4,540	Walker, E. W.	Henderson
8,140	Walker, Eli	Jefferson
17,202	Walker, H. O.	Loudon
18,346	Walker, Haywood	Shelby
10,966	Walker, Henry	Hamblen
13,978	Walker, Henry J.	Williamson
9,064	Walker, James G.	Grainger
19,701	Walker, John P.	Rhea
13,057	Walker, Joseph	Bedford
3,643	Walker, Lawrence W.	Sumner
18,168	Walker, Samuel	Blount
21,300	Walker, Sarah M.	Sevier
22,260	Walker, Thos.	Hamblen
21,883	Walker, Thos.	McMinn
21,889	Walker, Thos.	Sevier
22,179	Walker, Thos., Estate of	Grainger
10,099	Walker, Winton N.	Hamblen
15,950	Wallace, Ethelbert S.	Sumner
19,297	Wallace, Harbert	Sumner
16,593	Wallace, James E.	Bedford
14,743	Wallace, Joseph	Putnam
10,108	Wallace, Riley	Grainger
19,687	Wallace, Sam, Jr.	Monroe
19,687	Wallace, Sam, Jr.	Sumner
9,058	Wallace, Wm.	Hawkins
18,352	Wallace, Wm. H.	Shelby
17,695	Wallace, Wm. H.	Sumner
12,757	Waller, Amanda T.	Fayette
11,578	Walsh, James H.	Hamblen
3,419	Walt, R. P.	Shelby
5,076	Walters, Israel	Grainger
14,056	Walters, John	Washington
19,025	Walters, Laban L.	Williamson
12,586	Walton, Timothy	Davidson
11,345	Ward, James	Rutherford
10,654	Ward, John J.	Obion
5,396	Ware, Jane E.	Haywood
9,143	Ware, John D.	Haywood
7,874	Warenell, Charles	Grainger
1,782	Warfield, Thos., Estate of and Anderson, James	Wayne
3,032	Warner, Terisa	Davidson
9,144	Warren, John T. & Peyton S.	Gibson
10,236	Warren, Sam	Franklin
6,567	Washburn, West H.	Humphreys
7,731	Wasson, Richard F.	Rutherford
6,907	Waterman, Nelson	Rutherford
19,744	Watkins, John M.	Jefferson
15,438	Watkins, Mary & Robert	James
15,438	Watkins, Robert & Mary	James
17,995	Watkins, Sam B.	Rutherford
15,732	Watkins, Sam S.	James
7,045	Watson, Goodwin	Grainger
1,577	Watson, John G.	Henderson
17,436	Watson, John M.	Hamilton
9,260	Watson, Nimrod W.	Hardin
20,813	Watson, Sam	Shelby
15,566	Watson, Thos. S.	Sumner
7,919	Watson, Wm. K,	Jefferson
12,863	Watterson, Calvin	Hawkins
12,878	Waugh, Albert A.	Jefferson
4,539	Waugh, James W.	Carroll

13,429	Wayland, Felix G.	Blount
18,599	Wayland, Felix G.	Knox
13,484	Wayman, Charles	Loudon
15,733	Weas, Michael, Estate of	Hamilton
10,704	Weatherly, James M.	Madison
21,269	Weatherly, Robert	McNairy
15,361	Webb, Benj.	Sullivan
10,760	Webb, Henry	Giles
21,021	Webb, James C.	Davidson
12,759	Webb, James E.	Rutherford
7,915	Webb, James G.	Davidson
2,096	Webb, James W.	Gibson
19,644	Webb, John R.	Monroe
13,499	Webb, Wm.	Monroe
19,640	Webb, Wm. R.	Monroe
16,815	Webster, Cleveland & Robt. P.	Bedford
12,061	Webster, Cyrus & Chafin, Thorton	Maury
6,428	Webster, Margaret R.	Maury
17,793	Webster, Nancy	McNairy
16,815	Webster, Robert P. & Cleveland	Bedford
14,440	Weddington, Clemmontine	Franklin
21,283	Weir, Beverly	Bradley
15,168	Weisgerber, Jacob	Knox
9,479	Welch, Henry A.	Madison
10,100	Wellborn, A. C.	Shelby
15,791	Wellford, Elizabeth H. & Jackson, Jane H. T. (of Mississippi)	Shelby
20,193	Wells, Dan J.	Hardeman
17,085	Wendel, Aaron	Rutherford
6,761	West, John, Estate of	Madison
13,376	West, John J.	Loudon
21,712	West, John N.	Grainger
21,711	West, Sam	Grainger
19,545	West, Sam A., Estate of	Giles
21,708	West, Wm. C.	Grainger
7,984	Westar, Elias	Grainger
7,886	Wester, James L.	Grainger
20,384	Wester, Wm. C.	Grainger
14,642	Western, Pleasant	Hamblen
1,578	Wheeler, J. A.	Gibson
16,591	Wheeler, Jesse M., Estate of	Bedford
9,971	Wheless, Susan A.	Davidson
16,332	Wherry, John J.	Sumner
15,622	Whitaker, John H.	Putnam
7,354	White, Carr B.	Giles
14,570	White, Catharine	Grundy
18,795	White, Charles T.	Grundy
566	White, Clark C.	Shelby
8,667	White, Elbert A.	Shelby
12,845: 12,874:	White, James	Hawkins
21,913	White, James, Estate of	Washington
8,485	White, James M.	Shelby
19,015	White, M. A.	Bradley
10,909	White, Mahlon	Hawkins
11,956	White, Martha	Monroe
19,454	White, Meady, & Davy, Jehu L.	Hardin
4,541	White, D. P.	Henderson
19,727	White, Richard	Rutherford
10,471	White, Sam M.	Hamblen
7,359	White, Sanford M.	Giles
8,358	White, Sarah L.	Humphreys
21,909	White, Stephen	Grainger
15,800	White, Thomas C., Mrs.	Giles
12,875	White, Wm.	Hawkins
15,707	White, Wm.	McMinn
8,375	White, Wm. C., Estate of	Giles
5,011	White, Wm. H.	Obion
7,361	White, Wm. R.	Giles
1,581	Whitehorn, Joseph N.	Carroll
13,374	Whitlock, Sherwood	Loudon
14,237	Whitsett, Nancy A.	Hardin
8,995	Whittemore, Wm. B.	Davidson
19,775	Whitten, James M.	Hardeman
19,475	Whitworth, Ezekiel	Madison
714	Wiatt, Benj.	Monroe
2,831	Widner, Jacob	Sevier

4,511	Wiggans, Elijah	Monroe
15,858	Wiggin, Norris J.	Shelby
12,907	Wiggs, Martin H.	Madison
1,579	Wilder, China	Carroll
12,059	Wiley, Addie	Maury
21,533	Wiley, Thos. A.	
19,190	Wilhite, Wm. M.	Knox
12,835	Wilhoite, Wm.	Knox
21,657	Wilkerson, Caesar	Rutherford
14,875	Wilkerson, G. W.	Franklin
14,441	Wilkerson, Thos.	Coffee
11,225	Wilkes, Amelia	Maury
8,082	Wilkins, Washington	Tipton
15,620	Wilkinson, Cassandra	Rutherford
21,921	Willard, E. A.	Sullivan
13,983	Williams, Alfred O.	Lawrence
8,177	Williams, David P.	Haywood
18,791	Williams, Elijah S.	Loudon
14,129	Williams, John S.	Maury
17,800	Williams, Gaston D.	McNairy
21,931	Williams, Gideon J.	Shelby
21,320	Williams, Green B.	Sumner
19,197	Williams, Harvey S., Estate	Franklin
22,262	Williams, James S.	Williamson
10,135	Williams, James W.	Obion
4,395	Williams, John	Giles
15,482	Williams, Joseph J.	Dockson
16,470	Williams, Joseph R.	Shelby
14,124	Williams, Nathan T.	Washington
21,866	Williams, O. D., Estate of	DeKalb
5,843	Williams, Powell W.	Shelby
1,580	Williams, Robert C.	Carroll
11,746	Williams, Roland D.	Hickman
21,154	Williams, Sam	Hamilton
11,686	Williams, Samson B.	DeKalb
6,403	Williams, Samuel	DeKalb
22,069	Williams, Silas H.	Claiborne
22,189	Williams, Susan S.	Davidson
2,699	Williams, Thos. P.	Carroll
11,275	Williamson, Anthony	Madison
12,827	Williamson, Geo. S.	Wilson
8,849	Williamson, James M. & Mrs. James M.	Shelby
10,746	Williamson, Joseph	Giles
17,635	Williamson, Lewis T.	Madison
16,685	Willing, Geo.	Hamblen
1,675	Willingham, Thomas J.	Haywood
18,266	Willis, Wm. W.	Haywood
13,767	Willoughby, James G.	Hardin
14,109	Willoughby, John, Estate of	Greene
19,078	Willoughby, M. W. A.	Sullivan
19,686	Wilson, Alex H.	Bradley
10,804	Wilson, Alfred	Giles
1,582	Wilson, David	Henderson
17,397	Wilson, David W.	Meigs
716	Wilson, Frank	Giles
10,623	Wilson, Grandison	Giles
1,583	Wilson, Henry T.	Henderson
17,588	Wilson, Hezekiah	McNairy
13,380	Wilson, John	Loudon
18,236	Wilson, Oscar	Blount
9,126	Wilson, Richard	Monroe
15,421	Wilson, Wm. C.	James
11,278	Wilson, Wm. D.	Madison
11,698	Wilson, Wm. T.	Weakley
5,397	Winborne, Margaret L.	Fayette
18,486	Windham, Margaret	Sumner
20,739	Winkler, Abraham	Bradley
15,244	Winn, K. J. B. L.	Shelby
12,627: 13,868:	Winslow, Robert B.	Greene
17,435	Winters, James	Hamilton
19,729	Winton, James Jr.	Grundy
11,136	Wise, Wm. D.	Haywood
14,442	Wiseman, Joseph M.	Franklin
12,203	Wiseman, Wilson D.	Franklin
16,747: 19,380:	Witt, James	James
14,255	Witt, Mary I.	Jefferson
15,440	Witt, Nat	Meigs

10,286	Witt, Wm. R., Estate of	Polk
10,103	Wolfenbarger, Peter	Union
22,261	Wood, Geo. K., Estate of	Carroll
8,460	Wood, Eliza	Sullivan
17,064	Wood, Eliza	Washington
10,033	Wood, George & Wm. H.	Shelby
3,405	Wood, J. E.	Gibson
19,422	Wood, James	McMinn
6,908	Wood, John	McNairy
17,396	Wood, Sam O.	Meigs
10,915	Wood, Wm.	Jefferson
19,601	Wood, Wm. H.	Shelby
10,033	Wood, Wm. H. & George	Shelby
11,085	Wood, Wm. J.	Wilson
16,586	Wood, Wm. P.	Giles
15,868	Woodard, Benj.	Cheatham
13,932	Woodrough, Hall	Rutherford
9,071	Woodruff, Geo. G.	Coffee
8,183	Woods, Andrew J.	Jefferson
4,058	Woods, Montgomery	Hawkins
21,042	Woodside, Joseph	Maury
20,149	Wooldridge, Adine; and Sinnott, Della C.	Shelby
1,585	Woolen, A. T. M.	Carroll
14,132	Woolfolk, Julia C.	Madison
14,571	Wooten, Thos.	Grundy
18,248	Word, Edmund	Bedford
19,372	Word, Wm. H.	Bedford
17,107	Workman, Andrew M.	Washington
10,635	Worsham, Columbus C.	
2,934	Worthington, Hugh	Davidson
5,977	Worthy, George	Monroe
5,978	Worthy, J. H.	Monroe
5,317	Wray, Willis B.	Williamson
18,779	Wright, Demarcus L.	Morgan
16,974	Wright, John	Hamblen
12,873	Wright, John	Hawkins
11,998	Wright, John Franklin	Dickson
5,903	Wright, Mary	Maury
1,584	Wright, P. G.	Carroll
18,506	Wright, Paul Thompson	Shelby
4,057	Wright, Sarah	Davidson
5,505	Wright, Thos.	Henderson
10,486	Wright, Wm.	Hamblen
20,885	Wyant, Benj. F.	Shelby
16,616	Wyatt, Addison	Sullivan
15,543	Wyley, James J.	Humphreys
10,742	Wyninger, John	Giles
20,453	Wyrick, Sam	Bradley
21,256	Yancey, Martha L.	Shelby
10,638	Yancy, Edward G.	Giles
9,480	Yancy, Edwin T.	Fayette
17,039	Yandell, Eliza B.	Fayette
16,141	Yarborough, James H., and Robertson, W. D.	Davidson
17,305	Yarbrough, Sam	Humphreys
1,004: 16,885:	Yarnell, Dan	Hamilton & James
1,576	Yates, Allcey	Gibson
3,383	Ycuff, Wm.	Loudon
5,343	Yearwood, Thos.	Monroe
9,094	Yell, Francis M.	Coffee
20,526	Yett, John C.	Sevier
6,639	Yoakum, Aaron	Claiborne
6,640	Yoakum, George	Claiborne
19,924	Yoe, Pryor F.	Jefferson
13,991	Yost, Wm. K.	Sullivan
16,828	Young, Asa B.	Monroe
4,542	Young, B. J.	Henderson
14,125	Young, Catharine	Greene
17,198	Young, Strobridge	Washington
17,552	Young, Wm.	Bedford
19,320	Young, Wm.	Blount
7,351	Young, Wm. Conn	Monroe
13,418	Young, Wm. H.	Blount
10,121	Zachery, Gilbert	Grainger
12,344	Zerkel, Reuben	Jefferson
19,377	Zigler, Jacob, Estate of	Meigs
9,438	Zobrist, Barnhard	Morgan

TEXAS

2,425	Alexander, Esther	Walker
17,495	Barnett, John A.	Navarro
4,270	Bauer, Catharine	Calhoun
16,139	Brackenridge, Mary E. & Matthews, Leonora H.	Bexar
18,917	Braman, Don Egbert Erastus	Matagorda
12,685	Brown, Alex P.	Marion
1,430	Brown, Artemas H.	Cameron
4,271	Brown, James H.	Calhoun
10,496	Brown, Leander	Travis
19,930	Browne, James G.	Cameron
21,787	Bryant, Wm.	Dallas
21,624	Busick, Thos. C.	Bowie
12,964	Butler, Pauline V.	Cameron
21,743	Cain, Caroline A.	Smith
10,000	Catchings, Augustus	Kaufman
12,965	Champion, Nicholas	Cameron
17,634	Clark, Geo. M.	Hunt
12,358	Cleveland, Philemon	Matagorda
19,931	Cummings, Franklin & Mary M	Cameron
19,931	Cummings, Mary M & Franklin	Cameron
14,805	DuBois, Lucas	Calhoun
19,243	Dycus, Green B.	Galveston
18,351	Dyer, Alfred A.	Smith
13,325	English, Benj.	Lampasas
14,262	Erwin, Isaac	Tarrant
1,055	Flanagan, J. W.	Rusk
12,968	Garza, Ramijeo	Cameron
2,256	Gaudet, A.	Cameron
15,464	Giton, Elisha	Cameron
951	Guilbeau, Francis	Bexar
4,114	Halfin, Henry	Victoria
4,545	Harrison, Martha E.	Calhoun
11,237	Harrison, Thos.	Nueces
4,639	Hiller, Adam	Victoria
16,723	Hilliard, Z. W.	Shelby
2,268	Hogan, Wm.	Calhoun
14,356	Horst, Louis	Travis
2,016	Jenschke, August	Galveston
9,172	Johannes, Michael	Calhoun
11,688	Johnson, Ann O., Sam & Sidney	Calhoun
11,688	Johnson, Sidney	Bexar
14,263	Jones, Thomas	Denton
21,010	Lamon, G. W.	Burnet
12,963	Langdon, Sarah Ann	Cameron
1,742	Levi, Abraham	Victoria
11,238	Ley, Vallentine	Calhoun
13,637	Liveley, Charles S. & Mary B.	Nueces
14,366	Lockwood, Sylvester	Travis
21,254	Matthews, Elijah Doyel	Bowie
16,139	Matthews, Leonora H. & Brackenridge, Mary E.	Jackson
13,169	McCall, Altazara	Humt
948	McDonald, John	Calhoun
12,035	Menley, Margaret R.	Nueces
2,269	Merriman, Amos L.	Calhoun
14,810	Miller, Henry	Cameron
14,988	Miller, Richard	Duval
14,806	Morgan, Geo. A.	Calhoun
8,654	Morris, John, Estate of	Matagorda
4,129	Nickelson, J. L.	Victoria
12,966	Parisot, P. F.	Cameron
11,236	Peres, Jose A. & Rogers, Wm. L.	Nueces
7,905	Philip, John P.	Matagorda
1,435	Philips, Wm. C.	Travis
14,584	Plummer, Goen W.	Jefferson
8,902	Priest, Alvin C.	Nueces
3,235	Purnell, Mary E.	Marion
1,288	Rahn, Adam	Calhoun
4,139	Rapley, Wm.	Victoria
4,273	Rehner, Benedict	Calhoun
21,374	Riordan, Ellen	Kinney
11,236	Rogers, Wm. L. & Peres, Jose A.	Nueces
17,719	Ross, Newton J.	Hunt
15,656	Rouff, Lion	Calhoun
13,514	Saens, Antonio	Starr
1,743	Schuhmann, Valentine	Victoria
17,757	Scott, Hubert P.	Lamar
12,657	Shaffer, John H.	Cameron
14,685	Smith, Henry C.	Jefferson
12,967	Solis, Francisco	Cameron
4,275	Steinberg, Louisa	Calhoun
13,313	Sterling, Wm. H.	Matagorda
12,934	Stone, Henry L.	Nueces
4,274	Straube, Anton	Calhoun
17,633	Stroope, Elizabeth	Hunt
2,944	Vance, John	Medina
4,382	Volk, G. W.	Calhoun
949	Wagner, August	Calhoun
12,223	Wallace, Willis R.	Travis
7,906	Wilkins, Henry	Calhoun
20,315	Woodward, Horatio	Grimes
4,575	Zeigler, Jacob	Nueces
16,724	Zipprian, Wilhemina	Matagorda

VIRGINIA

14,702	Abbott, James, Estate of	Craig
7,323	Abbott, Wesley M.	Halifax
7,659	ABBOTT, W. K.	Rockingham
20,183	Abdell, George D.	Accomack
11,026	Abel, George F.	Loudoun
14,606	Ackiss, Harper, Estate of	Princess Anne
11,235	Acord, Andrew J.	Augusta
11,479	Adams, David C.	Loudoun
3,432	Adams, Feletia	Fauquier
2,903	Adams, Francis	Henrico
3	Adams, Geo. R.	Alexandria
183	Adams, Hiram	Frederick
21,603	Adams, James	Loudoun
2,902	Adams, Joseph	Hanover
15,241	Adams, Robert H.	Prince George
15,884	Adams, Wm. H. (Morrisonville)	Loudoun
21,600	Adams, Wm. H. (Mt. Gilead)	Loudoun
16,645	Adkins, Spottswell	Charles City
20,780	Ager, James B., Estate of	Alexandria
6,526	Agner, Andrew	Rockbridge
4,622	Agner, John	Rockbridge
13,783	Airington, Andrew & Mary M.	Alleghany
13,783	Airington, Mary M. & Andrew	Alleghany
14,626	Aistrop, Andrew J.	Washington
4,603	Akers, Osker	Washington
3,798	Akin, Albert M.	Henrico
20,802	Albermarle & Chesapeake Canal Company	Norfolk
11,750	Albert, Adam	Frederick
2,529	Albin, Alex W.	Frederick
11,484	Alder, James	Loudoun
11,515	Alder, James, Jr.	Loudoun
11,710	Alder, Mary C.	Loudoun
17,667	Alderman, James	Carroll
8,409	Alexander, John	Clarke
19,562	Alexander, Robert E.	Augusta
14,997	Alexander, Wm.	Loudoun
16,466	Alford, Robert	Spotsylvania
239	Allan, Patterson	Goochland
14,833	Allen, Catharine A. S.	Fauquier
3,264	Allen, Jane L.	Culpeper
17,156	Allen, Jospeh L.	Cumberland
14,529	Allen, Lavinia L.	Culpeper
11,106	Allen, Loftin D.	Henrico
21,821	Allen, Mary Ann	Culpeper
20,485	Allen, Robert H.	Henrico
17,155	Allen, Sarah	Rockingham

14,142	Allen, Wm.	Franklin
4,554	Alley, Crawford	Henrico
17,004: 20,999:	Allison, John W.	Fauquier
9,750	Allnutt, Robert G.	Loudoun
2,637	Almond, John F.	Orange
7,959	Ambrose, Sarah	Shenandoah
30	Ames, Hiram L.	Culpeper
11,293	Amidon, Daniel	Prince William
16,298	Anderson, Alex	Amelia
16,011	Anderson, Alfred	Amelia
1,910	Anderson, Chas. H.	Rockbridge
16,012	Anderson, Francis B.	Amelia
10,701	Anderson, Henry	Warren
19,267	Anderson, James	Rockingham
16,297	Anderson, James P.	Amelia
5,987	Anderson, John	King William
2,121	Anderson, John H.	Botetourt
12,775	Anderson, John P.	Fauquier
16,880	Anderson, Mary	Fauquier
1,725	Anderson, Richard	Augusta
13,147	Anderson, Richard	Prince William
5,988	Anderson, Sam	King William
16,296	Anderson, Wm.	Amelia
2,901	Anderson, Wm.	New Kent
20,789	Anderson, Wm. Hamilton	Frederick
2,113	Andrews, Alex	Augusta
11,071	Andrews, Elias	Warren
10,180	Andrews, Wm.	Frederick
15,785	Ansley, Wm.	Fairfax
21,606	Appel, Thos.	Loudoun
1,377	Arehart, Geo. L.	Augusta
5,245	Argyle, T. R.	Goochland
7,851	Armentrout, John	Rockingham
16,403	Armitage, Wm. H.	Lancaster
5,984	Armstrong, Ashbel	Dinwiddie
12,474	Armstrong, Benj.	Spotsylvania
5,985	Armstrong, E. J.	Dinwiddie
5,986	Armstrong, Erastus	Dinwiddie
224	Armstrong, John T.	Alexandria
6,004	Armstrong, Wm., Estate of	Dinwiddie
454	Arnold, Joseph	Loudoun
10,263	Arnold, Wm.	Halifax
20,929	Arrington, Francis C.	Prince William
6,114	Artes, Anderson	Southampton
14,164	Ashby, Mary	York
20,411	Ashor, Isaac, Estate of	Henrico
21,777	Ashton, Arthur	Fauquier
13,155	Ashton, Mary W.	Fauquier
20,471	Ashton, Wm. L.	Fairfax
16,642	Atkins, Elias	Charles City
17,877	Atkins, Isabella	Henrico
20,414	Atkins, Joseph	Henrico
9,510	Atkisson, Lucien B.	Hanover
199	Atlee, Jacob S.	Henrico
223	Auld, David & George	Fairfax
3,203	Austin, Valorus G.	Alexandria
7,329	Averett, Primus	Halifax
18,759	Avery, Wm. C.	Prince William
20,936	Avery, Wm. W.	Prince William
21,552	Axline, David	Loudoun
12,369	Ayler, James T.	Nansemond
658	Ayre, Thos.	Loudoun
13,926	Ayres, Elias, Estate of	Loudoun
21,160	Babcock, Lemuel E.	Charles City
1,482	Bacher, Anthony W.	Frederick
14,885	Bacon, Allen	Albemarle
17,424	Bacon, Joel S., Estate of	Fauquier
12,424	Bagent, Wm.	Loudoun
11,027	Bagent, Wm. & Crim, Susan	Loudoun
21,713	Baggot, Elizabeth, Estate of	Loudoun
15,503	Bagley, Benj.	Augusta
13,185	Bailey, Elizabeth & Jenks, W. S.	Alexandria

4,778	Bailey, Harvey	Alexandria
8: 1,291:	Bailey, Lewis	Fairfax
7,585	Bailey, Major Parker	New Kent
18,467	Bailey, Martha	Culpeper
17,489	Bailey, Nancy	Fauquier
7,585	Bailey, Parker, Major	New Kent
1,399	Bailey, Wm.	Hanover
3,992	Bailie, Robert	Washington
2,714	Baily, Francis	Prince William
21,203	Baker, Annie S., Chas. W., Cornelia E., Sam D. & W. H.	Frederick
2,527	Baker, Dan	Frederick
455	Baker, George	Loudoun
9,979	Baker, James	Nansemond
94	Baker, James	Rockingham
2,517	Baker, John H.	Rockingham
7,071	Baker, Mary	Augusta
21,826	Baker, Philip	Rockingham
15,986	Baker, Sam	Loudoun
21,203	Baker, Sam D., W. H., Annie S., Chas. W. & Cornelia E.	Frederick
17,682	Baker, Sam M.	Hanover
17,835	Baker, Savage	Norfolk
5,087	Baker, Thos.	Nansemond
2,502	Baker, Thos.	Shenandoah
21,203	Baker, W. H., Annie W., Chas. W., Cornelia E., & Sam D.	Frederick
11,647	Baker, Wm. A.	Loudoun
20,983	Balderston, John C. & Ward, James Henry ,	Fauquier
11,300	Baldwin, Isaac T.	Prince William
41	Baldwin, Joseph	Loudoun
15,703	Baldwin, Sam B.	Appomattox
13,241	Ball, Charity	Fauquier
20,263	Ball, Horatio, Estate of	Alexandria
21,061	Ball, Martha Corbin, Estate of	Fairfax
12,935	Ball, Mary Ann	Lee
1,403	Ball, Sallie	Stafford
20,262	Ball, Sam	Alexandria
18,003	Ball, Sam	Loudoun
13,724	Ball, Wm.	Lee
11,854	Balthrope, Rebecca E.	Fauquier
20,305	Banks, Wm.	Charles City
20,778	Banks, Wm.	Henrico
13,927	Barber, David, Estate of	Fairfax
2,051	Barber, Geo.	Fairfax
18,192	Barber, John	Stafford
4,754	Barbour, Daniel	Rappahannock
19,093	Barclay, Solomon T.	Norfolk
17,625	Barcroft, Ambrose	Fairfax
4,555	Barker, Chas.	Hanover
2,905	Barker, Jesse	Hanover
2,904	Barker, John	New Kent
11,104	Barker, Sam J.	Henrico
20,476	Barker, Ulom W.	Fairfax
4,508	Barker, Wm.	Washington
15,208	Barksley, Patterson	Spotsylvania
9,925	Barlow, James P.	Fairfax
4,779	Barnhart, George & James H.	Frederick
4,779	Barnhart, James H. & George	Frederick
21,825	Barr, Dan	Rockingham
727	Barrett, Dan H.	Fairfax
4,450	Barrett, Lucius J.	Northumberland
1,116	Bartley, Henry A.	Orange
1,115	Bartley, Oliver	Orange
4,737	Barton, John F.	Shenanhoah
20,918	Basey, Ruthy	Rappahannock
20,313	Bastable, Gilbert M.	Fauquier
22,112	Baston, Richard	Fairfax
16,245	Bates, John H., Estate of	Augusta
21,766	Batt, John H.	Prince George
410	Battley, G. W.	Norfolk
19,282	Baugher, Andrew J.	Rockingham
17,901	Baugher, Asa S.	Rockingham
22,150	Baugher, Winfield S.	Rockingham
8,451	Bauman, Frederick	Spotsylvania

18,420: 21,776:	Bauserman, Joseph	Shenandoah
11,974	Bayliss, Augustine	Fairfax
11,975	Bayliss, Ezra	Fairfax
1,076	Bayliss, George	Alexandria
19,590	Bayly, Jane O.	Henrico
18,206	Bayly, Marcus B.	Fauquier
44	Bayne, Wm. H., Trustee	Alexandria
17,303	Beahm, Henry A.	Roanoke
21,068	Beale, John G., Estate of	Fauquier
12,724	Beamer, Geo.	Loudoun
1,481	Bean, Mahlon	Loudoun
461	Beans, A. Humphrey	Loudoun
21,736	Beans, Amos	Loudoun
460	Beans, Isaiah B.	Loudoun
21,553	Beans, Uriah	Loudoun
3,166	Beans, Wm. H. H., Estate of	Loudoun
15,991	Beard, James W.	Augusta
5,066	Beasley, R. R., Heirs of	Brunswick
19,035	Beasley, Richard B., Heirs of	Prince George
21,568	Beavers, Francis A.	Loudoun
21,566	Beavers, Wm. M.	Loudoun
619	Beazley, Massena	Henrico
14,402	Beckelhimer, Levi	Montgomery
941	Beckett, Wm.	Alexandria
16,712	Beckham, Sarah A.	Orange
16,338	Beckley, Wm. C.	Alexandria
536	Beckner, Dan	Alleghany
3,406	Beemer, John W.	Clarke
18,421	Beery, Abraham, Estate of	Rockingham
7,852	Beery, Henry	Rockingham
8,698	Beery, John H.	Rockingham
8,941	Beery, Joseph	Rockingham
8,942	Beery, Solomon	Rockingham
4,463	Bell, Dan	Nansemond
12,456	Bell, Geo. H.	Clarke
2,028	Bell, Gilbert J. & Mears, John E.	Accomack
21,312	Bell, Joseph J.	Dinwiddie
11,749	Bently, Edgar L.	Loudoun
20,226	Benton, Wm.	Loudoun
4,471	Berry, Wm. S.	Prince Edward
4,918	Beydler, Amelia	Shenandoah
21,159	Bickers, Edmund, Estate of	Culpeper
20,786	Bickers, James	Culpeper
16,947	Bierley, Benj. S.	Rockingham
1,125	Bigelow, John R.	Fairfax
724	Biggs, Henry D.	Fairfax
18,576	Biggs, John	Fauquier
4,481	Biller, Ambrose	Shenandoah
8,945	Billhimer, Isaac G.	Rockingham
22,123	Birch, Almond	Fairfax
12,003	Birch, Jane C.	Alexandria
15,326	Birch, John C., Estate of	Alexandria
20,261	Birch, John T.	Alexandria
11,435	Birch, Mary	Alexandria
1,052	Birch, Randolph	Alexandria
221	Birch, Sam	Alexandria
11,437	Birch, Sam (of Caleb)	Alexandria
228	Birch, Wm. R.	Alexandria
10,097	Bird, Bennett M.	Accomack
13,784	Bird, Mary A.	Highland
14,824	Bird, Uriah	King & Queen
13,785	Bird, Wm. C.	Highland
1,904	Birdsall, Benj.	Loudoun
1,903	Birdsall, Benj., Jrs., Estate	Loudoun
6,136	Bishop, A. J.	Prince George
20,314	Bittinger, E. C., Rev.	Fairfax
8,410	Bitzer, James H.	Clarke
20,337	Blackburn, Manasseh; and Lewis, John R.	Rockingham
1,378	Blackburn, Mary	Augusta
5,350	Blackmore, Wm. F.	Fauquier
3,204	Blackstone, Thos. W.	Accomack
16,197	Blackwell, Elizabeth P.	Fauquier
19,266	Blackwell, Polly	Rockingham
2,990	Blackwell, Rebecca	Floyd
6,304	Bland, Peter R.	Amelia

5,528	Blankenship, Elis	Bland
16,114	Bleakly, Charles	Fauquier
11,833	Blick, Adelina T.	Dinwiddie
11,893	Blockley, Eugene	Frederick
9,780	Blosser, Jonas	Rockingham
16,500: 21,855:	Blosser, Peter	Rockingham
9,179	Blunt, John H.	Hanover
10,527	Blunt, Lewis T.	Hanover
8,154	Blunt, Temple J.	Hanover
4,915	Bly, Susannah	Shenandoah
46	Bodine, Theordore, Estate of	Prince William
4,721	Boehm, John W.	Shenandoah
20,814	Bogan, Martin V. B.	Fairfax
451: 11,648:	Boger, Jacob	Loudoun
21,161	Bolling, Anne F.	Dinwiddie
17,006	Bolon, Geo. H.	Loudoun
82	Bomar, John	Halifax
21,219	Bond, Abner	Frederick
6,915	Bonner, Jerry	Dinwiddie
6,913	Bonner, John	Dinwiddie
11,372	Bonner, Nelson	Prince George
6,911	Bonner, Robert	Dinwiddie
13,967	Bonnewell, Ann & James E.	Nansemond
13,967	Bonnewell, James E. & Ann	Nansemond
17,453	Bonney, Thos. W.	Princess Ann
12,372	Booth, Susan	Nansemond
2,907	Booze, Martha	Hanover
4,725	Borden, Joseph	Shenandoah
9,443	Bosham, Ellis L.	Floyd
9,440	Bosham, N., Estate of	Floyd
17,164	Bosserman, Wm.	Augusta
10,524	Boston, Wm. H.	Fairfax
393	Boswell, Charles	Fluvanna
18,187	Botts, Sam H.	Fauquier
18,209	Botts, Thornton S., Estate of	Fauquier
245	Bowden, Henry M.	Norfolk
20,775	Bowden, Lemuel J., Estate of	York
14,373	Bowen, G. W.	Culpeper
2,223	Bowen, James	Culpeper
10,332	Bowen, James J.	Fairfax
14,890	Bowen, Joseph, Estate of	Culpeper
1,379: 20,827:	Bowers, David	Augusta
22,116	Bowler, Thos.	Stafford
5,928	Bowles, J. H.	Goochland
12,353	Bowles, James L., Estate of	Frederick
21,222	Bowles, James L., Sr., Estate	Frederick
7,877	Bowman, Benj.	Rockingham
7,850	Bowman, Dan	Rockingham
15,511: 21,859:	Bowman, Isaac	Rockingham
17,165	Bowman, Jacob	Augusta
1,962	Bowman, John	Halifax
15,510: 21,853:	Bowman, John, Sr.	Rockingham
6,709	Bowman, John F.	Charles City
15,017	Bowman, John W.	Rockingham
7,983	Bowman, Joseph	Rockingham
19,350	Bowman, Josiah B.	Fairfax
634	Bowman, Leonard	Culpeper
15,903	Bowman, Michael W.	Rockingham
16,501	Bowman, Sam	Rockingham
571	Bowser, Thos.	Nansemond
4,172	Boxley, Joseph C.	Louisa
813	Boxley, Martha A., Estate of	Louisa
21,592	Brabham, F. M.	Louisa
20,304	Bradby, Allen	Charles City
14,976	Bradby, Edward	King William
14,852	Bradby, Evans	King William
14,977	Bradby, Pleasant	King William
15,494	Bradby, Sterling, Estate of	King William
15,142	Bradby, Thos.	King William
13,786	Bardley, Harriet	Bath
6,306	Bardley, Terrill	King William
5,063	Bradshaw, Willis	Southampton
7,742	Brally, Andrew J.	Wythe
2,759	Bramblee, Miles	Fairfax

21,180	Brandt, Mary & Randolph	Culpeper
21,180	Brandt, Randolph & Mary	Culpeper
8,470	Branham, Thos.	Rockingham
15,904	Branner, Geo., Estate of	Rockingham
2,571	Branner, James M.	Rockingham
7,944	Brannon, Mary	Clarke
13,473	Branson, Polly	Washington
21,731	Brawner, Henry C.	Prince William
1,335	Brawner, John C.	Prince William
19,168	Bray, Charles R.	King William
17,902	Breeden, Nicholas	Rockingham
15,512	Breneman, Abraham	Rockingham
9,123	Breneman, David C.	Rockingham
16,503	Breneman, Mary	Rockingham
14,014	Brent, Elias	Fauquier
8,645	Brice, Geo.	Fairfax
17,836	Brickhouse, Joseph B.	Norfolk
18,830	Bridger, James C.	Nansemond
20,930	Brill, Philip F.	Prince William
13,370	Brindle, Dan, Estate of	Frederick
456	Brisbin, Michael	Loudoun
19,204	Brisby, Wm. H.	New Kent
14,979	Brisby, Matilda, Estate of	King William
13,787	Briscoe, Jacob	Highland
12,608	Briscoe, Jane H.	Fairfax
10,261	Brittin, Mary W.	Halifax
21,637	Britton, Chadwell	Lee
20,553	Britton, James H., Estate of	Henrico
10,164	Brockwell, Josiah R.	Chesterfield
16,683	Bromley, G. W.	Frederick
17,050	Brooks, Caroline	Cumberland
19,835	Brooks, Chauncey, and Walter B.; Rogers, John A.; and Thrasher, Isaac	Prince Edward
317	Brooks, Francis J.	Rappahannock
167	Brooks, Jacob	Fairfax
3,433	Brooks, Peter	Fauquier
17,052	Brooks, Spencer	Prince Edward
15,285	Brooks, Thos. A.	Fauquier
19,835	Brooks, Walter B. & Chauncey; Rogers, John A.; and Trasher, Isaac	Prince Edward
100	Broughton, Lyman	Fairfax
18,761	Broughton, Wait, Estate of	Fairfax
6,468	Brown, Albert	Charles City
18,662	Brown, Alex H.	Alexandria
10,890	Brown, Alonzo D.	Loudoun
7,325	Brown, Ambrose E.	Halifax
8,025	Brown, Ann M.	Rappahannock
11,745	Brown, Archibald	Fairfax
6,137	Brown, Crawford C.	Charles City
17,509	Brown, Dan W.	Frederick
6,469	Brown, Edmund C.	Charles City
20,598	Brown, Edward W.	Culpeper
14,999	Brown, Edwin C.	Loudoun
19,512	Brown, Elison	Frederick
5,246	Brown, Elizabeth	Charles City
21,234	Brown, Ellen Ann	Alexandria
14,286	Brown, Ham	Fauquier
4,898	Brown, Henry	Appomattox
11,072	Brown, Joel T.	Culpeper
8,306	Brown, John	Alexandria
15,556	Brown, John	Culpeper
20,719	Brown, John B., Estate of	Alexandria
8,083	Brown, John N. & Wm.	Charles City
3,001	Brown, John W.	Culpeper
18,499	Brown, Joseph	New Kent
19,886	Brown, Joseph M.	Augusta
6,706	Brown, M., Major	Charles City
6,706	Brown, Major M.	Charles City
11,655	Brown, Mary A.	Loudoun
8,967	Brown, Mary Jane	Orange
16,135	Brown, Nancy	Norfolk

1,187	Brown, Nimrod	Spotsylvania
6,470	Brown, Oscar D.	Charles City
6,138	Brown, Robert S.	Charles City
7,724	Brown, S. T.	Charles City
6,710	Brown, Sam	Charles City
12,141	Brown, Sam T.	Fairfax
13,788	Brown, Sarah W.	Alleghany
20,181	Brown, Susan	Culpeper
17,488	Brown, Thos.	Fauquier
7,591	Brown, Warren A.	Charles City
303	Brown, Wm.	Frederick
19,209	Brown, Wm.	New Kent
8,083	Brown, Wm. & John N.	Charles City
9,917	Brown, Wm. M.	Clarke
14,731	Browning, John	Russell
15,280	Browning, Mary	Russell
20,980	Browning, Willis	Rappahannock
11,596	Brubaker, Benj.	Roanoke
11,595	Brubaker, Elias	Roanoke
2,566	Brubeck, Philip	Shenandoah
16,582	Bruce, James	Albemarle
11,322	Brumly, John	Frederick
9,733	Brunk, Christian	Rockingham
15,513	Brunk, Geo.	Rockingham
16,948: 17,903:	Brunk, Jacob	Rockingham
21,856	Brunk, John	Rockingham
1,404	Bryam, James	Stafford
10,530	Bryan, Landon C.	Washington
10	Bryan, Richard H.	Stafford
860	Bryan, Thos. M.	Stafford
15,209	Bryant, Alex, Estate of	Prince George
13,981	Bryant, Emily C.	Dinwiddie
14,149	Bryant, Francis O.	Buckingham
2,122	Bryant, Jesse L.	Bedford
2,760	Bryce, Matthew, Estate of	Fairfax
11,426	Bryhim, Alex O.	Stafford
2,906	Bryson, Marshall	New Kent
6,892	Buchanan, David	Augusta
6,893	Buchanan, John R.	Augusta
7,284	Buck, Lavinia	Shenandoah
17,089	Buckley, Bushrod, Estate of	Clarke
11,715	Buffin, Alfred R.	Henrico
20,176	Buffington, Armistead M.	Loudoun
2,587	Bull, Wm.	Augusta
21,684	Bullock, Wm. S.	Stafford
142	Bulman, John W.	King & Queen
2,134: 9,293:	Bumgardner, John	Augusta
11,603	Buncutter, John H.	Frederick
21,022	Bundy, Geo.	Spotsylvania
13,694	Bundy, Joseph H.	Lee
19,818	Bundy, Riban	Culpeper
19,817	Bundy, Warner	Culpeper
10,262	Buntin, John, Sr.	Halifax
572	Bunting, Edward J.	Norfolk
5,507	Buracker, Sam A.	Page
1,484	Burch, Isaac	Fairfax
15,673	Buren, Richard	Prince George
5,360	Burgess, Henry	Princess Anne
1,118	Burgess, Wm.	Dinwiddie
3,229	Burging, Christian	Henrico
13,789	Burk, James	Alleghany
21,184	Burke, Mary Ann	Fairfax
2,358	Burke, Mary E.	Fairfax
5,873	Burke, Wilson	Montgomery
21,857	Burkholder, Henry	Rockingham
9,730	Burkholder, Rebecca	Rockingham
11,980	Burley, Wm., Estate of	Alexandria
21,212	Burner, John A.	Page
2,908	Burnett, Isaac	Hanover
15,495	Burnett, James	Dinwiddie
15,242	Burrow, John C.	Prince George
15,367	Burton, Harris W.	Stafford
16,818	Burton, Millie Ann	Stafford

3,243	Burton, Nancy,	Richmond
4,889	Burton, Sallie & Chance, Joseph T.	Accomack
19,359	Bush, James	Lancaster
458	Bush, John C.	Loudoun
19,358	Bush, Nancy	Lancaster
18,271	Buxhrod, John T.	Fairfax
14,623	Bussey, Harman L.	Russell
2,798	Butler, Elisha	Nansemond
7,141	Butler, Isaac	Hanover
15,672	Butler, James C.	Spotsylvania
5,034	Butler, Jesse	Frederick
83	Butler, John	Halifax
20,815	Butler, John T.	Fauquier
58	Butler, Pierce	Fairfax
14,703	Butler, Robert	Fauquier
12,032	Butt, Rignal	Washington
18,200	Butts, Henry E.	Loudoun
457	Butts, Oliver G.	Loudoun
12,410	Butts, Wm., Estate of	Loudoun
2,549	Bydler, Hiram	Shenandoah
16,241	Byerly, Benj. F.	Roanoke
10,509	Byrd, Obid F.	Shenandoah
4,931	Byrd, Uriah	Nansemond
13,735	Byrd, Wm. S.	Accomack
8,331	Cadwallader, Joseph	Frederick
15,496	Cain, James H.	Prince George
9,912	Cain, John	Clarke
1,726	Calbreath, Thos.	Augusta
14,426	Calbreath, Zachariah F.	Augusta
11,570	Caldwell, John	Fauquier
20,931	Callahan, Allen T.	Prince William
3,410	Cammack, Wm. E.	Orange
20,025	Campbell, Alex	Middlesex
6,139	Campbell, John	Louisa
21,583	Campbell, Robert	Loudoun
10,778	Campbell, Sam C.	Shenandoah
3,265	Campbell, Wm.	Rockingham
11,474	Canada, Beverly	Halifax
84	Canada, Guilford	Halifax
20,802	Canal Co., Albermarle & Chesapeake	Norfolk
8,040	Cannady, Isaac Y.	Franklin
7,827	Cannady, Peter	Franklin
13,680	Cannell, Wm. L.	Louisa
4,782	Canter, Isaac W.	Frederick
13,891	Carden, James W.	Montgomery
13,889	Carden, John	Montgomery
13,893	Carden, Randolph	Montgomery
21,100	Carder, Chas. R.	Rappahanock
21,099	Carder, Wm.	Rappahanock
13,712	Carey, Geo.	Westmoreland
14,699	Carhart, Chas.	Westmoreland
6,313: 16,741:	Carhart, Wm. E.	Norfolk
2,428	Carleton, Nathan W.	Halifax
4	Carlin, Andrew W. F.	Alexandria
21,697	Carlin, Wesley	Alexandria
736	Carpenter, Benj. D. & Benj. F.	Fairfax
1,112	Carpenter, J. N.	Fairfax
131	Carpenter, Jonathan	Rappahanock
9,154	Carpenter, Marion H.	Clarke
10,435: 20,903:	Carpenter, Marshall W.	Loudoun
1,113	Carpenter, Mary F.	Fairfax
19,283: 21,773:	Carpenter, Sam	Rockingham
15,813	Carpenter, Tabitha	Madison
4,780	Carper, Annie L.	Frederick
7,945	Carper, James	Clarke
8,332	Carper, Julia Ann	Clarke
9,935	Carper, Philip W.	Frederick
15,134	Carper, Thos. J.	Fairfax
11,013	Carper, Wm.	Frederick
7,946	Carper, Wm. B.	Frederick
1,389	Carr, David	Loudoun
3,167	Carr, Joseph, Estate of	Loudoun

21,594	Carr, Sam	Loudoun
441	Carson, Jacob	Loudoun
22,125	Carter, Alfred	Fairfax
1,184	Carter, Benj. S.	Spotsylvania
21,181	Carter, Elizabeth	Stafford
4,781	Carter, Geo. H.	Frederick
18,465	Carter, John	Louisa
17,666	Carter, Johnson, Estate of	Stafford
11,573	Carter, Luke	Alexandria
17,487	Carter, Nat. G.	Fauquier
20,350	Carter, Robert	Fairfax
2,429	Carter, Ruth	Floyd
8,649	Carter, Susan M.	Fauquier
10,294	Carter, Wm. A.	Frederick
1,405	Carter, Wm. L., Estate of	Stafford
1,380	Carwell, Jacob B.	Augusta
1,381	Carwell, Michael	Augusta
17,135	Cary, Richard	Westmoreland
5,991	Casby, Caswell	King William
21,590	Cassaday, Wm. H.	Loudoun
13,899	Cathcart, T. J., Estate of	Alexandria
11,323	Cather, Wm.	Frederick
18,184	Catlett, James M.	Fauquier
20,361	Catlett, Martha	Warren
17,839	Cator, James	Stafford
8,940	Cave, Willis	Rockingham
964	Caywood, Benj.	Fairfax
4,558	Chadwick, Sarah E.	New Kent
4,557	Chadwick, Wm. T.	Hanover
2,715	Chamberlain, Oliver	Prince William
19,126	Chamberlain, Oswin	Frederick
11,890	Chamblin, E. B.	Loudoun
18,191	Chamblin, Ellzey	Loudoun
21,569	Chamblin, Jared, Estate of	Loudoun
11,859	Chamlin, Levin P.	Loudoun
11,711	Chamblin, Wm. B.	Loudoun
11,965	Chambliss, Thos. A.	Brunswick
4,889	Chance, Joseph T., & Burton, Sallie	Accomack
9,880	Chancellor, Sam	Rappahanock
79	Chandler, John J.	Halifax
9,395	Chaplin, J. C.	Fairfax
21,862	Chapman, Frank M.	Rockingham
13,068	Chapman, Sidney F., Estate of	Alexandria
21,383	Chappelear, Elias	Rappahanock
11,718	Chappell, John A.	Dinwiddie
4,116	Chappell, Mirander	Fairfax
12,088	Charity, Maria	Nansemond
20,400	Charity, Wm.	Charles City
2,909	Charles, John H.	Henrico
20,237	Cherry, Wm. R.	Norfolk
10,507	Chewning, Isham B.	Culpeper
21,024	Chewning, Parmelia	Spotsylvania
11,356	Chewning, Pereguin E.	Orange
1,396	Childress, B. F.	Dinwiddie
21,988	Childress, Stephen	Montgomery
18,324	Childs, Francis A.	Fauquier
8,966	Chisholm, Cleavers S.	Hanover
6,115	Chisum, Edward C.	Charlotte
1,185	Chivis, John	Spotsylvania
8,231	Chrisman, Crockett	Montgomery
9,729	Chrisman, Geo. H., Estate of	Rockingham
13,895	Chrisman, James W.	Montgomery
17,721	Christian, Isham	Appomattox
7,987	Christian, John J.	Augusta
15,963	Church, Indiana Methodist	Norfolk
217	Church, Manassas Presbyterian	Prince William
21,838	Church, Mount Crawford ME	Rockingham
18,201	Church, Mount Holly, Baptists	Fauquier
17,447	Church, Oak Grove Methodist	Norfolk
18,204	Chruch, Walnut Branch ME	Fauquier
6,715	Chutkawski, Ignatius F.	Alexandria
10,523	Claggett, Julia F.	Prince William
17,646	Clare, John	Alexandria
9,089	Clark, Benj., Estate of	Amelia
4,755	Clark, Benj. F.	Rappahanock
1,963	Clark, Eliza A.	Roanoke

15,671	Clark, Geo. J.	Amelia
11,374	Clark, Henry C.	Prince George
18,592	Clark, J. F., Heirs of; and Cocknell, John H. & William	Fairfax
21,625	Clarke, J. T., Estate of	Alexandria
13,330	Clark, John T.	Halifax
4,756	Clark, Jonas	Rappahanock
9,088	Clark, Martha A.	Amelia
2,109	Clark, Peter	Washington
2,426	Clark, Phebe	Charlotte
9,124	Clark, Robert M.	Prince William
16,421	Clark, Seymour B.	Fairfax
9,125	Clarke, Eldora, Richard & Robert, M.; and Force, Adolphus	Prince William
15,132	Clarke, Elizabeth	Richmond
597	Clarke, Ephraim	Fairfax
10,183	Clarke, G. W.	Madison
9,125	Clarke, Richard, Eldora & Robert M.; and Force, Adolphus	Prince William
8,169	Clarke, Robert	Dinwiddie
9,125	Clarke, Robert M., Eldora & Richard; and Force, Adolphus	Prince William
2,015	Clay, Elizabeth H.	Chesterfield
9,090	Clay, Peter F.	Henrico
1,215	Claypool, Abraham F.	Dinwiddie
9,309	Clem, Alex	Shenandoah
9,308	Clem, Mary Jane	Shenandoah
11,518	Clendening, John	Loudoun
11,622	Clendening, Ruth	Loudoun
397: 21,610:	Clendening, Sam	Loudoun
20,014	Clendening, Wm.	Loudoun
210	Cleveland, John H.	Fairfax
12,234	Cleveland, Wm.	Fairfax
3,217	Clevenger, Henry, Estate of	Fairfax
2,581	Click, Joseph	Augusta
2,522	Click, Joseph	Rockingham
2,580	Cline, Frederick K.	Augusta
2,583	Cline, Frederick M.	Augusta
2,533	Cline, John A.	Rockingham
2,578	Cline, Joseph M.	Augusta
16,511	Clore, Margaret A.	Madison
16,751	Clowser, Joseph	Frederick
14,324	Clubb, John W.	Fairfax
4,441	Coal & Iron Company, Cumberland	Alexandria
13,574	Cobb, Nathan F., Jr.	Northampton
18,861	Cobb, Warren D.; Doughty, E. B.; & Williams, John W.	Northampton
12,415	Coburn, Israel, Estate of	Frederick
14,722	Cochrane, Ellen	Loudoun
2,011	Cock, Ambrose	Fairfax
2,010	Cock, Ambrose, Jr.	Fairfax
9,997	Cocke, Martha	Prince George
1,916	Cockerville, Hiram	Alexandria
18,592	Cocknell, John H. & Willamena J.; and Clark, J. F., Heirs	Fairfax
952	Cochran, George L.	Roanoke
21,607	Cockrell, Absalom	Loudoun
21,735	Cockrell, Joseph H.	Fairfax
19,076	Cody, Edward	Fairfax
11,803	Coe, Aurelius & Maria	Loudoun
11,803	Coe, Maria & Aurelius	Loudoun
18,727	Coffman, Benj. F.	Page
2,579	Coffman, Isaac	Augusta
16,243	Coffman, Jacob, Estate of	Augusta
2,512	Coffman, Rebecca	Augusta
9,519	Coffman, Sam	Rockingham
13,683	Cohoon, Willis E.	Nansemond
2,785	Colbert, Geo. N.	Fauquier
21,727	Cole, Henry	Prince William
21,309	Coleman, Francis	Hanover

10,814: 22,122:	Coleman, James	Fairfax
19,719	Coleman, John	Dinwiddie
574	Coleman, John	Norfolk
2,492	Coleman, Robert G.	Fairfax
14,016	Coles, Mark	Fauquier
14,624	Colley, Wm. E.	Washington
15,814	Collins, Andrew J., Estate of	Prince George
6,777	Colson, Henry	Lee
6,778	Colson, James B.	Lee
11,772	Colter, Wm.	Botetourt
642	Colvin, John N.	Culpeper
18,469	Colvin, Lucy M.	Culpeper
21,015	Colvin, Wm.	Fauquier
13,733	Comer, Peter F.	Halifax
20,479	Commins, Moses A.	Fairfax
20,910	Compton, John A.	Rappahanock
11,028	Conard, Abner	Loudoun
11,029	Conard, Ebenezer J.	Loudoun
13,292	Conard, John D.	Loudoun
11,030	Conard, Joseph	Loudoun
12,776	Conard, Joseph M.	Loudoun
14,802	Conduff, S. G.	Floyd
20,482	Connell, Brice	Page
90	Conner, Chas. F.	Halifax
14,932	Conner, Joel	Appomattox
123	Conner, Nelson	Alexandria
8,732	Conrad, John W.	Loudoun
12,296	Conway, Wm. & Dixon, John	Alexandria
6,305	Cook, Thos.	King William
21,023	Cook, Wm.	Spotsylvania
21,816	Cooke, Major, Estate of	King & Queen
4,758	Cookey, Martha A.	Rappahanock
4,757	Cookey, Philip F.	Rappahanock
5,382	Cooksey, Sanford W.	Fairfax
12,465	Cooksey, Wm.	Loudoun
445	Cooper, Adam	Loudoun
11,737: 15,983:	Cooper, Elias	Loudoun
17,492	Cooper, Emeline	Loudoun
54	Cooper, Fannie A.	Norfolk
10,998	Cooper, George (of G.)	Loudoun
459	Cooper, George (of John)	Loudoun
15,985	Cooper, Geo. T.	Loudoun
9,913	Cooper, Harrison	Clarke
6,286	Cooper, Jacob	Montgomery
6,267	Cooper, John	Montgomery
15,886	Cooper, John (of P.)	Loudoun
17,400	Cooper, Levi	Frederick
1,214	Cooper, Sarah	Loudoun
18,193	Cooper, Wm. D.	Fauquier
11,031	Copeland, Harmon	Loudoun
13,466	Copeland, Milton	Norfolk
12,368	Copeland, Sarah A.	Nansemond
10,627	Copp, G. W.	Shenandoah
10,626	Copp, John E.	Shenandoah
1,041	Copp, Philip	Shenandoah
2,818	Copp, Sam	Shenandoah
4,736	Copp, Sarah	Shenandoah
7,844	Corbett, Cooper	Alexandria
4,440	Corbett, Frank E.	Alexandria
2,301	Corbett, Sewell B.	Alexandria
399: 1,905:	Corbett, Virgil P.	Alexandria
3,002	Corbin, Isaiah	Rappahanock
1,402	Corbin, Juliet A.	Rappahanock
12,459	Corbin, Silas	Loudoun
2,123	Corcoran, Thos.	Bedford
13,157	Cordell, Richard	Halifax
12,057	Cornick, Endymion	Princess Anne
1,138	Cornwall, Andrew	Clarke
8,486	Cornwall, John	Fairfax
573	Corprew, Geo.	Norfolk
18,211	Corum, James F.	Fauquier
2,996	Corvin, Ephraim & Francis	Wythe
18,864	Costen, Robert S.	Northampton
20,303	Cotman, Allen	Charles City

6,471	Cotman, Thos.	Charles City
11,598	Cottrell, Mary	Appomattox
3,991	Counts, Linick	Washington
8,965	Courtney, Wm. J.	Caroline
20,801	Courtright, M.	Princess Anne
17,482	Couse, Peter	Spotsylvania
21,156	Covell, Mildred S.	Orange
17,907	Cowdery, Alex A.	Norfolk
18,881	Cowgill, Alfred	Rappahanock
18,880	Cowgill, James M., Estate of	Rappahanock
13,131	Cowling, Mary	Norfolk
14,678	Cox, Cumberlon G.	Henrico
20,334	Cox, Ellen C.	Augusta
21,689	Cox, Fleet	Stafford
99	Cox, Geo. S.	Fairfax
18,199	Cox, Hugh	Fauquier
305	Cox, James	Smyth
15,001	Cox, James A.	Loudoun
117	Cox, Oliver	Alexandria
1,139	Coxen, Morgan	Clarke
3,222	Coyle, Jane E.	Fairfax
5,336	Crabb, Cyrus E.	Westmoreland
13,815	Craft, Mary	Campbell
17,908	Craig, Benj. J.	Augusta
10,321	Craig, Frederick	Shenandoah
7,648	Craig, Walter	Shenandoah
6,108	Crandol, Amanda F.	James City
18,944	Craun, Geo.	Augusta
8,943	Craun, Joseph H.	Augusta
21,861	Crawford, John, Estate of	Rockingham
21,860	Crawford, Lawrence	Rockingham
16,464	Crawford, Madison B.	Craig
17,559	Crawford, Zachariah	Frederick
230	Crawford, W. E.	Amherst
4,099	Creasy, Wm. O.	Patrick
13,103	Creekur, Bartlett	Norfolk
21,235	Creel, David	Rappahanock
17,906	Crickenberger, Sam	Augusta
11,787	Crim, John H.	Loudoun
15,883	Crim, Matilda	Loudoun
20,495	Crim, Sam	Loudoun
12,423	Crim, Susan	Loudoun
11,027	Crim, Susan & Bagent, Wm.	Loudoun
21,567	Crim, Wm.	Loudoun
4,789	Crinshaw, John B.	Henrico
19,469	Crippen, Minor A.	Fairfax
2,582	Crist, Jacob	Shenandoah
16,732	Crizer, Mary E.	Alleghany
20,353	Crocker, James H.	Fairfax
1,676	Crocker, John S.	Fairfax
10,525	Crocker, Jonathan D.	Fairfax
847	Crocker, Lott W.	Fairfax
11,785	Crockett, Sam	Loudoun
16,951	Cromer, Martin	Rockingham
11,492	Crone, David	Frederick
2,940	Cropley, Sam, Estate of	Prince William
14,340	Cropp, Carter B.	Culpeper
21,069	Cropp, Carter G.	Stafford
13,573	Cross, Benj., Estate of	Fairfax
11,780	Cross, James H.	Loudoun
11,763	Cross, Jefferson	Lee
9,866	Cross, John	Prince William
9,679	Crouse, J. N.	Augusta
20,796	Crow, Thos. H., Estate of	Clarke
12	Cruikshank, Richard	Fairfax
2,034	Cruise, David	Patrick
372	Cruit, Robert, Estate of	Alexandria
2,577	Crumbaker, Jacob	Augusta
113	Crump, Jane	Fairfax
13,946	Crump, John H.	Fauquier
11,129	Crump, Lewis A.	Fairfax
21,570	Crusen, Jacob, Estate of	Loudoun
9,311	Cullars, Dan	Shenandoah
11,798	Cullers, Isaac	Page
16,036	Culpeper, Josiah	Norfolk
19,208	Cumber, Warren C.	New Kent
4,441	Cumberland Coal & Iron Co.	Alexandria

3,486	Cumbie, John J.	Halifax
7,725	Cumbo, Walker	Charles City
12,544	Cummings, Harrison	Loudoun
13,152	Curtis, Francis F.	Fauquier
18,198	Curtis, Henry B.	Fauquier
2,857	Curtis, John J., Estate of	Culpeper
19,580	*Curtis, Wm. P., & Hopkins, Stephen (*also spelled Custis)	Accomack
10,154	Custer, Jacob, Heirs of	Roanoke
20,406	Dabney, Benj.	Dinwiddie
20,408	Dabney, Robert	Dinwiddie
17,234	Dade, Nace	Fairfax
22,174	Daily, Aaron	Loudoun
2,716	Dane, Henry	Prince William
76	Dangerfield, Sigismund	Clarke
6,459	Daniel, G. W.	Middlesex
10,207	Daniel, Wm.	Louisa
8,027	Danner, David	Rockingham
9,748	Danre, James W.	Loudoun
21,236	Darne, Robert	Fairfax
2,008	Darnell, John T. and Tennison, Whiting M.	Fairfax
12,058	Daughtrey, Fannie Emma	Isle of Wright
1,711	Daulton, Celia	Carroll
6,140	Davenport, David F.	Northumberland
21,896	Davidson, G. W.	Henrico
13,700	Davidson, Judith	Appomattox
9,415	Davidson, Wm.	Rockbridge
791	Davis, Alex G.	Loudoun
21,694	Davis, Diana, Estate of	Fairfax
8,964	Davis, Erastus P.	Cumberland
2,135	Davis, James F.	Augusta
15,545	Davis, James M.	King & Queen
1,117	Davis, John	Buckingham
14,347: 21,692:	Davis, John C.	Fairfax
10,149	Davis, John H.	Henry
12,571: 20,548:	Davis, Joseph	Loudoun
2,639	Davis, Josiah H., Heirs of	Alexandria
12,909	Davis, Mary E.	Fauquier
3,299	Davis, Matthew	Washington
584: 12,722:	Davis, Susan A.	Stafford
621	Davis, Thos. H.	Prince William
8,092	Dawson, Susan A.	Botetourt
11,621	Dawson, Thos. B.	Alexandria
2,858	Day, Delila	Culpeper
14,148	Day, John	Buckingham
20,816	Dean, James Seymout	Fauquier
2,009	Dean, John	Fairfax
130	Dean, Phebe A. E.	Rappahanock
12,416	Dean, Wm., Sr.	Frederick
3,266	Deane, Josiah C.	Amherst
17,684	Deans, Lydia	Norfolk
11,597	Deaton, Elisha	Roanoke
11,252	Defenbaugh, Lewis	Augusta
18,852	Degge, Geo. A.	Norfolk
9,734	Deihl, Mathias	Augusta
9,081	Delany, Dan F.	Loudoun
11,452	Demasters, Henry	Augusta
16,043	Deming, Eliza J.	Fairfax
11,032	Demory, Mahlon & Sophia E.	Loudoun
11,032	Demory, Sophia E. & Mahlon	Loudoun
1,917	Denning, Levi	Alexandria
1,964	Dennis, E. F., Mrs.	Halifax
20,582	Denny, Robert L.	Clarke
172	Densmore, Wm.	Loudoun
21,863	Derro, Henry, Estate of	Rockingham
11,033	Derry, Eli	Loudoun
11,034	Derry, G. W.	Loudoun
11,035	Derry, John P.	Loudoun
11,036	Derry, Louis W.	Loudoun
11,037: 11,038:	Derry, Philip	Loudoun
8,691	Dettor, James	Washington

511	Dettor, John	Augusta
5,288	Detwiler, John L.	Fairfax
17,090	Deutermany, Edward	Alexandria
5,860	Devere, Larkin	Floyd
14,841	Devers, John W.	Fairfax
14,325	Devers, Thos.	Fairfax
6,303	Dice, Margaret	Henrico
9,916	Dick, Edward	Clarke
9,842	Dickens, Amelia J., Maria M., and Eloise C.	Fairfax
1,406	Dickerson, Sarah	Stafford
17,157	Dickinson, Mary A. J.	Appomattox
15,872	Dickinson, Wm. T.	Hanover
15,042	Dillard, G. W.	Albermarle
3,402	Dillard, James M.	Nelson
2,910	Dillard, John	Goochland
17,668	Dillon, Wm.	Patrick
2,430	Dillon, Wm. J.	Floyd
4,899	Dinguid, Carlos H.	Appomatox
4,783	Dinkle, Enos	Frederick
21,238	Dison, Annie E.	Fauquier
19,207	Dixon, Beverly	New Kent
11,751	Dixon, Henry W.	Norfolk
15,179	Dixon, James G.	Rockbridge
12,296	Dixon, John; and Conway, Wm.	Alexandria
2,138: 18,581:	Dixon, John W.	Mathews
12,351	Dixon, Mary M.	Loudoun
13,911	Dixon, Solomon	Washington
4,509	Dixon, Wm.	Washington
22,275	Dobson, Wm.	King George
15,002	Dodd, John W.	Loudoun
13,309	Dodd, Mehethalem B.	Fauquier
16,647	Dodge, Allen & R. P.	Alexandria
16,647	Dodge, R. P. & Allen	Alexandria
381	Dodson, Francis E.	Fairfax
21,237	Dogan, Henry, Estate of	Prince William
17,472	Dogan, Robert Henry	Alexandria
5,700	Dogans, John M.	Page
6,866	Doggett, Wm.	Lancaster
5,441	Donaldson, Benedict	Fairfax
18,485	Donaldson, James	Alexandria
8,854	Donaldson, Robt. H.	Alexandria
18,186	Donnelly, Edward W.	Fauquier
20,460	Dorman, Orloff M.	Norfolk
12,192	Dorrel, Thos. W.	Loudoun
3,776	Dorton, Wm. C.	Scott
16,463	Doss, Robert R.	Craig
3,223	Dougherty, John	Fairfax
14,330	Dougherty, Thompson	Tazewell
18,861	Doughty, E. B.; Williams, John W.; Cobb, Warren D.	Northampton
20,720	Douglas, Malcolm	Alexandria
13,242	Douglass, Kitty	Fauquier
11,599	Dove, Ashford	Henry
3,225	Dove, Sam	Fairfax
9,091	Dovel, Thos., and Garber, David J.	Rockingham
3,775	Dowell, James	Washington
13,299	Dowell, Octavia	Fauquier
19,582	Downing, James W.	Accomack
9,520	Downs, Wm. S.	Rockingham
12,461	Downy, James M.	Loudoun
6,117	Drake, Wm.	Southampton
15,514	Driver, David & Louisa	Rockingham
18,422	Driver, Emanuel	Rockingham
16,920	Driver, Jacob	Rockingham
8,155	Driver, John W.	Rockingham
15,514	Driver, Louisa & David	Rockingham
19,563	Driver, Sam	Augusta
11,341	Duble, Aaron	Clarke
8,988	Dudley, Mary	Henrico
14,990	Duke, James	Henrico
10,338	Duke, Parker	Nansemond
170	Ducke, Thos. H.	Albermarle
1,925	Dulaney, Sam	Floyd
21,587	Dulin, Alfred	Loudoun
9,841	Dungey, Jesse	King William

10,630	Dunlap, Wm. W.	Washington
13,156	Dunn, Elizabeth	Halifax
5,442	Dunn, Fanny E.	Dinwiddie
5,651	Dunn, Mary	Chesterfield
4,442	Dunnington, Stephen	Louisa
2,911	Duval, Joseph F.	Goochland
14,625	Dye, Jefferson	Russell
4,040	Dyer, Robt.	Alexandria
10,317	Dyson, John	Nottoway
8,954	Eaches, Delilah	Louisa
13,474	Eads, Wm.	Washington
20,234	Eagle, Noah K.	York
16,218	Eakle, Henry K.	Augusta
8,337: 8,338:	Early, Abraham	Rockingham
8,937	Early, Henry	Rockingham
8,939	Early, John	Rockingham
8,198	Early, Jonas	Rockingham
8,338	Early, Joseph, Estate of	Rockingham
16,651: 21,830:	Early, Noah	Augusta
20,722	Easby, Wm., Estate of	Alexandria
16,877	East, James K.	Augusta
19,958	Eastham, J. B.	Rockingham
21,728	Eastman, Hiram, Estate of	Prince William
15,003	Eaton, Malinda	Loudoun
4,740	Ebert, Catharine A.	Shenandoah
13,127	Edmonds, Elias, Estate of	Fauquier
18,190	Edmonds, Sarah B.	Fauquier
20,099	Edmonds, Susan E.	Fauquier
13,811	Edmondson, Wm. C.	Washington
43	Edsall, Joseph E., Estate of	Culpeper
14,891	Edwards, A. T., Estate of	Culpeper
5,878	Edwards, Chas.	Wythe
11,039	Edwards, Elizabeth	Loudoun
6,141	Edwards, John W.	Prince George
11,719	Edwards, Joseph H.	Norfolk
7,606	Edwards, Joseph H.	Patrick
11,041	Edwards, Joseph L.	Loudoun
21,310	Edwards, Lewis	Isle of Wight
20,549	Edwards, Sam H., Estate of	Loudoun
18,207	Edwards, Wm. G.	Fauquier
15,674	Eichberg, Abram	Dinwiddie
19,351	Elgin, John W.	Fairfax
6,477	Elinger, Peter	Augusta
14,143	Eller, Abraham	Roanoke
4,177	Eller, John, Sr.	Roanoke
13,928	Ellicott, Thos.	Prince William
16,465	Ellington, Wm.	Stafford
10,212	Ellington, Wm. F.	Prince Edward
17,685	Elliott, Josiah	Norfolk
11,016	Elliott, Perry	Fairfax
3,535	Elliott, Robert & Wm.	Norfolk
8,307	Elliott, Wm.	Alexandria
21,216	Ellis, Martin	Page
9,751	Ellison, Wm. H.	Fairfax
15,468	Elly, Edward	Culpeper
21,361	Ellzey, Wm. W., Estate of	Loudoun
15,497	Elmore, Hartwell, Estate of	Dinwiddie
14,847	Elmore, Wm. M.	Richmond
15,535	Elsea, Delitha	Clarke
12,493	Ely, Eliza	Lee
22,110	Embrey, Dan	Stafford
6,919	Embrey, James M.	Stafford
21,071	Embrey, John James	Fauquier
18,194	Embrey, S. G.	Fauquier
21,070	Embrey, Sinclair A.	Fauquier
18,196	Embry, Robert, Estate of	Fauquier
848	Embry, Robert D.	Fauquier
14,676	Emmons, Oveil	Fairfax
1,382	Engleman, John	Augusta
1,104	Engleman, Philip	Rockbridge
21,730	Ennis, Richard	Prince William
7,590	Enruffty, Dorrita	Henrico

5,085	Eolly, Richard	Chesterfield
3,491	Epperly, Eli	Floyd
14,398	Epperly, Jacob C.	Floyd
20,397	Eppes, John W.	Prince George
9,672	Epps, Robert P.	Charles City
17,471	Erwin, Walter H.	Fairfax
20,005	Escridge, Henry	Fairfax
18,882	Eskridge, Meredith, Estate of	Fauquier
3,434	Essex, Victoria E.	Fauquier
4,480	Estep, John H.	Shenandoah
20,769	Estes, Ann	Orange
20,772	Estes, James W.	Orange
22,297	Estes, John, Heirs of	Spotsylvania
21,245	Etheridge, Coland, John, Lalla, Rooke & Percival	Norfolk
7,634	Etheridge, India V.	Norfolk
4,510: 16,733:	Etheridge, Sam	Norfolk
5,073	Evans, Davis D.	Shenandoah
21,813	Evans, Ellen E.	Henrico
21,584	Evans, Jonathan, Estate of	Loudoun
14,572	Evans, Richard	Lancaster
20,788	Evans, Wm. A.	Frederick
11,000	Everhart, Edmund S.	Clarke
10,439	Everhart, Elizabeth	Loudoun
11,229: 11,652:	Everhart, John	Loudoun
11,040	Everhart, John B.	Loudoun
11,517	Everhart, Joseph	Loudoun
11,653	Everhart, Joshua	Loudoun
2,576	Evers, Geo. W. M.	Rockingham
8,938	Evers, John (of Bridgewater)	Rockingham
16,504: 21,775:	Evers, John (of Cross Keys)	Rockingham
20,811	Ewbank, Emma S.	Lancaster
3,453	Ewing, Nathaniel	Lee
17,910	Ewing, Wm. D.	Augusta
21,641: 20,998:	Faggins, Robert	Henrico
12,534	Fahey, Thos.	Alexandria
15,933	Fahnestock, Wm.	Frederick
14,346	Falen, Wm. A.	Scott
16,919	Fallin, John Hobson, Estate of	Northumberland
1,287	Fant, Hamilton G.	Henrico
635	Farish, James	Culpeper
7,594	Farley, Helen T.	Dinwiddie
5,997	Farley, Isaiah	Hanover
21,812	Farrell, Thos., Estate of	Prince William
6,718	Farrow, Geo. A., Estate of	Albermarle
1,816	Fauber, Harrison	Shenandoah
2,819	Fauber, Valentine	Shenandoah
1,727	Fauber, Wm. T.	Augusta
21,841	Faught, Nancy	Rockingham
16,813	Faulk, Letitia	Norfolk
20,774	Faulkner, Richard J.	Fairfax
2,368	Fauntleroy, John M.	King William
1,383	Fauver, John B.	Augusta
304	Fawcett, Elkanah	Frederick
15,298	Fawley, Jeremiah	Loudoun
14,659	Feagles, John L.	Pulaski
52	Febrey, John E.	Fairfax
6,328	Feguson, Esther J.	Fairfax
12,414	Fenton, Mary J.	Frederick
11	Fenton, Sam	Fairfax
3,230	Fenwick, Thos.	Fairfax
19,994	Ferguson, Louisa & Wm.	Fairfax
13,701	Ferguson, Preston	Appomatox
13,704	Ferguson, Silburn P.	Appomatox
13,699	Ferguson, Stephen	Appomatox
8,742	Ferguson, Uriah	Fairfax
19,994	Ferguson, Wm. & Louisa	Fairfax
21,690	Ferrell, Orzey, Estate of	King George
846	Ferris, Wm.	Fairfax
20,728	Ferry Company, Norfolk	Norfolk
13,777	Fessenden, Sarah A.	Northumberland

21,793	Fetzer, Bernard	Frederick
9,722	Fetzer, Geo. H.	Rockingham
4,733	Fetzer, Sam	Shenandoah
5,365	Ficklen, Joseph B.	Stafford
4,559	Fiddler, Lindsey L.	Henrico
3,003	Field, Ira	Culpeper
14,208	Field, James W.	Loudoun
11,342	Fields, James & Young, Franklin	Loudoun
533	Fiendley, James	Norfolk
19	Finch, Davis L.	Fairfax
14,754	Finney, Reuben	Prince George
6,568	Firestone, David M.	Botetourt
532	Fish, Sam	Fairfax
2,136	Fishburn, Dan	Augusta
18,234	Fisher & Co.	Frederick
13,679	Fisher, David, Estate of	Shenandoah
13,678	Fisher, Isaac, Estate of	Shenandoah
14,070	Fisher, James H.	King William
11,105	Fisher, John	Henrico
4,724	Fisher, John	Shenandoah
14,809	Fisher, Martha A.	Fauquier
200	Fisher, Sam P.	Lousia
4,560	Fisher, Susan C.	Henrico
13,014	Fisher, Thos.	Alexandria
20,935	Fitzgerald, John	Prince William
14,013	Fitzhugh, Anna M.	Fairfax
14,896	Fitzhugh, Edwin C.	Alexandria
1,695	Fitzhugh, Henry	Spotsylvania
12,619	Fitzhugh, Sallie J.	Loudoun
20,787	Fitzhugh, Thos.	Culpeper
20,097	Fitzhugh, Wm. D.	Prince William
7,011	Fix, Adam	Augusta
1,384	Fix, John H.	Augusta
1,607	Flagher, Albert	Fairfax
8,093	Flaherty, Edward G.	Botetourt
3,777	Fleenor, Wesley	Washington
15,815	Fleshman, Fielding	Madison
16,113	Fletcher, E. A., Mrs.	Loudoun
10,708	Fletcher, Geo. R.	Frederick
6,711	Fletcher, John E.	Fauquier
216	Fletcher, John W.	Fauquier
20,917	Fletcher, Thos.	Rappahanock
1,468	Fletcher, Wm.	Fauquier
1,469	Fletcher, Wm. H.	Fauquier
19,588	Fletcher, Wm. S.	Accomack
14,573	Flippers, Elizabeth	Lancaster
2,573	Flory, Dan	Rockingham
8,411	Flory, John	Rockingham
2,585	Flory, Joseph	Augusta
2,575	Flory, Noah	Rockingham
5,351	Flowerree, G. Hanson	Fauquier
20,993	Foglesong, Margaret M.	Bland
20,926	Foley, Mary	Prince William
20,475	Follin, Joseph N.	Fairfax
21,654	Follin, Mary, Heirs of	Fairfax
15,327	Follin, Richard	Fairfax
21,291	Foltz, Noah	Page
10,184	Foltz, Sam	Culpeper
20,357	Foote, Francis T., Estate of	Prince William
8,452	Foote, Frederick	Fairfax
9,125	Force, Adolphus; Clark, Eldora, Robert M. & Richard	Prince William
6,337	Ford, Carter	Fauquier
14,374	Ford, Jane & Matthew	Culpeper
14,374	Ford, Matthew & Jane	Culpeper
17,448	Foreman, Alex N.	Norfolk
525	Foreman, Arthur	Norfolk
17,449	Foreman, Naharai	Norfolk
413	Forney, Abraham	Warren
5,443	Fornshill, John	Alexandria
5,013	Forrest, Josiah D.	Mathews
20,932	Foster, Edmund	Prince William
20,906	Foster, Geo.	Warren

10,199	Foster, J. H.	Shenandoah
17,912	Foster, Wm. R.	Augusta
11,284	Fouch, Temple	Loudoun
2,154	Foulke, Andrew	Fairfax
11,009	Foulkes, Joseph M.	Amelia
690	Foushee, John C.	Culpeper
9,918	Fowler, Wm.	Clarke
11,786	Fox, Alfred	Loudoun
21,580	Fox, Bushrod L.	Loudoun
14,803	Fox, John, Estate of	Fauquier
21,205	Fox, John (of Peter)	Page
21,218	Fox, John, Sr.	Page
19,206	Fox, Thos.	New Kent
20,496	Fox, Wm.	Loudoun
211	Francis, Emanuel	Alexandria
11,126	Francis, Wm.	Fauquier
2,554	Frank, Henry	Rockingham
175	Franklin, Benj. T.	Loudoun
8,738	Fraser, Anthony R.	Alexandria
5,179	Fraser, Wm.	Fauquier
5,728	Fravel, Catharine	Shenandoah
16,115	Fred, Thos. L.	Loudoun
20,627	Freeman, Harris	Fauquier
4,606	Freeman, Richard	Norfolk
20,610	Freeman, Sarah A.	Culpeper
13,311	Freeman, Stephen	Fauquier
6,119	Freeman, Thos. A.	Charlotte
95	French, Charles E.	Alexandria
501	Fritter, Gustavus	Stafford
442	Fry, Geo. M.	Loudoun
15,982	Fry, John D.	Loudoun
15,318	Fugett, John R.	Clarke
252	Fultz, David	Augusta
2,506	Funk, Jonathan (of Shem)	Rockingham
9,313	Funk, Timothy	Rockingham
2,952	Funkhouser, Abraham	Shenandoah
4,731	Funkhouser, Geo.	Shenandoah
15,905	Funkhouser, James W.	Shenandoah
18,883	Funkhouser, Joseph E.	Frederick
2,820	Funkhouser, John H.	Shenandoah
10,645	Funkhouser, Louis	Shenandoah
2,900	Funkhouser, Noah M.	Shenahdoah
3,635	Furguson, Edna A.	Fauquier
14,621	Furguson, Jacob	Russell
14,144	Furguson, John B.	Roanoke
5,710	Furr, Geo. M.	Augusta
21,613	Furr, Wm.	Loudoun
20,611	Gaines, Edwin R.	Culpeper
17,485	Gaines, Gustavus	Fauquier
17,263	Gaines, Hester	Lancaster
21,823	Gaines, Mary T.	Culpeper
22,066	Gaines, Thos. B., Estate of	Prince William
10,881	Gale, Alfred	Nansemond
12,089	Gale, Randall	Nansemond
147	Gallagher, Hugh L.	Augusta
5,289	Gallagher, Wm. J.	Fairfax
3,752	Galpin, Emma L. & Nourse, Ella J. and Alfred W.	Fairfax
3,411	Galpin, Josiah	Fairfax
8,996	Gangwer, John	Rockingham
2,504	Gangwer, John B.	Rockingham
8,936	Garber, Abraham	Rockingham
2,555	Garber, Abraham D.	Augusta
9,736	Garber, Christian, Estate of	Rockingham
21,845	Garber, Dan, Estate of	Rockingham
8,029	Garber, David	Rockingham
8,412	Garber, David J.	Rockingham
9,091	Garber, David J. & Dovel, Thos.	Rockingham
2,546	Garber, David W.	Augusta
2,560	Garber, Eli A.	Augusta
2,545	Garber, Elizabeth	Augusta
8,413	Garber, Joel	Rockingham
8,277	Garber, John J.	Rockingham
2,537	Garber, Martin	Augusta
11,096: 15,246:	Garber, Martin	Rockingham
2,505	Garber, Reuben A.	Augusta
2,508	Garber, Sam	Augusta
2,507	Garber, Sam	Shenandoah
8,028	Garber, Solomon	Rockingham
38	Gardiner, Alfred W.	Alexandria
11,055	Gardner, Albert G.	Fairfax
3,061	Gardner, James L.	Loudoun
21,025	Gardner, Nathan	Spotsylvania
171	Garland, Thos.	Albemarle
14,397	Garmong, Emanuel	Warren
14,574	Garner, Griffin	Lancaster
728	Garner, Wm. A.	Stafford
17,975	Garnett, Tabitha	Culpeper
14,209	Garrett, Burr W.	Loudoun
12,957	Garrett, John W.	Loudoun
6,920	Garrison, Alex E.	Stafford
1,745	Garrison, James B.	Stafford
20,770	Garrison, John L.	Stafford
220	Garrison, John R.	Stafford
14,168	Garst, Noah P.	Roanoke
13,713	Gaskins, Bartley	Washington
3,259	Gaskins, Glascoe	Fairfax
10,175	Gaskins, Jane P.	Fauquier
13,173	Gaskins, Nathaniel	Fairfax
20,919	Gaskins, Oliver 2d.	Prince William
18,173	Gaskins, Oliver, Sr.	Fairfax
20,920	Gaskins, Oliver, 3d	Prince William
11,299	Gaskins, Susan, Heirs of	Prince William
11,299: 11,298:	Gaskins, Thos.	Prince William
8,962	Gatewood, John N.	Caroline
16,875	Gatewood, Wright	Shenandoah
2,912	Gaulding, Ellison	Hanover
11,042	Gaver, C. C.	Loudoun
17,913	Gay, Gustavus A.	Rockingham
8,700	Geil, Abraham	Rockingham
16,921	Geil, Henry	Rockingham
21,844	Geil, Jacob	Rockingham
8,701	Geil, John	Rockingham
16,661	Gentry, Louisa A.	Hanover
4,371	George, Edwin E.	Lancaster
14,575	George, Joseph	Lancaster
19,471	George, Sam W.	Loudoun
463: 20,712:	George, Sam W., Jr.	Loudoun
20,711	George, Sam W., Jr. & Heirs of Solomon	Loudoun
14,576	George, Zamoth H.	Lancaster
600	Gerhardt, Christopher	Henrico
1,045	Getz, Wm.	Shenandoah
526	Gibbs, John T.	Norfolk
15,546	Gibson, Edward	King & Queen
4,027	Gibson, Elizabeth & James W.	Alexandria
4,027	Gibson, James W. & Elizabeth	Alexandria
57	Gibson, Sterling, Estate of	Fauquier
8,955	Gibson, Wm., Estate of	Augusta
20	Gilbert, John	Fairfax
6,539	Gilbert, Leroy C.	Rockbridge
7,264	Gilbert, Thos. J.	Augusta
11,857	Gilchrist, Walter	Prince George
11,950	Gill, John L.	Loudoun
11,952	Gill, Wm. H.	Loudoun
16,170	Gillan, John	Alexandria
12,487	Gilliam, Reuben	Prince George
14,615	Galliher, Wm. J.	Washington
18,463	Gillin, Catharine	Henrico
8,243	Gilmer, David	Rockingham
13,790	Gilmore, Alex	Highland
1,441	Gilmore, Sam	Montgomery
5,880	Gilmore, Wm. T.	Montgomery
1,442	Ginn, G. W.	Frederick
19,247	Ginn, James	Frederick
16,952: 17,915:	Gladden, Adam R.	Rockingham

10,946	Glascock, Wm. D.	Fauquier
21,059	Glass, David T., Estate of	Culpeper
15,515	Glick, Joel	Rockingham
14,090: 15,516:	Glick, John	Augusta
2,562	Glick, Sam	Augusta
18,488	Goddin, Adolphus	James City
20,924	Godfrey, Wm. Henry	Fauquier
15,934	Godwin, Wm.	Norfolk
17,722	Gion, Sam	Appomattox
5,998	Goldsby, Caleb	Hanover
1,426	Gollahorn, Elenor	Stafford
1,407	Gollahorn, Thos.	Stafford
2,731	Gomer, Thos.	Nansemond
21,843	Good, Dan J.	Rockingham
9,521	Good, Dan P.	Rockingham
215	Good, Elias	Prince William
9,307	Good, Jacob	Buckingham
7,643	Good, James Y.	Albemarle
1,064	Good, Kesiah	Henrico
15,518	Good, Michael J.	Shenandoah
19,284	Good, Sam	Rockingham
15,517	Good, Sam	Shenandoah
14,704	Goode, John	Craig
1,885	Goodin, Anna	Loudoun
13,572	Gooding, Amanda M.	Fairfax
21,820	Goodloe, Ann, Estate of	Albemarle
578	Goodloe, Benton H.	Nelson
16,644	Goodman, Christopher C.	Hanover
21,267	Goodwin, Geo. M.	Prince William
9,186	Gordon, Ella V.	Culpeper
15,393	Gordon, Ellen	Montgomery
20,904	Gore, Bushrod R.	Warren
13,918	Gorham, James T.	Fairfax
2,945	Gossom, Mary A.	Fairfax
2,551	Gouchenour, Isaac, Estate of	Shenandoah
194	Gould, Elizabeth A.	Alexandria
9,491	Gover, Henry T.	Loudoun
16,652: 16,953:	Gowl, Adam	Rockingham
2,547	Grady, G. W.	Rockingham
2,992	Graham, Amos A.	Floyd
21,788	Graham, Curtis B.	Alexandria
1,127: 1,126:	Graham, Michael	Shenandoah
21,948	Grant, Beverly	Fluvanna
20,360	Grant, Sarah	Warren
12,001	Grantham, Joseph	Clarke
20,768	Graves, Anna H.	Orange
8,963	Graves, Nancy H.	Orange
20,767	Gravis, Garrit	Spotsylvania
7,333	Gravitt, Wm.	Halifax
1,082	Gray, John T.	Nansemond
8,935	Gray, Robert A.	Rockinghan
17,127	Gray, Wm.	Alexandria
19,333	Graybill, Joseph	Botetourt
6,923	Grayson, John	Stafford
16,045	Grayson, Thos. Minor	Fauquier
17,560	Green, Fielding	Loudoun
11,438	Green, Israel	Rappahanock
18,595	Green, James W.	Fairfax
20,613	Green, John G., Heirs of	Culpeper
14,892	Green, Lexington	Culpeper
18,854	Green, Lucy	Charles City
19,819	Green, Richard A.	Frederick
15,284	Green, Robert	Fauquier
2,050	Green, Wm. E.	Spotsylvania
22,274	Greenlaw, Adelaide	Stafford
7,901	Gregg, John	Fauquier
22,050	Gregg, Margaret	Prince William
21,602	Gregg, Nathan, Estate of	Loudoun
7,902	Gregg, Sam	Fauquier
1,590	Griffin, John N.	Culpeper
2,859	Griffin, Sam A.	Culpeper
6,921	Griffis, Thos.	Stafford
8,993	Griffith, Aaron H.	Frederick

21,207	Griffith, John, Jr.	Page
98	Griffith, Lewis P.	Fairfax
16,266	Griffith, Meshack	Franklin
20,907	Grigsby, Bazil	Rappahanock
2,946	Grigsby, Casandra	Rappahanock
18,468	Grigsby, Geofrry	Warren
7,947	Grim. Lyles	Frederick
11,358	Grimes, Madison	Loudoun
12,706	Grimsley, John S.	Culpeper
21,842	Grove, Emanuel	Rockingham
1,397	Grover, Emily J.	Henrico
11,043: 20,101:	Grubb, Benj. H.	Loudoun
66	Grubb, Benj. J.	Loudoun
15,299	Grubb, Curtis	Loudoun
20,494	Grubb, Ebenezer, Jr.	Loudoun
1,331	Grubb, Ebenezer, Sr.	Loudoun
11,805: 21,615:	Grubb, John, Jr.	Loudoun
12,667	Grubb, Sam N.	Loudoun
11,044: 21,593:	Grubb, Wm.	Loudoun
17,262	Gulick, Derrick H.	Northumberland
21,614	Gulick, Sanford	Loudoun
13,791	Gum, Abraham	Highland
13,792	Gum, Isaac	Highland
19,836	Gunnel, Elizabeth	Fairfax
871	Gunnel, Robert	Fairfax
14,048	Gutherie, David	Augusta
15,228	Guy, Charles B.	Orange
15,519	Guyer, Mary	Rockingham
3,004	Gwinn, Mary	Culpeper
12,112	Haas, Judith	Campbell
2,824	Hahn, Elizabeth	Shenandoah
1,293	Haight, Alex	Fairfax
19,511	Hailey, Wm. W.	Augusta
21,187	Haines, Dan, Estate of	Fauquier
21,004	Haines, Harriet	Shenandoah
14,553	Haislip, John	Fairfax
14,555	Haislip, John & Trice, F. M.	Fairfax
9,976	Hale, Cherry	Nansemond
3,246	Hale, Elizabeth	Richmond
15,394	Hale, Robert	Roanoke
8,437	Haley, John	Culpeper
8,042	Hall, Alex	Floyd
22,282	Hall, Asa C.	Bland
2,422	Hall, Brazil	Alexandria
9,306	Hall, Geo. G.	Rockingham
610	Hall, John J.	Fairfax
2,964	Hall, Mary	Washington
11,669	Hall, Mary A.	Alexandria
6,120	Hall, Sam	Washington
21,186	Hall, Spencer	Fauquier
15,192	Hall, Susan P. W.	Culpeper
2,065	Hall, Thos. B.	Montgomery
14,250	Hall, Wesley	Fairfax
8,692	Hamilton, Brandon & William	Washington
12,489	Hamilton, E. B.	Clarke
1,121	Hamilton, Edward F.	Loudoun
20,420	Hamilton, Wm.	Washington
8,692	Hamilton, Wm. & Brandon	Washington
4,919	Hamman, Rebecca	Shenandoah
21,011	Hammerly, Chas. W.	Loudoun
18,565	Hammill, Hugh	Prince William
11,590	Hancock, Anthony	Appomattox
4,981	Hancock, Edwin	Craig
3,062	Hancock, Stephen	Craig
731	Hand, Thos.	Rappahanock
19,933	Hanger, Hannah M.	Augusta
15,321	Hansell, James W.	Frederick
6,059	Hansenfluck, Wm.	Warren
10,196	Hardesty, Isaac	Rockingham
10,130	Harding, Hiram	Northumberland
12,515	Harding, Wm. J.	Stafford
14,744	Hardwick, A. L.	Washington
15,856	Hardy, Henry M.	Loudoun
254	Harkader, Margaret	Wythe

8,230	Harless, Allen	Montgomery
13,369	Harmon, Manoah	Shenandoah
1,789	Harman, W. H.	Montgomery
2,431	Harmon, Benj.	Floyd
537	Harmon, Thos.	Alleghany
18,232	Harper, Ann E.; and Owings, Jesse	Alexandria
11,657	Harper, Chas. F.	Loudoun
9,673	Harper, John E.	Nottoway
10,210	Harper, Sarah	Nottoway
8,605	Harrell, Mary N.	Norfolk
14,403	Harris, Charlotte	Floyd
1,918	Harris, Chas. P.	Prince William
15,498	Harris, Emeline	Dinwiddie
242	Harris, Geo.	Fairfax
19,909	Harris, James, Estate of	Rockbridge
7,738	Harris, Jesse	Fairfax
16,198	Harris, Joseph, Estate of	Fairfax
20,921	Harris, Kittie	Fairfax
18,172	Harris, Moses	Fairfax
7,739	Harris, Obed	Fairfax
8,961	Harris, Octavus D.	Caroline
7,592	Harris, P. B.	Charles City
19,845	Harris, Wm.	Henrico
1,186	Harris, Wm.	Spotsylvania
16,364	Harrison, Henry F.	Amelia
21,847	Harrison, John	Rockingham
1,271	Harrison, John H.	Fairfax
2,913	Harrison, Richard	Dinwiddie
16,857	Harrison, Sam J.	Washington
17,916	Harrison, Wm. C.	Rockingham
2,584	Harshbarger, Jacob	Rockingham
2,567	Harshbarger, John & Jacob	Rockingham
21,846	Harshbarger, Joseph W.	Rockingham
18,574	Hart, John	Alexandria
19,862	Hart, Joseph S.	Fairfax
10,328	Hart, Mary	Clarke
9,731	Hartman, Christian	Rockingham
18,423: 21,852:	Hartman, David	Rockingham
21,851	Hartman, Sam	Rockingham
11,045	Hartman, Thos. J.	Loudoun
13,793	Harvy, James	Alleghany
2,973	Haskins, James O. C.	Fairfax
12,958	Hatcher, Thos. E.	Loudoun
8,443	Hatchen, Wm.	Franklin
11,861	Hauling, Sidney, Estate of	Loudoun
15,300	Havener, Joseph	Loudoun
21,612	Havener, Thos. Al	Loudoun
11,514	Hawes, Oliver	Loudoun
444	Hawes, Wm.	Loudoun
810	Hawhrustt, John & Job	Fairfax
21,824	Hawkins, John W.	Culpeper
15,520	Hawse, John	Rockingham
4,452	Hayden, Richard H.	Lancaster
10,259	Hayden, Thos.	Augusta
286	Hayes, Alonzo G., Annie M., and Malvina A. G.	Alexandria
20,937	Hayes, Electy	Fauquier
18,863	Hayman, John	Norfolk
11,594	Hays, Elvira	Campbell
16,334	Hazen, Abraham N.	Prince William
16,335	Hazen, Chas. W. & Issac L. N.	Prince William
16,333	Hazen, Levi, Estate of	Prince William
9,932	Headley, Jonathan	Frederick
251	Heater, Caroline	Frederick
12,466	Heater, John	Loudoun
10,095	Heath, Augustine B.	Dinwiddie
8,997	Heatwole, Abraham D.	Rockingham
21,831	Heatwole, Gabriel D.	Rockingham
8,699	Heatwole, J. G., Estate of	Rockingham
14,705	Heavner, Strother	Montgomery
1,953: 20,543:	Hedgeman, Francis	Alexandria
1,123	Hedgman, Peter D. G.	Stafford
8,335	Hedrick, John	Rockingham

12,129	Heflen, James	Stafford
312	Heflin, G. W.	Fauquier
12,942	Heflin, Mary Ann	Fauquier
20,597	Heflin, Wm.	Culpeper
16,563	Heflin, Wm. H.	Fauquier
3,050	Herlybower, Mary	Clarke
465	Hefner, Andrew	Loudoun
21,097	Heller, Theresia E.	Rockingham
18,203	Helm, James H.	Fauquier
14,616	Helvey, John J.	Montgomery
1,385	Hemp, Wm. D.	Augusta
10,996	Henderson, Chas. W.	Loudoun
1,408	Henderson, Edward G.	Stafford
14,825	Henderson, Robert	King & Queen
9,127	Hendricks, A. L.	Washington
2,289	Henry, Sam	Scott
9,208	Henry, Theodore B.	Fauquier
620	Henson, John	Fluvanna
20,550	Hern, Wm.	Loudoun
2,369	Herndon, Esther H.	Madison
17,248	Herndon, Ludwell	Stafford
20,752	Herrick, Geo. R.	Alexandria
1,386	Hess, G. W. & Jacob	Augusta
1,386	Hess, Jacob & G. W.	Augusta
15,881	Hewitt, Horace B.	Stafford
16,123	Hibbs, Solomon	Fauquier
11,654	Hickman, Ann E.	Loudoun
447	Hickman, Geo., Estate of	Loudoun
5,247	Hicks, Cassandra C.	Goochland
1,006	Hicks, John T.	Culpeper
509	Hicks, Wm. R., Estate of	Albemarle
509	Hicks, Wm. R., Estate of	Augusta
4,727	Hide, Joseph	Shenandoah
2,915	Higgins, Chas. J.	New Kent
4,561	Higgins, John	New Kent
2,914	Higgins, Joseph F.	New Kent
1,398	Higgins, Thaddeus	Hanover
15,906	Hildebrand, John	Rockingham
868	Hiler, G. W.	Washington
9,128	Hill, Gabriel	Prince George
11,486	Hill, James W.	Loudoun
2,936	Hill, J. M.	Dinwiddie
8,609	Hill, Robert	Dinwiddie
12,407	Hill, Thos. Jefferson	King William
6,912	Hill, Willis P.	Dinwiddie
11,784	Hilleary, Wm. P.	Loudoun
15,970	Hilliard, Cynthia	New Kent
8,340	Hinegardner, Nancy	Rockingham
6,449	Hines, Rachel	Patrick
2,947	Hines, Thos.	Fairfax
16,653	Hinkle, Wm.	Rockingham
3,208	Hipkins, James W.	Richmond
11,451	Hiser, Henry & John	Shenandoah
11,451	Hiser, John & Henry	Shenandoah
12,042	Hisey, Abraham	Shenandoah
13,367	Hite, Isaac R.	Shenandoah
2,717	Hixon, Noah	Prince William
13,177	Hoage, Shelden J., Estate of	Fairfax
3,309	Hobbs, Hanson	Washington
7,646	Hockman, Isaac	Shenandoah
21,220	Hockman, Jacob	Shenandoah
4,720	Hockman, John	Shenandoah
4,728	Hockman, Michael	Shenandoah
2,826	Hockman, Noah	Shenandoah
247	Hodges, Ann Eliza	Norfolk
2,336	Hodges, James G.	Norfolk
22	Hodges, Oliver	Fairfax
13,702	Hodges, Wm.	Franklin
2,633	Hodgson, Abner	Frederick
11,888	Hodgson, Caroline O.	Loudoun
12,440	Hodgson, Elijah	Frederick
2,632	Hodgson, Sam	Frederick
126	Hoff, Lydia and Updike, Hannah	Rappahanock
3,005	Hoffman, Aaron B.	Culpeper
13,436	Hoffman, Wm. D.	Stafford
1,294	Hoge, Solomon	Fauquier
20,412	Holladay, Wm.	Dinwiddie

7,038	Holland, Ahab	Nansemond
19,285	Holland, Archibald	Rockingham
20,928	Holland, Chas. W.	Prince William
12,508	Holland, Jacob	Nansemond
5,170	Holland, John R.	Fauquier
12,091	Holland, Wiley	Nansemond
17,091	Holland, Wm.	Fairfax
21,827	Hollar, G. W.	Augusta
9,361	Holler, Philip	Rockingham
436	Hollingsworth, Chas. L.	Loudoun
4,784	Hollingsworth, Harriet B.	Frederick
21,072	Holmes, James E.	Fauquier
3,006	Holmes, John Henry	Culpeper
12,693	Holsapple, Wm. M.	Fairfax
2,124	Holt, Sam P.	Campbell
15,812	Holtzman, Augustine & Mary Louisa	Frederick
15,812	Holtzman, Mary Louisa & Augustine	Frederick
9,362	Homan, Mary L.	Rockingham
15,907	Homan, Michael, Estate of	Rockingham
92	Hooe, George Anna S.	Spotsylvania
1,181	Hoomes, Dan	Spotsylvania
15,521	Hoover, Emanuel M.	Rockingham
21,848	Hoover, Jacob	Rockingham
15,908: 21,849:	Hoover, John, Estate of	Rockingham
21,794	Hoover, John H.	Frederick
21,616	Hope, John A.	Loudoun
13,153	Hope, Sallie	Fauquier
10,098	Hope, S. Wm.	Accomack
2,360	Hopkins, Chas. A.	Fairfax
2,361	Hopkins, John H.	Fairfax
9,065	Hopkins, John P. L. & Wm. H.	Accomack
19,580	Hopkins, Stephen & Curtis, Wm. P.	Accomack
2,362	Hopkins, Wm.	Fairfax
9,065	Hopkins, Wm. H. & John P.L.	Accomack
14,886	Hoppe, Theodore	Albemarle
12,708	Hoppe, Wm. A.	Prince Edward
13,154	Hord, Elizabeth	Fauquier
11,550	Hord, Sam	Fauquier
214	Hornbaker, John R.	Prince William
870	Horne, Isaac	Washington
19,825	Horner, Frederick	Fauquier
15,752	Horner, Inman	Fauquier
19,583	Horsey, Wm. S.	Accomack
4,723	Hottle, J. T.	Shenandoah
2,821	Hottle, Sam	Shenandoah
7,881	Houff, Erasmus Leroy	Augusta
7,880	Houff, Wm. A.	Augusta
21,579	Hough, Amasa, Estate of	Loudoun
21,578	Hough, Amasa, Jr.	Loudoun
174	Hough, Wm.	Loudoun
11,645	Hough, Wm. N.	Loudoun
7,586	Howell, John	New Knet
2,899	Hughes, James M.	Nelson
2,897	Hughes, Lucien	Nelson
448: 10,886:	Householder, Gideon	Loudoun
11,070	Houser, Jacob H.	Warren
440	Houser, Richard	Loudoun
4,372	Houston, John	Cumberland
14,554	Howard, Beverly W.	Fauquier
2,718	Howard, Chas. F.	Prince William
20,923	Howard, John R.	Prince William
3,221	Howard, Maria	Fairfax
21,012	Howell, Craven	Loudoun
15,058	Hoyer, Paul	Stafford
15,522	Huddle, Abraham	Rockingham
19,286	Hudlow, Elias	Rockingham
15,754	Hudnall, Blucker	Fauquier
390	Hudnall, Drayton	Fauquier
21,179	Hudnall, Westward	Fauquier

2,705	Hudson, Augustine G.	Alexandria
15,193	Hudson, Lucy	Culpeper
15,194	Hudson, Matilda G.	Culpeper
8,333	Huff, Dan	Frederick
8,359	Huff, Esom	Floyd
14,404	Huff, Isaac M	Franklin
8,442	Huff, Jacob	Franklin
7,948	Huff, Joseph H.	Shenandoah
11,175	Huff, Thos. G.	Roanoke
20,000	Huffman, Abraham	Page
17,918	Huffman, Edward	Rockingham
8,339	Huffman, Elijah	Rockingham
19,997	Huffman, Isaac, Sr.	Page
19,945	Huffman, James A.	Giles
19,268	Huffman, John	Rockingham
17,919	Huffman, Sam, Estate of	Augusta
13,067	Hughes, Joseph H. et al	Alexandria
11,251	Hughes, Sallie P.	Halifax
15,278	Hughes, Thos., Estate of	Alexandria
13,929	Hughlett, Elizabeth	Alexandria
14,287	Hughs, Jerry	Fauquier
240	Hull, Sam V.	Frederick
1,728	Hulvey, Ephraim	Augusta
2,524	Humbert, Jacob L.	Augusta
2,563	Humbert, John M.	Augusta
2,553	Humbert, Sam D.	Augusta
18,879	Hume, Jacob	Fauquier
3,218	Hummer, Benj. A.	Fairfax
11,889	Humphrey, Phebe	Loudoun
11,485	Humphrey, Thos. L.	Loudoun
11,862	Humphrey, Thos. M.	Loudoun
13,794	Humphries, Jesse	Alleghany
13,795	Humphries, Wm.	Alleghany
6,121	Hunt, John	Southampton
15,990	Hunter, Alex B.	Madison
9,289	Hunter, Lavinia G.	Alexandria
8,334	Hunter, Sawney	Clarke
812	Huntington, Thos.	Alexandria
19,561	Hupman, Valentine	Augusta
18,464	Hupp, Catharine, Estate of	Shenandoah
16,876	Hurley, Julia	Augusta
20,477	Hurley, Lucinda	Alexandria
13,796	Hurley, Thos.	Alleghany
2,125	Hurt, Meredith E.	Nottoway
20,890	Hutchinson, Elizabeth	Loudoun
11,535	Hutchinson, John	Prince William
11,951	Hutchinson, Joseph A.	Loudoun
21,003	Hutchinson, Wm.	Alexandria
2,898	Hutter, Henry W.	Nelson
1,858	Huyett, Henry	Clarke
17,170	Hylton, Elijah W.	Floyd
20,754	Hyson, James S.	Alexandria
20,755	Hyson, John E.	Alexandria
20,098	Iden, Elizabeth	Fauquier
2,156	Ihms, Anthony	Alexandria
12,111	Ikenberry, Benj.	Franklin
15,963	Indiana Methodist Church	Norfolk
10,150	Inge, Willis	Appomatox
3,007	Inskeep, Mary Ann	Culpeper
4,441	Iron Company, Cumberland Coal &	Alexandria
17,093	Irwin, James W.	Clarke
10,322	Irwin, Joseph S.	Shenandoah
19,021	Irwin, Thos., Estate of	Fairfax
11,593	Isbell, Charles	Appomattox
11,592	Isbell, Joseph	Appomattox
845	Ives, A. Henry	Alexandria
12,300	Ives, Mary	Fairfax
287	Ives, Reuben	Fairfax
4,983	Ivirson, Savory	Clarke
3,008	Jackson, Alex	Culpeper
13,797	Jackson, Croppord	Alleghany
6,916	Jackson, Eliza	Dinwiddie
709	Jackson, George	Fauquier
11,328	Jackson, J. Fenton	Frederick
12,526	Jackson, John	Fairfax
19,246	Jackson, John	Fairfax
11,717	Jackson, Joseph	Prince George

19,264	Jackson, Richard F.	Fairfax
12,473	Jackson, Walter	Spotsylvania
16,295	Jackson, Walter C., Estate of	Amelia
9,978	Jackson, Wm.	Nansemond
1,183	Jackson, Wm.	Spotsylvania
14,025	Jacobs, Edward N.	Loudoun
2,827	Jacobs, John	Shenandoah
11,111	Jacobs, Lytha	Fauquier
3,237	James, Aldridge	Fauquier
15,499	James, Alfred	Prince George
13,323	James, Amanda M.	Fauquier
12,787	James, Duncan	Fauquier
1,486	James, Mahlon	Fauquier
446	James, Richard	Loudoun
18,280	James, Robert	Henrico
12,427	James, Wm.	Henrico
20,405	James, Wm., Estate of	Henrico
4,759	Jamison, G. W.	Culpeper
1,247	Janney, James C.	Loudoun
9,536	Janney, Joseph T. & Smoot, Thos	Prince Wm.
4,762	Jayne, Robert, Estate of	Scott
15,385	Jefferson, Nancy & Thos.	Augusta
14,899: 21,729:	Jeffries, Robert L.	Fauquier
6,648	Jenkins, James H.	Fairfax
19,831	Jenkins, Jonathan	Frederick
21,013	Jenkins, Reuben	Loudoun
4,562	Jenkins, Robert L.	Hanover
18,355	Jenks , Augustus A., Estate of	Chesterfield
13,185	Jenks, W. S. & Bailey, Eliz.	Alexandria
12,704	Jenks, Wm., Heirs of	Alexandria
18,365	Jennings, Ahaz R.	New Kent
13,069	Jennings, Geo. T.	Culpeper
2,917	Jennings, James F.	Goochland
18,366	Jennings, John W.	New Kent
18,470	Jennings, Joseph L., Heirs of	Fauquier
85	Jennings,, Wm. R.	Halifax
427	Jett, James, Estate of	Rappahanock
9,183	Jett, John	Rappahanock
15,368	Jett , Norvell W.	Spotsylvania
1,180	Jett, Thos.	Spotsylvania
179	Jewell, Francis	Montgomery
20,356	Jewell, Henry C.	Alexandria
14,405	Jewell, Wm.	Floyd
20,709	Jewell, Wm., Estate of	Alexandria
11,588	Johns, Sam	Appomattox
10,151	Johnson, Albert	Appomattox
21,582	Johnson, Alex	Loudoun
19,587	Johnson, Alfred F., Estate of	Accomack
11,253	Johnson, Annie M.	Alexandria
11,782	Johnson, Armistead M.	Loudoun
14,622	Johnson, Benj. E.	Russell
10,094	Johnson, Betsey	Fairfax
14,015	Johnson, Charles	Fauquier
21,018	Johnson, Chas . E.	Fairfax
21,577	Johnson, Chas. W.	Loudoun
15,533	Johnson, Cloe	Nansemond
17,126	Johnson, Court H.	Fairfax
19,993	Johnson, G.W.	Fairfax
17,921	Johnson, Harvey	Rockingham
17,628	Johnson, Henry	Fairfax
1,046	Johnson, John	Shenandoah
3,300	Johnson, John	Smyth
4,444	Johnson, John P.A.	Louisa
17,837	Johnson, John R.	Accomack
15,007	Johnson, Joseph L.	Loudoun
6,339	Johnson, Lewis	Hanover
570	Johnson, Luke, F.	Norfolk
16,125	Johnson, Melvin	Loudoun
21,017	Johnson, Mildred H.	Fairfax
2,918	Johnson, Mildred M.	Louisa

17,510	Johnson, Meshack	Frederick
10,699	Johnson, Ray	Warren
3,409	Johnson, Richard	Orange
10,195	Johnson, Robert	Loudoun
11,589	Johnson, Spencer	Appomattox
17,385	Johnson, Thos.	Halifax
21,121	Johnston, John R.	Fairfax
18,010	Jolliffe, Joseph N.	Frederick
21,832	Jones, Absalom W.	Rockingham
17,723	Jones, Albert	Appomattox
18,493	Jones, Benj. D.M.	Nottoway
469	Jones, Bransom G.	Rappahanock
16,654	Jones, David S., Estate of	Rockingham
18,197	Jones, Diadenia, Estate of	Fauquier
6,473	Jones, E.W.	Charles City
21,937	Jones, Edward	Fauquier
2,700	Jones, Fielding	Culpepper
22,106	Jones, Fred	Fairfax
19,434	Jones, Gabriel	Fairfax
19,671	Jones, Gabriel	Spotsylvania
5,980	Jones, Isaac	Elizabeth City
16,643	Jones, James H.	Charles City
21,989	Jones, Joel	Bedford
13,970	Jones, John A.	Nansemond
7,726	Jones, John D.	Charles City
1,409	Jones, John W.	Stafford
18,495	Jones, Joseph M.	Henry
12,805	Jones, Levi	Alexandria
15,301	Jones, Lewin F.	Loudoun
470	Jones, Lucy A.M.	Rappahanock
11,180	Jones, Lydia H.	Loudoun
21,622	Jones, Mary W.	Fairfax
19,362	Jones, Milford	Frederick
9,522	Jones, Morrison	Rockingham
13,467	Jones, Owen	Washington
7,727	Jones, Ruby	Charles City
8,960	Jones, Robert	Orange
2,719	Jones, Thos.	Prince Wm.
6,474	Jones, Thos. C.	Hanover
3,227	Jones, Wm.	Alexandria
1,218	Jones, Wm.	Mecklenburg
1,410	Jones, Wm. A.	Stafford
9,087	Jones, Wm. W.	Amelia
14,826	Jordon, G. W.	King & Queen
19,564	Jordan, James	Augusta
16,789	Jordan, Lucy, Estate of	Rockbridge
16,154	Jordan, Nathan	Nansemond
21,734	Joy, G. W.	Prince Wm.
4,563	Joyce, John	Dinwiddie
21,211	Judy, Abraham, Estate of	Page
19,559	Judy, Henry	Rockbridge
2,521	Kagey, Mary	Rockingham
1,122: 11,285:	Kalb, John G. R.	Loudoun
10,889	Kalb, Sam J.	Loudoun
13,947	Kane, Mary	Caroline
449	Karn, Michael	Loudoun
15	Karner, Lanslet, Sir; and Millard, Josiah	Fairfax & Loudoun
10,174: 11,172:	Kase, Elijah L.	Prince Wm.
14,827	Kauffman, Jeremiah, Estate of	King & Queen
11,800	Kauffman, Joseph	Page
314	Kay, Joseph W.	Alexandria
16,621	Keagy, John R.	Rockingham
820	Kealey, John	Norfolk
976	Kearney, Louisa	Alexandria
10,331	Keeler, G. W.	Frederick
13,469	Keeler, Leander J.	Washington
14,733	Keeling, Thos.	Princess Anne
16,117	Keen, John	Loudoun
4,213	Keens, Richard	Fairfax
17,367	Keiser, John K.	Augusta
16,092	Keith, Mary V. & Susan P.	Fauquier
16,092	Keith, Susan P. & Mary V.	Fauquier

20,182	Kellam, Sallie R.	Accomack
19,287	Keller, Dan	Shenandoah
10,316	Kelley, Fannie	Hanover
19,295	Kelley, Lewis	King William
4,445	Kelly, Ellen, John & John L.; and Williams, Warren & Hannah	Alexandria
1,702	Kelly, G. W.	Patrick
528	Kelly, John	Alleghany
59	Kelly, John	Norfolk
8,469	Kelly, John	Rockingham
4,445	Kelly, John, John L. & Ellen; and Williams, Warren W. & Hannah	Alexandria
18,233	Kelly, Sylvester	Elizabeth City
18,550	Kelso, Joseph W.	Rockbridge
18,878	Kemper, Adaline S.	Fauquier
21,073	Kemper, Peter	Fauquier
11,296	Kemper, Thos. J.	Prince Wm.
1,295	Kendall, Claiborne	Fauquier
9,908	Kennan, James H.	Clarke
19,602	Kennedy, Dan W.	Nelson
20,934	Kenner, Sam	Warren
9,431	Kenney, John	Louisa
20,762	Kenney, Robert H.	Louisa
20,905	Kenny, John W.	Warren
4,453	Kent, Drury, C.	Northumberland
564	Kent, Horace L.	Henrico
12,020	Kent, John	Botetourt
17,384	Kern, Nimrod	Frederick
20,550	Kern, Wm.	Loudoun
8,228	Kesler, Christian	Montgomery
3,308	Kesner, Philip	Washington
11,770	Kessler, John	Botetourt
12,609	Keys, David	Fairfax
5,444	Keys, James	Fairfax
21,208	Keyser, Benj. F.	Page
21,655	Keyser, Joseph R.	Page
21,206	Kibler, David	Page
13,896	Kiester, David, Sr.	Montgomery
13,892	Kiester, Harman S.	Montgomery
15,252	Kiester, Henry L.	Montgomery
13,798	Kincaid, James S.	Alleghany
13,799	Kincaid, Sam	Alleghany
19,885	Kindig, Elias M.	Augusta
8,610	King, Allen	Prince George
5,293	King, Craven J.	Prince Wm.
14,251	King, George P.	Stafford
11,475	King, James J.	Halifax
6,142	King, John F.	Orange
11,127	King, Matthew	Prince Wm.
22,114	King, Sam	Spotsylvania
641	King, Sarah	Norfolk
8,740	Kinsey, Oty T.	Floyd
434	Kirby, Chas.	Fairfax
636	Kirk, James B.	Culpeper
15,715	Kirkpatrick, Thos.	Rockingham
645	Kirtly, Francis W. & St. Clair D.	Rockingham
13,977	Kitchen, Chas. W.	Fairfax
17,295	Kite, Reuben	Page
742	Kite, Wm. H.	Orange
2,503	Kline, Christian	Augusta
21,828	Kline, David	Rockingham
15,250	Kline, Geo.	Rockingham
2,538	Kline, John B.	Rockingham
2,550	Kline, Joseph F.	Rockingham
962	Kline, Mary A.	Prince Wm.
8,157	Kline, Michael B. E.	Rockingham
1,147	Kline, Sam	Augusta
2,523: 8,468:	Kline, Sam	Rockingham
18,424	Knighting, Meredith	Rockingham
11,373	Knox, James	Prince George
1,411	Knoxville, Mary	Stafford
17,820	Krantz, Wm. H.	Loudoun
2,951	Kronck, Sam	Shenandoah

9,523	Kyger, Alex	Rockingham
8,242	Kyger, Nicholas	Rockingham
19,961	Lacey, Richard P.	Fairfax
222: 17,407:	Lacey, Robert S.	Alexandria
1,273	Lacey, Wm. B. & Ware, Chas.A.	Alexandria
11,879	Lackey, Moses	Fairfax
1,976	Lacks, R.B.	Halifax
8,170	Ladd, James A.	Charles City
10,208	Ladd, Joseph H.	Charles City
16,787	Lam, James	Rockbridge
18,551	Lam, John	Rockbridge
2,706	Lamb, Harriet	Fairfax
19,277	Lamb, John C.	Carroll
21,829	Lamb, Mary	Rockingham
9,749: 16,336:	Lamb, Thos, K., Heirs of	Prince Wm.
8,032	Lambert, Isaac	Shenandoah
20,922	Lambert, John	Prince Wm.
19,992	Lambden, John	Alexandria
15,871	Lancaster, Richard	Madison
12,639	Landers, John, Jr.	Bath
17,923	Landes, Christian	Augusta
19,565	Landes, David W.	Augusta
17,922	Landes, John W.	Augusta
8,414	Landes, Noah	Rockingham
16,924	Landes, Sam	Fairfax
596	Landes, Wm. A.	Augusta
15,143	Lane, G.W.	Hanover
13,303	Lane, Indiana	Montgomery
3,241	Lane, Ira	Alexandria
1,401	Lange, Francis	Henrico
15,144	Langston, Holt	King Wm.
15,415	Langston, James, Estate of	King Wm.
14,978	Langston, John	King Wm.
14,980	Langston, Thos. W.	King Wm.
21,949	Langston, Wm. C.	New Kent
2,638	Larell, Abraham	Augusta
56	Larry, James	Hanover
4,984	Latham, Mary C.	Rappahanock
17,508	Latham, Thos.	Frederick
2,004	Lavery, Wm.	Norfolk
20,721	Law, Abner W.	Alexandria
4,619	Lawrence, Alex	Culpeper
20,421	Lawrence, Lewis	Fauquier
12,371	Lawrence, Sarah E.	Nansemond
7,903	Lawson, James	Fauquier
947	Lawson, James W.	Fauquier
16,938	Lawson, Rebecca	Rockingham
16,467	Lawson, Robert & Washington, Peyton	Stafford
12,468	Lawson, Thos.	Alexandria
650	Layton, Morgan	Rockingham
13,780	Leary, Thos. H.	Henrico
4,985	Leavell, Mary J.	Rappahanock
8,094	Ledgerwood, Wm. J.	Roanoke
13,800	Lee, Arthur	Alleghany
14,994	Lee, Jesse	Frederick
6,340	Lee, John	Fairfax
8,364	Lee, Littleton L.	Prince George
1,673	Lee, Margaret G., Heirs of	Fauquier
21,688	Lee, Mary A.	Stafford
2,068	Lee, Mary Jane	Montgomery
13,716	Lee, Susan A.	Washington
2,761	Le Ferre, Sarah E.	Fairfax
17,882	Leitch, James	Hanover
16,110	Leith, Theodoric, Estate of	Loudoun
4,373	Leland, Lucius C.	Lancaster
11,814	Leonard, John	Madison
21,850	Leopold, Lewis	Rockingham
21,586	Leslie, Benj.	Loudoun
11,230	Leslie, John	Loudoun
15,969	Lester, John B.	New Kent
22,109	Lettrell, Wm.	Spotsylvania
15,211	Levy, Leon	Spotsylvania
21,737	Lewis, Benj. D.	Fairfax
1,805	Lewis, Betsy	Culpeper

19,020	Lewis, Edwin, Estate of	Spotsylvania
10,344	Lewis, Eliza M. & James	Frederick
3,244	Lewis, Elizabeth T.	Richmond
9,129	Lewis, Fleming E.	New Kent
9,934	Lewis, James	Frederick
10,344	Lewis, James & Eliza M.	Frederick
12,114	Lewis, James W.	Frederick
11,970	Lewis, John E.	Frederick
20,337	Lewis, John F. & Blackburn, Manesseh	Rockingham
16,037	Lewis, John W.	Norfolk
9,763	Lewis, Joseph B.	Northumber-land
20,473	Lewis, Margaret & Wm. B.	Fairfax
7,949	Lewis, Mary Francis	Clarke
11,227	Lewis, S. H., Estate of	Culpeper
9,524	Lewis, Sam H.	Rockingham
1,704	Lewis, Wm.	Fairfax
20,473	Lewis, Wm. B. & Margaret	Fairfax
19,585	Lewis, Wm. J.	Accomack
21,595	Lickey, Sampson, Estate of	Loudoun
10,776	Lickletter, Jacob	Shenandoah
13,371	Liggitt, Wm.	Shenandoah
1,977	Light, Dalbin	Halifax
8,901	Light, James	Patrick
3,009	Lightfoot, James	Culpeper
16,752	Limbrick, Landon	Stafford
643	Linane, Patrick	Culpeper
8,933	Lindsey, Jacob H.	Rockingham
1,300	Lindsey, John T.	Clarke
8,415	Lineweaver, Wm.	Rockingham
19,335	Linkenpoker, James R.	Botetourt
10,152	Lipes, Sam	Botetourt
21,716	Lipscomb, Wm. C.	Fairfax
93	Little, Mary Jane	Frederick
16,124	Littleton, John R.	Loudoun
16,090	Lively, Eliza A.	Elizabeth City
13,302	Livesey, Chas. T.	Dinwiddie
17,183	Lloyd, John I., Heirs of	Alexandria
8,472	Lloyd, Spencer	Fairfax
10,887	Locker, Jarrett	Loudoun
20,523	Lockwood, H. A.	Fairfax
5,445	Loehr, Geo. P.	Henrico
992	Lohmann, John	Fairfax
8,104	Long, Abraham C.	Rockingham
2,415	Long, Elder Isaac	Rockingham
9,784	Long, Jacob	Rockingham
6,123	Long, John J.	Caroline
1,178	Long, Mary E.	Spotsylvania
16,622: 17,298:	Long, Sam E.	Rockingham
16,519	Long, Willis	Fauquier
9,511	Love, Eli A.	Loudoun
22,113	Love, Henry	Spotsylvania
22,113	Love, Henry	Stafford
11,295	Love, Leonard	Prince Wm.
21,585	Loveless, John W.	Loudoun
7,041	Lovett, Mary B.	Frederick
8,958	Loving, Sam B. R.	Amelia
5,078	Lovitt, Erasmus	Princess Anne
15,822	Lowe, John T.	Loudoun
15,981	Lowe, Thos.	Loudoun
528	Lowe, Wm.	Norfolk
8,702	Lowenback, Jonas A.	Rockingham
8,467	Lowenback, Morritz & Jonas	Rockingham
6,329	Lown, L. M.	Fairfax
1,412	Lowry, James L.	Stafford
1,413	Lowry, John	Stafford
1,414	Lowry, Thos.	Stafford
4,726	Loyde, Sam	Shenandoah
13,692	Lucas, Edwin	Spotsylvania
14,679	Lucas, John S.	Prince George
6,922	Luckett, G. W.	Stafford
3,435	Lunceford, Harriet	Fauquier
19,932	Lushbaugh, Adams	Augusta
7,889	Lutholtz, Mary	Shenandoah
7,647	Lutz, Alex	Shenandoah
8,914	Lutz, Morris	Shenandoah
7,645	Lutz, Wm.	Shenandoah
20,351	Lynch, John Wm.	Fairfax
15,821	Lyne, Thos. H.	Loudoun
21,817	Lyons, Wm.	Fairfax
14,026	Lytle, Lydia P.	Loudoun
18,768	Machier, Philip A.	Shenandoah
20,472	Macy, Wm. D.	Warwick
13,673	Madden, Slaughter	Culpeper
128	Madden, Willis	Culpeper
15,212	Madowney, Geo.	Spotsylvania
17,483	Magee, Absalom	Spotsylvania
20,584	Magill, John S.	Frederick
2,363	Magner, Peter	Fairfax
21,301	Mahaney, Joseph P., Estate of	Frederick
18,425	Maiden, James G.	Rockingham
22,151	Maiden, Wm. D.	Rockingham
19,460	Major, Charles J.	Charles City
20,415	Mallory, John E. F.	Hanover
20,409	Malone, Anderson	Dinwiddie
19,715	Malone, Peyton	Dinwiddie
19,834	Malvin, John	Fauquier
217	Manassas Presbyterian Church	Prince Wm.
19,960: 21,732:	Manchester, F. Mason	Prince Wm.
13,468	Mann, Henry A.	Washington
11,651	Mann, Jacob	Loudoun
644	Mann, Joel	Culpeper
20,294	Mann, John A.	Augusta
3,503	Mann, Joseph G.	Halifax
1,054	Mansfield, David	Loudoun
2,528	Maphis, John	Shenandoah
10,644	Maphis, Joseph	Shenandoah
7,728	Marable, Major	Charles City
18,278	Marcey, James & Lewis	Alexandria
18,278	Marcey, Lewis & James	Alexandria
313	Marcy, Wm.	Alexandria
22,097	Mark, Wm. E. N.	Lee
15,500	Marks, Wm. R.	Prince George
12,707	Mars, Geo.	Culpeper
15,059	Marshall, A. C.	Fairfax
4,990	Marshall, Alex	Clarke
12,298	Marshall, John	Fauquier
3,094	Marsteller, Elise	Prince Wm.
1,837	Martain, Mary E.	Fairfax
11,095	Martin, Adam	Fairfax
16,410	Martin, Alex	Fauquier
22,253	Martin, David	Craig
11,788	Martin, John W.	Loudoun
12,921	Martin, Jonathan (of Deep Creek)	Norfolk
575	Martin, Jonathan (of Portsmouth)	Norfolk
7	Martin, Robert L.	Fauquier
648	Martz, Sam	Rockingham
20,989	Masincup, Wm. L.	Augusta
29,621	Mason, Elizabeth	Gloucester
2,302	Mason, John H.	Fairfax
3,407	Mason, Sanders	Orange
15,235	Massoletti, Vincent	Fauquier
17,058	Masson, Ellenor	Gloucester
149	Massy, Dan	Clarke
18,500	Masters, Henry, B.	New Kent
1,415	Masters, Wm. J.	Stafford
607	Matthews, Wm. W.	Montgomery
17,724	Matthews, Beverly	Appomattox
653	Mauzy, Jacob K.	Rockingham
7,269	Maxwell, Thos.	Fauquier
20,552	Mayar, John, Philip, Richard & Simon	Dinwiddie
21,639	Mayes, Stephen F.	Dinwiddie
5,701	Mayhew, Polly	Fairfax
20,260	Maynard, James	Fairfax
18,491	Mays, Martha	Halifax
17,014	McBee, John R.	Fauquier
17,491	McBee, Wm.	Fauquier
11,326	McCardell, Thos.	Frederick
19,991	McCauley, James B.	Henrico
9,936	McCauley, Joshua, Estate of	Frederick
9,937	McCauley, Margaret	Frederick

13,801	McClintock, Alex H.	Bath
6,544	McCorkle, Sam	Rockbridge
21,274	McCormick, John	Henrico
3,646	McCormick, Margaret A.	Clarke
1,063	McCormick, Matthew	Henrico
11,425	McCowan, Geo.	Fluvanna
6,898	McCray, Amelia	Augusta
16,873	McCue, James C.	Albermarle
9,184	McDonald, Thos. M.C.	Culpeper
6,703	McDowell, Andrew J.	King Wm.
12,426	McDowell, John	Henrico
15,279	McElyea, Emily	Russell
177	McGavick, John	Loudoun
15,382	McGhee, John A., Estate of	Smyth
13,041	McGregor, John R.	Stafford
9,310	McInterff, Hiram, Estate of	Shenandoah
16,505	McInturff, Wm.	Rockingham
12,441	McKay, Esther Ann	Warren
1,103	McKenney, Wm. M.	Rockbridge
552	McKenzie, Lewis	Alexandria
1,919	McKerichar, Alex	Alexandria
13,912	McKie, Rodham	Washington
15,254	McKinney, Alex G., Estate of	Caroline
4,707	McKown, Matthew	Fairfax
16,735	McMann, John	Alleghany
15,523	McMullen, Joseph	Shenandoah
3,306	McNew, David	Washington
376	McPhail, Matilda H.	Norfolk
13,170	McReynolds, John	Washington
225	McWilliams, Henry	Alexandria
11,864	McWilliams, Henry	Fairfax
14,926	McWilliams, James	Fairfax
17,294	McWilliams, Wm.	Rockingham
15,243	Meade, John	Prince George
12,677	Meads, John	Norfolk
2,028	Mears, John E. & Bell, Gilbert J.	Accomack
914	Meeks, James W. C.	Nelson
17,371	Meltier, Geo.	Nansemond
9,185	Menefee, James A.	Fauquier
4,760	Menifee, Alex F.	Rappahanock
15,880	Merchant, Archibald	Fairfax
7,950	Meredith, Chas. B.	Frederick
17,927	Merrick, Gasner, Estate of	Rockingham
22,124	Merry, Lucretia C.	Fairfax
17,049	Mettaner, John P.	Prince Edward
21,285	Michaels, Robert	Dinwiddie
11,306	Middleton, Thos. J.	Frederick
18,320	Milbourn, Anderew	Lee
21,814	Miles, Archie, Estate of	King & Queen
18,049	Miles, Frankey, Estate of	Amelia
20,399	Miles, Harris	Charles City
15,146	Miles, Isaac	King Wm.
17,490	Miles, Wm.	Fauquier
14,981	Miles, Wm. P.	King Wm.
4,916	Miley, Mary E.	Shenandoah
15	Millard, Josiah; and Karner, Lanslet, Sir.	Fairfax & Loudoun
20,002	Millard, Squire	Fairfax
21,903	Millegan, Wm. B.	Shenandoah
8,365	Miller, Abraham	Dinwiddie
17,291	Miller, Abraham	Rockingham
11,473: 21,576:	Miller, Armstead M.	Loudoun
647	Miller, Barbara	Rockingham
2,525	Miller, Benj.	Rockingham
2,541	Miller, Dan	Augusta
19,288	Miller, Dan, Estate of	Rockingham
21,854	Miller, David	Rockingham
10,779	Miller, Geo. E.	Shenandoah
651	Miller, Henry	Rockingham
8,084	Miller, Isaiah	Henrico
9,783	Miller, Jacob	Rockingham
17,288	Miller, Jacob (of Joseph)	Rockingham
8,998	Miller, James J.	Rockingham
18,466	Miller, James L., Estate of	Warren

2,544	Miller, John	Augusta
14,620	Miller, John	Smyth
17,292	Miller, John A.	Rockingham
2,552	Miller, John D.	Rockingham
11,128	Miller, John G.	Spotsylvania
9,092	Miller, John J., Sr.	Rockingham
8,932	Miller, John M.	Rockingham
8,878	Miller, Joseph	Montgomery
21,215	Miller, Joseph	Page
10,528: 19,289:	Miller, Joseph M.	Rockingham
11,441	Miller, Lewis M.	Frederick
8,877	Miller, Mary A.	Montgomery
9,732	Miller, Michael M.	Rockingham
1,277	Miller, Robert	Augusta
20,331	Miller, Sam	Page
2,518	Miller, Sam	Rockingham
14,210	Miller, Thos.	Loudoun
966	Miller, Wm.	Rappahanock
21,564	Miller, Wm. C.	Loudoun
16,524	Miller, Wm. J.	Rockingham
2,982	Milligan, Jane	Norfolk
2,921	Mills, Catharine C.	Louisa
2,922	Mills, James	Louisa
21,281	Mills, Silas E.	Prince George
1,834	Mills, Susan E.	Spotsylvania
20,771	Mills, Thos. M.	Orange
20,933	Milsted, Isaac	Prince Wm.
21,311	Minger, Geo.	Isle of Wight
2,962	Minnick, John, Estate of	Rockingham
2,963	Minnick, Noah	Rockingham
18,335	Minor, Catharine Ann	Fairfax
466	Minor, Jackson M.	Loudoun
18,760	Minor, John R.	Alexandria
20,878	Minor, Mary L., Heirs of	Alexandria
20,877	Minor, Philip H., Estate of	Fairfax
1,387	Mish, Henry	Augusta
3,303	Misselwhite, Worley	Washington
7,904: 21,185:	Mitchell, Benj. E.	Fauquier
13,897	Mitchell, Dan	Montgomery
47	Mitchell, G. W.	Prince Wm.
16,010	Mirchell, Gustavus A.	Smyth
20,551	Mitchell, Horace	Dinwiddie
15,248	Mitchell, Jacob A.	Rockingham
9,910	Mitchell, Joseph T.	Augusta
75	Mitchell, London	Clarke
19,173	Mitchell, Mary, Estate of	Clarke
13,538	Mtchell, Parker	Nansemond
15,709	Mitchell, Richard D.	Henrico
21,008	Mix, Chas. E.	Alexandria
15,469	Moffett, Hays	Augusta
3,695	Monch, Wm. H.	Fairfax
1,677	Money, Elijah	Fairfax
21,019	Money, John	Fairfax
1,678	Money, Lawson	Fairfax
11,294	Monney, Olmstead	Prince Wm.
16,359	Monroe, James	Stafford
21,739	Monroe, Narcissa	Fairfax
21,686	Monteith, John A.	Stafford
21,687	Monteith, Fenton, Lucy & Marion; and Willoughby, Jennie	Stafford
15,019	Montgomery, Granville	Montgomery
48	Montgomery, Morris	Spotsylvania
15,395	Mooman, Benj. F.	Roanoke
14,145	Mooman, John C.	Roanoke
14,933	Moon, Parham, Estate of	Halifax
2,923	Mooney, Robert M.	Goochland
9,899	Moore, Alfred	Loudoun
15,147	Moore, Certis	Hanover
20,174	Moore, G. W., Estate of	Loudoun
21,565	Moore, Isaac	Loudoun
11,860	Moore, James W.	Loudoun
4,454	Moore, John W.	Lancaster
9,878	Moore, Mary C.	Alexandria

12,124	Moore, Medley	Augusta
20,505	Moore, Sylvester B.	Norfolk
3,506	Moore, Wm. H.	Halifax
19,589	Moore, Wm. P.	Northampton
19,592	Moore, Wm. P., Estate of	Northampton
87	Morefield, Susan A.	Halifax
13,366	Moreland, Wm.	Shenandoah
6,003	Moren, John	Caroline
3,301	Morgan, Henry Lewis	Washington
4,574	Morgan, John Bakeman	Stafford
18,212	Morgan, John W.	Loudoun
2,126	Morgan, Louisa J.	Appomattox
10,209	Morgan, Thos.	Prince Edward
4,927	Morgan, Verlin	Washington
2,939	Morrell, Abraham	Norfolk
14,406	Morricle, Sam	Floyd
1,077	Morrison, Archibald	Loudoun
21,002	Morrow, Robert, Estate of	Fauquier
11,613	Morson, Hugh	Caroline
20,765	Morton, Fannie E. & Young, Mary E.	Orange
17,016	Morton, James, Estate of	Stafford
8,095	Mosby, Elizabeth F.	Amherst
15,396	Mosby, Henry	Roanoke
3,069	Mosby, John	Albermarle
4,901	Mosby, Thos. Y.	Bedford
1,979	Moseley, R. E.	Charlotte
1,978	Moseley, Wm.	Charlotte
2,993	Moses, Jaçob B.	Floyd
21,838	Mount Crawford ME Church	Rockingham
18,201	Mount Holly Baptist Church	Fauquier
17,293	Mowbry, Tazewell	Rockingham
2,574	Moyers, Jacob	Rockingham
17,928	Moyers, Joseph B.	Rockingham
2,364	Mulholland, John, Patrick, & Peter	Fairfax
9,316	Mummaw, Elizabeth	Frederick
8,913	Munch, Silas	Shenandoah
993	Munson , T. B., Estate of	Fairfax
18,497	Munt, John L., Estate of	Prince George
2,924	Murphy, Alfred	Prince Wm.
257	Murray, James E.	Fairfax
17,929	Murray, Stephen H.	Rockingham
9,678	Murry, John	Alexandria
3,049	Murry, John F.	Alexandria
17,072	Murtaugh, Andrew, Estate of	Fairfax
19,880	Murtaugh, James	Fairfax
11,878	Muschett, J. C.	Prince Wm.
20,404	Musgrove, James V.	Charlotte
1,416	Musselman, Albert	Stafford
209	Mutesbaugh, David M. & John B.	Fairfax
12,509	Myers, Chas. W.	Loudoun
2,526	Myers, Christian	Rockingham
12,113	Myers, David	Augusta
15,302	Myers, Elijah P.	Loudoun
12,126	Myers, Franklin H.	Augusta
12,125	Myers, Isaac S.	Augusta
2,557	Myers, Jacob	Augusta
1,608	Myers, Jacob	Loudoun
2,825	Myers, Joel T.	Shenandoah
17,629	Myers, Peter	Shenandoah
8,197	Myers, Sam H.	Rockingham
2,511	Nair, Peter	Augusta
18,568	Nalls, Wm. B.	Culpeper
6,707	Nance, Benj. A.	Charles City
6,924	Nash, Geo.	Stafford
6,925	Nash, John E.	Stafford
17,272	Nash, Nathaniel	Norfolk
21,209	Nauman, John	Page
20,927	Naylor, Sam, Estate of	Prince Wm.
320	Nearville, John C.	Norfolk
11,046	Neer, Geo.	Loudoun
2,534	Neff, Abraham	Shenandoah
1,114	Nelson, Thos. H.	Fairfax
3,656	Nelson, Wm.	Essex
19,210	New, Joseph S.	Charles City
16,641	New, Robert, Estate of	Charles City
11,113	Newcome, Leroy	Frederick
9,304	Newham, Wesley, Dr.	Rockingham
14,247	Newlon, Chas. A.	Loudoun
657	Newlon, John F.	Loudon
22,120	Newman, Geo.	Orange
42	Newman, Wm. H.; and Von Hoffman, Louis A.	Alexandria
2,515	Nicewander, Joseph F.	Augusta
4,917	Nicholous, Elizabeth I.	Shenandoah
478	Nichols, Coleman G.	Halifax
116	Nichols, Joseph	Loudoun
86	Nichols, Sallie A.	Halifax
115	Nichols, Sam E.	Loudoun
1,279	Nichols, Sam H.	Loudoun
2,516	Nichter, Philip	Rockingham
16,506	Niswander, Henry, Estate of	Rockingham
15,524: 16,939:	Niswander, Joseph E.	Rockingham
15,018	Niswander, Sam	Rockingham
11,047	Nisewaner, John	Loudoun
21,572	Nixon, James W., Estate of	Loudoun
21,605	Nixon, John W.	Loudoun
21,588	Nixon, Jonah	Loudoun
62	Noakes, James	Prince Wm.
18,552	Norcross, Sallie J.	Rockbridge
20,728	Norfolk Ferry Co.	Norfolk
4,902	North, John	Appomattox
17,643	Northam, Geo. H.	Washington
3,783	Nottingham, Wm. D.	Scott
3,752	Nourse, Alfred W. & Ella J.; and Galpin, Emma L.	Fairfax
1,717	Nowlen, Christopher C.	Patrick
18,948	Nunn, Joseph A.	Louisa
17,447	Oak Grove Methodist Church	Norfolk
19,334	Obensham, Peter	Botetourt
13	O'Brien, John	Fairfax
3,219	O'Conner, Pat	Fairfax
19,721	O'Dea, Dennis	Henrico
8,999	Odor, Waller	Augusta
13,464	Old, Geo. T.	Norfolk
15,328	Oliver, Aaron	Fairfax
10,941	Oliver, James	Fairfax
4,374	Oliver, John D.	Lancaster
14,146	Oliver, Julius	Roanoke
21,074	Oliver, Susan T.	Fauquier
2,132	Oliver, Wm. R.	Fauquier
11,115	O'Neal, J. C.	Alexandria
20,554	Orange, Wm. R.	Amelia
12,128	Orcutt, Albert	Fairfax
19,820	O'Rear, Elizabeth	Fauquier
10,345	Orindorff, Hezekiah	Shenandoah
11,714	Orme, Maria W. D.	Fairfax
11,318	Orrick,, John	Frederick
21,563	Orrison, David L.	Loudoun
20,524	Orrison, John W.	Loudoun
21,573	Orrison, Sam	Loudoun
97	Osborn, Cyrus & Seth	Fairfax
10,246	Osborn, Scarum	Halifax
97	Osborn, Seth & Cyrus	Fairfax
2,365	Osgood, Amos D.	Fairfax
11,732	Osmun, Joseph	Fairfax
17,372	Osmun, L. C.	Prince Wm.
2,498	Ostrander, E. C.	Fairfax
21,249	Otis, Harrison G.	Fairfax
17,163	Ott, Wm. H.	Rockbridge
10,197	Overton, Joseph	Norfolk
20,583	Owen, John W.	Frederick
81	Owen, Peter	Halifax
18,232	Owings, Jesse; and Harper, Ann E.	Alexandria
16,872	Page, Horace	Fauquier
9,130	Page, Lambert C.	King Wm.
19,169	Page, Thos. S.	Clarke
20,001	Painter, Joseph, Sr.	Page
19,860	Palmer, Andrew J.	Augusta
15,854	Palmer, Christian	Augusta
5,599	Palmer, David P.	Fairfax
10,181	Palmer, John	Rappahanock

16,865	Palmer, Levick	Alexandria
622	Pancoast, John L.	Loudoun
12,408	Parham, Alex	Dinwiddie
6,917	Parham, Fanny	Prince George
6,914	Parham, Thos.	Dinwiddie
13,304	Parker, John	Montgomery
96	Parker, Levi	Fairfax
3,224	Parker, Moses	Fairfax
598	Parr, Joel E.	Prince George
9,735	Parret, Bransen M.	Rockingham
762	Parsons, Maria, Mildred & Sophia	Campbell
3,779	Parsons, Stephen J.	Wise
16,565	Patterson, Eli S.	Stafford
632	Patterson, Richard L.	Culpeper
6,633	Patterson, Sam	Nelson
19,205	Patterson, Wm. H.	New Kent
18,185	Pattie, Wm. A.	Fauquier
861	Patton, Elliott, Sr.	Stafford
1,457	Patton, John T.	Frederick
6,909	Patton, Thos.	Stafford
443	Paxson, Cornelias W.	Loudoun
21,558	Paxson, Griffith W.	Loudoun
12,457	Paxson, Townsend M.	Loudoun
4,999	Paxton, Wm.	Craig
1,417	Payne, Catharine	Stafford
11,434	Payne, Chas. W.	Alexandria
14,752	Payne, Henry L.	Loudoun
13,756	Payne, James	Fairfax
14,323	Payne, John A.	Stafford
20,480	Payne, Lavinia M.	Fairfax
22,128	Payne, Mary L.	Culpeper
15,369	Payne, Spottswood S.	Stafford
13,149	Payne, Thornton	Fauquier
10,940	Peacock, Albert	Fairfax
23	Peacock, Thos. J.	Fairfax
17,466	Pearce, Allan	Alexandria
12,090	Pearce, James	Nansemond
9,080	Pearl, Elijah C., Estate of	Alexandria
7,589	Pearman, John	New Kent
7,588	Pearman, Jones	New Kent
7,587	Pearman, Thos.	New Kent
1,679	Pearson, Chas., John, Joshua, Phillis & Wm.	Fairfax
15,324	Peck, Harvey J.	Alexandria
1,994	Peden, John	Stafford
20,590	Pegram, E. Oscar	Dinwiddie
20,293	Pelter, Samson, Jr.	Augusta
2,513	Pence, David	Rockingham
8,615	Pence, Lewis	Rockingham
21,380	Pendleton, John, Estate of	Culpeper
20,106	Perkins, Andrew J.	Louisa
22,276	Perkins, M. Ringgold	Stafford
1,981	Perkins, Peter P.	Halifax
380	Perry, Anna	Fairfax
18,426	Perry, Wm. S.	Rockingham
13,802	Persinger, Annie	Alleghany
12,050	Peterman, John W.	Montgomery
16,222	Peters, Geo.	Augusta
1,334	Peters, John	Fauquier
19,036	Peters, Wm.	Rockingham
9,312	Peters, Wm.	Shenandoah
1,449	Peterson, Eli	Montgomery
20,909	Peterson, Susan W.	Warren
14,150	Peticrew, Sam B.	Campbell
4,903	Pettigrew, James W.	Campbell
13,734	Petty, Isaac, Jr.	Pittsylvania
22,119	Petty, Lucy Kate & Mollie B.	Culpeper
129	Peyton, Benj.	Rappahanock
16,518	Peyton, Elias	Fauquier
11,254	Peyton, Eugene, John & Mary A.; and Tuttle, J. M. & Laura	Alexandria
5,649	Phares, Joseph	Floyd
14,708	Phillips, John	Fauquier
10,211	Phillips, Joseph W.	Prince Edward
20,378	Phillips, Robert A.	Alexandria
3,437	Phillips, Sam C.	Fauquier
3,439	Phillips, Thos., Estate of	Fauquier
3,438	Phillips, Wm. W.	Fauquier
13,336	Phipps, Hiram	Smyth
646	Pickering, Martha	Rockingham
15,616	Pidgeon, Sam	Clarke
19,863	Pierce, Abner, Estate of	Fairfax
3,637	Pierce, Elizabeth T.	Fauquier
9,497	Pierpoint, Eli	Loudoun
1,588	Pierpont, John W.	Fairfax
737	Pierpont, Joseph	Loudoun
1,587	Piggott, Hannah J.	Loudoun
11,513	Piggott, Jesse	Loudoun
20,817	Pilcher, Alex S.	Fauquier
11,489	Pingley, James A.	Frederick
14,579	Pinn, David	Lancaster
2,720	Pinn, Howson, Sr.	Prince Wm.
18,460	Pinn, Richard	Fauquier
21,075	Pinn, Sally	Fauquier
17,932	Pinner, Peter	Norfolk
2,159	Pintler, Emma C.	Alexandria
18,112	Piper, James E. & Sarah	Alexandria
3,307	Pippin, Elisha	Washington
2,721	Pitkin, George	Prince Wm.
15,320	Pitman, Jonathan E.	Frederick
4,564	Pitts, Atwell F.	Henrico
51	Pitts, Benj.	Nansemond
4,188	Plaine, David H.	Roanoke
16,121	Plaster, Henry	Loudoun
16,122	Plaster, Michael, Estate of	Loudoun
16,341	Plats, Telam, Estate of	Fauquier
2,556	Plaugher, Sam H.	Rockingham
20,403	Pleasants, Isaac	Henrico
13,907	Poage, Elijah	Roanoke
9,526	Poindexter, St. Clair	Rockingham
20,632	Pollard, Letitia	Shenandoah
14,687	Pollard, Reuben	Fauquier
14,288	Pollard, Thornton	Fauquier
18,915	Porterfield, Lewis S.	Giles
6,903	Post, Emily F.	Norfolk
11,483	Poston, Wm. W.	Loudoun
5,652	Potter, James	Rockbridge
21,561	Potts, Edwin H.	Loudoun
21,601	Potta, Ezekiel	Loudoun
21,618	Potts, Fred M.	Loudoun
11,048	Potts, Jonas	Loudoun
11,863	Powell, Maria L.	Loudoun
6,125	Powell, Wm.	Southampton
4,601	Prater, Carington	Washington
5,702	Presgraves, Albert R.	Page
21,210	Presgraves, John H.	Page
11,842	Preston, Edward T.	Loudoun
14,211	Preston, G. W.	Loudoun
407	Price, Asa	Norfolk
6,083	Price, Charles H.	Albermarle
3,781	Price, Dan E.	Washington
5,552	Price, Isaiah K.	Bland
12,049	Price, Jacob, Sr.	Montgomery
6,902	Price, John	Augusta
21,597	Price, John	Loudoun
6,901	Price, John D.	Augusta
14,619	Price, Martha	Russell
19,996	Price, Morgan	Page
20,555	Price, Noah	Madison
14,653	Prichard, Sam R.	Frederick
15,010	Priest, John H.	Loudoun
21,217	Printz, Aaron S.	Page
16,412	Proctor, Sam K., Estate of	Fauquier
15,893	Proctor, Sam S.	Culpeper
3,071	Propst, Emanuel	Highland
17,484	Prunmer, Abraham	Stafford
527	Pugh, Wm.	Norfolk
14,755	Pulley, Whitmel	Prince George
1,993	Pulman, Sam	Fairfax
18,059	Pulman, Thos.	Fairfax
6,124	Pulmer, Thos. C.	Charlotte
8,703	Pulse, Henry	Rockingham
12,418	Purcell, John	Frederick
1,982	Purcell, Matilda H.	Halifax

John & Jane Weil

GRAPEVINE GRAPHICS

Metro (817) 481-1498

14,027	Purcell, Mordecai	Frederick
1,228	Purcell, Wm. F.	Fairfax
6,714	Purdy, James S.	Fairfax
2,856	Purks, Wm.	Culpeper
11,110	Pursell, Enos	Loudoun
11,587	Purvis, James M.	Nelson
20,766	Quarles, Harry W.	Louisa
16,753	Quarles, John T., Estate of	Orange
7,885	Quick, James S.	Augusta
22,108	Quigg, Henry	Fairfax
12,370	Quillin, Richard	Nansemond
5,001	Quinn, James	Fairfax
21,026	Quisenberry, Wm.	Spotsylvania
9,566	Quisenberry, Wm. P., Estate of	Alexandria
14,757	Quisenbury, Wm.	Floyd
21,214	Racer, John A.	Page
14,530	Radford, Elener	Franklin
6 330	Raines, Edward	Norfolk
1,418	Rains, John M., Estate of	Stafford
21,839	Ralston, Fannie	Rockingham
11,231	Ramey, Ann M. M.	King George
8,366	Ramey, Micajah	Prince George
13,693	Ramey, Thos. A.	Rappahanock
17,486	Ramy, Wm. P.	Rappahanock
13,176	Randall, Hager	Fairfax
13,690	Randolph, Abner S.	Stafford
17,003	Randolph, C.C., Heris of	Fauquier
11,791	Randolph, John P.	Stafford
1,786	Ransdell, Mary E.	Fauquier
4,904	Ransom, Absalom	Appomattox
4,905	Ransom, Robert	Appomattox
8,741	Ratliff, Philip	Floyd
726	Ray, Euphan W.	Mathews
1,188	Rea, James	Frederick
17	Read, Hiram Walter	Fairfax
11,855	Read, James	Nansemond
12,956	Read, John D., Estate of	Fairfax
11,468	Read, Wm. C.	Culpeper
11,327	Reather, Robert	Frederick
18,183	Rector, Alfred, Estate of	Fauquier
1,785	Rector, Dan	Fauquier
1,883	Rector, Wm.	Fauquier
9,442	Redinger, Amos	Floyd
15,668	Redman, Arthur	Culpeper
2,994	Reed, Madison D.	Floyd
2,434	Reed, Mariah	Floyd
18,060	Reed, W. S., Estate of	Fairfax
14,134	Reed, Wm.	Washington
4,739	Reedy, David	Shenandoah
17,473	Rees, Elias	Prince Wm.
20,628	Reese, Mary Ann	Fauquier
12,027	Reeser, John W.	Shenandoah
15,303	Reeves, Walter C.	Loudoun
13,310	Reid, Coleman	Fauquier
12,507	Reid, Dempsey	Nansemond
1,420	Reid, Gustavus	Stafford
16,824	Reid, Horatio, Estate of	Fairfax
12,087	Reid, John Q. A.	Nansemond
9,776	Reid, Oliver W.	Madison
12,013	Reid, Richard S., Estate of	Fairfax
16,811	Relph, N. J.	Prince George
14,887	Remeley, C. F.	Albermarle
17,233	Rennoe, Chapman	Prince Wm.
10,194: 13,331:	Reynolds, Alex	Amherst
3,782	Reynolds, Hamilton	Scott
9,728	Rhodes, Anthony	Rockingham
9,314	Rhodes, David B.	Rockingham
21,837	Rhodes, Fred S.	Rockingham
9,527	Rhodes, Margaret H.	Rockingham
5,729	Richard, A. W.	Shenandoah
17,319	Richards, Jesse	Loudoun
18,052	Richards, Moses R.	Frederick
16,116	Richards, Washington L., Estate	Loudoun
894	Richards, Zalmon	Alexandria
22,126	Richardson, Elizabeth A.	Warren
20,807	Richardson, Geo.,Estate of	Norfolk
13,465	Richardson, James S.	Norfolk
6,649	Richardson, Mary A.	Fauquier
8,759	Richardson, Sam E.	Mathews
22,127	Richardson, Wm., Estate of	Warren
9,131	Richardson, Wm. E.	Prince George
11,302	Richmond, Perry	Prince Wm.
1,044	Rickard, Abraham	Shenandoah
12,025	Rickard, Asher	Page
21,598	Rickard, Geo.	Loudoun
3,263	Rickard, Isaac & Jacob	Shenandoah
1,042	Rickard, John	Shenandoah
1,043	Rickard, Martha E.	Shenandoah
14,614	Ricketts, Eliza D.	Washington
1,983	Rickman, Henry	Halifax
4,602	Rickman, James G.	Washington
89	Rickman, Thos. V.	Halifax
534	Ricks, Geo.	Norfolk
21,599	Ridgeway, G. W.	Loudoun
12,490: 20,803:	Riely, Betty B.	Frederick
11,771	Rieley, Geo.	Botetourt
16,246	Riffey, Annie	Roanoke
11,880	Riker, Alfred	Fairfax
11,049	Riley, Absalom	Loudoun
1,419	Riley, Ransom	Stafford
17,494	Riley, Thos.	Culpeper
5,248	Riley, Thos.	Fauquier
16,517	Riley, Wm.	Fauquier
14,331	Rimmer, Joseph S.	Smyth
20,908	Rinker, Geo. S.	Frederick
12,412	Rinker, Josiah	Frederick
8,096	Ripley, John	Botetourt
19,461	Risby, Richard R.	Chesterfield
15,247: 21,840:	Ritche, James	Rockingham
16,089	Ritche, Peter	Rockingham
2,570	Ritchie, Jacob	Augusta
3,010	Ritenour, Frances	Rappahanock
2,531	Ritnour, Henry	Shenandoah
19,514	Ritter, John	Frederick
11,658	Ritter, Walker	Frederick
11,656	Rivers, Joseph	Loudoun
581	Rivers, Wm. M.	Henry
16,564	Rives, John E.	Sussex
15,501	Rives, Sam B.	Dinwiddie
9,980	Rix, John	Nansemond
132	Rixey, Smith H.	Culpeper
20,612	Rixey, Thos. R.	Culpeper
1,688	Roberson, Barcellus	Stafford
18,171	Roberson, John	Prince Wm.
6,647	Roberson, Joseph W.	Fairfax
21,221	Robert, Felix, Heirs of	Frederick
20,407	Roberts, Elizabeth	Dinwiddie
165	Roberts, G. W.	Fairfax
19,720	Roberts, Levy	Dinwiddie
8,311	Roberts, Robert F.	Alexandria
946	Robertson, A. H.	Nottoway
21,268	Robertson, G. W.	Prince Wm.
9,867	Robertson, James	Fairfax
20,484	Robertson, James C.	Page
11,877	Robey, Chas.	Fairfax
10,093	Robey, Priscilla D.	Fiarfax
12,417	Robinson, Alex	Frederick
14,829	Robinson, Archie	King & Queen
2,722	Robinson, Baily	Prince Wm.
241	Robinson, James	Prince Wm.
17,763	Robinson, John	Stafford
197	Robinson, John J.	Madison
14,828	Robinson, Lorenzo D.	King & Queen
1,689	Robinson, Ruth	Stafford
13,172	Robinson, Sanford	Fairfax
12,454	Robinson, Wm. H.	Clarke
3,476	Roby, Gabriel A.	Fairfax
13,174	Roby, Tobias	Fairfax
2,569	Rodehafer, Wm.	Rockingham
16,950	Rodes, David E.	Rockingham
21,836	Rodes, Henry L.	Rockingham

16,949: 21,858:	Rodes, John, Estate of	Rockingham
12,130	Rodgers, Robert C.	Stafford
11,648	Roger, Jacob	Loudoun
4,141	Rogers, Geo. S.	Patrick
16,112	Rogers, Hugh	Fauquier
19,835	Rogers, John A.; Thrasher, Isaac; and Brooks, Chauncey & Walter B.	Prince Edward
21,904	Rohr, Philip	Washington
15,525	Roller, Sam	Shenandoah
16,120	Rollins, John H.	Loudoun
21,183	Rollins, Thos. H.	Rappahanock
15,180	Rorrer, Thos. D.	Patrick
3,310	Rose, J. D. & J. M.	Washington
3,998	Rose, John D.	Washington
11,457	Rose, Patrick; and Scott, Claiborne	Roanoke & Campbell
18,757	Roseberry, G.W.	Prince Wm.
18,758	Roseberry, Joseph W.	Prince Wm.
1,428	Roseberry, Michael	Prince Wm.
18,490	Ross, Chas.	Halifax
17,320	Ross, James F.	Loudoun
16,111	Ross, John T.	Loudoun
8,754	Ross, Wm.	Culpeper
10,341	Rosser, Geo. N.	Shenandoah
20,474	Rotchford, Christopher & John I; Tynan, Nancy	Fairfax
9,192	Rout, Sarah	Lancaster
13,308	Routt, Alphonso	Fauquier
21,8685	Rowe, S. Eliza	Stafford
17,215	Rowell, Alfred W.	Fairfax
6,667	Rowland, Andrew L.	Charles City
9,871	Rowland, Wm. H.	Henrico
13,672	Rowles, Millie	Culpeper
2,160	Rowley, Wm. S.	Surry
7,650	Rowsey, Kilburn H.	Augusta
8,602	Roy, Harry	Warren
2,127	Rucker, A.T.B.	Campbell
2,568	Rudy, James	Shenandoah
17,934	Ruebush, John	Augusta
1,388	Ruebush, Peter	Augusta
8,931	Ruebush, Sam	Rockingham
4,519	Ruffin, Robert D.	York
163	Rumsey, Wm. F.	Fairfax
450	Ruse, Joseph	Loudoun
9,572	Rushmore, Thos.	Prince George
16,874	Russell, James	Frederick
11,334	Russell, James	Norfolk
11,050	Russell, Joseph L.	Loudoun
16,411	Russell, Mark	Fauquier
14,190	Russell, Robert	Loudoun
12,455	Russell, Thos. W.	Clarke
4,761	Ryan, James A.	Rappahanock
21,575	Ryan, Robert	Loudoun
18,011	Ryley, John R.	Clarke
21,733	Safford, Chas.	Prince Wm.
166	Sager, Wm.	Fairfax
17,158	St. Clair, Francis M.	Appomattox
80	Salmon, John	Halifax
21,815	Sampson, Lewis, Estate of	King & Queen
14,982	Sampson, Thos.	King Wm.
14,341	Samuel, Susan T.	Culpeper
15,304	Sanbower, Simon	Loudoun
16,941	Sandy, Annie	Rockingham
8,278	Sandy, Silas	Rockingham
5,783	Sanford, Geo. T.	Page
8,614	Sanger, Joel	Rockingham
6,904	Sansabaugh, David	Augusta
21,591	Saunders, Benj.	Loudoun
15,305	Saunders, Henry, Jr.	Loudoun
15,753	Saunders, James L.	Fauquier
15,3056	Saunders, John	Loudoun
1,984	Saunders, Jourdon M.	Fauquier
15,823	Saunders, Mary D.	Loudoun
2,948	Saunders, Robert J.	Norfolk
11,007	Savage, Lycurgus E.	Frederick
9,975	Sawyer. Lemuel J.	Nansemond

11,876	Sawyer, Matthew	Nanesmond
9,528	Sayer, Abraham	Rockingham
11,170	Scanlon, John	Rockingham
11,802	Schaffer, Henry	Page
8,186	Shaffer, Mary	Page
21,650	Schank, Benj.	Dinwiddie
17,084	Schenck, John & Peter	Alexandria
1,053	Schneider, Augustus & Frederick	Alexandria
741	Schooler, John	Stafford
437	Schooley, Milton	Loudoun
1,680	Scisson, Robert T.	Fairfax
3,012	Scott, Alex	Culpeper
17,010	Scott, Amos	Rockingham
11,457	Scott, Claiborne & Rose, Patrick	Campbell
11,457	Scott, Claiborne & Rose, Patrick	Roanoke
12,536	Scott, Dan S.	Patrick
19,935	Scott, Edward	Henrico
3,655	Scott, Fanny S. & Mary A.	Stafford
14,407	Scott, Fleming	Franklin
17,878	Scott, G.W. & Margaret A.	Norfolk
3,519: 15,887:	Scott, Harold S.	Smyth
13,326	Scott, Jacob	Nansemond
14,342	Scott, John	Culpeper
17,878	Scott, Margaret A. & G.W.	Norfolk
3,655	Scott, Mary A. & Fanny S.	Stafford
17,051	Scott, Robert T.	Prince Edward
231	Scott, Virginia	Fairfax
14,166	Scott, Wm.	York
12,898	Scranage, Richard, Heirs of	Caroline
8,408	Seal, Alfred	Frederick
20,359	Sealock, Davis	Fauquier
13,171	Seals, Ferdinand	Fairfax
3,638	Seaton, Elmiras F.	Fauquier
3,440	Seaton, John W.	Fauquier
16,426	Seaton, Martha J.	Norfolk
21,555	Seaton,T. D.	Loudoun
21,596	Seaton, Wm.	Loudoun
1,987	Seay, Abram	Halifax
8,957	Seay, C. R. F.	Fluvanna
16,640	Seay, Cornelia	Chesterfield
12,131	Segar, Joseph	Elizabeth City
16,396	Seitz, Andrew	Loudoun
9,000	Sellers, Silem	Rockingham
16,926	Semans, Wm.	Alexandria
18,270	Semms, Wm. H.	Fairfax
17,935	Senger, Jacob	Rockingham
2,530	Senger, Sam	Rockingham
1,732	Setszer, Henry	Shenandoah
3,441	Settle, Frank	Fauquier
8,026	Settle, John H.	Rappahanock
15,371	Settle, Thos.	Loudoun
13,813	Sewell, Joseph Wm.	Fairfax
1,395	Sewell, Philip, Jr. & Sr.	Dinwiddie
11,297	Sexsmith, Rebecca	Prince Wm.
20,925	Sexsmith, Sally, Heirs of	Prince Wm.
14,375	Shackelford, Robert	Culpeper
14,756	Shackleford, Wm. L.	Prince George
3,477	Shacklett, B.C.	Fauquier
3,478	Shacklett, Elizabeth	Fauquier
8,384	Shacklett, Harriet	Fauquier
9,876	Shafer, John M.	Fairfax
19,340	Shands, M.C., Mrs. & Children	Prince George
11,228	Shane, John	Culpeper
9,738: 21,833:	Shank, Abraham	Rockingham
9,529	Shank, Anna	Rockingham
9,782	Shank, Jacob, Estate of	Rockingham
7,781	Shank, Jacob, Jr.	Rockingham
19,059	Shank, Michael	Rockingham
9,739	Shank, Sam	Rockingham

13,804	Sharp, Andrew	Bath
15,675	Sharp, Joseph	Dinwiddie
17,108	Sharpe, James H.	Charles City
16,700	Sharper, Sam	Fairfax
18,501	Sharpley, Joseph	New Kent
17,011	Shaull, David	Clarke
17,162	Shaver, Andrew (also 4,657)	Rockbridge
2,510	Shaver, Emanuel B.	Shenandoah
2,532	Shaver, Geo. H.	Shenandoah
15,526	Shaver, John, Estate of	Rockingham
9,721	Shaver, John E.	Rockingham
15,527	Shaver, Milton H.	Augusta
21,774	Shaver, Sam A.	Shenandoah
14,137	Shaw, Amanda M.	Culpeper
14,135	Shaw, Archibald	Culpeper
14,136	Shaw, Simeon	Culpeper
8,743	Shaw, Wm. D.	Fairfax
9,191	Shay, Martin	Lancaster
7,951	Shearer, Barbary Ann	Frederick
19,887	Sheets, Albert	Augusta
1,729	Sheets, Peter	Augusta
2,501	Sheets, Sam	Rockingham
16,944	Shefflett, James E.	Rockingham
15,253	Shell, Floyd C.	Montgomery
13,894	Shell, John H.	Montgomery
21,213	Shelton, Morgan	Page
1,421	Shelton, Richard M.	Stafford
1,422	Shelton, Rodney J.	Stafford
12,917	Shelton, Thos.	Patrick
1,400	Sheppard, F.L.	Henrico
20,308	Sherman, James	Frederick
18,496	Sherman, Reuben, Estate of	Prince George
15,669	Sherman, Thos.	Culpeper
22,111	Sherwood, Wm.	Fairfax
14,315	Shipley, Henry C.	Frederick
19,927	Shipman, John J.	Fairfax
318	Shipman, Mason	Fairfax
17,772	Shoemaker, Basil W.	Loudoun
15,528	Showalter, Adam	Rockingham
17,936	Showalter, Christian	Rockingham
15,909	Showalter, G.W.	Rockingham
9,530	Showalter, Henry J.	Rockingham
9,305	Showalter, Jackson	Rockingham
9,742	Showalter, Maria	Rockingham
9,737	Showalter, Peter	Rockingham
19,290	Showalter, Philip H.	Rockingham
178	Shufflebarger, David	Montgomery
4,738	Shultz, Benj.	Shenandoah
2,509	Shultz, John	Rockingham
2,572	Shumake, Abner	Augusta
15,063	Shumate, James H.	Fauquier
14,913	Shumate, Lewis	Fauquier
11,357	Shumate, M. E., Mrs.	Clarke
20,818	Shumate, Shelton	Fauquier
18,202	Shumate, Virginia A.	Fauquier
867	Shupe, David F.	Washington
17,009	Sibert, Elija W.	Rockingham
4,503	Sibley, John G.	Norfolk
2,548	Sibruce, Jacob	Rockingham
5,897	Sifford, John	Pulaski
11,481	Silcott, Norval	loudoun
14,2452	Silver, Isaac	Stafford
8,697	Silver, Zephaniah	Frederick
16,943	Simmers, Abram C.	Rockingham
16,945	Simmers, Wm. C.	Rockingham
11,620	Simmons, Treca A.	Alexandria
19,728	Simms, G. W.	Alexandria
21,714	Simms, Lewis	Loudoun
18,270	Simms, Wm. H.	Fairfax
8,814	Simpers, Henry	Fauquier
12,051	Simpkins, James H.	Montgomery
20,912	Simpson, James	Warren
11,891	Simpson, John W.	Loudoun
9,155	Simpson, Silas	Fairfax
17,937	Sims, Mary F.	Greene
9,539	Sinclair, Charity, Estate of	Fauquier
19,034	Sines, Dan D.	Fairfax
17,192	Singhass, Henry S.	Frederick
17,193	Singhass, Sam, Estate of	Frederick
13,913	Singleton, G. W.	Nansemond
20,100	Singleton, Robert, Estate of	Fauquier
12,021	Sink, Jonathan	Franklin
17,554	Sisson, Joseph	Richmond
569	Skeeter, Jason	Nansemond
15,910	Skelton, G. W.	Rockingham
5,233	Skinker, John H., Estate of	Stafford
4,455	Slacum, Margaret C. land	Northumber-land
2,925	Slater, Bartine	Lancaster
10,437	Slater, Geo., Estate of	Lancaster
17,725	Slaughter, James C.	Bedford
6,126	Sledge, Merit P.	Surry
11,610	Sledge, Powhatan B.	Surry
17,720	Slemaker, Ellen G.	Alexandria
20,992	Slight, Robert, Estate of	Alexandria
9,911	Slow, Charles H.	Clarke
9,914	Slow, Thos.	Clarke
5,704	Slusher, Geo. B.	Page
16,946	Sluss, Dan	Rockingham
14,191	Smallwood, Wm.	Loudoun
8,855	Smart, Moses B.	Augusta
3,304	Smith,braham	Washington
22,115	Smith, Annie; Turner, J. Bettie	Stafford
19,586	Smith, Annie M.	Accomack
15,012	Smith, Augustus G.	Loudoun
19,916	Smith, Bennett H.	Loudoun
14,948	Smith, Cain	Fauquier
17,428	Smith, David	Mecklenburg
7,191	Smith, Downing	Greene
5,249	Smith, Dudley	Fauquier
3,302	Smith, Francis	Smyth
10,318	Smith, Geo.	Culpeper
10,326	Smith, Hiram Jackson, Estate	Frederick
16,166	Smith, Isaac	Rockingham
21,835	Smith, James	Rockingham
14,408	Smith, James H.	Floyd
15,885	Smith, Job	Loudoun
12,943	Smith, John	Fauquier
649	Smith, John B.	Rockingham
10,888	Smith, John F.	Loudoun
16,337	Smith, John J.	Fairfax
17,159	Smith, Lyon O.	Cumberland
11,875	Smith, Mary A.	Loudoun
11,051: 21,557:	Smith, Mary J.	Loudoun
22,191	Smith, Mildred J.	Culpeper
13,671	Smith, Robert A.	Culpeper
18,659	Smith, Sam	Alexandria
10,775	Smith, Sam	Frederick
464	Smith, Sam	Loudoun
21,293	Smith, Sam T.	Prince George
11,534	Smith, Sarah E.	Fairfax
21,292	Smith, Thos., Estate of	Prince George
18,407	Smith, Thos., M.; Wilson, J.C.; and Snow, Wm. R.	Prince Wm.
188	Smith, Wm. D.	Alexandria
9,999	Smith, Willmorth, Estate of	Floyd
9,536	Smoot, Thos; Janney, Joseph T.	Prince Wm.
7,644	Smootz, Elizabeth	Shenandoah
8,200	Smootz, Henry	Shenandoah
10,642	Smootz, Reuben	Shenandoah
2,383	Snapp, Henry H.	Frederick
13,368	Snapp, Jacob B.	Shenandoah
16,942	Snell ,Christian, Estate of	Rockingham
11,488	Snider, John	Frederick
14,617	Snider, John, Sr.	Montgomery

14,618	Snider, John H.	Montgomery
2,540	Sniteman, Henry	Augusta
10,436	Snoots, Susan A.	Loudoun
18,407	Snow, Wm. R.; Smith, Thos. M.; and Wilson, J.C.	Prince Wm.
11,008	Snyder, Alex W.	Dinwiddie
20,483	Snyder, Emanuel	Page
8,361	Snyder, John F.	Culpeper
11,801	Somers, Isaac	Page
11,796	Somers, Reuben	Page
11,166	Sommers, A.H., Adelina, & E.	Alexandria
7,888	Sonner, Geo. M.	Shenandoah
8,863	Sonner, Sam H.	Shenandoah
11,644	Souder, John	Loudoun
11,794	Sours, John	Page
11,795	Sours, Wm. H.	Page
198	Southall, Geo. H.	Nottoway
5	Southern, Richard	Fairfax
19,039	Southward, Bettie C.	New Kent
17,756	Soutter, Wm. A.	Culpeper
12,413	Sowers, G.W.	Clarke
12,022	Sowers, John A.	Roanoke
9,559	Sowers, John H.	Floyd
17,604	Spangler, Hannah J.	Floyd
21,834	Spangler, Harrison C.	Rockingham
2,435	Spangler, Mary	Floyd
14,399	Spangler, Sam	Floyd
18,384	Sparrow, Wm.	Norfolk
18,862	Spence, Lemos J.	Accomack
11,491	Spencer, Abraham	Frederick
8,097	Spessard, Ann M.	Roanoke
14,343	Spicer, Happy A.	Culpeper
945	Spiers, John W.	Dinwiddie
12,040	Spiggle, Rebecca	Shenandoah
4,735	Spigle, Joel	Shenandoah
2,823	Spika, Ezra	Shenandoah
20,307	Spillman, Jacob	Frederick
5,705	Spitler, Joseph	Page
11,799	Spitler, Nathan	Page
2,535	Spitzer, Davis	Rockingham
15,911	Spitzer, Emanuel	Rockingham
15,529	Spitzer, Jacob	Rockingham
15,245	Spitzer, Noah	Rockingham
4,565	Spriggs, Thos.	Lancaster
15,307	Spring, Jefferson	Loudoun
16,376	Sprinkle, Sylvester D.	Smyth
524	Stafford, John	Norfolk
2,942	Stake, John M.	Alexandria
17,160	Stansbury, Mary J.	Prince Edward
1,701	Staples, Wm. C.	Patrick
11,304	Starbuck, Gideon M.	Prince Wm.
19,816	Starkey, Benj.	Clarke
476	Starrett, Andrew T.	Nansemond
11,797	Steckler, Benj.	Page
9,537	Steele, G. W.	Fairfax
112	Steers, Edward	Fairfax
1,140	Stene, Frank	Clarke
2,259	Stephens, Briant	Fauquier
1,179	Stephens, Eliza C.	Spotsylvania
21,589	Stephenson, Wm. H.	Loudoun
2,128	Stevens, Elizabeth A.V.	Campbell
15,131	Stevens, Sophronia	Norfolk
1,423	Stewart, Barnett	Stafford
21,150	Stewart, Charles, Estate of	Fairfax
21,381	Stewart, Dan K.	Henrico
18,189	Stewart, Emily E. & Nancy B.	Fauquier
10,688	Stewart, Sam, Estate of	Fauquier
9,538	Stewart, Thos. B.	Fauquier
20,309	Stewart, Thos. N.	Fairfax
2,926	Stewart, Wm. H.	New Kent
12,937	Stewart, Wm. K.	Prince Wm.
978	Stickley, Simon	Augusta
977	Stickley, Wm.	Augusta
2,436	Stigleman, Andrew F.	Floyd
20,629	Stigler, Susan J.	Fauquier
21,294	Stiles, Mary E.	Prince George

18,553	Stine, Joseph	Frederick
8,704	Stinespring, John	Rockingham
2,371	Stockdale, Benj. S.H., Estate	Greene
5,292	Stokes, Richard	Prince Wm.
11,301	Stokes, Warner	Prince Wm.
9,909	Stolle, Wm. F.	Clarke
21,195	Stone, Anne, Elizabeth & Louisa	Loudoun
1,424	Stone, Geo. T.	Stafford
4,477	Stone, Isaac S.	Fauquier
21,195	Stone, Louisa, Anne & Elizabeth	Loudoun
9,575	Stone, Richard	Fauquier
20,556	Stone, Wm. B.	Dinwiddie
12,464	Stoneburner, Christopher	Loudoun
6,448	Stoops, Wm. W.	Patrick
10,526	Storm, Susannah H.	Fairfax
11,450	Storrs, Peter	Hanover
15,308	Stout, John L.	Loudoun
20,478	Stoutenburg, James A.	Alexandria
212	Stover, Charles	Fauquier
2,520	Stover, Dan	Augusta
14,147	Stover, J. C.	Roanoke
19,888	Stover, Jacob	Augusta
15,563	Stover, Sam D.	Augusta
15,855	Stover, Simon P.	Augusta
11,736	Stream, G. W.	Loudoun
3,011	Street, Wm.	Culpeper
18,427	Strickler, Lewis	Rockingham
14,894	Stringfellow, Mary	Culpeper
19,912	Stroman, Henry C.	Fairfax
18,494	Strong, Mildred	Hanover
1,819	Strong, Robert	Fairfax
20,422	Strother, Elizabeth M.	Fauquier
2,791	Strother, James P.	Washington
20,481	Strother, Letitia	Fairfax
19,265	Strother, Mary	Rockingham
19,717	Stroud, Elizabeth	Dinwiddie
17,938	Strough, Wm. V.	Augusta
13,012	Studds, Henry, Estate of	Fairfax
13,805	Stull, Hannah	Alleghany
4,730	Stump, Joshua E.	Shenandoah
20,902	Stunkle, Chas. H.	Loudoun
14,947	Sudduth, Elizabeth, Estate of	Fauquier
19,248	Sudduth, Harriet	Fauquier
1,453	Sullivan, Edward J.	Rockingham
16,819	Sullivan, Geo.	Stafford
19,032	Sullivan, Wm.	Stafford
11,561	Summers, Benj.	Norfolk
3,226	Summers, Eliza J.	Fairfax
3,259	Summers, Geo.	Page
8,103	Summers, Simon P.	Rockbridge
19,830	Summerville, Geo.	Alexandria
3,073	Sumner, Owen	Floyd
16,940	Sunnafrank, Mary	Rockingham
2,822	Supinger, Joseph	Shenandoah
13,898	Surface, Geo.	Montgomery
8,336	Suter, Emanuel	Rockingham
11,292	Sutherland, John	Prince Wm.
14,893	Sutphin,Barnett	Rappahanock
10,019	Sutphin, Celie	Floyd
12,458	Swank, Wm.	Loudoun
1,817	Swartz, Geo.	Shenandoah
17,827	Swartz, James	Frederick
1,040	Swartz, Noah	Shenandoah
4,732	Swartz, Wm.	Shenandoah
18,498	Sweat, Frank	New Kent
11,056	Sweeney, Jerry	Fauquier
2,007	Sweeney, John H.	Fairfax
15,370	Swetnam, Sarah	Stafford
9,001	Swisher, Philip D.	Augusta
9,002	Swisher, Sam H.	Augusta
12,428	Sykes, Henry	Henrico
12,429	Sykes, Isaac	Henrico
12,430	Sykes, Richard	Henrico
8,956	Synan, Elizabeth E.	Louisa

3,045	Tabb, Thos. T.T.	Goochland
16,512	Tabb, Wm.	Spotsylvania
1,790	Tabor, Davidson	Montgomery
19,203	Talifero, Randall	King & Queen
17,540	Talliaferro, Spotsworth	Culpeper
3,657	Tally, Boulding	Hanover
18,110	Talmage, Job A.	Dinwiddie
18,188	Tannehill, Geo.	Fauquier
18,489	Tanstall, Francis A.	New Kent
16,419	Tarter, Elijah	Wythe
21,060	Tate, Caroline & Washington	Culpeper
21,386	Tate, Randall G.	Culpeper
21,060	Tate, Washington & Caroline	Culpeper
16,038	Tatem, Mary Louisa	Norfolk
17,445	Tatem, Stephen B.	Norfolk
7,593	Tatum, Ann E.H.	Prince George
21,604	Tavenner, F.H.	Loudoun
21,617	Tavenner, Richard	Loudoun
89,915	Taylor, Belford	Frederick
13,670	Taylor, Burgess	Culpeper
21,239	Taylor, Catharine E.	Alexandria
16,142	Taylor, Chas.	Fairfax
11,789	Taylor, Chas. N.	Loudoun
7,679	Taylor, Edmund C.	Hanover
11,319	Taylor, G. W.	Frederick
16,788	Taylor, G. W.	Rockbridge
16,118	Taylor, Geo. B.	Loudoun
12,350	Taylor, James W.	Loudoun
3,175	Taylor, Lewis	Loudoun
16,682	Taylor, Mariah	Fauquier
8,085	Taylor, Martin S.	Henrico
12,127	Taylor, Theron W.	Stafford
14,376	Taylor, Wm. B.	Culpeper
258: 17,819:	Taylor, Wm. H.	Fairfax
20,764	Taylor, Wm. J.	Spotsylvania
20,352	Taylor, Wm. P., Heirs of	Alexandria
11,303	Teasdale, Sidney	Prince Wm.
16	Tennent, Harriet	Fairfax
14,248	Tennison, Lucinda	Fairfax
2,008	Tennison, Whiting M. & Darnell, John T.	Fairfax
18,658	Terrill, Robert	Culpeper
12,225	Territt, Martha A. F.	Alexandria
17,829	Terry, John W.	Hanover
12,109	Terry, Wm.	Fairfax
15,148	Thacker, Wm. A.	Hanover
20,362	Thatcher, Branon	Frederick
16,339	Thatcher, Chas.	Prince Wm.
9,740	Thomas, Adam	Rockingham
9,779	Thomas, Dan, Estate of	Rockingham
6	Thomas, Henry C. & Lorenzo, Jr.	Alexandria
17,321	Thomas, Herod	Loudoun
15,397	Thomas, Jane	Roanoke
13,965	Thomas, John	Campbell
22,049	Thomas, Joseph, Richard & Wm.	Prince Wm.
6	Thomas, Lorenzo, Jr. & Henry C.	Alexandria
2,439	Thomas, Lucinda	Halifax
633	Thomas, Peyton L.	Culpeper
22,049	Thomas, Richard, Wm. & Joseph	Prince Wm.
13,821	Thomas, Robert, Estate of	Culpeper
22,049	Thomas, Wm., Richard & Joseph	Prince Wm.
11,480	Thomas, Wm. P.	Loudoun
20,332	Thompson, Amanda C.	Rockingham
17,137	Thompson, Bennett	Washington
21,559	Thompson, Edward	Loudoun
9,806	Thompson, Hiram	Augusta
8,611	Thompson, Jack	Dinwiddie
13,471	Thompson, James H.	Washington

20,589	Thompson, Jane M.	Hanover
21,581	Thompson, John H.	Loudoun
2,440	Thompson, Levi	Floyd
3,687	Thompson, Sylvester	Lee
20,997	Thompson, Thos. H.	Alexandria
17,136	Thompson, Wm.	Washington
10,777	Thompson, Wm. C.	Shenandoah
15,249	Thompson, Wm. G.	Rockingham
17,446	Thompson, Willis	Northampton
12,535	Thornhill, Bluford	Rappahanock
6,479	Thornton, David	Augusta
150	Thornton, Taylor	Clarke
13,150	Thorpe, Geo. L.	Fauquier
13,151	Thorpe, John E.	Fauquier
19,835	Thrasher, Isaac; Rogers, John A.; and Brooks, Walter B. & Chauncey	Prince Edward
11,716	Thrift, Ann T.	Dinwiddie
3,245	Thrift, Richard F.	Richmond
9	Throckmorton, Hugh W.	Fairfax
8,829	Tice, Cynthia	Floyd
16,137	Timberlake, John H.	Albemarle
5,450	Timberlake, Wm. H.	Hanover
21,076	Timmons, Chas. M.	Fauquier
13,175	Timmons, John R.	Stafford
2,860	Stimson, Lucinda	Culpeper
20,982	Tinder, Ann G.	Orange
3,408	Tinder, John T.	Orange
3,390	Tinder, Thos.	Orange
5,006	Tingler, Henry	Craig
7,651	Tisdale, Matthew	Augusta
6,128	Toombs, Charles	Charlotte
577	Topping, Wm. R.	Norfolk
16,469	Torreyson, John N.	Fairfax
253	Torreyson, Sam	Fairfax
10,295	Touchstone, Sampson	Frederick
19,390	Travers, Rachel C.	Alexandria
2,129	Trent, Wm.	Appomattox
14,555	Trice, F.M. & Haislip, John	Fairfax
811	Trice, G. W.	Louisa
13,470	Trigg, John	Washington
213	Trimmer, Geo.	Prince Wm.
3,442	Triplett, Alva	Fauquier
5,352	Triplett, Feston	Fauquier
2,152	Triplett, Leven	Fauquier
21,653	Triplett, Thos. M.	Loudoun
5,799	Trisler, Lewis	Alexandria
15,309	Tritipoe, Geo. C.	Loudoun
2,012	Troth, P. Hillman	Fairfax
16,809	Trundle, Horatio, Estate of	Loudoun
4,785	Trussell, Margaret	Frederick
18,492	Tuck, Allen	Halifax
21,640	Tucker, Asa	Dinwiddie
18,484	Tucker, James W.	Alexandria
942	Tucker, John Henry	Alexandria
15,816	Tucker, John R.	Madison
11,979	Tucker, Sam, Estate of	Alexandria
5,007	Tucker, Wm. H.	Craig
19,567	Tunis, John E., Estate of	Norfolk
20,236	Tunis, Rebecca B.	Norfolk
21,693	Turberville, Margaret V.	Fairfax
2,991	Turman, Rebecca E.	Floyd
523	Turner, Benj.	Nansemond
5,716	Turner, Edward C.	Fauquier
21,387	Turner, Horace C.	Alexandria
22,115	Turner, J. Bettie & Smith, Annie	Stafford
9,315	Turner, Jacob	Buckingham
4,887	Turner, John	Fairfax
3,216	Turner, Louisa H.	Fauquier
764	Turner, Sam F.	Amherst
8,444	Turner, Sam F.	Franklin
11,254	Tuttle, J.M. & Laura; and Peyton, John, Mary A. & Eugene	Alexandria

17,939	Tutwiler, Henry	Augusta
17,493	Tyler, Dan	Fauquier
19,074	Tyler, Hiram W.	Henrico
4,375	Tyler, Madison V.	Hanover
2,927	Tyler, Wm. E.	Hanover
20,474	Tynan, Nancy; and Rotchford, John I. & Christopher	Fairfax
9,977	Tynes, Archer	Nansemond
522	Tynes, Richard, Jr.	Nansemond
13,806	Tyre, John	Alleghany
15,286	Tyson, James W.	Fauquier
2,997	Umbarger, J.P. & Wm.	Wythe
16,816	Umbarger, Michael, Estate of	Wythe
2,997	Umbarger, Wm. & J.P.	Wythe
14,409	Underwood, Elizabeth	Franklin
21,658	Underwood, John C.	Alexandria
3,520	Underwood, Noah B.	Floyd
127	Updike, Dan J.	Rappahanock
126	Updike, Hannah & Hoff, Lydia	Rappahanock
20,265	Urquhart, Mary	Fairfax
13,822	Utz, John	Rappahanock
16,510	Utz, Peachy E.	Madison
1,056	Valeantine, Edward H.	Henrico
45	Vandenburgh, Gilbert	Alexandria
13,314	Vanderwerken, Gilbert	Alexandria
2,768	Van Deusen, Wm.	Fairfax
965	Van Lone, Louisa	Culpeper
17,566	Van Pelt, Alvam, Estate of	Prince Wm.
3,075	Varner, Mary	Highland
19,998	Varner, Sam	Page
389	Vassar, John A.	Halifax
40	Vaughan, Wm. H.	Caroline
14,344	Vaughn, Walker	Culpeper
40	Vaughn, Wm. H.	Spotsylvania
14,693	Veney, David	Richmond
7,828	Vest, John	Franklin
1,691	Viands, Geo.	Page
12,673	Vietch, John W.	Alexandria
453	Vinsel, Philip	Loudoun
13,703	Vinyard, J.W.	Roanoke
11,053	Virts, Geo. W.	Loudoun
21,608	Virts, Virginia	Loudoun
585	Virts, Wm. Henry	Loudoun
10,438	Virtz, Peter, Estate of	Loudoun
42	Von Hoffman, Louis A.; and Newman, Wm. H.	Alexandria
11,131	Von Patton, Maria	Fairfax
21,384	Vorce, Nelson	Alexandria
20,004	Vorhees, Nelson	Fairfax
11,240	Vowells, Newton	Fauquier
13,808	Wade, Henry S.	Bath
13,809	Wade, James	Highland
12,658	Waddle, Julius C.	Augusta
1,278	Waggaman, John H.	Fairfax
4,734	Wakeman, Jonas W.	Shenandoah
12,547	Wale, Patsey	Culpeper
21,092	Walker, Eli	Loudoun
21	Walker, James M.	Loudoun
7,023	Walker, Mary Ann	Fauquier
11,436	Walker, Wm.	Alexandria
20,810	Walker, Wm. B.	Lancaster
13,128	Wall, Dan	Floyd
20,558	Wall, John	Prince George
2,615	Wall, Mary M.	Wythe
11,748	Wallace, James M.	Loudoun
3,658	Wallace, John P.	Albermarle
14,377	Wallace, Stephen	Culpeper
10,182	Wallach, Margaret, Estate of	Culpeper
18,204	Walnut Branch M.E. Church	Fauquier
2,002	Walter, Geo. A.	Loudoun
8,024	Walter, Harriet J.	Rappahanock
13,305	Walters, Annie	Montgomery
506	Walters, Geo. F.M.	Fairfax
5,861	Walters, Jacob	Floyd
1,730	Walters, Wm.	Fairfax

763	Walthall, John B.	Prince Wm.
2,565	Wampler, Benj. F.	Augusta
2,559: 8,102:	Wampler, David	Augusta
2,558	Wampler, John	Augusta
2,561	Wampler, Jonas	Augusta
2,542	Wampler, Joseph	Rockingham
2,543	Wampler, Joshua	Rockingham
2,536	Wampler, Sam	Rockingham
9,777: 15,530:	Wampler, Sam H.	Rockingham
8,471	Wanger, Eve	Rockingham
16,344	Wanger, Joseph	Augusta
20,983	Ward, James Henry; and Balderston, John C.	Fauquier
19,458	Ward, John, Estate of	James City
20,493	Ward, John T.	Accomack
1,272	Ware, Chas. A.	Alexandria
1,273	Ware, Chas. A. & Lacy, Wm. B.	Alexandria
8,755	Ware, Geo.	Augusta
12,671	Ware, Isaac	Augusta
18,170	Warne, Gideon	Prince Wm.
21,554	Warner, Israel	Loudoun
9,363	Warren, Charles H.	Stafford
169	Warwick, A. J.	Albermarle
20,180	Warwick, Jacob	Amherst
13,849	Washburn, Cyrus	Warwick
12,555	Washington, Euphan M.	Prince Wm.
3,013	Washington, Henry	Culpeper
16,467	Washington, Peyton; and Lawson, Robert	Stafford
18,566	Waterman, Emilie S.	Rockingham
11,052	Waters, John F.	Loudoun
20,177	Waters, Levi, Estate of	Loudoun
11,291	Waters, Robert	Prince Wm.
18,210	Waddell, John & Wm.	Fauquier
13,807	Wade, Elizabeth	Highland
8,086	Watkins, John E. W.	New Kent
2,762	Watkins, Rachel	Fairfax
16,420	Watkins, Sawyer	Norfolk
1,425	Watson, James W.	Stafford
521	Watts, Benj.	Norfolk
16,378	Watts, James W.	Norfolk
18,195	Waugh, Tabitha A., Estate of	Fauquier
11,783	Weadon, Ashford	Loudoun
11,516	Weadon, Wm. H.	Loudoun
12,250	Weaver, Alfred H.	Fauquier
12,251	Weaver, Elizabeth & Octavius A.	Fauquier
5,862	Weaver, Jacob	Floyd
12,252	Weaver, Margaret L.	Fauquier
5,863	Weaver, Mary	Floyd
15,817	Weaver, Moses S.	Madison
12,251	Weaver, Octavius A. & Elizabeth	Fauquier
14,367	Weaver, Sam, Estate of	Fauquier
16,044	Webb, Albert	Alexandria
19,897	Webb, E.M.	Prince George
10,329	Webb, Edward	Frederick
10,325	Webb, James M.	Orange
1,363	Webb, John F.	Fairfax
2,130	Webb, Martin	Appomattox
17,161	Webb, Mary M.	Cumberland
18,302	Webber, Wm. G.	Norfolk
3,456	Webster, Francis B.	Fairfax
21,822	Webster, Isaac C.	Culpeper
15,398	Webster, Julia	Roanoke
623	Webster, Nathan	Fairfax
2,441	Weddle, David	Floyd
17,764	Weddle, John	Floyd
14,698	Weddle, John, Sr.	Floyd
2,995	Weddle, Joshua	Floyd
843	Welch, David	Spotsylvania
14,925	Wells, Fontaine M.	Albermarle
21,652	Wells, James M.	Fairfax
20,413	Wells, James Peterson	Dinwiddie

10,153	Wells, John L.	Henry
11,082	Wells, Washington	Warren
9,525	Wenger, Benj.	Rockingham
8,934	Wenger, Henry	Rockingham
9,788	Wenger, Isaac	Rockingham
15,912	Wenger, Jacob	Rockingham
9,741	Wenger, John B.	Rockingham
15,531	Wenger, Noah C.	Rockingham
11,845	Wenner, Emanuel	Loudoun
12,703: 20,799:	Wenner, Geo. H.	Loudoun
20,797	Wenner, Geo. S.	Loudoun
17,818	Wenner, Jacob	Loudoun
20,798	Wenner, Mary, Estate of	Loudoun
15,390	Wertz, John, Sr.	Roanoke
18,428	West, James W.	Rockingham
20,609	West, Malcolm	Culpeper
20,596	West, Wm.	Culpeper
2,255	Weston, Charles T.	Warren
16,613	Whaley, Gilson R.	Fairfax
20,184	Whealton, John A.M.	Accomack
14,677	Wheden, Ansel	Fairfax
168	Wheeler, Joel N.	Albermarle
19,202	Wheely, Wm.	King Wm.
8,124	Whipple, Edward A., Estate of	Alexandria
8,367	White, Benj. K.	Dinwiddie
12,110	White, C.A., Mrs.	Fauquier
1,700	White, Cornelius	Fairfax
535	White, David	Nansemond
531	White, Edwin F.	Nansemond
21,560	White, Elizabeth R., Estate of	Loudoun
529	White, Exum	Nansemond
639	White, Henry	Norfolk
3,305	White, Jane	Washington
15,195	White, Jane F.	Culpeper
10,631	White, John	Washington
13,324	White, John B.	Fauquier
640	White, Joseph	Norfolk
21,574	White, Joshua, Estate of	Loudoun
21,556	White, Josiah T.	Loudoun
8,087	White, Mary A.	Henrico
14,332	White, Spencer, Sr.	Washington
15,470	White, W.L., Estate of	Albermarle
530	White, Warren	Norfolk
5,451	White, Wm.	Henrico
769	White, Wm. H.	York
10,817	Whitehurst, Edward	Elizabeth City
20,633	Whitehurst, John F.	Norfolk
8,379	Whitehurst, Peter H.	Norfolk
2,001	Whitlow, R.W.	Floyd
18,430	Whitmer, P.W.	Rockingham
18,429	Whitmor, Martin	Rockingham
8,930	Whitmore, Sam	Rockingham
21,609	Whitmore, Wm. W.	Loudoun
8,229	Whittaker, Joseph	Montgomery
1,886	Wibbirt, Isaac	Alexandria
12,908	Wierman, Hiram C.	Lee
18,877	Wigfield, John J., Estate of	Fauquier
21,562	Wightman, Joseph L.M.	Loudoun
88	Wilborn, James R.	Halifax
21,726	Wilcoxon, Josiah, Estate of	Prince Wm.
15,210	Wilder, Thos.	Dinwiddie
4,446	Wilkerson, Henry	Louisa
2,796	Wilkinson, Wm.	Alexandria
20,911	Wilkinson, Wm. C.	Warren
11,490: 16,617:	Williams, Elijah	Frederick
8,959	Williams, H. W.	Dinwiddie
4,445	Williams, Hannah & Warren W.; Kelley, John, John L. & Ellen	Alexandria
16,509	Williams, Harrison	Prince Wm.
11,650	Williams, Henry S.	Loudoun
11,571	Williams, John	Fairfax
11,649	Williams, John C.	Loudoun
18,861	Williams, John W.; Cobb, Warren D.; and Doughty, E. B.	Northampton
2,303	Williams, Joseph	Augusta
3,696	Williams, Joseph L.	Frederick
11,572	Williams, Sanford	Alexandria
7,952	Williams, Sarah R.	Shenandoah
4,445	Williams, Warren W. & Hannah; Kelley, Ellen, John & John L.	Alexandria
7,671	Williamson, Dan	Fairfax
5,904	Williamson, Geo., Sr.	Montgomery
568	Williamson, Henry	Norfolk
20,559	Williamson, Robert C.	Hanover
3,688	Willis, Susan, Estate of	Lee
21,687	Willoughby, Jennie; and Monteith, Lucy, Marion & Fenton	Stafford
765	Wills, Geo. E.	Amherst
13,478	Wills, Lovenia	Washington
10,031	Wilson, Annie E. & Fannie V.	Norfolk
10,427	Wilson, Charles H.	Dinwiddie
12,100	Wilson, Elijah, Estate of	Floyd
10,031	Wilson, Fannie V. & Annie E.	Norfolk
3,014	Wilson, Isaac N.	Rappahanock
18,407	Wilson, J.C.; Snow, Wm. R.; and Smith, Thos. M.	Prince Wm.
6,331	Wilson, James T.	Norfolk
10,324	Wilson, Joseph	Elizabeth City
12,411	Wiltshire, Philip	Loudoun
3,389	Wiltshire, Weeden	Orange
14,495	Wimmer, Hosea	Floyd
21,713	Wimsatt, Mary V.	Loudoun
12,409	Wince, Henry L.	Loudoun
1,047	Windel, Amos	Shenandoah
4,729	Windel, Benj.	Shenandoah
1,733	Windel, Joseph	Shenandoah
4,722	Windel, Sam	Shenandoah
5,871	Winder, Wm. H.	Mathews
12,041	Windle, Jacob, Estate of	Shenandoah
8,199	Wine, Elder Jacob	Shenandoah
2,519	Wine, Geo.	Rockingham
8,199	Wine, Jacob, Elder	Shenandoah
1,589	Wine, James M.	Fauquier
18,728	Wine, John	Augusta
2,539	Wine, John	Rockingham
8,202	Wine, John H.	Shenandoah
16,507	Wine, Michael, Jr.	Shenandoah
8,201	Wine, Michael, Sr.	Shenandoah
20,410	Wingfield, Elizabeth	Dinwiddie
10,265	Winn, Wm. J.	Halifax
9,981	Winslow, John	Nansemond
10,997	Wire, Peter	Loudoun
435	Wirtz, Wm.	Loudoun
8,168	Wise, Peter	Rockingham
4,666	Wiseman, Lucy J.	Prince George
2,131	Witherite, Sally Ann	Campbell
3,015	Withers, Adelaide	Culpeper
14,898	Withers, Thornton	Fauquier
1,371	Wolford, John	Loudoun
2,723	Wolverton, Sam	Prince Wm.
19,339	Wood, Ann C.	Prince Geo.
20,398	Wood, Dan. L.	Dinwiddie
20,265	Wood, Dan T.	Frederick
761	Wood, Jaquelin M.	Campbell
11,012	Wood, Robert B., Heirs of	Clarke
14,345	Wood, Wesley	Culpeper
14,830	Wood, Wm.	Norfolk
10,200	Woodard, Wm. H.	Princess Ann
18,205	Woodward, Eliza A.	Fauquier
1,391	Woodyard, Arthur F.	Prince Wm.
3,215	Woodyard, Geo.	Fairfax
1,390	Woodyard, Matthew	Prince Wm.
1,489	Woolwine, Philip	Montgomery

14,761	Wooster, Nancy	Fairfax
4,906	Wright, David M.	Bedford
9,441	Wright, James A.	Floyd
10,891	Wright, James T.	Loudoun
8,368	Wright, John	Dinwiddie
10,999	Wright, John P.	Loudoun
462	Wright, Sam	Loudoun
20,557	Wright, Thos., Estate of	Fairfax
11,591	Wright, York	Appomattox
110	Wunder, Geo. Ott	Alexandria
5,709	Wyatt, John B.	Elizabeth City
22,117	Wyatt, Joseph	Albermarle
9,535	Wylie, Andrew	Fairfax
10,330	Wyndham, Thornton O.	Clark
19,718	Wynn, Ephraim	Dinwiddie
19,374	Wynn, Ferdinand	Charles City
2,998	Wyrick, Joseph	Wythe
21,885	Wysong, John	Giles
20,819	Yager, Francis C.	Culpeper
15,670	Yancy, Henry	Culpeper
2,979	Yarrington, Mildred Ann	Henrico
652	Yates, Curtis	Rockingham
12,012	Yeatman, John H.	Prince Wm
20,158	Yerby, Wm. G.	Fauquier
970	Yerion, James W.	Wythe
8,341	Young, Abraham	Rockingham
8,341	Young, Abraham	Rockingham
64: 953:	Young, Amos	Fairfax
11,781	Young, Benj. F.	Loudoun
10,327	Young, Dan	Orange
20,763	Young, Edward, Sr.	Orange
11,342	Young, Franklin; and Fields, James	Loudoun
173	Young, Henson	Loudoun
12,705	Young, John M.	Alexandria
20,765	Young, Mary E. & Morton, Fannie E.	Orange
7,649	Zehring, Mathias	Shenandoah
17,290	Zeiler, Ferdinand	Shenandoah
15,532	Zerkle, John B.	Rockingham
16,954: 18,431:	Zettee, Peter	Rockingham
17,726	Ziegler, Augustus	Campbell
7,658	Zigler, John	Rockingham
2,564	Zigler, Sam	Rockingham
3,079	Zimmerman, David	Craig
14,009	Zimmerman, G.W.	Botetourt
16,955	Zirkle, Jacob W.	Rockingham
12,034	Zirkle, Monroe	Shenandoah
10,643	Zirkle, Moses A.	Shenandoah

WEST VIRGINIA

14,627	Aglionby, Charles	Jefferson
4,259	Andrews, Linton N.	Jefferson
8,617	Atkinson, John H.	Hancock
14,998	Bain, Robert M.	Berkeley
1,114	Baker, Wm. C.	Hardy
16,145	Ballard, Beverly	Monroe
15,589	Bane, Garrett W.	Jefferson
15,980	Baylor, Moses	Jefferson
17,007	Beck, John	Jefferson
12,425	Beeson, Lewis R., Estate of	Berkeley
15,591	Bell, Hector	Jefferson
19,342	Bickett, James H.	Monroe
14,534	Boltz, John H.	Berkeley
11,317	Bond, John S.	Pendleton
17,280	Borror, Simon	Pendleton
15,534	Boyers, G.W.	Jefferson
16,397	Bowers, Christian S.	Pendleton
13,289	Brotherton, Lee G.	Jefferson
13,291	Brown, Thos.	Jefferson
15,592	Burns, Caleb	Jefferson
13,207	Burns, Isaac V.	Jefferson
11,324	Cain, Augustine	Jefferson
11,428	Caldwell, Joseph F.	Greenbrier
19,343	Campbell, Allan	Monroe
13,025	Chamberlain, John	Jefferson
16,146	Clark, Sam M.	Monroe
15,000	Coalman, Dan	Jefferson
14,308	Cockrell, G.W.	Jefferson
14,428	Cockrell, John G.	Jefferson
17,008	Colbert, Hezekiah	Jefferson
13,211	Cook, John	Jefferson
13,530	Copeland, Nathan H.	Jefferson
8,607	Craigen, Jacob J.	Hampshire
15,196	Criswell, James	Berkeley
12,740	Crow, Wm., Estate of	Jefferson
12,726	Custer, Randolph	Jefferson
21,976	Daley, Patrick H.	Jefferson
21,378	Dalwick, John, Estate of	Berkeley
13,501	Daniels, Eliza J.	Hampshire
18,058	Day, Leonard	Pendelton
15,197	Detter, Joseph	Berkeley
15,593	Dixon, Wm. A.	Jefferson
11,712	Dixon, Wm. H.	Jefferson
15,594	Dust, Isaac	Jefferson
17,281	Eagle, Julia A.	Pendleton
15,595	Eckels, Benj.	Jefferson
13,287	Engle, Edwin C.	Jefferson
576	Frank, (Foulk?), Joshua	Randolph
13,212	Freese, John W.	Berkeley
11,320	Frye, Henry W.	Hardy
12,664	Fulk, Frederick A.	Jefferson
17,282	Full, Jacob	Pendleton
12,727	Goen, John F.	Jefferson
15,319	Gordon, Philip	Jefferson
16,833	Graham, Isaac	Grant
16,836	Graham, James H.	Pendleton
14,628	Green, Wm.	Jefferson
14,394	Grove, Wm., Estate of	Jefferson
5,092	Haines, Edward V.	Jefferson
13,020	Hamill, Alleria A.	Jefferson
20,179	Hawk, Elijah	Jefferson
15,004	Havslett, John	Berkeley
17,013	Hazlewood, James T.	Jefferson
16,849	Hellms, Leonard W.	Monroe
15,005	Henson, G.W.	Berkeley
5,093	Herring, Ezra	Berkeley
14,395	Hill, John W.	Jefferson
15,006	Hoffman, Joseph	Berkeley
14,844	Hooff, Francis R.	Jefferson
20,076	Hopkins, E.C.	Jefferson
353	Huff, Harrison	Jefferson
15,590	Hurst, Wm., Estate of	Jefferson
16,144	Jackson, Thos.	Monroe
14,437	Jewett, Mary S.	Jefferson
13,018	Johnson, Andrew J.	Jefferson
8,462	Johnson, Zachariah	Hampshire
16,838	Judy, Mary Ann, Estate of	Pendleton
16,834	Judy, Zebulon	Grant
12,355	Kanode, John H.	Jefferson
15,008	Keiter, Hamilton J.	Berkeley
20,178	Kennedy, Anna	Jefferson
12,665	Kerny, A.H., Mrs., Estate of	Jefferson
21,767	Kidwiler, Adam	Jefferson
20,229	Kidwiler, Isaac	Jefferson
20,175	Kirwin, Thos.	Jefferson
11,321	Kotz, Francis	Hardy
15,009	Lamon, John W.	Berkeley
14,629	Langdon, Charles	Jefferson
15,373	Largent, Benj.	Morgan
15,374	Larkin, Michael	Morgan
10,707	Laudaker, Jesse	Hardy
5,341	Lemen, Robert	Berkeley

13,118: 13,479:	Lemen, Wm. M.	Jefferson
12,545	Lemen, Willoughby N.	Jefferson
13,523	Lewis, Sam	Jefferson
13,288	Licklider, Thos.	Jefferson
9,933	Light, Wm.	Hampshire
13,213	Lindsey, Sam K.	Berkeley
14,845	Lloyd, Dangerfield	Jefferson
14,369	Lloyd, James	Berkeley
13,481	Lloyd, Wm.	Jefferson
17,314	Lock, Benj.	Berkeley
15,984	Lock, Remington S.	Jefferson
8,464	Malcolm, James	Hampshire
8,463	Malcolm, Robert	Hampshire
15,987	McCloy, James W.	Jefferson
14,370	McCurdy, John W.	Jefferson
13,532	McSherry, Wm.	Jefferson
17,012	Melvin, Joseph, Estate of	Jefferson
15,536	Menifee, Joseph	Jefferson
13,019	Merritt, Jacob	Jefferson
21,619	Miles, Thos. H.	Jefferson
17,507	Miller, Edward W.	Jefferson
13,022	Miller, Jacob J.	Jefferson
14,309	Miller, Lydia	Jefferson
12,364	Miller, Robert M.	Jefferson
12,191	Mock, G.W.	Jefferson
1,925	Moler, Dan	Jefferson
13,023	Moler, Philip R.	Jefferson
15,537	Moler, Wm. J.	Jefferson
243: 14,371:	Moreland, Sam	Jefferson
10,709	Morrison, Amos	Berkeley
17,315	Morrow, James W.	Berkeley
16,398	Mowery, Anthony	Pendleton
18,208	Myers, Aaron, Estate of	Berkeley
13,209	Myers, James W.	Jefferson
17,316	Myers, Lucinda	Jefferson
14,431	Neer, John W.	Jefferson
1,696	Nisewaner, John	Jefferson
15,538	Osborne, Mary, Estate of	Jefferson
14,433	Osburn, Logan	Jefferson
15,185	Ott, Barney, Estate of	Jefferson
14,310	Ott, Dan	Jefferson
12,666	Ott, John W.	Jefferson
16,837	Ours, Elizabeth	Grant
14,434	Packett, John B.	Jefferson
17,317	Packett, John W.	Jefferson
14,435	Pane, Wm.	Jefferson
17,318	Pettit, Jonathan J.	Jefferson
5,342	Pitzer, Geo. J.	Berkeley
14,535	Pitzer, James S.	Berkeley
1,213	Pool, Richard N.	Jefferson
13,531	Ramey, Wm. C.	Jefferson
13,024	Ramsbury, John J.	Jefferson
14,543	Reed, Henry	Jefferson
14,436	Ridenour, Sam	Jefferson
13,017	Roberts, Joseph L.	Jefferson
15,011	Roberts, Wm. H.	Berkeley
15,198	Robinson, James H.	Berkeley
14,311	Rockenbaugh, John	Jefferson
14,372	Roper, James, Estate of	Jefferson
13,117: 13,290:	Ruckle, Sam	Jefferson
12,723	Rutherford, Uriah, Estate of	Jefferson
21,305	Russell, Wm.	Hardy
11,464	Seaman, Mary B.	Jefferson
19,341	Sears, Wm.	Monroe
18,585	Seymour, Jonathan	Grant
13,480	Shaull, Geo. E.	Jefferson
13,522	Shaull, John F.	Jefferson
13,482	Shaull, Nicholas S.	Jefferson
14,536	Shepherd, Francis R.	Berkeley
13,210	Show, Geo.	Jefferson
15,199	Snapp, Jacob H.	Berkeley
13,021	Snyer, James W.	Jefferson
14,438	Spotts, G.W.	Jefferson
15,539	Staley, Jacob W.	Jefferson
12,725	Staley, Stephen	Jefferson
20,173	Stipes, Anna	Jefferson
13,119	Straith, John J.H.	Jefferson
21,715	Strother, David H.	Jefferson
17,283	Teter, John A.	Pendleton
1,959	Thompson, Carey	Jefferson
13,519	Thompson, David	Berkeley
5,006	Tingler, Henry	Monroe
14,537	Turner, Anthony	Berkeley
17,313	Turner, John, Estate of	Berkeley
14,312	Urton, John	Jefferson
12,546	Wageley, David A.	Jefferson
13,520	Walker, James	Jefferson
12,354	Ware, John W.	Jefferson
14,630	Welcome, John	Jefferson
14,313	Welsh, Elizabeth P.	Jefferson
13,521	Welshams, Joseph	Jefferson
13,208	Welshans, Philip H.	Berkeley
14,544	Weshans, Henry C.	Berkeley
10,446	West, Joseph	Berkeley
15,596	West, Thos.	Jefferson
14,545	Whittington, Francis A.	Jefferson
21,379	Williams, Geo. T.	Hardy
11,949	Willis, Thos. H.	Jefferson
16,835	Wise, Zebulon	Pendleton
11,325	Woodward, Thos. E.	Jefferson
15,013	Wright, Dan	Berkeley
15,597	Yates, Francis	Jefferson
1,182	Zepp, G. W.	Berkeley
14,546	Zepp, Henry	Berkeley
15,375	Ziler, Jacob	Morgan
13,518	Zombro, Geo. P.	Jefferson

ADDENDA

Arkansas

3,037	Allen, Russel	Crawford
20,244	Boren, Joshua	Madison
21,516	Brazil, Moses	Saline
4,875	Cochran, Ned	Crittendon
2.202	Edens, Landon C.	Benton
21,512	Johnson, Thos.	Pulaski
21,514	Kurtz, John	Conway
21,515	Laferre, Mary	Pulaski
21,510	Lindsay, John Y.	Saline
21,517	Mitchell, Joshua	Saline
21,518	Prilliman, E.N., Mrs.	Saline
21,509	Prilliman, J. G.	Saline
16,034	Seigrist, Charles H.	Crittendon
21,354	Shepperd, James, Estate of	Jefferson
18,851	Wade, Henry G., Estate of	Drew

Florida

18,896	Falconer, Wm.	Escambia